Business
Management

13e

JAMES L. BURROW, PH.D.

BRAD KLEINDL, PH.D.

SOUTH-WESTERN
CENGAGE Learning

Australia • Brazil • Japan • Korea • Mexico • Singapore • Spain • United Kingdom • United States

SOUTH-WESTERN
CENGAGE Learning

Business Management, Thirteenth Edition

James L. Burrow and Brad Kleindl

Vice President of Editorial, Business:
Jack W. Calhoun

Vice President/Editor-in-Chief: Karen Schmohe

Executive Editor: Eve Lewis

Marketing Program Manager: Linda Kuper

Sr. Content Project Manager: Colleen A. Farmer

Sr. Media Editor: Sally Nieman

Manufacturing Planner: Kevin Kluck

Editorial Assistant: Anne Merrill

Production Service: diacriTech

Consulting Editor: Hyde Park Publishing
Services LLC

Cover and Internal Designer: PreMediaGlobal

Cover Images:
1. © Gala/shutterstock
2. © iStockphoto.com/kristian sekulic

Rights Acquisition Specialist: (Text and Photo):
Amber Hosea

For product information and technology assistance, contact us at
Cengage Learning Customer & Sales Support, 1-800-354-9706

For permission to use material from this text or product,
submit all requests online at **www.cengage.com/permissions**
Further permissions questions can be emailed to
permissionrequest@cengage.com

Exam_View_® is a registered trademark of eInstruction Corp. Windows is a registered trademark of the Microsoft Corporation used herein under license. Macintosh and Power Macintosh are registered trademarks of Apple Computer, Inc. used herein under license.

© 2008 Cengage Learning. All Rights Reserved.

ISBN-13: 978-1-111-57172-6
ISBN-10: 1-111-57172-4

South-Western
5191 Natorp Boulevard
Mason, OH 45040
USA

Cengage Learning products are represented in Canada by Nelson Education, Ltd.

For your course and learning solutions, visit **www.cengage.com/school**
Visit our company website at **www.cengage.com**

Printed in the United States of America
3 4 5 17 16 15

Reviewers

Lisa Brooks
Business and Information Technology Teacher
Henderson High School
Henderson, Texas

Deb Brunett
Business Education Teacher
Merrill High School
Merrill, Wisconsin

Martha J. Burrell
Business Education Teacher
Blue Ridge Early College
Cashiers, North Carolina

Tricia Valiquette Gross
Business Education Teacher
De Pere High School
De Pere, Wisconsin

Jan Imhoff
Business and Information Technology Teacher
Portage High School
Portage, Wisconsin

Katy Morgan
Business and Information Technology Teacher
Palmyra-Eagle High School
Palmyra, Wisconsin

Regina M. Stelma
Career and Technology Education Teacher
Walkersville High School
Walkersville, Maryland

Charisse Woodward
Business Teacher
Frederick County Public Schools
Stephens City, Virginia

About the Authors

James L. Burrow, Ph.D., has a background in marketing and human resource development. He works regularly with the business community and other organizations as a consultant on marketing and performance improvement strategies including the use of the Internet as an education and training resource. He recently retired from the faculty of North Carolina State University, where he served as the coordinator of the graduate Training and Development Program for more than fifteen years. Dr. Burrow received degrees from the University of Northern Iowa and the University of Nebraska in marketing and marketing education.

Brad A. Kleindl, Ph.D., is dean of the School of Business at Park University in Kansas City, Missouri. He previously served as dean and professor of marketing of The Robert W. Plaster College of Business Administration at Missouri Southern State University. He has authored and co-authored six books and more than 60 articles and conference papers. Dr. Kleindl has served twice as a Senior Fulbright Scholar, during 2007 in Austria and 2003 in South Africa. He has taught courses in consumer behavior, marketing research, principles of marketing, Internet marketing, and international marketing, and has presented at conferences and industry meetings across the United States, Europe, Africa, and Asia.

Contents

UNIT 4
Financial Management 390

FEATURES IN UNIT 4

UNIT 6
Human Resources Management   620

FEATURES IN UNIT 6

CHAPTER 23
Managing Human Resources   621

CHAPTER 24
Rewarding and Developing Employees   646

CHAPTER 25
Developing an Effective Organization   670

Helping You Build a Solid Foundation of Business Management Skills for Success in Today's Business World!

Business Management, 13e offers comprehensive coverage of higher level business management content including production and operations management in a realistic, investigative and enriching manner. All the functions of business management are covered extensively, including the use of technology and communication as tools of business.

Chapters are broken into several class-length lessons. The Lesson Numbers and Titles provide an overview of the chapter content.

Reality Check presents a story written to introduce concepts in the chapter using real-world examples.

Previewing the **Goals** and **Terms** helps you read each lesson effectively.

Key Terms, first introduced in the Lesson Openers, are bold in the text, emphasizing their importance and allowing you to find them easily.

Focus On... features take a look at current events, technology topics, international trends, innovation, change and other important issues that impact the business environment to give you a larger view of the business community.

The Changing Nature of Management

A new introductory chapter, **Managers and Managing**, has been added to provide an overview of management. It discusses the history of management and compares management approaches and philosophies.

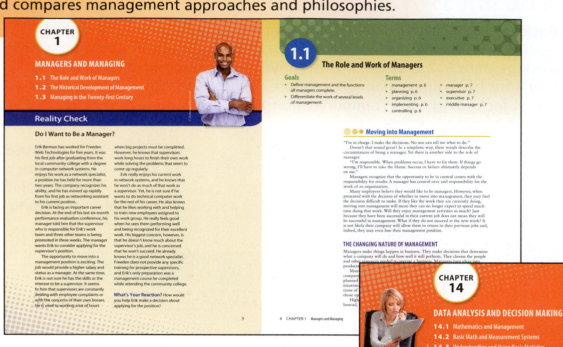

A new chapter, **Data Analysis and Decision Making**, demonstrates the importance of math, statistics, and quantitative decision making.

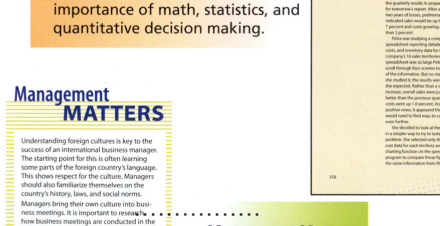

Management MATTERS

Understanding foreign cultures is key to the success of an international business manager. The starting point for this is often learning some parts of the foreign country's language. This shows respect for the culture. Managers should also familiarize themselves on the country's history, laws, and social norms.

Managers bring their own culture into business meetings. It is important to research how business meetings are conducted in the each culture where an international manager does business.

What Do You Think? Why is it important to learn a foreign language? How should a manager prepare for a cross cultural meeting?

Mangement Matters provides interesting business scenarios for you to consider as you apply higher order thinking skills.

Special Features Enhance Learning

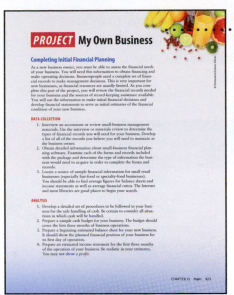

Project: My Own Business is an ongoing project where you apply the concepts you've learned while running a juice bar, building on previous knowledge as you build your business.

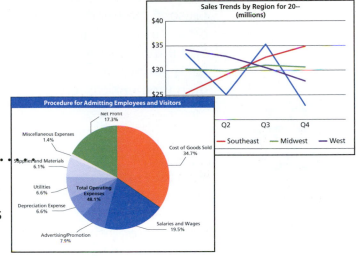

Figures visually organize information and detail the links and associations between data and corresponding analysis.

Winning Edge activities help you prepare for BPA, DECA, and FBLA competitive events.

21st CENTURY SKILLS content applies valued skills, such as problem solving, critical thinking, and technology use, as defined by the *Partnership for 21st Century Skills.*

21st CENTURY SKILLS

Communication Skills

Most Americans have a limited understanding of the factors related to international business. To be a successful international communicator, Americans must learn the history, culture, and language of the countries where they want to do business. Learning a foreign language is a good starting point. Even if you do not become fluent, people appreciate the effort you take to understand their language and culture.

Engaging and Relevant Features

MAKE ACADEMIC CONNECTIONS

Complete the following activities.

25. **Math** The current accounts of the imaginary nation of Utopia f
the past three years are given below in millions of dollars.

	Year 1	Year 2	Year 3
Exports of goods	$100	$120	$125
Imports of goods	$175	$195	$205

Make Academic Connections provides the integrated curriculum activities that show how business management concepts relate to other courses of study.

Career Cluster features present the needed skills, education, work experience and industry opportunities for a variety of management careers.

Tax Accountant

Tax accountants work with businesses and individuals to reduce their taxes by developing strategies that maximize deductions and minimize taxable revenue. They also help develop investment strategies. Tax accountants must understand federal and state tax laws. Some work for federal and state tax agencies.

Employment Outlook

Employment for accountants and auditors is expected to grow by 22 percent between 2008 and 2018. This growth is much faster than the average for all other occupations. This job expansion is linked to changing financial laws and regulations, increased scrutiny of company finances due to accounting scandals, and legislation designed to curb corporate accounting fraud.

Job Titles

Accounting Trainee
Junior Tax Accountant
Tax Accountant
Tax Accounting Manager
Chief Tax Accountant

Needed Skills

- Must possess a bachelor's degree in accounting from an accredited college or university.
- Should have an aptitude for mathematics and be able to analyze, compare, and interpret facts and figures quickly.
- Public accountants must pass the Certified Public Accounting (CPA) exam.
- Forty-six states and the District of Columbia require CPA candidates to have an additional 30 hours of coursework beyond a bachelor's degree. Many colleges

and universities now offer five-year combined bachelor's degree and master's degree program to meet these requirements.

Working in an Accounting Firm

Ryan completed his bachelor's degree in accounting. As a student, he worked as a volunteer helping people fill out personal tax forms. After graduating, he started working for a medium-size accounting firm as a trainee. After passing the CPA exam, he worked for three years as a junior tax accountant. He was then promoted to tax accounting, supervising a team of accountants helping businesses develop tax strategies. Ryan hopes to become a tax accounting manager, then a chief tax accountant, and ultimately a partner in the firm.

Career Assessment

Why are tax accountants important to businesses and individuals? Why do they need years of training? What do you like and dislike about this career area?

CAREER CLUSTER

CHAPTER 14   Career Cluster   387

Annual Reporting

Corporations whose stock is publicly traded must provide an annual report to stockholders and file financial information with the Securities and Exchange Commission. Annual reports contain financial statements, including an end-of-year balance sheet. Most corporations post the annual report on the corporate website.

Facts & Figures offers interesting information, statistics, and numerical representations to help you understand the breadth and scope of business enterprises and activities.

CASE IN POINT

CASE 15-1: The Value of Budgeting

Karen Kline and Joe Kim are both staff accountants in a manufacturing firm. The accounting manager, Brooke Shenker, has asked Karen to prepare the sales budget for next month's annual budget meeting. Brooke asked Joe to construct the cash budget. Both Karen and Joe had prepared similar budgets in the past. They were surprised when the budgets were returned with changes made to their projections. As they started to work on the budgets, Karen expressed her feelings about the process to Joe.

Karen: *We spend weeks developing these budgets and then the budget committee discusses it for two days and changes our estimates. It makes me wonder why they don't trust the figures we submit.*

Joe: *I agree. But no matter where the budgets end up, the actual results never come in on target with the budget. When the collections on customer accounts don't match the budgeted amounts, it throws the cash budget off. Last year they projected sales to be $350,000 for the first quarter, and they were only $315,000.*

Karen: *May be if they would ask us to come to the meeting and explain how we develop the budgets it would save them time and discussion and we would understand how they arrive at the final budget.*

Joe: *Last year they argued for three days and look what happened. With the way the economy changed, we were so far off budget that I heard Brooke say we could have used a dartboard to forecast. Budgeting this way makes it hard to get close to the actual results.*

Karen: *I'll start on the sales budget tomorrow, but I wish the committee would let us come up with a better process to arrive at the final numbers.*

THINK CRITICALLY

1. If Karen and Joe prepared budget figures, why is it necessary for management to discuss them?
2. How serious is the variance between forecasted and actual sales from last year? Do you agree with Joe that it is a problem when budgeted amounts and actual figures do not match? Explain.
3. How do you believe the company's budgeting process could be improved?

CASE 15-2: The Value of a New Business

Anneika Lafferty and her friend Bernie Williams started an Internet business 15 months ago selling affordable musical instruments for beginners. They named it A&B Musical Instruments. Because they live near each other, Bernie keeps the inventory in his garage and Anneika has the computer system, phones, and office space in her home. While the business has done well financially, it requires more time than either expected and affordable instruments for resale are not easy to find. They have decided to try to sell the business and create a different type of online business. A larger Internet music company wants to buy them but the $50,000

CHAPTER 15   Assessment   421

Case in Point includes engaging in-depth scenarios related to the chapter content followed by high level critical thinking questions.

Integrated Assessment...
Putting Your Knowledge to the Test

End of Lesson ongoing assessment is found at the conclusion of each lesson to ensure you can apply what you've learned.

9.3 ASSESSMENT

UNDERSTAND MANAGEMENT CONCEPTS

Determine the best answer for each of the following questions.

1. The theory that a country should specialize in products or services that it can provide more efficiently than can other countries is called
   a. international specialization
   b. competitive advantage theory
   c. comparative advantage theory
   d. specialization theory.

2. Which of the following is not part of the balance of payments?
   a. current account
   b. capital account
   c. economic surplus
   d. All are included as part of the balance of payments.

THINK CRITICALLY

Answer the following questions as completely as possible.

3. If a country regularly has a trade surplus, what will happen to its international business?

4. Explain the situations under which a multinational firm will use [...] country, host-country, and third-country nationals in its foreign [...]

End of Chapter Assessment provides a summary of the main points. Questions and activities test your knowledge.

CourseMate helps you make the grade!

- Interactive eBook
- Learning Objectives
- Study Tools — Games
- Interactive Quizzes - with eBook rejoinders
- Net Bookmarks
- Flashcards
- Crossword Puzzles
- Template Files
- Management Videos
- Spanish Glossary

You can access interactive study tools in a dynamic, online learning environment. An enhanced eBook provides you with an interactive, online-version of the textbook. A Student Learning Pathway features a variety of integrated digital media with a simple, user-friendly interface.

Engagement Tracker allows teachers to assess their students' preparation and engagement. This intuitive, online reporting tool makes it easy to evaluate use of study resources, monitor time-on-task, and track progress for the entire class or for individual students. Instantly see what concepts are the most difficult for your class and identify which students are at risk throughout the semester.

1

UNIT 1

Managing and Management Responsibilities

MANAGERS AND MANAGING

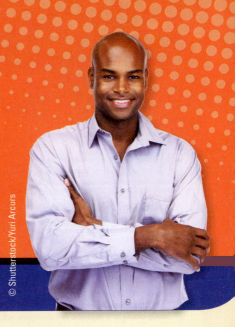

© Shutterstock/Yuri Arcurs

Reality Check

Do I Want to Be a Manager?

Erik Berman has worked for Freeden Web Technologies for five years. It was his first job after graduating from the local community college with a degree in computer network systems. He enjoys his work as a network specialist, a position he has held for more than two years. The company recognizes his ability, and he has moved up rapidly from his first job as networking assistant to his current position.

Erik is facing an important career decision. At the end of his last six-month performance evaluation conference, his manager told him that the supervisor who is responsible for Erik's work team and three other teams is being promoted in three weeks. The manager wants Erik to consider applying for the supervisor's position.

The opportunity to move into a management position is exciting. The job would provide a higher salary and status as a manager. At the same time, Erik is not sure he has the skills or the interest to be a supervisor. It seems to him that supervisors are constantly dealing with employee complaints or with the concerns of their own bosses. He is used to working a lot of hours

when big projects must be completed. However, he knows that supervisors work long hours to finish their own work while solving the problems that seem to come up regularly.

Erik really enjoys his current work in network systems, and he knows that he won't do as much of that work as a supervisor. Yet, he is not sure if he wants to do technical computer work for the rest of his career. He also knows that he likes working with and helping to train new employees assigned to his work group. He really feels good when he sees them performing well and being recognized for their excellent work. His biggest concern, however, is that he doesn't know much about the supervisor's job, and he is concerned that he won't succeed. He already knows he is a good network specialist. Freeden does not provide any specific training for prospective supervisors, and Erik's only preparation was a management course he completed while attending the community college.

What's Your Reaction? How would you help Erik make a decision about applying for the position?

The Role and Work of Managers

Goals

- Define management and the functions all managers complete.
- Differentiate the work of several levels of management.

Terms

- management p. 6
- planning p. 6
- organizing p. 6
- implementing p. 6
- controlling p. 6
- manager p. 7
- supervisor p. 7
- executive p. 7
- middle manager p. 7

●●● Moving into Management

"I'm in charge. I make the decisions. No one can tell me what to do."

Doesn't that sound great? In a simplistic way, these words describe the circumstances of being a manager. Yet there is another side to the role of manager.

"I'm responsible. When problems occur, I have to fix them. If things go wrong, I'll have to take the blame. Success or failure ultimately depends on me."

Managers recognize that the opportunity to be in control comes with the responsibility for results. A manager has control over and responsibility for the work of an organization.

Many employees believe they would like to be managers. However, when presented with the decision of whether to move into management, they may find the decision difficult to make. If they like the work they are currently doing, moving into management will mean they can no longer expect to spend much time doing that work. Will they enjoy management activities as much? Just because they have been successful in their current job does not mean they will be successful in management. What if they do not succeed at the new work? It is not likely their company will allow them to return to their previous jobs and, indeed, they may even lose their management position.

THE CHANGING NATURE OF MANAGEMENT

Managers make things happen in business. They make decisions that determine what a company will do and how well it will perform. They choose the people and other resources needed to operate a business. Managers turn ideas into products and services.

Managers make up only a small percentage of all employees in a company. The larger number of employees actually complete the work planned by managers. There are often several levels of managers in an organization. Some managers are directly responsible for the day-to-day operations of a part of the business and the work of employees who complete those operations.

Higher-level managers are not directly involved in day-to-day operations. Instead, they spend their time planning, problem solving, and making decisions about how to make the business more successful. Nonmanagement employees often do not recognize the contributions that managers make to the business. In addition, these workers may not understand the challenges of being a manager.

The daily work of managers is quite different from the work of employees. Yet both types of work are necessary for a business to succeed. Mutual understanding and respect are important. Managers must understand and appreciate the work of employees. Employees who understand what managers do and why management is important to business success tend to be motivated and cooperative.

The nature of management and the way managers interact with employees has changed in recent years. In the past, many managers exerted a great deal of authority and control, expected employees to follow orders without question, and provided little information about the company to workers. Employees and managers did not always share the same views and attitudes about the company and the work that needed to be done. Relationships between managers and employees were formal and sometimes antagonistic.

Today's managers work more closely with employees. They keep employees informed about company performance and upcoming changes. They also involve employees in important decisions. Employees have greater responsibilities in many companies, and employee teams now complete some work previously done by managers. Businesses in which managers and employees respect each other, communicate effectively, and cooperate are usually more successful than businesses that use traditional management techniques.

MANAGEMENT ACTIVITIES

There are many different kinds of managers. The president of an international corporation with facilities around the world and thousands of employees is a manager. The owner of a small service business with one location and only a few employees is also a manager. Managers are in charge of many different

© iStockphoto/Abel Mitja Varela

Employees may not be aware of the contributions managers make. Name some responsibilities of managers.

aspects of business including purchasing, sales, communication, and technology. People who supervise workers on an assembly line, in a warehouse, or in a customer service center are all managers.

Because there are so many types of managers, it is difficult to identify exactly what managers do. However, there are a number of activities that all managers must perform. The type of business, size of company, or department within the organization do not matter—all managers perform some of the same activities.

Management is the process of accomplishing the goals of an organization through the effective use of people and other resources. Those resources include money, facilities, equipment, and materials. The primary work of all managers falls within four functions: planning, organizing, implementing, and controlling.

- **Planning** involves analyzing information and making decisions about what needs to be done.
- **Organizing** is concerned with determining how plans can be accomplished most effectively and arranging resources to complete work.
- **Implementing** focuses on carrying out the plans and helping employees to work effectively.
- **Controlling** involves evaluating results to determine if the company's objectives have been accomplished as planned.

Operating any business is a complex process. Regardless of the size of the business, all managers make decisions about operations, marketing, personnel, and finances every day. If managers are not well prepared to operate the business, problems soon develop. The manager who knows how to plan, organize, implement, and control is ready to make the decisions needed to operate a business successfully.

CHECKPOINT

What are the four management functions that all managers complete?

The Work of Managers

All managers perform the same four broad functions as a part of their jobs, but the specific activities they perform and the amount of time they spend on each function varies. The functions of management may even seem to describe work activities of some employees who are not classified as managers.

MANAGERS AND NONMANAGEMENT EMPLOYEES

Many employees of a business complete tasks that could be considered management activities. They might develop plans to accomplish the work assigned to them. They may organize their workspace and the materials they use to complete their work efficiently. An experienced employee may lead a group project, and the group members may help evaluate the completed project. The increasing use of teams in organizations provides opportunities for employees to participate in activities that previously have been the domain of managers.

In each of these examples, the employee gains valuable experience. New knowledge and skills help employees understand the work of managers and prepare for possible promotion to a management position. Even though employees perform some work that is similar to work performed by managers, the employees are not managers. There are important differences in the nature of managers' work and that of nonmanagerial employees.

A **manager** completes all four management functions on a regular basis and has authority over other jobs and people. In each of the situations above, where employees were completing what seemed to be management functions, they were doing those tasks infrequently, were not completing all of the management functions, or were completing them for their job only. Seldom do nonmanagement employees have authority over other employees for more than a short period. Final authority and responsibility remains with the manager.

LEVELS OF MANAGEMENT

Most companies have more than one level of management. Small companies may have two or three levels. Large companies may have five or six management classifications. The levels of management in an organization can be described as a *management pyramid*. There are more managers at the lower levels and fewer at higher levels. The chief executive or owner who heads the business is at the top of the pyramid. Figure 1-1 illustrates the management pyramid.

A **supervisor** is a manager whose main job is to direct the work of employees. Supervisors are the first, or beginning, level of management in a company. They often perform nonmanagerial activities in addition to overseeing the work of others. Supervisors are at the bottom of the management pyramid.

An **executive** is a top-level manager who spends almost all of his or her time on management functions and decisions that affect the entire company. Executives have other managers reporting to them. Executives are at the top of the management pyramid.

Between executives and supervisors in larger organizations, there will be one or more levels of middle managers. A **middle manager** completes all of the management functions, but spends most of the time completing specialized work in one management function or is responsible for a specific part of the company's operations. A middle manager may complete detailed planning activities, may manage a specific product line, or be responsible for a specialized division such as information security.

The amount of time devoted to each function of management differs depending on the level of management. Supervisors work most directly with employees and are involved primarily in ensuring that the day-to-day work of the business is completed. Therefore, they devote most of their management time to implementing and monitoring results of their work team. Executives work with other managers and are responsible for the long-term direction and overall success of the business. They spend most of their time on planning and organizing.

Figure 1-2, shows how the time spent on management functions changes for different levels of managers in a business. You can see from the figure that as a manager moves up in the organization, responsibilities change.

Management Pyramid

Executives

Middle Managers

Supervisors

© Cengage Learning 2013.

Figure 1-1 The management pyramid illustrates the levels of management within an organization.

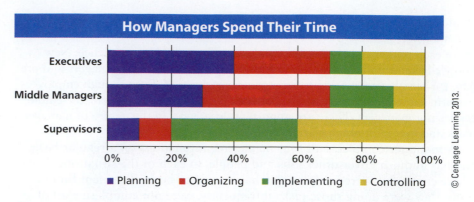

Figure 1-2 The amount of time spent on each management function depends on the level of management.

 **CHECKPOINT**

How is the work of supervisors different from the work of middle managers and executives?

1.1 ASSESSMENT

UNDERSTAND MANAGEMENT CONCEPTS

Determine the best answer for each of the following questions.

1. Which of the following is *not* one of the four functions of management?
   a. planning
   b. budgeting
   c. implementing
   d. controlling

2. The level of management that devotes the greatest amount of time to planning is
   a. supervisors
   b. middle managers
   c. executives
   d. All levels spend equal amounts of time on planning.

THINK CRITICALLY

Answer the following questions as completely as possible.

3. What can employees do both on and off the job to prepare to be effective managers?

4. Why are businesses reducing the number of management levels?

The Historical Development of Management

Goals

- Describe historical changes in management that led to the beginning of management science.
- Describe four different philosophies that have been used to manage organizations.

Terms

- Industrial Revolution p. 10
- management science p. 11
- classical management p. 11
- administrative management p. 12
- behavioral management p. 12
- quality management p. 13

Management through the Ages

Management has been needed since civilizations first began organizing work. Individuals and groups had to make decisions about how work would be completed. They had to ask questions such as

- What resources do we need to complete the work?
- How and where will we get the resources?
- Who will be responsible for various tasks?
- How will we decide if the completed work is satisfactory?

Today, the smallest part-time businesses, the newest entrepreneurial business ventures, and the largest global corporations require management. Small business owners decide how much time to devote to their work, how much work can be done from home, how much personal money must be invested, and how to price and market products and services. Entrepreneurs with visions of building the next Subway or Facebook develop business plans, secure investors, hire talented employees, and manage the growth of their businesses. Giant international businesses require managers versed in the cultures and laws of many countries. These same managers need to be able to harness the skills of diverse work teams. They also need to be prepared to manage a large portfolio of products and compete with other businesses to satisfy the ever-changing demands of customers.

THE EARLIEST FORMS OF MANAGEMENT

The first managers had to rely on their instincts, intuition, and experience to decide how to organize work and operate their businesses. Some of the earliest civilizations organized large numbers of people to accomplish seemingly impossible tasks. The Incas in South America, Egyptians in northern Africa, and Chinese in eastern Asia are a few examples. These remarkable societies accomplished great feats of engineering and construction. They organized vast agricultural enterprises and developed systems of commerce and finance. These efforts required planning and the management of people and other resources. Often the work involved large numbers of workers completing difficult tasks. In most cases the emphasis was on getting the job done with little concern for the health and safety of the workers.

Until the development of technology and machines began near the end of the seventeenth century, most work was completed using manual labor. Governments often undertook the large-scale projects of the society that required massive numbers of laborers or vast amounts of resources to complete. On the other end of the spectrum, individuals and families worked to provide goods and services needed for everyday living. Small businesses developed in many societies as transportation and trade allowed people to specialize in their work. Whether working alone, in family groups, or operating large government projects, management was required to plan and complete the work with the available resources.

THE INDUSTRIAL REVOLUTION

The invention of advanced machines that allowed for the faster processing of raw materials began the transformation of work and business leading to the Industrial Revolution. The **Industrial Revolution** was the era of the eighteenth and nineteenth centuries in which machine power replaced human and animal power in the production process, leading to major business and social changes. Rather than individual artisans completing work on each product, businesses could hire workers to operate the new machines. The result was greater production and a larger number of products for sale. The invention of the steam engine and the harnessing of waterpower contributed to the development and expansion of businesses that produced a variety of new products.

The Industrial Revolution had its beginnings in Western Europe and then spread to the United States and around the world. It had particular impact on the textile industry, coal and metal mining, and agriculture. With the use of machines, people could complete much more work in the same amount of time. Factories developed to house the machines, provide workspace for the employees, and store the raw materials and finished products. When completed, the products needed to be transported to businesses that used them in their own production or to customers who purchased them for personal use. Products were moved first by road and river, and then by large ships at sea. The invention of the steam and gasoline engines increased transportation choices to include railroads, steam-powered ships, automobiles, and trucks. The transportation industry and retail trade expanded as a result.

The economic expansion spawned by the Industrial Revolution required a new approach to business operations. Money was needed to build the factories, buy the equipment, and obtain the materials needed for production. Employees needed to be hired and prepared for the new types of work as machine operators rather than craftsmen. Finished products had to be sold and transported to customers. A small number of people were needed to make the decisions, supervise the employees, and ensure the factories operated efficiently and profitably. These were the business managers.

The Industrial Revolution changed business practices and businesses. Many people were needed to mine the coal and minerals and to operate the mills and factories. The goal of the business owners was to produce as many products as could be sold. As they organized the new factories and other businesses, they often had little concern for working conditions or safety.

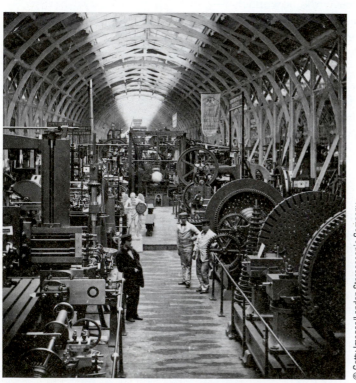

In 1862, an exhibit of machines was an attraction at the International Exhibition in London. How did the invention of advanced machines affect workers?

© Getty Images/London Stereoscopic Company

Employees worked long 12-14 hour days, six or seven days a week. They worked in hot, dark, crowded spaces without breaks or vacations. They were inadequately trained to operate the new and sometimes dangerous equipment, resulting in frequent worker injuries. If the business owners could not find enough adults to operate their business, they would turn to younger and younger children to do the work. The Industrial Revolution resulted in new types of business and employment opportunities, the growth of cities, and a higher standard of living for many. However, it also created large, complex businesses that were difficult to manage and a growing set of economic and social problems.

 **CHECKPOINT**

How did the Industrial Revolution change the way work was done?

Changing Approaches to Management

As the economy expanded and as problems emerged, some business leaders recognized that their operating practices were not good for either employees or businesses. They were interested in learning how businesses could be run more effectively and efficiently. They began to examine ways to improve business practices and to pass on that knowledge to the people who were running the business. Those efforts to improve business management lead to the beginning of management science. **Management science** is the careful, objective study of management decisions and procedures in order to improve the operation of businesses and organizations.

THEORIES OF MANAGEMENT

Managing is not easy. Determining the best ways to manage an organization has been an issue facing business leaders for nearly two centuries. Business leaders and researchers began to study management practices shortly after the Industrial Revolution began, and that study continues today. Several theories of management have been developed and tested. Among the most widely accepted are classical management, administrative management, behavioral management, and most recently, quality management.

CLASSICAL MANAGEMENT Classical management was the first effort to apply scientific study to business activities. **Classical management** studies the way work is organized and the procedures used to complete a job in order to increase worker productivity. Work areas are arranged to make parts and materials readily accessible in order to speed work. The most efficient employees are studied to identify the best assembly or work methods that are then taught to other employees.

NETBookmark

As businesses and industries grow and decline, employment opportunities change. As you think about a possible future in management, you will need information to help you make a career decision. The U.S. Bureau of Labor Statistics publishes estimates of job growth.

Access the website for this textbook and choose the link for Chapter 1 Net Bookmark. Review the estimates of management job opportunities in major occupational areas. Look at the most recent data and the 10-year projection. Select three management jobs that may be of interest to you. Compare the projected job growth by total number of jobs and percentage increase or decrease. Prepare a bar graph that illustrates your findings. In addition to job growth, what other types of information are important to you as you make career plans?

www.cengage.com/school/bizmgmt

© iStockphoto/Skip ODonnell

21st CENTURY SKILLS

Organizations using classical management may use experiments to try to develop ways to improve the organization of workspace and work procedures to increase efficiency.

One of the early leaders in the development of classical management was Frederick W. Taylor. An engineer by training, Taylor worked in factories and steel mills in the United States during the late 1800s. He believed most workers would not choose the most productive methods of working. They would need clear instructions and close supervision to work efficiently.

Taylor believed there was one best way to do every job. In order to determine the best way, he observed workers completing tasks. Using precise time and motion measurements, Taylor and his researchers worked to identify the least number of steps, the most efficient layout of work, and the fastest work procedures to complete a task. Taylor developed the idea of compensating employees using a *piece rate* where employees are paid based on the amount of work they produce.

Classical management was widely accepted and implemented in businesses in the late 1800s and through the first two decades of the 1900s.

ADMINISTRATIVE MANAGEMENT While classical management experts focused on increasing worker productivity, another group of experts was concentrating on improving the overall management of growing businesses. Their ideas became known as administrative management. **Administrative management** identifies the most effective practices for organizing and managing a business. From administrative management came the concepts of multiple levels of management, organizing businesses into specialized departments, and defining the type of work all managers must complete for an organization to operate effectively.

An early proponent of administrative management was Henri Fayol, a French businessman. Fayol first described the common functions of management—planning, organizing, commanding, coordinating, and controlling. He also identified 14 characteristics of an effective organization. Many of those characteristics are still recognized in organizations today, including:

- *Authority and responsibility*—managers have the authority to assign tasks. They can delegate responsibility to others but must give the needed authority as well.
- *Unity of command*—each employee must receive direction from only one manager to avoid conflicts and to maintain a clear line of authority.
- *Unity of purpose*—the goals and direction of an organization must be clear and supported by everyone.
- *Adequate compensation*—the wages and benefits for every employee should be fair and satisfactory to both the individual and the organization.
- *Esprit de corps*—organizations should work to build good interpersonal relationships, a sense of teamwork and harmony.

BEHAVIORAL MANAGEMENT The earliest approaches to management were directed at organizing work and efficient procedures. They had little concern for the effects of changes on employees. Recognizing the growing worker dissatisfaction in many companies, a group of management experts began to focus on the relationship between managers and employees and developed the principles of behavioral management. **Behavioral management** is directed at organizational improvement through understanding employee motivation and behavior. Behavioral management is sometimes called *human relations management*.

The focus of behavioral management is developing a work environment in which workers believe they are a valuable part of the organization and they are motivated to do their best. That is most likely to occur when there are positive relationships between managers and employees. This approach suggests that managers should find ways to improve working conditions and increase worker satisfaction, which will lead to better performance.

The first efforts to implement behavioral management began in U.S. factories in the 1920s. Researchers led by Elton Mayo experimented with changing the amount of light in employee work areas. They found that increasing the light resulted in higher productivity. Surprisingly however, they also found that if they then began decreasing the light, productivity continued to climb. They conducted several related experiments and obtained similar results. They concluded that when employees felt managers were concerned about them and were attempting to improve working conditions, they were willing to work harder. This response of people behaving differently when they are receiving attention is known as the *Hawthorne effect*. The name comes from Western Electric's Hawthorne Works factory where the first experiments were conducted.

Another important contributor to behavioral management was Douglas McGregor, who developed Theory X and Theory Y. Theory X managers think that employees will not work to their greatest potential without close supervision. Theory Y managers believe that employees will work hard if they are involved in decisions about their work and are assigned meaningful tasks. McGregor believed managers interact differently with their employees depending on which of the theories they accept.

Management MATTERS

Involvement Equals Profits

A study of Fortune 1000 companies found that the use of employee involvement has a greater return on investment than other management approaches. Involvement works because employees are often in the best position to identify problems and offer solutions. They quickly spot quality issues and waste. Experienced employees find effective shortcuts and other ways to save time. Employee involvement is most effective when businesses follow three guidelines:

- Improvements cannot lead to job loss for current employees.
- Employees should benefit from savings or increases in profits.
- Businesses should publicly recognize employees for the improvements they suggest.

What Do You Think? Why might some employees be reluctant to get involved when first asked by their manager?

QUALITY MANAGEMENT In the second half of the twentieth century, businesses were growing rapidly, expanding the number of products they produced, and looking for methods to speed production and cut costs. Assembly lines and modern technology allowed for the production of many products in a short period. Along with increased production, however, these advances caused some problems. The number of product defects increased and production resources were wasted. This resulted in losses of time and money required to correct mistakes.

Japanese manufacturers were the first to take note of the growing problems. At the time, the image of Japanese products was low cost and even lower quality. Japanese companies brought an American engineer, W. Edward Deming, to Japan to teach quality management, a new approach to management and operations. **Quality management** is a total commitment by everyone in an organization to improve the quality of procedures and products by reducing waste, errors, and defects. Quality management involves using facts and data to make decisions, and continually looking for ways to make improvements. Training, participation, and commitment are hallmarks of quality management.

CHECKPOINT

What are the differences among the four theories of management?

1.2 ASSESSMENT

UNDERSTAND MANAGEMENT CONCEPTS

Determine the best answer for each of the following questions.

1. The Industrial Revolution began primarily because of
   a. large numbers of people unable to find work
   b. the growth of corporations in the U.S.
   c. the invention of machines allowing the faster processing of raw materials
   d. managers using practices to improve productivity of employees

2. The first effort to apply scientific study to the management of businesses was
   a. behavioral management
   b. classical management
   c. quality management
   d. administrative management

THINK CRITICALLY

Answer the following questions as completely as possible.

3. Why did management become so important to businesses as a result of the Industrial Revolution?

4. Why might employees not like to work in a business where managers use classical management?

Management Innovation

Putting Employees First

What kind of company would put employees first and customers second? What kind of executive would consider employees more important than managers? These are some of the innovative views of Vineet Nayar, Chief Executive Officer of HCL Technologies. Located near New Delhi, India, HCL employs 30,000 people in the competitive information technology outsourcing business.

Employee empowerment comes first with Nayar. He is a strong believer that effective teamwork and motivated employees build a great company. He trusts employees so much that management evaluation is put in their hands. Every employee rates not only his or her own boss but also any three other managers in the company. Employees fill out an 18-item questionnaire and the results are posted online where all employees and managers can review them.

Another innovation in employee empowerment is the employee "ticket." Whenever employees see a problem or want managers to take some action, they can immediately fill out an electronic form. The issue can be as simple as a problem with the menu in the cafeteria or as major as a product defect. The "ticket" is immediately routed to a manager who becomes responsible for the solution. And when is the solution satisfactory? Not until the employee who filed the original form is satisfied.

A public question-and-answer space is provided on the company's intranet, where any employee can post a question and receive a reply from management. Again, all questions and answers can be reviewed by every employee. Over 400 questions are posted each month. Managers are actually rewarded by the number of employee tickets and questions submitted—the more, the better. HCL managers receive regular training in how to be effective in an empowered work environment. Key courses are negotiation skills and expectation management—how to meet the expectations of employees.

The results of the company's employee empowerment program have been outstanding. Employee retention rates have doubled in an industry where highly skilled employees change jobs regularly to increase their pay. At the same time, sales, profits, and the company's stock price are climbing.

"I want to be the company that gives superior service to my employees compared to everybody else," Nayar says.

THINK CRITICALLY

1. Do you agree or disagree with Vineet Nayar's management philosophy? Why or why not?
2. Would you like to work as a manager in that type of company? Why or why not?
3. How do you believe customers feel about Nayar's views that employees are first and customers are second?

1.3

Managing in the Twenty-first Century

Goals

- Describe ways that the workforce and work are changing.
- Discuss important factors that influence the management strategy of an organization.

Terms

- business competition p. 18
- management strategy p. 19

 CHANGES AND CHALLENGES FOR MANAGERS

If anything characterizes business, it is change. While businesses have always faced change, the change facing business today has three characteristics. The pace of change is extremely fast. The number of changes that must be addressed at one time is challenging. Finally, the impact of change is often dramatic.

Change affects managers in many ways. The most significant challenges include the changing workforce, the nature of work itself, competition, and technology.

WORKERS

The best description of the changing American workforce is *diverse*. The makeup of the workforce is becoming increasingly diverse based on a number of factors including age, ethnic background, gender, and education.

There are some indications that the United States workforce will become much younger as baby boomers move into retirement. Other indicators suggest that as people live longer, they will remain in the workforce longer. This may be due to financial need brought on by a longer life span as well as the desire to stay active and involved.

The U.S. Department of Labor estimates that people over the age of 55 will make up 23 percent of the workforce by 2050 compared to just 13 percent in 2000. The largest component of the workforce will continue to be those between the ages of 25 and 54. Figure 1-3 shows the age diversity of the U.S. workforce of 2000 compared to projections for 2050.

The ethnic composition of the U.S. workforce will change as the proportion of white workers declines to about 50 percent by 2050. The biggest percentage increase will be Hispanic workers. Figure 1-4 shows the ethnic makeup of the U.S. workforce in 2000 and projections for 2050.

The percentage of women in the workforce increased a great deal in the last three decades of the twentieth century. Men and women will be represented almost equally in the workforce in the future. However, women are increasingly filling important positions in businesses as well as becoming key managers and top executives of many organizations. The total U.S. workforce is anticipated to grow from just over 150 million workers today to 195 million by 2050.

Businesses will employ a workforce that is much more educated. Young people continue to enroll in education beyond high school in greater numbers as they recognize the jobs of the future will require advanced education and

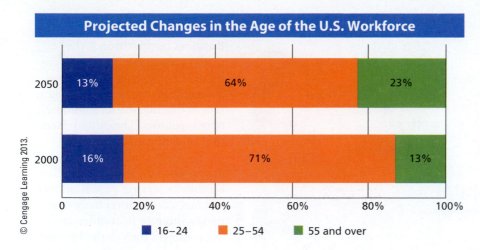

Projected Changes in the Age of the U.S. Workforce

Year	16–24	25–54	55 and over
2050	13%	64%	23%
2000	16%	71%	13%

■ 16–24 ■ 25–54 ■ 55 and over

© Cengage Learning 2013.

Figure 1-3 Although the percentage of workers age 25 to 54 will drop between 2000 and 2050, this group will remain the largest component of the workforce.

training. In the next ten years, over 60 percent of the anticipated 47 million job openings in the U.S. will require some education beyond high school. Few options will be available for anyone without a high school diploma, and those jobs will offer little job security and low pay.

WORK

Just as the workforce is changing, so is the way work is accomplished. Fewer jobs today require individuals to work on specialized tasks in isolation from other employees. Instead, work is organized around processes or projects where teams of employees collaborate. Technology is quickly reshaping organizations. More work tasks are completed by automated machines or by workers using technology. While many production and service jobs still require physical labor, more jobs are less physically demanding and more intellectually challenging. Jobs require workers to think critically, solve problems, and make decisions.

Jobs require effective communication and interpersonal skills. Communication often occurs virtually rather than face-to-face. This requires workers and managers to choose the appropriate technology, learn new procedures, and conduct themselves professionally.

Business competition has changed as well. Today businesses compete globally rather than just with businesses in the same city or country. Small businesses invested in the latest technologies and linked via the Internet can compete effectively with even the largest businesses. It is common for international businesses to have work locations and employees in many different countries. A small business in one country can partner with businesses in other countries to have an international presence. Managers and employees must be able to work effectively across time zones and country borders. They need to be able to respond to different economic and political systems as well as unique cultural and social needs.

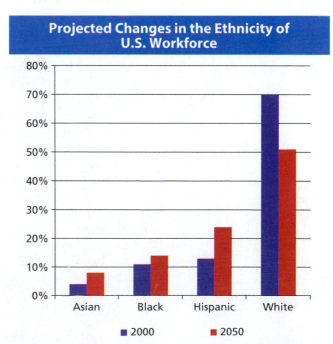

Projected Changes in the Ethnicity of U.S. Workforce

■ 2000 ■ 2050

© Cengage Learning 2013.

Figure 1-4 The percentage of Asian, black, and Hispanic workers will increase as the percentage of white workers declines.

© iStockphoto/Kristian Sekulic

Why are many businesses facing competition from around the globe?

COMPETITION

Business competition is the rivalry among companies for customers. Two aspects of business competition are changing rapidly. One is the location and number of competitors. The other relates to production efficiency.

Today business competition has no borders. Even the smallest businesses serving a local market can face competition from companies thousands of miles away as customers turn to the Internet to make purchases. E-commerce retail sales in the United States were estimated at $165 billion in 2010. That was an increase of nearly 15 percent from the previous year. Yet e-commerce retail sales represented less than 5 percent of total retail sales for 2010. Managers need to understand how competition is changing and how these changes affect their business.

When it comes to production efficiency, some businesses located outside the United States have an advantage. These companies may have access to a lower-cost workforce and less expensive production and distribution alternatives. Laws, regulations, and financial incentives in other countries also may create advantages for some companies.

TECHNOLOGY

Internet and telecommunications technologies are driving changes in business and management. Most businesses today cannot compete without a website to promote their businesses, communicate with customers, and sell their products and services. In addition to a website, companies are adding social media access and a variety of mobile applications for instant communication and interaction with customers.

The same access and technologies makes it possible for employees to communicate with each other and with their managers in a virtual environment. Employees no longer need to work at the same physical location or even in a business environment. Internet technology has given rise to the virtual employee, who may work from home, a hotel, or the local coffee shop.

New technologies also have led to major changes in accessing and using data. Specialized software tracks, analyzes, and reports information to managers. Managers can access information about all aspects of the business. For example, they might want production schedules, sales figures, customer characteristics, competitive analysis, or market data. Managers can also access information about individual employee work activities and performance.

 CHECKPOINT

How will the U.S. workforce be different in 2050 than it was in 2000?

●●●● DEVELOPING A MANAGEMENT STRATEGY

Effective management cannot be arbitrary. Managers cannot just do what they believe is best based on their own instincts and experience. An effective business has a management strategy that is planned, consistent, and understood. A **management strategy** is a carefully developed overall approach to leading an organization.

Determining the best approach to manage an organization can be a complicated procedure. Every business has a unique set of characteristics. It can be large or small, offer goods or services, and operate locally or globally. The management strategy must be appropriate for each business. Resources and the environment in which a business operates affect the way a business is managed. Given all of the characteristics and options, each organization must develop its own management strategy. Figure 1-5 shows the major factors a company considers when determining its management strategy.

THE BUSINESS Management will be quite different if the business is small or large, new or old, or operating in one or multiple locations. Managing retail businesses is not the same as managing manufacturing or transportation companies. A service business may need large numbers of personnel, while a computer manufacturer relies more on technology.

THE WORK Managers must be prepared to manage the work and the employees doing the work. Different kinds of work require different kinds of management. Managing routine tasks is different from managing work in a stressful and ever-changing environment. For example, managing an assembly line is different from managing a hospital emergency room.

Today's managers usually work with employees who have different backgrounds and different aspirations. They will manage experienced workers as well as new hires. Some workers are full-time employees, while others are part-time or temporary. Employees in a small company with one location will require different approaches to management than a multinational company with locations in ten countries where employees come from different cultures and speak multiple languages.

Figure 1-5 All aspects of a business must be considered when developing a management strategy.

Many companies have facilities, suppliers, and customers all over the world. What are some challenges managers face when operating in an international environment?

THE BUSINESS ENVIRONMENT

Some industries are highly regulated. Examples include pharmaceuticals, nuclear power, and airlines. Others have fewer restrictions and can operate more freely. Many companies face intense competition from businesses offering similar products or services. The environment for businesses that offer unique products and services is much less competitive. An effective management strategy must recognize the nature of competition; be able to effectively respond to any political, legal, and regulatory issues; and demonstrate the level of social responsibility expected by customers and the communities in which the business operates.

THE MANAGEMENT The fourth factor that affects a business's management strategy is the characteristics of its management. The management of an organization determines the overall approach and philosophy it will follow. Will it be more traditional, administrative, behavioral, or quality-focused? The levels of management and the numbers of managers in business affect the approach to management. If the levels and numbers shift up or down, the strategy may need to change. Finally, the management strategy affects the responsibilities of managers. This includes their relationships with nonmanagement employees and their approach to the completion of the four management functions.

MOVING INTO MANAGEMENT

At the beginning of the chapter, Erik Berman was trying to decide if he wanted to move into management as a supervisor. He knows he will spend most of his time on management activities—planning, organizing, implementing, and controlling. As a supervisor, he will become a part of the company's management team and will be the link between the employees he supervises and upper management. He and the other supervisors and managers will work as a team to plan the future and guide the business. They will be responsible for the wise use of resources, the jobs of employees, and—ultimately—the success or failure of the business.

Management is challenging and exciting, but it is also demanding and pressure-filled work. Management is increasingly complex and requires people who are energetic, well prepared, and committed to their company and their career. Regardless of your career goals, you benefit from understanding about how businesses manage production, marketing, finance, operations, and other important activities. This is true if you plan to operate a business of your own, move into a top management position in a large company, or work as a valuable and valued employee for a company.

If you plan to be an entrepreneur or executive, you will need a complete understanding of all phases of business planning and operations. If you expect to become a supervisor or an executive, you must fully grasp how the activities of all departments are coordinated in a smoothly operating business. This same knowledge will help you as an employee in organizations that empower workers to take responsibility for managing their own work and participating in teams. Understanding management principles and practices will help you contribute as an employee or as a manager in any organization.

 CHECKPOINT

What is a management strategy?

1.3 ASSESSMENT

UNDERSTAND MANAGEMENT CONCEPTS

Determine the best answer for each of the following questions.

1. Which of the following is *not* a projected change in the U.S. workforce by 2050?
   a. a greater percentage of younger workers
   b. more women filling key management and executive positions in business
   c. the percentage of white workers will increase
   d. the fastest growing percentage based on age will be older workers

2. The major factors that should be considered by a company when developing a management strategy include all of the following except the
   a. cost
   b. business
   c. work
   d. business environment

THINK CRITICALLY

Answer the following questions as completely as possible.

3. What are several ways that managers' jobs will be different as a result of the fast pace of change they will be facing in the future?

4. Why should an organization develop a management strategy rather than allow each manager to do what he or she chooses?

Manager's Perspective on
CAREERS

Now that you have been introduced to management, you might be wondering if a career in management is what you want. You don't have to decide just yet. In the remaining chapters you will develop understanding and skills in business management that will be valuable whether they are an employee or choose to move into management.

CHAPTER CONCEPTS

- The decisions of managers determine what a company will do and how well it will perform. The work of managers can be grouped within four functions: planning, organizing, implementing, and controlling.

- There is typically more than one level of management in most companies. There are more managers at the lower levels and fewer at higher levels.

- The Industrial Revolution changed business practices and businesses. It resulted in large, complex businesses that were difficult to manage and a growing set of economic and social problems.

- Determining the best ways to manage an organization has been an issue facing business leaders throughout history. Four widely accepted management theories are classical management, administrative management, behavioral management, and quality management.

- Managers are affected by change in many ways. Technology, competition, the changing workforce, and the nature of work itself are all important factors that must be addressed.

- An effective business has a management strategy that is planned, consistent, and understood. Every business has a unique set of characteristics that affect its management strategy.

REVIEW BUSINESS MANAGEMENT TERMS

Write the letter of the term that matches each definition. Some terms will not be used.

a. administrative management
b. behavioral management
c. business competition
d. classical management
e. controlling
f. executive
g. implementing
h. Industrial Revolution
i. management
j. management science
k. management strategy
l. manager
m. middle manager
n. organizing
o. planning
p. quality management
q. supervisor

1. Person who completes all four management functions on a regular basis and has authority over other jobs and people.
2. Management theory directed at organizational improvement through understanding employee motivation and behavior.
3. Management theory that studies the way work is organized and the procedures used to complete a job in order to increase worker productivity.
4. The process of accomplishing the goals of an organization through the effective use of people and other resources.
5. Evaluating results to determine if the company's objectives have been accomplished as planned.
6. The careful, objective study of management decisions and procedures in order to improve the operation of businesses and organizations.
7. A manager whose main job is to direct the work of employees.
8. A carefully developed overall approach to leading an organization.
9. Management theory that identifies the most effective practices for organizing and managing a business.
10. Analyzing information and making decisions about what needs to be done.

REVIEW BUSINESS MANAGEMENT CONCEPTS

Determine the best answer.

11. Which of the following statements about the role of managers is true?
    a. Managers are responsible for the success or failure of the company.
    b. Managers make up the greatest percentage of employees in a business.
    c. Managers are responsible for completing the day-to-day work of a business.
    d. Managers spend most of their time planning for the future.

12. The first level of management in a company is typically
    a. executives
    b. supervisors
    c. middle managers
    d. work coaches

13. Executives are likely to spend most of their time
    a. controlling
    b. implementing
    c. organizing
    d. planning

14. The invention of machines that allowed for the faster processing of raw materials began the transformation of work and business and led to
    a. the need for fewer managers
    b. a change from classical management to quality management
    c. the Industrial Revolution
    d. the decline of labor unions

15. The management theory that is directed at organizational improvement through understanding employee motivation and behavior is
    a. quality management
    b. behavioral management
    c. administrative management
    d. classical management

16. Which age group is projected to increase in the workforce by the greatest percentage between 2000 and 2050?
    a. 16–24
    b. 25–40
    c. 41–54
    d. 55 and over

17. Which of the following factors should be considered by a company when developing its management strategy?
    a. the type and characteristics of the business
    b. the type of work and the workers in the company
    c. the business environment
    d. All of the factors should be considered.

APPLY WHAT YOU KNOW

Answer the following questions.

18. Explain the following quote: "Managers make things happen in business."

19. Which of the four management functions most directly affects the daily work of employees? Justify your choice.

20. What is the major difference between the classical theory of management and the administrative theory?

21. How will the changing diversity in the U.S. workforce affect the characteristics of managers in the future?

22. What are some ways to prepare for management careers of the future?

MAKE ACADEMIC CONNECTIONS

Complete the following activities.

23. **Math** During one month, three managers recorded the number of hours they spent on each of the four management functions. Ms. Perez spent 42 hours on planning activities, 26 on organizing activities, 83 on implementing activities, and 57 on controlling activities. Mr. Patton used 65 hours on planning, 24 hours on organizing, 36 hours on implementing, and 59 hours on controlling. Ms. Matsumi spent 18 hours planning, 40 hours organizing, 60 hours implementing, and 74 hours controlling. For each manager, determine the total hours worked during the month and the percentage of time devoted to each management function. Then determine the total percentage of time spent by the three managers on each of the functions. Develop a chart to illustrate the results. What conclusions can you draw from the information in the chart?

24. **History** Use library and Internet resources to gather information about the Industrial Revolution. Identify two positive effects and two negative effects of the Industrial Revolution on business and society. Write a report and include reference citations.

25. **Technology** Use a computer program to create a table with four columns and five rows. Label each of the rows with one of the management theories discussed in lesson 1.2. Then label the first column "Business Advantage," the second column "Business Disadvantage," the third "Employee Advantage," and the fourth "Employee Disadvantage." Think carefully about each approach to management and complete the table by describing an advantage and disadvantage each theory offers to the business and to the employees of the business.

26. **Communication** As a human resources manager at Freedon Web Technologies, the company described in the Reality Check at the beginning of the chapter, you have developed a plan for preparing employees like Eric Berman for the possibility of moving into management. Develop a short presentation that you can give to Freedon's current supervisors identifying several things they can do to help their employees prepare for that possibility.

CASE IN POINT

CASE 1-1: What Makes An Effective Manager?

Amber and Travis are considering careers in business and have hopes of becoming managers someday. Both hold part-time jobs and have seen a number of managers at their work. Amber was even selected to fill in for a short time as the shift supervisor for her work team when the full-time supervisor was on vacation. That gave her a closer view of some of the work managers do and how their job is different from that of employees. Amber shared her experiences with Travis, which led to a discussion of their views of a manager's work.

Travis: *A manager's job is easy if the company hires good employees. All a manager has to do is make sure the work gets done.*

Amber: *Do you really think it is that easy? First, I don't think companies can always find employees who can do the work well. Also, a manager's job involves much more than working with employees.*

Travis: *I think a manager just has to be a good communicator. If a manager can explain clearly what needs to be done, good employees will take it from there.*

Amber: *But what about all of the things that can go wrong in a company that a manager can't plan for? Equipment can break down, new employees may not be well trained, or a big order may require everyone to work overtime.*

Travis: *I read that companies spend a large amount of their training budgets on management development. If you ask me, either you're a good manager or you aren't. I don't think taking classes on how to manage will do much good if you aren't the right type of person.*

Amber: *I might have agreed with you a few years ago, but today it seems that management is much more complicated. In fact, I believe that the problems each manager faces are so different it would be difficult to develop training programs that would benefit all of the managers in a company.*

THINK CRITICALLY

1. Analyze the views of Amber and Travis toward management. With what do you agree or disagree?
2. Do you believe that managers spend most of their time working with employees? Justify your answer.
3. What characteristics are common to all managers' jobs? What are the types of things that would be quite different from one manager's job to another?
4. If you were responsible for developing a training program for managers, what would you include?

CASE 1-2: Improving Quality

Olivia and Leo were returning to their jobs on the production line after completing the first class in the company's Total Quality Management training program.

> Olivia: *That's the first time I've ever been in the same training session with supervisors and managers as well as employees. The trainer said that total quality won't happen without the cooperation of everyone. I hope management believes that.*

> Leo: *I agree. We were told that managers and employees alike can improve the quality of the products we make. Most of the problems I see occur because the materials we use are defective or a production machine breaks down. I'm not sure how we employees can solve those problems.*

> Olivia: *Well, the trainers did say that we would be able to stop production if we spot a quality problem. That will get our manager's attention. However, I'm not sure they will be happy about that. Don't you think we will have problems if we try to stop production?*

> Leo: *Well, the information we were provided showed companies have been very successful when they implemented TQM. Certainly in these times, if we can find ways to be more profitable it will be good for all of us. It seems like management is willing to value our ideas, and I think both you and I can make suggestions on how to improve production procedures.*

> Olivia: *I agree. They told us that at our next training session we would learn new ways to work effectively as a team. That might be interesting if it includes our managers as well. If I see managers doing their part, I'm willing to give it a try.*

THINK CRITICALLY

1. Why might it be unusual for managers and supervisors to be in the same training session as employees?
2. Do you believe that improving quality in a company is more the responsibility of management, employees, or that both share the responsibility? Justify your choice.
3. Why might Olivia be concerned about actually stopping production for a quality issue even when employees were told in training they should do that?
4. What types of suggestions do you believe employees working on a production line could make that might improve the quality of the products?
5. Why would team training that involves managers and employees working together be important for a program like Total Quality Management?

PROJECT My Own Business

First Decisions

Throughout this course, you will participate in a continuing project in which you will plan your own business—a juice bar. This project will require you to gather and analyze information and make decisions about your new business. The section called "My Own Business" at the end of each chapter will guide you through business planning, as you apply what you learned in the chapter to a new business venture.

Juice bars are a part of two industries—fast food and health foods. Although juice bars are popular today, you will want your business to be successful in the future. In this project, you will study information to help you determine the future of your business and make the first specific decisions about it.

DATA COLLECTION

1. Gather information about the size and growth of the health and fitness market as well as the fast-food industry from the Internet, newspapers, magazines, and other publications.
2. In your neighborhood, identify the types of businesses that exist in the areas of fast food and health foods. (Try to include small businesses that operate as part of a larger business, such as a supermarket or health club.) List the name and location of each business, a brief description of the business, and the type of products offered.
3. Find information that identifies the failure rate of new fast-food businesses and health and fitness businesses.
4. Using the Internet and the library or by visiting businesses, identify the common types of products offered by juice bar businesses.

ANALYSIS

1. What factors have led to the growth of juice bars? Is there any evidence that juice bars may not be as successful in the future?
2. What are the advantages and disadvantages of starting a small juice bar business in your community?
3. Create a name for your business. A good business name is short and easy to remember. It should relate to the type of business being operated, should be appealing to prospective customers, and should be different from other similar businesses. You may want to create an interesting design for your business name that could be used on signs and in promotion.
4. Develop an initial business concept. Write a one- to two-paragraph statement that describes the business and a possible location, the most likely customers, and the primary products and services that could be offered.

CHAPTER 2

MANAGEMENT, SUPERVISION, AND DECISION MAKING

2.1 Increasing Management Effectiveness

2.2 Effective Supervision

2.3 Managing with Information

© Shutterstock/Blaj Gabriel

Reality Check

What Does It Take?

Catherine recently applied for a management position at her company. Before her interview, she asked her friend Pia to help her get ready. Pia had been promoted recently and Catherine knew that Pia researched frequently asked questions in management interviews. Pia suggested they meet at their favorite coffee shop so she could share what she knew about interviewing for jobs in management.

"Congratulations on getting an interview," Pia said as she slid into the booth and sat down across from Catherine.

"Thanks. I'm excited, but I'm also nervous. I hope you remember some of the frequently asked interview questions from that list you found. And I really hope you remember some questions from your own interview," Catherine said as she unwrapped a straw and put it in her iced tea.

Pia smiled and said, "What is the most important contribution you could make to this organization as a manager?"

"That's not an easy question to answer," said Catherine as she thought about a number of possibilities.

"It will be even harder if some asks it during an interview and you haven't thought about an answer," cautioned Pia.

Catherine sat up straight and answered the question, "I would be effective at getting the employees I manage to work as a team. I get along well with all of my current co-workers, and I'm often chosen as the leader for special projects."

"Is that your final answer?" Pia asked.

Catherine frowned and said, "I think companies really want managers who can get their employees to work well and not create problems."

"I agree that businesses count on employees doing a good job," said Pia. "But today it seems that many businesses are really concerned about the bottom line. Don't you think it might be more important to a business to have a manager who is good with budgets and who can control costs?"

"You might be right, Pia. Some managers only work with a few employees but all of them must meet their budget and help the business make a profit. I'm not sure what the best answer for that question might be."

What's Your Reaction? How would you answer the question Pia posed about the most important contribution?

Increasing Management Effectiveness

Goals

- Identify three important roles successful managers play in organizations.
- Explain how managers use resources to accomplish the work of an organization.
- List and explain accepted management principles.

Terms

- management role   p. 29
- management principles   p. 32

Management Roles

Managers are responsible for getting the work of an organization accomplished through the efforts of other people. Whether you are a club president, the captain of an athletic team, a parent, or a business manager, it is not easy to get other people to do what you want.

Some managers use threats and punishment to motivate workers. Although these tactics work in some situations and with some workers, they are not always effective. Even if the work is done, it might not be done properly or meet quality standards.

Think about your own experiences with chores, school assignments, and other activities. What motivates you to do your best? One of the main challenges you will face if you decide to be a manager is determining the best ways to work with employees so they will be prepared and motivated to do their jobs well.

Management scientists have studied successful managers to determine what makes them different from those who were not successful. By observing the daily work schedules of managers, the scientists were able to identify important activities of successful managers and group them within three management roles. A **management role** is a common set of activities that make up an important part of a manager's job. Successful managers are communicators, relationship builders, and decision makers.

COMMUNICATORS As communicators, managers need to make sure important information is gathered, used appropriately, and shared with those who need it. They identify important information sources and maintain many communication channels. As a spokesperson, they communicate frequently and clearly within and outside their organization.

RELATIONSHIP BUILDERS As relationship builders, managers represent their organization and maintain effective relationships with others. Within the organization, they work to develop a positive, motivating environment. They interact effectively with other managers, develop and support subordinates, and work to resolve conflicts.

DECISION MAKERS In the role of decision maker, effective managers are constantly on the lookout for new opportunities and areas for improvement. They determine the best way to allocate resources to meet the needs of the organization. They solve problems and take corrective action but also recognize and reward success.

✓ CHECKPOINT

What are the three roles of successful managers?

 **Getting Work Accomplished**

Managers' jobs are organized around four functions—planning, organizing, implementing, and controlling. Every manager determines what needs to be done, who will do it, and what resources will be needed. Just as workers use tools and equipment to complete their jobs, managers have access to resources to get work accomplished. The resources of an organization include people, money, facilities, equipment, and materials.

The most important resource available to managers is the company's employees. Managers determine the work that employees will do. Then they must make sure employees have the things they need to complete that work. Figure 2-1 shows that managers must carefully consider how each of the types of resources can be most effectively used as they plan, organize, implement, and control the work of the organization.

The first step for managers is to develop a plan. The plan shows how each of the types of resources will be used to accomplish the goals of the company. Once the plan is in place, the next management decision is how to organize each type of resource to make sure the plan can be accomplished. Each resource must be available where and when it will be needed. Managers then implement the plan using those resources to complete the work of the company. The last step is controlling. Here, managers check to see whether each of the resources was used effectively or whether changes need to be made.

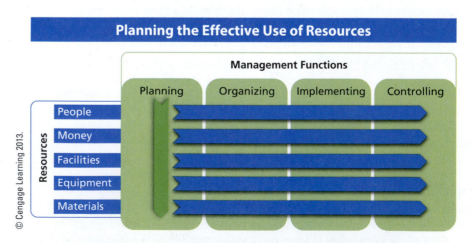

Figure 2-1 Managers make decisions about how the company's resources are used while completing each of the four functions of management.

As an example, consider how an organization manages its resources. The goal of a large preschool is to offer the best educational programs and care possible for the children it serves. The work is completed by teachers, aides, cooks, drivers, and maintenance workers, but the managers must make sure the right people are hired and that every employee has the resources they need to do their jobs. Managers are continually involved in planning, organizing, implementing, and controlling activities.

As a part of planning, managers determine the type and number of people needed to operate the center. A budget is established as well as plans for facilities, equipment, and materials required for all parts of the operation.

In organizing, employees are divided into work teams based on the types of activities they will be completing. Indoor and outdoor space will be planned where children will study, play, eat, and rest. In addition, office space, an employee break room, and perhaps a parking lot will be needed. Money from the budget must be allocated for each of the major activities.

Managers and their work teams then implement the plans using the resources available to them—money, facilities, equipment and materials. Employees must be well trained and work well together. Each job must be done correctly and on schedule to make sure the children, learn, play, eat, and rest. As a part of the controlling function, managers monitor the work of employees and the use of all resources to make sure they are being used as planned. When necessary, changes and improvements will be made. Different menus may need to be developed to control costs while providing nutritious meals and snacks. The play area may need to be reorganized to reduce the chance of accidents.

As you can see, while other employees will complete most of the activities in the operation of the preschool, managers are responsible for their work and the success of the business. They must make sure the employees have the resources they need and that those resources are used as planned.

 CHECKPOINT

How can managers make effective decisions about how the work of an organization is accomplished?

Principles of Effective Management

Businesses are quite different today compared to those of one hundred, fifty, and even twenty years ago. As businesses change, what it takes to be an effective manager has changed as well. Along the way, scientists and business people have studied the changes and effective management practices. They have identified things effective managers do well and ways managers can develop and improve their management skills.

Project plans help managers coordinate their work. What types of planning would a major construction project require?

© iStockphoto/Goodluz

From the studies of effective organizations and managers, a number of management principles have been identified. **Management principles** are the fundamental guidelines for the decisions and actions of managers. The following six principles of management are well accepted as effective practices.

- Effective managers demonstrate commitment to the current and future success of the organization.
- Effective managers take responsibility for developing and implementing plans to achieve the organization's goals.
- Effective managers identify the resources the organization needs and ensure they are available when and where needed.
- Effective managers organize and coordinate the work of the organization in a way that achieves efficient and effective operations.
- Effective managers recognize the importance of employees and balance those needs with the goals and work of the organization.
- Effective managers monitor activities and results to identify ways the organization can be improved.

Managers need to be consistent and objective in their work. They cannot rush to judgments, let biases affect their decisions, or act in their own self-interests rather than those of the organization and its employees.

Effective managers prepare carefully for their work. They spend time gathering and reviewing information before they act. They consider the possible effects of their decisions on other parts of the organization as well as the area they manage. They think about the possible long-term effects of their actions as well as the immediate results. They consult with other managers and their employees to get additional views and ideas.

Managers want the very best for their organization and the people they work with. They know that, as managers, the decisions they make and the work they do affect not only themselves but many other people and resources. They take their work seriously and find ways to improve their own effectiveness as well as the effectiveness of their employees.

CHECKPOINT

What are management principles?

2.1 ASSESSMENT

UNDERSTAND MANAGEMENT CONCEPTS

Determine the best answer for each of the following questions.

1. Which of the following is *not* one of the roles of successful managers?
   a. rule enforcer
   b. relationship builder
   c. decision maker
   d. communicator

2. People, money, facilities, equipment, and materials are the _____ of an organization.
   a. tools
   b. resources
   c. work
   d. operations

THINK CRITICALLY

Answer the following questions as completely as possible.

3. Why is it difficult to get employees to do their best work using threats and punishment?

4. Why should managers be concerned about how the decisions they make affect others?

2.2

Effective Supervision

Goals

- Identify the responsibilities of supervisors.
- Describe the day-to-day management activities of supervisors.
- Discuss ways that businesses can improve the skills of supervisors.

Terms

●●● The Supervisor's Job

Supervisors are critical to the success of a business. They are the managers who work directly with nonmanagement employees and are responsible for translating the company's plans into the every day work of the business. One of their most important tasks is to create a work environment that motivates employees to do their best. They make sure all of the work assigned to their area of responsibility is completed on time and that it meets established standards of quality.

As first-level managers, supervisors are responsible for the day-to-day activities of the company's employees. They need to understand and work with both employees and management. They serve as the communication link between management and nonmanagement employees. Supervisors must implement the decisions of management. At the same time, they must solve employee problems and present employee concerns to management.

Supervisors are often promoted into management in the same part of the business where they work. Usually, supervisors are selected from among the most experienced and most skilled employees in an area. However, they will probably have little or no management training.

The job of supervisor will be quite different from the work they had been doing. They may not have the level of confidence or immediately have the same success they were used to as experienced employees. They often need to develop different working relationships with employees than in their previous job. In the past, the employees they worked with were their co-workers. Now employees are their subordinates. A **subordinate** is subject to the authority and control of another person. Supervisors must command respect from the employees who report to them but in a way that encourages employees to do their best. Moving from the role of co-worker to the role of boss is not an easy change. Many supervisors fail due to their inability to make the change.

The effectiveness of a supervisor's job is determined by three factors: (1) the quality of the work of the supervised employees, (2) the efficient use of the company's resources, and (3) the satisfaction of the supervisor's employees. If the employees are not doing the work well, management will not be pleased with the supervisor's performance. If they are not using resources efficiently, a company may not be able to make a profit. And if the employees are not happy with their work, they may not perform their jobs well and may decide to leave the company.

RESPONSIBILITIES OF SUPERVISORS

Supervisors often divide their time between management activities and other work. They are responsible for implementing the plans developed by the company's executives. Supervisors must use the plans to determine what needs to be done and who will be assigned to complete the needed work. Then they must explain the work plans and assignments to their employees. Finally, they need to be able to motivate employees to perform effectively on a day-to-day basis.

One supervisor's job may be very different from another's, especially from those of supervisors in other departments and companies. Employees have different levels of education, training, and experience. Some supervisors manage mostly experienced employees, whereas others may work more with new employees. In spite of the differences in their jobs, however, supervisors still have a common set of responsibilities in all companies.

COMMUNICATE THE GOALS AND DIRECTIONS OF MANAGEMENT TO EMPLOYEES For employees to complete work effectively, they must understand what needs to be done and why. Supervisors must be able to communicate effectively with employees. Good supervisors can show employees the importance of the company's goals and help them see how they can accomplish their own goals by helping the company to be successful. They must use language and actions that are understandable and meaningful.

EXPLAIN EMPLOYEE CONCERNS AND IDEAS TO MANAGEMENT Employees want to feel that they are a part of the company and that management considers their ideas and opinions. Therefore, supervisors must take the time to talk with the people they supervise in order to learn about their concerns and ideas. Then they must communicate what they learn to management and follow up to find out what action was taken. Employees like to work for a supervisor who is interested in them and their ideas. They will work hard for a company that is concerned about them, involves employees in planning and decision making, and takes their ideas and suggestions seriously.

EVALUATE AND IMPROVE EMPLOYEE PERFORMANCE Supervisors get work done through individual employees and work teams. They need to be sure that each employee is performing as effectively as possible. Supervisors regularly conduct performance reviews on each employee. A **performance review** is a procedure that evaluates the work and accomplishment of an employee and provides feedback on performance.

Formal and informal performance reviews can reveal the employee's strengths and weaknesses. Supervisors must be both positive and objective when they complete employee evaluations. Good supervisors discuss evaluations with their employees in ways that contribute to effective understanding, not conflict. They provide rewards and recognition for employees who perform well. They also provide help for employees who are not performing well, so that their skills can be improved. This help might be in the form of advice and coaching, or it might involve additional training. When serious problems occur, supervisors may be required to discipline employees or even recommend termination.

Reasons Employees Leave

Keeping the best employees is a wise business decision. Lack of recognition is a common reason employees give for leaving a company. Other reasons include low wages, lack of opportunities for advancement, and not being asked for input by managers.

ENCOURAGE EMPLOYEES TO DO THEIR BEST WORK How employees feel about their jobs affects their performance. If they are unsure about what they are doing or if the work environment is filled with conflict, employees will not be able to perform well. Supervisors can help to create a comfortable atmosphere in which employees can enjoy their work and do a good job. Employees want to feel accepted and respected. They want to know that they can get help if they have problems. They want others to realize that what they do is important and that they will be recognized for good work.

Supervisors are sometimes called the most important managers in a business. Do you agree or disagree with that statement? Why?

USE RESOURCES EFFICIENTLY Companies won't operate long if they are unable to make a profit. An important part of earning a profit is controlling the costs of the business. Because supervisors are responsible for the day-to-day activities of a business, they have a great deal of control over whether a company makes a profit or suffers a loss. Good supervisors continually look for ways to operate more efficiently and to use resources more effectively. They seek advice from employees and make suggestions to managers on how processes can be improved and costs can be controlled.

 **CHECKPOINT**

List the responsibilities that are common to all supervisors.

●●●● MANAGING DAY-TO-DAY ACTIVITIES

Supervisors are essential to most businesses, because they are directly responsible for the work of employees. Each employee gets direction from a supervisor, and the supervisor is responsible for the work of each employee. Supervisors must be able to complete their own work as well as manage the work of the employees for whom they are responsible. Supervisors are responsible for planning, organizing, implementing, and controlling the daily work of their units. Several management activities are important for day-to-day management. Those activities are described below and some management tools used to complete the activities are shown in Figure 2-2.

SCHEDULING WORK

Supervisors complete daily planning through the use of work schedules. **Work schedules** identify the tasks to be done, employees assigned to the work, and the time frame for completion of each task. Supervisors may be responsible for both full-time and part-time employees. The business may operate 7 days a week and 24 hours a day. Supervisors will have to decide what days of the

Common Tools Used by Supervisors

Memos and Reports

ARBOR SHOES
MEMORANDUM

TO: Peter, Isabelle, Anita
CC: Philip, Marie
FROM: Adam
DATE: 10/25/--
SUBJECT: Holiday Promotions

Just a quick update on the plans for Holiday 20--. As you know, the marketing mix for fourth quarter will depend more heavily than ever on in-store promotions to gain that all-important impulse purchase.

Women's Dress and Evening Shoe Promotion

The tentative theme for the women's dress and evening shoe promotion is lights: Styles to light up your holidays. Components of the promotion include:

• Special lighted display
• 4-color flyer featuring sequined evening wear
• Sparkle-in-the-dark earrings with purchase

Evaluation Checklists

Personnel Evaluation

Work Schedules

Employee Weekly Time Sheet

Figure 2-2 Common tools used by supervisors for day-to-day management include schedules, memos, and forms.

week employees will work and which projects each person will complete. If they schedule too few people, the work will not get done. If they schedule too many employees, costs will increase. Projects may be assigned to individuals or to groups. The people assigned must have the skills to complete the work as well as the motivation to do it and must work well together if they are part of a work team.

Managing time is an important management skill for supervisors. **Time management** involves managing work schedules to achieve maximum productivity. In other words, not wasting time. Supervisors must be able to determine the work to be done, set priorities for the most important work, and ensure that it is completed properly and on time. They must not only use their time effectively, but also help their employees determine how to use their time most effectively each day.

COMMUNICATING WITH EMPLOYEES

Supervisors communicate every day with their employees. Some communications are with individual employees, while others are with the entire work group. Though much of the communication between supervisors and employees is oral, they communicate in writing as well. Increasingly, electronic communications such as e-mail and text messaging are used.

Whether oral or written, communications must be specific and clear. Supervisors need to plan the content of their communications and determine the best method, place, and time to communicate the information. Supervisors should follow up on communications and ask for feedback to make sure the receivers understood the messages. Listening is an important communication skill for supervisors.

CONTROLLING QUALITY

The final daily management skill for supervisors relates to the quality of the work produced. **Quality control** is the process of making sure work meets acceptable standards. In some companies, employees spend a great deal of time correcting errors and redoing work that was not done well the first time. Supervisors can reduce those problems by planning work carefully, developing

21st CENTURY SKILLS

Productivity

Time management is a key to productivity. Managers must know how to develop and implement realistic schedules to achieve short- and long-term goals. They also need to understand the importance of helping employees develop their own time management skills. Many people who have good time management skills at work use the same skills to manage their time away from work.

quality standards, and regularly checking the quality of the work being done. Also, supervisors can help employees recognize the importance of quality work, so the employees will take responsibility for reducing errors and controlling costs.

CHECKPOINT

What are some common management tools used by supervisors and how does each help with day-to-day management responsibilities?

IMPROVING SUPERVISORY SKILLS

One of the most difficult challenges facing new supervisors is understanding the need to spend less time on nonmanagerial activities and more time on management functions. Because supervisors are usually skilled employees, they often want to continue to do the work they were doing before being promoted. At times, they may think that their employees are not doing the job as well as it can be done. Therefore, new supervisors are often tempted to step in and do the job themselves.

If a supervisor spends a little time helping an employee improve his or her work procedures, the employee will usually value the supervisor's support. However, if the supervisor steps in and takes over the employee's task, the employee will resent that action. Both the quality and quantity of the employee's work will suffer and the supervisor will have less time for important management work. Supervisors must rely on their employees to get the work done, so they can concentrate on management activities and use the talents of the people with whom they work.

Today, more companies help supervisors develop and improve their management skills. Many companies provide formal training programs for new supervisors. Employees moving into supervisor positions might, for instance, participate in management classes full-time for a few weeks and then continue training through a series of meetings and short training sessions during their first weeks and months in the new job. Or, they might study training materials, such as books, podcasts, and videos, for several months after they begin their supervisory duties.

Other companies help supervisors develop their skills by paying for them to attend management classes at a nearby college or sending them to management development programs offered by companies specializing in training and development. A newer method of helping supervisors is to provide an experienced supervisor or another manager to serve as a work coach for the new supervisor. A **work coach** is an experienced manager who meets regularly with a new manager to provide feedback and advice.

If companies do not provide training, the new supervisor needs to develop management skills individually by enrolling in classes, attending meetings, reading management books and magazines, participating in professional associations for managers, and other similar activities.

Management MATTERS

Executive Summary

Managers are expected to read a large number of business reports that provide important information. Often reports are long and complex. To help managers recognize, understand, and remember the important information in a report, an executive summary is placed at the beginning. An *executive summary* is a concise overview of the full report. It highlights each major section and summarizes key information.

By reading the executive summary, managers understand what the report is about and what they will learn from it. They can read the full report faster and with greater understanding. They can also use the executive summary as a way to remember the important information at a later date without having to read the entire report again.

What Do You Think? What are some of the advantages to having an executive summary? What are some possible disadvantages?

Supervisors can also use personal computers to access training programs on CDs and online to continue their development. Talking with and observing the work of experienced supervisors is another way to improve management skills.

CHECKPOINT

How does a work coach help a new supervisor?

2.2 ASSESSMENT

UNDERSTAND MANAGEMENT CONCEPTS

Determine the best answer for each of the following questions.

1. As first-level managers, supervisors are responsible for
   a. developing company plans
   b. designing new products and services
   c. day-to-day operations of the business
   d. the overall profit or loss of the business

2. Which of the following is not found in a work schedule?
   a. a list of tasks to be completed
   b. the employees assigned to complete work tasks
   c. the time required to complete work tasks
   d. the way the work tasks will be evaluated

THINK CRITICALLY

Answer the following questions as completely as possible.

3. What are some ways that supervisors can increase the motivation and satisfaction of their employees?

4. Because supervisors are typically among the most experienced and effective employees, why are additional training and education so important?

Total Quality Management

For many years, the approach to business management did not change. Managers believed the best way to be successful was to focus exclusively on the efficient operation of the business. To achieve that goal, managers tried to get more and more work out of employees, make as few changes in products as possible, and find ways to reduce costs, often at the expense of quality.

W. Edwards Deming developed 14 guiding principles for managers that taught them to view their management role in a different way. He suggested that a long-term commitment to quality, customer satisfaction, and employee morale would lead to success. His process led to the development of Total Quality Management (TQM).

TQM touches all aspects of a business. Businesses committed to TQM do the following:

- Look for ways to increase effectiveness and quality.
- Care about customer satisfaction and employee motivation.
- View employees as valuable contributors to success.
- Rely on leadership and cooperation in dealing with employees.
- Encourage teamwork and employee involvement in decision making.
- Use training to improve employee effectiveness and motivation.

A number of tools has been developed to help businesses implement Total Quality Management. A few examples of the tools are:

Flow charts. These identify each step in a procedure and how the steps are related to each other. They can be used to compare how work is being done to how it is supposed to be done in order to reduce errors.

Cause-and-effect analysis. Employee and management teams brainstorm about problems to find solutions. They develop a diagram that lists problems and possible causes and link them together until they discover and agree on the basic problem. Then they can develop solutions.

Scatter diagrams. Data from two different factors are visually plotted on a chart and analyzed to discover relationships. For example, the number of employee absences over a six-month period is compared to the number of product defects to see if the use of temporary employees is related to a reduction in product quality.

Today, quality, customer satisfaction, teamwork, and process improvement are making a difference in business competitiveness.

THINK CRITICALLY

1. Why do many managers find it so difficult to change from traditional approaches to TQM?

2. Many schools are now implementing TQM and teaching students to use its tools. What types of procedures in schools could benefit from TQM?

3. If a school was facing a problem with students regularly being late for classes, how could the school use one of the TQM tools to help solve that problem?

© Shutterstock/Rick Becker-Leckrone

Managing with Information

Goals

- Explain how management information systems and business research help managers with planning and controlling activities.
- Identify the four steps in the problem-solving process and how the process supports decision making.

Terms

- management information system p. 41
- what-if analysis p. 41
- problem p. 43
- symptom p. 44
- contingency plan p. 45

●●●● Using Management Information

Managers must have access to information to do a good job of planning, organizing, implementing, and controlling. They need records on production and sales, personnel, expenses, and profit or loss to make decisions. Data must be collected, organized, and made available to managers so they can make decisions quickly and efficiently.

Even in very small businesses, managers cannot remember all of the information needed to make decisions. In large companies with many managers and hundreds of employees, it is impossible to operate without a systematic way to gather information for managers to use in decision making.

USING MANAGEMENT INFORMATION SYSTEMS

To make information readily available to managers when and where they need it, companies develop management information systems. A **management information system (MIS)** is a computer-based system that stores, organizes, and provides information about a business. Management information systems are discussed in detail in Chapter 12. Every company needs such a system as an important management tool. Computerized information systems help managers develop effective plans and control business operations.

Planning involves making choices. Plans should be based on information from past experience as well as anticipated changes. With an effective management information system, managers can use information to answer "what-if" questions. **What-if analysis** is a systematic way to explore the consequences of specific choices using computer software. A sales manager may ask, "*What if* we increased sales by 5 percent?" Using a computer to analyze the records of past costs and sales will show the manager whether the additional sales will generate more profit or not. An operations manager may ask, "*What if* we replaced our aging fleet of trucks with new, more fuel-efficient models?" Again, the computer analysis will provide the needed information to determine whether the purchase would be cost-effective.

Managers can also use information systems to reduce the amount of time spent on controlling activities. If managers took the time to review all of the information collected on business operations, they would have little time for other activities. Computers can be used to monitor the performance of activities in a

Because of computers and the Internet, managers have much more information available today than ever before. How can too much information actually decrease a manager's effectiveness?

company. If activities are performed as planned and standards are met, no management attention is needed. Managers should become involved only when activities do not occur as planned or results do not meet standards. When managers want to evaluate performance, they can quickly access data from the management information system related to that performance. The data can be used to compare performance to previously established standards or to the performance of a similar group or a previous time period.

BUSINESS RESEARCH

Managers must be careful not to make decisions without sufficient information about the problem or possible solutions. When they need more information to make a good decision, they may need to conduct research. Research is conducted to gather new information not yet included in the management information system. The results of business research can be added to the information available to managers and then used for future decisions.

Business research is conducted in many areas. Wherever and whenever managers need information to make decisions and the needed information is not available, business research should be considered.

Marketing research and product development research are two common areas of study. A marketing manager may want to determine why certain groups of customers are purchasing a product whereas others are not. A proposed new product should not be developed unless research shows that the product can be produced at a profit and that customers are likely to purchase it.

Human resources studies are conducted on such topics as the supply and demand of labor, employee motivation, and training techniques. Financial executives need the results of research that deals with borrowing and investing money. These managers also need research results regarding economic factors, such as the expected economic performance of specific companies or of the industry in which a company operates. The research described as well as other types of research helps executives make important decisions relative to the growth and development of their companies.

Much of the needed business research is done by the business itself. Most large companies have research departments that plan and complete studies related to the specific problems of the company. Because research departments are expensive to maintain, small companies often depend on professional research organizations.

Research centers and faculty members at universities conduct studies that are often helpful to businesses. Various agencies of the federal government undertake extensive research, and much of this information is available to and useful for business. Trade and professional associations conduct research studies that are useful to the particular industries they serve. Companies may also pay research organizations or individual consultants to gather and analyze information to help solve problems or improve decision making.

CHECKPOINT

In addition to conducting their own research, what other sources of business research are available to companies?

●●● Decision Making

In the process of planning, organizing, implementing, and controlling, managers encounter problems that require them to make decisions. Top-level managers make some of the decisions, such as new products to be developed or new markets that the business will enter. Middle managers make other decisions that may result in new ways of organizing work, how to prepare employees for the use of new technology, or improved procedures to reduce the time and cost of a work procedure. First-level supervisors make decisions about the daily operations of their units including work schedules and project assignments. It is important to the overall success of any business that the decisions be made as carefully as possible at every level of management.

PROBLEMS AND DECISION MAKING

Generally, a **problem** is a difficult situation requiring a solution. Problems usually do not have single solutions. Often many possible solutions can be identified. There may be several good solutions, but there may also be several poor solutions. For example, the problem may be to find the most effective and efficient method to ship products from a manufacturing plant in Texas to customers in Montreal, Canada. Possible solutions are to ship by airplane, ship, train, or truck. Depending on the circumstances, any one of the shipping methods could be the best or the worst solution. To find the best solution, managers should follow a systematic approach to solving problems. That problem-solving procedure is outlined in Figure 2-3.

STEPS IN PROBLEM SOLVING

Most problems can be analyzed by completing a series of steps. You may have learned this problem-solving process in other classes, such as a science class. The procedure works as well in business as it does in scientific problem solving.

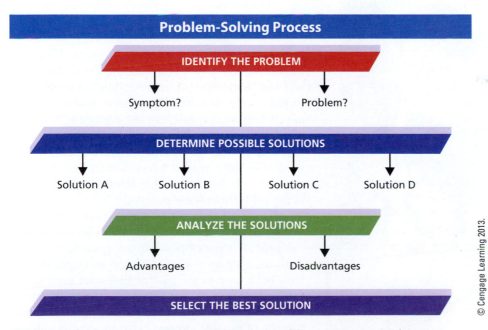

Figure 2-3 Developing an effective solution to a problem requires a step-by-step process.

The four steps in problem solving are (1) identify the problem, (2) list possible solutions, (3) carefully analyze the possible solutions, and (4) select the best solution using the results of the analysis.

IDENTIFY THE PROBLEM Before a manager can make a decision to solve a problem, the problem must first be identified. Often, a manager may not even be aware that a problem exists. For example, employees may be unhappy about a co-worker. The manager may not know about the problem unless employees communicate this concern or it begins to affect their work.

A manager must also be careful not to identify a symptom as the problem. A **symptom** is a sign or indication of something that appears to be the problem. When a patient complains of a headache, the headache may be a symptom. The problem could be high blood pressure, a cold, or another illness. Falling sales of a brand of small appliances for a retailer is a symptom. The problem could be ineffective advertising, a bad product location in the store, untrained salespeople, quality problems in the products, poor service, and so on. Therefore, it will be difficult to change the symptom until the problem can be correctly identified and corrected.

What are some reasons that sales are declining? Are fewer customers entering the store? Are customers shopping but deciding not to buy? Are customers buying but then returning the products because they are not performing as expected? Or, are customers using the Internet to buy small appliances rather than buying from the store? Managers can often identify the problem by asking questions and gathering information. They can use the symptom to help determine what type of information needs to be gathered in order to isolate the problem.

Sometimes managers are unaware that problems exist until it is too late. They need to review plans and performance regularly to determine if operations are proceeding as planned. When any evidence appears that suggests a problem, they should study the evidence carefully rather than ignore it. It is better to review symptoms and determine that there is no problem than to wait until problems are so big that they are difficult to correct.

LIST POSSIBLE SOLUTIONS Once they identify a problem, managers should begin to list all possible solutions. For example, if the problem is ineffective advertising, they should list all possible ways to change the advertising. The list might include better advertising design, a change in the advertising media used, the frequency and timing of advertising, as well as other possibilities. Every problem has more than one solution. Managers need to identify at least two solutions and should not overlook any reasonable solution at this point in the problem-solving process.

There are many ways to identify possible solutions. Having a group participate in brainstorming can provide a list of possible solutions for later analysis. Managers should review solutions that have been used in the past or that were used to solve related problems. Discussing the problems with other managers, experienced employees, customers, or outside experts helps to identify solutions. Reading and studying can keep managers aware of new types of solutions.

Good managers follow a clear problem-solving process to handle various kinds of problems that arise in any business. What is your problem-solving style?

© Getty Images/Photodisc

ANALYZE THE SOLUTIONS The third step in problem solving is to analyze the solutions. Managers do this by studying each possible solution separately, then comparing the solutions, and reducing the number of solutions to the best two or three. To study each solution thoroughly and objectively, managers may need information from business records, trade associations, libraries, consultants, government sources, or the Internet. The use of management information systems and business research may be an important part of this step.

After collecting all of the necessary information, managers should examine the strengths and weaknesses of each solution individually. Then they should compare solutions and classify them in some way, such as very desirable, some-what desirable, and least desirable. Some solutions may be too costly or imprac-tical, whereas others may be inexpensive or very practical. For example, in a list of solutions comparing advertising media the business is considering, managers may find that the cost of television advertising is more than is available in the budget, whereas newspaper advertising is affordable. Managers need to compare the solutions on how effectively each will solve the problem, not just how well they treat the symptom. After all the analyses have been completed, two or three solutions may appear to most effectively solve the problem.

For very important decisions, managers may want to conduct an experiment to test one or more solutions before making a final choice. A likely solution may be tested in one part of the organization to see how it works. The results are then compared with those from other tests to determine which was more effective in solving the problem before using it throughout the business. The results of the experiment may eliminate some solutions and identify those that seem be effective.

SELECT THE BEST SOLUTION The last step in problem solving is to make the final decision from among the remaining solutions. Some problems must be solved quickly, but for very important decisions, managers take more time before selecting the solution. Only after careful consideration do they make the final decision and put it into action. For certain problems, managers may be able to make the decision and implement the solution. For others, managers may need to seek the approval or cooperation of other managers before taking action.

After selecting a solution, the managers must determine the best way to implement it and who will be part of the implementation. The problem is not solved just because the solution has been selected and implemented. As imple-mentation proceeds, the managers should gather information to determine if the solution is solving the problem or if they need additional efforts or another solution.

Once again, management information systems will be very helpful in monitor-ing the implementation of the solution and the results. Studying and evaluating the results of solutions to problems is a part of the controlling function for managers.

CONTINGENCY PLANNING

In some situations, managers do not wait for problems to occur. Instead, they anticipate problems and work in advance to develop contingency plans. A **contingency plan** is an alternative course of action to be followed if a specific problem arises.

Contingency planning is similar to problem solving, but the timing is dif-ferent. Rather than waiting for problems to emerge or symptoms to be identi-fied, managers are proactive. They work to identify possible problems that may occur. Then they develop alternative approaches that could be followed if the problem begins to emerge. In contingency planning, more than one problem can be identified. For each problem, just as in problem solving, several alternative solutions should be proposed and evaluated. Based on careful study, managers

Manager's Perspective on

SUCCESS

Take a Time Out
Experts in creative problem solving recommend the use of "incubation," which is a "time-out" stage to let the mind wander, without forcing it to think about any particular aspect of the problem or solution. This stage could be as simple as a lunch break or a good night's sleep. Some of the world's most creative think-ers say some of their best ideas come to them during unfocused quiet time.

choose the best possible alternative. The next step is developing procedures to use if the problem begins to occur.

Contingency plans are not prepared for all possible problems. Businesses often develop contingency plans for new procedures or expensive changes. The development of contingency plans requires an investment of time and money. However, effective contingency plans can be a cost effective way to prevent or quickly solve problems.

 **CHECKPOINT**

List the four steps in problem solving.

2.3 ASSESSMENT

UNDERSTAND MANAGEMENT CONCEPTS

Determine the best answer for each of the following questions.

1. When managers use a management information system, no management action is needed if
   a. activities are performed as planned and standards are met
   b. all employee performance reviews are completed on schedule
   c. there are no changes in the organization
   d. None of the answers is correct.

2. Which of the following is not a step in the problem-solving process?
   a. Analyze the solutions.
   b. Identify the symptoms.
   c. List possible solutions.
   d. Select the best solution.

THINK CRITICALLY

Answer the following questions as completely as possible.

3. Why should managers ask what-if questions when developing plans?

4. How might a business benefit if employees are trained in the decision-making process and encouraged to use that process in their work?

CHAPTER CONCEPTS

- Successful managers are communicators, relationship builders, and decision makers.

- Managers must carefully consider how each of the types of resources can be most effectively used as they plan, organize, implement, and control the work of the organization. Successful managers understand, believe in, and follow a set of principles to guide their decisions and actions.

- As first-level managers, supervisors are responsible for the day-to-day activities of the company's employees. One of their most important tasks is to create a work environment that motivates employees to do their best. They also serve as a communications link between employees and management.

- Every company needs a management information system to help managers reduce the amount of time they spend on controlling activities. Data must be collected, organized, and made available to managers so they can make decisions quickly and efficiently.

- Effective problem solving involves identifying the problem, listing possible solutions, analyzing the possible solutions, and selecting the best solution based on the results of the analysis.

REVIEW BUSINESS MANAGEMENT TERMS

Write the letter of the term that matches each definition.

1. A common set of activities that make up an important part of a manager's job.
2. A computer-based system that stores, organizes, and provides information about a business.
3. A difficult situation requiring a solution.
4. A procedure that evaluates the work and accomplishment of an employee and provides feedback on performance.
5. A sign or indication of something that appears to be the problem.
6. A systematic way to explore the consequences of specific choices using computer software.
7. An experienced manager who meets regularly with a new manager to provide feedback and advice.
8. Schedules identifying the tasks to be done, employees assigned to the work, and the time frame for completion of each task.
9. Someone who is subject to the authority and control of another person.
10. The fundamental guidelines for the decisions and actions of managers.

a. management information system (MIS)
b. management principles
c. management role
d. performance review
e. problem
f. subordinate
g. symptom
h. what-if analysis
i. work coach
j. work schedules

REVIEW BUSINESS MANAGEMENT CONCEPTS

Determine the best answer.

11. Which of the following statements about the roles of managers is true?
    a. They should avoid sharing most information with others in the organization.
    b. They avoid getting in the middle of conflicts between employees.
    c. They solve problems and take corrective action but also recognize and reward success.
    d. None of the statements are true.

12. The first level of management in a company is typically
    a. executives
    b. supervisors
    c. middle managers
    d. work coaches

13. Which of the following is *not* one of the factors that determines the effectiveness of a supervisor's job?
    a. the quality of work of the supervised employees
    b. the efficient use of the company's resources
    c. increases in the company's total profits
    d. the satisfaction of the supervisor's employees

14. An appropriate way to improve the quality of work accomplished in a supervisor's work area is for the supervisor to
    a. spend a short amount of time helping an employee improve their work procedures
    b. step in and take over the work of an employee who is not performing correctly
    c. schedule more employees than are required to complete the work
    d. All of the answers are correct.

15. New information not yet included in a management information system can be gathered by
    a. conducting research
    b. asking what-if questions
    c. reviewing company records
    d. asking employees

16. The first step in the problem-solving procedure is to
    a. conduct research
    b. identify possible symptoms
    c. analyze several solutions
    d. locate and identify the problem

APPLY WHAT YOU KNOW

Answer the following questions.

17. Why is it sometimes difficult for managers to get others to do what they want them to do?

18. Which of the three management roles do you believe is the most important? Which is the most difficult?

19. Why is it important for managers to consider all of the types of resources needed when completing planning activities?

20. What are some reasons the best employee in a job may not make the best supervisor for other people in that job?

21. Why are most supervisors required to divide their time between supervisory responsibilities and other work?

22. Of the five areas of responsibility of supervisors, which do you believe is the most important to the success of the company, and why?

23. What are some ways that supervisors can help employees manage their time better?

24. What skills do supervisors and other managers need in order to manage business information effectively?

MAKE ACADEMIC CONNECTIONS

Complete the following activities.

25. **Math** Elisha supervises three full time employees: Jack, Samantha, and Pope. Each work 7 hours a day for 35 hours each week. Elisha also has two part-time employees: Jaysun, who can work Tuesday and Thursday for a total of 10 hours; and Sonji, who can work Monday, Wednesday, and Friday for a total of 15 hours. Elisha has three projects that must be completed next week. Project 1 will requires 55 hours and must be completed by the end of the week. Project 2 requires 38 hours and must be completed by Tuesday night. Project 3 requires 42 hours and must be completed by Thursday night. No more than three people can work on a project at one time. Elisha can devote 10 hours during the week to project work if needed. Use a computer to prepare a chart or table of a daily work schedule for Elisha's team. Show the employees assigned to each project and the amount of time each will work on the project.

26. **Reading** Many supervisors are using small tablet computers as a daily part of their work. They can access production records, performance data, and even individual employee information as needed on the job to speed decision making. Read several articles and blogs on the Internet that discuss the use of tablet computers by managers. Write a summary of your findings that includes the advantages and problems of using the technology.

27. **Writing** A list of symptoms of business problems follows. For each symptom, write a question that could be used to help identify the actual problem.

    a. The number of products returned by customers has increased greatly in the last six months for an e-commerce company.

    b. Three employees who have worked for the company less than a month quit without giving notice.

    c. Advertising costs have increased by 10 percent this year.

    d. The number of customers who have overdue credit accounts has doubled in the past six months.

    e. Employees have been given the authority to stop the assembly line anytime they notice a defective product. Since that decision was made, work stoppages have increased by four per week.

CASE IN POINT

CASE 2-1: FRUSTRATIONS OF A NEW SUPERVISOR

Steve was leaving the supervisors' meeting when his work coach, Fran, caught up with him and asked, "Do you have time for a quick break?"

When they were settled in the break room, Fran said, "Is something bothering you, Steve? I noticed you were unusually quiet in today's meeting."

Steve sighed, "I've been a supervisor now for almost a year but sometimes I don't think the older managers believe I can do the job."

"As I recall, you got a very good performance review last month with only a few suggestions for improvement." Fran responded. "What happened to cause your current feelings?"

"I like to get input from my employees about ways we can do our work better," Steve explained. "But when I share those ideas with other supervisors, they often say things like, 'It's probably not a good time to make changes since we are on such a tight schedule.' Or, 'My employees don't say much so I think they are pretty satisfied with the way we are doing things now.' Sometimes I get so frustrated I just want to go ahead and make the change with my employees and show the other supervisors it can work."

"It's often easier for experienced managers to keep doing things the way they've always been done rather than trying to make changes. And, they may not try to get the type of input from their employees that you do," responded Fran. "You're a younger supervisor and closer to the age of many of the employees you work with. Also, your team members know you just moved up from an employee position, so they may believe you have a better understanding of their experiences."

"I really am enjoying my new work," said Steve. "Moving into a management job certainly isn't easy and I know I have a lot to learn. I do try to listen carefully to the more experienced supervisors. But I also believe I have some good ideas and want to share them as well. I would be happy with constructive criticism, but usually it seems like outright rejection. It is so frustrating."

"I can see how that would be frustrating for you. Let's talk about ways you might gain their support."

THINK CRITICALLY

1. What are some reasons that the experienced managers don't respond positively to Steve's suggestions?
2. Do you think other managers may be right when they advise Steve that it isn't the right time to make changes? Why or why not?
3. What might happen if Steve goes ahead with his plan to make changes with his employees rather than getting approval and cooperation from other supervisors?
4. If you were Steve's work coach, what advice would you give him on how to get his employees' ideas accepted by others?

CASE 2-2: MEETING THE STANDARD

A'yanna Lyons is the manager of the accounting department for the Hemmerle Supply Company, an office supplies wholesaler. As the manager, she is responsible for all of the work completed by the employees in the accounting department, including its quality and quantity. A'yanna was proud of the work her employees did. They had a high level of motivation and always seemed to do their best to complete the work assigned to them. The entire department seemed committed to being an asset for the company. Therefore, she was surprised by feedback she received on a work issue that affected her department.

Hemmerle had recently established a new standard that invoices would be prepared, printed, and mailed to customers within 24 hours of receiving the order. Although the new standard presented a big challenge to the accounting department, A'yanna had worked with her teams to do their part to meet the standard. By reorganizing the way they did their work and using a new computer tracking system for each order, the department was able to complete the invoice process within half a day from the time they received the information from the shipping department.

After the new procedures were in place, A'yanna had carefully checked the work of her department. Although there had been a few times when an employee absence or a problem with the new computer software had slowed the work, the department was meeting its standard of processing invoices in half a day 93 percent of the time. However, in the first productivity report she received that tracked the company's progress in meeting the 24-hour standard, A'yanna learned that 25 percent of the invoices were being mailed three days after the order was received. Upon checking further, she discovered two things. First, her department did not always receive the necessary information from the shipping department on schedule. Second, the mail room was having trouble meeting its goal of making sure that invoices received before noon went out the same day.

THINK CRITICALLY

1. What are some possible problems in this situation? Identify problems that could be occurring in the accounting department as well as in other departments of the company.
2. List the symptoms of the problems. Explain why you believe the things you listed are symptoms rather than problems.
3. What are some alternative solutions?
4. How would you suggest that A'yanna proceed in this situation?
5. How can a management information system contribute to resolving this situation?

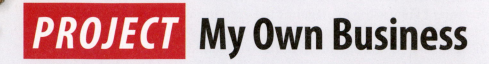

PROJECT My Own Business

Preparing for the Management Function

The failure rate for new small businesses is fairly high. Many people start a business without considering the difficulty of the process, the time required to manage a business, and the costs of starting a new business and operating it until it can become profitable. One of the major reasons for failure is that the owner does not practice effective management skills. Many new business owners have never been managers or have managed only a specialized part of another business. They have not had the experience of being responsible for all aspects of managing. Few new business owners have undertaken any type of management training to prepare themselves for their new role.

To increase the chances of success for your new business, you need to prepare yourself for your new role as owner and manager. Through your study of management, you are now aware of all of the functions that top managers and executives perform. You know that you will have to devote much of your time to management activities in order to complete all the major management functions. In addition, you must be prepared to identify and solve problems before they negatively affect the business.

DATA COLLECTION

1. Survey five managers of small businesses. Ask them to identify the types of activities they commonly perform during the day and estimate the amount of time they spend on each activity during the typical day. Use your own judgment to classify the activities within the four management functions. You may also need a category for nonmanagement activities. Prepare a chart to illustrate your findings on how small-business managers spend their time.
2. Identify two problems you expect to face in operating your business. Complete the steps in problem solving to develop an appropriate solution. As you analyze possible solutions, identify several sources of useful information, including business research.

ANALYSIS

1. Develop a chart with four headings: Planning, Organizing, Implementing, and Controlling. Under each heading, list the activities you will need to complete to manage your juice bar effectively.
2. Under the list of activities developed above, estimate (a) how much time you will need to devote to each activity and (b) when you will need to complete each activity during a typical month. Then develop a sample monthly calendar on which you schedule management activities.
3. For each problem identified in the data collection section above, select the solution you believe is likely to be most effective. Then develop a contingency plan listing the procedures to follow to accomplish each solution and prevent the problem from occurring.

© Getty Images/Huntstock

Reality Check

Can a Leader Be Popular?

Brittany and Foster shared their thoughts after attending a political debate. Because the election for the city's mayor and council members was only three weeks away, their government and economics teachers asked students to attend the debate and then discuss the candidates the next day in class. Each student was asked to identify the characteristics they believed were most important for the office of mayor and be prepared to discuss each candidate using those characteristics.

Brittany: *Our city is growing rapidly and has a lot of problems. We need a mayor who's a problem solver and willing to make tough decisions. I don't know if any of the candidates showed me they were willing to do that.*

Foster: *I think as politicians they want people to like them. They all seem to be effective communicators but don't want to say anything that will upset voters. Do you really think they can do what has to be done for the city without making some people upset with them?*

Brittany: *Running a city is just like managing a large company. If you're a good manager and the business is successful, people will be satisfied.*

Foster: *I'm not sure. Being mayor of a city and manager of a large business may be similar in some ways. But a manager can make decisions that are best for the business and still have dissatisfied employees and customers. I don't think a mayor can risk upsetting voters even if a decision seems to be best for the city's future.*

Brittany: *I think we both agree that it's not easy to lead a large organization, whether it's a city or a business. It's hard to decide what the most important characteristics of an effective manager or mayor should be.*

What's Your Reaction? Does it take the same type of leadership to be the mayor of a city as it does to manage a large business?

3.1

The Importance of Leadership

Goals

- Recognize the importance of leadership and human relations.
- Identify important leadership characteristics and types of power.
- Describe four types of power available to leaders.

Terms

- leader p. 54
- leadership p. 54
- human relations p. 54
- power p. 57
- position power p. 57
- reward power p. 57
- expert power p. 57
- identity power p. 57

●●● The Importance of Leadership

Anyone who holds a responsible position in an organization must have a number of qualities to meet his or her responsibilities successfully. One of the key qualities for a manager at any level is effective leadership. If you plan a career in business, you need to develop your leadership skills.

Many years ago, managers were totally responsible for all decisions in a business. Today, many businesses seek input from employees and want them to be involved in problem solving and decision making. Managers need to be leaders of their employees as well as managers of the business. Employees who are interested in moving into management positions in the future can look for opportunities to take on leadership roles as a way to develop important skills needed by managers.

LEADERSHIP IN BUSINESS

Managing a business, whether large or small, is certainly not simple. Managers are responsible for getting the work of an organization accomplished through its employees. To be most productive, employees must understand why their work is important and be motivated to do the work. Generally, employees want to contribute to the success of the business. They appreciate managers who value their ideas as well as their work. Employees respond well to managers who are also effective leaders. A **leader** earns the respect and cooperation of employees to effectively accomplish the work of the organization. **Leadership** is the ability to influence individuals and groups to cooperatively achieve common goals.

Leaders have excellent human relations skills. **Human relations** refers to how well people get along with each other when working together. A group of people who respect each other and work well together will likely do better work than groups characterized by negative feelings, misunderstandings, hostility, and a lack of respect for each other. In a negative group atmosphere, individuals—and often the entire group—will do things that interfere with the group's success rather than contributing to it. You can probably think of groups that do not work well together. How do the members treat each other? How do they spend their time when the group is together? Usually it is not enjoyable to be part of a group with poor human relations. A leader not only demonstrates effective human relations skills but also helps others to develop these skills.

DEVELOPING AS A LEADER

A manager can contribute to effective or ineffective human relations. Because managers have a responsibility for getting work done through others, relationships are important. Not every manager is currently an effective leader, but leadership skills can be developed. Because leadership is so important in business, most management training programs today emphasize leadership and effective human relations.

✓ CHECKPOINT

Why do leaders need human relations skills?

●●●● Leadership Characteristics

Although managers have many responsibilities, one of the most important is creating an atmosphere that encourages employees to do their best work to make the business successful. Individual employees, however, have their own goals and needs. Employees will be most productive when the work meets their needs as well as those of the company. Managers should recognize and help to meet important needs of each employee while also accomplishing the goals of the business. Success in this task requires leadership.

Because leadership is directly related to the success of an organization, it is important that managers develop leadership characteristics. Leaders help employees get work done correctly and willingly. A poor manager may be able to get employees to perform the necessary tasks, but the work may be done poorly and inefficiently. A good manager, on the other hand, creates a work environment in which employees enjoy their work and want to do a good job.

Researchers have studied leaders in order to identify the characteristics that make them successful. Common characteristics of effective leaders are described in Figure 3-1. Having those characteristics does not ensure that a person will be a good manager. Leaders must also understand the work to be done, and the business must be well organized with the resources needed to accomplish the work. In addition, managers must be able to plan, organize, implement, and control the work and employees for which they are responsible.

Leadership characteristics are personal qualities rather than specific ways that managers behave. Each company, each job, and each situation is different. Leadership characteristics prepare managers to be responsible yet flexible and able to adjust to changes. Two managers who possess the same leadership qualities will probably respond in different ways to specific situations but will be able to work well with people to get the necessary work accomplished.

Think of someone you know in a leadership position. What makes that person effective? How could his or her leadership be improved?

© Getty Images/Digital Vision

Common Leadership Traits

INTELLIGENCE

Leaders use their intelligence to study, learn, and improve their management skills. They also help the people they work with to develop new skills. Leaders must use their intelligence effectively.

JUDGMENT

Leaders must make many decisions. They consider facts carefully, gather new information, and apply knowledge and experience.

OBJECTIVITY

Leaders must be able to look at all sides of a problem and not make biased judgments or statements. They gather information and do not rush into actions before considering the possible results. They value individual differences, and try to avoid reacting to stereotypes or first impressions.

INITIATIVE

Leaders have ambition and persistence in reaching goals. They are self-starters who plan what they want to do and then do it. They have drive and are highly motivated. They encourage others to be involved, take actions, and make decisions when appropriate.

DEPENDABILITY

Those who lead are consistent in their actions, and others can rely on them. They do not make promises that cannot be fulfilled. When they make a commitment, they follow through, and expect others to do the same. The people they work with can count on them for help when needed.

COOPERATION

Leaders understand the importance of other people and enjoy being with them. They strive to work well with others. They understand that people working together can accomplish more than the same people working alone. They devote time and effort to building cooperative relations.

HONESTY

Leaders are honest and have high standards of personal integrity. They are ethical in decisions and their treatment of others.

COURAGE

Leaders possess the courage to make unpopular decisions and try new approaches in solving problems. They are willing to take risks to support others.

CONFIDENCE

Leaders have a great deal of self-confidence. They attempt to make the best decisions possible and trust their own judgment. They respect others and expect quality work.

STABILITY

Leaders are not highly emotional. You can depend on their reactions. They work with others to solve problems and reduce conflicts.

UNDERSTANDING

Leaders recognize that the feelings and ideas of others are important. They try to understand the people they work with. They encourage others to share their ideas, experiences, and opinions and show that each person is a valuable member of the organization.

© Cengage Learning 2013.

Figure 3-1 Effective leaders possess many of the characteristics listed above.

21st CENTURY SKILLS

Leadership

If you want your team to be successful, the team will need both an effective leader and cooperative and supportive team members. Many of the traits of effective leaders are needed by team members as well.

 **CHECKPOINT**

How do leadership characteristics help managers do their work?

●●● Influencing People

Managers influence people to accomplish the work of the organization. However, there are both negative and positive ways to influence others. Just because managers can get others to do what they want does not mean that the managers are effective leaders.

MANAGEMENT POWER

Managers can influence employees because of their power. **Power** is the ability to control behavior. There are several ways that managers obtain power. The type of power will determine how employees respond to managers. Four types of power available to managers and the source of each type are summarized in Figure 3-2.

Position power comes from the position the manager holds in the organization. If a manager is an employee's boss, the manager has the power to give directions and expect the employee to complete that work. If the manager does not directly supervise the employee, the manager's directions are more requests than orders. The manager does not have the position power to tell that employee what to do.

Reward power is power based on the ability to control rewards and punishments. If a manager can determine who receives new equipment, preferred work schedules, or pay increases, or can penalize people for poor work or inappropriate performance, employees are likely to respond to that manager's requests.

Expert power is power given to people because of their superior knowledge about the work. When workers are unsure of how to perform a task or need information to solve a problem, they may turn to an expert. Experts are able to influence behavior because of the knowledge and skill they have.

Identity power is power given to people because others identify with and want to be accepted by them. If an employee respects a manager and wants recognition and support from that person, the employee will likely do what the manager requests. Experienced or well-liked employees often have identity power. Those people can influence the work of others in the organization even though they are not managers.

Types of Management Power	
TYPE OF POWER	**RESULTS FROM**
Position	The manager's position in the organization
Reward	The manager's control of rewards/punishments
Expert	The manager's knowledge and skill
Identity	The employee's perception of the manager

© Cengage Learning 2013.

Figure 3-2 Managers use power to influence the behavior of employees.

USING POWER EFFECTIVELY

An analysis of the types of power shows that managers can influence employees because of their position or because of the rewards and punishments they control. However, those types of power are not related to leadership characteristics. Employees do not grant those types of power to managers. Position and reward power come from the manager's position in the company. If a manager has only position and reward power, employees may do the requested work but may not do it willingly or well.

However, expert and identity power come from employees, not position in the company. Employees grant these kinds of power to managers they believe deserve it. If employees consider the manager to be an expert, they will seek the manager's advice and help. If employees want the approval or positive recognition of the manager, they will work cooperatively and support the requests of the manager. Both expert and identity power are related to effective leadership characteristics.

Sometimes people other than managers have power in an organization. Other employees can influence people's behavior because they can control rewards and punishments, they are considered experts, or other employees identify with them and want their approval. If those powerful employees support the work of the organization, they can have a positive influence on other employees. On the other hand, employees

Employees are willing to work hard when they are satisfied with their jobs. Do employees as well as managers have a responsibility for increasing job satisfaction?

© Getty Images/Photodisc

with power can be disruptive if their needs and goals differ from those of the organization. Employees may choose to be influenced by those people rather than by their managers.

 CHECKPOINT

Which types of power are related to effective leadership characteristics?

3.1 ASSESSMENT

UNDERSTAND MANAGEMENT CONCEPTS

Determine the best answer for each of the following questions.

1. Leadership ability is important to managers because
   a. a manager without leadership skills has no way to influence employee behavior
   b. businesses will not hire a manager without leadership skills
   c. leadership helps managers satisfy employees' needs while also meeting the goals of the business
   d. managers must get work done whether employees want to do it or not.

2. Power given to people because of their superior knowledge about the work is
   a. identity power
   b. expert power
   c. reward power
   d. position power

THINK CRITICALLY

Answer the following questions as completely as possible.

3. Why are leadership characteristics important for employees to develop as well as for managers?

4. How can the inappropriate use of power by managers have a negative effect on employees? How might it negatively affect the business?

3.2

Developing Leadership Skills

Goals

- Discuss why businesses value leadership skills of managers and employees.
- Identify and define five important human relations skills.

Terms

- self-understanding p. 61
- team building p. 62

 **Leadership in Business**

People are not born leaders. People develop their leadership qualities through experience, training, and personal development. For example, anyone can learn to be dependable, to take initiative, and to cooperate with others. Becoming an effective leader requires commitment, preparation and practice.

Managers need to be leaders. However, they are not the only people in an organization who need leadership skills. Many businesses are using employee teams to plan work and make decisions. The team may include a manager, although many do not. Even when a manager is a part of the team, the leader of the group will not always be the manager. As the team completes various projects, individual team members may assume leadership for specific activities. If the team is well organized, the leaders often have expert and identity power that help to get individual projects completed. The entire team may be given position and reward power by the organization that they can use as they plan and implement team activities and to encourage the achievement of the team goals.

Today, companies frequently evaluate applicants' leadership abilities before hiring them. Companies often prefer to hire employees who have already developed many leadership characteristics and have had leadership experience. Training programs for employees often emphasize team building and leadership development. Some companies allow employees to volunteer for leadership training, whereas others expect everyone to participate. Companies recognize that employees with leadership skills can make valuable contributions to a business's success. It is important to take advantage of leadership development opportunities whenever they occur.

✓ CHECKPOINT

What are ways that businesses develop the leadership skills of employees?

 **Human Relations**

Managers are continually interacting with employees, other managers, customers, and others who have interest in the work of the business. Because of these contacts, managers need human relations skills. They must maintain good working relationships with others both inside and outside the business and help employees work well together.

Human relations involve several skills. Those skills may be just as important to the success of a business as the ability to make decisions or operate a complicated piece of equipment. Important human relations skills include (1) self-understanding, (2) understanding others, (3) communication, (4) team building, and (5) developing job satisfaction.

SELF-UNDERSTANDING

To work well with others, managers must have self-understanding. **Self-understanding** involves an awareness of your attitudes and opinions, your leadership style, your decision-making style, and your relationships with other people.

Employees look to managers for information and direction. They want managers to be able to make decisions, solve problems, and communicate expectations. If managers understand themselves and what other people expect of them, they can decide on the best way to work with people and the type of leadership to use. They can use the understanding of their strengths, weaknesses, and how others perceive them to improve their skills as managers.

UNDERSTANDING OTHERS

Every individual is different. Each person has a different background as well as different attitudes, skills, and needs. A manager cannot treat everyone the same way. Some people want a great deal of support and regular communication from their supervisor; others do not. Some employees want managers to consult them when making important decisions, whereas others do not care to be involved in decision making. Some people work harder when praised; others expect managers to tell them when their work needs improvement.

Managers need to know the best way to work with each employee. They need to be able to satisfy individual workers' needs and, at the same time, accomplish the goals of the company. The leader who works hard to get to know each person and his or her needs will be a better manager.

Many human relations problems occur when managers fail to recognize the unique qualities and differences among employees. Should all employees be treated the same by a manager? Why or why not?

COMMUNICATION

Effective communication is essential in business. Managers spend much of their time communicating. When communication breakdowns occur, human relations problems will likely develop.

Managers must understand what information needs to be communicated and what methods to use. They need to know when too much communication is occurring and when there is not enough. Managers need to understand and use official lines of communication. They need to communicate effectively with other managers, employees, and other individuals and groups within and outside of the business.

Managers do not just provide information, although they must be skilled in both written and oral communications. Listening is an important communication skill as well. By listening to employee concerns, managers can identify problems, determine needs, and respond to them more effectively.

© Getty Images/Photodisc

Management MATTERS

Diversity

Most workforces are diverse in terms of age, gender, education, race, nationality, and culture. Managers are responsible for establishing and maintaining a work environment where effective interactions and communication occur among employees who may have quite different backgrounds and experiences. As a manager you should:

- Be aware that your background may cause you to misunderstand others. At the same time, others might misinterpret your actions or statements.
- Get to know each person you work with. Treat all employees and their work with respect and high expectations.
- Communicate with employees in ways that they understand and make them most comfortable.
- Encourage open dialogue about diversity issues within your workgroup and across the business.
- Avoid offensive actions and language and don't tolerate them from anyone.
- Continue to learn more about others' cultures and backgrounds by broadening your interests, reading, travel, and participating in cultural events.

What Do You Think? Do you think managers are solely responsible for creating an effective work environment with a diverse workforce? What are the responsibilities of employees?

The language and methods used in communication are both important. Managers must communicate with employees in language they can understand. They must use methods employees expect and are comfortable with. When employees are involved in planning and decision making, managers are responsible for communicating their employees' ideas and concerns to upper management.

TEAM BUILDING

People want to feel that they are a part of a team, that they are important, and that they can count on other team members. **Team building** means getting people to support the same goals and work well together to accomplish them. Teams that take responsibility for work and pride in the results reduce the amount of time managers must spend monitoring the team's work.

DEVELOPING JOB SATISFACTION

Most people who work at a job for any length of time are not totally satisfied or dissatisfied with their jobs. However, some people enjoy their work much more than others. An employee's feelings about work may be very different from one day to the next. There are many reasons for these differences. Job satisfaction can be influenced by factors such as the personal characteristics of employees and managers, individual needs, the people with whom the employees work, and the actual work itself. Factors outside the job can also have an influence on job satisfaction.

Managers must be aware of the differences among their employees to help them maintain a high level of job satisfaction. For example, when two people with different backgrounds, values, and needs must work together, they may initially have difficulty relating to each other. Managers may want to develop activities that help employees get to know each other. Companies should offer training and development opportunities to improve the human relations skills of employees and managers.

People should be carefully matched with the kind of work they perform, because personal characteristics can affect job performance. A shy person, or one who enjoys working alone, might perform better as a computer maintenance tech than as a computer salesperson. A person who does not pay close attention to details may not be an effective quality inspector on a production line. Human resources departments often test new employees or those seeking a promotion in order to match people with appropriate jobs. Whenever possible, managers should match the job tasks with the needs and interests of the employees and watch people when they begin new tasks to identify possible problems.

 **CHECKPOINT**

What are five important human relations skills?

A satisfied employee is a more productive employee. How can employees be matched to the jobs they will enjoy?

3.2 ASSESSMENT

UNDERSTAND MANAGEMENT CONCEPTS

Determine the best answer for each of the following questions.

1. Which of the following statements about leadership is true?
   a. For the most part, effective leaders are "born" with many leadership skills.
   b. Businesses prefer to develop the leadership skills of employees rather than hire people with those skills.
   c. The leader of a work team is usually the employees' manager.
   d. With proper training, most people can become effective leaders.

2. Getting people to support the same goals of the company and work well together to accomplish them is called
   a. human relations
   b. team building
   c. management
   d. leadership

THINK CRITICALLY

Answer the following questions as completely as possible.

3. How would you demonstrate to a prospective employer that you have already developed some important leadership skills?

4. Which of the human relations skills do you believe are most important for a manager in working with employees? Justify your choice.

Focus On...Ethics

Costs Versus Jobs

EndCore is a packaging manufacturer. The third production unit produces cardboard boxes. EndCore led the industry in total box sales for 20 years. However, during the past five years, it fell to fifth place in sales. Competing businesses have gradually increased the quality of their products while still undercutting EndCore in product prices.

EndCore employees are trained for specific production jobs that have changed little over time. Because of the declining performance, EndCore management determined it had to cut costs and improve sales. They decided to involve employees in the process, hoping that would encourage employees to accept any changes that needed to be made. The company made a commitment to the new approach and the teams were formed and trained for their new roles.

The unit three team had to find ways to reduce production costs. After considerable study, the team was able to develop an improved method to assemble the boxes. The process increased production using the same number of employees and cut the amount of cardboard waste resulting in a cost savings of about 4 percent. This still left the company's costs just slightly higher than those of competitors.

While looking for other ways to reduce costs, the team learned of a new automatic glue machine that was coming on the market. EndCore always hand-glued its boxes because the quality of the seals was much better. Gluing was a major part of the process, involving more than 15 percent of the employees. The new machine completely automated the gluing process and increased the speed with which boxes could be assembled. It had a 98 percent reliability rating—equal to that of the hand-gluing method. The cost of the machines was just under $3 million. However, the cost would be recovered in three years because production could be increased by 5 percent, with a reduction in labor costs of 12 percent. Using the gluing machines would put EndCore's costs below the competitor's by more than 2 percent without sacrificing quality.

The employee team had found a way to make the company competitive. But implementing it would mean at least 30 employees would lose their jobs. The team had to decide whether to recommend the improved assembly process or purchasing the new gluing machine.

THINK CRITICALLY

1. What are advantages and disadvantages of the two solutions identified by the employee team from management's viewpoint and from employees' viewpoint?
2. What responsibility does the employee team have to management and to other employees in making a recommendation?
3. What recommendation do you believe the employee team should make? Why?

© Shutterstock/Rick Becker-Leckrone

Leadership Styles

Goals

- Describe three views of employees that affect the type and amount of management supervision.
- Differentiate among three leadership styles.

Terms

- leadership style p. 66
- autocratic leader p. 66
- democratic leader p. 67
- open leader p. 68
- situational leader p. 69

●●●● Management Views of Employees

Individual managers often deal with employees in very different ways. Managers' attitudes about people and work affect the way they do their jobs and treat the people they supervise. Good managers are able to adjust their management style to the characteristics of the people they supervise and to the situation.

CLOSE MANAGEMENT

Some managers believe employees will not perform their work well unless they are closely managed. This attitude results from a feeling that employees are not very interested or motivated and work only because they have to. With this attitude, managers are likely to assume that employees will not work any harder than necessary and will try to avoid responsibility. These managers expect that they will have to find ways to force employees to put forth the effort necessary to complete the work assigned to them. They do not assume that employees will take individual initiative or have concern for the quality of their work. Managers with these beliefs closely supervise and control employees and make all important decisions. They are likely to use rewards and penalties regularly to try to influence worker performance. They spend much of their time in close supervision of employees rather than on other management responsibilities.

LIMITED MANAGEMENT

Managers who believe employees generally enjoy their work relate to people in a very different way. These managers believe that employees are interested in their work because the job meets many of their personal needs. Employees who enjoy their work are motivated to do a good job. With this set of beliefs, managers assume that employees like personal responsibility and will take the initiative to solve problems, help others, and perform quality work. Employees with those characteristics do not need close supervision and control.

Managers with this set of beliefs ask people for their ideas on how to perform the work. They allow employees a great deal of control over their own work and do not feel they need to apply immediate punishments or rewards. These managers spend more time on other management activities and less on close employee supervision.

FLEXIBLE MANAGEMENT

Studies have found that neither of these management views is correct for all employees and all jobs. Although many managers tend to favor one view over the other, managers who adjust their approach as circumstances change are likely to be more effective. For example, if there is some work that employees strongly dislike, closer supervision may be required. When employees are doing work they enjoy, managers may not need to supervise as closely. Flexibility in managers' views of employees permits flexibility in their treatment. Employees tend to prefer managers who are flexible enough to increase or decrease the amount of supervision as needed.

Managers can influence whether employees like or dislike their work. New employees are often nervous and unsure about some of their job assignments. However, they are usually excited about the work and want to do a good job. If they have a negative experience, decide they don't like the work, or believe their manager does not care about them, they may be less motivated and enthused. New employees will feel better if their supervisor is available and willing to provide help and feedback until the employees are comfortable with the work.

Experienced employees who have demonstrated they can perform their jobs well may resent close supervision. They will believe their manager lacks confidence in them and expects them to make errors or work too slowly. Employees who have demonstrated they can perform their work well will have a positive view of their manager when they see their manager's trust.

If the employees do not seem to enjoy the work they are doing, rather than increasing the amount of supervision, managers can try things to change their attitudes. Managers can work with the employees to determine the reasons for their feelings and to find out what they like and dislike about that type of work. The managers can develop ways to involve employees, encourage and respect their ideas, and offer opportunities to do more of the type of work they enjoy when possible.

CHECKPOINT

What are the beliefs about employees that lead to close management and to limited management?

Leadership Styles

The general way a manager treats and supervises employees is called **leadership style**. It includes the way a manager gives directions, handles problems, and makes decisions. Leadership style is influenced by many factors, including the manager's preparation, experience, and beliefs about whether employees like or dislike work. Every manager approaches leadership in a slightly different way. However, leadership styles fall into three general categories: autocratic, democratic, and open leadership.

AUTOCRATIC LEADERSHIP

The **autocratic leader** gives direct, clear, and precise orders with detailed instructions as to what, when, and how work is to be done. With an autocratic leader, employees usually do not make decisions about the work they perform.

When questions or problems arise, employees look to the manager to handle them. The autocratic manager seldom consults with employees about what should be done or the decisions to be made.

Efficiency is one of the reasons for using the autocratic style. The employees are supposed to do the work exactly the way the manager says—no surprises. Employees generally know what the manager expects. If they are in doubt about what to do or how to do it, they consult the manager. The autocratic leader believes that managers are in the best position to determine how to achieve the goals of the organization. They also assume that workers cannot or do not want to make decisions about their work.

Some workers prefer leaders with autocratic styles, but many do not. A major disadvantage of the autocratic style is that it discourages employees from thinking about better ways of doing their work. As a result, some employees become bored or frustrated. This type of leadership may lead to employee dissatisfaction and a decline in their work performance. Human relations problems arise, especially between managers and employees, when managers use an autocratic leadership style extensively. Finally, the autocratic style does not prepare employees for leadership opportunities or promotion, because they do not gain experience or confidence in decision making or problem solving.

The autocratic style is effective in some situations. For example, it is often the best style to use in emergencies. Getting out a large rush order, for example, may not allow time for a supervisor to discuss the necessary procedures with employees. It is much more efficient for a supervisor to give specific orders and expect a rapid response. Managers may also need to use an autocratic style with temporary employees, such as part-time workers hired for short periods of time. The effective leader is one who knows when a situation calls for an autocratic style of leadership and uses it only until that situation is over.

Can you think of a business situation in which an autocratic leader may be more effective than a democratic or open leader? Explain why.

DEMOCRATIC LEADERSHIP

The **democratic leader** is one who encourages workers to share in making decisions about their work and work-related problems. When using the democratic style, managers communicate openly with employees and discuss problems and solutions with them rather than merely announcing decisions. The manager may still make the final decision, but only after discussing possible solutions with employees and seeking their advice. Even when a decision is not involved, the democratic manager provides workers assistance or encouragement and offers reasons about why certain work changes must occur. The principal characteristic of the democratic style, however, is that it encourages employees to participate in planning work, solving work problems, and making decisions.

Many people say they prefer a manager who uses a democratic style of leadership. Involvement in planning and decision making helps employees feel like active members of a team striving to reach common goals, rather than just workers putting in their time. They are more likely to carry out plans and decisions they helped to develop. Employees who see that managers have confidence in them are often highly motivated and, as a result, need not be as closely supervised.

As good as the democratic style may sound, however, it has limitations. Not all people like to participate in decisions. Some prefer to just do the work for which they were hired. Also, planning and discussing problems is time consuming. Furthermore, many jobs are fairly routine, with little opportunity for sharing in decision making. Employees will certainly be upset if managers ask them to help make only unimportant decisions or if they don't see management carefully considering their ideas.

The democratic leadership style is effective in many situations, especially when employees are committed to their jobs and want more responsibility. It is also effective with experienced, well-trained workers. When special problems arise and the manager wants as many helpful ideas as possible, the democratic style is particularly effective.

OPEN LEADERSHIP

The **open leader** gives little or no direction to employees. Employees are expected to understand the work that needs to be done, and methods, details, and decisions are left to individual employees or teams. Employees are generally allowed to do their work with little management oversight or involvement. Only when problems occur or major changes are implemented will the manager take a leadership role. Generally, employees concentrate on specific tasks and are not involved in the tasks of others.

The open style works best with experienced workers and in businesses where few major changes occur. If people have their own specialized jobs and are experts at them, the manager might use this style of leadership. If people work in many different locations, such as salespeople or home-based employees, the open style may work well. Managers will not be able to closely control employees' work because of their location, and getting together to make decisions may not be feasible.

Managers should be careful when using the open style of leadership with inexperienced employees or employees who are not used to making their own decisions. When employees are not confident in their abilities or do not trust that managers will let them make their own decisions, they are likely to be ineffective with the open style. When effective teamwork is required without training in team responsibilities, the open style can lead to confusion and lack of direction. Open leadership should be used very carefully and only after ensuring that employees are prepared for it and comfortable with the individual responsibility.

Examples of Leadership Qualities

Employees prefer a manager who:
1. Encourages employee participation and suggestions.
2. Keeps employees informed and shares employee ideas with upper management.
3. Works to build and maintain morale.
4. Is available to employees and easy to talk to.
5. Supports employee training and development.
6. Communicates effectively with employees.
7. Considers the ideas and feelings of others.
8. Makes changes when needed rather than relying on past practices.
9. Supports employees who are doing their best even when mistakes are made.
10. Shows appreciation and provides recognition for good work.

© Cengage Learning 2013.

Figure 3-3 Employees prefer managers who demonstrate these leadership qualities.

SITUATIONAL LEADERSHIP

Effective managers understand the four management functions, demonstrate leadership, use human relations skills, and choose the most appropriate management style. The most effective managers use situational leadership. A **situational leader** understands employees and job requirements and matches actions and decisions to the circumstances. For example, if a situational leader forms a team of experienced employees to work on a task, the leader will use an open style. If the team were composed of new employees, the leader might be more involved and provide more direction, using a more democratic or autocratic style.

Employees have different expectations of managers and want to work for an effective manager who understands them and their needs. Figure 3-3 lists the qualities most employees would like to see in their managers.

 CHECKPOINT

Under what circumstances could an autocratic leadership style be used effectively?

3.3 ASSESSMENT

UNDERSTAND MANAGEMENT CONCEPTS

Determine the best answer for each of the following questions.

1. Managers who use close management believe that
   a. employees generally enjoy their work
   b. experienced employees are able to perform their jobs well
   c. employees work only because they have to
   d. employees want to be a part of a team

2. Of the four leadership styles, the one in which managers are the most flexible in their approach is
   a. autocratic
   b. democratic
   c. open
   d. situational

THINK CRITICALLY

Answer the following questions as completely as possible.

3. Do you believe younger workers generally prefer a different leadership style from their supervisor than do older employees? Why or why not?

4. As a supervisor, which leadership style would work best for you?

3.4

Employee Issues and Work Rules

Goals

- Understand the manager's role in recognizing and dealing with employees' personal issues.
- Describe the importance of establishing and enforcing work rules.

Terms

- employee assistance programs p. 70
- rules p. 71
- work rules p. 71
- labor union p. 71
- labor agreement p. 71

●●●● Managing Personal Issues

Employees have full lives with responsibilities beyond work. Young people may be trying to balance work, completing additional education, and starting a family. Families with children may be juggling two careers, school and activity schedules for children, and normal daily activities including meals, errands, and appointments. Some workers are caring for elderly parents or family members with long-term illnesses. Personal interests, hobbies, volunteer activities, and social needs take additional time and compete for the attention of employees and managers alike.

BALANCING WORK AND PERSONAL LIFE

Personal and family issues are important to employees. These issues cannot be forgotten or ignored when the employee comes to work. While most people are able to balance their work life with their personal life, occasionally personal issues arise that can affect their work. In most cases, the employee is able to resolve the problem and the manager doesn't need to take any action. At other times, the manager just needs to be understanding and sympathetic. These situations occur infrequently, such as when an employee has an ill child or is late to work because of a transportation problem. Many businesses develop procedures that allow employees to deal with those types of problems.

HANDLING DIFFICULT PERSONAL PROBLEMS

Managers are increasingly confronted with some personal problems of employees that are more serious. Problems such as drug or alcohol abuse, conflicts in personal relationships, or serious financial difficulties may result in employees being unable to perform their jobs well. Some of the personal problems have effects beyond the individual employee and begin to affect the performance and morale of co-workers. In those situations, managers must do more than give the employee an opportunity to resolve the personal issues.

Managers need to be aware of employees who are having difficulty on the job and try to determine the reasons for it. Then they need to work with the employee to get the necessary help to resolve the problem even if it is a personal issue.

Most managers are not trained to solve difficult personal problems, and they should not attempt to do so. But they should not ignore the problems either. Many businesses provide employee assistance programs. **Employee assistance programs** provide confidential individual assistance including counseling and support services for employees experiencing serious personal or family issues. The services range from treatment for substance abuse; professional counseling for family, personal, or financial difficulties; and support through major life events such as the birth of a child, death of a family member, serious illness, or divorce.

Managers need to make employees aware of those services and the importance of solving personal problems before they affect job performance. Managers should encourage employees to use the services available in the company when the problem first occurs. Then the manager should support the employee's decision to seek help. That usually means treating the problem confidentially and providing some accommodation for the employee's schedule while he or she works to solve the problem.

CHECKPOINT

What should managers do when confronting an employee's difficult personal problem?

● ● ● ● The Need for Work Rules

When we play a game, we follow a set of rules. **Rules** are prescribed guides for actions and conduct. Without rules, each person could decide how he or she wanted to play the game. Soon there would be disagreements and arguments. Everyone would soon become dissatisfied with playing the game. In the same way, when people work together in a business, rules are needed to describe expectations and offer guidance for acceptable actions and conduct. The rules of a business are known as work rules. **Work rules** are regulations created to maintain an effective working environment in a business.

DEVELOPING WORK RULES

Employees must meet certain expectations if a business is to operate effectively. Those expectations might deal with hours of work, care of equipment, worker safety, and relationships among employees and between employees and management.

Companies develop work rules to identify expected behaviors. There are usual company-wide rule that must be observed by all employees. Then unique sets of rules are developed for workers in different divisions or job categories in the business to meet the unique requirements of those areas. Those specific rules may be needed because of safety issues in operating machinery, unique work responsibilities or schedules, or the needs for confidentiality and security when handling information.

The employees in some businesses are represented by labor unions. A **labor union** is an organization of workers formed to represent their common interests in improving wages, benefits, and working conditions. The contract between management and the union identifying rights and responsibilities of the business and its employees is a **labor agreement**. The labor agreement often specifies important work rules and the procedures to be followed if there are violations of the rules.

Managers need to make sure each employee is aware of and understands all work rules that apply to the job. In addition to the work rules, each manager needs to clearly communicate to all employees what is expected of them and how the manager will resolve problems if they occur. If managers do not communicate expectations to employees and do not handle problems in a reasonable and

FACTS &FIGURES

Substance Abuse

Recent studies have shown that rates of illicit drug and heavy alcohol use were higher among workers age 18–25 than among older workers, and higher among males than females. Rates were also higher among white non-Hispanics than among black non-Hispanics or Hispanics. In addition, rates were higher among those with less than a high school education than among those with a high school diploma or more education.

equitable way, they soon lose the respect of the employees. Managers who involve employees in developing rules and procedures usually find greater support for those rules and fewer problems when penalties need to be applied for rules violations. Guidelines for managers to follow in enforcing work rules are listed in Figure 3-4.

RESPONDING TO RULES VIOLATIONS

In addition to developing work rules, companies must have procedures for responding to violations of those rules. The procedures should be clear and specific, communicated to all employees, and enforced fairly and equitably.

Procedures sometimes include an oral warning for the first violation, a written warning for the second violation, a short suspension, and finally termination if the problem continues. Penalties are usually more severe for serious violations of work rules. Some rules are so important that any violation results in termination. As a part of the procedures for dealing with rules violations, employees should be provided protections. Those protections might include hearings, appeals of penalties, and labor union representation.

It is not easy for managers to handle difficult employee situations, especially if they must reprimand or discipline an employee. Managers do not want employees to dislike them or perceive their actions negatively. However, it is important that managers deal with those situations in a direct way rather than postponing or ignoring them. The result of not dealing with an obvious rule violation or other employee problem is that employees will not have clear expectations and will not know whether the manager intends to enforce the rules or not.

If work rules and procedures for responding to violations are clear, well communicated, and reasonably enforced, employees will understand and respect the process. If employees have been involved in developing the rules and believe their rights are protected from unfair treatment, they will support the use of work rules that contribute to a positive work environment.

Reacting immediately, objectively, and firmly to rules violations is sometimes referred to as the "hot stove principle." We may remember as small children that if we touched a hot stove we got immediate feedback in the form of a burn and probably an immediate reprimand from an adult. Because of that feedback, we learned not to touch the hot stove again. In the same way, if an employee gets an

---

Management Guidelines for Enforcing Work Rules

1. Explain work rules and provide written copies of the rules to all employees.
2. Acquaint employees with penalties for work rule violations and make sure they understand the penalties as well as when and how they will be applied.
3. Investigate possible rules violations thoroughly before taking action.
4. Consider any special circumstances before determining the violation and the penalty.
5. Act as soon as possible after investigating a violation and deciding on the action to be taken.
6. Inform the employee who violated a work rule of the rule that was violated, the penalty that will be applied, and the reason for the penalty.
7. Treat similar violations consistently.
8. Punish in private and praise in public.
9. Encourage employees to follow work rules by rewarding those who consistently follow the rules.

© Cengage Learning 2013.

Figure 3-4 Managers must be objective, fair, and consistent when enforcing established work rules.

immediate reprimand from a manager for a violation of the rules, the employee will pay more careful attention to the rules in the future.

Effective leaders handle many types of work-related problems confidently. Successful leaders understand human behavior and apply good management and human relations principles in working with people. They also continue to study and learn to improve their management skills. When conflicts and problems occur, leaders work to solve them before they create larger problems. They understand that they must help employees satisfy their own needs while also accomplishing the goals of the business.

 **CHECKPOINT**

Why should managers deal with difficult employee situations in a direct way rather than postponing or ignoring them?

3.4 ASSESSMENT

UNDERSTAND MANAGEMENT CONCEPTS

Determine the best answer for each of the following questions.

1. When confronted with an employee's personal problem that affects the employee's work or that of other employees, the manager should
   a. allow the employee to work through the problem alone
   b. help the employee identify services offered by the business that will help solve the problem
   c. take personal responsibility for counseling the employee
   d. begin termination proceedings on the employee

2. Appropriate procedures for handling violations of work rules would include all of the following except
   a. provide a verbal warning for the first infraction
   b. ignore minor violations but respond to major violations
   c. put a written reprimand in the employee's file
   d. give the employee a short suspension

THINK CRITICALLY

Answer the following questions as completely as possible.

3. Why should employee participation in a company's counseling program or other services to help with personal problems remain confidential?

4. Do you believe employees should be involved in establishing work rules? In developing penalties for violations of work rules? Justify your decisions.

CHAPTER CONCEPTS

- One of the key qualities for managers at any level is effective leadership. Effective leaders exhibit a number of common personal characteristics.

- Employees are most productive when work meets their needs as well as those of the company. Managers must work to satisfy important needs of each employee while also meeting the goals of the business.

- Four types of power available to managers are position power, reward power, expert power, and identity power.

- Important human relations skills are self-understanding, understanding others, communication, team building, and developing job satisfaction.

- The general way a manager treats and supervises employees is called leadership style. Leadership styles fall into three general categories: autocratic, democratic, and open leadership.

- Work rules are regulations created to maintain an effective working environment in a business. Employees must meet certain expectations if a business is to operate effectively. Effective leaders confidently handle work-related issues with employees. When conflicts and problems occur, leaders work to solve them before they create larger problems.

REVIEW BUSINESS MANAGEMENT TERMS

Write the letter of the term that matches each definition. Some terms will not be used.

a. autocratic leader
b. democratic leader
c. employee assistance program
d. expert power
e. human relations
f. identity power
g. labor agreement
h. labor union
i. leader
j. leadership
k. leadership style
l. open leader
m. position power
n. power
o. reward power
p. rules
q. self-understanding
r. situational leader
s. team building
t. work rules

1. The general way a manager treats and supervises employees.
2. Power given to people because of their superior knowledge about the work.
3. One who encourages workers to share in making decisions about their work and work-related problems.
4. An awareness of your attitudes and opinions, your leadership style, your decision-making style, and your relationships with other people.
5. Contract between management and the union identifying rights and responsibilities of the business and its employees.
6. Employer programs that provide confidential individual assistance including counseling and support services for employees experiencing serious personal or family issues.
7. Getting people to support the same goals and work well together to accomplish them.
8. How well people get along with each other when working together.
9. Manager who gives little or no direction to employees.
10. Power that comes from the position the manager holds in the organization.
11. One who gives direct, clear, and precise orders with detailed instructions as to what, when, and how work is to be done.

12. Organization of workers formed to represent their common interests in improving wages, benefits, and working conditions.
13. One who understands employees and job requirements and matches actions and decisions to the circumstances.
14. Power given to people because others identify with and want to be accepted by them.
15. Regulations created to maintain an effective working environment in a business.
16. The ability to influence individuals and groups to cooperatively achieve common goals.

REVIEW BUSINESS MANAGEMENT CONCEPTS

Determine the best answer.

17. An employee who understands a particular work procedure very well and uses that information to help other employees has
    a. position power
    b. reward power
    c. expert power
    d. identity power
18. Which type of power is not related to leadership characteristics?
    a. expert
    b. position
    c. identity
    d. none of the above
19. Which of the following statements about leadership in business is *not* true?
    a. Leadership qualities can be improved through training and personal development.
    b. Employees as well as managers need leadership skills.
    c. Even when a manager is a part of a work group, the leader of the group will not always be the manager.
    d. Leadership and management mean the same thing.
20. An effective work team has all of the following characteristics except
    a. the manager monitors the work of the team closely
    b. employees feel that they are a part of the team
    c. an employee can count on other team members for help
    d. team members work well with each other
21. A manager who believes that employees are not very interested or motivated by their work will use
    a. close management
    b. limited management
    c. flexible management
    d. democratic management
22. A manager who discusses possible solutions with employees and seeks their advice before making a decision is a(n)
    a. democratic leader
    b. autocratic leader
    c. open leader
    d. situational leader

APPLY WHAT YOU KNOW

Answer the following questions.

23. Based on the Reality Check scenario at the beginning of the chapter, do you believe the executive of a large company and the mayor of a large city need the same leadership characteristics? Why or why not?

24. How is effective human relations related to effective leadership?

25. Using Figure 3-1, select the five most important leadership characteristics you believe are needed by business managers. Justify your choices.

26. Provide two examples of a manager using power inappropriately. Now provide two other examples of how a manager uses power appropriately.

27. What are several things businesses and managers can do to help employees prevent or eliminate problems on the job that result from trying to balance work and personal life?

28. Do you believe each manager should develop work rules that apply only to his or her employees? Why or why not?

MAKE ACADEMIC CONNECTIONS

Complete the following activities.

29. **Communication** Form a team of at least three classmates or join a team assigned by your teacher. Select one of the five human relations skills discussed in the chapter. Think of a business situation that demonstrates the effective or ineffective use of that skill. Then prepare a written script of dialogue between a manager and one or more employees that illustrates the situation. Role-play the situation for your classmates using the script. Students from other teams should attempt to determine which human relations skill you are demonstrating.

30. **Technology** Identify someone you believe is a good manager. Interview the person to determine his or her beliefs about (a) the use of power by a manager, (b) whether people need close or limited supervision, and (c) leadership style. Using a computer, prepare three or more slides that list the major points on these topics from the textbook and compare these points with the viewpoints of the manager you interviewed. Share your findings with your class.

31. **Decision Making** With a group of your class members, brainstorm things supervisors can do to increase the job satisfaction of workers. Identify the things that would have a direct cost to the business and those that could be provided with no real cost to the business. Compare the list developed by your group with those of other groups in your class. Try to reach agreement among the groups on the top five factors that your class believes would work for teenage employees. Then see if you can agree on five factors that the class believes would be most effective for employees over 30 years of age. Discuss reasons for any differences between the two lists.

CASE IN POINT

CASE 3-1: Supervising a New Work Group

Rita Meyers had been a supervisor of five research specialists in her company's marketing department for nearly two years. She had been promoted to the position after working as an employee in marketing for eight years. At the time of her promotion, she had more experience than the specialists she supervised. She had even helped train three of them when they were first hired by the company. The workers thought a great deal of Rita. In fact, many of them said she was the best supervisor they had ever had.

Rita's work coach, Jesse Suarez, was most impressed with the good relations among the employees and with the excellent work Rita's department did. Mr. Suarez was so impressed he encouraged Rita to consider advancing into middle management. He believed that supervising a larger work team would be an important step in Rita's development. There was an opening for a supervisor of 10 data entry specialists in the accounting department. Even though Rita had not worked in accounting, she did have experience with computer systems and data entry as part of her marketing work. Jesse told her she would be perfect in the new job and would enjoy working with a new group of employees. Rita applied for and received the promotion.

After only two months, however, Rita had already received several complaints from the employees she was supervising in the accounting department. She knew her relationships with the new group were not as positive as with the employees in the marketing department. Also the work output had declined steadily since she had taken over as supervisor.

"What's happening, Rita?" Jesse asked when they met to discuss the problem. "Why isn't it working out? You're the same person who was an effective supervisor in the marketing department. What has changed?"

Rita responded, "I don't know. In the marketing department, I always discussed problems with the workers, and as a group we worked out solutions acceptable to everyone. Those employees wanted to be involved. In accounting, no one wants to discuss problems and solutions. They say they don't have time to meet as a group. They say solving problems is what a manager is for. You know that's not my style. I like to spend time with employees, help them, and get them to feel like a team. I don't feel I should make decisions on important problems without at least talking with them."

THINK CRITICALLY

1. Is it possible that a person might be an effective leader in one situation but not in another? Explain.
2. What type of leadership style does Rita practice?
3. What do you recommend that Jesse and Rita do to improve the situation in the accounting department?
4. If you could have talked to Rita before she moved from marketing to accounting, what recommendations would you have made to help her avoid the problem she encountered?

CASE 3-2: Enforcing Company Policies

Mikayla Fletcher was very upset because she had just suspended one of the employees she supervised, Dylan Holcomb. Although Dylan was a good worker, he had begun to develop a problem with coming to work on time. Once and sometimes twice a week, he was 5 to 10 minutes late. Although he was usually not very late, the tardiness was frequent and caused negative feelings among Dylan's co-workers. They often had to wait for him to show up before they could continue with projects in which he was involved.

The company had a policy on employee tardiness: a half-hour of pay was deducted for any part of 15 minutes the employee was late. If the employee was late more than 30 minutes, a verbal warning was given the first time, a written warning was given the second time, and the employee would be suspended for one week without pay the third time.

Dylan didn't seem to mind losing the money when he was late, and he had never been tardy to the point Mikayla had to issue a warning. However, because it was a continuing issue, Mikayla decided to talk with him informally about the problem. Dylan didn't seem overly concerned and simply said he would try to do better. Following the conversation, he had been on time for several weeks. Then, two weeks ago, he was 35 minutes late one day. Last Thursday he was late by 50 minutes. Following company policy, Mikayla gave him a verbal warning first, followed by a written warning.

Yesterday the city was hit by a heavy snowstorm. Because roads in the area were very slippery early in the morning, the company decided that employees who were late would not be penalized. Mikayla was surprised when Dylan showed up on time. He said he had used his new four-wheel-drive vehicle and had fun driving to work through the snow.

Today Mikayla was furious when Dylan walked in 40 minutes late. She confronted him and told him he was suspended. Dylan accused Mikayla of being unfair. He said the battery on his new vehicle had failed; otherwise, he would have been on time. Besides, the company hadn't penalized employees for tardiness yesterday when he had been on time. Because of that, he didn't feel he should be penalized today.

THINK CRITICALLY

1. What are the advantages and disadvantages of a rule violation policy such as the one described in the case?
2. Do you believe Mikayla should have suspended Dylan under the circumstances? Why or why not?
3. Do you believe Dylan was justified in his claim that Mikayla was being unfair? Support your answer.
4. What do you think Mikayla should do after Dylan returns from his suspension?

PROJECT My Own Business

Your Leadership Style

If your business is successful, it will grow and you will likely add employees. When you are the sole employee of a business, your primary responsibilities will be as a manager. However, as you add employees, you will take on the role of leader as well as manager. With more employees, leadership responsibilities become more complex and more important. You will need to earn the respect, confidence, and support of employees so they will want to do a good job. All employees will recognize you as their manager, although they may not view you as an effective leader unless you develop effective leadership skills.

Some new business owners have a difficult time developing and enforcing work rules. They didn't need rules when they were the sole employee or when the first few employees were hired. Many new managers try to avoid conflicts and don't want to have to reprimand or fire employees. They see work rules as difficult to develop and enforce and believe they build a wall between the business owner and the employees.

The activities below focus on analyzing your leadership style and preparing for your role as leader. You will prepare a plan to increase your leadership skills. You will also consider an initial set of work rules that you can use as you expand your business.

DATA COLLECTION

1. Provide a brief description of each leadership style to five people who know you well. Ask them to identify the description that best expresses the way you work with people. Summarize their responses. Do you have a clear-cut leadership style?
2. Contact the owner of a small business. Ask to review the company's employee handbook. Identify the work rules. Discuss the rules with the owner to determine how effective the rules are in helping the person manage the business.

ANALYSIS

1. Using the information you collected on your leadership style, do you agree or disagree with the responses of others? If you disagree, why do you believe others' view of your style differs from your own view? Develop a written statement of what you can do during this school year to increase your leadership skills. Include useful leadership or career development activities available through your local career and technical student organization or other school or community organization.
2. Develop at least five work rules for your business. Consider attendance and absences, relationships with others, safety, care of equipment, and other employee responsibilities.

PLANNING AND ORGANIZING

© Shutterstock/svry

Reality Check

Not So Fast!

Eldron Huntley was excited after attending a seminar titled "Moving Your Small Business to the Internet." He believed he had discovered a whole new idea for expanding his successful 10-year-old catering business.

People told Eldron that he offered menu items they could not find anywhere else. In addition, they could always count on the quality and great taste of the meals. Customers who had moved from the area, frequently called his business to ask if there was a way to purchase menu items for special occasions. Eldron had been looking for ways to serve those customers and others like them.

At the seminar Eldron attended, the speaker explained the growth of Internet commerce. He explained that any business with a successful product could use the Internet to expand its market. That was just the idea Eldron was looking for. The Internet provided a way to affordably get his business name and menu to people all over the country.

Eldron estimated it would take about $80,000 for website development and reliable Internet service. He also figured he would need an additional $200,000 to expand his food preparation and shipping facilities. Finally, he calculated the expansion would require $50,000 to pay the expenses of additional personnel for several months until adequate sales were generated to meet the payroll costs. He anticipated the new business would quickly provide a nice profit. He scheduled a meeting with his banker to request a loan for the expansion.

The banker was not quite as excited as Eldron. She explained, "Everyone seems to want to use the Internet for their business. I agree it has a lot of potential, but there are no guarantees you'll be successful. Before I can approve a loan, I'll need to see a business plan that demonstrates how you'll repay the loan. Who will be your customers and competitors? How much will each customer buy and what will they be willing to pay? Will this new business affect your ability to serve your current customers? What will it cost to ship the food to customers so that it arrives in perfect condition? When do you expect the new part of your business to start making a profit?" Eldron recognized that the answers to those questions were important, but he had not thought about preparing a written plan.

What's Your Reaction? Do you believe Eldron's banker was justified in her response? Why or why not?

The Planning Function

Goals

- Recognize the importance of planning to business success.
- Differentiate between strategic and operational planning.

Terms

- business plan p. 81
- strategic planning p. 83
- operational planning p. 83
- SWOT analysis p. 83
- mission p. 84
- vision p. 84

 **Why Plan?**

New businesses are started every day, and existing businesses regularly look for opportunities to expand. At the same time, many new and existing businesses fail. Lack of planning is often one of the reasons for business failures. Owners and managers who can effectively plan for a business's future are much more likely to be successful than those who concentrate only on day-to-day operations. Planning is a specific management activity and needs to be done carefully. Managers need to know how to plan and how to use some specific planning tools and procedures.

THE VALUE OF A BUSINESS PLAN

Eldron's banker reminded him that he had to plan carefully in order to make the best decisions about developing and managing the new Internet business. Poor planning could result in huge losses and the possible failure of his existing successful business. However, the correct decision could result in a much larger business, higher profits, and a great deal of personal satisfaction.

Eldron's banker asked him to develop a business plan before she would consider approving the loan. A **business plan** is a written description of the nature of the business, its goals and objectives, and how they will be achieved. A business plan is an important tool for any business that is planning an important change. Planning how to achieve objectives includes analyzing the opportunities and risks the business faces. A business plan includes a detailed financial analysis showing the potential profitability that should result from the planned operations.

Business plans may be brief and simple for a new small business. On the other hand, written plans for a large, existing business may be very long and complex. Large multinational businesses generally have more than one business plan. Each part of the business develops its own plan to guide its operations. However, all of the plans must work toward the same overall objectives. The top corporate executives and planning specialists work with all parts of the business to coordinate planning and to approve each unit's plans.

Elements of a Business Plan

NATURE OF THE BUSINESS

Detailed description of products and/or services
Estimation of risk based on analysis of the industry
Size of business
Location of business
Background of entrepreneur(s)

GOALS AND OBJECTIVES

Basic results expected in the short and long run
Results expressed in terms of sales volume or profits

MARKETING PLAN

Customers and their demand for the product or service
Pricing, distribution, and promotion activities
Comparison of product or service with competitors

FINANCIAL PLAN

Investment needed to start and maintain the business
Projected income, expenses, and profit
Cash start-up and cash flow needs

ORGANIZATIONAL PLAN

Legal form of ownership
Legal factors—licenses, leases, contracts
Organization chart
Job descriptions and employee skills needed
Physical facilities—buildings, equipment, tools

© Cengage Learning 2013.

Figure 4-1 A business plan provides goals, direction, and detailed plans for all parts of the business.

When Eldron Huntley develops a written business plan, he will have long-range goals and direction for the new Internet business as well as specific plans for operations, marketing, financial management, and human resource decisions. The plan will address the new Internet business activities but also provide plans for the continuing operation of the existing business. As a result of completing the business plan, Eldron will have given much more thought to both the new and current business activities. He will have a greater understanding of what will be required to make both parts successful. His banker will have the information needed to determine if granting the requested loan is a wise business decision. The business plan will give the banker greater confidence that Eldron has carefully considered the new opportunity and knows what needs to be done to add it to his business. The banker is much more likely to make a positive decision about the loan when there is a carefully developed written plan. Figure 4-1 outlines important elements of a business plan.

THE IMPORTANCE OF PLANNING

Not all managers are responsible for preparing a business plan. However, all managers are involved in planning in some way. Some managers make complex, expensive decisions, such as whether to build a new $20 million factory or expand operations into another country. Other managers develop very short-term plans, such as an employee work schedule for the next week.

Planning is probably the most important management activity. It sets the direction for the business and establishes specific goals. Plans serve as guides for making decisions about business operations. Managers use plans to determine whether the business is making progress. Planning helps managers communicate with each other and with employees to coordinate activities. Careful planning encourages managers to be more precise and objective in their decisions.

Planning in a large business is somewhat like assembling a jigsaw puzzle. Each piece must mesh with the others around it in order to assemble the entire puzzle. One missing or broken piece affects the look of the entire puzzle. Large businesses require a great deal of coordination to avoid problems, conflicts, and missed opportunities. Shared planning allows managers from various parts of the business to understand how their work affects other parts of the business. They are also able to recognize when coordinated efforts are needed. Each part of the organization's plan must "fit together" for a successful business.

 **CHECKPOINT**

How is planning in a large organization similar to assembling a jigsaw puzzle?

●●●● Levels of Planning

Managers plan on two levels—strategic planning and operational planning. **Strategic planning** is long-term and provides broad goals and direction for the entire business. **Operational planning** is short-term and identifies specific goals and activities for each part of the business.

STRATEGIC PLANNING

Many important changes in a business require planning over a long period of time. Developing and producing a new product line can take more than a year. Building a new factory may require several years for planning and construction.

When Eldron Huntley prepares his business plan, he will be involved in strategic planning. The banker was telling him that he should not make the decision to expand his business quickly without carefully considering how to do it. Managers need a great deal of information to determine if a particular decision will be profitable. Strategic planning provides the needed information and procedures for making effective decisions about the direction and goals of a business. Figure 4-2 describes the steps in strategic planning.

The external and internal analyses, steps 1 and 2 of Figure 4-2, are often referred to as SWOT analysis. **SWOT analysis** is the examination of the organization's internal **S**trengths and **W**eaknesses as well as the external **O**pportunities and **T**hreats. *Internal factors* are all of those things within a business that managers can influence and control to help accomplish business plans. *External factors* are those things operating outside of the business that managers cannot control but that may influence the success of business plans.

Steps in Strategic Planning

STEP 1: EXTERNAL ANALYSIS

Managers study factors outside the firm that can affect effective operations: customers, competitors, the economy, government.

STEP 2: INTERNAL ANALYSIS

Managers study factors inside the business that can affect success: operations, finances, personnel, other resources.

STEP 3: MISSION

Managers agree on the most important purposes or direction for the firm based on the information collected.

STEP 4: GOALS

Managers develop outcomes for the business to achieve that fit within the mission.

STEP 5: STRATEGIES

Managers identify the efforts expected from each area of the firm if goals are to be achieved.

© Cengage Learning 2013.

Figure 4-2 Strategic planning sets the direction for a business.

Manager's Perspective on

TECHNOLOGY

Collaboration software makes it easy for planning to take place virtually rather than requiring face-to-face meetings. Using computers, computer tablets, or even smartphones team members view the same information and discuss it via typed comments or voice communication.

In step 1 of the analysis, managers identify any opportunities for expanding and improving the business and any threats the company faces from competition, changes in the economy, new laws and regulations, technology improvements, and other factors outside the company. For example, Eldron Huntley identified an opportunity when he noticed that customers from outside his operating area wanted to have meals shipped to them. The seminar helped him recognize that Internet technology provided a low-cost way to communicate with those customers.

In step 2, managers evaluate the organization's own capabilities to determine strengths and potential weaknesses. A company has successful products, experienced employees, financial resources, and well-organized operations. On the other hand, it may be experiencing low sales or may have outdated facilities and equipment. Each factor can contribute to the success or failure of business plans. Eldron Huntley identified his company's strengths as the unique menu items along with dependable quality and taste. His banker questioned whether Eldron currently had the capability to distribute his products to a large number of customers across the country while maintaining the quality. Managers want to build on the company's strengths and reduce its weaknesses whenever possible.

In step 3, managers describe and agree on the business's mission. A **mission** (or *mission statement*) is a short, specific statement of the business's purpose and direction. The mission flows out of a broad, long-term, and often inspirational **vision**, the company's reason for existing. For example, Huntley's vision statement for his company might be "to conveniently provide memorable meals to celebrate life's special occasions." His mission statement, then, might be "to prepare high-quality, memorable meals from unique recipes to satisfy the tastes of our customers no matter when or where they want them." Steps 4 and 5 then use the planning information and the mission to set specific goals for the company and descriptions of activities and resources needed to achieve the goals.

The top executives in a business are responsible for strategic planning. A careful and objective process is followed to prepare the strategic plan. The executives use information collected from lower-level managers, from the company's employees and operations, and from other sources. Large companies may have a special planning and research department to collect and analyze information and to develop proposals for executives to consider. Smaller companies may hire research firms or consultants to help with strategic planning. New and small businesses may be able to obtain planning assistance from government agencies such as the Small Business Administration and local economic development offices. The business departments of area colleges and universities are also a useful resource for planning assistance.

OPERATIONAL PLANNING

A strategic plan tells managers where the business is going. The managers must then take action to move the business toward those goals. Operational planning determines how work will be done, who will do it, and what resources will be needed to get the work done in each area of the business.

Operational plans in a factory could include developing department budgets, planning inventory levels and purchases of raw materials, setting production levels for each month, and preparing employee work schedules. Operational planning in a marketing department might include the development of promotional plans, identifying training needed by salespeople, deciding how to support retailers who will handle the product, and selecting pricing methods. A great deal of the operational planning in a business is the responsibility of middle-level managers and supervisors and even some experienced employees.

Operational plans are based on the business's strategic plan and are developed after the strategic plan is completed. Operational plans determine what resources will be required and how they will be used. Therefore, operational planning influences the amount and type of equipment and supplies needed, the number of employees and the training they require, work schedules, payroll, operating budgets, and many other factors. Operational plans direct the day-to-day activities of a business and largely determine whether the strategic plan of the business will be successful or not.

 **CHECKPOINT**

What is the difference between strategic and operational planning?

4.1 ASSESSMENT

UNDERSTAND MANAGEMENT CONCEPTS

Determine the best answer for each of the following questions.

1. Planning provides all of the following benefits to a company except
   a. encouraging managers to be more specific and objective in their decisions
   b. helping managers to determine whether the business is making progress
   c. ensuring a business will be successful and profitable
   d. provides a guide for managers when making important decisions

2. The internal and external analysis completed by businesses as a part of planning is often referred to as
   a. PERT
   b. SWOT
   c. ABCD
   d. KISS

THINK CRITICALLY

Answer the following questions as completely as possible.

3. Why should top executives in a company be responsible for strategic planning but involve lower-level managers and employees in the planning process?

4. How can a clear and meaningful vision and mission help increase employee motivation and enthusiasm for a business?

4.2

Using Planning Tools

Goals

- Identify the characteristics of effective goals.
- Describe several business planning tools and how they are used.

Terms

- goal p. 86
- budget p. 87
- schedule p. 87
- standard p. 88
- policies p. 88
- procedure p. 89

●●● Establishing Direction

It has been said that you will never know when you have arrived if you don't know where you are going. Goals provide direction for a business. A **goal** is a specific statement of a result the business expects to achieve. All types and sizes of businesses and all parts of a business need to develop goals.

Goals keep the business focused on where it wants to be in the future and the results it expects to accomplish. Managers and employees may overreact to short-term problems or the actions of competitors if goals are not clearly stated and communicated. Managers in large companies may take actions that conflict with those of other managers if they are not aware of goals. Here are several characteristics of effective goals:

1. *Goals must be specific and meaningful.* The goal "to make a profit" is vague. However, the goal "to increase sales from new customers by $25,000 in the next six months" is much more specific. Goals should relate to the activities and operations of the business so that employees see how their work relates to the goals.

   Managers must be careful in setting goals and must consider such factors as (1) the general economic conditions facing the business, (2) past sales and profits, (3) the demand for products and services, (4) the reactions of current and prospective customers, (5) the resources of the business, (6) the actions of competitors, and (7) any other factors that can influence the achievement of the goals.

2. *Goals must be achievable.* It is important that goals move the company forward, but they must also be realistic. It is not useful to set a goal "to increase unit sales by 5 percent" if the company does not have the capability of manufacturing that many more units. If telemarketing salespeople are already completing many more calls each day than the industry average, it may not be realistic to set a higher goal for completing calls without increasing the number of salespeople.

3. *Goals should be clearly communicated.* Company and departmental goals should be communicated to all employees, because they will be responsible for accomplishing those goals. Communicating the company's goals will help employees understand that they are part of a team effort working together for a common purpose. Usually, they will work harder to achieve goals they understand.

4. *Goals should be consistent with each other and with overall company goals.* Each department within a business has its own specific goals, but the goals must be coordinated with those of other departments. Assume, for example, that the sales manager sets a goal of increasing sales in a specific area of the country. The advertising manager, however, sets a goal of reducing expenditures in the same area to use the money for a new product introduction that will occur in another part of the country. If advertising is needed to support the sales efforts, the managers have conflicting goals. Managers must work together so that their goals will complement each other and support the overall company goals.

CHECKPOINT

Identify the four characteristics of effective goals.

Planning Tools

Managers must be skilled and efficient in planning. A number of planning tools are available to help them with their work. Using tools such as budgets, schedules, standards, policies, procedures and research will improve the results of planning.

BUDGETS

The most widely used planning tool is the budget. A **budget** is a written financial plan for business operations developed for a specific period of time. Financial budgets assist managers in determining the best way to use available money to reach goals. As a part of Eldron Huntley's business plan, his banker will require him to develop a budget for the new Internet business. This budget will help both the banker and Eldron see how much money he will need as well as if and when the new part of the business could be profitable. When department managers complete operational planning, they prepare budgets for their departments. In addition to the operating budget, the managers often prepare specific budgets for personnel expenses, equipment, costs of materials and supplies, sales, and many others.

SCHEDULES

Just as budgets help in financial planning, schedules are valuable in planning for the most effective use of time. For most business purposes, a **schedule** is a time plan for reaching objectives. Schedules identify the tasks to be completed, the sequence of related tasks, and the time allotted to complete each task. A supervisor may develop a schedule to organize the work done by each employee for a day or a week (see Figure 4-3). Production managers use

Management MATTERS

Trend Spotting

A trend is a current style of preference that may have a major impact on individual and business behavior. Trend spotting is a new business planning activity that analyzes a number of business sources to identify emerging trends. Businesses use information from trend spotting to plan new products, delete older products, and find ways to tie existing products to the budding trends in order to develop customer interest and excitement. Trend spotting researchers are increasingly monitoring social media to identify trends that may provide opportunities for businesses. They are interested in what opinion leaders are communicating through social media about what is new, hot, in, or out.

What Do You Think? What are some advantages and possible problems for businesses that use trend spotting as a part of their planning? What are some current trends you believe businesses should be "spotting" today?

Department Work Schedule

DEPARTMENT	Special Order Department					
DATE	July 27					
EMPLOYEE		ORDERS				
Name	Number	Order 532	Order 533	Order 534	Order 535	Order 536
Duffy, P.	50531	532				
Gaston, S.	50540		533			
Kingston, C.	20896			534		
Robinson, J.	10765			534		
Shenker, M.	50592		533			
Tamborski, Q.	10573				535	
Ziegler, L.	50243					536

© Cengage Learning 2013.

Figure 4-3 A work schedule is an important planning tool for supervisors and employees.

schedules to plan the completion and shipment of orders. Salespeople use schedules to plan their sales calls efficiently, and advertising people use schedules to make sure the ads appear at the correct time and in the proper media. Administrative managers need to schedule the preparation and printing of mailings and reports to make sure they are completed on time.

STANDARDS

Another planning tool for managers is the use of standards. A **standard** is a specific measure against which something is judged. Businesses set quality standards for the products and services they produce. Completed products are examined using the standards to judge whether or not the quality is acceptable. Companies also set standards for the amount of time that tasks should take. For example, a fast-food restaurant may set a standard that customers will receive their food within three minutes of placing their orders. If managers see that customers are getting their food five minutes after ordering, then the service time is not meeting company standards and is therefore not acceptable. Companies may also set standards for the number of defective products allowed on an assembly line or the number of calls a salesperson must make during a day.

Managers are responsible for setting realistic standards and for using those standards to judge performance. They also must know when to revise outdated standards.

POLICIES

As part of planning, managers frequently establish policies. **Policies** are guidelines used in making decisions regarding specific, recurring situations. A policy is often a general rule to be followed by the entire business or by specific departments. Work rules are examples of business policies.

A broad policy may state that the performance of each employee must be evaluated at least twice a year using the company's performance review procedures. Because of that policy, even an employee who has been with the company for 10 years must be evaluated. Policies help to reduce misunderstandings and encourage consistent decisions for similar conditions by all managers and employees.

PROCEDURES

A **procedure** is a sequence of steps to be followed for performing a specific task. In order to implement the policy described in the previous paragraph, the company must develop a specific performance review procedure. Procedures for both routine and complex tasks that are completed by many employees improve business efficiency and are of special help to employees who are learning a new job. The procedure shown in Figure 4-4 would be helpful to a new employee assigned to monitor the secured entrance for a company headquarters. Experienced employees can help managers design new procedures and improve existing ones.

RESEARCH

To do a good job of planning, managers need a great deal of information. To develop budgets, they need to know how money was spent in past years, what certain tasks will cost, and how competitors are spending their money. Managers can improve schedules if they know how long certain jobs take to complete. They can establish better standards and procedures by analyzing carefully collected information on the way jobs are performed. Research is done to collect data for managers and to provide the information needed to improve their planning decisions.

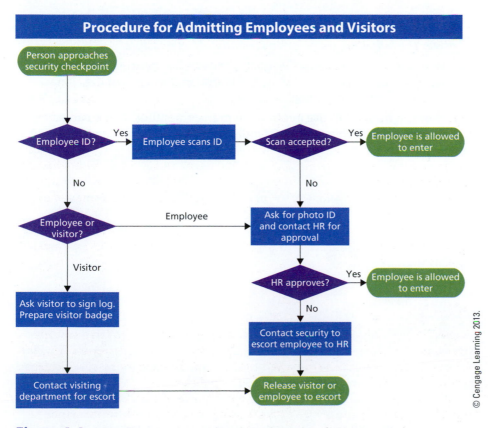

Figure 4-4 A flowchart can be used to show the order of steps in a work procedure.

CHECKPOINT

What is the difference between a policy and a standard?

4.2 ASSESSMENT

UNDERSTAND MANAGEMENT CONCEPTS

Determine the best answer for each of the following questions.

1. The goal "to increase the average productivity of all work teams by 3 percent within six months" is an example of which characteristic of an effective goal?
   a. specific and meaningful
   b. achievable
   c. clearly communicated
   d. consistent with each other

2. Guidelines used in making decisions regarding specific, recurring situations are called
   a. standards
   b. policies
   c. procedures
   d. goals

THINK CRITICALLY

Answer the following questions as completely as possible.

3. How does the use of effective goals increase the chances that business plans will be successful? Discuss the importance of each of the characteristics of an effective goal.

4. How can businesses use information from competitors and customers when establishing quality standards for their products and services?

The Organizing Function

Goals

- Describe factors that managers should consider when organizing work.
- Discuss how the characteristics of good organization contribute to a more effective work environment.

Terms

- organization chart p. 91
- responsibility p. 95
- authority p. 95
- empowerment p. 96
- accountability p. 96
- unity of command p. 96
- span of control p. 97

●●●● Organizing Work

Before a plan can be put into operation, the company must be organized to carry out the plan and perform work effectively. *Organizing* is concerned with determining how plans can be accomplished most effectively and arranging resources to complete work. More specifically, it involves arranging resources and relationships between departments and employees and defining the responsibility each has for accomplishing work. For example, when the plan is to start manufacturing a new product, specific activities will be determined and assigned to the appropriate departments. Making a new product involves several departments: research, manufacturing, human resources, marketing and sales, finance, and information management. Each department manager organizes the assigned activities so the work will be accomplished on a schedule that matches the work of the other departments.

THE ROLE OF ORGANIZATION CHARTS

An **organization chart** is an illustration of the structure of an organization, major job classifications, and the reporting relationships among the organization's personnel. The purposes of an organization chart are to (1) show the major work units that make up the business, (2) allow employees to identify which unit they are affiliated with, how it relates to other units, and to whom they are accountable, and (3) identify lines of authority and formal communication within the organization. Figure 4-5 is an example of an organization chart for part of a retail business.

Large organizations usually provide new employees information through an employee handbook or on the company's website that explains the organization of the business and shows an organization chart. By understanding an organization chart, employees have some idea of where and how they fit into the company, how the organization works, and possible promotion opportunities. As changes occur in an organization through reorganization of work or when major operating units are bought and sold, the company's organization chart can become outdated. To be a useful management and communication tool, the chart should be revised when changes occur in the organizational structure.

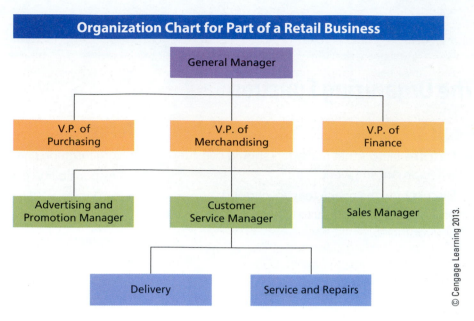

Organization Chart for Part of a Retail Business

```
                          General Manager
                                │
        ┌───────────────────────┼───────────────────────┐
   V.P. of                  V.P. of                  V.P. of
   Purchasing              Merchandising              Finance
                                │
        ┌───────────────────────┼───────────────────────┐
 Advertising and            Customer                Sales Manager
 Promotion Manager       Service Manager
                                │
                 ┌──────────────┴──────────────┐
              Delivery               Service and Repairs
```

© Cengage Learning 2013.

Figure 4-5 An organization chart provides a visual picture of how work is structured in a business.

THE PROCESS OF ORGANIZING WORK

As a new small business grows, the owner has the complicated task of organizing the entire structure of the business. However, just because an established business is already organized, the managers cannot ignore the organization function. The organization may need to change when goals are revised or when the business expands. Using the example from the beginning of the chapter, if Eldron Huntley is successful in developing the new Internet business, he will have a very different organization than before the expansion. It is not likely that the current organizational structure and employees will be able to accommodate all of the new activities and the extra workload. He will need to carefully organize the business to perform the new activities efficiently while still maintaining the existing business activities. If he does not pay attention to the organization of the work, the business may not be able to adjust to the changes.

Whether the focus is on a new or existing department, division, or an entire business, the process of organizing involves three elements: (1) the division of work, (2) the facilities and working conditions, and (3) the employees.

DIVISION OF WORK In establishing an organization structure, the total work to be done must be divided into units, such as departments. The first consideration is the grouping of activities into broad, natural divisions, such as buying and selling or production, marketing, and administration. For small businesses, only two or three divisions may be needed to separate the work into manageable units. For large businesses with many employees and activities, the major divisions will need to be divided several times into departments or work units of reasonable size. Departments should be organized around meaningful and related work, work should flow smoothly within and among departments, and employees should be assigned to the units where they have expertise to complete that work.

Major divisions of work vary with the type of industry and business. A small retailer will usually organize around the major activities of purchasing and selling. Manufacturing will have purchasing, production, and marketing. Most businesses have departments or work units for administration, information management, and human resources. For effective management and control, even small businesses benefit from organizing work into related and manageable units.

As a business grows, the number of major divisions will increase or existing divisions will be reorganized. When the small retailer expands, the basic selling division may be subdivided. A larger marketing division may be established and subdivided into advertising and promotion, personal selling, and customer service. Determining how to divide work into efficient units is based on (1) the type of work to be done in each unit and (2) the amount of work to be done. The organization charts shown in Figure 4-6, 4-7, and 4-8 point out how the organization of a business may change as the company grows.

A small business needs good organization just as much as a large organization. Management problems often begin to occur in a small business when employees are added but work responsibilities and relationships are not clear. Making organizing decisions as a small business expands may not at first result in a formal organization chart. However, the business's work should be carefully studied and assigned to specific employees. If there is not an organization chart, the work responsibilities, the relationships among employees, and their authority should be clearly communicated to everyone.

For example, the owner of a retail business that sells and services home appliances hires two employees, A and B. The owner is responsible for management of the business and is involved in both selling and service as time permits. Employee A is given responsibility for appliance sales and is the contact with the suppliers from which the company purchases appliances. Employee A is also in charge of the business when the owner is absent. Employee B is responsible for appliance service and repair and has the authority to make decisions related to customer relationships after the customer has purchased a product from the business. These organizational decisions clearly identify the work to be done by and the relationships among the people involved. The example illustrates how even very small organizations can develop an effective organizational structure and manage work.

FACILITIES AND WORKING CONDITIONS While divisions of work are being established, the physical aspects of organizing must also be considered. The business must provide the necessary equipment and materials for employees to be able to complete their work. The layout of the facilities needs to be arranged so that all work flows smoothly with little waste while providing the best and safest working conditions possible.

Work should move through the business as efficiently as possible. Employees should not have to waste time, and the work of one group should not delay the work of others. A mechanic repairing an automobile, for example, should have ready access to the needed tools and parts close to the work area. If special parts are needed, a system to quickly order and obtain the parts should be in place so the repairs are not delayed. Most auto repair companies have computer systems that can quickly locate auto parts from area suppliers and an express pickup and delivery service to immediately obtain the needed parts. When a customer comes in for service, an expert service writer will consult with the customer to identify problems and write a service order that identifies the work needed, the time and personnel required to perform the repairs, and the parts and supplies required. If the items are not in stock in the repair facility, an emergency order will be placed and quickly filled.

Physical working conditions also have an effect on the morale of workers. Job satisfaction is influenced by lighting, temperature, ventilation, and cleanliness of the work areas, as well as the quality and maintenance of tools and equipment. Even facilities outside the work area should be carefully planned, such as convenient and safe parking facilities and easy access to cafeterias and break rooms.

FACTS & FIGURES

A Great Place to Work

Analysis of companies ranked by employees as the best places to work shows the companies have some common characteristics. The companies do the following:

- Perform better financially
- Have more qualified applicants for open positions
- Experience less turnover
- See lower levels of employee stress
- Have higher customer satisfaction and loyalty
- Demonstrate more innovation, creativity, and risk-taking
- Achieve greater productivity

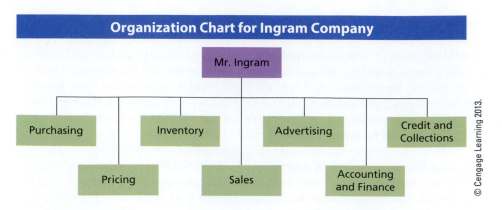

Figure 4-6 The owner of a small business might perform all of the work.

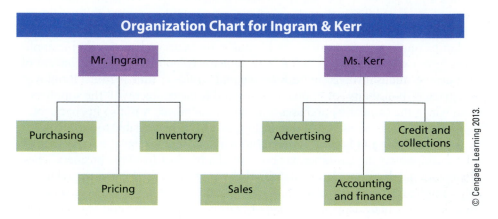

Figure 4-7 Two owners allow for a division of work.

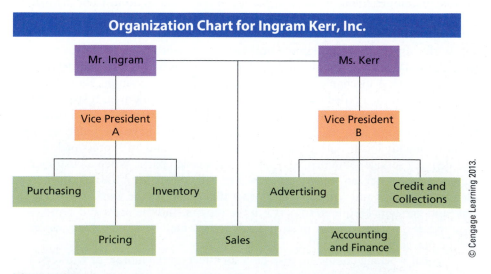

Figure 4-8 As the business expands, there can be a further division of work with a clear delegation of responsibility and authority.

EMPLOYEES Dividing the work into manageable units and providing adequate equipment and facilities must be done with employees in mind. In fact, organizing involves establishing good relationships among the employees, the work to be performed, and the facilities needed, so that productivity will be high. In part, organization is a successful matching of the employee and the employee's materials and work. Employees should be matched to work that they are prepared to do. That means that they have the necessary preparation and skill to complete the assigned tasks. If employees are members of work teams, the total skills of the team should match the work requirements.

In addition, employees should be assigned to work that they enjoy. If employees are dissatisfied with their work assignment, problems with the quality and quantity of their work will result. Although not all work is enjoyable, managers should look for opportunities to make the best work assignments possible, to spread less desirable assignments among employees so a few people do not have to spend all of their time doing that work, and to work closely with employees to establish a positive working environment.

CHECKPOINT

What are the three elements that should be considered when organizing work?

Characteristics of Good Organization

When one person operates a business, there is little need for an organization chart—that person performs all the work. The need for organization increases when two or more people work together. When people engage in any kind of cooperative activity, whether as members of an athletic team or as construction workers building a house, they can accomplish better results if the overall task is planned and organized. In that way, each person knows what is expected and how they are expected to work together to accomplish the necessary work. Several characteristics of good organization apply to the management of work.

RESPONSIBILITY AND AUTHORITY

Responsibility is the obligation to do an assigned task. In a good organization, the assigned tasks are clearly identified so all employees know exactly the work for which they are responsible. **Authority** is the right to make decisions about work assignments and to require other employees to perform assigned tasks. Authority is delegated from the top of the organization to others at lower levels.

One of the greatest mistakes in business is to assign responsibilities to employees without giving them sufficient authority to carry out those responsibilities. Consider the situation of an employee at an auto rental counter. The employee is responsible for providing a car to a customer standing at the counter who has a reservation, but the type of car requested is currently unavailable. The employee must have the authority to rent another car that will meet the customer's needs or the customer will be very upset. Each employee and each manager should know specifically (1) the description and duties of each job, (2) what authority accompanies the job, (3) the manager in charge, (4) who reports to the manager, and (5) what is considered satisfactory performance.

A growing practice in many organizations today is employee empowerment. **Empowerment** is the authority given to individual employees to make decisions and solve problems they encounter on their jobs with the resources available to them. Empowered employees need to be well trained and be effective decision makers and problem solvers. They need to understand the effects of their decisions on the business, other employees, and customers. Empowered employees have the confidence that their managers will support the decisions they make. Some companies have been reluctant to empower their employees, believing that managers will lose control of the organization. However, experience has shown that empowerment improves employee morale, produces more satisfied customers, reduces work problems, and increases work efficiency.

Unless employees know their specific responsibilities, duties, and authority, they are likely to be unsure about the work they are to do. Furthermore, conflicts may arise due to misunderstandings about what needs to be done and who makes decisions about work assignments and satisfactory performance. When employees understand responsibility and authority, overlapping duties can be eliminated. Effective organization is helpful in eliminating conflicts between managers, employees, and departments and in increasing cooperation and collaboration.

ACCOUNTABILITY

Accountability is the obligation to accept responsibility for the outcomes of assigned tasks. When any manager assigns responsibility and delegates authority to an employee, the manager does not give away the responsibility for ensuring that the work is completed and for evaluating the quality of that employee's performance. Although the manager is ultimately responsible for the work, the employee is accountable to the manager for performing the assigned work properly, including the quality, quantity, and completion time. The manager, in turn, is accountable to his or her boss for the outcomes of all work done in the unit. Figure 4-9 shows how the owner of a rental business might assign responsibilities and delegate authority to two employees. Use the figure to identify the accountability of each person for the work of the organization.

Managers evaluate employees' work by comparing the work to established goals and work standards. For the assigned work, each employee is accountable for achieving the quality and quantity defined by the goals and standards. Managers need to communicate the goals and expected standards when assigning work and then use those same goals and standards when evaluating the employee's work.

21st CENTURY SKILLS

Accountability

In every business, people are accountable for the quality, quantity, and timeliness of their work. Being accountable requires you to understand what is expected of you and working to achieve the standards that have been set. If also requires you to admit mistakes and seek help when you need it.

UNITY OF COMMAND

An important principle of good organization is unity of command. **Unity of command** means that no employee reports to more than one supervisor at a time or for a particular task. Confusion and poor work relations result when a person has work assigned by and is accountable to more than one supervisor. The person may not know which assignment to perform first or may receive conflicting instructions regarding the same work assignment. With the increasing use of teams, problems with unity of command are more likely to occur. Teams and their supervisors must practice the same careful organization of work as when more traditional structures are used. Teams need clear assignments of responsibility and authority for their tasks, and all team members need to be aware of who is in charge of each activity. Ultimately the entire team and its supervisor are responsible and accountable for the results produced. A team

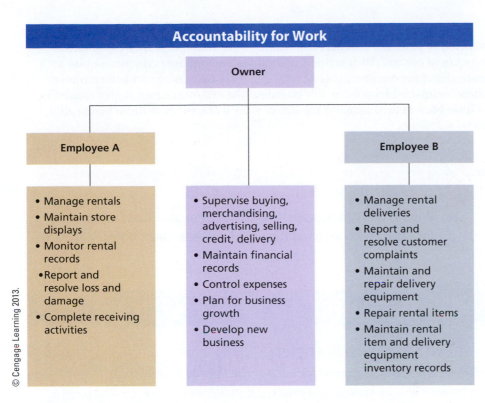

Accountability for Work

Owner

Employee A

- Manage rentals
- Maintain store displays
- Monitor rental records
- Report and resolve loss and damage
- Complete receiving activities

- Supervise buying, merchandising, advertising, selling, credit, delivery
- Maintain financial records
- Control expenses
- Plan for business growth
- Develop new business

Employee B

- Manage rental deliveries
- Report and resolve customer complaints
- Maintain and repair delivery equipment
- Repair rental items
- Maintain rental item and delivery equipment inventory records

© Cengage Learning 2013.

Figure 4-9 When a manager assigns work to an employee, authority and accountability must be given as well.

member cannot shift the blame to someone else or fail to take on a share of the workload if that organizational structure is to work successfully.

SPAN OF CONTROL

Span of control is the number of employees that any one manager supervises directly. Organizations must establish a reasonable span of control for each manager. The manager who supervises too many people is overworked and unable to perform all duties effectively. Employees may not have access to the manager when help is needed. On the other hand, time and money are wasted if a manager supervises too few people. That manager may supervise each person too closely or spend too much time in nonmanagement work. In general, the span of control is larger at the lower levels of an organization than at the higher levels. For example, the head nurse in charge of a floor unit in a hospital may supervise 15 or more employees, whereas only three vice presidents report to the chief executive of the hospital.

How can a business define what is a reasonable span of control for a manager?

© Getty Images/Photodisc

Companies that use work teams and encourage employees to be more involved in planning and decision making have found that they can increase the span of control. Well-trained and motivated employees do not require as much direct supervision as those who must rely on managers for direction. These companies have been able to reduce the numbers of managers required or have been able to increase the size of their workforces without hiring additional managers.

 **CHECKPOINT**

What is likely to happen if employees are assigned responsibility for work tasks but are not given the needed authority?

4.3 ASSESSMENT

UNDERSTAND MANAGEMENT CONCEPTS

Determine the best answer for each of the following questions.

1. A well-designed organizational chart shows all of the following except
   a. the major work units that make up the business
   b. which unit each employee is affiliated with, how it relates to other units, and to whom employees are accountable
   c. lines of authority and formal communication within the organization
   d. the primary groups of customers to whom the business sells its products

2. The number of employees that any one manager supervises directly is the
   a. span of control
   b. unity of command
   c. division of work
   d. assignment of responsibility and authority

THINK CRITICALLY

Answer the following questions as completely as possible.

3. Do you believe that a large business will operate more efficiently and effectively with more or fewer organizational units? Justify your answer.

4. If you were a supervisor, what would you do to make sure each employee is aware of his or her responsibilities and authority? What could you do to make your employees feel empowered to make decisions and solve problems associated with their work?

F☉cus On... Innovation

Betting on Employee Ideas

To remain competitive, businesses need to look for product improvements and new product ideas. Top company executives or a research and product development department usually develop these ideas. That procedure often results in a few ideas that are good enough to develop into profitable opportunities for the company.

Rite-Solutions, a company in the competitive gaming and computer simulation industry, involves all employees in product development. At Rite-Solutions, success means having a regular supply of new products as well as responding quickly to new technology and changing customer expectations for challenging and exciting game experiences.

Jim Lavoie and Joe Marino, the entrepreneurs who started Rite-Solutions, wanted an organization that would "make it happen," not just "make us money." They developed a culture that attracts optimistic, energetic people who have both technical skills and an interest in collaboration. Employees are called F.E.W.—friends enjoying work.

The inspiration for a way to generate new product ideas is a result of Rite-Solutions' culture. The owners knew their employees were creative, wanted to be involved, and would work hard to make the company successful. With that in mind, they developed a process called Mutual Fun, modeled after the stock market. Mutual Fun has three components: Savings Bonds, for ideas that could save money or increase efficiency; Bow Jones, ideas for new products or services; and Spazdaq, ideas for new and improved technologies.

Any employee can prepare a proposal for a new idea using a format called an "expectus" on the company's website. Each expectus is placed on the Bow Jones at an initial stock price of $10 for everyone in the company to review. Each person has $10,000 in "opinion money" to invest in ideas they support. Investments result in higher stock prices, signaling employee choices for the best ideas. Employees can volunteer time to help turn an idea into an actual product. If it becomes successful, resulting in a profit or saving for the company, those who participated are paid in real money.

The result has been a number of innovative products. One new military simulation now accounts for nearly 30 percent of company sales. Another idea, suggested by an employee with no software development expertise, turned an existing technology used in casino gaming into a successful educational game for students.

THINK CRITICALLY

1. Do you think most company owners and executives would embrace the idea of "friends enjoying work"? Why or why not?

2. What do you believe makes the Mutual Fun process a successful way to develop new product ideas?

3. If you were a Rite-Solutions employee, would you volunteer to work on a product idea without assurance of being paid for your time? Explain.

4.4

Developing Effective Organizations

Goals

- Describe the strengths and weaknesses of four types of organizational structures.
- Make recommendations for improving business organization.

Terms

- line organization   p. 100
- line-and-staff organization p. 101
- matrix organization   p. 101
- team organization   p. 103
- self-directed work teams p. 103
- centralized organization p. 104
- decentralized organization p. 104
- flattened organization   p. 104

 Types of Organizational Structures

A business's organizational structure identifies the relationships among departments and personnel and indicates the lines of communication and decision making. Two principal types of organizational structures are (1) line and (2) line-and-staff organizations. Two newer structures in companies today are matrix and team organizations.

LINE ORGANIZATION

In a **line organization**, all authority and responsibility can be traced in a direct line from the top executive down to the lowest employee level in the organization. A line organization is shown in Figure 4-10 (sales is the only area for which the complete organization is shown). The lines connecting the individual boxes indicate the lines of authority. The lines show, for example, that the president has authority over the sales manager, the sales manager has authority over the assistant sales manager, the assistant sales manager has authority over the branch managers, and the branch managers have authority over the sales representatives. In addition, the lines describe how formal communications are expected to flow up and down the organization.

In a line organization, the top executive has direct control over all units of the business, but responsibility, authority, and accountability are passed along from one person to another, down to the lowest level. Under this form of organization, each person is responsible to only one manager, who, in turn, is responsible to someone else. This type of organization can be very efficient, because new plans and ideas can be put into effect immediately in one area of the business without involvement from other areas. However, it often leads to many layers of management and isolation or lack of communication between departments and divisions. There is no direct way that managers of different departments not in the same line of authority can communicate and work together. This type of isolation and focus on only one part of the organization is known as the *silo effect*.

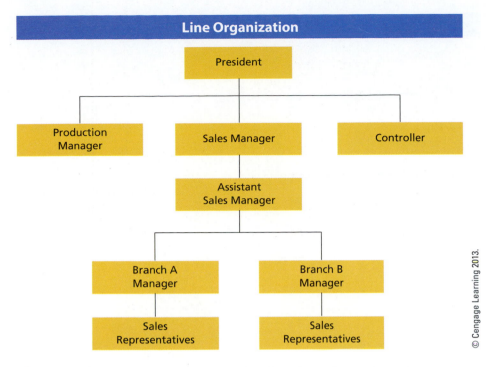

Line Organization

President

Production Manager | Sales Manager | Controller

Assistant Sales Manager

Branch A Manager | Branch B Manager

Sales Representatives | Sales Representatives

© Cengage Learning 2013.

Figure 4-10 A line organization establishes direct lines of authority and responsibility from top to bottom.

LINE-AND-STAFF ORGANIZATION

Large and complex businesses need a great deal of expertise to operate well. Managers have greater difficulty mastering all of the knowledge and skills they need in every area of responsibility. In the **line-and-staff organization**, managers have direct control over the units and employees they supervise but have access to staff specialists for assistance. Specifically, the line-and-staff organization adds staff specialists to a line organization. It is designed to solve the problem of complexity and still retain the advantages of direct and definite lines of authority. Staff specialists give advice and assistance when needed. They have no authority over line personnel to require them to perform any task. They are there to help with specialized expertise. Thus, line personnel are still responsible to only one manager.

The line-and-staff organization shown in Figure 4-11 is like the line organization in Figure 4-10 except for the addition of the advertising specialist and the marketing research specialist. Their responsibility is to give specialized advice and assistance to the sales organization. This relationship is indicated in the organization chart by broken lines. Other examples of staff positions in some organizations are legal, technology planning, and human resources specialists.

MATRIX ORGANIZATION

A newer, more flexible structure is the matrix organization, sometimes called a *project organization*. A **matrix organization** organizes employees into temporary work teams to complete specific projects. Employees report to a project manager with authority and responsibility for the project. When a new project must be done, employees with the needed skills are assigned to work on the project team. They work for that manager until the project is finished. Then they are assigned to a new project and another project manager. Work assignments and relationships in a matrix organization are clear but temporary.

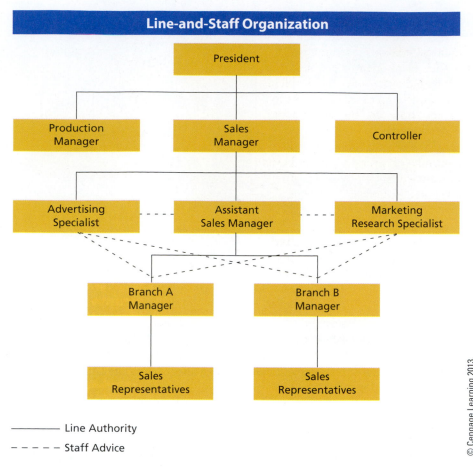

Line-and-Staff Organization

President

Production Manager | Sales Manager | Controller

Advertising Specialist | Assistant Sales Manager | Marketing Research Specialist

Branch A Manager | Branch B Manager

Sales Representatives | Sales Representatives

———— Line Authority

– – – – – Staff Advice

© Cengage Learning 2013.

Figure 4-11 In a line-and-staff organization, staff specialists are available to provide needed advice and assistance to line managers.

In the matrix organization, there is no permanent organizational structure in which an employee continues to report to the same manager and works in only one functional area. It is difficult to develop an organizational chart for this type of organization because it changes regularly. Typically, the company prepares an organization chart for each project, so that employees know the current project structure and the management and employee relationships. The company prepares a new chart when that project ends and a new one begins.

The matrix organization is used successfully in research firms, advertising agencies, and construction companies, but it is being considered by other types of businesses because it provides flexibility and allows for rapid change. This structure uses the specific skills of managers and employees as effectively as possible by bringing together people with the right skills for each project. When employees are given new project assignments, managers must be careful to define authority and responsibility so as not to violate unity of command. They also need to encourage good working relationships with new project members.

TEAM ORGANIZATION

The newest type of organization structure is known as team organization. A **team organization** divides employees into permanent work teams. The teams have responsibility and authority for important business activities with limited management control over their daily work. Teams often have team leaders who are likely to be experienced employees rather than managers. Team leaders replace the traditional position of supervisor and act as facilitators more than as traditional managers. Team leaders help their teams identify problems and work with them to solve the problems as a group. Team members report to the team leader, and the team leader makes some management decisions for the team. A full-time manager is responsible for several teams and meets with team leaders for planning, progress reports, and problem solving.

© Getty Images/Digital Vision

What are some advantages of team organization to employees and to management?

Sometimes teams are organized without a permanently designated team leader. These are **self-directed work teams**, in which team members together are responsible for the work assigned to the team. Self-directed work teams have a manager to whom they can turn with unusual or very difficult problems, but most of the time they work together to establish goals and to plan and organize their work. Often members take turns as team leader or facilitator. A self-directed team has full authority over planning, performing, and evaluating its work. For ideas and assistance, the team may talk to other teams or draw on the support of specialists available to work with all teams in the organization. In addition, the team is expected to talk to suppliers and customers from inside or outside the business to get their input and feedback.

In self-directed work teams, the team decides who will do which types of work and how they will do it. Each worker must be able to perform the tasks of other team members to cover for absent members or additional workloads. Teams can hire, train, and even remove team members, evaluate individual and team performance, and handle most of the traditional management tasks. The role of the manager is to serve as the team's consultant and to concentrate on higher-level management tasks. Some differences between self-directed work teams and traditional work teams are shown in Figure 4-12.

Effective work teams, whether self-directed or not, have been shown to increase productivity and improve quality. Individual team members work hard to support their team and make sure the team meets its goals. Companies that have developed effective team structures have a better record of keeping customers happy, reducing absenteeism, reducing turnover, and keeping motivation high.

Teams require certain ingredients for success. Managers must support the idea and assist the teams as needed. Team members must become competent in three areas:

1. Technical job skills
2. Interpersonal skills, such as writing, speaking, discussing, and negotiating
3. Administrative skills, such as leading meetings, thinking analytically, and maintaining records

NETBookmark

Employee satisfaction must be an important concern of every manager. Dissatisfied employees are likely to leave if another job becomes available. They will also be less productive than those who like their work. The Gallup Organization has identified twelve things that are different about employees who are engaged in their work and those who are not.

Access the website for this textbook and choose the link for Chapter 4 Net Bookmark. Read the article that summarizes the research and lists the twelve factors. Which of the twelve items surprises you the most and which match your expectations? If you were the top executive of a company, how would you use this information to improve employee satisfaction in your company? Develop three recommendations that you would make to the managers who report to you.

www.cengage.com/school/bizmgmt

A Comparison of Traditional and Self-Directed Work Teams		
	Traditional Work Team	**Self-Directed Work Team**
Work Categories	Many narrow tasks	One or two broad tasks
Worker Authority	Team leader controls all routine tasks	Team controls tasks through group decisions
Effectiveness	Determined by manager and team leader evaluations, individual member performance	Based on team performance plus breadth of skills of individual team members

© Cengage Learning 2013.

Figure 4-12 Self-directed work teams have more authority and responsibility for their work than do traditional teams.

Teams need top management support as well as skills in these three areas to do well. New teams must have both time and support to be able to develop to their full potential.

CHECKPOINT

Who is responsible for traditional management functions in a team organization?

Improving Business Organization

Traditionally, businesses have used **centralized organization**, in which a few top managers do all major planning and decision making. Studies of the effect of business organization on quality and productivity have discovered that companies with centralized organizations often experience some common problems. Large companies often develop very complex centralized organizational structures. Those structures may cause communication problems and the need for many policies and rules to control the organization. Individual managers and employees then begin to feel like unimportant parts of the business. They get frustrated when rules keep them from doing things they consider important or when it takes a long time to get decisions made.

To overcome these types of problems, companies are decentralizing. With **decentralized organization**, a large business is divided into smaller operating units, and managers who head the units have almost total responsibility and authority for operations. In many ways, the units operate as if they were independent companies. For example, a large computer manufacturer could be decentralized into operating units by categories of products (mainframes, personal computers, portables and accessories) or by types of customers (business, government, and consumers).

Another major type of reorganization occurring in businesses today is known as *flattening*. A **flattened organization** is one with fewer levels of management than traditional structures. To achieve a flattened organization, the remaining managers and employees assume many of the responsibilities previously assigned to other levels of management. A flattened organization should have improved communication, because information has to flow through fewer levels. There should also be more coordination and cooperation because there is less specialization within the organization. As competition increases and customers expect businesses to improve quality and service, the organization of a business becomes very important. A complex organizational structure that requires a great deal of time for making decisions and for communicating information will not be as competitive as one that is more flexible and responsive.

 CHECKPOINT

How can business organization be made more effective?

4.4 ASSESSMENT

UNDERSTAND MANAGEMENT CONCEPTS

Determine the best answer for each of the following questions.

1. If managers in large organizations have difficulty mastering the knowledge and skills they need in all of their areas of responsibility, which type of organizational structure would be most helpful?
   a. line
   b. line-and-staff
   c. matrix
   d. team

2. For work teams to be successful in an organization, team members must become competent in all of the following areas except
   a. technical job skills
   b. interpersonal skills
   c. administrative skills
   d. financial skills

THINK CRITICALLY

Answer the following questions as completely as possible.

3. Why does the line organizational structure often create problems in sharing information and communicating among employees and managers from different parts of the organization?

4. Flattened organizations provide benefits in improved communications, coordination, and cooperation. Why does that occur? What problems do you believe might result from the flattened organization structure?

CHAPTER CONCEPTS

- Managers who can effectively plan for a business's future will be more successful than those who focus on day-to-day operations. Planning sets the direction for the business and establishes specific goals. Plans are guides for making decisions. Strategic plans tell where the business is going. Operational plans determine how work will be done, who will do it, and what resources will be needed to get the work done.

- Goals keep a business focused on where it wants to go and the results to be accomplished. Tools that can help develop effective plans include budgets, schedules, standards, policies, procedures, and research.

- Companies must be organized to carry out plans and complete work effectively. The process of organizing involves three elements: division of work, facilities and working conditions, and employees. Characteristics of good organization include responsibility and authority, accountability, unity of command, and span of control.

- The type of organizational structure identifies the relationships among departments and personnel as well as lines of communication and decision making. Types of organizational structures are line, line-and-staff, matrix, and team organizations. Recently, traditional organizations have become more decentralized and flattened.

REVIEW BUSINESS MANAGEMENT TERMS

Write the letter of the term that matches each definition. Some terms will not be used.

a. accountability
b. authority
c. budget
d. business plan
e. empowerment
f. goal
g. line organization
h. matrix organization
i. mission
j. operational planning
k. organization chart
l. policies
m. procedure
n. responsibility
o. span of control
p. standard
q. strategic planning
r. SWOT analysis
s. unity of command
t. vision

1. Broad, lasting, and often inspirational view of a company's reason for existing.
2. Principle which states that no employee has more than one supervisor at a time.
3. Obligation to do an assigned task.
4. Specific measure by which something is judged.
5. Written financial plan for business operations developed for a specific period of time.
6. Organization which combines workers into temporary work teams to complete specific projects.
7. Authority given to individual employees to make decisions and solve problems they encounter on their jobs with the resources available to them.
8. Business structure in which all authority and responsibility can be traced in a direct line from the top executive down to the lowest employee level.
9. Guidelines used in making decisions regarding specific, recurring situations.
10. Short-term planning that identifies specific activities for each area of the business.
11. Number of employees who that any one manager supervises directly.
12. Obligation to accept responsibility for the outcomes of assigned tasks.
13. Sequence of steps to be followed for performing specific task.

REVIEW BUSINESS MANAGEMENT CONCEPTS

Determine the best answer.

14. Strategic planning in an organization is followed by
    a. operational planning
    b. organizational planning
    c. hiring and training employees
    d. management planning
15. Which of the following is *not* a characteristic of an effective goal?
    a. Goals must be specific and meaningful.
    b. Goals must be achievable.
    c. Goals must be clearly communicated.
    d. Each goal must focus on one company activity.
16. Businesses measure the quality of products and services by comparing them against
    a. procedures
    b. standards
    c. policies
    d. goals
17. The span of control at the top of an organization is usually _____ at the lower levels.
    a. greater than
    b. about the same as
    c. smaller than
    d. There is no span of control at the top of an organization.
18. The most efficient organizational structure is a
    a. line organization
    b. line-and-staff organization
    c. team organization
    d. decentralized organization

APPLY WHAT YOU KNOW

Answer the following questions.

19. Based on the Reality Check scenario at the beginning of the chapter, identify one example of strategic planning and one example of operational planning that you believe Eldron Huntley should complete.
20. It is recommended that a new business develop a business plan. Do you believe large, well-established businesses need a business plan as well? Why or why not?
21. What is the difference between a business strength and a business opportunity? For a business in your community, provide an example of a strength of the business and an opportunity for the business.
22. Write a list of procedures that another person can follow to copy a computer file from the hard drive to a removable storage device. The procedures should be complete and in the order they need to be performed.

23. Do you believe employees prefer to work in organizations where they have very specialized work that they do over and over, or in organizations where they have a broader set of responsibilities and work changes regularly? Justify your answer.
24. What is the difference between responsibility and authority? Provide examples of each from your role as a family member and your role as a student.
25. Compare the line organization with the matrix organization in terms of how it affects the work, relationships, and communication of managers and employees.

MAKE ACADEMIC CONNECTIONS

Complete the following activities.
26. **Communication** Review the information from the beginning of the chapter about Eldron Huntley's idea to expand his catering business using the Internet. Write two goals that Mr. Huntley could set for the business—one that should be achieved in three months and one that should be achieved by the end of the first year. Write the goals to include the four characteristics of an effective goal.
27. **Visual Arts** Your class decides to hold a student recognition and parent appreciation event at the end of the school year. All students will participate in planning and managing the event. A matrix organization structure will be used. Identify the major divisions of work that need to be completed for a successful event. Using a computer drawing program, design an organization chart you believe will be most effective for getting the work done. Assign each student in your class to a particular role in the organization chart. Be prepared to discuss your decisions with other students.
28. **Technology** Use the Internet to locate an example of a business use of each of the planning tools identified in the chapter: budget, schedule, standard, policy, procedure, and research. Construct a 3 × 6 table. In the first column, identify the planning tool. In the second column, briefly describe its use. In the third column, identify how the use of the tool supports business planning.
29. **Research** Use a library or the Internet to locate three articles from business magazines on the effects of flattening (reducing the levels of management) on businesses and their employees. Take notes on the articles as you read. Then prepare a one-page analysis of your research, presenting the advantages and disadvantages of the use of flattening and downsizing.
30. **Mathematics** Research is an important tool businesses use for strategic planning. On average, businesses spend about 3.8 percent of sales on research activities each year. In a recent year, the top businesses worldwide in terms of research expenditures were Rosche, Microsoft, and Nokia. Roche invested $9.1 billion on research with sales of $45.4 billion. Microsoft's investment was $9.0 billion for research with $58.5 billion in sales. Nokia's research budget was $8.2 billion and sales were $57.2 billion. Calculate the percentage of annual sales each company invested in research. Determine the percentage of sales invested in research by all three companies combined. Compare it with the average of all businesses.

CASE IN POINT

CASE 4-1: Solving Planning Conflicts

The ToyTime Company makes and sells a line of popular children's toys. In two months, retail stores will begin buying the company's products in large quantities in preparation for the holiday shopping season. Every year, ToyTime introduces one or two new toys designed to attract the attention and interest of children and their parents and get them into the stores at holiday time. Then they design in-store displays and promotions for the company's new toys as well as those that have been popular for many years, bringing in a high volume of sales of both new and traditional toys.

Jacob Marks, the marketing manager, has recently reviewed the results of research on this year's newest toy. The toy received the most positive customer response of any toy they have introduced in the past five years. Based on that research, Marks and his staff have projected that sales will be 10 percent higher this year than last. As a result of these estimates, he has committed funds for an advertising blitz to introduce the new toy. Several additional salespeople have been hired to begin early work with retailers to make sure both the national chains and independent stores are prepared with adequate inventory for the upcoming holiday sales period.

At the same time Jacob Marks has been working on the expanded marketing efforts, Janice McConklin, the production manager, has been running into problems. She has had difficulty getting an adequate supply of one of the key raw materials from the firm's only supplier. Production levels for the new toy have been 10 percent below plans during the last two months. It would be possible for Ms. McConklin to devote additional production time to increasing the inventory of the company's traditional products. However, she was not aware of the recent marketing research or marketing plans. The production plans, developed three months ago, were to keep inventory levels of those toys just slightly above last year's level. In discussions with the raw-materials supplier, it appears that the supply problem may be solved in two weeks. If so, she might be able to meet the production goals for the new toys but labor costs will have to increase and product deliveries will be delayed to retailers. She knows that retailers like to have the new toys early, but there is little she can do about it right now.

THINK CRITICALLY

1. What management problems are apparent in the ToyTime Company? Why have these problems occurred? Are the reasons related more to planning issues or to organizing issues in the company?
2. What is likely to happen to the company this year and in future years if the problem is not resolved quickly?
3. Using the management tools discussed in the chapter, give examples of how each could be used to help solve the company's problems.
4. What would you recommend right now that can help resolve the problems being faced by ToyTime? What should they do to avoid the same type of problem in the future?

CASE 1-2: Reorganizing a Business

Hector Fuego had just been hired by the board of directors to become the new CEO of You Build, Inc. You Build is a 50-year-old building supply company that operates in the southwestern United States. The company has a very successful history and has seen expansion to 50 stores in 23 cities. However, in the past three years, operations have been much less successful because the largest retailer in the industry, Home Warehouse, began to expand into the areas served by You Build. Home Warehouse built larger stores in very convenient locations with a broader set of products and low prices. It was clear the Home Warehouse was threatening the success of You Build. The board of directors made it clear to Mr. Fuego as they discussed their expectations with him that his most important priority was to find ways to meet the competition and maintain the success of You Build, Inc.

Because of its history, You Build had developed a very traditional line organizational structure. All strategic planning and major decisions are made by the CEO and a team of three vice presidents. There are two more levels of management at the corporate level; four regional offices with managers who report to the corporate level; a management team in every city that has three or more stores; and a store management team. Most of the managers has many years of experience with You Build and worked their way up through the system. Mr. Fuego believes most of the managers are very good at their jobs and work hard to make the company successful. However, it seems that the current organizational structure makes decision making very slow, and the many employees at the store level who work with customers have little input into store operations. He learned that the previous CEO had little contact with managers or employees of individual stores.

Hector Fuego wants to change the organizational structure of You Build, Inc. He believes the business will be more effective if the organization is flattened and the line organization is replaced with a team organization. The executives would set an example by forming a team to do corporate-level planning, advised by regional teams of experienced employees and store managers. City management positions would be eliminated, and each store would develop teams of employees to make decisions for the store's departments. He knew the change would not be easy because the company had used the traditional organizational structure for 50 years.

THINK CRITICALLY

1. What are the advantages and disadvantages of the change in organizational structure Hector Fuego is planning?
2. How do you believe You Build's managers will feel about the change? How do you believe the employees will feel?
3. What steps do you recommend that Mr. Fuego follow to prepare managers for the change? What should he do to prepare employees for their new role in the organization?

PROJECT My Own Business

Planning and Organizing Your Business

As you prepare to become a new business owner, you will spend the majority of your time on planning and organizing activities. If you recognize the importance of planning to the success of a new business, you will be willing to devote the necessary time to it. Starting with a business plan, you must develop goals, budgets, schedules, policies, and procedures. As you add employees, you will have to make decisions on how to organize and divide work so that it will be completed effectively. In the project activities for this chapter, you will plan and organize your business.

DATA COLLECTION

1. Meet with your business mentor and discuss the importance of planning and the types of planning tools he or she uses.
2. Go to several company or organization websites and read their vision and mission statements. Note several points you would like to include in your own company's vision and mission.
3. Using the Internet or your library, find and read several articles on ways that businesses are reorganizing work for more effective operations. Summarize the key points from those articles that you believe are useful to small businesses.
4. Locate several examples of organization charts for small businesses. Look for common elements and unique features. Consider how you can use the information in planning an organizational structure for your business that will support planned business growth.

ANALYSIS

1. Divide a sheet of paper or word-processing document into two columns. Label one column "Strategic Planning" and the other "Operational Planning." In each column, list as many areas of planning as you can that must be completed for your business.
2. Write a brief vision statement that reflects your vision of your company's reason for existing. Then write a mission statement that gives your company purpose and direction.
3. For each of the planning tools discussed in this chapter, identify how and when you will use the tool in your business. Prepare a one-month planning schedule in which you list when you will use each tool.
4. Assume you have hired two full-time and four part-time employees to help you operate your business. Consider the operations and activities that must be completed and prepare an organizational chart in which you list job titles and duties for each employee. Identify whether the organizational structure is line, line-and-staff, or some other type. Why do you believe that structure will be most effective?

CHAPTER 5

© Shutterstock/Yuri Arcurs

IMPLEMENTING AND CONTROLLING

5.1 The Implementing Function

5.2 Motivation and Change Management

5.3 The Controlling Function

5.4 Gathering and Using Performance Information

Reality Check

Losing Control

An office supply company developed a strategy to sell office supplies to the local business market through Internet and telephone sales. Jasmine Marsh was hired as the manager of a new telemarketing department that included computerized telephone and order-processing systems. She was given a large budget to retrain current employees and to hire and train new employees for telephone sales. A sales brochure highlighting the company's online catalog was personally delivered to all businesses in the city by company managers to introduce the new business and explain the ordering process. Follow-up telephone calls were made, promoting the company's delivery guarantee. The promise was that any order placed by 10 p.m. would be delivered by 10 a.m. the next day.

There was a real excitement among the employees when they made the sales calls to the new business customers. They were able to reinforce the company's service guarantee. Soon, orders began to come in. However, the rapidly expanding sales volume was putting pressure on Jasmine's department. The

workload was increasing rapidly as the telephone sales associates took orders, answered questions about products and existing orders, and attempted to solve customer problems. Technical difficulties resulted in unanswered calls and slow computers. Although individual problems were solved as quickly as possible, customers and sales associates were frustrated. After the first month of operations, it was clear that a growing number of problems were leading to employee dissatisfaction and a high turnover rate. Experienced employees, especially those who had worked for the company before the change, were quitting or asking for transfers because of the pressure they were facing on the job.

Jasmine knew that her department was essential to the success of the company. If the department was not able to maintain and increase the level of sales and process orders efficiently, the new business strategy would fail.

What's Your Reaction? What are the primary reasons for problems in the new department? What might Jasmine do to help employees?

112

The Implementing Function

Goals

- Recognize problems that can occur when plans are implemented.
- Identify important implementing activities performed by managers.

Terms

- motivation p. 115
- work team p. 115
- operations p. 116
- operations management p. 116
- process improvement p. 117

●●●● The Challenge of Implementing

The implementing function of management involves carrying out the organization's plans and helping employees to work effectively. The controlling function involves evaluating results to determine if the company's objectives have been accomplished as planned. The majority of managers, especially supervisors and middle-level managers, spend a great deal of their time on implementing and controlling activities.

Implementing involves guiding employee work toward achieving the company's goals. For example, a manager may communicate important goals to an employee team, provide leadership to help them determine how to complete the necessary work, and make sure that rewards and recognition are provided to everyone involved when their work achieves the goals.

You will remember from the scenario at the beginning of the chapter that Jasmine had many activities for which she was responsible in the new department. She was spending a great deal of time implementing the company's plans. Jasmine discovered what many experienced managers have learned. Plans are not effective unless they are implemented well. Changing conditions in a business create problems in the way work is accomplished. Here is what Jasmine learned about the implementing function as she continued to study the problems she was facing as a manager.

At the beginning, employees seemed to enjoy using the new computer equipment and making calls to customers. Jasmine had an excellent training budget and three months to prepare employees for their new work. The preparation time and training made them comfortable with their new work. The careful planning to personally deliver the brochures to customers and make follow-up calls resulted in immediate orders. Employees were pleased with their initial success. Customers liked the rapid delivery guarantee and the service-oriented approach of the local business. But as Jasmine looked back, that was where the problems started.

The first problem occurred when Jasmine established sales quotas for each employee. With sales growing rapidly, she didn't think it would be difficult for most employees to make their quotas. Jasmine believed the quotas would encourage everyone to emphasize selling rather than just waiting for customers to call in orders. However, some people easily exceeded their sales quotas whereas others seldom reached theirs. Several employees complained that the quotas emphasized selling too much and didn't allow them adequate time to answer customers' questions and solve their problems.

Supervisors must implement the plans that have been developed. What types of information are available in business plans to help supervisors direct the work of employees?

© iStockphoto/Daniel Laflo

The department began to experience some computer difficulties. When a high volume of calls came in, the computers would slow down. Employees would have to wait to get information on their screens, and occasionally all of the information entered would be lost before the order could be processed. Also, Jasmine was learning that when sales volume was high, the company sometimes was not able to meet its goal of overnight delivery. Although sales volume was higher than anticipated, Jasmine's department and the delivery department were still operating with the same number of employees as when the new wholesale business started. As a result, the telemarketing employees were starting to receive customer complaints that they were not prepared to handle.

While Jasmine was struggling with the computer problems and the sales quota issue, she was also facing the growing employee turnover problem. Even though she was hiring and training new employees, it seemed there were never enough employees to replace those who left and to handle the growing amount of business. To get new employees on the job faster, training time was reduced. That seemed to result in more errors in the orders processed. Veteran employees were being asked to work overtime to meet the demand and to help inexperienced telemarketers. That created even more employee dissatisfaction. Jasmine couldn't believe that a plan that seemed so good and had initially been successful could result in so many problems.

21st CENTURY SKILLS

Collaboration

Work teams require collaboration by all members. It is not enough to just do your job; you need to understand the goals of the team and how your role affects the work of other team members. Learning how to collaborate with others is helpful in every work environment, but it is especially important when you are a member of any sort of team.

 CHECKPOINT

Identify several types of changes that can occur in an organization that can create problems in accomplishing plans.

 Implementing Activities

To implement successfully, managers must complete a number of activities designed to channel employee efforts in the right direction to achieve the goals. These activities include effective communications, motivating employees, developing effective work teams, and operations management.

EFFECTIVE COMMUNICATIONS

Communication is an essential part of implementing work in a business. Managers must be able to communicate plans and directions, gather feedback from employees, and identify and resolve communication problems. Both personal and organizational communications are important. Because so many forms of communications media exist in organizations today, managing communications technology is an important responsibility.

Communication is much more than telling employees what to do. In fact, if employees believe managers are being too directive, they will likely be dissatisfied and not work as hard or effectively as they could. An important communication skill for managers is to listen to employees and involve them in deciding how work should be done. A manager should use both formal and informal communications. Encouraging employees to contribute their ideas and involving them in deciding the best way to do the work will help gain their commitment to achieving the goals.

EMPLOYEE MOTIVATION

Motivation is a set of factors that influence an individual's actions toward accomplishing a goal. Employees may be motivated to achieve company goals, or they may be motivated to pursue other goals that do not benefit the company. Managers don't actually "motivate" employees, but they can use rewards and punishments to encourage employees to motivate themselves toward pursuing company objectives. A key to motivation is to know what employees value and give them those things for achieving company goals. A reward is not motivating unless it is something the employee values. The reward does not always have to be monetary. People also value things such as praise, respect, an interesting job assignment, or extended breaks after hard work.

Motivation comes from influences both inside and outside the individual. *Internal motivation* stems from a person's beliefs, feelings, and attitudes that influence the person's actions. For example, many workers are motivated to do a good job because they get a feeling of satisfaction from a job well done. *External motivation* comes from rewards and punishments supplied by other people. For example, performing well on a difficult task may result in a bonus in the employee's paycheck, praise from the boss, or promotion to a team leadership position.

For many people, internal factors have the most influence on behavior. If employees consider work boring, they will not be motivated to do a good job. For others, external factors have the strongest influence on performance. An employee who values recognition will likely be motivated by the challenge of a competition to obtain the highest customer service rating. Keeping work areas clean, clutter free, and repaired can motivate employees who value a pleasant work environment.

All people have their own needs, and whenever possible will choose to do things that satisfy their needs and avoid doing things that don't. Managers can influence employee performance by understanding individual needs and providing rewards that satisfy those needs when employees accomplish work goals.

WORK TEAMS

Seldom do people complete all of their work alone. Most people are part of a work group and rely on cooperation from others to perform their work. Well organized groups can accomplish more than the same number of people working independently. Managers need to be able to develop effective work teams. A **work team** is a group of individuals who cooperate to achieve a common goal.

Effective work teams have several characteristics. First, the members of the group understand and support its purpose. They clearly understand the activities to be completed, know which activities they must perform, and have the knowledge and skills necessary to complete them. Group members are committed to meeting the expectations of others in the group and helping the group succeed. Finally, group members communicate well with each other and work to resolve problems within the group.

Managers can motivate employees with their actions even when they can't provide monetary rewards. Provide lots of encouragement, don't harshly criticize one-time errors, add fun and variety to routine work, offer leadership opportunities, allow employee input and choice when possible, and provide opportunities for social interaction as part of the job.

Team members must be able to work well together. How can an individual employee contribute to team effectiveness?

© Shutterstock/Alexander Raths

Just because several people work together, however, does not guarantee that they will be an effective work team. In fact, there are many reasons why they may not be an effective team. They may not know each other well or trust each other. They may have biases or stereotypes about other group members. They may not be prepared to cooperate in completing a task or know how to make effective team decisions.

Managers can play an important role in developing team effectiveness. To develop effective teams, they must understand the characteristics that make groups effective, help to organize the team and develop needed team skills, create a work environment that supports teamwork, and help the group resolve problems when they occur.

OPERATIONS MANAGEMENT

Operations are the major ongoing activities of a business. **Operations management** involves effectively directing the major activities of a business to achieve its goals. Several activities are part of operations management. Facilities, equipment, materials, and supplies must be available and in good operating condition so employees can perform their work. Employees must have the knowledge and skills to do their work. Managers must make sure that employees complete their tasks on schedule, and work to resolve problems that could interfere with the successful completion of the job.

Effective planning and organizing are important parts of operations management. Planning helps employees know what to do. In the same way, well-organized work space and procedures for completing work tasks help operations run smoothly. If problems occur in the operations of a business, managers should examine the planning and organizing of the work.

Managers must be prepared to implement the activities assigned to their area of responsibility. Some activities are common to most management areas. For example, managers must hire new employees, monitor work schedules, and communicate policies and procedures. In addition, most departments are organized to perform specialized operations. The manager of the marketing department may be responsible for advertising and sales. The information systems manager must ensure that computer systems are operational, the company's Internet sites are up-to-date, and software is problem-free. Managers need to understand the unique work of their departments in order to help employees complete that work.

In the past several years, organizations have paid a great deal of attention to improving the way work is done. Due to increasing competition, companies must operate efficiently to keep costs low so that they can compete successfully. Customers are demanding improved quality, so the company must produce products free of defects. The efforts to increase the effectiveness and efficiency of specific business operations are known as **process improvement**.

CHECKPOINT

What are the primary activities managers must perform as part of the implementing function?

5.1 ASSESSMENT

UNDERSTAND MANAGEMENT CONCEPTS

Determine the best answer for each of the following questions.

1. An example of an internal motivation factor is
   a. praise from your supervisor
   b. a pay increase
   c. personal satisfaction
   d. the admiration of co-workers

2. The efforts to increase the effectiveness and efficiency of specific business operations are known as
   a. organizational change
   b. team effectiveness
   c. the implementing function of management
   d. process improvement

THINK CRITICALLY

Answer the following questions as completely as possible.

3. What are some reasons that managers with well-developed plans may still have problems when implementing those plans?

4. Why do some employees work well in teams and others do not?

Motivation and Change Management

Goals

- Describe the main points of three theories of motivation.
- Identify the steps managers should follow when implementing change.

Terms

- physiological needs p. 118
- security needs p. 118
- social needs p. 118
- need for esteem p. 118
- self-actualization p. 118
- achievement need p. 119
- affiliation need p. 119
- power need p. 119
- hygiene factors p. 119
- motivators p. 119

●●● Motivation Theories

Think of the days when you are excited to get up and go to school or work. You enjoy the day and work hard. Time seems to move faster than usual. Compare that to the days when it is impossible to get up and you dread going to work or school. The day seems to go on forever, and you don't seem to be able to get anything done.

In the same way, you probably can identify teachers, coaches, or business-people for whom you enjoy working and who seem to be able to encourage your best efforts. You also know others whom you would prefer to avoid and for whom it is a struggle to perform well. What causes the differences?

You learned earlier that internal and external factors motivate people to act in certain ways. Psychologists have developed theories about what factors motivate people to behave as they do. Managers can influence employees to behave in ways that help achieve company goals by understanding and applying theories of motivation.

MASLOW'S HIERARCHY OF NEEDS

Abraham Maslow described motivation in terms of a hierarchy of needs. The first level is physiological needs, followed by security, social, esteem, and self-actualization needs. **Physiological needs** are things required to sustain life, such as food and shelter. **Security needs** involve making sure you and those you care about are safe and free from harm. **Social needs** include the need to belong, to interact with others, to have friends, and to love and be loved. The **need for esteem** includes the need for recognition and respect from others. Finally, **self-actualization** is the need to grow emotionally and intellectually, to be creative, and to achieve your full potential.

According to the theory, people seek to satisfy these needs in order, from lowest to highest. If a lower level of need is not satisfied, a person will have little motivation related to higher levels. For example, starving people will be more motivated to find food than to be concerned about friendships. But once people have reasonably satisfied their physiological and security needs, the need for social interaction will have more influence on their behavior. Applying Maslow's theory, managers can influence employee behavior by recognizing the levels of the hierarchy that are currently most important to an employee and then try to use things such as job assignments, praise and support, and financial rewards that best meet those needs.

MCCLELLAND'S ACHIEVEMENT MOTIVATION

Whereas Maslow's theory is based on a set of needs common to all people, David McClelland believed that people are influenced most strongly by one of three specific needs: the need for achievement, the need for affiliation, and the need for power.

McClelland suggested that people with a high **achievement need** take personal responsibility for their own work, set personal goals, and want immediate feedback on their work. People with a strong **affiliation need** are concerned about their relationships with others and work to get along well and fit in with a group. Finally, those with a strong **power need** want to influence and control others and to be responsible for a group's activities. You can probably think of people who fit into each of these three need classifications.

Managers who believe in McClelland's theory recognize that various jobs provide greater or fewer opportunities for achievement, affiliation, or power. Managers working with individuals with a high achievement need should provide opportunities for them to make decisions and control their own work. When managers see a high affiliation need in their employees, they should assign them to group projects and teams. These employees will respond well if socializing opportunities are provided. Finally, people with a high need for power will work best when given the opportunity to be project leaders or to be involved in planning and decision making. McClelland's theory suggests that the strength of the three needs can be changed over time with careful development.

HERZBERG'S TWO-FACTOR THEORY

A third important motivation theory was developed by Frederick Herzberg. He conducted studies of employees to identify what satisfied and dissatisfied them in their work. His research resulted in the identification of two distinct groups of factors related to motivation. Therefore his theory is known as the *two-factor theory*.

Herzberg called one group hygiene factors. **Hygiene factors** are job factors that dissatisfy when absent but do not contribute to satisfaction when they are present. Examples of hygiene factors are the amount of pay and fringe benefits, working conditions, rules, and the amount and type of supervision. For example, a good company-sponsored health care plan will not motivate employees to do a better job. But the lack of a good health plan could cause employees to be dissatisfied with their jobs.

Herzberg called the second group motivators. **Motivators** are factors that increase job satisfaction. The people whom Herzberg studied were motivated by factors such as challenging work, recognition, achievement, accomplishment, increased responsibility, and personal development.

The interesting part of Herzberg's theory is that the two types of factors and their results are separate from each other. In other words, hygiene factors can create dissatisfaction but cannot improve satisfaction. For example, people can be dissatisfied with the level of their pay and fringe benefits, but pay increases will not increase satisfaction very much or for any length of time. So, providing hygiene factors, such as pay increases and better working conditions, will only prevent employees from being dissatisfied. It will not motivate employees to perform at a higher level for more than a short time.

On the other hand, motivators increase satisfaction. To stimulate workers to higher achievement, managers should provide motivators such as opportunities

FACTS & FIGURES

Employee Retention

Managers are challenged to find ways to retain their best employees. From surveys of over 100,000 employees, the Gallup organization reported the key reasons employees choose to leave their jobs are lack of respect for management, stress or job burnout, lack of challenge, poor work environment, insensitivity to personal needs, poor quality of work life, and feeling out of the loop on information.

for interesting work, greater individual control and responsibility, and recognition for good work.

Managers are often surprised by Herzberg's studies. It is easy to believe that a pay increase will motivate employees to perform better. However, people are often dissatisfied when they compare their pay to that of others, or they believe they are worth more than they are currently being paid. Factors such as fair pay, flexible work hours, and good fringe benefits can keep people from being dissatisfied but seldom are the major reason people are motivated to perform well.

CHECKPOINT

Why should managers understand motivation theories?

●●● Managing Change

The only thing that seems certain in business is change. Global competition, downsizing, mergers, and many other organizational changes affect workers and their jobs.

People are not always comfortable with change. Consider changes you have experienced. Examples could include moving, changing schools, relationships with family or friends, or an important decision you may be facing. How did you react to that change? When it appears that things will be different, those affected by the change are likely to be very concerned.

When people's jobs are threatened, when they are uncertain about how a change will affect them, or when they do not trust those responsible for planning the change, they will probably resist the change. They are likely to resist most when change occurs suddenly, when they are not prepared, or when they don't understand the reasons for the change.

To implement organizational change, managers must work to reduce that resistance and to make change as comfortable as possible for the employees affected. Careful planning that involves the people affected will make the transition smoother, and employees will be more likely to support the change. The steps in an effective change appear in Figure 5-1.

Implementing Change
STEP 1: PLANNING Carefully plan for the change.
STEP 2: COMMUNICATING Communicate with people, so that change does not surprise them.
STEP 3: INVOLVING Involve people, so they feel a part of the change.
STEP 4: EDUCATING Educate people, so they understand the change.
STEP 5: SUPPORTING Support people in their efforts to change.

© Cengage Learning 2013.

Figure 5-1 Managers should follow these steps when making changes that affect employees.

Change occurs regularly in business today. What are some examples of recent changes that have occurred in businesses in your community?

© Getty Images/Altrendo

PLANNING

Whenever possible, managers should not move too rapidly to make changes. They must be certain that change is needed and that the organization will be better off as a result of the change. Then they should follow a careful procedure to gather information, identify and study alternatives, and determine the consequences of change. A well-considered plan will help to assure the best results and will give confidence to those most affected by the change. Taking a bit more time to plan will save time and reduce problems later.

COMMUNICATING

Sometimes managers believe it is best not to say anything to employees about possible changes until they are ready to take action. They believe that early information will raise unnecessary concerns and misunderstanding. People who study the change process recognize that it is almost impossible to conceal information about pending changes. Based on informal communication and limited information, rumors and misinformation will spread. If people are surprised by a change or believe they have been misled, the result is usually more damaging to the organization than the result of early, direct communications.

Managers who have previously established open communications with employees are in the best position to communicate with them about possible changes. Because change occurs frequently in business, employees who are used to regular communications with their managers will not be surprised by information about potential changes, even if the changes may appear to be negative. Regular, open, two-way communications between managers and employees are part of an effective change process.

NETBookmark

One of the most highly respected awards in business is the Malcolm Baldrige Quality Award. Established by the federal government in 1987, it recognizes the achievements of companies that improve the quality of their goods and services and provide an example of high quality and productivity.

Access the website for this textbook and choose the link for Chapter 5 Net Bookmark. Watch the video highlighting the reasons organizations participate in this award program and the results they have achieved. How do employees benefit when their company works to identify and achieve quality goals?

www.cengage.com/school/bizmgmt

INVOLVING

People are more likely to support changes when they have been involved in planning. Managers must recognize that employees can be a good source of ideas for effective solutions and how to make changes. Most effective change processes involve the people who will be affected in gathering information, considering alternatives, and testing solutions. It is usually not possible to involve everyone in all parts of the change process or to use a majority vote to decide on a change. However, employees will be more supportive when they know their voices will be heard and that they have input into plans that result in change.

Managers need to respect and seek the input of employees. Sometimes managers say they want employees' ideas but then ignore their input. That will frustrate employees and make them reluctant to participate in the future. Managers must make it clear that not every idea contributed by an employee can be implemented but will be carefully considered in the planning process.

EDUCATING

Change in business does not just happen. New products, new technology, or redesigned jobs require people to prepare. Usually, that means information and training. As plans for change develop, managers must determine who will be affected and what new knowledge and skills those employees will need. Then managers should implement information meetings and training programs to prepare employees for the required changes.

Many companies have had to reduce the number of employees through downsizing. That type of change is very difficult for managers to implement and employees to accept. Some companies try to help the people who will no longer have jobs by offering training for other positions available in the company or to develop skills that will help them get jobs with another company.

SUPPORTING

How willing are you to make a change if you are uncertain of the result? When people believe they will receive support from their organization, they are more willing to accept changes. All changes involve some amount of risk, and organizations cannot guarantee success. However, managers need to assure employees that there is support available to help them adjust to the change.

The support can take many forms, such as allowing employees time to adjust to change. Managers may provide more feedback on employee performance and be less critical of mistakes early in the new process. Counseling, training, additional information and advice from employees who have already experienced the change are other methods of support.

Sometimes changes have negative effects on employees that cannot be avoided. Jobs may be eliminated or restructured. Employees may have to deal with major job changes that can require reduction in pay, different working conditions, additional training, or a move to another location. Support is especially needed under these circumstances. Employees who lose their jobs need time to adjust. Companies may provide full or partial salary for several weeks or months while the people affected look for new jobs. The companies may identify open positions in the organization and help employees retrain or relocate. They can give preference to those employees when new positions open. Many companies now provide personal and career counseling, help with job-seeking skills, and even pay for employment services for employees who are terminated due to change.

CHECKPOINT

What steps should managers follow to help employees understand and adjust to a major change?

5.2 ASSESSMENT

UNDERSTAND MANAGEMENT CONCEPTS

Determine the best answer for each of the following questions.

1. The motivation theory that people are influenced most strongly by one of three specific needs—achievement, affiliation, or power—was developed by
   a. Maslow
   b. McClelland
   c. Pavlov
   d. Herzberg

2. Which of the following is not an effective way for a manager to implement change?
   a. Do not move too rapidly to implement change.
   b. Don't communicate with employees about the change until a final decision has been made.
   c. Ask employees for ideas on effective solutions and procedures.
   d. Be less critical of mistakes made by employees while changes are being made.

THINK CRITICALLY

Answer the following questions as completely as possible.

3. Do you agree or disagree that increases in pay and other financial benefits are not good long-term motivators for most employees? Explain your answer.

4. How do you believe a manager should involve employees in planning for a change that will result in some of them losing their jobs?

The Controlling Function

Goals

- List the three basic steps in the controlling function.
- Identify and describe four types of standards.

Terms

- quantity standard p. 126
- quality standard p. 126
- time standard p. 126
- profit p. 126
- cost standard p. 126
- variance p. 127

 Understanding Controlling

"Employee absences have increased by 3 percent this year."

"Maintenance costs are down an average of $150 per vehicle."

"Salespeople in the southern district have increased new customer orders by 12.3 percent in a three-year period."

"An average of 16 additional employees per month are enrolling in the company's wellness program."

"The adjustments to the welding robot's computer program have reduced the variations in the seam to 0.0004 mm."

These statements provide very valuable information to managers. With the proper information, managers can tell how well activities are being performed. Reviewing performance is one part of the fourth management function—controlling. Managers must be able to determine if performance meets expectations. When expectations are being met, the manager can recognize employees for their success and even reward them when possible. If performance problems are occurring, managers need problem-solving skills to develop good solutions.

MANAGEMENT AS A CONTINUOUS PROCESS

All managers perform four management functions. Planning involves setting goals and directions for the business. Organizing deals with obtaining and arranging resources so the goals can be met. Implementing is the responsibility for carrying out the work of the organization. Controlling is determining whether goals are being met and what actions to take if performance falls short of the goals.

Although each of the functions has a unique purpose and includes a specific set of activities, they are all related. Planning improves if there is an effective organization to provide information to managers. Without effective planning, it is difficult to decide how to organize a business and what resources are needed. Implementation is impossible without plans and difficult with a poorly designed organization. Controlling cannot be completed unless the company has specific goals and plans. Figure 5-2 shows that management is a continuous process and that each function supports the others. Controlling is the final function and provides the information needed to improve the management process and business operations.

THE STEPS IN CONTROLLING

Controlling involves three basic steps: (1) establishing standards for each of the company's goals, (2) measuring and comparing performance against the established standards to see if performance met the goals, and (3) taking corrective action when performance falls short of the standards.

Consider the following example. A business has a goal to manufacture and deliver to a customer 1,000 made-to-order blankets by a specific date. The standard is to produce 25 blankets each day for 40 consecutive days. During the first 10 days, only 200 blankets are produced, or an average of 20 blankets a day. Because production is 50 blankets below the standard—250 blankets in 10 days—the managers must take action to increase production during the remaining 30 days. The corrective action may include scheduling overtime work or assigning more workers to the task. Even as they take action, the managers should carefully study the manufacturing process to see why the standard that was originally set could not be met.

As another example, the manager of a shoe store wants to make sure that new styles of shoes sell rapidly. The standard is to sell 30 percent of all shoes in a new style within one month. If the store sells only 20 percent, the manager must take corrective action. The manager may choose to increase the advertising for the shoes, give salespeople a higher commission for selling that style, or mark down the price to sell more. The manager will also want to use this information when planning purchases in the future.

In each example, the managers set a standard based on the work to be accomplished. Then they compared performance against the standard to see if the company's goals could be met. Finally, if performance was not meeting the standard, the managers had to determine how to correct the problem. Note that in both examples the managers did not wait very long to begin measuring performance. Controlling activities should be completed before the problem is too big or too expensive to correct.

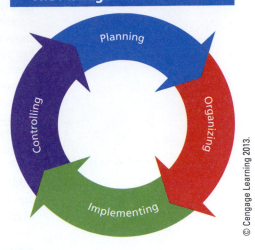

The Management Functions

© Cengage Learning 2013.

Figure 5-2 The four functions of management are directly related. The way in which one is completed affects each of the others.

 **CHECKPOINT**

What are the three basic steps in controlling?

●●● Setting Standards

Managers establish standards in the planning stage. They need to set high but achievable standards. Managers can determine reasonable standards by studying the task, using their past experience, gathering industry information, and asking for input from experienced workers. The standards become the means for judging success and for applying controls.

TYPES OF STANDARDS

The standards used to control business operations depend on the type of business, its size, and the activities being controlled. The major types of standards are quantity, quality, time, and cost standards.

QUANTITY STANDARDS A **quantity standard** establishes the expected amount of work to be completed. Quantity standards take different forms, depending on the tasks. Production managers may specify the minimum number of units to be produced each hour, day, or month by individual workers or groups of workers. Sales managers may establish the number of prospective customers that sales representatives must contact daily or weekly. A manager of administrative services may establish a minimum number of forms to be completed or number of lines of information to be keyed in an hour by information-processing personnel. The quotas Jasmine established for her employees in the telemarketing department described at the beginning of the chapter are examples of quantity standards.

QUALITY STANDARDS Quantity standards alone are often not enough to judge an employee, a product, or a service. A fast worker, for example, can be very careless, or a slow worker can be extremely careful. Thus, the quality of the work performed is often just as important as the quantity produced. A **quality standard** describes expected consistency in production or performance.

Perfection—having no errors—may be the only acceptable standard for some products and services. An automobile battery that does not work cannot be sold. An invoice with pricing errors cannot be sent to a customer. An accountant cannot calculate a client's taxes incorrectly. Perfection is the standard, but it may not always be practical or cost-effective to develop procedures to check every finished product. On an assembly line where thousands of products are produced every hour, sampling a few products each hour may be enough to identify when quality problems occur so corrective action can be taken.

TIME STANDARDS Time standards are closely related to quantity and quality standards. Most business activities can be measured by time. A **time standard** is the established amount of time needed to complete an activity. The amount of time it takes to complete an activity has an effect on costs, the quantity of work completed, and often on the quality of the work. Time standards are more important to some businesses than to others. Building contractors and bakeries are examples of businesses that normally have strict time schedules. If they do not meet the schedules, they suffer an immediate financial loss. If an office tower is not completed on time, the builder usually must pay a financial penalty. A baker who does not have doughnuts and bagels ready for the breakfast rush will lose a major portion of the day's sales. Other businesses may not see the immediate financial loss, but failure to maintain time standards will result in fewer products being produced, poor coordination of activities between departments, or other problems.

COST STANDARDS An important measure of the success or failure of a firm is financial profit or loss. **Profit** equals income minus costs. Therefore, managers can increase profits by either (1) increasing sales revenue or (2) decreasing costs. Not all managers or employees are directly connected with work that increases sales. However, most employees and managers do influence costs. Wasting material or taking more time than necessary to perform a task adds to the cost of doing business. Increased costs, without a proportionate increase in sales dollars, decrease profit. Businesses must be cost-conscious at all times. **Cost standards**, or the predetermined cost of performing an operation or producing a good or service, are an effective way of helping businesses maintain profitability.

Generally, businesses pay more attention to cost controls than to any other type of control. The control devices used, as a result, are numerous. One of the main purposes of the accounting department is to provide detailed cost information. This is why the head of an accounting department is often called a *controller*. Most managers, however, act as cost controllers in some way. Increasingly, employee work teams and individual employees are assigned responsibility for cost controls.

The most widely used tool for controlling costs is the budget. Like schedules and standards, budgets are also planning devices. When a budget is prepared, it is a planning device; after that, it is a controlling device. Actual cost information is collected and compared with budgeted amounts. These comparisons permit judgments about the success of planning efforts and provide clues for making changes that will help the company reach its financial goals. Managers need to monitor costs regularly. When budget problems are identified early, managers have time to take corrective action.

MEASURING AND COMPARING PERFORMANCE

Once standards have been established, they are used to determine effective performance. Managers gather information on all parts of business operations for which they are responsible. They compare that information against the standards to determine if performance is meeting the standards. A **variance** is a difference between current performance and the standard. A variance can be positive (performance exceeds the standard) or negative (performance falls short of the standard). Whenever a variance exists, managers must identify the reasons for the difference.

Actual performance exceeding the standard may seem to be an ideal situation that requires no corrective action. However, it is important to understand why the higher-than-expected performance occurred so that it can be repeated. Or, perhaps the positive performance in one area of the business is having a negative effect on another area. In addition, managers should review the process for developing standards to see why they set the standard lower than the performance that could actually be achieved.

The greatest concern occurs when performance is lower than the standard. That means that the company is not performing at the expected level. It also says that there are problems between planning and implementing activities. Managers not only need to take corrective action as soon as possible to improve performance but must review procedures carefully to avoid the same problem in the future. Managers must be careful in the way they communicate the problem to employees and how they take corrective action. If employees believe the manager is blaming them for their role in the substandard performance, they may not be motivated to help solve the problem. On the other hand, if employees do not recognize the seriousness of the problem, they will not make the changes needed for improvement to occur.

Management MATTERS

There's an app for that, too

On a large scale, computer applications can instantaneously track everything in a business from the hourly production of oil wells to the sales of specific colors of sweaters in each store of a worldwide retail business. At any time, managers can access that information to make production decisions and update sales forecasts.

In the same way, cell phone users can track minutes used, text messages sent, or amount of data downloaded by their phone. Some plans require users to pay for each service while others set limits and charge customers when they exceed their plan. Some plans allow users to check their usage online or directly on their phones. The information can be used in controlling expenses. Knowing the current status of your account can help you make better decisions on whether to send a text message to all your friends or download a new song.

What Do You Think? Does access to information help you make better decisions? What types of information can help you stick to a budget, better schedule your time, or improve your physical health?

Monitoring all activities for which managers are responsible can take a great deal of time. Managers can use information systems to reduce the amount of time spent on controlling. Computers can monitor performance and compare it to the standard. When the computer identifies a variance, it generates a variance report for the manager. Through the use of computer monitoring and variance reports, managers can identify problems quickly and begin to take immediate corrective action.

 **CHECKPOINT**

Provide an example of each of the four types of standards.

5.3 ASSESSMENT

UNDERSTAND MANAGEMENT CONCEPTS

Determine the best answer for each of the following questions.

1. The final step managers take in the controlling process is
   a. establishing performance standards for company goals
   b. measuring performance using established standards
   c. establishing new goals
   d. taking corrective action when standards are not met

2. Consistency in products and performance is measured with a
   a. quantity standard
   b. quality standard
   c. time standard
   d. cost standard

THINK CRITICALLY

Answer the following questions as completely as possible.

3. Do you believe managers should perform each of the management functions in order? Why or why not?

4. Which type of standard do you believe is most important to improving the overall effectiveness of a business? Justify your choice.

Changing the Face of Manufacturing

You can't make a mistake when building airplane engines. The jet engines produced by the General Electric Aircraft Engines plant in Durham, North Carolina, have more than 10,000 parts. When completely assembled, they weigh more than eight tons. Yet a bolt not tightened, a tool left inside the engine, or a safety procedure not followed can cost hundreds of lives.

Approximately 200 people assemble the huge engines. But there is only one boss, the plant manager, and one instruction to guide the work of the plant—the date each engine needs to be finished. Beyond that instruction, employees make every decision about how the work will be completed. They hold a record for delivering every engine ordered on schedule for over three years. During that time, they were able to reduce the cost of producing the engine by nearly one-third.

How was this GE plant able to achieve its amazing record with only one manager? Here are some unique characteristics of the organization:

- Employees are organized into fourteen work teams that make almost all decisions. Everyone is on a team, and team meetings are scheduled when all employees are available.
- There are three pay levels for employees, based on skill levels. As employees increase their skills, they can advance into a higher pay level.
- There is no time clock. If someone has a doctor's appointment or needs to go to their child's school activities, they work with team members to be able to leave.
- Everyone learns how to do many of the assembly tasks so they can help each other.
- Teams are responsible for hiring new team members. They do the interviewing, and they have to agree on the right person.
- Teams solve problems and often come up with unique but simple solutions.

The team environment in Durham works. The plant has the lowest turnover rate and lowest production costs of any of General Electric's engine assembly plants. Its unique organization demonstrates that when employees are given the opportunity to work together to manage their work, they do it better than anyone could have imagined.

THINK CRITICALLY

1. How do you believe the pay plan affects employee motivation? What are the advantages and disadvantages of that plan?

2. Discuss reasons why the team problem-solving process seems to result in unique but effective solutions. Are there reasons a solution developed by employees is likely to be more successful than if the same solution was developed by a manager without the input of employees?

© Shutterstock/Rick Becker-Leckrone

Gathering and Using Performance Information

Goals

- Describe three corrective actions managers can take as part of controlling performance.
- Discuss several important areas of cost control in businesses.

Terms

- inventory p. 131
- just-in-time (JIT) inventory control p. 132
- credit p. 132

●●●● Taking Corrective Action

When managers discover that performance is not meeting standards, they can take three possible actions:

1. Take steps to improve performance.
2. Change policies and procedures.
3. Revise the standard.

If managers have planned carefully, they should be reluctant to change standards. In the blanket-manufacturing business discussed earlier, managers should know from past experience whether producing 25 blankets a day is reasonable. Only under unusual circumstances (major equipment breakdown, problems with suppliers, employee strikes, etc.) would the blanket managers reduce the standard. However, failure to meet the goal of 1,000 blankets by the specified date will not please the customer and may result in a loss of sales.

Most often, managers need to improve performance of activities when standards are not being met. This usually means making sure that the work is well organized, that supplies and materials are available when needed, that equipment is in good working order, and that employees are well trained and motivated.

Occasionally, standards are not met because activities cannot be accomplished as planned, or policies and procedures are not appropriate. This is likely to happen when a business begins a new procedure, starts to use new equipment, or has other major changes. In this situation, managers may need to change the policies or procedures that are not working in order to meet the standards. Process improvement discussed earlier usually results in policy or procedure changes.

Finally, when the managers have explored all possibilities to improve performance and it still does not meet the standards, they need to evaluate the standards themselves. Planning is usually not exact. Conditions can change between the time plans and standards are developed and the time activities are performed. Managers cannot expect that all standards will be appropriate. Managers like to raise standards when they believe workers can achieve higher performance. It is difficult to make the decision to reduce standards, but that may be necessary from time to time. If a group of new employees is doing the task, performance standards may need to be reduced until the employees have had the necessary training and opportunity to perfect their skills.

When new planning procedures are used or new activities are implemented, planning is less likely to be accurate. Standards developed in those situations should be studied more carefully than the standards for ongoing activities or standards that have been developed in the same way for a long period of time.

Standards should be revised when it is clear they will not accurately reflect performance and attempts to improve performance have been unsuccessful. When standards are changed, the new standards and the reasons for the changes should be clearly communicated to the employees affected. Also, the procedures for setting standards should be revised so that standards developed in the future are more accurate.

CHECKPOINT

Why should managers be reluctant to change standards even when performance does not meet those standards?

CONTROLLING COSTS

All managers need to watch constantly for ways to reduce costs. Excessive costs reduce the company's profit. There are several areas in a business where managers can anticipate cost problems and develop ways to reduce costs. They are inventory, credit, theft, and employee health and safety.

INVENTORY All the materials and products a business has on hand for use in production and available for sale is called **inventory**. Manufacturers need to produce enough of each product to fill the orders they receive. They need enough raw materials to produce those products. Wholesalers and retailers must maintain inventories to meet their customers' needs. In all types of businesses, if inventories are too low, sales will be lost. If inventories are too high, costs of storage and handling will increase. There may be products remaining in inventory that are never used or sold. In that situation, the company loses all of the money invested in those products.

Inventory control requires managers to walk a fine line. They must maintain sufficient inventory to meet their production and sales needs yet not so much

© Shutterstock/Dmitry Kalinovsky

Inventory control is a kind of balancing act. What factors need to be in place for just-in-time inventory controls to be successful?

FACTS & FIGURES

Consumer Credit

According to the U.S. Census Bureau, 181 million Americans hold a total of 1.5 billion credit cards. Credit cards are used to complete more than $2.5 trillion in transactions each year. The National Foundation of Credit Counseling reports that 26 percent of Americans admit to not paying their bills on time. At any time, about 4 percent of credit card payments are more than 30 days past due.

that it is too costly to handle and store. They must select products to purchase that can be sold quickly at a profit. They must purchase products at the right time and in the correct quantities to minimize the company's inventory cost.

Many companies use **just-in-time (JIT) inventory control**. JIT is a method of inventory control in which the company maintains very small inventories and obtains materials just in time for use. To set up a JIT system, managers carefully study production time, sales activity, and purchasing requirements to determine the lowest possible inventory levels. They then place orders for materials so that they arrive just as they are needed for production or to fill sales orders. Production levels are set so the company has only enough products to fill orders as they are received. Effective inventory control methods can be very complicated. JIT inventory management requires the close support and cooperation of a company's suppliers as well as the companies providing transportation services to resupply inventories. If an order is not delivered on time, production will be delayed and sales will be lost.

CREDIT Most businesses must be able to extend credit to customers. Businesses also use credit when buying products from suppliers. **Credit** is the provision of goods or services to a customer with an agreement for future payment. If the company extends credit to customers who do not pay their bills, the company loses money. Also, businesses that use credit too often when making purchases may spend a great deal of money on interest payments. Those payments add to the total cost of the product and reduce profits.

Businesses must develop credit policies to reduce the amount of losses from credit sales. They must check each customer's credit history carefully before offering them credit. They must develop billing and collection procedures that will collect most accounts on time. The age of an account is the number of days that payment is past due. Managers need to watch the age of each credit account. The longer an account goes unpaid, the greater the chance that the company will never collect the full payment.

Companies should buy on credit when they will lose money if they don't make the purchase. If a production schedule cannot be maintained without the credit purchase and if the price that can be charged for the sale of the product is high enough to cover the added cost, the credit purchase should be made. Companies may also need credit to purchase expensive equipment or large orders of products and materials. But managers responsible for purchasing must control the amount of money the company owes to other businesses. It is easy to make too many purchases on credit. When this happens, the interest charges will often be high, and the company may not have enough money to pay all of its debts on time.

Managers must be sure bills are paid on time to protect the credit reputation of the business. If the supplier offers a discount for paying cash, managers should check to see if the company will benefit from taking advantage of the discount. Before using credit, managers should study the credit terms to see what the final cost will be. Credit can be a good business tool if used carefully but can harm the business if not controlled.

THEFT Businesses can lose a great deal of money if products are stolen. Thefts can occur in many parts of a business and can be done by employees as well as by customers and others. Businesses can lose cash, merchandise, supplies, and other resources due to theft. By establishing theft controls, businesses usually are able to reduce losses.

The theft of merchandise from warehouses and stores is a major business concern. Retail stores are the hardest hit by such losses. Retailers lose billions of dollars annually due to crime, much of which is from theft of merchandise.

Businesses and individual computer users must apply security measures to protect data and personal information. Have you ever experienced identity theft?

© Getty Images/Photodisc

Shoplifting by customers and employees equals 6 percent or more of total sales each year for the typical retailer. Much of the loss occurs during the end-of-year holiday shopping season when stores are crowded and part-time workers are employed, but it is an ongoing and serious problem throughout the year.

Many stores, warehouses, and trucks are burglarized during the night or when merchandise is being transported. Security guards and a variety of security equipment are frequently used to reduce the chances of such thefts. Many companies carry insurance against losses, but with high loss rates the cost of insurance is very expensive.

A rapidly growing area of concern to businesses and consumers alike is computer and Internet fraud. Business data and personal information are held in large and small computer files. Financial records and personal identity information are moved back and forth via the Internet. Data are exchanged online as part of many business transactions. Businesses increasingly contract with specialized companies to handle activities such as order processing, customer billing, accounting, and human resource management. Businesses must carefully plan and review all procedures for gathering, storing, and exchanging data to ensure the highest level of security and to prevent data and identity theft.

HEALTH AND SAFETY Even when employees are absent from work because of sickness or injury, the company must continue to operate. Other employees must be available to fill in for the absent employee or the work will go undone. The salary of both the absent employee and the replacement employee must be paid. A share of employee health insurance costs and other benefits are often paid by the company as well. Studies estimate that the annual costs to many businesses of employee absence and health care now exceed 20 percent of the salary paid to each employee. An employee paid at the rate of $17.00 per hour requires an additional $3.40 each hour to pay those costs. A person earning $45,000 will add $9,000 or more to the costs of the business just for health expenses and employee absences.

The rising cost of health insurance is causing many businesses to increase the percentage of the insurance costs employees must contribute and offer coverage only to full-time employees. Businesses are working with insurance companies to find lower-cost insurance alternatives that may reduce benefits and add to the out-of-pocket costs for employees. Many companies offer no health insurance benefits at all. The cost of health insurance is one of the major issues facing business managers and employees today.

Businesses can control or even reduce the costs associated with health and safety programs if managed carefully. These companies provide safety training for all employees. Work areas and equipment are inspected regularly to make sure they operate correctly and safely. Employees are provided information on ways to improve their health. Investments in fitness centers and wellness programs have resulted in lower costs for the business due to fewer medical claims and reduced employee absences.

 **CHECKPOINT**

What are the main areas in a business where managers can anticipate cost problems and develop ways to reduce costs?

5.4 ASSESSMENT

UNDERSTAND MANAGEMENT CONCEPTS

Determine the best answer for each of the following questions.

1. Which of the following is not one of the actions managers should take if they discover that performance is not meeting standards?
    a. Take steps to improve performance.
    b. Change policies and procedures.
    c. Revise the standard.
    d. Assign the problem to a trusted employee.

2. The best credit policy for a company is to
    a. never make purchases on credit
    b. charge very high interest rates to customers to increase profits
    c. only buy on credit when it will lose money if the purchase isn't made
    d. pay for credit purchases well before payment is due

THINK CRITICALLY

Answer the following questions as completely as possible.

3. Explain the meaning of the statement "planning is usually not exact" as it applies to evaluating performance and standards.

4. What recommendations would you make to a business to increase computer and Internet security for the business and its customers?

CHAPTER CONCEPTS

- Implementing involves communicating effectively, motivating employees to do their best work, developing work teams, and managing company operations.

- People choose to do things that will satisfy their needs and avoid things that don't. Managers influence performance by providing rewards when employees accomplish work goals. Theories of motivation developed by Maslow, McClelland, and Herzberg describe factors that influence employee behavior.

- Change is common in organizations and managers need to help employees accept change. The steps in an effective change process are planning, communicating, involving, educating, and supporting.

- Controlling ensures that company operations meet expectations. Controlling steps are: establishing standards for goals, measuring and comparing performance against standards, and taking corrective action when performance falls short of standards. Common types of standards are quantity, quality, time, and cost standards.

- To help the company make a profit, managers must control costs. Areas commonly monitored for cost control are inventory, credit, theft, and employee health and safety.

REVIEW BUSINESS MANAGEMENT TERMS

Write the letter of the term that matches each definition. Some terms will not be used.

1. A specific measure that describes expected consistency in production or performance.
2. The predetermined cost of performing an operation or producing a good or service.
3. A specific measure that establishes the expected amount of work to be completed.
4. Job factors that increase job satisfaction.
5. A specific measure that establishes the amount of time needed to complete an activity.
6. Job factors that dissatisfy when absent but do not contribute to satisfaction when they are present.
7. All the materials and products a business has on hand for use in production and available for sale.
8. Effectively directing the major activities of a business to achieve its goals.
9. Efforts to increase the effectiveness and efficiency of specific business operations.
10. The difference between current performance and the standard.

a. achievement need
b. affiliation need
c. cost standard
d. hygiene factors
e. inventory
f. motivation
g. motivators
h. need for esteem
i. operations management
j. physiological needs
k. power need
l. process improvement
m. quality standard
n. quantity standard
o. security needs
p. self-actualization
q. social needs
r. time standard
s. variance

REVIEW BUSINESS MANAGEMENT CONCEPTS

Determine the best answer.

11. Effective work teams have all of the following characteristics *except*
    a. all members understand and support the group's purpose
    b. the team does not need to have a group leader
    c. members work to resolve problems in the group
    d. The team's activities are clear.

12. The person who described motivation in terms of a hierarchy of needs was
    a. Maslow
    b. Herzberg
    c. McClelland
    d. Jacobs

13. Employees are more likely to support what they
    a. find to be the easiest
    b. are paid for
    c. are involved in planning
    d. have been told to support by their manager

14. The first step in the controlling process is
    a. establishing standards for each of the company's goals
    b. communicating with employees about the importance of controlling
    c. taking corrective action when performance falls short of standards
    d. organizing employees into work groups

15. Which of the following is *not* a way managers can increase profits?
    a. Increase sales revenues.
    b. Decrease costs.
    c. Add more employees.
    d. Reduce waste.

16. A production manager who specifies the minimum number of units to be produced each hour, day, or month is establishing a
    a. variance
    b. time standard
    c. quality standard
    d. quantity standard

APPLY WHAT YOU KNOW

Answer the following questions.

17. Based on the Reality Check scenario at the beginning of the chapter, do you believe most of the problems were the result of poor planning or poor implementation? Justify your answer.

18. Why are businesses paying much more attention to developing effective work teams today than in the past?

19. What differences in implementation and controlling activities, if any, would there be for a manager of a small business and a manager in a large business?

20. What should a manager do if it is clear that many employees will view a planned change negatively?
21. What are some examples of business activities where perfection is the only acceptable standard for performance?
22. Should managers delegate controlling activities to employees and employee teams? Why or why not?

MAKE ACADEMIC CONNECTIONS

Complete the following activities.

23. **Technology** Form a team with three or four other students in your class to analyze motivation theories. As a team, develop a list of at least 15 things you believe motivate employees to perform well. After completing the list, prepare diagrams using a computer graphics program that illustrate each of the three motivation theories discussed in the chapter. Then add your team's motivating items in the appropriate locations on each of the three illustrations. Present your diagrams to the other teams and provide reasons for your decisions about the motivating items and the theories.

24. **Mathematics** The following chart shows several items from a company's budget. Column 1 shows the categories for which a budget amount has been determined. The budgeted amounts are shown in Column 2 and the actual amounts are shown in Column 3. Complete the chart by calculating the variance between the budgeted and actual amounts (Column 4) and the percentage increase or decrease (Column 5).

Budget Category	Budget	Actual	Variance	% + or −
Sales	$680,000	$720,000		
Merchandise returns	11,000	12,500		
Cost of goods	229,400	240,000		
Operating expenses	52,000	46,500		
Administrative costs	34,000	31,500		
Marketing expenses	306,000	350,500		
Net profit	47,600	39,000		

25. **Research** Gather information on the Internet about the growing problem of identity theft. Identify five specific actions individuals can take to prevent identify theft and five steps businesses can take to protect personal information of their customers. Use a computer and presentation software to report your findings. Make sure to reference the sources of your information.

CASE IN POINT

CASE 5-1: Preparing For Change

Kane's Buy-Rite Used Cars had experienced its third straight year of declining profits. Although a few more cars were sold each year, the profit per sale was down. Kane Shouk, the owner, had traditionally relied on a loyal group of customers who returned to buy a second and even third car, demonstrating their satisfaction with the company. Fewer customers were returning each year, however, and the company had to increase its promotional budget. Although the promotional activities were attracting prospective customers to the business, salespeople were finding it difficult to convince them to buy. There were fewer new customers than there were former customers who were not returning.

Kane believed two factors were contributing to the declining business. First, new-car dealers were now leasing many of their cars rather than selling them. This meant customers needed very low or no down payments and paid lower monthly payments. New-car payments were now comparable to used-car payments. Second, Kane's salespeople were getting more aggressive in order to sell cars. Because profits were down, more cars needed to be sold. Some customers, especially those who had purchased from the business before, were complaining they felt pressured by salespeople.

Kane decided the procedures for selling automobiles had to change. He knew that several of the new-auto dealers had gone to a one-price, no-negotiation strategy. A low but fair price was put on each car, and the car would be sold at that price so there would be no pressure from the salesperson regarding the price to be paid. Kane hoped the salespeople would help the customer select the best car rather than worrying about negotiating the best price. He wanted customers to find a good value but also to have a very positive experience when they came to Kane's Buy-Rite to shop for a used car.

Kane expected two problems in convincing the salespeople that the new sales strategy would be effective. First, it would require a different type of selling relationship with the customer, and some salespeople might have a hard time adjusting. They were already having greater difficulty selling the number of automobiles they were able to sell in the past. Now, Kane was asking them not to pressure customers to buy. Second, the salespeople would be paid a salary rather than a commission. Several of the top salespeople would not be able to make as much money as they could when sales were good, but all salespeople should be able to make a decent salary if the new strategy worked.

THINK CRITICALLY

1. How can Kane motivate the salespeople now that commissions will not be paid on sales?
2. What controlling activities could Kane undertake to be able to specifically determine why profits have been declining?
3. Do you agree with Kane's approach to trying to resolve the problem? Why or why not?

CASE 5-2: Cutting Employee Compensation

The TieDown Company has been an established company in the United States since 1938. It manufactures specialty fastening materials used by trucking, storage, and construction firms. It is increasingly facing competition from companies that have manufacturing facilities around the world. Many of those companies have lower production costs, allowing them to undercut TieDown's prices to customers. Several of TieDown's U.S. competitors have moved manufacturing facilities to other countries where wage rates are lower, whereas others have faced bankruptcy and have either been bought out by foreign firms or have gone out of business. TieDown's management wants to remain in the United States and retain its loyal employees, but it has to find a way to reduce costs. Though it is still profitable, profits have been declining and it is clear the future is not bright unless major changes are undertaken. After careful thought and study, the company's executive team has developed a strategy they believe will allow them to remain in their current location, become competitive once again, and return to their previous level of profitability over a period of five years.

As a part of its new strategy, the company will implement a major change in the way it produces its belts and fasteners. In the past, most production was handled by skilled machine operators who completed a three-year apprenticeship program before operating the manufacturing equipment on their own. A new computerized manufacturing process will allow the main production activities to be performed by people with fewer skills who require only a very short training period. That means the company will reduce the number of machine operators by 20 percent and will cut the pay rate for machine operators by $6 per hour. However, the company will need a number of computer programmers and computer technicians for the new equipment. Those jobs will pay $5 per hour more than the average skilled machine operator is currently making.

TieDown will encourage the current operators to switch jobs and will provide the needed training for the new computer jobs. It is expected that nearly half of the current machine operators will be able to switch jobs if they choose to do so. The rest can be employed in the new production jobs but will have to take the lower pay rate for the job. To make the change easier for those operators, TieDown will provide a one-time payment equal to one month's wages to help them with the adjustment to the new job and pay rate.

THINK CRITICALLY

1. What is your opinion of TieDown's plans for the change to the new production equipment and jobs?
2. What would you recommend that the company do, if anything, for the machine operators who are not hired for the computer positions and choose not to accept the pay reduction?
3. As the production manager for TieDown, outline the procedure you would follow to implement the changes described so that most employees will support them.
4. In small groups, play the role of TieDown's managers and prepare a presentation about the change, using presentation software. As each group presents, the rest of the class should play the role of employees and ask questions of the presenters.

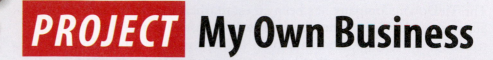

PROJECT My Own Business

Motivating Employees and Controlling Business Performance

Many small-business owners are very good at performing the work required to run a new business. The business is their idea, may have been a lifetime goal, and involves work that they enjoy. The owner is very willing to work hard and spend long hours each day and week in making sure the business is successful.

As employees are added, the owner is sometimes disappointed that they are not as committed to the business and seem less motivated. A whole new area of management skill is required when the number of employees starts to increase.

Managers must also use controlling activities determine if decisions are working well or if changes must be made. In this part of the project, you will study employee motivation and controlling activities and develop plans to use those skills as a business manager.

DATA COLLECTION

1. Survey 10 people who are employed full- or part-time. Ask them to list the factors related to their work that motivate them to perform well and the factors that dissatisfy them. Classify each person based on the three motivation theories discussed in this chapter.
2. Identify sources of information on these areas of cost control: inventory, cash and credit management, theft, and personnel health and safety. Make a list of the resources you locate, along with a brief description of the information available from each resource.

ANALYSIS

1. Assume that you have several employees working for your business. Identify the factors you would use to motivate them to maintain effective performance. Estimate the cost of each of the motivation methods. (Many effective motivation strategies have no real cost.)
2. Develop a standard to evaluate each of the following activities in your business: (a) daily sales of each product, (b) amount of product spoilage and loss, and (c) customer satisfaction. Then describe the data collection and analysis procedure you would follow to determine if the standard is being met.

Administrative services managers are responsible for all the support services needed to maintain a company's operations: secretarial and clerical services; mail, telephone, and electronic communications services; operating supplies procurement and management; conference and meeting planning; employee travel; printing and reproduction; records management; and security services.

Employment Outlook

Administrative services careers will grow at an average rate over the next 10 years. The greatest demand will be in service industries, government, and health care. Demand for managers with special knowledge of security and safety issues and facilities management will increase.

Job Titles

Facilities Manager

Office Manager

Operations Manager

Procurement Specialist

Property Manager

Support Services Manager

Needed Skills

- Must be analytical, detail-oriented, flexible, with good communication skills.
- In small businesses, may need only a high school degree and significant work experience. In large organizations and at higher levels, need at least a bachelor's degree, often in a specialized area such as information management, office technology, human resources, or accounting. For most positions, advanced computer and technology skills are increasingly important.

Working in Administrative Services

As executive vice president for administrative services, Janeen ensures that every department in the company has the support services it needs. She has just met with an architect who is designing an addition to the offices. She must make sure the building meets the requirements for communications and computer technologies and has adequate space for all the necessary administrative support activities. She is now on her way to meet with the CEO to discuss new information security procedures that will protect employee and customer data stored in the company's computers. She was called into work late last night to deal with a burst water line that flooded the first floor. She had to negotiate a contract for temporary work space and arrange for materials to be shipped overnight.

Career Assessment

Why is administrative services management important to the success of a business? What do you like and dislike about the career area?

Business, Management & Administration

© Getty Images/Photodisc

Case Study

SOUTHWEST AIRLINES: PROFILE OF A LEADER

Airlines have faced economic difficulties with rising fuel costs and increased security standards. While many airlines have faced bankruptcy and corporate restructuring, Southwest Airlines has consistently maintained profitability and a high level of success. Starting as a small airline serving three Texas cities in 1971, it is now the largest domestic airline in the U.S. based on the number of passengers served.

The mission of Southwest Airlines is "dedication to the highest quality of customer service delivered with a sense of warmth, friendliness, individual pride, and company spirit." The airline's mission statement has always guided the way the corporation conducts business. It highlights the company's commitment to serve customers, act ethically, and practice good citizenship in all decisions and actions. Southwest Airlines wants customers and investors to have confidence in the airline and its employees. The airline has a strong commitment to providing customers with safe, affordable, reliable, timely, courteous, and efficient air transportation and baggage handling on every flight it operates. Southwest is equally concerned with providing a fair return on its shareholders' investments. Southwest's mission statement has led the way to the best cumulative consumer satisfaction record in the airline industry.

Southwest Airlines is also committed to providing employees a stable work environment with many opportunities for learning and personal growth. Since its beginning, the airline has developed a culture that encourages an entrepreneurial spirit in its employees. It emphasizes personal responsibility, initiative, creativity, innovation, and the use of independent judgment. Southwest Airlines management is committed to providing employees the same concern, respect, and caring attitude within the organization that they are expected to share with every Southwest customer.

Southwest is widely recognized as an outstanding corporate citizen. Southwest Airlines ranked fourth on *Fortune* magazine's World's Most Admired Company list. It was named to MSN Money's "10 Companies That Treat You Right." The American Customer Satisfaction Index has ranked Southwest Airlines number one among all airlines for 17 years.

THINK CRITICALLY

1. Which groups of people are addressed by the Southwest mission statement?
2. Why is it important for a company to have a strong reputation for community service?
3. Why does Southwest Airlines pay so much attention to its employees?
4. What are important factors to customers when considering the value of an airline?

Prepared Speech Event

PROCEDURE   The BPA Speech Event requires participants to select a topic related to management and develop an oral presentation of no less than five and no more than seven minutes. Participants will be allowed one minute to set up their presentation. Participants must use a scholarly approach to secure information that emphasizes content and research. The speech and works cited must be prepared using the format provided in the Style & Reference Manual. Participants must provide two word-processed copies of the speech outline and works cited before giving the speech.

SCENARIO   The CEO of a successful national retailer has asked you to prepare a presentation for new managers devoted to an important management concept of your choice. Examples include one of the management functions (planning, organizing, implementing, controlling), decision making, and leadership. Your speech should include examples of management strategies used by successful businesses. The CEO has asked you to focus on successful managing during challenging economic times. The speech should provide a road map for new managers to follow as they begin their management careers.

YOUR ASSIGNMENT

Your assignment is to prepare a speech that gives valuable guidance for new managers of a large national retailer. The content of your speech should provide important guidelines for management responsibilities.

SCORING CRITERIA

- **Content** Appropriate, accurate, well developed, and well researched
- **Organization** Coherent, logical, understandable, and suitable for topic
- **Voice** Pitch, tempo, volume, and enthusiasm
- **Deportment** Appearance, eye contact, gestures, mannerisms, and poise
- **Effectiveness** Clear purpose, interesting examples, practical advice

> ### Think Critically
>
> 1. Choose a topic for your speech and explain why you chose it.
> 2. What can you do to make sure that you achieve the highest possible score based on the criteria presented?
> 3. Why is it important to research successful companies when preparing your presentation?

www.bpa.org

For more information about competitive events and performance indicators, go to the BPA website

The Environment of Business Management

2 UNIT

CHAPTERS

CHARACTERISTICS OF BUSINESS

6.1 The Nature of Business

6.2 Changes Affecting Business

6.3 The Contributions of Business

© Shutterstock/Kurhan

Reality Check

Income and Expenses: Maintaining a Balance

Sean Mackin stood at the curb waiting for the school bus with his son, Jake. Jake was growing up so fast. It seemed Sean had to buy something new for him every week—clothes, shoes, school supplies, sports equipment, and, most recently, his own computer. His daughter, Bella, had similar demands. Last week it was golf shoes; this week, her first visit to the orthodontist; and next week, supplying cupcakes for Bella's softball team.

"Is there ever an end to expenses?" Sean wondered.

"What did you say, Dad?" asked Jake.

"I'm just thinking out loud, Jake. Here comes your bus. Don't forget you have baseball practice after school. I packed your glove and shoes in your backpack."

Jake shrugged. "After practice, can we stop and get that new game for my computer? Remember, it's on sale."

Sean had forgotten, but he could always rely on Jake and Bella to remind him of things they wanted him to buy. That was on top of the regular purchases to run the household. Of course, he and his wife, Nora, both had things they regularly needed to buy as well. Fortunately, with

Nora's management job at the new manufacturing plant and his job as a physical therapist, the family's income was adequate to meet their ongoing expenses, with some set aside in a small but growing savings account. However, they had to budget carefully and watch what they spent. Sean and Nora always hoped they would not face an unexpected large expense.

Waving good-bye to Jake as the bus pulled away, Sean thought about the family vacation he and Nora were planning for late June. The children had never been on a plane and Sean wanted to make the vacation special. Nora was leaning toward a drive to the mountains for the kids' first camping experience. "Maybe Nora is right. Not paying for a hotel and airline tickets would help keep costs down," he mused. "We can use our old tent, but Jake and Bella will need sleeping bags, and we'll need to save extra money for the higher cost of gas for the car. Either way, we need to organize a garage sale if we want to go on vacation."

What's Your Reaction? What do Jake and Nora need to consider as they make vacation plans?

The Nature of Business

Goals
- Explain the nature of business activities.
- Describe the general types of businesses.

Terms
- business p. 146
- production p. 146
- marketing p. 146
- finance p. 146
- goods-producing businesses p. 147
- service businesses p. 147
- industry p. 147

●●●● Management of Business Activities

American businesses work for Nora and Sean Mackin and their family as well as for millions of other people in the United States and around the world. As the family's financial manager, Nora budgets the family's money and pays the bills. She and her husband, Sean, along with Jake and Bella, are consumers. They buy goods such as clothes, computers, food, and sporting goods. Likewise, they buy services such as trips to the orthodontist and repairs for their automobile. Businesses work very hard to provide the goods and services needed by consumers.

The story of American business is a fascinating one. Products found in most homes come from countless types and sizes of businesses. The flowering plant growing on the Mackin's front porch could have been purchased from a vendor at the local farmers' market. The new sleeping bags could have been produced by a business with 10 manufacturing plants and over 100,000 employees. Jake's computer may have been assembled by a company that purchases hundreds of computer parts from several other companies around the world. The cupcakes for Bella's softball team may be baked by one of the 15 employees of the neighborhood bakery. These and scores of other products found in homes, offices, shops, and factories are produced and sold by many kinds of businesses.

An organization that produces or distributes a good or service for profit is called a **business**. Profit is the difference between earned income and costs. Every business must manage at least three major activities. The first activity, **production**, involves making a product or providing a service. Manufacturing firms create products that customers purchase to satisfy needs, whereas service firms use the skills of employees to offer activities and assistance to satisfy customer needs. Examples of service firms are doctors' offices, airlines, restaurants, and home repair businesses. Today the number of service firms far exceeds the number of manufacturing firms. For this reason, it is sometimes said that we live in a service society.

The second activity that businesses must manage is marketing. **Marketing** includes the activities between business and customers involved in buying and selling goods and services. The third management activity, **finance**, deals with all of the money matters involved in running a business. Whether a business has one worker or thousands of workers, it must manage its production, marketing, and finance activities.

The price that Nora and Sean pays for Jake's computer game will be based in large part on supply and demand for the game. Supply of a product refers to the number of similar products that will be offered for sale at a particular time and at a particular price. If there are many similar products available, the price is likely to be lower. Demand, on the other hand, refers to the number of similar products that will be bought at a given time at a given price. If there are many people looking to buy the same computer game, the price is likely to be higher.

CHECKPOINT

What is the difference between a manufacturing firm and a service firm?

●●● Types of Businesses

This chapter will focus on the various types of businesses and business activities and what it takes to manage a business successfully. Management is influenced by the type of business, its size, and the resources it needs.

Generally, there are two major kinds of businesses—goods-producing businesses and service businesses. **Goods-producing businesses** produce goods used by other businesses, organizations, or consumers. Companies that mine coal and extract oil from the earth provide resources that are used by other companies and consumers. Automotive companies sell to businesses as well as consumers. Goods-producing companies construct buildings, build bridges, manufacture airplanes, and assemble televisions. Farmers and other agricultural producers are considered goods-producing businesses because they grow crops and raise livestock needed for the food we eat and used in the manufacture of a variety of products we use every day.

Unlike goods-producing businesses, **service businesses** are a type of business that use mostly labor to offer mostly intangible products to satisfy consumer needs. Service business examples include firms engaged in marketing (wholesalers and retailers), in finance (banks and investment companies), and in providing services (medical offices, fitness centers, and hotels) as their primary business activities.

Industry is a word often used to refer to all businesses within a category doing similar work. For example, the publishing industry includes any business that deals with producing and selling books, magazines, newspapers, and other printed documents prepared by authors. The automotive industry includes all manufacturers of automobiles, trucks, and other vehicles as well as the producers of related automotive products. Even government can be considered an industry, because it provides fire and police protection, libraries and schools, and many other services required by the citizens the government serves. Figure 6-1 shows the number of people employed in selected industries.

CHECKPOINT

Name an example of a goods-producing business and an example of a service business.

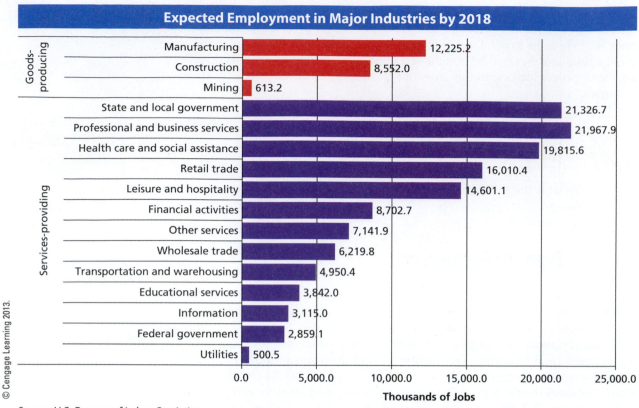

Expected Employment in Major Industries by 2018

Goods-producing

Industry	Thousands of Jobs
Manufacturing	12,225.2
Construction	8,552.0
Mining	613.2

Services-providing

Industry	Thousands of Jobs
State and local government	21,326.7
Professional and business services	21,967.9
Health care and social assistance	19,815.6
Retail trade	16,010.4
Leisure and hospitality	14,601.1
Financial activities	8,702.7
Other services	7,141.9
Wholesale trade	6,219.8
Transportation and warehousing	4,950.4
Educational services	3,842.0
Information	3,115.0
Federal government	2,859.1
Utilities	500.5

Thousands of Jobs (axis: 0.0, 5,000.0, 10,000.0, 15,000.0, 20,000.0, 25,000.0)

Source: U.S. Bureau of Labor Statistics

Figure 6-1 All aspects of a business must be considered when developing a management strategy.

6.1 ASSESSMENT

UNDERSTAND MANAGEMENT CONCEPTS

Determine the best answer for each of the following questions.

1. An organization that produces or distributes goods or services for a profit is a(n)
   a. producer
   b. manufacturer
   c. business
   d. industry

2. A lawn-mowing business is an example of a(n)
   a. service business
   b. industrial business
   c. manufacturing business
   d. marketing business

THINK CRITICALLY

Answer the following questions as completely as possible.

3. Why are service businesses growing faster than other types of businesses in the United States?

4. How do service businesses support the work of goods-producing businesses?

Changes Affecting Businesses

Goals

- Describe how innovations affect businesses.
- Identify the impact global competition has had on U.S. businesses.
- Discuss ways in which businesses can improve their business practices.

Terms

- innovation p. 149
- global competition p. 150
- effectiveness p. 151
- efficiency p. 151
- domestic goods p. 151
- foreign goods p. 151
- output p. 152
- productivity p. 152
- downsize p. 153
- empowerment p. 153

Innovation's Impact on Management

Management decisions are made in a dynamic environment—an atmosphere of constant change. To be successful, a manager must guide a business to react quickly to the changing nature of society. Managers need to understand the impact of innovation.

An **innovation** is something entirely new. Innovations affect the kinds of products and services offered for sale by other businesses. For example, telephones have been around since the late 1800s. Basic telephone technology did not change much until the innovation of cellular phone systems in the 1980s. Today, change is even faster with the growth of smartphones. These phones combine wireless communication with computing power allowing software applications to provide digital assistance at almost any location. Now customers have more choices in how to communicate with others.

Innovations also affect business operations. For example, since Apple Computer built one of the first personal computers about 35 years ago, computers operated by individual employees have increasingly influenced the way companies do business. Computers help businesses design and manufacture products as well as keep track of billing, inventory, and customer information. Computers are now involved in most key business functions. The Internet is an innovation that has literally changed the relationships between businesses, employees and their customers. Customers have 24-hour access to businesses without leaving their homes. Employees can work for a business by linking in with others from all over the country and even around the world. Modern innovations are allowing for instant and constant contact between managers, employees, and customers. Managers can now keep in contact by cell phones, e-mail, social networks, and text messaging.

 CHECKPOINT

What are two ways that innovations affect businesses?

●●●● Impact of Global Competition on Business Management

For hundreds of years, American businesses led the way in producing new goods and services for sale around the world. Consumers worldwide eagerly purchased exciting new products that were invented and made in the United States. Factories hummed with activity, workers from other countries arrived by the thousands to find jobs, and people spent their wages buying the goods that the firms produced. Many businesspeople and government leaders from foreign countries also arrived to find out how American businesses were managed.

During the past half-century, however, other countries have become more industrialized and have learned how to invent and produce new products for consumers. Often the products were cheaper than similar products produced in the United States and, over time, many of the products were judged to be of equal or better quality. Americans gradually began to purchase these foreign products.

Foreign companies learned to produce innovative designs for products ranging from cell phones to MP3 players and flat-screen televisions. American business leaders soon realized it was time for change. They had to find ways to use the abundant resources of the United States and the human talent of their managers and employees to meet the challenge of global competition. **Global competition** is the ability of businesses from one country to compete with similar businesses in other countries. One of the biggest challenges facing American businesses today is competing in the global economy.

 CHECKPOINT

Identify two major types of changes that present challenges to business.

In what types of consumer goods does the U.S. face serious global competition?

© Getty Images/Digital Vision

●●●● Focusing Management on the Right Things

Managers often study their own operations to determine whether they are doing the right things and doing the right things well. Two terms are used to describe the best management practices. First, **effectiveness** means making the right decisions about what products or services to offer customers and the best ways to produce and deliver them. Second, **efficiency** means producing products and services quickly, at low cost, without wasting time and materials. Firms that provide products at the lowest cost while maintaining the quality customers expect will usually succeed. Some companies are extremely efficient but very ineffective, whereas others are effective but inefficient. Good managers focus on both effectiveness and efficiency and are able to achieve both.

ACHIEVING EFFECTIVENESS

Making the right decisions requires both common sense and skill. Knowing what customers want is critical to business success and to achieving effectiveness. What kind of sleeping bags, for example, will best satisfy the needs of the Mackin family when they take their summer vacation in the mountains? In the early days of manufacturing, customers bought whatever was available because there were few brands, colors, and styles from which to select. Today, the choices for most products have increased because many businesses provide similar products. Consumers can usually choose among the products offered by both domestic and foreign firms. **Domestic goods** (products made by firms in the United States) must compete with **foreign goods** (products made by firms in other countries).

Businesses today focus efforts on gathering information from consumers, studying their buying habits, testing new products with prospective customers, and adding new features to existing products. New designs, different materials and colors, understandable instructions, and ease of product use are features customers like. Large businesses spend millions of dollars examining customers' preferences. Equally important, businesses also invest heavily in keeping customers satisfied after products are sold. Product guarantees and follow-up with customers to make sure the product is working well help keep customers loyal.

American car producers have learned to equal or exceed foreign car makers in the quality of their products. Is quality an important factor when you buy a car or other expensive product?

To meet their needs, customers increasingly are concerned about the quality of products they buy. They want them to work well and last a long time. A growing emphasis of American producers is to improve the quality of the products they produce. Japanese car makers are an excellent example of how foreign producers captured a large portion of the market worldwide by providing customers with reliable and attractive cars. In the past, American car producers were not meeting quality needs as well as Japanese producers in the view of many buyers.

© Getty Images/Photodisc

Too many new cars had defects that required numerous trips to car dealers to correct. On the other hand, Japanese cars had fewer initial problems and required little service.

American producers learned important lessons about quality from the Japanese. Today, American car producers are building products that are equaling their Japanese and European counterparts. American car manufacturers and producers of many other products vigorously stress to their workers the importance of using procedures that result in the highest quality. The concept is called *total quality management (TQM)*, which is a commitment to excellence that is accomplished by teamwork and continual improvement of work procedures and products. Where TQM is practiced, managers and employees receive a great deal of training on the topic of quality from experts. The result is a return to what customers want—well-made products.

ACHIEVING EFFICIENCY

Not only must firms do the right things, such as offering high-quality products, but they must also produce their products efficiently. Efficiency is measured by **output**—the quantity produced within a given time. **Productivity**, on the other hand, refers to producing the largest quantity in the least amount of time by using efficient methods and modern equipment. Workers are more productive when they are well equipped, well trained, and well managed. Employee productivity in the United States has grown over the years; however, Americans are working longer than employees in other countries.

Efficiency—including improved productivity—can be achieved in three ways:

1. Specialization of effort
2. Better technology and innovation
3. Reorganization of work activities

SPECIALIZATION In any business with more than a few employees, work can be performed more efficiently by having workers become specialists. In a large automobile repair shop, for example, not all workers are general mechanics. Rather, some workers specialize in body repair work whereas others specialize in repairing transmissions or engines. When workers specialize, they become expert at their assigned tasks. As a result, specialization improves quality while increasing the amount produced. Because specialization improves efficiency, it is no wonder that businesses hire or train employees for many specialized jobs.

Efficiency can also be improved through mass production. Mass production is a manufacturing procedure actually started in the early 1900s. It combines the use of technology, specialized equipment, and an assembly line. Employees perform efficient repetitive assembly methods to produce large quantities of identical goods. Through mass production, the cost of goods manufactured decreases because it is possible to produce more items in less time. Today, computer-driven equipment and robots make it possible to mass-produce large numbers of items with fewer workers.

TECHNOLOGY AND INNOVATION Efficiency can also be improved through the application of advanced technology. Technology includes equipment, manufacturing processes, and materials from which products are made. Because of new discoveries and inventions, better-quality goods and services are built at a faster pace and often at a lower cost. Improved materials, for example, may weigh less, last longer, and permit faster product assembly. Examples of new technology are found in everyday items such as cars, clothing, computers, and electronic appliances. Advanced technology helps companies stay ahead of competitors. And because technology has a significant impact on productivity, businesses spend billions of dollars annually on inventing, buying, and using new technology.

REORGANIZATION OF WORK   The third and quite challenging way to increase efficiency is through reorganizing the way work gets done. When companies experience slow growth or negative growth, a typical reaction is to try to cut back on production costs. Businesses **downsize** by reducing the amount and variety of goods and services produced and the number of employees needed to produce them. Laying off workers, dropping unprofitable products, or even increasing the use of technology helps firms cut their costs, but producing the right products inexpensively is still a problem. To address this problem, some firms choose bold actions similar to tearing down the business and rebuilding it.

Many firms believe employees are their most important resource. Further, managers have learned that by empowering workers, businesses can become more productive. **Empowerment** is letting workers participate in determining how to perform their work tasks and offer ideas on how to improve the work process. Empowerment dramatically changed the role of the worker. In the past, workers performed narrow tasks on assembly lines and had little decision-making power. After empowering workers, firms find that the quality of work often improves, as does the efficiency of production. Although better-trained and highly skilled workers are required, fewer managers are needed. Companies reduce the number of levels of management by pushing down the day-to-day decisions directly to workers rather than to managers. Workers learn to use new technology, to work in teams, and to be responsible for quality.

While practicing empowerment, some managers also redesign the work flow throughout their organizations—a concept sometimes called *re-engineering*. Instead of typical assembly lines found in factories and offices, production steps are eliminated, abbreviated, or placed entirely in the hands of a team of employees. Fewer well-trained workers, with the help of advanced technology and streamlined work processes, are able to better satisfy customers. Firms that adopt these practices find that customer satisfaction rises along with productivity.

As a result of the recession of 2007, companies experienced slow and sometimes negative growth. At the same time, businesses were facing competition from growing economies such as China. Many companies reacted by trying to cut production costs by laying off workers and freezing hiring. In turn, the rate of unemployment in the U.S. and around the world rose dramatically.

Investing in advanced technology helps businesses achieve greater efficiency. How does technology contribute to greater customer satisfaction?

© Jupiter Images/Comstock

Recessions don't last forever. The American economy recovered by the actions of both the U.S. government and businesses across the country. American firms renewed their position as strong competitors in the global marketplace as a result of restructuring their work processes and a more intensive focus on quality and customers' needs. Businesses became more innovative by using technology and by empowering workers to be innovative. Furthermore, both large and small businesses are no longer thinking only about customers in their own countries. They see prospective customers located all around the world.

 **CHECKPOINT**

Why must companies be concerned about both effectiveness and efficiency?

6.2 ASSESSMENT

UNDERSTAND MANAGEMENT CONCEPTS

Determine the best answer for each of the following questions.

1. The ability of businesses from one country to compete with similar businesses in other countries is known as
   a. domestic competition
   b. foreign competition
   c. global competition
   d. fair competition

2. Which of the following is *not* one of the ways companies can achieve efficiency?
   a. specialization of effort
   b. reducing prices charged to customers
   c. better technology and innovation
   d. reorganization of all work activities

THINK CRITICALLY

Answer the following questions as completely as possible.

3. Why were Japanese automobile manufacturers able to compete effectively with U.S. manufacturers who were considered world leaders?

4. What are some reasons that quality increases when employees are empowered to make decisions about their work?

Dell Direct

Companies can satisfy customers in many ways. Most buyers want a high-quality product at the lowest possible price and immediate help when trouble occurs with a product. Successful firms in recent years have introduced innovative ways to meet customer expectations. Not only pizza businesses make home deliveries; now many furniture companies make deliveries to the customer's home on the day of purchase. United Parcel Service and Federal Express not only make door-to-door deliveries but also pick up packages to be shipped from customers' homes. Best Buy offers home repairs of computers and other electronic equipment using their Geek Squad.

Dell Computer Corporation, however, was the first to do what everyone said would surely fail—sell computers using a toll-free phone number. Michael Dell, the founder of the firm, was told that people want to see, touch, and try highly technical products before they buy. However, those critics were proven wrong.

Michael Dell, who had always looked for easier and faster ways to get things done, got an idea while in college that he believed would serve the computer customer well. He would provide customers with a catalog of computers and computer parts. When they knew what they wanted, they could call his toll-free number, place the order with a credit card, and expect to have the computer shipped directly to their homes or offices within a brief period. Dell worked with computer parts suppliers and assemblers to quickly build the specific computer for each customer once the order was received. Because he didn't incur the expense of maintaining a physical store or a large inventory of parts and supplies, Dell was able to keep prices low.

To further make customers happy, he provided a guarantee, and later an extended repair contract offering efficient mail-in or local service if anything went wrong. The idea worked beyond anyone's imagination. Within a few years, his business was profitable and growing rapidly. With the development of the Internet as a method for customers to quickly locate and purchase products, Dell extended its direct sales efforts through an interactive website. Dell is now one of America's largest firms, with computers sold around the world using many of the same ideas that Michael Dell created in 1983, when the business was launched.

Many other computer firms have copied his low cost, fast service, and customer satisfaction guarantee and have initiated direct-sales efforts. Many other firms in different businesses soon adopted Michael Dell's ideas to gain the effectiveness and efficiency that lead to satisfied customers.

THINK CRITICALLY

1. Why do you think buyers like to purchase from Dell Computer Corporation using the Internet or telephone?

2. What specific actions did Michael Dell take to make his company effective?

3. What specific actions did he take to make his company efficient?

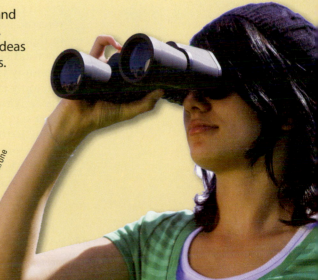

© Shutterstock/Rick Becker-Leckrone

6.3

The Contributions of Business

Goals

- Identify two ways a nation measures its economic growth and prosperity.
- Describe the benefits of business ownership to the nation and individuals.

Terms

- gross domestic product (GDP) p. 156
- underground economy p. 156
- entrepreneur p. 158
- franchise p. 159
- franchisor p. 159
- franchisee p. 159

●●● Business Growth and Prosperity

Overall, the United States is a prosperous nation. Much of its prosperity is due to business growth. Around the world, people admire and envy this country's economic strength. Let's look at two ways in which a nation measures its economic wealth and its benefits to citizens.

GROSS DOMESTIC PRODUCT

The chief measure of a nation's economic wealth is the **gross domestic product (GDP)**. The GDP is the total market value of all goods and services produced in a country in a year. Whenever products or services are purchased, the total dollar amount is reported to the federal government. The GDP of the United States is compared from year to year and is also compared with the GDP of other countries. These comparisons provide an ongoing measure of economic success.

Certain types of transactions, however, are never included in the GDP. These transactions are not recorded because they are unlawful or do not occur as part of normal business operations. For example, when a student is hired by a homeowner to mow lawns, formal business records are not normally prepared and the income is usually unrecorded. Some adults work part- or full-time for cash and never report that income or pay taxes on it. When drugs or counterfeit merchandise are sold illegally, such transactions are of course unreported. Income that escapes being recorded in the GDP is referred to as the **underground economy**. Business transactions that occur in the underground economy have increased in recent years in relation to the total GDP. Estimates range between 5 percent of the GDP during a brisk economy to 20 percent during a slow economy. The size of the underground economy concerns government officials due to its illegal nature and because the activities are not taxed although the people involved still require government services.

In 2010, the total known and recorded GDP for the United States reached the staggering $14.7 trillion mark, as shown in Figure 6-2. As a comparison, the GDP of the United States is just slightly less than the combined total GDP of the 27 countries that make up the European Union (EU). China is a developing country that comes close to America in terms of GDP. That country's rapidly growing economy produces a GDP now totaling almost $10 trillion. The rate of growth and the current size of the U.S. GDP indicate, in a rather striking way, its economic strength.

INDIVIDUAL WELL-BEING

A second measure of a nation's wealth is the individual well-being of its citizens. Although GDP figures are helpful in judging the overall growth of an economy, such figures by themselves tell little about the economic worth of individuals. However, the U.S. Department of Commerce gathers information that reveals the financial well-being of U.S. citizens.

With increased income, an average family improves its level of living. Over 66 percent of all families live in homes they own. Many families now own items that less than 50 years ago were considered luxuries by most households. More than 80 percent of all adults in the United States carry cell phones today and some families give cell phones to their children before they are 10 years old. Of course, possessions alone do not necessary make a good measure of quality of life. A Human Development Index (HDI) has been developed by the United Nations that measures life expectancy, education, and the gross national product. By this measure, the U.S. ranked fourth in 2010 after Norway, Australia, and New Zealand.

In addition to consumer products, Americans also invest money in self-improvement, including education, exercise and fitness, and personal-care products. They participate in life-enrichment activities by attending the theater and concerts and by traveling in this country and abroad. Despite these large expenditures on material goods and services, Americans also put some of their money into savings. Since the recession of 2007, Americans have increased their saving levels, reaching more than $677 billion by January 1011.

Even though the typical American has done well financially compared to people in other countries, economic and social problems still exist. For example, slow economic periods may create job shortages, layoffs, and reduced incomes. Some people cannot find employment because of inadequate skills or reductions in the supply of jobs caused by business failures or relocation of companies to other states and other countries. When incomes drop, it becomes more difficult to buy homes, to send children to college, and to save for retirement. Increasing costs for medical care, insurance, gasoline, and electricity put pressures on many people, especially those with low or fixed incomes. Although the United States is a prosperous nation, many people live in poverty. In recent years, over 14 percent of all American families had incomes below the poverty level of about $22,000 for a family of four. Among the results of poverty are poor housing conditions, inadequate nutrition, and lack of access to health care and quality education. You will learn more about these and similar problems in later chapters. The health and well-being of both a country's businesses and its citizens are important to its long-term success.

Gross Domestic Product Largest Economies in 2010	
World	$ 74,430,000,000,000
1 European Union*	14,900,000,000,000
2 United States	14,720,000,000,000
3 China	9,872,000,000,000
4 Japan	4,338,000,000,000
5 India	4,046,000,000,000
6 Germany	2,960,000,000,000
7 Russia	2,229,000,000,000
8 Brazil	2,194,000,000,000
9 United Kingdom	2,189,000,000,000
10 France	2,160,000,000,000

© Cengage Learning 2013.

*Combined GDP of all EU countries
Source: CIA World Factbook..

Figure 6-2 Comparing the GDP of the United States to other countries is a way to measure of economic success.

 **CHECKPOINT**

What does gross domestic product (GDP) measure?

 Business Ownership

The successful growth of business in the United States has resulted from many factors. Two reasons for business growth are the strong desire by individuals to own their own businesses and the ease with which a business can be started. Someone who starts, manages, and owns a business is called an **entrepreneur**.

POPULARITY OF SMALL BUSINESS

It is the tradition of this country to encourage individuals to become entrepreneurs. Few government controls, for example, prevent a person from launching a new business. Almost anyone who wishes to do so may start a business. Some require almost no money to start and can be operated on a part-time basis. As a result, many new businesses spring up each year. These new businesses may have physical facilities, such as a store in a mall or a small rented space used for manufacturing or service activities. On the other hand, new business owners may work from home offices or even operate businesses that exist only on the Internet.

Small business is a term used to describe companies that are operated by one or a few individuals. Small businesses have always been an important part of our economy. By far the largest number of businesses operating in the United States are considered small, and about half of all employed people work for small businesses. In economic slowdowns, it is not uncommon for laid off workers to start their own small businesses. Often these new entrepreneurs are highly skilled managers who have been displaced by large firms that were downsizing. During recessions, the number of applicants hired by small firms often exceeds the number laid off by large firms. It is often believed that small businesses pay lower wages than larger businesses. Contrary to that belief, many of these small firms, especially those providing technical and professional services, were offering high-paying jobs.

Many small businesses are one-person or family managed operations with only a few employees. Examples include restaurants, gift shops, gas stations, and bakeries. Computers have made it possible for small businesses to operate from homes and on the Internet. For example, consultants working from their homes can do much of their work by e-mail with clients, and craftspeople can offer their products for sale on the Internet, without the expense of a storefront.

Most large businesses today began as very small businesses. Because they were well managed and supplied products and services consumers desired, they grew larger and larger. For example, Subway began as a small business and now is the largest restaurant chain in the world with more than 33,000 locations. The first Kinko's copy center was opened by a new college graduate in 1970 to serve students and faculty at the University of California at Santa Barbara. Due to its popularity and success, it expanded into more than 1,200 locations with 20,000 employees. In 2003, it was purchased by FedEx for over $2 billion.

 **FACTS & FIGURES**

Millions of Businesses

More than 25 million businesses currently exist in the United States. They vary in size from one part-time employee to over 1 million employees worldwide and in assets from a few dollars to billions of dollars. Some of these businesses have only a few customers, whereas others have millions of customers located throughout the world.

GROWTH OF FRANCHISE BUSINESS

For the person with an entrepreneurial spirit, a popular way to launch a small business is through a franchise. A **franchise** is a legal agreement in which an individual or small group of investors purchases the right to sell a company's product or service under the company's name and trademark. Wireless Zone, Supercuts, and Bruegger's Bagels are examples of franchises operated by small-business owners under such agreements. The two parties to a franchise agreement are the **franchisor**, the parent company of a franchise agreement that provides the product or service, and the **franchisee**, the distributor of a franchised product or service.

In a typical franchise agreement, the franchisee pays an initial fee— often $100,000 or more—to the franchisor, and a percentage—usually 3 to 8 percent—of sales. In return, the franchisee gets assistance in selecting a location for the store or building and exclusive rights to sell the franchised product or service in a specified geographic area. The franchisor also provides tested policies and procedures to follow as well as special training and advice in how to manage the franchise efficiently. These services are particularly valuable to inexperienced business owners. They give a franchise business a far greater chance of success than a firm starting on its own has. Although 5 to 10 percent of franchised businesses fail, the failure rate is far lower than the failure rate of nonfranchised new businesses.

Prospective franchisees should carefully check out the franchisor. Fraudulent dealers have deceived many innocent people. Franchise agreements may require franchisees to buy all items needed to operate the business from the franchisor, often at a price substantially higher than available elsewhere. Some franchisors have been charged with allowing other franchisees to open businesses too close to each other, reducing the amount of possible revenues. To avoid these problems, some states have passed laws to protect franchisees. Potential franchisees should seek the help of lawyers and accountants and even experienced business-people before signing franchising agreements.

In spite of the possible dangers, the number of franchises has grown steadily. Although they make up fewer than 5 percent of all businesses, there are more than 800,000 franchise businesses in the United States. Figure 6-3 lists the variety of businesses operating under franchise agreements. Franchising is especially popular in the retail and service industries. Franchise businesses account for over $1.2 trillion of the GDP in the United States.

21st CENTURY SKILLS

Self-Direction

People use self-direction skills in their daily lives and at work as they plan how they will spend their time and energy to accomplish goals. Small business owners, including franchisees, are usually self-directed because they are responsible for the success of their business. Employers value workers who are self-directed and understand the relationship between their contributions and the success of the business.

Examples of Franchises A to Z		
Agway	Gotcha Covered	Orange Julius
Budget Rent a Car	Howard Johnson	Pizza Hut
Cartridge World	Jiffy Lube	Roy Rogers
Century 21	Kona Ice	Sbarro
Dairy Queen	Kwik Kopy	TCBY
Denny's	Lawn Doctor	Wendy's
Fairfield Inn by Marriott	Midas	Yogi Bear's Jellystone Park
Goodyear Tire Centers	Nathan's Famous	Ziebart

© Cengage Learning 2013.

Figure 6-3 You can find all types of businesses represented by franchises.

RISKS OF OWNERSHIP

The success of a business depends greatly on managerial effectiveness. If a business is well managed, it will likely earn an adequate income from which it can pay all expenses and earn a profit. If it does not earn a profit, it cannot continue for long. An entrepreneur assumes the risk of success or failure.

Risk—the possibility of failure—is one of the characteristics of business that all entrepreneurs must face. Risk involves competition from other businesses, changes in prices, changes in style, competition from new products, and changes that arise from economic conditions. Whenever risks are high, the risk of business failure is also high.

Businesses close for a number of reasons. The Service Core of Retired Executives (SCORE) reports that up to 70 percent of new firms with employees survive at least two years, and about half survive for five years. Business failure can be causes by external factors such as the economy and competition, but it is often the result of management failure.

OBLIGATIONS OF OWNERSHIP

Anyone who starts a business has a responsibility to the entire community in which the business operates. Customers, employees, suppliers, and even competitors are affected by a single business. Therefore, a business that fails creates an economic loss that is shared by others in society. For example, an unsuccessful business probably owes money to other firms that will also suffer a loss because they cannot collect. In fact, a business that cannot collect from several other businesses may be placed in a weakened financial condition and it, too, may fail.

Successful businesses also have economic and social responsibilities. The privilege of operating a business with the potential of making a profit also carries a number of obligations to a variety of groups that serve and are served by the company. These groups include customers, employees, investors, competitors, and the public. In free market systems, it is socially responsible to provide profits to investors. This helps to ensure employment and a sustainable business. At the same time, a business must meet customers' needs and treat competitors fairly. Businesses will survive if they balance the needs of all of their stakeholders.

Just as every business has an obligation to the community, the community has an obligation to each business. Society should be aware that owners face many risks while trying to earn a fair profit on the investment made in the business. Consumers should realize that the prices of goods and services are affected by expenses that arise from operating a business. Employees should realize that a business cannot operate successfully, and thereby provide jobs, unless each worker is properly trained and motivated to work. The economic health of a community is improved when groups in the community are aware of each other's obligations.

CHECKPOINT

Describe the groups to whom business owners are responsible.

6.3 ASSESSMENT

UNDERSTAND MANAGEMENT CONCEPTS

Determine the best answer for each of the following questions.

1. An example of income that would be included in the underground economy but not included in the GDP is
   a. small-business profits
   b. income generated by oil and gas production
   c. income from the sale of services
   d. cash paid for work that is not reported on taxes

2. Which of the following is *not* offered to a franchisee by a franchisor?
   a. help in finding a location for the business
   b. operating procedures and policies
   c. a guaranteed minimum profit
   d. the use of the company's name and trademark

THINK CRITICALLY

Answer the following questions as completely as possible.

3. What factors do you believe have contributed to the very large GDP of the United States compared to that of most other countries?

4. What are a business's responsibilities to the community in which it operates? What are the community's responsibilities to businesses?

CHAPTER CONCEPTS

- Goods-producing businesses produce goods used by other businesses, organizations, or consumers. Service businesses are a type of business that use mostly labor to offer mostly intangible products to satisfy consumer needs. Every business engages in at least three major activities: production, marketing, and finance.

- The increased global competition of recent years has required firms to become more efficient and effective at providing goods and services of high quality at low prices to customers around the world. Innovations such as computer technology and the Internet have changed the way businesses run.

- A country's economic growth is seen in a continuously expanding GDP and the variety of goods and services that people are able to afford. The ease of starting a small business has allowed many people to become entrepreneurs. Although many small firms fail, many others are highly successful as independent enterprises, franchisees, or large international firms.

REVIEW BUSINESS MANAGEMENT TERMS

Write the letter of the term that matches each definition. Some terms will not be used.

a. domestic goods
b. downsize
c. efficiency
d. entrepreneur
e. foreign goods
f. franchisee
g. franchisor
h. goods-producing business
i. global competition
j. gross domestic product (GDP)
k. industrial businesses
l. industry
m. innovation
n. output
o. production
p. productivity
q. service businesses

1. Businesses that produce goods used by other businesses or organizations to make things
2. A business that produces goods used by other businesses, organizations, or consumers.
3. Producing products and services quickly, at low cost, without wasting time and materials
4. Something entirely new
5. Businesses that use mostly labor to offer mostly intangible products to satisfy consumer needs
6. Activity that involves making a product or providing a service
7. Ability of businesses from one country to compete with similar businesses in other countries
8. Parent company of a franchise agreement that provides the product or service
9. Quantity produced within a given time
10. All businesses within a category doing similar work
11. Total market value of all goods and services produced in a country in a year
12. Products made by firms in other countries
13. Someone who starts, manages, and owns a business
14. To reduce the amount and variety of goods and services produced and the number of employees needed to produce them

15. The difference between earned income and costs is
    a. finance
    b. start-up costs
    c. profit
    d. revenue

16. Coal-mining and construction companies are examples of
    a. industrial businesses
    b. goods-producing businesses
    c. service businesses
    d. domestic businesses

17. When Apple Computer built a personal computer, it was an example of
    a. global competition
    b. a new-product franchise
    c. a marketing activity
    d. an innovation

18. A result of global competition on the U.S. auto industry was that
    a. laws were passed to prevent foreign auto sales in America
    b. U.S. manufacturers improved quality and efficiency
    c. consumers preferred U.S. brands over foreign brands of cars
    d. no companies were able to make a profit

19. A company that is committed to total quality management
    a. hires managers with college degrees
    b. asks employees to emphasize efficiency rather than effectiveness
    c. uses teamwork and improved work procedures
    d. all of the answers are correct

20. Efficiency can be achieved in all of the following ways **except**
    a. specialization of effort
    b. setting a lower price than competitors
    c. using better technology and innovation
    d. reorganizing work activities

21. The gross domestic product (GDP) of the United States is approximately equal to that of
    a. China
    b. all of the countries in the European Union
    c. England and France
    d. the rest of the world

22. An important measure of individual well-being is
    a. the poverty rate
    b. average family income
    c. the standard of living
    d. All the answers are correct.

Answer the following questions.

23. Why is the supply and demand of products important to both businesses and consumers?
24. Why do you believe some innovations are successful whereas others are not?
25. Do you believe that most U.S. businesses are getting better at meeting the challenges of global competition? Why or why not?
26. Do you believe it is more important for a business to be more effective, be more efficient, or try to balance both? Justify your choice.
27. Why do you believe employees would want to work in a business that believes in empowerment even when it often means more work and responsibility?

MAKE ACADEMIC CONNECTIONS

Complete the following activities.

28. **Research** Use your school library or the Internet to identify the top 10 industries in the United States based on the number of businesses in the industry. Prepare a bar chart to report your findings. Make sure to carefully label all of the information.
29. **Math** Use the U.S. GDP figures shown below to answer these questions: (a) What is the percent of increase for each decade? (b) Calculate the total percent of increase from 1970 to 2010. (c) Project the U.S. GDP for 2010 based on the growth factor from 2000 to 2010.

Year	GDP ($)
1970	1.036 trillion
1980	2.784
1990	5.744
2000	9.963
2010	14.660

30. **Technology** Use a word processing or desktop publishing program to create a historic timeline that illustrates every decade from 1950 to the present. Use the Internet to identify an important innovation that had a major impact on businesses and consumers for each decade. Complete the timeline by listing the innovation, the inventor of the innovation, and the year it was developed.
31. **Speaking** You are a manager at a company that is implementing a program to empower employees. Prepare a speech that could be presented to the employees that will inform them about the pro gram and the benefits to them and to the business. You may want to prepare a slide presentation using a computer to support your speech.
32. **Writing** At a library or on the Internet, find a recent article about problems a U.S. company or industry is having in competing with foreign companies. Write a report describing the problems and what the U.S. companies are doing to compete more successfully.

CASE IN POINT

CASE 6-1: Staying Competitive

The Kirk family came to this country early in the twentieth century and made a bicycle that soon developed a reputation for its quality. Through much of the century, Kirk was the "Cadillac" of American bicycles. In the 1980s, it ran circles around numerous competitors; one in four bikes was a Kirk. Throughout this time, three generations of the Kirk family managed the company.

The success of Kirk's line of bicycles gave the company great confidence—perhaps too much confidence. During the last three years sales dropped, slipping from 1 million bikes sold yearly to 800,000 the next year and 650,000 last year. Three major competitors with well-designed but much lower-priced bikes who sold through discount stores and large sporting goods stores were stealing customers. When the Kirks saw competitors offering new and innovative bicycle styles, they ridiculed them as fads that only added to the companies' costs.

To compensate for the lower sales, Kirk began to cut costs. Some longtime employees were let go and lower-quality parts were bought from foreign firms. The company tried to keep its higher prices even as customers complained, believing that people who really knew bikes would want to buy Kirks as they always had done. Kirk managers made no attempt to talk to biking customers. Neither did the managers listen to the hundreds of dealers who sold Kirk bicycles in specialty shops. Loyal dealers started adding competitors' products to survive. Bike deliveries were running late. The changes made to cut costs did not correct the situation. For the last three years, Kirk operated at a loss. Something drastic had to occur.

Recently, Kirk was purchased by another company. Headquarters for the company were set up in Colorado, where biking is popular. Kirk's new managers talked to customers and dealers. As a result, new products rolled off the assembly line that satisfied loyal dealers and older bikers who recalled the excellent quality of the Kirk two-wheelers. But can the new Kirk adequately rebuild itself to compete in a tough market? Quality Kirk bikes sold only at specialty shops cost $550 to $2,500, which is far more than most bikes purchased at discount stores cost. Plenty of persuading will be needed to convert price-conscious casual bikers or more serious riders who put on 25 to 100 miles a week.

Signs of success appear on the horizon. A small profit is expected this year for the struggling firm. Whether the new managers can reestablish Kirk's earlier lead in the marketplace is yet to be determined.

THINK CRITICALLY

1. What was the main reason the old Kirk company failed? Explain your answer.
2. What should the new managers do to help improve Kirk's effectiveness?
3. What might the company do to help improve its efficiency?
4. Form a group with two other students to discuss and make recommendations for how the Kirk company might regain its former success.

CASE 6-2: Know Your Franchise

Fast Snacks is a food franchise that sells outlets to entrepreneurs interested in opening their own businesses. The business sells a variety of healthy snacks and drinks that can be prepared rapidly. It requires only a small, inexpensive location for the food preparation area and a sales counter. The franchisees are usually quite successful because of the strict rules set by the franchisor. Start-up costs are not as high as those of sandwich shops and small restaurants. Because the franchisor is very careful about who owns a Fast Snacks franchise in order to maintain a low failure rate, many applications are rejected.

Emi Tanaka and Rosa Lopez, two friends who have known each other for years, decided they would like to quit their jobs and go into business for themselves. Neither friend had been a manager or run a business before, but Rosa had worked several years at a large full-service restaurant and Emi's parents ran a small clothing shop where she had worked part-time until she graduated from high school. Both agreed that a new, unique fast-food business would be an excellent idea for their community and even agreed on a downtown location. Both liked to cook at home and had visited many restaurants. They agreed that a nice place in the business district of their town would attract shoppers, workers, and others. Both believed they could raise enough money to get started.

Emi and Rosa believed that a franchise business would be the best choice, and both seemed to have adequate money to invest. They checked the local library and Internet resources for franchising information and found a long list of possibilities. They studied the list and decided Fast Snacks was their favorite. They gathered as much information as possible, contacted the Fast Snacks headquarters, and obtained and mailed an application. They were excited when the manager called them for a meeting. However, they were surprised to learn that although the start-up costs were low, the franchisor collected 8 percent of sales. After thinking about it for a few days, they decided that because the franchise business had a great reputation, it could not fail. There was no need to check with other franchisors.

THINK CRITICALLY

1. Did Emi and Rosa make any mistakes in how they made their decision to select Fast Snacks? Give reasons for your answer. (With directions from your instructor, you may prefer to form groups of three to five students. Half the groups should argue that Emi and Rosa made the right decision, whereas the others should argue that they made the wrong decision. Each group should then provide reasons for the decisions.)
2. What advice would you give Rosa and Emi as they prepare to open their business to help them become successful and make adequate profits?
3. The franchisor of Fast Snacks is considering selling franchises in locations that are much nearer to each other in order to have more franchises. That might result in lower sales and profits for each franchisee, but higher franchise fees as well. What are the advantages and disadvantages of the current policy for new franchise locations?

PROJECT My Own Business

Investigate Both Sides of Franchising

As you plan your juice bar, you should investigate franchise businesses similar to the business you want to open. Before investing time, money, and effort into your new business, you should determine if franchise opportunities for juice bars exist. Depending on what you discover, you could decide that buying a franchise has advantages over starting your business from the bottom up. Even if you decide to continue with your plans for an independent business, investigating franchise opportunities will allow you to learn about potential competitors.

In addition to starting businesses, entrepreneurs think about how a business will thrive and grow. Some businesses thrive and grow in a single location while others expand with additional locations. Franchising is another avenue to growth. If your ideas for your juice bar business are significantly different from existing juice bar franchises, you may want to consider how you could become a franchisor.

DATA COLLECTION

1. Use the Internet and library research to learn about the pros and cons of buying a franchise.
2. Research five franchise opportunities that are similar to the juice bar business you are planning. Examples include Juice It Up and Juice Zone. Identify the differences between your business plan and each of the franchises. Identify differences in your business plan that would give your franchise a competitive advantage.
3. Interview the owners of two local franchises. Choose one franchise in the food and beverage industry and another in an unrelated industry. Ask the franchisees about the benefits of owning a franchise. Also, ask if they have any specific advice for someone who is considering buying a franchise.

ANALYSIS

1. What are the advantages of purchasing a franchise rather than opening an independent business? What are the advantages of starting your own juice bar business?
2. Design a spreadsheet to record the data you collect about existing juice bar franchises.
3. If you were going to buy a franchise, which one would you most like to buy? Create a presentation explaining your decision.

CHAPTER 7

SOCIAL AND ETHICAL ENVIRONMENT OF BUSINESS

7.1 Human Resources

7.2 Societal Values

7.3 Ethical Issues and Social Responsibility

© iStockphoto/Michal Kowalski

Reality Check

The Supervisor's Secret

Tyler Eastman picked up the file folder and walked to his supervisor's office. He had finally saved enough money for the down payment and closing costs for a small stone house on the lake that he had long wanted. He now needed his supervisor's signature on several documents that the bank required in order to approve the loan money.

The Quest Company, where Tyler worked, was the main employer in this small Ohio town. Because the firm paid high wages, the town had nice stores and good restaurants. Taxes paid by the company supported the police and fire departments, the public school, and the recreation center.

Recently, however, Quest had fallen on hard times. Sales declined and unsold goods piled up. Some employees were let go. To survive, Quest had to cut costs. Rather than continue operations in Ohio, Quest decided to relocate to Georgia, where costs for taxes, wages, utilities, and raw materials were lower.

Only yesterday, Tyler's supervisor, Rayshawn Clark, had been informed that the town's factory would shut down over the next 12 months. He was being promoted but would move to the new Georgia plant. Many workers, like Tyler, would lose their jobs.

Therefore, when Tyler excitedly asked Rayshawn to sign the bank papers for his new home, Rayshawn was disturbed. Should he sign the loan papers when he knew Tyler's job would barely last a year? If he doesn't sign, everyone would soon find out why. Morale among the employees would drop, and they would look for jobs elsewhere. It is important to keep the plant closure decision a secret as long as possible. The town will be devastated when the news about Quest comes out. Rayshawn ponders his choices.

What's Your Reaction? What would you do if you were Rayshawn?

Human Resources

Goals

- Describe the changing nature of the U.S. worker characteristics.
- Explain the issues that businesses face with the U.S. labor force.

Terms

- baby boom p. 170
- Generation X p. 170
- Generation Z p. 170
- Frost Belt p. 171
- Sun Belt p. 171
- Rust Belt p. 171
- labor force p. 171
- labor participation rate p. 171
- glass ceiling p. 174
- sticky floor syndrome p. 174
- comparable worth p. 174

●●● Characteristics of the Workers

Since its establishment more than 235 years ago, the United States has become the world's leading economic, technical, and political power. The U.S. has the world's largest single country economy and relies on highly sophisticated and modern means of production, transportation, and communication. Americans enjoy a very high standard of living. All these achievements can be attributed to the enormous resources that the country possesses: the ingenuity of its people, a democratic form of government, a social system that rewards individual initiative, and public policies that encourage innovation.

Despite the many successes, however, problems persist with regard to discrimination, crime and violence, environmental protection, ethical conduct, and social responsibility. Because businesses are a part of the total society in which they operate, social changes affect how they operate. Similarly, businesses affect society in different ways, as Tyler Eastman will soon discover. Thus, one cannot study business principles and management without also having an understanding of the social forces that shape business.

People are a firm's most important resource. A recent study of top managers found that finding and retaining qualified workers was more important than finance, technology, product innovation, or international business. The workers help businesses achieve their organizational goals. The challenges faced by businesses are closely interwoven with those experienced by the workers. In particular, such issues as those caused by changes in population and life-styles have a direct bearing on business operations and on the well-being of the nation.

The gross domestic product (GDP) of a country cannot increase unless there are enough people to provide the necessary labor and to purchase the goods and services produced. Population statistics enable businesses to plan how much and what kinds of goods and services to offer. However, the GDP of a country must grow at a faster rate than its population in order to improve living standards. Both the size and the characteristics of the population are important in business planning. Information about the size and characteristics of the American population can be found at the website of the U.S. Census Bureau.

GROWING POPULATION

The population of the United States has grown steadily over the years, as shown in Figure 7-1. The growth rate is largely determined by the birth rate, the death rate, and the level of immigration into the country. Generally, as the standard of living increases, the birth rate falls, and this has been the case in the United States. At the same time, because of better health care and an improved public health system, people are living much longer.

Much of the population increase takes place through immigration. The United States annually accepts more legal immigrants than any other country in the world, with large numbers coming from Asian and Latin American nations. Many immigrants also enter the country illegally to seek a better life.

CHANGING POPULATION

The nature of the population has been changing, too. Currently, more than 25 percent of Americans can be racially classified as non-white. Because of higher birth rates among non-white Hispanics and African-Americans, and recent immigration, their proportions in the population have been growing. This growing diversity of the workforce increases the need for better cross-cultural communication and sensitivity to the interests and concerns of various groups.

Population size and birth rate affect businesses because they influence the number of people available to work and to consume goods and services. The U.S. population is rising as illustrated by the bars in Figure 7-1. The number of people living in the United States has more than doubled between 1940 and 2010. The fluctuation in birth rate contributes to the percent of change in the population as illustrated by the line connecting the data points in the figure.

The high birth rate between 1945 and 1965 created a generation called the **baby boom**. The low birth-rate period between 1960 and 1980 is called the *baby bust*. People born during this period are **Generation X**. The higher birth rate between 1991 and the end of the millennium resulted in **Generation Z**, or the *millennials*.

Fluctuations in population growth create bubbles and busts. The baby boomer bubble created a large pool of workers who are now facing retirement. The *baby bust* period, between baby boomers and the millennials, created a

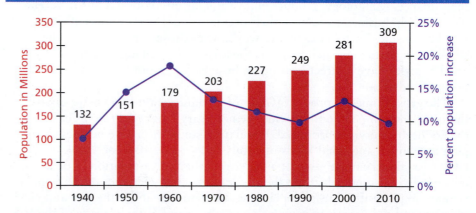

Population and Growth Rate in the United States 1940 to 2010

Figure 7-1 Between 1940 and 2010, the U.S. population increased while the growth rate fluctuated.

shortage of workers. The larger number of millennials represents a larger pool of potential employees.

Managers must deal with workers from multiple generations. These workers are influenced by the time in which they were raised. Baby boomers grew up in a time of limited technology and narrow global perspective. Millennials, who are children of the baby boomers and baby busters, do not know a world without the Internet and global competition.

MOVING POPULATION

Americans are people on the move. Every year, on average, one out of seven Americans changes his or her address. People move short distances, often from cities to suburbs. They also move long distances, such as from the **Frost Belt**, the colder states in the north and northeast, to the **Sun Belt**, the warmer states in the south and southwest. As businesses relocate to where customers are located, they affect where other people move to in order to find jobs. For example, factories have relocated to the southeastern states, where wage rates are lower than in the **Rust Belt**—the north central and northeastern states where major manufacturing firms once dominated. As illustrated at the beginning of this chapter, the Quest Company decided to move from Ohio to Georgia to lower its labor and other costs.

CHECKPOINT

What factors are influencing shifts in the U.S. worker characteristics?

The continuing movement of people from the city to the suburbs and from the north to the south has led to many unintended consequences. When families and businesses leave cities in large numbers, the cities lose the financial ability to provide high-quality services. As a result, crime and poverty have increased in some large cities. Many southern states such as Georgia and Florida have experienced rapid economic and industrial growth. When businesses move from the Rust Belt, they leave behind unemployed workers, closed factories, decaying towns, and homeless people. However, in recent years, political and business leaders have taken bold steps to revitalize cities and communities in the northern states.

 **Labor Force**

As the population grows, so does the labor force. The **labor force** includes most people aged 16 or over who are available for work, whether employed or unemployed. People who are actively looking for work are included in the labor force. Full-time students, full-time homemakers, and retirees are not part of the labor force. Figure 7-2 shows the growth of the labor force from 2001 to 2011.

The **labor participation rate** is the percentage of the adult population that is in the labor force. The labor participation rate is calculated by dividing the labor force by the adult population. The labor participation rate for the first decade of this century is shown in Figure 7-2.

21st CENTURY SKILLS

Workplace Skills

Job competition can be very intense. Consider yourself to be a bundle of skills that businesses will buy. Think about all your skills including job-specific skills required for the position as well as soft skills that can make you a valued employee. For example, employers need workers who can show up on time, follow directions, work well with others. Identify the skills that make you unique and appealing to a business.

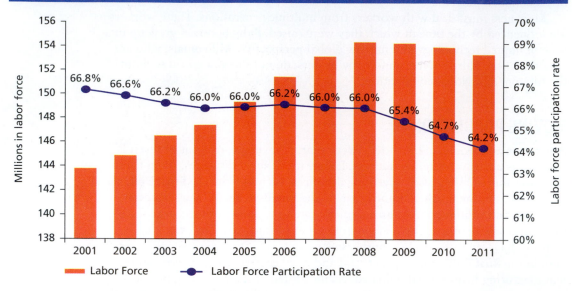

U.S. Labor Force and Labor Force Participation 2001 to 2011

© Cengage Learning 2013.

Figure 7-2 Although the U.S. labor force increased by more than 9 million between 2001 and 2011, the labor force participation rate fell by 2.6 percent.

Pay Equity

In 1966, women earned 58 cents for every dollar earned by men for comparable work. That gap has closed by an average of half a penny each year since then. In 2009, women earned 77 cents for every dollar earned by men for comparable work. Nearly every year the difference in earnings narrows somewhat.

While the overall labor participation rate hovers around 65 percent, the participation rate is higher for men than for woman. However, the gap between men and women participating in the labor force has narrowed over time, as shown in Figure 7-3. In 1950, around 35 percent of women worked outside the home. By 2010, the figure had risen to nearly 60 percent. Some reasons for the increase are that women have been choosing not to marry, to delay marriage, or to marry and pursue careers before or while raising children. Figure 7-3 shows the trend in the labor participation rates for males and females.

The expansion of the economy from the mid 1980s until 2001 coaxed many people, such as retirees, people with disabilities, and homemakers, to enter the labor force. As the economy slowed and entered a recessionary period in 2007, some workers left the workforce.

The job market is influenced by fluctuations in the economy, changes in the population and where people live, and technological advances. One of the great strengths of the American economy is the flexibility of the workforce and an entrepreneurial culture allowing for the creation of new jobs. Most of these new jobs have been in service industries, such as computer services, banking and insurance, leisure, food services, and health care.

In the United States, workers are free to travel across the country to pursue new opportunities. A loss of a job can be an opportunity for a career change. New technologies are allowing workers the flexibility of maintaining contact with an office from any location, including working from home. For the millennial generation, the use of technology and multiple changes in careers may come easier than it has for their parents.

Many of the new jobs require more skills, which means workers have to be educated. As a result, more people are going to college or acquiring training in new skills. As technology changes and old jobs disappear, many workers need retraining. At the same time, technology has simplified jobs, such as short-order cook or bank teller. These jobs now require little training and therefore pay low wages. Some jobs, such as telephone operator, have been eliminated since the work has been automated. A large number of workers are in dead-end jobs and are not earning an adequate income to maintain a reasonable standard of living.

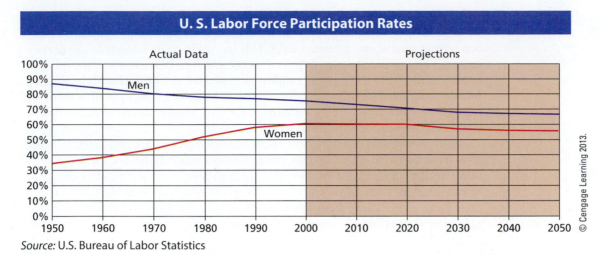

U. S. Labor Force Participation Rates

Source: U.S. Bureau of Labor Statistics

Figure 7-3 The labor force participation rate for women in the United States increased dramatically between 1950 and 2000.

The labor force participation rate for women in the United States increased dramatically between 1950 and 2000.

For various reasons, including lack of financial resources, public schools in many areas are failing to provide the quality of education historically expected of high school graduates. High school graduates are particularly deficient in math, computer, social, and communication skills. Businesses are sometimes forced to provide remedial education in basic skills for newly hired workers.

POVERTY

The prosperity of Americans is not equally distributed among the population. According to the Bureau of the Census, between 13 and 15 percent of the population in any given year live in poverty. This means that these people are poorly housed, clothed, and fed. Many live in inner-city slums or in rural areas. Statistics suggest that the richest 20 percent of American families have continued to earn more over the past 30 years, whereas the income of the lowest fifth has remained about the same. Thus, the gap between the rich and poor is widening.

Due to such programs as Social Security, poverty among elderly people is much lower today than previously. However, many children live in poverty because they reside in households where one or more parents do not have the education and skills to hold high-paying jobs. Many parents cannot participate fully in the labor force because they don't have access to good-quality, affordable child care. The strongest influence on increased income is increased education.

The government has several programs to reduce poverty. Minimum wage rates, unemployment benefits, financial or food aid, and subsidized medical care provide a basic safety net for the economically disadvantaged. Businesses increasingly offer training programs to provide skills that enable people to find and hold jobs.

EQUAL EMPLOYMENT

Equality for all is one of the basic principles on which the United States was founded. Yet, some groups of Americans have found it difficult to obtain jobs or be promoted on an equal basis. Several laws have been passed to outlaw discrimination on the basis of race, gender, national origin, color, religion, age, handicap, and other characteristics.

In many occupations, the numbers of women and racial minorities are few. Even when they find jobs, people in these groups may encounter difficulties in being promoted above a certain level. This has come to be known as the **glass ceiling**—an invisible barrier to job advancement. The barriers are often difficult to detect. For example, if employees expressed discomfort with having a female or African-American supervisor, this may make promotion of women and African-Americans less likely. Employers are now legally obligated to provide equal employment opportunities for all.

Many women and members of racial minority groups are employed in entry-level positions with little hope for career advancement. These are low-paying jobs requiring little skill and education, such as restaurant server, sales clerk, or nurse's aide. The inability of these workers to move up from these jobs is referred to as the **sticky floor syndrome**. Higher education and redesigning the jobs offer the best opportunities for workers to escape from this predicament.

COMPARABLE WORTH

Studies show that men tend to earn more than women. It is not clear if this difference is due to discrimination against women or to the nature of the jobs women do. There are a few professions in which women predominate. Wages tend to be lower in jobs that employ lots of women than in jobs held primarily by men. For instance, most dental hygienists are women, whereas most airline pilots are men. Pilots tend to earn more money than dental hygienists.

But what happens when the jobs are not the same but require similar levels of training and responsibility? **Comparable worth** means paying workers equally for jobs with similar but not identical job requirements. The concept is also called "equal pay for comparable work." Jobs compared may be distinctly different, such as legal secretary and carpenter. However, if it can be determined that the two jobs require about the same level of training and responsibility, the pay scale for the two jobs should be the same. That is, legal secretaries should be paid more than what they currently earn to bring their pay up to that of carpenters. To determine whether work is of equal value, analysts compare factors such as special skills, physical strength, job dangers, responsibility, and education.

However, it is not easy to determine the specific factors that measure the worth of jobs. Should physical strength, for instance, be used to compare the worth of a legal secretary to a carpenter? And if few applicants are available for the carpenter's position and many are available for legal secretaries, is it fair to pay legal secretaries more than carpenters? These and other factors make it difficult for employers to design and implement comparable worth plans. But businesses are trying. Many states have passed laws that promote using comparable worth for determining wages in government jobs.

In the United States most women work in service industries. Identify several reasons why this is true.

© Shutterstock/Tracy Whiteside

✓ CHECKPOINT

List the factors influencing the U.S. labor force.

UNDERSTAND MANAGEMENT CONCEPTS

Determine the best answer for each of the following questions.

1. The U.S. labor force includes
   a. people aged 16 and over who are available for work
   b. employed people aged 16 and over
   c. unemployed people aged 16 and over
   d. all of the above

2. When people encounter difficulties in being promoted to management above a certain level, they have encountered
   a. a glass ceiling
   b. a promotion ceiling
   c. a sticky floor
   d. a legal barrier

THINK CRITICALLY

Answer the following questions as completely as possible.

3. What factors are contributing to the growth of the U.S. population?

4. What has caused the growth in the number of young workers in recent years?

7.2

Societal Values

Goals

- Discuss how the values of Americans have changed.
- Explain how businesses have adapted to changing values.
- Describe the dilemma posed by the need for business to grow and the need to protect the natural environment.

Terms

- values p. 176
- telecommute p. 178
- sustainability p. 178
- recycling p. 179

●●● Changing American Values

Change is constant in our society. We produce a steady stream of new products, new ideas, new ways of doing things, and new attitudes. **Values** are underlying beliefs and attitudes. Just as it is common for members of a family to share similar values, there are some values that are shared by society as a whole. In recent decades, societal values have been undergoing change at a fast pace.

An especially striking development has been the transformation of the family. The number of children living with both parents continues to fall because of rising divorce rates and the rising number of single parents. The birth rate, too, has declined, as women delay marriage and pursue careers outside the home. The typical family depicted in television shows in the 1950s consisting of a working husband, a homemaker wife, two children, and a dog is now the exception. Fewer than one fourth of America's families fit this picture. Today, blended families, stay-at-home dads, and multi-generational households are all common. Businesses have responded to the needs of modern family life with a whole array of time-saving products and services from day care to lawn service to salad in a bag.

Because of increased competition in the economy, managers are striving to produce more while keeping costs low. Employers have increased their demands on employees. Many employees find the pace and demands of work stressful. For dual-career couples and especially those with children, the quality of home life often suffers. Job insecurity discourages workers from taking vacations or time off, and instead they work longer hours to meet their job requirements. Factors such as these have strained the employer–employee relationship. Workers from Generation X feel less loyal to a particular employer than did earlier generations. They expect to change jobs many times during their careers, as do younger workers.

According to the U.S. Government Accountability Office, in 2007, women only accounted for about 40 percent of managers. Full-time female managers earned 81 cents for every dollar earned by male managers and managerial mothers earned 79 cents for every dollar paid to managerial fathers. These differences may change in the future. Women are currently earning almost 66 percent of all associate degrees and 57 percent of all bachelor's degrees. Also, competent women stopped by the glass ceiling often quit their jobs to start their own businesses. Women now operate a majority of new small businesses.

With so many men and women working side by side, workplace romance has blossomed, but so have incidents of sexual harassment. As the number of single adults and working couples has grown, dining at home is being replaced by dining out. American consumers spend more on restaurant meals than on groceries. People are placing more emphasis on safety and active lifestyles. This is reflected in airbags in cars, larger cars, and sporty vehicles.

A disturbing aspect in some parts of contemporary American society is the incidence of unpredictable and unprovoked violence through the use of guns, often by young people. Workplaces, schools, shopping centers, entertainment venues, and transportation systems are all susceptible to the random gunfire killing and injuring of innocent people. This concern over violent crime has led to an expanding personal-security business in the form of personal and home protective gadgets, guns, guards, gated communities, and prison construction.

The United States also has the dubious distinction of being lawsuit-happy. Individuals, groups, and organizations are quick to file lawsuits. Damage awards can run into millions of dollars. To avoid such expensive legal liabilities, businesses try to be very careful with respect to the safety of their products and the impact of their operations on employees, customers, and the overall society.

Employer Responses

A changing society affects individuals as well as organizations. Many social issues transfer to work settings. Managers and employees leave home each workday thinking about personal problems. Responsibilities may be enormous for workers with preschool children, aging parents, family illnesses, and financial burdens. Concerns such as these follow employees to their work sites and affect their job performance. Competition for quality employees can be intense. To attract and retain competent workers, employers have responded to these social changes by taking action to improve the way work is done, to assure healthier and safer working conditions, and to help workers deal with some personal problems.

REDESIGNING JOBS

As you will learn in other chapters, when jobs consist of mainly repetitive tasks, workers get bored, productivity drops, and morale declines. Many workers come late to work, call in sick, or even quit their jobs to find more interesting jobs elsewhere. Thus, to retain workers, employers redesign jobs to make them varied and challenging. In some cases, employees learn a variety of jobs and regularly switch jobs within the same organization. Such job rotation increases workers' interest in their jobs and enables employees to fill in for co-workers who may be absent.

Workers now often participate in job decisions, provide suggestions, and serve on committees that look for ways to improve work quality. Today's employees often work in teams. Work teams can improve morale as well as the quality of work. Businesses also try to improve job satisfaction through empowering workers to make important decisions.

Management MATTERS

Understanding Values

An individual's personal values are developed within a family, social, and historical context. Many baby boomers were raised by a stay-at-home mother and a working father. They ate home-cooked meals at the kitchen table with their families. Television was limited to a few channels, and there was no FM radio.

Raised around the turn of the century, many millennials grew up in homes with both parents working or with a single-parent provider. Meals in front of the television and channel surfing were common. These individuals do not know a world without computers, the Internet, or cellular phones.

Generational differences have an impact on career choices and attitudes toward work. These differences also influence how managers manage and their expectations of employees.

What Do You Think? List the values you find important. Identify how they may change over time. List the jobs you think will match your personal values and why.

IMPROVING HEALTH AND SAFETY

The United States is facing an obesity epidemic that is negatively affecting employees' health. In response to concerns over health and safety, businesses operate wellness and fitness programs. A physically unfit employee is absent more and is less productive than a fit employee. Many businesses encourage a healthy lifestyle by providing incentives for smokers to quit, membership to health clubs, counseling services where workers can receive support for stress or emotional problems, and payment for treatment of drug, alcohol, and other forms of addiction. Employers thereby reduce medical and insurance costs.

FAMILY-FRIENDLY PRACTICES

Given the changes in the family structure, employers are making efforts to address this aspect of their employees' lives. By law, employers provide unpaid leave to employees to take care of their sick children or parents, or to give birth to, adopt, or take care of newborn children. Many progressive businesses provide day-care facilities for the young children of employees. Some employers provide flexible scheduling so that workers can avoid commuting to and from work during hectic rush hour traffic as well as accommodate their family needs and lifestyle. Advances in communication technology in the form of the Internet, e-mail, mobile phones, and fax have led many businesses to allow workers to **telecommute**. Telecommuters work from home or on the road, staying in contact with their employers electronically.

 **CHECKPOINT**

Describe how employers are reacting to changing societal issues.

Sustainability Issues

A growing population means more people to buy more things. More purchases mean more boxes and packaging, plus worn-out products to throw away. Discarded plastic, chemical, and metal products take many years to break down in landfills. Moreover, some products, such as medical waste, may be harmful if not disposed of properly. The increasing demand for products places great pressure on natural resources, such as land, water, air, minerals, and forests. It also affects the habitats of wild animals and the lives of native peoples.

Both business and society must address these resource issues. When developing strategies, managers are responding to government and social concerns by focusing on sustainable strategies. **Sustainability** involves using strategies that consider the needs of the environment, society, and the economy to meet present needs without compromising the ability of future generations to meet their needs.

Many companies, including Walmart, have made a commitment to sustainable practices. Walmart has set goals to operate using 100 percent renewable energy, create zero waste, and sell products that sustain people and the environment. Walmart is using its influence to motivate its more than 100,000 global suppliers to evaluate their own companies' sustainability in areas of energy and climate, material efficiency, and natural resources.

MANAGING THE ENVIRONMENT

Preserving the natural environment and properly disposing of consumer and industrial waste have become major sustainability concerns in our society. As landfills become full, we have shifted our focus to reducing the growth of waste and to **recycling**— reusing products and packaging whenever possible. We are trying to conserve nonrenewable resources, such as oil, natural gas, and iron ore. At the same time, we are using more renewable resources, such as electricity generated from the sun (solar power), from water, and from wind.

© Shutterstock/Picsfive

According to the Annenberg Foundation, each year the United States generates 230 million tons of trash. Less than 25 percent is recycled although 70 percent could be recycled. How many tons of trash are recycled and how many tons could be recycled?

At times, pollution-control goals, such as improvement of air quality, may be at odds with energy conservation goals. For example, the use of coal, which is currently in great supply, generally pollutes air more than natural gas, which is in short supply. A business changing from coal to natural gas meets environmental goals but violates conservation goals. In contrast, a business changing from natural gas to coal conserves natural gas but creates pollution. In time, scientists may discover ways to use coal without creating a great deal of pollution. Until then, people have to decide how best to conserve natural resources and protect the environment.

Pollution dangers have become more and more apparent. Large cities are often covered by smog that contains pollutants from motor vehicles. As a result, many residents suffer from breathing problems. In numerous rivers and lakes, pollutants have killed fish and other marine life. Chemical products used to destroy insects and plant life have especially endangered waterways and farmlands, and in some places entered the food chain.

CONTROLLING ENVIRONMENTAL POLLUTION

Many groups have pressured governments and employers to tighten pollution standards and to conserve natural resources. The federal government created the Environmental Protection Agency (EPA) in 1974 to help control and reduce pollution in the basic areas of air, water, solid waste, pesticides, noise, and radiation. Laws enforced by the EPA include the Clean Air Act, Clean Water Act, Resource Recovery Act, Federal Water Pollution Control Act, Federal Environmental Pesticide Control Act, Noise Control Act, and Resource Conservation and Recovery Act. The EPA is planning on making sustainability a goal of environmental protection by using advances in science and technology and government regulations to develop policies to protect public health and welfare, and promoting innovative green business practices.

Some EPA regulations require that engines in cars be both fuel-efficient and less polluting. New waste disposal rules, especially for hazardous materials like medical and nuclear waste, are very strictly enforced and often costly to carry out. These high costs also encourage illegal dumping in bodies of water or on remote land areas. To conserve resources and to protect the environment, more and more companies are using recycled materials in their production processes.

Laws against pollution and demands for conserving natural resources are costly to businesses. An issue arises when other countries show less concern about the environment or less commitment to conservation than the United States. Some countries have weaker laws or lax enforcement. As a result, companies in these countries can make goods more cheaply than companies in America. One of the objections to increasing trade with Mexico, for example, is that laws against pollution in Mexico are much weaker than in the United States.

CHECKPOINT

What are some sustainability issues businesses face and how are they responding?

7.2 ASSESSMENT

UNDERSTAND MANAGEMENT CONCEPTS

Determine the best answer for each of the following questions.

1. What percentage of all bachelor's degrees are earned by women?
   a. 42 percent
   b. 51 percent
   c. 57 percent
   d. 66 percent

2. Pollution can, in part, be controlled through
   a. recycling
   b. EPA regulations
   c. following the sustainability principles
   d. all of the above

THINK CRITICALLY

Answer the following questions as completely as possible.

3. Identify a list of employer practices that have enhanced the quality of work life for employees.

4. Give at least two examples of how environmental goals can be at odds with energy conservation goals.

Ethical Issues and Social Responsibility

Goals

- Describe how ethics relates to business practice.
- Suggest ways in which businesses can be socially responsible.

Terms

- ethics p. 181
- business ethics p. 181
- code of ethics p. 181
- social responsibility p. 182
- stakeholders p. 182
- nongovernmental organizations (NGOs) p. 183

Business Ethics

Laws provide a minimum standard of behavior for people and businesses to follow. However, many behaviors are neither allowed nor disallowed by law. The guide that then comes into play is ethics. **Ethics** refers to standards of moral conduct that individuals and groups set for themselves, defining what behavior they value as right or wrong.

Ethical behavior is closely linked to personal values—underlying beliefs and attitudes that individuals or groups possess. To decide whether a particular action is ethical or not, we have to ask questions such as: Is the action right or is it wrong, regardless of what the laws state? Therefore, ethical conduct goes beyond state and federal laws.

A collection of principles and rules that define right and wrong conduct for an organization is called **business ethics**. Any action that does not conform to these moral principles is unethical behavior. Not all firms have the same rules of ethical conduct, however. Notions of right and wrong vary from manager to manager, business to business, and country to country. Generally, moral conduct that is favorable to the largest number of people is considered ethically desirable.

The business scandals at companies such as Tyco International, Enron, and MCI have placed considerable importance on business ethics. This has led some companies to hire chief ethics officers. Their job is to ensure that workers are trained in how to comply with a company's ethics policies. Many businesses have created codes of ethics to guide managers and workers in their behavior. A **code of ethics** is a formal, published collection of values and rules that reflect the firm's philosophy and goals. Having such a code removes or reduces opportunities for unethical conduct. These codes deal with such issues as accepting business gifts, respecting employee privacy, using company property for personal use, and maintaining confidentiality. Business confidentiality means keeping sensitive company information secret.

Ethical codes are communicated to employees through memos, newsletters, posters, and employee manuals. Organizations establish procedures to handle situations that arise when employees violate the codes. To be effective, codes of ethics must have the full support of the organization's top-level managers. Codes are ineffective if they are not enforced.

Manager's Perspective on
ETHICS

Businesses want workers who are honest, have a strong work ethic, and do not have substance abuse problems. As part of the hiring process, managers frequently check references, conduct Internet searches, and require employees to consent to a background check. Some businesses ask job candidates to submit to a lie detector test or take a personality test before employment is offered.

Offshore drilling is an important source of crude oil. Can you name some environmental drawbacks of offshore drills?

ETHICAL DILEMMAS

The issue of ethics often arises when it is not clear whether a particular action is legal or illegal. As the opening story illustrated, the supervisor, Rayshawn Clark, is caught in the dilemma of revealing the future plans of the company versus ensuring business as usual. Philosophers have debated the issue of right and wrong for centuries. One well-known approach is to ask the question: What is the value or worth of a specific behavior for society as a whole? The best behavior is that which does the most good for the most people. For example, assume a company employed 200 people and it eliminated 50 people so that it could continue to operate. Although 50 people were left jobless, 150 benefited by retaining their jobs.

Businesses are constantly faced with ethical dilemmas of various kinds. Should a lumber company cut down a forest if doing so would endanger a rare species of bird that nests there? Should oil drilling be permitted off a coast, thus destroying its natural beauty? Should a manager accept a request by a foreign official to arrange for his daughter's admission to an American university if the company wants to land a contract? Should a business hire a woman to win support from women's groups? How businesses handle these issues determines whether they are acting in an ethical manner. Notions of what is right or wrong change over time. Answers often are not clear-cut.

Because values also differ among nations, problems sometimes arise for firms involved in international business. Firms have to choose between the ethical practices of the foreign country and of their home country. For instance, it is an accepted business practice in Japan for employees to give expensive gifts to their bosses. Such behavior in the United States is generally discouraged. Should an American company behave in Japan as it does in the United States, or should it follow the Japanese practice? Answers to such questions are not readily apparent, and managers have to find ways to reconcile conflicting goals.

 **CHECKPOINT**

Describe why ethics is important to a business.

●●● Social Responsibility of Business

A question often raised is: What is business's responsibility to help solve society's problems? The answer is not simple, because the profit motive of a business often collides with what is good for society. Should businesses accept lower profit, for instance, in order to keep jobs in a declining community? In such cases, businesses must decide for themselves what is right and wrong.

The primary goal of business is to make a profit for the owners. Businesses cannot survive for long if their owners are not rewarded for their investment. Although profit plays a key role in our business system, businesses today also emphasize another business goal—social responsibility. **Social responsibility** refers to the duty of a business to contribute to the well-being of society. Because businesses depend on society for resources, opportunities, and rights, they have an obligation to the communities in which they operate. **Stakeholders** are any individuals or groups that are affected by the firm's actions, such as owners, customers, suppliers, employees, creditors, government, and the public. Stakeholders expect a business to be responsible and responsive to their interests. Such responsibility may mean a variety of things. Examples include donating money to flood victims, sponsoring an exhibition on Hindu art at a local museum, providing college scholarships to needy students, training gang members in job-related skills, and setting up day-care centers for employees' children.

Stakeholders usually believe that a business has the resources to contribute to a community's well-being. Also, good deeds translate into favorable publicity for the business, which, in turn, means more sales and profits. The founders of Ben and Jerry's, the ice cream makers, for example, commit themselves to buying expensive milk from hormone-free Vermont dairy farms and giving 7 percent of pretax profits to charity. Such actions endear them to the residents of Vermont, where their operations are based.

Milton Friedman, a renowned economist and Nobel laureate, once said, "The business of business is business." People who follow his view believe that if a business uses some of its profits for social causes rather than using all of its profits to grow the business, the company will not remain very profitable. Thus, workers will get lower wages, customers will pay higher prices, and the owners will make less profit. Questions are also raised about the ability of a business to solve social problems. Does a manager know how to solve drug abuse? Should a business be responsible for promoting sporting events in the community? Are these not roles for the government or others to perform?

Despite these serious concerns, it is now widely recognized that business has an important responsibility to its stakeholders. Business has also realized that by getting involved socially, it advances its own interests. Enhancing goodwill in the community reduces government's desire to regulate the business.

Some businesses review their social programs regularly. The reviews show what the business is doing to fulfill its social responsibilities, its success in accomplishing its goals, and its plans for pursuing future activities.

The conduct of businesses is being increasingly and closely examined by various independent groups known as **nongovernmental organizations (NGOs)**. Examples of such organizations are the American Civil Liberties Union and the Sierra Club. They specialize in particular issues, such as workplace discrimination or environmental protection. NGOs influence businesses through lobbying, publicity, and pressure tactics to alter their activities.

THE FUTURE

Given the fast pace of change in the world today, society and business will face different issues in the future. Although it is difficult to predict the future, current trends provide hints of what may be in store in the years to come.

Various economic and social data provide an in-depth picture of changes occurring in American society. The racial and ethnic mix of the labor force will continue to change. The Internet is dramatically altering how people communicate and businesses operate. Computer-related jobs are multiplying as entrepreneurs establish Internet companies to find new applications for this new technology.

Businesses are apt to become more and more involved in providing social services to the community that, in the past, have been provided by families, funded by the government, or purchased

NETBookmark

Businesses are concerned about social responsibility. The organization, Business for Social Responsibility (BSR), helps companies demonstrate their respect for ethical values, people, communities, and the environment.

Access the website for this textbook and choose the link for Chapter 7 Net Bookmark. Go to the BSR Issue Brief to view a list of corporate social responsibility issues. Choose two topics, summarize the major issues related to them, and list at least three reasons businesses should practice social responsibility. Write a short paragraph describing how you are personally affected by corporations for whom social responsibility is a priority.

www.cengage.com/school/bizmgmt

Wind power is considered a clean source of energy that does not add to environmental pollution. What are some other ways businesses can demonstrate social responsibility?

by individuals. The general public has become more conscious of environmental and human rights issues, and there is growing concern over balancing family and work life. Businesses have to ensure that their activities do not harm the natural environment and that they respect the individual rights of a rapidly diversifying workforce. As societal values change, each business will continue to shape and be shaped by the society in which it functions.

Business innovations often transform societies in indirect ways. Henry Ford's mass-marketed automobiles led to paved roads and highways across the United States, the eventual growth of suburbs, and a highly mobile culture based on the car. Modern innovations, including the Internet, have allowed for computer applications such as social networks. Facebook, LinkedIn, and other social networking sites allow individuals to connect and share information with others in their social network. Cell phones are replacing land line telephones in homes and are allowing individuals to have immediate access to the Internet and to networks of individuals through systems such as Twitter. Social networks and cell phones have helped people draw attention to social issues and organize protests against repressive governments.

 **CHECKPOINT**

List the reasons that a business needs to be concerned about social responsibility issues.

7.3 ASSESSMENT

UNDERSTAND MANAGEMENT CONCEPTS

Determine the best answer for each of the following questions.

1. Which of the following is not related to the concept of ethics?
   a. Ethics refers to standards of moral conduct.
   b. Ethical behavior is closely linked to personal values.
   c. Ethics always shows what is right and what is wrong.
   d. Ethics helps define what behavior is seen as right or wrong.

2. The duty of a business to contribute to the well-being of society is called
   a. business ethics
   b. social responsibility
   c. constituency analysis
   d. business responsibility

THINK CRITICALLY

Answer the following questions as completely as possible.

3. Because businesses are established for making profits, the only way to ensure that they behave ethically is to have strong laws that require them to do so. Do you agree with this statement? Justify your answer.

4. Explain how a business can ensure that its code of ethics will be effective.

F⊕cus On...Ethics

The Wage Issue

One of the most famous names in sports shoes, Nike is based in Beaverton, Oregon. Sports shoes of all kinds carrying the swoosh logo are sold throughout the world, often at prices of more than $100. But how much does it cost to make these shoes?

Nike does not manufacture any of its shoes. Instead, they are made by private contractors in countries such as China, India, Indonesia and Vietnam. Nike provides design and quality specifications and places orders for millions of pairs of shoes. In 2010, Nike reported revenues of $19 billion.

Although Nike is successful, it has faced criticism. In recent years, various NGOs alleged that Nike's shoes and apparel were made under unacceptable working conditions. Workers as young as 14 worked over 60 hours a week and received wages of about $1 a day. Safety and health standards were minimal. The cost of labor was estimated at less than 4 percent of the price that the consumer paid for a pair of shoes. Thus, shoes sold for $100 had a labor cost of less than $4. Even after paying the manufacturers and the distributors, Nike makes a profit of $15 on the pair. Nike argued that its profits were comparable to those made by Reebok, Adidas, and others in the industry. It also claimed that the company had little control over the manufacturers, though Nike tried to ensure that these companies followed the employment laws of the respective countries with regard to minimum wages, hours of work, and working conditions.

Nike argued that it was incorrect to compare working conditions in the United States with those in less prosperous countries. The company pointed out that not too long ago, working conditions in the United States were also harsh, and only economic growth led to the enlightened work conditions prevalent today.

Labor unions and human rights groups in the United States began a campaign to draw attention to the conditions in which Nike's shoes were made. Pressure mounted on Nike's shareholders, bankers, retailers, and other stakeholders to force Nike to make changes in the working conditions at the foreign factories. The negative publicity led to sharp declines in sales and profits.

Nike reacted to the demand for change by establishing an office to monitor working conditions in its foreign factories. Nike set four goals to address the labor issues. First, they would eliminate excessive overtime in factories. Second, they would develop human resource systems and provide educational training for workers. Third, they would implement a freedom of association education program. Finally, Nike would collaborate with other brands to implement these changes.

THINK CRITICALLY

1. Were Nike and its suppliers reacting in socially responsible ways? Why or why not?

2. What was the motivation of the protestors against Nike? Why couldn't Nike ignore them?

3. Should one society force its work standards and wage rates on another? Why or why not?

CHAPTER CONCEPTS

- The U.S. population has been growing largely because of immigration and because Americans are living longer. It is also becoming more diverse. The trend has been for people and businesses to locate in the southern part of the country.

- Changes in American society and its values affect how businesses function. Changes can be seen in the growing number of women in the workforce, the changing nature of the family, and rising job insecurity, stress, and violence. Poverty and discrimination persist. Businesses are becoming more environmentally conscious.

- Businesses are responding to employee needs by redesigning jobs, improving workplace health and safety, and providing flexible scheduling and family-friendly benefits.

- Ethical conduct in business requires doing more than the law prescribes. Businesses establish codes of ethics to identify right and wrong behavior for employees.

- The goal of business extends beyond merely making profits to being socially responsible to various stakeholders.

REVIEW BUSINESS MANAGEMENT TERMS

Write the letter of the term that matches each definition. Some terms will not be used.

a. baby boom
b. business ethics
c. code of ethics
d. comparable worth
e. ethics
f. glass ceiling
g. labor force
h. labor participation rate
i. nongovernmental organizations (NGOs)
j. recycling
k. social responsibility
l. stakeholders
m. sticky floor syndrome
n. sustainability
o. telecommute
p. values

1. Collection of principles and rules that define right and wrong conduct for an organization
2. Invisible barrier to job advancement
3. Considering the needs of the environment, society, and the economy to meet present needs without compromising the ability of future generations to meet their needs
4. Independent groups which influence businesses through lobbying, publicity, and pressure tactics to alter their activities
5. Group that includes most people aged 16 or over who are available for work, whether employed or unemployed
6. Paying workers equally for jobs with similar but not identical job requirements
7. Staying in contact with the employer electronically while working from home or on the road
8. Duty of a business to contribute to the well-being of society
9. Inability of workers to move up from low-paying jobs that require little skill and education
10. Owners, customers, suppliers, employees, creditors, government, general public, and other groups who are affected by a firm's action
11. Percentage of the adult population that is in the labor force
12. Underlying beliefs and attitudes

REVIEW BUSINESS MANAGEMENT CONCEPTS

Determine the best answer.

13. The north central and northeastern states where the major manufacturing firms once dominated is called the
    a. Rust Belt
    b. Frost Belt
    c. Sun Belt
    d. Snow Belt

14. A person born in 1959 is part of the
    a. Baby boom
    b. Generation Y
    c. Generation X
    d. Net Generation

15. How is the labor participation rate calculated?
    a. Employed workers divided by the total number of people in the labor force.
    b. 100 percent minus the unemployment rate.
    c. Labor force divided by the adult population.
    d. Labor force divided by the total population.

16. Businesses are reacting to a changing society by all of the following except
    a. job redesign
    b. increasing all worker's salaries
    c. improving health and safety
    d. putting in place family-friendly practices

17. The American Civil Liberties Union and the Sierra Club are examples of
    a. nongovernmental organizations (NGOs)
    b. quasi-governmental organizations (QGOs)
    c. legal-governmental organizations (LGOs)
    d. environmental-governmental organizations (EGOs)

18. Telecommuting means
    a. selling by telephone
    b. working via communication technology instead of showing up at an office
    c. selling over the Internet
    d. using an office as a telecommunications center

19. Stakeholders could include
    a. business owners
    b. customers
    c. creditors
    d. all of the above

20. Generally, as the standard of living increases, the birth rate
    a. increases
    b. stays the same
    c. falls
    d. fluctuates

APPLY WHAT YOU KNOW

Answer the following questions.

21. Explain how the movement of people from cities to suburbs and from the Frost Belt to the Sun Belt has affected cities and businesses.
22. Describe the actions that the federal government has taken to protect the environment.
23. Describe why the age and ethnic makeup of the U.S. population is important to business.
24. List at least two examples of how values have changed in the United States in the past 20 years. Explain how these changes have affected businesses.
25. List at least two reasons why businesses should be socially responsible.

MAKE ACADEMIC CONNECTIONS

Complete the following activities.

26. **Research** Use your school library or the Internet to identify the differences in values between baby boomers and younger workers. Relate these findings to changing business practices. Use examples from your own life.
27. **Math** Use the data from the period 2010–2050 to answer each of the following questions. Round off to one decimal place. (a) What is the percentage increase in population for the United States? (b) What is the percentage increase for each ethnic category? (c) Determine the percentage of each ethnic group to the total population in 2010. (d) Determine the percentage of each ethnic group to the total population in 2050.

Population in Millions	2010	2050
TOTAL	309	439
White (non-Hispanic)	200	203
Black	38	52
Asian	14	33
Other races	8	18
Hispanic (of any race)	49	133

28. **Technology** Use presentation software such as PowerPoint to show how a variety of communication technology tools can be used to support telecommuting. Use the Internet to find content on how companies use these tools to support business operations.
29. **Speaking** Develop an argument for or against the concept of comparable worth. Include measuring levels of training and responsibility, comparing job value, and how to analyze special skills, physical strength, job dangers, responsibility, and education. Find someone in your class with the opposite view. Debate that person based on your analysis.
30. **Writing** Create a list of sustainability issues. Use your library or the Internet to find articles that show how businesses are reacting to each of these issues. Explain the reasons that businesses are reacting positively or negatively to these issues.

CASE IN POINT

CASE 7-1: Corporate Generosity or Tax Deduction?

Greengrocers, a major food company in the United States, stores packaged foods such as vegetables, fruits, cereal, and meats in its warehouses. The quality of the food in the cans, bottles, and boxes declines over time. Therefore, an expiration date is stamped on each container, after which the product cannot be sold, even though the food is not spoiled and is still edible. Were it not for strict rules laid down by the government, the expiration date could easily be pushed to the future and the food would still be fit for human consumption.

Packages with expired dates are returned to Greengrocers, where they are destroyed. Recently an opportunity appeared for Greengrocers to use the expired food packages. A hurricane had devastated parts of Mexico, leaving people homeless and without food. Greengrocers decided to make a generous donation of free packaged food to the destitute Mexicans, and this was announced with great fanfare. The U.S. military transported the food on one of its relief flights. The donation was reported in the national media, and Greengrocers received favorable publicity as a socially responsible firm stepping in to lessen human misery in the highest tradition of American generosity.

The donated packages, of course, had expired dates. Mexico's laws on selling food products with expired dates were very weak and rarely enforced. Greengrocers' managers assumed that starving people would rather have food with expired dates than no food. In any case, the food was still edible. In addition, Greengrocers could claim a charitable-contribution tax deduction in the United States.

Once the relief flight arrived in Mexico, the donated food was turned over to a relief organization, Save the Children Fund, for distribution to the hungry. As several young American volunteers unpacked the boxes, they noticed that the packages had expired dates. A huge group of starving Mexicans was waiting for the packages and the correspondent of a television network was waiting to broadcast the event in the United States. What was broadcast instead was news about the expired dates on the donated food.

THINK CRITICALLY

1. Because Mexico has weak laws on food dates and the food was still edible, do you think Greengrocers acted in a socially responsible manner? Explain.
2. If you were the president of Greengrocers, how would you explain your conduct now that the details of the donation have been revealed?
3. Do you believe the American volunteers acted ethically when they made an issue of the expiration dates on the food?
4. Suggest some ways by which Greengrocers can discourage unethical conduct by its employees in the future.

CASE 7-2: Tobacco Rights?

Cigarettes are a lawful product in the United States. Many farmers grow tobacco, and big companies such as Philip Morris process the leaves into cigarettes. Thousands of people are employed in the industry, and local, state, and federal governments earn billions of dollars in taxes on the sale of tobacco products.

Although the Surgeon General of the United States has long required that cigarette packages carry a warning stating that smoking is injurious to health, it was only in the 1990s that a concerted campaign was mounted to discourage smoking and to punish tobacco companies. After denying it for decades, senior managers of the tobacco companies admitted that smoking was addictive and dangerous to human health. Lawsuits were filed against the company by state governments that claimed compensation for the extra medical costs that had to be incurred for treating people suffering from smoking-related illnesses. Individuals who had become ill from smoking sued the tobacco firms for seducing them into the habit through aggressive advertising. Groups such as flight attendants claimed that they were subjected to secondhand smoke from passengers and thus needed to be compensated for their suffering. In addition, the government drew up plans to ban advertising of tobacco products and ultimately to ban the product itself.

Faced with such opposition, the tobacco companies agreed to pay the government billions of dollars, reduce their active advertising of the product, and accept stringent laws on how the product would be described and distributed. Philip Morris recognized that the United States was no longer going to be a viable market for its cigarettes. The cost of doing business was only going to rise as individual Americans began filing lawsuits. The company instead turned its attention to countries in Asia, such as China, Thailand, and Turkey. In those countries, health concerns over smoking were not yet fully recognized, and the governments earned lots of money through taxing tobacco products. The quality of locally produced cigarettes was not high, and American cigarettes were highly valued. Through creative advertising, American cigarettes had acquired an image of success, glamour, and independence, all of which made a strong mark on young Asian consumers, a huge market. Philip Morris agreed to build cigarette factories in several foreign countries to create jobs, a move welcomed by their governments. Sales of Philip Morris in foreign countries rose sharply while they stagnated in the United States.

THINK CRITICALLY

1. Is the behavior of Philip Morris to aggressively sell cigarettes abroad socially responsible? Explain.
2. Should other governments be as concerned about tobacco smoking as the American government is?
3. Should individual Americans sue tobacco companies because they smoke, although they have been warned through cigarette labels that smoking is harmful?
4. Should Philip Morris have disclosed to the public that cigarette smoking was addictive as soon as it found out?

PROJECT My Own Business

Social Responsibility

The way people in a community view a business can often determine whether it will be successful or not. A business owner must consider changes in population, income, attitudes, and values. In this project, you will study the social environment in which your business will operate and the importance of socially responsible and ethical operations.

DATA COLLECTION

1. Collect newspaper and magazine articles or information from the Internet that describe social and environmental changes that could affect your business. Try to identify issues that have national/international implications as well as those that are currently important to your own community.

2. Interview five people of various ages and backgrounds. Ask them to describe their positive and negative feelings about fast-food businesses. Ask them the same questions about the health/fitness industry. Create a table comparing the positive and negative responses for each type of business.

3. Discuss the importance of business ethics with a businessperson. Ask the person to identify the areas of business operations where he or she believes ethics is most important.

ANALYSIS

1. Using information from the Internet or business publications, try to describe the typical customers for health and fitness products. Develop charts that illustrate the information you gathered.

2. Develop at least four business operating procedures that show how you will operate in an ethical and socially responsible manner. Examples are use of resources, pollution, product quality, and employment practices.

3. Analyze the information collected from #2 of the Data Collection activities. What can you do in your business operation to take advantage of the positive factors and overcome the negative factors?

4. Some juice bars add supplements such as vitamins to their juices at an additional charge. These supplements may be unhealthy for some people, and the price charged is very high compared to their cost. Each of these is an ethical dilemma for a business owner. Select either the health dilemma or the pricing dilemma. Complete an analysis, describing both sides of the issue and deciding how you would respond as the business owner.

ECONOMIC ENVIRONMENT OF BUSINESS

© Shutterstock/Yuri Arcurs

Reality Check

Hard Work Pays Off

Juan Guevara grew up in a small Mexican village. His parents were "dirt-poor shopkeepers," as he would often say, but Juan's dad was intent on going to America. And that's what the family did when Juan was 19. They moved to a large village in the state of New Mexico.

Upon arrival his parents bought a small neighborhood grocery store that had several acres of land behind it. Juan entered a technical college where he learned about agricultural methods. One day after graduation his father said, "Join me in running the store, Juan. Maybe together we can expand with this growing neighborhood." Juan smiled and told his dad he would use the land behind the store and his new knowledge to experiment with raising and selling vegetables. Within a year, customers from other neighborhoods were stopping by the Guevaras' store to buy Juan's fresh produce.

By the second year, the family decided to expand the store and move to a nearby shopping area. Juan's dad had already bought a farm to expand the popular vegetable department and to add a homegrown fruit department as well. Juan was made manager of the farm. He was responsible for quality control, managing workers, and product shipment.

The store would now be called the Guevara Fruit and Vegetable Market. Within a short time, the store was prospering. Like so many people before them, another family of motivated and hardworking immigrants had succeeded in a country known for its prosperous economic system. The Guevara family had become an active part of the country's growing economy.

What's Your Reaction? What economic factors allowed for the Guevara family's success?

Economic Wants

Goals

- Describe economic concepts that apply to satisfying economic wants.
- Explain the role of capital formation in an economy.

Terms

- economics p. 193
- economic wants p. 193
- noneconomic wants p. 193
- utility p. 193
- producer p. 194
- factors of production p. 194
- natural resources p. 194
- labor p. 194
- human capital p. 194
- capital goods p. 194
- capital formation p. 195
- consumer goods and services p. 195

Satisfying Our Economic Wants

All societies face the problem of trying to satisfy the wants of their citizens for goods and services. Although all societies share this problem, different societies developed different systems for producing and using goods and services. The body of knowledge that relates to producing and using goods and services that satisfy human wants is called **economics**.

At the beginning of this chapter, you will study the concepts that are essential to understanding any economic system. You will then learn about the world's economic systems, along with political-economy systems. The chapter concludes with fundamentals of capitalism and factors related to economic growth.

Businesses help to make the economic system work by producing and distributing the particular goods and services that people want. A good place to begin the study of economics is with the two broad categories of wants found throughout an economic system: economic wants and noneconomic wants.

People have many wants. The economic system, however, operates on the basis of **economic wants**—the desire for scarce material goods and services. People want material goods, such as clothing, housing, and cars. They also want services, such as hair care, medical attention, and public transportation. Items such as these are scarce because no economic system has the resources to satisfy all the wants of all people for all material goods and services. People also have noneconomic wants. **Noneconomic wants** are desires for nonmaterial things that are not scarce, such as air, sunshine, friendship, and happiness.

The goods and services that people want have to be produced. Clothes must be made. Homes must be built. Personal services must be supplied. And as you learned in the opening scenario, the Guevara family expects their customers to want fruit, vegetables, and other basic foods.

UTILITY

Utility is the ability of a good or a service to satisfy a want. In other words, a good or a service that has utility is a useful good or service. Something is not useful, however, unless it is available for use in the right form and place and at the right time. As a result, four common types of utility exist: form, place, time, and possession. Definitions of the four types of utility, with examples, appear in Figure 8-1.

Types of Economic Utility		
	Description	**Example**
Form utility	Created by changes in the form or shape of a product to make it useful. (Form utility usually applies only to goods and not to services.)	Is the jacket you desire to buy available in a particular fabric and style?
Place utility	Created by having a good or service at the place where it is needed or wanted.	Is the jacket you desire available in a nearby store where it can be purchased, or can it be shipped from an online purchase?
Possession utility	Created when ownership of a good or service is transferred from one person to another, but may also occur through renting and borrowing.	Is the jacket available at a price you can afford and are willing to pay?
Time utility	Created when a product or service is available when it is needed or wanted.	Is the store open when you are ready to buy and use your jacket?

Figure 8-1 Satisfying wants involves four common types of utility.

Anyone who creates utility is a **producer**. Producers are entitled to a reward for the usefulness that they add to a good or service. Hairstylists are entitled to a reward for the usefulness of their services. The price you pay for a pen includes a reward for the manufacturer who made the pen, the shipping company that delivered it to the merchant, and the retailer who made it possible for you to buy the pen at the time you wanted it.

FACTORS OF PRODUCTION

In creating useful goods and services, a producer uses four basic resources. These resources, called **factors of production**, are land (natural resources), labor, capital goods, and entrepreneurship.

NATURAL RESOURCES The extent to which a country is able to produce goods and services is, in part, determined by the natural resources that its land provides. **Natural resources** are anything provided by nature that affects the productive ability of a country. The productive ability of the United States, for example, depends on its fertile soil, minerals, water and timber resources, and mild climate.

LABOR **Labor** is the human effort, either physical or mental, that goes into the production of goods and services. In today's world of technology and special equipment such as computers, physical effort is much less important than mental effort—knowing what tasks to complete and how to complete them. A part of labor is **human capital**, the accumulated knowledge and skills of human beings—the total value of each person's education and acquired skills. In a highly technological world, the need for human capital has increased significantly. Juan's expertise at growing fruit and vegetables and his father's knowledge and skill needed to operate a store are examples of labor and human capital.

CAPITAL GOODS To produce goods that people want, producers need capital goods. **Capital goods** are buildings, tools, machines, and other equipment that are used to produce other goods but do not directly satisfy human wants. A robot on a car assembly line is an example of a capital good. The robot does not directly satisfy human wants. Instead, it helps make the cars that do satisfy human wants. Capital goods allow the production of goods in large quantities which, in turn, should decrease production costs and increase the productivity of labor.

ENTREPRENEURSHIP For the production of goods, more is needed than the mere availability of natural resources, labor, and capital goods. Someone, or some group, must take the risks involved in starting a business and plan and manage the production of the final product. Entrepreneurship, the fourth factor of production, brings together the other three factors—land (natural resources), labor, and capital. By starting and managing a business, Juan and his father are acting as entrepreneurs.

Because government provides many services that are essential to the operation of a business, economists often list it as a fifth factor of production. Some of the essential services provided by government are streets and highways, police and fire protection, and courts that settle disputes.

21st CENTURY SKILLS

Interpersonal Skills
Many people are much happier working for themselves than they are working for others. Entrepreneurs do work for themselves, but successful entrepreneurs must know how to work with others. They must be able to form partnerships, work with employees, and work with customers. Entrepreneurs must develop strong interpersonal skills.

✓ CHECKPOINT

What are the four basic resources used by a producer?

 ## Capital Formation

The production of capital goods is called **capital formation**. Capital goods, such as buildings and equipment, are needed to produce consumer goods and services. The Ford truck that Juan uses to deliver farm products to the store is a capital good. Unlike capital goods, **consumer goods and services** are goods and services that directly satisfy people's economic wants. The foods that Juan's father sells to customers are consumer goods.

A country is capable of producing a fixed quantity of goods and services at any one time. As a result, total production is divided between capital goods and consumer goods and services. When the production of consumer goods and services increases, the production of capital goods decreases. On the other hand, when the production of consumer goods and services decreases, the production of capital goods increases. New capital goods must be made—capital formation—in order to add to the total supply and to replace worn-out capital goods. Capital formation takes place, for example, when steel is used to produce the tools and machinery (capital goods) needed to make cars rather than to produce the cars themselves (consumer goods).

When productive resources are used for capital formation, it becomes possible to produce more consumer goods. For example, when robots and other tools and machinery are produced for making trucks, it is then possible to increase the production of trucks.

However, using steel, labor, and management to produce tools and machinery (capital goods) means that these same resources cannot also be used for automobiles (consumer goods). The immediate result is that consumers have fewer automobiles to buy. But, because the tools and machinery were made, consumers will have more automobiles to buy in the future. Developing countries often use large portions of their resources in capital formation. China for example, used its economic resources to obtain capital goods to produce consumer goods for export. Many developing nations take this first step before they satisfy their own consumers with consumer products.

 **CHECKPOINT**

Create a list of capital goods and a list of consumer goods.

8.1 ASSESSMENT

UNDERSTAND MANAGEMENT CONCEPTS

Determine the best answer for each of the following questions.

1. The body of knowledge that relates to producing and using goods and services that satisfy human wants is called
   a. needs analysis
   b. marketing
   c. economics
   d. none of the above

2. The ability of a good or a service to satisfy a want is called
   a. economizing wants
   b. utility
   c. production
   d. benefiting

THINK CRITICALLY

Answer the following questions as completely as possible.

3. What are the four most common types of utility?

4. What is the difference between capital goods and consumer goods?

Economic Systems

Goals

- Discuss three economic systems and three political-economy systems.
- Explain why a business considers the political-economy system of a country.

Terms

- economic system 197
- market economy 197
- command economy 197
- mixed economy 198
- privatization 198
- capitalism 199
- socialism 200
- communism 200

●●● Economic Systems

Remember that no country has enough resources to satisfy all the wants of all people for material goods and services. Because productive resources are scarce, difficult decisions must be made about how to use these limited resources. For example, somehow countries must decide whether to produce more capital goods and fewer consumer goods or more consumer goods and fewer capital goods.

All countries have an economic system. An **economic system** is an organized way for a country to decide how to use its productive resources; that is, to decide what, how, and for whom goods and services will be produced. While there are many countries in the world, all economies operate under some form of three basic economic systems, described below.

TYPES OF ECONOMIC SYSTEMS

The primary types of economic systems are a market economy, a command economy, and a mixed economy. All countries' economic systems have characteristics of these basic three types.

A **market economy** is an economic system in which individual buying decisions in the marketplace together determine what, how, and for whom goods and services will be produced. For example, if more consumers choose to buy whole-grain bread than white bread, their buying decisions will influence bread producers to use their productive resources to produce more whole-grain and less white bread. Thus, individual consumers, making their own decisions about what to buy, collectively determine how the society's productive resources will be used. In a market economy, individual citizens, rather than the government, own most of the factors of production, such as land and manufacturing facilities. The free-enterprise system found in the United States is the best example of a market economy.

A **command economy** is an economic system in which a central planning authority, under the control of the country's government, owns most of the factors of production and determines what, how, and for whom goods and services will be produced. Countries that adopt a command economy are often dictatorships. The government, rather than consumers, decides how the factors of production will be used. Forms of command economies exist in Cuba, Iran, North Korea, and Vietnam.

Manager's Perspective on ETHICS

Economists play an important role in helping government regulators manage the economy. They help identify companies who engage in monopolistic practices or illegal pricing strategies to drive out competition. As economic watchdogs, they help ensure ethical behavior.

Each nation decides whether to have a market, command, or mixed economic system. These same nations may change economic systems from time to time. Can you name any countries that have changed their economic systems in recent years?

© Getty Images/Photodisc

A **mixed economy** is an economic system that uses aspects of a market and a command economy to make decisions about what, how, and for whom goods and services will be produced. In a mixed economy, the national government makes production decisions for certain goods and services. For example, the post office, telephone system, schools, health care facilities, and public utilities are often owned and operated by governments.

No country has a pure market economy or command economy. All have mixed economies, although some have more elements of a market economy and others have more elements of a command economy. In the United States and Canada, for example, the government plays a smaller role in the economy than it does in the more command-oriented economies of Cuba and North Korea. Even countries of the former Soviet Union, once a predominantly command economy, now allow some privately owned businesses to operate freely and make their own economic decisions, such as what to offer for sale and at what prices. Vietnam and Iran do as well.

Today most countries are moving more toward market economies. For example, England, France, Sweden, Mexico, and Eastern European countries have restricted the number of goods and services owned and controlled by national governments. China also has been making major attempts to move more toward a market economy.

Privatization is the transfer of authority to provide a good or service from a government to individuals or privately owned businesses. Some governments of former Soviet countries have sold telephone and transportation services to private firms. Some states and cities in these countries have privatized by paying businesses to operate jails, collect trash, run cafeterias in government buildings, and perform data processing. The governments' incentive is to reduce costs for taxpayers and to increase efficiency.

 **CHECKPOINT**

Explain how a market economy differs from a command economy.

●●●● Types of Political-Economy Systems

Each country has a political system and an economic system. The political system nearly always determines the economic system. Because the two systems cannot be separated, we refer to them as a political-economy system.

The importance of the individual citizen has always been emphasized in the United States. Therefore, the United States developed a political-economy system that permits a great deal of individual freedom. History tells us that there is a relationship between political and economic freedom; that is, political freedom usually is found in countries where individuals and businesses have economic freedom. And political freedom is quite limited in countries that do not give people and organizations much economic freedom.

All political-economy systems are forms of three basic types: capitalism, socialism, and communism. As you read about these three political-economy systems, compare their features as shown in Figure 8-2.

CAPITALISM

The political-economy system in the United States is called **capitalism**, or the free-enterprise system, which operates in a democracy. Capitalism is an economic-political system in which private citizens are free to go into business for themselves, to produce whatever they choose to produce, and to distribute what they produce. Also included is the right to own property.

This strict definition of capitalism would have accurately described our economic system during much of the nineteenth century and the early part of the twentieth century. In recent decades, however, government has assumed an important economic role in the United States. As the economy developed without

Comparison of Political-Economy Systems			
	Capitalism	**Socialism**	**Communism**
	Market/ Mixed Economy	Mixed Economy	Command/ Mixed Economy
Who may own natural resources and capital goods?	Businesses and individuals	Government for some, but not all	Government for most
How are resources allocated?	By customers based on competition	By government for some and customers for others	By government only
To what extent does government attempt to control business decisions?	Limited	Extensive over the allocation of some resources, but little over distribution	Extensive
How are marketing decisions made?	By market conditions	By market conditions	By government
What one country is a good example of this economic system?	United States	Sweden	North Korea

© Cengage Learning 2013.

Figure 8-2 Three main political-economy systems exist throughout the world.

Without government control, some businesses might engage in activities that hurt both the environment and employees. What type of harm could result without government oversight of businesses?

© Shutterstock/puwanai

controls by government, certain abuses took place. For example, some people began to interfere with the economic freedom of others. Some large businesses began to exploit small businesses. In addition, manufacturing firms did not take into account the cost of pollution. In essence, these costs were passed on to the public. For example, assume a firm produced a new type of pesticide and sold it to farmers and gardeners. Several years after some pesticide had washed into streams and lakes, it was found to kill fish and harm swimmers. Neither the producer nor the buyers of the pesticide were required to pay for damages. The public ultimately pays in the form of poor health and medical costs as well as in the inability to safely swim in lakes and other bodies of water. To protect the public and to correct such abuses, Congress passed laws, many of which require producers to avoid harm to the public or reduce the costs to the public of the producers' operations.

SOCIALISM

Socialism is a political-economy system in which the government controls the use of the country's factors of production. How scarce resources are used to satisfy the many wants of people is decided, in part, by the government.

Socialists do not agree as to how much of the productive resources government should own. The most extreme socialists want government to own all natural resources and capital goods. Middle-of-the-road socialists believe that planning production for the whole economy can be achieved if government owns certain key industries, but they also believe that other productive resources should be owned by individuals and businesses. As a result, socialism is often associated with mixed economies.

Socialism is generally disliked in the United States because it limits the right of the individual to own property for productive purposes. The right to own property, however, exists in socialistic economies in different degrees, depending upon the amount of government ownership and control. Socialism in its different forms exists in many countries, particularly in the Western European countries of Sweden and France.

COMMUNISM

Communism is extreme socialism, in which all or almost all of a nation's factors of production are owned by the government. Decisions regarding what to produce, how much to produce, and how to divide the results of production among the citizens are made by government agencies on the basis of a government plan. Government measures how well producers perform on the basis of volume of goods and services produced, without much regard for the quality of or demand for the goods or services. A command economy is most often practiced by communist countries.

Consumer goods are often in short supply in communist countries such as Cuba and North Korea, because the government channels a large proportion of the factors of production toward capital formation. Even Chinese leaders have recognized the shortcomings of the system when it comes to meeting the needs of consumers. As a result, they are making adjustments that introduce market economy principles. Two such adjustments are judging the performance of producers by the demand for their products and permitting consumer demand to influence production.

Workers in a communist system cannot move easily from one job to another. And managers of businesses do not decide what is to be produced. A communist country's central planning agency makes most such decisions. Capitalism relies, instead, on consumers and managers to make these decisions. People in a pure communist society do not own property. All economic decisions are made by government leaders. These leaders decide how scarce resources will be used. The members of a communist country have few of the economic freedoms that Americans believe are important.

 **CHECKPOINT**

List three types of political-economy systems.

8.2 ASSESSMENT

UNDERSTAND MANAGEMENT CONCEPTS

Determine the best answer for each of the following questions.

1. An organized way for a country to decide how to use its productive resources is called a(n)
   a. economic system
   b. political system
   c. political-economy system
   d. political economy

2. Jax lives in a country where only individual buying decisions in the marketplace determine what, how, and for whom goods and services will be produced. Jax lives in a country that has primarily a
   a. market economy
   b. command economy
   c. socialist economy
   d. none of the above

THINK CRITICALLY

Answer the following questions as completely as possible.

3. Describe why most countries can be seen as having a mixed economy.

4. Describe the goals of privatizing government services.

8.3

Fundamentals of Capitalism

Goals

- Describe why private property is important to capitalism.
- Describe how prices are set in a capitalistic system.

Terms

- private property p. 202
- profit p. 202
- demand p. 203
- supply p. 203
- competition p. 205

● ● ● Private Property

Some political-economy systems either do not permit ownership of property (communism) or may impose limitations on ownership (socialism). One of the basic features of capitalism is the right to private property, a right reserved to the people by the Constitution. Other features include the right of each business to make a profit, to set its own prices, to compete, and to determine the wages paid to workers.

The principle of **private property** is essential to our capitalistic system. Private property consists of items of value that individuals have the right to own, use, and sell. Thus, individuals can control productive resources. They can own land, hire labor, and own capital goods. They can use these resources to produce goods and services. Also, individuals own the products made from their use of land, labor, and capital goods. Thus, the company that produces furniture owns the furniture it makes. The furniture company may sell its furniture, and it owns the money received from the buyer. The Guevara family owns its store, the farm it purchased, and the food it produces and buys before selling it. And the family is entitled to make and keep its profits.

PROFIT

In a capitalist system, the incentive as well as the reward for producing goods and services is **profit**, which is computed by subtracting the total costs of producing the products from the total received from customers who buy them. The company making furniture, for example, has costs for land, labor, capital goods, and materials. Profit is what the furniture company has left after subtracting these costs from the amount received from selling its furniture.

The profit earned by a business is often overestimated by society. The average profit is about 5 percent of total receipts while the remainder, 95 percent, represents costs. Consider a motel with yearly receipts of $500,000. If the profit amounts to 5 percent, then the owner earns $25,000; that is, $500,000 times 0.05. Costs for the year are 0.95 times $500,000, or $475,000. Some types of businesses have higher average profit percentages, but many have lower ones or even losses. Owners, of course, try to earn a profit percentage that is better than average.

One of the basic features of capitalism is the right to private property. How is property ownership handled in socialist and communist systems?

© Getty Images/Photodisc

Being in business does not guarantee that a company will make a profit. Among other things, to be successful a company must produce goods or services that people want at a price they are willing to pay. Other fundamental features of capitalism covered next deal with competition and the distribution of income.

✓ CHECKPOINT

Explain why private property is essential to a capitalistic system.

 ## Price Setting

Demand for a product refers to the number of products that will be bought at a given time at a given price. Thus, demand is not the same as want. Wanting an expensive luxury car without having the money to buy one does not represent demand. Demand for a Mercedes Benz is represented by the people who want it, have the money to buy it, and are willing to spend the money for it.

There is a relationship between price and demand. With increased demand, prices generally rise in the short run. Later, when demand decreases, prices generally fall. For example, if a new large-screen TV suddenly becomes popular, its price may rise. However, when the TV is no longer in high demand, its price will likely drop.

The supply of a product also influences its price. **Supply** of a product refers to the number of like products that will be offered for sale at a particular time and at a certain price. If there is a current shortage in

Management MATTERS

Management Practice

Management practice will vary based on the political-economy system. For example, employees in capitalistic countries such as the United States are often motivated by the ability to own personal property. The harder one works, the higher their income will be. In socialist countries, income can be taxed at a high rate to support social causes. This could limit an individual's motivation to increase income. In communist countries, workers may have no motivation to follow management directives. The workers may not be able buy and own personal property. They may receive the same benefits as someone who doesn't work very hard.

Supply and Demand

Economic math concepts have very concrete uses in business decision making. The concept of supply and demand is very important in understanding economic events and developing business strategies. For example, when the price of oil and gasoline increase significantly it is due to shifts in both supply and demand. Businesses need to decide future energy strategies based on projected changes in supply and demand. They need to determine if prices will go up or go down.

the supply of a product, its price will usually rise as consumers bid against one another to obtain the product. For example, if bad weather damages an apple crop and apples are in short supply, the price of apples will go up. When apples become more abundant, their price will go down. Thus, price changes are the result of changes in both the demand for and the supply of a product.

Generally, changes in prices determine what is produced and how much is produced in our economy. Price changes indicate to businesses what is profitable or not profitable to produce. If consumers want more sports shoes than are being produced, they will bid up the price of sports shoes. The increase in the price of the shoes makes it more profitable to make them and provides the incentive for manufacturers to increase the production of sports shoes. As the supply of the shoes increases to satisfy the demand for more shoes, the price of the shoes will fall. Because it is now less profitable to make sports shoes, manufacturers will decrease their production of them.

Prices, then, are determined by the forces of supply and demand; that is, prices are the result of the decisions of individual consumers to buy products and of individual producers to make and sell products. Therefore, consumers help decide what will be produced and how much will be produced.

Here is how supply and demand work in setting prices. Refer to Figure 8-3 as you study this example of a producer planning to sell a sweatshirt. In Figure 8-3, the market price for the sweatshirt, $30, is shown where the supply line crosses the demand line. The market price is the price at which the producer can meet costs and make a reasonable profit. It is also the price at which consumers will buy enough of the product for the producer to make a reasonable profit.

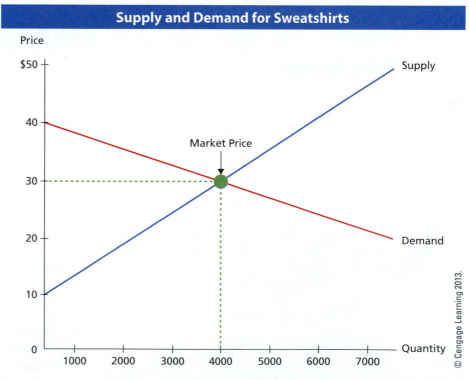

Figure 8-3 Supply and demand for a producer's sweatshirts determine market price.

Prices for many products and services are determined by the forces of supply and demand. What causes the price of gasoline to change from time to time?

If demand drops, profit drops; but if demand increases, the producer's profits will increase. If the profit gets quite large, other producers will enter into production with similar sweatshirts, which will then increase the total supply and lower the price. If the supply and demand lines never cross, the producer will not make the goods, because not enough consumers will want the product at the offered price and the profit reward disappears. If Juan Guevara grows a new type of apple but only a small number of people buy them, he will lose money and stop growing those apples.

COMPETITION

In our free-enterprise system, sellers try to make a profit and buyers try to buy quality goods at the lowest possible prices. This conflict of interest between buyers and sellers is settled to the benefit of society by competition. **Competition** is the rivalry among sellers for consumers' dollars.

Competition in a free-enterprise system benefits society in many ways. To attract customers away from other sellers, a business must improve the quality of its products, develop new products, and operate efficiently in order to keep its prices down. Thus, competition serves to ensure that consumers will get the quality products they want at fair prices. In addition to benefiting consumers, competition benefits the country because it tends to make all businesses use our scarce productive resources efficiently. If a firm does not operate efficiently, it will fail because customers will buy lower-priced or higher-quality products from a firm that is operating efficiently. Often these competing firms are from foreign countries. Competition in our economic system also provides the chance for people to go into business for themselves and to share in the profits being made by those already in business.

One aspect of competition is price competition. Price competition occurs when a firm takes business away from its competitors by lowering prices for identical goods. Today, however, more and more competition takes place in the form of nonprice competition. For example, a company attracts customers away from other sellers by providing products of better quality or by adding features to the product that competitors do not have. Or a company may attract customers away from competitors with unusual and colorful product packaging.

Another company may conduct an extensive advertising campaign to convince the public that its product is better than all other brands. All these are effective devices used in nonprice competition.

Competition is the opposite of monopoly. Monopoly is the existence of only one seller of a product. With no competition, a monopolist can charge unreasonably high prices and make extraordinary profits. For example, if a seller does not have to compete with other sellers for consumer dollars, it can usually increase profit by raising the price. Consumers have no choice. If they want that product, they must pay whatever price the monopolist sets.

INCOME DISTRIBUTION

Not only must all countries decide how scarce productive resources are to be used, but they must also decide how the goods produced will be divided among the people in the society. In a free-enterprise economy, the share of goods produced that an individual receives is determined by the amount of money that person has to purchase goods and services.

People receive income—wages and salaries—by contributing their labor to the production of goods and services. People also receive income as interest on money that they lend to others, as rent for land or buildings that they own, and as profit if they are owners of businesses.

The amount of money an individual receives in wages or salary is determined by many factors, including personal traits and abilities. The same factors that determine the prices of goods are also important factors in determining wages and salaries; that is, the amount of wages paid for a particular kind of labor is affected by the supply of and demand for that kind of labor. The demand is low and the supply is high for unskilled workers. Thus, the price (income) of unskilled workers is low. On the other hand, the demand for brain surgeons

How do supply and demand affect the wages or salaries in the types of business you are most interested in?

is high in terms of the supply of brain surgeons and the services they provide; therefore, their price (income) is high.

CHECKPOINT

What special feature of a free-enterprise system helps keep the prices of goods and services down?

8.3 ASSESSMENT

UNDERSTAND MANAGEMENT CONCEPTS

Determine the best answer for each of the following questions.

1. Items of value that individuals have the right to own, use, and sell are known as
   a. public goods
   b. product utility
   c. private property
   d. all of the above

2. The number of products that will be bought at a given time at a given price is called
   a. supply
   b. demand
   c. price
   d. quantity

THINK CRITICALLY

Answer the following questions as completely as possible.

3. Explain how the overestimation of profits earned by a business can affect a society.

4. Explain how supply and demand help determine the price of goods and services.

India's Changing Economy

More than a billion people live in India and about 50 percent are under the age of 25. Although the national average income is only $1,000 per person, this youth group will shift the old India to a new India for themselves, their families, and their country. Traditionally a socialist country, India is moving toward capitalism as young people open new businesses and change the way business is conducted.

Cell phones, the Internet, and computers have already had a dramatic impact on India's culture. Young people are buying cellular phones, computers, and other electronic gear and they are connecting with relatives, friends, and the world's citizens.

Prior to 2000, the Indian government controlled telecommunication access. There was limited Internet access and the rates were some of the highest in the world. In 1998, there were only about 1.5 million Internet users in India. That all changed when the state monopoly on telecommunications ended. By 2010, the number of Internet users had grown to 100 million. The cellular industry saw similar growth. There were only about 32 million handsets in India in 2000. Today, there are more than 700 million.

Technology is enabling India's youth to become a powerful force in producing rapid economic advances. Young people are attending technology schools and have a strong desire to start and run their own businesses. They admire entrepreneurs, such as Sunil Bharti Mittal, who have started their own companies. At 18 Mittal started as a bicycle parts entrepreneur, and by 23 he was importing telephones from Taiwan. In the 1990s, he won the bid for a mobile phone network license from the Indian government. His personal wealth grew with the cellular phone industry to over $8.3 billion. Through the Bharti Foundation, Mittal has helped to educate India's youth by establishing over 200 schools.

THINK CRITICALLY

1. India's population is about 1.2 billion. Approximately how many people are under 25 years of age?

2. From your knowledge of political-economy systems and the content of this feature, what indicates India is moving from socialism to capitalism?

3. How will India's youth contribute to making the country more capitalistic than it currently is?

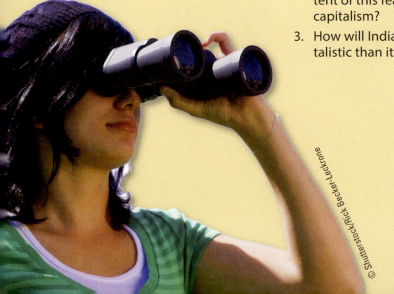

© Shutterstock/Rick Becker-Leckrone

Managing the Economy

Goals

- Explain how economic growth can be promoted and measured.
- List basic economic problems that exist and state what government can do to correct the problems.

Terms

- economic growth p. 209
- consumer price index (CPI) p. 210
- recession p. 211
- inflation p. 211
- business cycles p. 212
- depression p. 213

●●● Promoting Economic Growth

The strength of a nation depends upon its economic growth. Economic growth is measured by an annual increase in the gross domestic product, increased employment opportunities, and the continuous development of new and improved goods and services. However, growth cannot always be at the most desired rate. As you will soon learn, when the economy grows too fast or too slow, businesses and consumers suffer. Of concern to everyone is the promotion and measurement of such growth along with the identification and control of growth problems.

Economic growth occurs when a country's output exceeds its population growth. As a result, more goods and services are available for each person. Growth has occurred and must continue if a nation is to remain economically strong.

The following are basic ways to increase the production of goods and services in order to encourage economic growth:

1. Increase the number of people in the workforce.
2. Increase the productivity of the workforce by improving human capital through education and job training.
3. Increase the supply of capital goods, such as more tools and machines, in order to increase production and sales.
4. Improve technology by inventing new and better machines and better methods for producing goods and services.
5. Redesign work processes in factories and offices to improve efficiency.
6. Increase the sale of goods and services to foreign countries.
7. Decrease the purchase of goods and services from foreign countries.

For economic growth to occur, more is required than just increasing the production of goods and services. More goods and services must also be consumed. The incentive for producing goods and services in a free-enterprise economy is profit. If the goods and services produced are in demand and are profitable, business has the incentive to increase production.

FACTS & FIGURES

The Great Depression

The Great Depression of the 1930s resulted in tremendous economic difficulties around the world. In the United States, the prices of stock fell 40 percent; 9,000 banks went out of business; 9 million savings accounts were wiped out; 86,000 businesses failed; and wages were decreased by an average of 60 percent. The unemployment rate went from 9 percent to 25 percent—about 15 million jobless people.

Economic growth is basic to a healthy economy. Through such growth more and better products become available, such as a new drug that cures a disease, a battery that runs a small computer for months, and fuel-efficient cars. More and better services also become available, such as those provided by hospitals, travel agencies, and banks. But more important, economic growth is needed to provide jobs for those who wish to work.

MEASURING ECONOMIC GROWTH

To know whether the economy is growing at a desirable rate, statistics must be gathered. The federal government collects vast amounts of information and uses a variety of figures to keep track of the economy. The gross domestic product (GDP) that was discussed in Chapter 1 is an extremely valuable statistic. Figure 8-4 shows GDP growth rates over a 40-year time period.

The **consumer price index (CPI)** indicates what is happening in general to prices in the country. It is a measure of the average change in prices of consumer goods and services typically purchased by people living in urban areas. To calculate the CPI, the government tracks price changes for hundreds of items, including food, gasoline, housing, and even cellular phones. With the CPI, comparisons can be made in the cost of living from month to month or from year to year.

Some commonly used indicators for tracking the economy are shown in Figure 8-5. Government economists and business leaders examine the CPI, GDP, and other statistics each month to evaluate the condition of the economy. If the growth rate appears to be undesirable, the government can take corrective action.

CHECKPOINT

List the basic ways of encouraging economic growth.

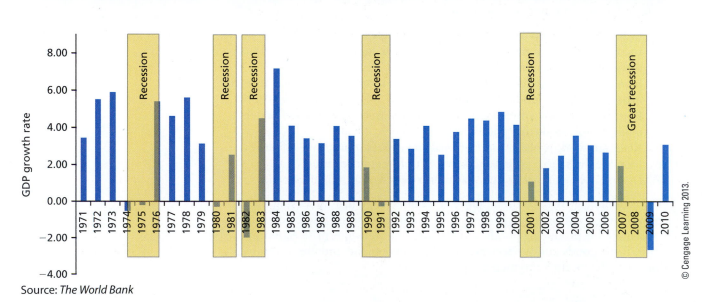

U.S. GDP Growth Rate and Recession History 1971–2010

Source: *The World Bank*

© Cengage Learning 2013.

Figure 8-4 Recessions are a common component of a business cycle. They also are typically short lived.

Sample of Economic Reports

Economic report	Description	Release organization
Consumer Price Index	Measures inflation at the retail level	Department of Labor, Bureau of Labor Statistics
Gross Domestic Product	Measures the total goods and services produced	Department of Commerce, Bureau of Economic Analysis
Index of Leading Economic Indicators	Measures the economy's strength for the next six to nine months using a variety of forward-looking indicators	The Conference Board
National Employment	Reports provide measures of occupational employment and wages, labor demand and turnover, and the dynamic state of the labor market.	Department of Labor, Bureau of Labor Statistics
Personal Income Consumption	Measures growth in personal income and consumer spending	Department of Commerce, Bureau of Economic Analysis
Retail Sales	Measures consumer spending	Census Bureau

© Cengage Learning 2013.

Figure 8-5 The federal government and other organizations issue many statistics throughout the year to help determine whether the economy is growing or declining.

Identifying Economic Problems

Problems occur with the economy when the growth rate jumps ahead or drops back too quickly. One problem that occurs is a **recession**, which is a decline in the GDP that continues for six months or more. A recession occurs when demand for the total goods and services available is less than the supply. Sales drop, production of goods and services declines, and unemployment occurs during recessions. In most recessions, the rate of increase in prices is reduced greatly, and in some cases prices may actually decline slightly. Figure 8-4 shows the growth and decline in GDP and recessionary periods since 1971. During this time, there were six recessions, including the Great Recession of 2007–2009.

Another problem arises when consumers want to buy goods and services that are not readily available. As revealed in the consumer price index, this increased demand causes prices for existing goods and services to rise. **Inflation** is the rapid rise in prices caused by an inadequate supply of goods and services. In other words, total demand exceeds supply. Inflation results in a decline in the purchasing power of money; that is, a dollar does not buy as much as it did before inflation. Retired people and those with fixed incomes are financially hurt the most, because their incomes don't increase fast enough to keep up with rising prices. Therefore, their buying power decreases faster during inflation than does the buying power of workers who receive raises from their employers. The effect of inflation on the purchasing power of the dollar is shown in Figure 8-6.

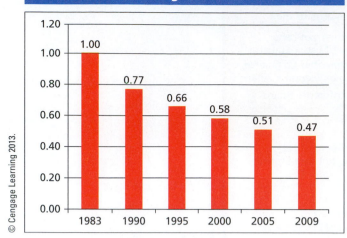

Purchasing Power Index

© Cengage Learning 2013.

Source: U.S. Bureau of Labor Statistics

Figure 8-6 Purchasing power is inversely related to CPI. Inflation has reduced the purchasing power of a dollar over time. From 1983 to 2009, the dollar lost 63 percent of its buying power.

CORRECTING ECONOMIC PROBLEMS

Most industrialized nations experience **business cycles**, a pattern of irregular but repeated expansion and contraction of the GDP. Business cycles, on average, last about five years and pass through four phases, as shown in Figure 8-7. These four phases—expansion, peak, contraction, and trough—can vary in length and in intensity, with many lasting only a few years. Some, however, can be severe. When statistics show that the economy may be about to enter a recessionary period (a contraction) or an inflationary period (an expansion), the government can take certain actions. Several specific devices used include controlling taxes, regulating government expenditures, and adjusting interest rates.

One way to control economic growth is to raise or lower taxes. Taxes are raised to slow growth and lowered to encourage growth. When taxes are raised, there is less money to spend, which discourages economic growth. When taxes are lowered, people and businesses have more money to spend, which encourages economic growth.

Government expenditures also influence economic growth. The federal government operates by spending billions of dollars each year to pay salaries and to buy equipment. Government can increase its spending to stimulate a slow economy or reduce spending to slow economic growth.

In addition, economic growth is regulated through interest rates, the money paid to borrow money. Borrowing by businesses and consumers generates spending. Spending stimulates economic growth. When interest rates are lowered, businesses are encouraged to borrow. This stimulates business activity and, in turn, the economy. When interest rates are raised to discourage borrowing, a slowdown occurs.

© Getty Images/Photodisc

What are some of the indicators that an economy may be heading for a recession?

Through interest rates, government spending, taxes, and other devices, the rate of economic growth can be controlled somewhat. Control, however, is usually kept to a minimum in a free-enterprise system. Furthermore, in a complex economic system the results of such controls are not always clearly visible in the short run. Economists do not always know exactly when control devices should be used, for how long they should be applied, or how effective they may be. Although the nature of controls can be debated, some control is needed to prevent a destructive runaway inflationary period or a **depression**—a long and severe drop in the GDP. Such conditions affect not only U.S. citizens but also the economic climate of foreign countries.

Because most nations engage in international trade and because of the impact of global competition on nations, a major recession or depression in one country usually impacts negatively on other countries. For example, during the Great Recession the United States experienced a period of recession and slow growth. Other countries in Europe, such as Ireland, Greece, France, England, also faced similar circumstances.

Business Cycle Phases		
Phase	Economic condition	Explanation
Expansion	Low inflation	Modest rise in GDP, profits, and employment
Peak	Modest to runaway inflation	Growth reaches its highest level, as do profit and employment
Contraction	Modest inflation	Growth begins to decline, as does employment
Trough	No growth, recession, or depression	Lowest point in the cycle, with increased unemployment

© Cengage Learning 2013.

Figure 8-7 Business cycles are irregular in length and in severity.

CHECKPOINT

Describe the two problems that occur when the economic growth rate jumps ahead or drops back too quickly.

NETBookmark

Many industry trade organizations try to maintain demand for their products. They do this by creating advertising to influence consumer consumption and lobbying governments to influence trade policies. Access the website for this textbook and choose the link for Chapter 8 Net Bookmark. Visit the website for USApple, the U.S. Apple Association. Explain how industry groups help to maintain demand for apples. Consider the impact on both consumer demand and government actions. Explain how high demand affects the price of apples. Visit the website for the trade organization for another product such as milk, orange juice, or beef. Explain what actions the organization is taking to increase the demand for its products.

www.cengage.com/school/bizmgmt

8.4 ASSESSMENT

UNDERSTAND MANAGEMENT CONCEPTS

Determine the best answer for each of the following questions.

1. Which of the following are basic ways to increase the production of goods and services in order to encourage economic growth?
   a. Increase the number of people in the workforce.
   b. Decrease the purchase of goods and services from foreign countries.
   c. Improve technology by inventing new and better machines.
   d. All are ways to increase the production of goods and services.

2. A(n) _____ occurs when demand for the total goods and services available is less than the supply.
   a. inflation
   b. recession
   c. depression
   d. business cycle

THINK CRITICALLY

Answer the following questions as completely as possible.

3. Explain the three problems that can occur within an economy when the growth rate is too fast or too slow.

4. Explain how an economic system can control its business cycles.

CHAPTER CONCEPTS

- To produce goods and services, businesses use land (natural resources), labor, capital goods, and entrepreneurship. Because a nation does not have enough resources to satisfy everyone's wants, it must decide what goods or services will be produced, how they will be produced, and who will get them.

- There are three basic economic systems. A market economy in a capitalistic society makes decisions through the forces of supply and demand. In a command economy, generally in a communist society, government makes these decisions. A mixed system has characteristics of both market and command economies.

- Capitalism is founded on basic principles: the right of individuals and businesses to own private property and produce goods and services; compete with other producers, set prices, and earn a profit; and buy whatever goods or services they like.

- In all political-economy systems, governments reserve the right to control unfair competition and to correct undesirable inflation and recession problems that occur in business cycles.

REVIEW BUSINESS MANAGEMENT TERMS

Write the letter of the term that matches each definition. Some terms will not be used.

1. Political-economy system in which the government controls the use of the country's factors of production
2. Human effort, either physical or mental, that goes into the production of goods and services
3. Anything provided by nature that affects the productive ability of a country
4. Rapid rise in prices caused by an inadequate supply of goods and services
5. Transfer of authority to provide a good or service from a government to individuals or privately owned businesses
6. Items of value that individuals have the right to own, use, and sell
7. Decline in the GDP that continues for six months or more
8. Ability of a good or a service to satisfy a want
9. Number of like products that will be offered for sale at a particular time and at a certain price
10. Desire for scarce material goods and services
11. Pattern of irregular but repeated expansion and contraction of the GDP
12. Buildings, tools, machines, and other equipment that are used to produce other goods but do not directly satisfy human wants

a. business cycles
b capital goods
c. capitalism
d. command economy
e. communism
f. demand
g. depression
h. economic wants
i. human capital
j. inflation
k. labor
l. mixed economy
m. natural resources
n. private property
o. privatization
p. recession
q. socialism
r. supply
s. utility

Determine the best answer.

13. The free-enterprise system, which operates in a democracy, is called
    a. capitalism
    b. communism
    c. socialism
    d. free market

14. The average change in prices of consumer goods and services typically purchased by people living in urban areas is known as the
    a. capital price index
    b. consumer price index
    c. national price index
    d. product price index

15. When a country's output exceeds its population growth it will have
    a. inflation
    b. economic growth
    c. a recession
    d. none of the above

16. Factors of production include
    a. money only
    b. labor and capital goods only
    c. land (natural resources), labor, and capital goods only
    d. land (natural resources), labor, capital goods, and entrepreneurship

17. Which of the following is true about labor in today's world?
    a. Low-cost labor is the key to U.S. competitiveness.
    b. Physical effort is much less important than mental effort.
    c. Computers will be able to take the place of mental effort.
    d. All of the above are true.

18. The accumulated knowledge and skills of human beings and the total value of each person's education and acquired skills are called
    a. human capital
    b. human potential
    c. human knowledge
    d. human labor

19. An economic system that uses aspects of a market economy and a command economy to make decisions about what, how, and for whom goods and services will be produced is called a(n)
    a. average economy
    b. market economy
    c. mixed economy
    d. socialist economy

20. People have
    a. economic wants
    b. noneconomic wants
    c. both economic and noneconomic wants
    d. no wants

APPLY WHAT YOU KNOW

Answer the following questions.

21. Describe how an economic want differs from a noneconomic want. Give an example of each.

22. Compare capitalism, socialism, and communism as to (a) how each allocates scarce resources among alternative wants and (b) the existence of private property.

23. Describe how form, place, and time utility apply to a small pizza business that just opened in your community.

24. Discuss why the following statement might be true: Economic decisions in a capitalist country are influenced by the federal government about 10 percent of the time; in a socialist country about 50 percent of the time; and in a communist country about 90 percent of the time.

25. Compare the three basic economic systems in terms of the economic opportunities available to businesses.

MAKE ACADEMIC CONNECTIONS

Complete the following activities.

26. **Research** Use your school library or the Internet to research the Great Depression. Identify the causes and the impact of the Great Depression on the economy of the United States. List the strategies that were used to move the U.S. economy out of the Great Depression.

27. **Math** Use the purchasing power information provided in figure 8-6 to determine the following.
    a. What was the percentage of decrease between 1983 and 1995?
    b. What was the percentage of decrease between 1995 and 2005?
    c. If the percentage of decrease between 1983 and 2009 remains the same between 2009 and 2035, what will the purchasing power be in 2035?

28. **Technology** Use presentation software such as PowerPoint to show how a variety of technology tools are being used to increase labor productivity. Be specific with your examples.

29. **Speaking** Develop an argument in favor of or against one type of economic system outlined in the chapter. Relate your arguments to other points brought up in the chapter such as how economic wants are met, how utility is decided, how factors of production are distributed, and how capital is formed. Find someone in the class who has chosen a different economic system and debate the advantages and disadvantages of each system.

30. **Writing** Assume you are working for a politician who is running for office based on increasing economic growth in the United States. Write a speech indicating how the United States can obtain economic growth and what specifically the politician will do to create this growth.

CASE IN POINT

CASE 8-1: Using Information

Marsha and Carlos sat on a bench, looking at a newspaper. "Cuba Experiments with Capitalism," one headline read, while another shouted, "Headwinds in China's Nudge to Market Economy." "Brazil's Inflation Out of Control," read still another. Lower on the page could be seen "CPI Inches Downward."

Marsha and Carlos read on. They were thinking about whether these stories had any bearing on their jobs and their lives. Finally, Carlos broke the silence.

Carlos: *Now I know why I never liked reading newspapers. The headlines don't make any sense—nothing in common. The same stuff appears on the Internet. They jump all over the place, and most of the news is bad. And half of it isn't understandable. Then we have to hear it again on TV and on the radio.*

Marsha: *I try to read some of the articles, but it's true many are unclear. For example, yesterday I saw "County Privatizes Trash Collection." The headlines aren't always clear, but fortunately things usually are explained in the stories. By reading each day, you learn more than you think you can, especially about economics.*

Carlos: *The sports pages are what I read. You get the "stats" like team won/lost records and learn about how much the superstars are paid in contracts. Some of them make as much in one year as you and I will make in a lifetime. You don't have to worry about inflation when you make $2 million.*

Marsha: *Today's headlines deal with economics and you're talking economics when you deal with how much people are paid. If you like "stats," you'll like looking at the economic indicators. You have a contract with your employer, Carlos. Someday when you have more knowledge and skills to sell, your "contracts" will get larger, too.*

Carlos: *Maybe I'll take this paper and read some of those headline details later ... after I find out who won last night's big game between the Cowboys and the Bears. See you after work.*

THINK CRITICALLY

1. Is the headline that reads "CPI Inches Downward" good news or bad news? Explain your answer.
2. What did all the headlines have in common?
3. Explain to Marsha what the county did when it "privatized" the trash service.
4. Bring the business section of a newspaper to class. Determine what economic ideas presented in this chapter are directly or indirectly revealed in one or more of the headlines. If your instructor decides to divide the class into groups, pick the two best stories in your group that cover the most important chapter ideas.

CASE 8-2: The Fruits Of Economic Progress

Meiling and Yi Cheng and their four children live on a farm in China located near the large city of Shanghai. Life on the farm today is unlike it was when they were younger. Less than 10 years ago, the family was quite poor and lived in a run-down small home with no plumbing. There were seldom good times. Raising enough food to eat and to sell barely made ends meet, and the economy was not at all like today's, with the GDP growing so rapidly.

Many people have moved to the city in order to earn more money and to learn new skills while working in new or growing businesses. Some of the factories are owned by foreign firms such as those based in Germany, Japan, and the United States. Yi travels to the city each day to work in one of the new plants, whereas Meiling runs the farm with her oldest son and other children when they are not in school. The family cannot afford to live in the city.

During the last few years, the Chengs have made improvements to their small home, adding indoor plumbing, a telephone, and a small television. Yi even has a cell phone that he uses with pride when bicycling the seven miles to and from work. The days are long, but life is getting easier. If things continue to improve, Yi may consider buying a motor scooter. The children want a computer but even a used one is an unaffordable luxury for now. The Chengs have learned that good times do not last forever. They must save for bad times, for the children's education, and for retirement. There is no social security system to depend upon when Yi retires. And if someone becomes ill or injured, the government can provide only limited help. Yi is also concerned that his foreign employer might leave China because of government regulations that are often unfair to foreign competitors. For now, the happy times continue for the Chengs, who consider themselves somewhat well-off for a rural family.

THINK CRITICALLY

1. How does the current life of the Chengs compare with that of the average American family? By American standards, would they be classified at the poverty level? Explain your answer.
2. Do the Chengs live more under a capitalistic or a communistic system? Explain your answer.
3. Using the library or the Internet, find out whether the Chinese people who live in large cities have a better quality of life than do people like the Chengs who live in rural areas. Report your findings to the class.
4. What conditions exist or could occur that would cause Yi's employer to leave China? Obtain information from your library or the Internet to make a report to the class.

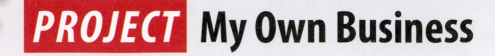

PROJECT My Own Business

Study the Competition

As a new business owner, you must be aware of the type of competition the business will face and the strengths and weaknesses of that competition. Also, you must determine customer demand for the business's products. Competition affects the prices you can charge for your products. You will study these factors in this segment of your project.

DATA COLLECTION

1. Identify five businesses in your area that could be considered competitors for your juice bar. Review the information from your work in Chapter 1 to help you. Rate each business on the basis of variety of products, location, prices, service, and image. Use a 1–5 scale, with 1 indicating the most competitive and 5 the least competitive.
2. Identify five products that would typically be offered on the menus of juice bars. Visit businesses in your area and determine the highest and lowest prices being charged for each of the products you identified.
3. Interview 10 people to determine how price affects their purchase decisions. Ask the following questions and summarize the responses
   a. How much would you usually expect to pay for a freshly prepared frozen juice drink?
   b. How important is the price when you decide to purchase that drink?
   c. What factors would cause you to pay a higher-than-normal price for a fresh juice drink?

ANALYSIS

1. A business must be able to satisfy consumer needs in order to be successful. Describe how your new business will provide the four basic utilities discussed in the textbook: form, place, time, and possession.
2. Identify four specific ways you can reduce the level of competition or increase the customer demand for your products.
3. Analyze the data you collected in the interviews for Data Collection #3 above. How important do you think the prices of your products will be to the success of your business? What is the evidence to support your decision? What nonprice factors do you believe will be important in attracting and keeping customers?
4. Identify five products you plan to offer at your juice bar. The products may be five varieties of juice drinks or other food products such as muffins and bagels. Make initial pricing decisions for each of your products. (You may decide to change the prices later.) If you will serve different sizes of drinks, make sure to price each size. Justify why you selected those prices.

CHAPTER 9

INTERNATIONAL ENVIRONMENT OF BUSINESS

9.1 Importance of International Business

9.2 Forms of International Business

9.3 Theories of International Trade and Investment

© Shutterstock/Goodluz

Reality Check

Not Made in America

Jake Applegate owned a fly-fishing and tackle shop called Jake's in Ely in northern Minnesota, just outside a region famous for fly-fishing. Jake's employed 10 seasonal workers every summer and was known for its handmade fly-fishing rods. In addition, Jake's carried a full line of fishing-related products. They were good quality, American-made products.

During the long summer season, anglers—professional and amateur—from all over the country stopped by Jake's to purchase fly rods and to stock up on flies, lures, baits, and other supplies as they headed to their favorite fishing spots. Sales were usually quite brisk until after Labor Day. By late September, when Jake boarded up the building for the cold season, he usually had made enough to pay his workers and provide an income for himself and his family.

This summer, Jake noticed that fewer fishers and tourists were stopping by his store. His sales were falling and he knew it wasn't because people had given up fishing. In fact, based on what he read and people he talked to, interest in the sport was growing. In particular, it was becoming more popular with women. Jake was concerned about his business and wondered what had caused the downturn in sales.

Jake soon found out what was happening. A national big box retailer had opened just outside Ely, and it had a huge sporting goods department. It carried a complete range of fishing gear including many new varieties of colorful and inexpensive lures. Checking out the prices, Jake found that they were all cheaper than comparable products that he carried. A close look at the packaging and boxes of the products told the story. In small print were the words "Made in Thailand."

Jake has some decisions to make. Should he continue to sell higher priced American made products? Could he specialize as a higher priced top-of-the-line fly-fishing shop? His management decisions would affect not only his business and family, but also the 10 summer workers.

What's Your Reaction? What do you think are the advantages and disadvantages of Jake promoting his business as "Made in America"?

221

The Importance of International Business

Goals

- Describe the nature, growth, and importance of international trade and investment.
- Explain the reasons for the growth of international business.

Terms

- international business p. 222
- World Trade Organization (WTO) p. 226
- trading bloc p. 226
- European Union (EU) p. 226
- euro p. 226
- North American Free Trade Agreement (NAFTA) p. 226
- International Monetary Fund (IMF) p. 226
- World Bank p. 226

●●● The Scope of International Business

International business is not new. People around the world have been trading since the beginning of history. Phoenician and Greek merchants were sailing the seas to sell and buy products in Africa and Europe long before recorded history. In 1600, the British East India Company was formed in order to establish branches and trade with countries in Asia. As Europeans discovered sea routes around the world, trade flourished among the nations of Europe and countries such as China, India, and Indonesia. American colonial traders began operating in a similar way.

Similarly, people throughout the world were investing in businesses abroad. An early example of successful American investment abroad was a factory built in Scotland by the Singer Sewing Machine Company in 1868. By 1880, Singer had become a worldwide organization with several sales offices and factories in other countries. During the eighteenth and nineteenth centuries, a great economic expansion occurred in the United States. Largely financed by foreign money, businesses laid railway lines, opened mines to extract coal and iron ore, and built factories.

International business typically means business activities that occur between two or more countries. Every country has its own laws and rules, its own currency, and its own traditions of doing business. When a restaurant manager in New Jersey buys lobsters from Maine, everyone understands the rules of business, because they are similar from state to state. When the restaurant manager buys salmon caught by Chilean fishermen, the rules of business are not as clear, because they differ from country to country.

Only since the end of World War II in 1945 has international business become a dominant aspect of economic life. Foreign trade has flourished. Companies have grown rapidly and operate on a global scale. Countries have become highly interdependent, so that events in one place have an impact in another place. Almost every business and individual is affected directly or indirectly by international business. As you saw in the opening vignette, although Jake was not directly involved in international business, his business was being hurt by the availability of cheaper products from Thailand.

Examples of Brand Names Owned by Foreign Companies			
Brand Name	**Product**	**Company**	**Country**
7-Eleven	Convenience stores	Ito-Yokado	Japan
Clearasil®	Skincare products	Reckitt Benckiser Group	United Kingdom
Dannon®	Yogurt	Danone	France
Firestone	Tires	Bridgestone Group	Japan
Frigidaire®	Home appliances	AB Electrolux	Sweden
Friskies®	Cat food	Nestlé S.A	Switzerland
LensCrafters®	Eyeglasses	Luxottica Group	Italy
PlayStation®	Game console	Sony	Japan
Popsicle®	Frozen confection	Unilever	United Kingdom
Right Guard®	Deodorant	Henkel KGaA	Germany

Figure 9-1 Foreign companies own many familiar brand names.

EXTENT OF INTERNATIONAL TRADE

Look around and you will see names you are sure are foreign: Honda cars, Sony televisions, Benetton clothes, and Chanel perfume. But what about names such as Clearasil, Dannon, and LensCrafters? They are the brand names of products of foreign companies. See Figure 9-1 for more information about these brands. Also, think of familiar American companies such as McDonald's, General Motors, IBM, Coca-Cola, and Apple. A growing portion of their total sales occurs in foreign countries.

Business activities are not confined by country borders. Foreigners buy American products (computers, wheat, airplanes) and services (banking, insurance, data processing) just as Americans buy foreign products (petroleum, cars, clothes) and services (vacations, shipping, construction). The United States trades with many countries. A list of the major U.S. trading partners appears in Figure 9-2. American firms make many products in factories in foreign countries just as foreign companies make products in the United States. In a recent year, world trade in goods exceeded $12 trillion.

Most of the world's trade takes place among developed countries. This group includes Japan and countries in North America and Western Europe. Over the past 35 years, countries in Asia have emerged as big trading nations. China, in particular, has become a trade powerhouse. Figure 9-3 lists the leading exporters and importers of goods and services.

Trade patterns have shifted from goods to services. Although goods remain dominant, service industries now represent more than one-fifth of international trade. When service industries emerged as an important segment of the American economy, more and more trade and investments occurred in businesses such as tourism, banking, accounting, advertising, and computer services.

TRADE, INVESTMENT, AND THE ECONOMY

As with trade, most investments are made within and by the world's most industrialized economies. Annual foreign investment by businesses in these countries exceeded $340 billion. In recent years, though, China has become

U.S. Trading Partners			
Exports		**Imports**	
Canada	19.37%	China	19.30%
Mexico	12.21%	Canada	14.24%
China	6.58%	Mexico	11.12%
Japan	4.84%	Japan	6.14%
UK	4.33%	Germany	4.53%
Germany	4.10%		

Source: CIA World Factbook

Figure 9-2 The top export trading partners for the United Sates are on its borders.

Leading Exporters and Importers (Billions of Dollars)

Leading Exporters of Merchandise

Rank	Exporters	Value	Share
1	China	$1,201.53	9.6%
2	Germany	1,126.38	9.0%
3	United States	1,056.04	8.5%
4	Japan	580.72	4.6%
5	Netherlands	498.33	4.0%
6	France	484.73	3.9%
7	Italy	405.78	3.2%
8	Belgium	369.85	3.0%
9	Korea, Republic of	363.53	2.9%
10	United Kingdom	352.49	2.8%
11	Hong Kong, China	329.42	2.6%
12	Canada	316.71	2.5%
13	Russian Federation	303.39	2.4%
14	Singapore	269.83	2.2%
15	Mexico	229.64	1.8%

Leading Importers of Merchandise

Rank	Exporters	Value	Share
1	United States	$1,605.30	12.7%
2	China	1,005.69	7.9%
3	Germany	938.30	7.4%
4	France	559.82	4.4%
5	Japan	551.96	4.4%
6	United Kingdom	481.71	3.8%
7	Netherlands	445.50	3.5%
8	Italy	412.72	3.3%
9	Hong Kong, China	352.24	2.8%
10	Belgium	351.95	2.8%
11	Canada	329.90	2.6%
12	Korea, Republic of	323.09	2.5%
13	Spain	287.57	2.3%
14	India	249.59	2.0%
15	Singapore	245.79	1.9%

Leading Exporters of Commercial Services

Rank	Exporters	Value	Share
1	United States	$473.90	14.1%
2	United Kingdom	233.30	7.0%
3	Germany	226.60	6.8%
4	France	142.50	4.3%
5	China	128.60	3.8%
6	Japan	125.90	3.8%
7	Spain	122.10	3.6%
8	Italy	101.20	3.0%
9	Ireland	96.70	2.9%
10	Netherlands	90.90	2.7%
11	Singapore	87.80	2.6%
12	India	87.40	2.6%
13	Hong Kong, China	86.30	2.6%
14	Belgium	78.80	2.4%
15	Switzerland	68.80	2.1%

Leading Importers of Commercial Services

Rank	Exporters	Value	Share
1	United States	$330.60	10.5%
2	Germany	253.10	8.1%
3	United Kingdom	160.90	5.1%
4	China	158.20	5.0%
5	Japan	146.90	4.7%
6	France	126.40	4.0%
7	Italy	114.60	3.6%
8	Ireland	103.40	3.3%
9	Spain	86.50	2.8%
10	Netherlands	84.70	2.7%
11	Singapore	81.40	2.6%
12	India	79.80	2.5%
13	Canada	77.60	2.5%
14	Korea, Republic of	75.00	2.4%
15	Belgium	74.10	2.4%

Source: World Trade Organization

Figure 9-3 For manufacturing and services, the United States imports more that it exports. China and Germany are net exporters.

U.S. Foreign Direct Investment, 2008			
Foreign Direct Investment in the United States		**Reciprocal U.S. Foreign Direct Investment Abroad**	
Country	**Millions**	**Country**	**Millions**
United Kingdom	$2,302,076	United Kingdom	$1,727,600
Germany	1,705,228	Germany	600,177
Switzerland	1,671,263	Switzerland	447,230
France	1,308,792	France	352,752
Canada	1,161,937	Canada	955,514
Total	$8,149,296	Total	$4,083,273

Source: U.S. Department of Commerce, Bureau of Economic Analysis

Figure 9-4 There is more direct investment in the United States from the top five countries than U.S. reciprocal investment abroad.

a major recipient of foreign investment, mostly from Taiwan, Japan, and the United States. Foreign investment occurs when firms of one country build new plants and facilities or buy existing businesses in another country. An example of such investment would be the investment in Chrysler in the United States by Fiat of Italy in 2009.

International trade and investment are a big and growing part of the American economy. In a recent year, America sold over $1.8 trillion of its goods and services to foreign customers. Almost 20 percent of all jobs depend on foreign trade, and nearly 5 percent of workers are employed by foreign companies operating in the United States. Foreign firms have invested nearly $2.1 trillion in the United States. Total American investment abroad exceeds $3.5 trillion over 20 years. Figure 9-4 shows the top countries that have invested in the United States and the reciprocal investment of American companies to those counties.

 **CHECKPOINT**

Explain why international trade is important to the United States.

Reasons for Growth in International Business

Why would McDonald's want to open a restaurant in Beijing, or Nokia sell mobile telephones in the United States, or Volkswagen build its Beetles in Mexico? For that matter, why would Macy's buy the jeans it sells from a garment maker in Hong Kong? Firms enter international business for many good reasons.

The main reason is profit. Businesses may be able to earn more profit from selling abroad or may be able to charge higher prices abroad than at home, where competition could be more intense. When the cost of making goods is lower in foreign countries than at home, it becomes cost effective for companies to buy goods made abroad or even set up their own factories abroad. The potential for sales abroad, when combined with the size of the domestic market, increases the overall size of the market. Using mass-production techniques, production costs should drop and profits should rise.

The International Language of Business

English is currently considered to be the world's business language. With over 250 million, the largest number of English speakers are in the United States. This is followed by India with 100 million, Nigeria with 79 million, and the United Kingdom with around 60 million. China has over 10 million English speakers, but is closing the gap. Some project that by 2025 China will have the largest number of English speakers.

In many cases, a company goes international in reaction to what other companies are doing or because of changes in the domestic market. If some firms are making large profits by selling abroad, other companies may be encouraged to do the same. When a large foreign market opens up, as in China in recent years, an American company may lose the market to firms from other countries if it does not act quickly.

Similarly, sales at home may be small, stagnant, or declining, whereas opportunities to sell abroad may be abundant. A company may have overproduced, and the only way to possibly dispose of its surplus goods profitably is to sell them abroad. It could also be that a company is physically close to foreign customers and markets. For example, Argentine firms can sell easily to Brazilian firms because they are neighbors.

Several factors help firms engage in international business. One key factor is treaties on trade and investment signed by different countries. The **World Trade Organization (WTO)** is an international organization that creates and enforces the rules governing trade among countries. Trade agreements negotiated under the authority of the WTO have led to huge cuts in tariffs. These cuts have boosted exports and imports among the almost 150 member countries.

Development of trading blocs has also stimulated global trade and investment. A **trading bloc** is a group of two or more countries that agree to remove all restrictions between them on the sales of goods and services, while imposing barriers on trade with and investment from countries that are not part of the bloc.

There are many forms of trading blocs. The best example of an advanced form of trading bloc is the **European Union (EU)**. The EU currently has 27 members, as shown in Figure 9-5. Since it was formed in 1957 as the European Economic Community, the EU has gone beyond free trade among its members. It is trying to create a "United States of Europe," where there will also be free movement of capital and labor and where common economic and monetary policies will be followed. On January 1, 1999, 11 EU members took a major step toward integrating their economies by merging their national currencies into a single new currency called the **euro**. With a single currency, international firms can look at these European countries as a single market and do not have to worry about exchange rate changes.

In 1989, the United States signed a free-trade agreement with Canada. In 1992, Canada and the United States signed a similar agreement with Mexico, called the **North American Free Trade Agreement (NAFTA)**, which created the world's largest trading bloc by removing tariffs and other barriers to trade among the three nations. Many American firms have relocated to Mexico to take advantage of the lower costs of production in that country. Unlike the EU, under NAFTA there is no move yet to allow unrestricted movement of people among the three countries or to integrate the three economies with common monetary or economic policies.

International business is also facilitated by two major international institutions—the **International Monetary Fund (IMF)** and the **World Bank**. The IMF's main purpose is to help countries that are facing serious financial difficulties in paying for their imports or repaying loans. The World Bank provides low-cost, long-term loans to less-developed

Member State of the European Union			
Austria	Finland	Latvia	Romania
Belgium	France	Lithuania	Slovakia
Bulgaria	Germany	Luxembourg	Slovenia
Cyprus	Greece	Malta	Spain
Czech Republic	Hungary	Netherlands	Sweden
Denmark	Ireland	Poland	United Kingdom
Estonia	Italy	Portugal	

Source: European Union, 2011

Figure 9-5 Twenty-seven countries are currently members of the European Union.

countries to develop basic industries and facilities, such as roads and electric power plants.

Another factor that has helped international business is the tremendous advances in communication and transportation. Telephone, fax, and the Internet have made it cheaper and quicker to obtain information from around the world and conduct business round the clock. The Internet and television broadcasts enable firms to advertise their products worldwide and create a global consumer culture. Faster and cheaper transportation has meant that firms can easily ship goods long distances. For example, thanks to air transport, tulips grown in the Netherlands are shipped daily to florists in New York City.

Since the fall of the Iron Curtain in Europe and the opening of China in the early 1990s, the world has seen a move toward free-enterprise practices. Many governments have reduced their control over the economy. Several types of businesses that were strictly regulated by the government, such as telecommunications and airlines, have been opened up to competition. In many foreign countries, business enterprises owned by the government have been sold to private owners—both domestic and foreign. All these changes have opened up new investment and trading opportunities for foreign firms.

CHECKPOINT

Explain why there has been growth in international business.

9.1 ASSESSMENT

UNDERSTAND MANAGEMENT CONCEPTS

Determine the best answer for each of the following questions.

1. International business has become more dominant in the United States since
   a. 1900
   b. World War I
   c. World War II
   d. 2000

2. NAFTA includes
   a. the United States and the EU
   b. the United States and Canada
   c. the United States and Mexico
   d. the United States, Canada, and Mexico

THINK CRITICALLY

Answer the following questions as completely as possible.

3. List the countries that are major trading partners with the United States.

4. Give four reasons why a firm may go into international business.

Forms of International Business

Goals

- Distinguish between the different forms through which international business is conducted.
- Describe the policies, rules, and laws that governments use to affect international trade and investment.

Terms

- exporting p. 228
- importing p. 228
- international licensing p. 228
- joint ventures p. 228
- wholly owned subsidiary p. 228
- strategic alliances p. 229
- multinational firm p. 229
- home country p. 229
- host country p. 229
- parent firm p. 229
- subsidiaries p. 229
- tariffs p. 229
- dumping p. 230
- quota p. 230
- nontariff barriers p. 230
- embargo p. 231
- sanctions p. 231
- exchange rate p. 231
- culture p. 232
- low-context culture p. 232
- high-context culture p. 232

●●● Forms of International Business

International business takes place in many forms. Usually, when a firm decides to enter into international business, it starts by selling its products or services to buyers in another country. This is known as **exporting**. For example, Boeing makes airplanes in the United States and sells some of them to Qantas, an Australian airline. **Importing** refers to buying goods or services made in a foreign country. When Americans buy Darjeeling tea, they are buying goods imported from India. Exporting and importing are usually the simplest forms of international business. Both can be done with limited resources and relatively risk free.

International business also takes place through licensing. **International licensing** occurs when one company allows a company in another country to make and sell products according to certain specifications. Thus, when an American pharmaceutical company allows a German firm to make and sell in Germany a medicine the American company has invented, this is licensing. The American company receives a royalty from the German company for any medicines the latter sells. Licensing and its related concept, franchising, are relatively more costly and risky methods of expanding abroad, compared to exporting.

Firms may set up businesses in foreign countries by forming **joint ventures** with other companies. In joint ventures, two or more firms share the costs of doing business and also share the profits. When the firm sets up a business abroad on its own without any partners, it is known as a **wholly owned subsidiary**. These are more expensive to set up and also more risky should the business fail.

© Getty Images/Photodisc

What factors make exporting and importing the simplest forms of international business?

In recent years, many competitors have entered into strategic alliances with each other. Under **strategic alliances**, firms agree to cooperate on certain aspects of business while remaining competitors on other aspects. Thus, because of the high cost of developing new medicines for curing cancer, two pharmaceutical companies may agree to share research information and costs while competing with each other in selling other medicines.

The expansion of international business has created multinational firms. A **multinational firm** is a firm that owns or controls production or service facilities in more than one country. The country in which the business has its headquarters is referred to as the **home country**. The foreign location where it has facilities is referred to as the **host country**. Company headquarters is called the **parent firm**; and the foreign branches, if registered as independent legal entities, are referred to as **subsidiaries**. Most of the world's largest businesses are multinational firms. However, many small firms, too, are multinational businesses.

Trade and investment in the international environment have some unique complications. Businesses must consider government policies toward foreign firms and products, the value of foreign currencies, and the contrast of cultures when doing business abroad.

 CHECKPOINT

List the different forms of international businesses.

●●● Government Policies

Because international business takes place between two or more countries, the policies, rules, and laws of more than one national government affect trade and investment. Although economists consider free trade desirable for a society, on occasion governments impose **tariffs**. These are taxes on foreign goods to

FACTS & FIGURES

Understanding Cultural Differences

The Japanese find it hard to answer a definite "no" to either a question or a statement. They signal that they "don't know" or "don't understand" by waving their own hand in front of their face, with the palm outward.

Dubai Ports

Many international companies buy businesses in the United States. In 2006, a Dubai company, Dubai Ports World, purchased a British firm that operated six U.S. ocean ports. This led to an outcry from the U.S. public and politicians. U.S. protestors did not want a company from the Middle East to buy these U.S. assets. Dubai Ports World finally transferred ownership of the U.S. ports to a U.S. entity. Each year, the United States buys billions of dollars of oil from the Middle East. These actions hurt the United States' image as a good country to invest in.

The decision not to sell U.S. ports to Dubai Ports World increased our trade deficit with Dubai. The U.S. continues to buy oil from Dubai but does not sell U.S. products to Dubai.

protect domestic industries and to earn revenue. For instance, assume that the U.S. government sets a tariff of 10 percent on a pair of jeans made in Colombia, South America. If the jeans are valued at $30, the American customs department will collect a tax of $3 ($30 × 0.10), and the price per pair will rise to $33.

Governments also impose tariffs when a foreign supplier is guilty of "dumping" its products. **Dumping** refers to the practice of selling goods in a foreign market at a price that is below cost or below what it charges in its home country. When a company dumps, it is trying to win more customers by driving domestic producers out of the market. The government prevents dumping by setting tariffs that increase the price of goods being dumped. For example, if Brazilian firms tried dumping steel in the United States, a tariff might be levied to sufficiently raise the price of that steel to permit domestic producers to compete successfully.

Another way by which governments restrict the availability of foreign goods is to create quotas. A **quota** limits the quantity or value of units permitted to enter a country. For instance, the U.S. government may allow only 10,000 tons of salmon to enter the country annually from Chile, although much more salmon could be sold. Alternatively, the government could allow salmon worth up to $100 million into the United States from Chile annually. In either case, quotas limit the number or dollar value of foreign goods that can be sold in a country. Quotas are designed to protect the market share of domestic producers. However, both tariffs and quotas increase the price of foreign goods to consumers.

In addition to tariffs and quotas, it may be difficult to sell goods and services abroad because of **nontariff barriers**. These are nontax methods of discouraging trade. In many cases, such barriers do not target specific foreign companies or products, but have the practical effect of keeping them out. In other cases, barriers are deliberately created to protect domestic producers.

Almost all countries have nontariff barriers of one sort or another. For example, in the United States, steering wheels are on the left side of motor vehicles, whereas in Ireland, the steering wheel is on the right side. Thus, before an

© Getty Images/Digital Vision

Many of the clothes you buy are made in foreign countries. Do they generally cost more or less than similar clothes made in the United States? What factors affect the pricing of foreign-made clothing?

American company can sell cars in Ireland, it would have to make changes to the vehicle. Another example of nontariff barriers would be a public campaign to "Buy American." This is clearly designed to discourage the buying of foreign goods and services. Nontariff barriers are difficult to remove because they are often part of a country's culture and tradition.

Governments may place restrictions on what goods and services can be exported or imported. The goals are again to protect domestic businesses, citizens, or cultures and to ensure national security. American firms need government licenses to sell high-technology or military products abroad. For political reasons, a government may bar companies from doing business with particular countries. Such a restriction is known as an **embargo**. For instance, the U.S. government has established an embargo that bars U.S. companies from conducting business with Cuba.

Sanctions are a milder form of embargo that bans specific business ties with a foreign country. For instance, it is illegal for an American company to sell nuclear technology to Pakistan, which tested atomic bombs in 1998.

Governments place restrictions on what domestic companies foreigners are allowed to buy or invest in. In the United States, foreign firms are not allowed to have a majority control of airlines or television stations. The government fears that allowing that to happen might endanger national security. In extreme cases, a government may seize foreign firms with or without compensation, if such businesses are thought to be harmful to the national interests.

CURRENCY VALUES

International business involves dealing with the money, or currency, of foreign countries. Currencies have different names, such as the dollar in the United States, peso in Mexico, and yen in Japan, but more important, they differ in value. This is a key difference between doing business domestically and doing business internationally. The **exchange rate** is the value of one country's currency expressed in the currency of another country. For example, one U.S. dollar might be worth eleven Mexican pesos right now. If you were traveling to Mexico and wanted some Mexican money, you would receive eleven pesos for every dollar you turned in to the bank at this exchange rate. The value of each currency in terms of another can change every minute, depending on many factors, such as the demand for a particular currency, interest rates, inflation rates, and government policies. Major newspapers and several websites publish exchange rates for most currencies. In addition, there are online calculators that convert one currency to another.

Managers must closely watch exchange rates, as they affect profits and investment decisions in a big way. For example, assume the value of one American dollar is equal to 80 Japanese yen. A camera made in Japan for 8,000 yen would sell in the United States for $100 (8,000/80). If the exchange rate changes to 75 yen to the dollar, that same camera will now cost $107 (8,000/75). Thus, the Japanese camera becomes more expensive in the United States entirely because of exchange rate changes. To protect firms against adverse changes in the exchange rates, international business managers use many techniques.

Management MATTERS

Understanding foreign cultures is key to the success of an international business manager. The starting point for this is often learning some parts of the foreign country's language. This shows respect for the culture. Managers should also familiarize themselves on the country's history, laws, and social norms.

Managers bring their own culture into business meetings. It is important to research how business meetings are conducted in the each culture where an international manager does business.

What Do You Think? Why is it important to learn a foreign language? How should a manager prepare for a cross cultural meeting?

CULTURAL DIFFERENCES

International business also requires understanding and coping with cultural values and traits in foreign countries that are different from those of the home country. **Culture** refers to the customs, beliefs, values, and patterns of behavior of the people of a country or group. It also includes language; religion; attitudes toward work, authority, and family; practices regarding courtship, etiquette, gestures, and joking; and manners and traditions. In many countries, especially large ones like India, Russia, and South Africa, numerous cultural differences exist within their own populations. Likewise, in the United States, there are cultural differences, such as among various racial and ethnic groups.

Some cultures may be more familiar to Americans, such as those of Canada and Great Britain. Others seem very unfamiliar to Americans, such as those of India and Thailand. Managers who work in foreign countries need to be aware of cultural differences in order to be successful in their assignments. The greater the cultural gap, the more the businessperson will have to adjust.

Culture affects how people communicate in a country. In a **low-context culture** such as the United States, people communicate directly and explicitly. A person is expected to come to the point directly and not beat around the bush. An American manager might say, "Do this task immediately." The receiver of this message is not expected to read between the lines. In contrast, in a **high-context culture** such as Japan, communication tends to occur through nonverbal signs and indirect suggestions. Ambiguity and indirect suggestions are expected and highly valued. A person is not supposed to come right out and say it. A Japanese manager might say, "This task is very important, and your attention to it will be greatly appreciated." The difference between high- and low-context cultures can cause communication misunderstandings.

English has become the language of international business. In general, business English is taught the same way in most business programs and within businesses. However, communication problems can arise outside of the office where relationships are built between individuals. Word usage and terminology vary across the world. This is even true for English-speaking countries. For example, individuals from the United Kingdom have a tendency to be more formal and keep a "stiff upper lip" or be more reserved and restrained. Individuals from Australia can be the direct opposite. They are very informal and self-deprecating.

Learning to communicate in other cultures is vital for international business managers. Even body language differs between cultures. What should you study before you negotiate with foreign managers?

© Shutterstock/ArTono

 **CHECKPOINT**

Describe the government policies that can be used to control international trade.

9.2 ASSESSMENT

UNDERSTAND MANAGEMENT CONCEPTS

Determine the best answer for each of the following questions.

1. When a company ships a product to a buyer in another country it is engaging in
   a. exporting
   b. importing
   c. international licensing
   d. a joint venture

2. Which of the following is *not* a barrier to free trade?
   a. tariffs
   b. dumping
   c. quota
   d. importing

THINK CRITICALLY

Answer the following questions as completely as possible.

3. What policies can a government adopt to protect domestic businesses from foreign competition?

4. How do changes in currency exchange rates affect international business?

Business Via the Internet

When the Lee Hung Fat Garment Factory started in 1975, overseas orders usually came by messenger from one of the big Hong Kong trading houses. Today, customers send in specifications for denim jeans and leather jackets directly to a computer on the desk of Mr. Eddy Wong Fun-Ming, the company's operations director. "What we do in one day used to take five weeks in the 1970s," says Mr. Wong.

This small Hong Kong company with annual sales of $40 million is using the Internet to completely change the way it does business. With the click of a mouse, Mr. Wong pulls up a customer's order on the screen. He can see all the details—from production at his factories in China and Bangladesh to shipping schedules to individual customers' accounts. So can many of his staff. Each order is simultaneously sent to any department involved in getting it filled.

Lee Hung Fat supplies apparel to about 60 companies in Europe. Most of these customers have gone online. So the decision to wire the company into the Internet was driven partly by customers wanting to do e-commerce, and partly by his own desire to cut costs.

Using the Internet to communicate has saved the company on phone bills. Before the company went online, fax and telephone calls to customers and factories overseas cost about $10,000 a month. With electronic mail, "You can have 50 messages to your buyer in a day and it doesn't really cost you anything," says Mr. Wong, who often checks his e-mails on the golf course using a smart phone. He also applies over the Internet for required documents to ship his goods. Before, he had to send someone to the government office and apply for the export license in person.

The company saves money in other ways, too. Before, the company sent a mockup of a garment to buyers overseas by courier or by mail. Now, Mr. Wong holds the item in front of a camera mounted on his PC and sends it over the Internet. He can scan a picture of a sample and transmit that to the customers, who can play with the cloth pattern or the stitching and then zap back a new version. This means samples are approved three to four times faster. Even after paying for the costs of installing computers, Mr. Wong estimates he saves about 15 to 20 percent in costs.

THINK CRITICALLY

1. How does the Internet help the Lee Hung Fat Garment Factory remain globally competitive?

2. Are there some aspects of the business that cannot be handled by the Internet?

3. What problems could the company encounter because of its heavy reliance on the Internet?

Theories of International Trade Investment

Goals

- Explain two theories of international trade.
- Discuss the concepts of balance of payments and current accounts.
- Consider career opportunities in international business and understand the factors related to being sent abroad on assignment.

Terms

- comparative advantage theory p. 235
- product life cycle theory p. 236
- balance of payments p. 236
- current account p. 236
- capital account p. 236

Theories of International Trade

Business transactions between countries have been steadily increasing for over 60 years. This is, in part, due to the realization that international trade can benefit all participants. In this section, you will learn about two well-known theories that explain why international trade and investment occur.

COMPARATIVE ADVANTAGE THEORY

The **comparative advantage theory** states that to gain a trade advantage, a country should specialize in products or services that it can provide more efficiently than can other countries. For instance, because of climate and soil conditions, Brazil is better able to grow coffee than India, whose soil and climate favor the growing of tea. Each country could gain by specializing—Brazil in coffee and India in tea—and then trading with each other.

What if one country can produce both coffee and tea at a lower cost than another country? The comparative advantage theory says that the focus should be on comparing the cost of producing both products in each country. For example, it is possible that India may be able to produce more tea than coffee for the same cost, whereas Brazil may find that it can produce coffee at a lower cost than it can produce tea. In such a case, Brazilians should specialize in producing and selling coffee to the Indians and buying tea from India. Similarly, the Indians should produce tea and sell some to the Brazilians to pay for the coffee they need. This theory explains why the United States produces computers, Saudi Arabia extracts oil from the earth, and Indonesia makes athletic shoes.

PRODUCT LIFE CYCLE THEORY

Another explanation for trade and investment relates to product life cycle. During its life cycle, a product or service goes through four stages: introduction, growth, maturity, and decline. Consider black-and-white televisions, for example. When they were first introduced in the 1940s and 1950s, they were the only televisions available. As more people in the country started buying TVs, their sales grew—the growth stage. When most households owned a TV, sales leveled off—the maturity stage. When color TVs appeared, the sales of black-and-white sets started falling—the decline stage.

The **product life cycle theory** states that companies look for new markets when products are in the maturity and decline stages of the product life cycle. When sales begin to slow in a country (the mature stage), Company A that makes the product starts selling it to foreign countries where the product may be in the introductory or growth stage. However, selling abroad is expensive because of transportation, tariffs, quotas, and other nontariff barriers. Companies in the foreign country find it attractive to make and sell the product at lower prices. To counteract this action, Company A sets up a factory in the foreign country where it makes and sells the product. Company A may even sell some of the products back to the home country.

Many American companies move to foreign countries when sales at home start lagging. Examples are fast-food restaurants and soft-drink companies. Because of technological changes, the life cycle of new products is much shorter. New products are regularly introduced. Their sales grow, then flatten, and eventually decline. To prolong the life of the product, firms first ship their products abroad, and later build factories there.

✓ CHECKPOINT

Explain the comparative advantage theory and product life cycle theory.

●●● Balance of Payments

Why has the United States usually had an advantage when it comes to trade?

© Getty Images/Photodisc

Goods and services sold abroad by American companies bring money into the United States. Money also comes from foreigners who buy American companies or set up new businesses in the United States or lend money to Americans. At the same time, money leaves the country when Americans buy foreign products, vacation abroad, invest in foreign businesses, or donate money to aid people in other countries. National governments and international organizations such as the United Nations and WTO keep records of international transactions, and governments use these to develop economic policies.

All international transactions are recorded in an accounting statement called the **balance of payments**. The balance-of-payments statement has two parts: the current account and the capital account. The **current account** records the value of goods and services exported and those imported from foreigners, as well as other income and payments. The **capital account** records investment funds coming into and going out of a country. Investment funds include bank loans or deposits, purchase and sale of a business, and investing in a new business.

For several decades, the United States has had a consistent deficit on its current account. Figure 9-6 shows how the deficit has ballooned over time. The balance-of-payments deficit means that Americans have been buying more goods and services made abroad than they have been selling to foreigners. How long can a country continue to buy more than it sells? Not indefinitely, of course. However, the United States has several advantages.

Countries everywhere value its currency, the dollar, because the United States is a stable society, government policies are pro-business, and its economy is the world's largest and richest. Foreign banks and governments are willing to lend money to the United States to enable it to pay for the excess product it buys.

Not all countries are so fortunate. Countries with prolonged trade deficits may not be able to pay their bills or may have to limit international trade. In addition, their governments may have to place restrictions on the outward flow of money or on the activities of foreign businesses in their countries. At such times, they may obtain financial assistance and economic advice from the International Monetary Fund.

When deficits continue, it means that companies and individuals are demanding more foreign currency to buy the foreign goods. For instance, if Americans buy more Korean toys, the demand for the Korean currency—the won—goes up, because American toy companies will need won to pay the Koreans. When demand increases for won, more dollars are needed to buy won. Thus, the value of the dollar declines in relation to the won. In turn, Korean products become more expensive for Americans, whereas American products become less expensive for Koreans. Theoretically, at this stage, higher prices discourage the sale of Korean products in America, and lower prices encourage the sale of American products abroad. In this way, the deficits can be reduced and eventually eliminated.

To illustrate this process, consider Apple computers made in the United States and sold in Korea. Assuming an exchange rate of $1 = 1,000 won, a $1,200 computer would sell in Korea for 1,200,000 won (1,200 × 1,000). As more Koreans buy Apple computers, they will need more and more U.S. dollars to pay for the computers. This will increase the demand for dollars, and more won will be needed to buy a dollar. Thus, if $1 is now worth 1,200 won, the Apple computer will cost the Koreans 1,440,000 won (1,200 × 1,200).

With the computers costing more, Koreans will buy fewer of them and U.S. exports will decline. Contrast this situation with what happens to a Korean product—say, a Samsung mobile phone costing 120,000 won. The phone will

FACTS & FIGURES

Voting with Dollars

Americans vote with their dollars. In a free-market system, customers are free to buy whatever goods and services they want. For many Americans, this means buying foreign products that are perceived as cheaper and/or of higher quality. Americans will buy domestic products if they offer a greater value than imported products, or they can vote to pay more for domestic products.

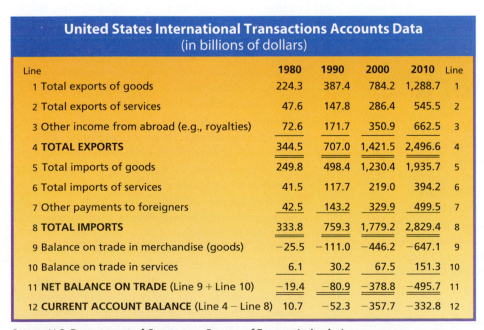

Line		1980	1990	2000	2010	Line
United States International Transactions Accounts Data (in billions of dollars)						
1	Total exports of goods	224.3	387.4	784.2	1,288.7	1
2	Total exports of services	47.6	147.8	286.4	545.5	2
3	Other income from abroad (e.g., royalties)	72.6	171.7	350.9	662.5	3
4	**TOTAL EXPORTS**	344.5	707.0	1,421.5	2,496.6	4
5	Total imports of goods	249.8	498.4	1,230.4	1,935.7	5
6	Total imports of services	41.5	117.7	219.0	394.2	6
7	Other payments to foreigners	42.5	143.2	329.9	499.5	7
8	**TOTAL IMPORTS**	333.8	759.3	1,779.2	2,829.4	8
9	Balance on trade in merchandise (goods)	−25.5	−111.0	−446.2	−647.1	9
10	Balance on trade in services	6.1	30.2	67.5	151.3	10
11	**NET BALANCE ON TRADE** (Line 9 + Line 10)	−19.4	−80.9	−378.8	−495.7	11
12	**CURRENT ACCOUNT BALANCE** (Line 4 − Line 8)	10.7	−52.3	−357.7	−332.8	12

Source: U.S. Department of Commerce, Bureau of Economic Analysis

Figure 9-6 The United States has been running current account deficits for more than 20 years.

sell in the United States initially for $120 (120,000/1,000). When the exchange rate becomes $1 = 1,200 won, the same phone will now cost Americans less: 120,000/1,200, or $100. This decline in price will lead Americans to buy more Samsung phones, which will lead to an increasing demand for won and raise the value of the won in terms of dollars. In turn, American goods will become less expensive to Koreans, and they will buy more American products. Thus, the trade deficits work out over the long run.

In the example above, the exchange rate of the currency fluctuates because of market conditions that impact supply and demand for the dollar and the Korean won. This type of flexible exchange rate is a result of free markets.

Some countries do not allow their currency to fluctuate on international markets. Instead the government sets a fixed exchange rate. China is the largest economy with a fixed exchange rate. In recent years, the Yuan has been fixed at about 6.5 to the dollar. As a result, China can keep the price of Chinese products low compared to products made in other countries. Low prices make it easier for China to export products. China's control of its currency creates an unfair advantage.

China has faced pressure to allow the Yuan to float against other international currencies. China has considered allowing this. A stronger Yuan could bring down Chinese inflation and make Chinese savers more wealthy in the international marketplace.

CHECKPOINT

Explain the difference between current and capital accounts.

● ● ● ● Career Opportunities in International Business

The growth of international business has created many new types of jobs. In addition to those who work for foreign firms in the United States, over 150,000 Americans work abroad for American or foreign firms.

Many people work in various aspects of international business, such as exporting and importing, teaching and translating languages, administering trade laws, managing offices and operations in foreign countries, and in banking and insurance firms. Others work in international trade organizations such as the WTO and the IMF, or in federal and state government agencies. As countries become economically interdependent, more and more jobs will require a knowledge of international business.

Most international companies hire at the entry level, but usually they send workers abroad who are very skilled, mature, and experienced. Studies show that the average salary in foreign companies located in the United States is higher than for similar jobs in American companies. As firms gain experience in doing business globally, they employ more and more people from various backgrounds and countries. However, although working several

NETBookmark

The world is becoming more competitive. Many countries produce more goods and services than the U.S. in specific product categories.

Access the website for this textbook and choose the link for Chapter 9 Net Bookmark. Use the NationMaster menu system to view "Economy," then choose at least four product categories (world trade > exports > product) to determine which countries are the top 10 producers of each product. Determine where the United States places in these product categories. Investigate the background of three high producers and explain why they are able to produce at such a high level.

www.cengage.com/school/bizmgmt

years overseas may promote workers' careers in many companies, it may hurt their careers in others. Workers abroad lose close contact with people and developments in the parent firm.

Today, both businesses and government agencies recruit extensively for jobs that require skills useful for international business. These include not only knowledge of business but also foreign-language ability, familiarity with foreign countries, and being comfortable with and in a foreign culture. Many colleges and universities provide coursework and academic degrees in international business. Many offer programs that allow students to do part of their studies in a foreign country or even in a foreign company.

EMPLOYMENT OF INTERNATIONAL MANAGERS

Firms need managers who can work successfully in a wide variety of countries. Such managers adapt readily to other cultures and are competent, socially flexible, and receptive to new ideas. Managers benefit from knowing the foreign language and from having strong self-confidence, a motivation to live abroad, and a skill for innovative problem solving.

During the start-up phase of foreign operations, firms tend to rely on managers sent from headquarters. However, most managers are citizens of the host country where the business is situated. Occasionally, businesses hire citizens of other countries (neither the home nor the host countries) because they are exceptionally qualified or because host country managers are not available. Sending managers abroad is expensive, because companies must provide extra benefits (such as housing, airfare for families, and cost-of-living allowances). Managers sent to a country that is culturally different from their own may experience culture shock. Many firms provide cross-cultural training to managers before sending them abroad.

The support of the entire family is often necessary for the manager to succeed in the foreign location. With more and more spouses of managers having careers of their own, many firms are finding it difficult to persuade managers to take long-term transfers to a foreign location. Instead, they are

© Getty Images/Photodisc

Jobs in international business take many forms. What kinds of international careers appeal to you?

using frequent short business trips, bringing in host-country managers to headquarters, and using teleconferencing and the Internet to manage their foreign operations.

CHECKPOINT

Describe the skills international managers need to be successful.

9.3 ASSESSMENT

UNDERSTAND MANAGEMENT CONCEPTS

Determine the best answer for each of the following questions.

1. The theory that a country should specialize in products or services that it can provide more efficiently than can other countries is called
   a. international specialization
   b. competitive advantage theory
   c. comparative advantage theory
   d. specialization theory

2. Which of the following is *not* part of the balance of payments?
   a. current account
   b. capital account
   c. economic surplus
   d. All are included as part of the balance of payments.

THINK CRITICALLY

Answer the following questions as completely as possible.

3. If a country regularly has a trade surplus, what will happen to its international business?

4. Explain the situations under which a multinational firm will use home-country, host-country, and third-country nationals in its foreign operations.

CHAPTER CONCEPTS

- Firms go into international business because of the potential for larger profits and limited opportunities in the home market. Removal of barriers to trade and investment, creation of trading blocs, and technological advances in communication and transportation have created a positive environment for conducting international business.

- International business occurs in various forms, such as exporting and importing, licensing, joint ventures, wholly owned subsidiaries, strategic alliances, and multinational firms.

- International business faces unique challenges, such as the need to work within the rules set by more than one government, currency exchange rates, and cultural differences.

- Two theories explain international trade and investments. The theory of comparative advantage explains why a particular country specializes in producing a particular product or service. The product life cycle theory explains how a product's life stage encourages international business.

- Data on trade and investment are used to set business and economic policies. The current account balance between countries is evidence of a nation's financial strength or weakness.

REVIEW BUSINESS MANAGEMENT TERMS

Write the letter of the term that matches each definition. Some terms will not be used.

1. Business activities that occur between two or more countries
2. Buying goods or services made in a foreign country
3. Business arrangement in which two or more firms share the costs of doing business and also share the profits
4. Type of business in which a firm sets up a business abroad on its own without any partners
5. Firm that owns or controls production or service facilities in more than one country
6. Foreign location where a firm has facilities
7. Value of one country's currency expressed in the currency of another
8. Taxes on foreign goods to protect domestic industries and to earn revenue
9. Nontax methods of discouraging trade
10. Government block preventing companies from doing business with particular countries
11. Selling goods in a foreign market at a price that is below cost or below what is charged in the home country
12. Record of investment funds coming into and going out of a country

a. capital account
b. dumping
c. embargo
d. exchange rate
e. home country
f. host country
g. importing
h. international business
i. joint venture
j. multinational firm
k. nontariff barrier
l. parent firm
m. tariffs
n. wholly owned subsidiary

Determine the best answer.

13. The foreign location where a multinational company has a manufacturing facility is known as the
   a. home country
   b. host country
   c. guest country
   d. parent country

14. The arrangement in which one international company allows another international company in another country to make and sell products according to certain specifications is called
   a. international franchise
   b. international joint venture
   c. international licensing
   d. international partnership

15. Culture includes all of the following except
   a. laws
   b. customs
   c. beliefs
   d. values

16. A type of culture in which people communicate directly and explicitly, and a person is expected to come to the point directly and not beat around the bush is a/an
   a. direct culture
   b. explicit culture
   c. low-context culture
   d. high-context culture

17. The international organization that creates and enforces the rules governing trade among countries is the
   a. International Monetary Fund
   b. United Nations
   c. World Bank
   d. World Trade Organization

18. An agreement between two or more countries to remove all restrictions between them on the sales of goods and services, while imposing barriers on trade and investment from countries that are not part of it, creates a/an
   a. free-trade zone
   b. economic union
   c. trade agreement
   d. trading bloc

19. The way by which governments restrict the availability of foreign goods, limiting the quantity or value of units permitted to enter a country, is called
   a. quota
   b. sanction
   c. limitation
   d. restriction

APPLY WHAT YOU KNOW

Answer the following questions.

20. Why is it easier for a firm to export instead of setting up a wholly owned foreign subsidiary?
21. Explain the purposes of the WTO, IMF, and World Bank.
22. How can a person from a low-context culture communicate with a person from a high-context culture and avoid misunderstandings?
23. If the value of the Canadian dollar continues to rise in relation to the American dollar, what can a Canadian exporter do to keep the price of the goods it sells in the U.S. market competitive?
24. Explain how it is possible for the United States to have a deficit in its current account year after year.

MAKE ACADEMIC CONNECTIONS

Complete the following activities.

25. **Math** The current accounts of the imaginary nation of Utopia for the past three years are given below in millions of dollars.

	Year 1	Year 2	Year 3
Exports of goods	$100	$120	$125
Imports of goods	$175	$195	$205
Exports of services	$80	$100	$150
Imports of services	$40	$60	$80
Other income from abroad	$30	$25	$40
Other payments abroad	$50	$70	$70

Given the above information, answer the following questions: Does Utopia have a deficit or surplus in its current account in Year 1, Year 2, and Year 3? Calculate the balance on merchandise trade for Year 1, Year 2, and Year 3. If you were the president of an American company, would you set up a business in Utopia? Why or why not? Suggest ways by which Utopia can reduce its deficit or surplus.

26. **Technology** An Australian sheep farmer who sells much of his wool in the United States has seen the exchange rate for the Australian dollar (AUD) change from U.S. $1 = AUD $1.20 to U.S. $1 = AUD $1.45 over the past six months. Use spreadsheet software to answer the following questions, assuming the farmer sells 1,000 AUDs worth of wool:
    a. Will this change in currency rates help or hurt his sales in the United States?
    b. What may be some of the reasons for the change in the currency rates?
    c. Do American consumers gain or suffer with the change in the currency rates?

CASE IN POINT

CASE 9-1: Country of Manufacturing Decision

Alexander's Electronics has its headquarters in Kansas City, Missouri. Alexander's manufactures and sells high-end surround sound systems for home entertainment. In 1991, the company moved its manufacturing to Taiwan. Now, given the increase in wages in Taiwan and expected increases in shipping costs to send products back to the United States, Alexander's Electronics is considering moving its manufacturing operations again.

Alexander's Electronics is evaluating China and Vietnam. Another option is moving manufacturing back to the United States. Each of these choices has advantages and disadvantages.

China has cheaper labor costs, but weaker legal protection to prevent the stealing of trade secrets. Alexander's does have managers in Taiwan who speak Mandarin Chinese, but these managers are native Taiwanese who may not be accepted in China because of the political problems between the two countries. Wages in China have also been moving up over time. Given the strong international pressure, China soon may have to increase its exchange rate, making it even more expensive to manufacture there.

Although Vietnam has cheap labor, there are concerns about staffing an operation in Vietnam. Vietnamese workers are not as highly skilled as workers in China and Taiwan. In addition, it is difficult to find well-qualified Vietnamese managers. The Vietnamese government is still communistic and there are high levels of corruption. Vietnam is even further from the United States than Taiwan, which would increase shipping costs. Distance is also an issue if Alexander's moves its operations to China.

Moving manufacturing options back to the United States would decrease shipping costs and there would be no import duties. The company could also advertise that their products are "made in the U.S.A." Highly skilled and motivated managers and workers are available in the United States, but higher wages could make Alexander's products less competitive against cheaper imports.

Alexander's managers are meeting to evaluate their alternatives. Each country has advantages and disadvantages.

THINK CRITICALLY

1. What should be considered when a manufacturer choices a manufacturing location?
2. Is being "made in the U.S.A." an important consideration for this type of product?
3. Should Alexander's Electronics consider manufacturing in Mexico? What are the advantages and disadvantages of manufacturing in Mexico?
4. What other countries should Alexander's Electronics consider?
5. What should Alexander's Electronics do? Why?

CASE 9-2: NAFTA's Impact on a Mexican Business

Despite intense lobbying by Mexican frozen-food companies against NAFTA, the Mexican government approved the treaty. Hidalgo Tortilla Company is a small firm based in Guadalajara, Mexico's second-largest city. It makes frozen taco and enchilada products for Mexico's rapidly growing middle class. The company was against the trade treaty, because it feared that American competitors would come to Mexico and drive smaller Mexican firms like itself out of business. American food companies, such as Sara Lee and Swanson, are very large and resourceful. They have huge modern factories with low production costs. Because the frozen-foods market is well developed in the United States, the American companies produce a wide range of products and use sophisticated marketing techniques.

Once NAFTA became a reality, Hidalgo began to prepare for competition in Mexico from American frozen-food companies. It was clear that Hidalgo could not go head-to-head in competition with larger and well-off American companies. However, the company's brand name is well known to Mexicans, and the company produces frozen food that appeals to the Mexican palate. There is a very large population of Mexicans in the American states just across the Mexican border.

Hidalgo Tortilla Company's management is exploring a number of options, such as focusing only on the Mexican market, using NAFTA to expand into the U.S. market, expanding into other Central and South American countries, or selling their current business to a large U.S.-based company.

THINK CRITICALLY

1. Does the fact that no tariffs and quotas will exist under NAFTA necessarily mean that American companies will be successful in Mexico? Explain.
2. Does NAFTA provide any opportunities for Hidalgo Tortilla Company to grow? Explain.
3. If Hidalgo proves to be a tough competitor to the American companies, what may the American companies do?
4. What should Hidalgo do to prepare itself for possible competition from American products?
5. How might cultural differences work to Hidalgo's competitive advantage?
6. How likely would it be for an American company to buy Hidalgo?
7. Explain how increased competition from American companies would help or hinder the competitiveness of Mexican businesses.

© Shutterstock/Dudarev Mikhail

PROJECT My Own Business

Going International

New small businesses seldom consider the impact of international business on their operations, yet almost all businesses today operate in an international business environment. Many suppliers of products and services purchased by small businesses are international or are owned by businesses located in other countries. A foreign market becomes less foreign as you learn more about it. As a business owner, you need to study those markets in order to understand potential foreign business opportunities. A small business that carefully researches a foreign market can be just as successful in international markets as a large business.

DATA COLLECTION

1. Fresh fruits are often imported from other countries. Using the Internet or the library, locate information that identifies the major international suppliers of fruits to the United States. Prepare one or more pie charts that illustrate your findings.
2. Using the Internet or the library, collect information on recent trade agreements and legislation that deal with international business. Summarize what experts are predicting will be the effect of the agreements and laws on U.S. businesses.
3. If you have access to people who have lived in other countries, discuss the types of health and wellness businesses, including juice bars, they are familiar with in the country in which they lived. Identify similarities to and differences from the ways businesses operate in the United States.

ANALYSIS

1. Identify three ways that international trade by U.S. businesses can have a positive effect on small businesses and three ways it can have a negative effect on those businesses.
2. Identify several food products popular in other countries and cultures that you would consider adding to your product line in the juice bar. Remember that the products should fit the image of health and fitness.
3. Assume that you have operated your business for 15 years, and it has been very successful in the United States. You now have franchises in 30 states. You want to test the international market to see if the business will work in other countries. Identify at least two countries in which you would consider introducing your business and justify your choices. Base your justification on information you have collected from the Internet or the library about the countries you chose.

Customs Inspector

Customs inspectors enforce laws governing imports and exports. Stationed in the United States and overseas at airports, seaports, and border crossing points, they examine, count, weigh, and measure cargoes entering and leaving the United States to determine whether the shipments are legal and how much duty must be paid. They determine whether people, ships, planes, and anything used to import or export cargo comply with all necessary regulations.

Employment Outlook

National security concerns and growing international trade are increasing the demand for customs inspectors, which is expected to rise 10 to 20 percent over the next 10 years. Customs inspecting is a federal job and less susceptible to economic conditions.

Job Titles

Customs and Border Protection Officer
Customs Agricultural Agent
Import Specialist
Compliance Inspector
Facility Operations Specialist
Intelligence Analyst

Needed Skills

- Must be a U.S. citizen and pass an extensive background investigation and medical examination.
- Must possess a bachelor's degree from an accredited college or university or possess three years of generalized experience.
- Must be willing to accept temporary or permanent assignments in a variety of geographical areas.

Working in Customs Services

Leopoldo began his career as a police officer in a small Texas town. After three years, he applied for a job as a customs inspector. His first assignment was on the U.S.–Mexico border, where he inspected cargo, baggage, people, cars, and trains entering the United States for contraband. This experience led to a new opportunity as an intelligence analyst. He will work with larger cases related to narcotics smuggling, money laundering, child pornography, and customs fraud. His goal is to move eventually into top management at the Customs Service.

Career Assessment

Why are customs agents important to international business? Why are they important to national security? What do you like and dislike about this career area?

Transportation, Distribution & Logistics

© Getty Images/Digital Vision

Case Study

ILLEGALS EXPLOITED IN KATRINA CLEANUP

Hurricane Katrina devastated New Orleans and the Gulf Coast of Mississippi. Post-Katrina reconstruction in New Orleans has depended heavily upon illegal workers from Mexico who appear at dawn and wait to be picked up for 14-hour shifts of hauling debris, ripping out drywall, and nailing walls.

Before Hurricane Katrina, Louisiana had one of the smallest Hispanic populations in the country. Hispanics represented 2.5 percent of residents, compared with 12.5 percent nationally. Nearly 100,000 Hispanics moved to the Gulf Coast region after Katrina, lured by promises of plentiful work and high wages. Nearly one-fourth of the construction workers in New Orleans are illegal immigrants.

Since many of the workers rebuilding New Orleans are in the U.S. illegally, they are vulnerable to exploitation. They work in hazardous conditions without protective gear and earn much less than their legal counterparts. Documented workers in New Orleans are paid $16.50 per hour, while illegal immigrants are paid $10 per hour.

Workers from Mexico have responded to a national priority to rebuild the city while their rights to safety are being violated. Under federal labor laws, illegal immigrants are given the same health and safety protections as documented workers.

Fewer than one-third of illegal immigrants said that they understood the hazards of removing asbestos or mold, compared with more than 65 percent of documented laborers. Many immigrant workers are afraid to raise their concerns to employers for fear they will be deported to Mexico.

Protecting the border between the United States and Mexico has become a hot political topic. Numerous illegal immigrants are performing important work in construction, agriculture, food processing, and the reconstruction of areas devastated by Hurricane Katrina. Opinion polls indicate that Americans want the borders tightened to shut down the pipeline of illegal immigrants coming into the United States.

THINK CRITICALLY

1. Why are illegal workers likely candidates for rebuilding the areas devastated by Hurricane Katrina?
2. Why do workers from Mexico risk coming to the United States for employment?
3. What are two ethical issues involved with this case?
4. What types of jobs provide popular employment for illegal immigrants? Why?

Emerging Business Issues Team Event

PROCEDURE Fifteen minutes before your presentation time, you will draw to determine whether you will present an affirmative or negative argument for your emerging business issue. Each presentation may last no more than five minutes. Following each oral presentation, the judges have five minutes to ask questions. Each team should be prepared to defend its argument. Any presentation that lasts more than five minutes will receive a five-point deduction.

YOUR ASSIGNMENT

This team event (two or three members) challenges FBLA members to develop and demonstrate research and presentation skills for an emerging business issue. Your research should help you develop affirmative and negative arguments for one of the following topics:

- Government incentives for green initiatives
- Consumer credit in the economy
- Conducting trade throughout the world
- Tax cuts in the market economy
- Investment in the development of alternative fuel products

PERFORMANCE INDICATORS EVALUATED

- Understand the given emerging business issue.
- Present an affirmative or negative argument for the topic.
- Conduct research to support your argument.
- Demonstrate persuasive speaking and oral presentation skills.
- Involve all team members in the research and presentation.

THINK CRITICALLY

1. Why is it important to consider both sides of an issue before presenting your viewpoint?
2. Why is it important to list pros and cons for an issue when trying to sell your viewpoint?
3. Why is it important to determine the demographics of your audience before presenting a speech?

UNIT 3

Business Organization and Management

CHAPTERS

© Shutterstock/Andresr

MANAGING THE FORM OF BUSINESS OWNERSHIP

© Shutterstock/auremar

Reality Check

One Way to Start a Business

Nancy Wakefield wondered about the rest of her life as she sat in front of her computer. Was she too young to consider starting her own business? Was the whole idea of opening an event planning business ridiculous for a 20-year-old college student? "My parents support my dream of investing my money to start a business," she thought to herself. "Both of them are entrepreneurs and can share their experiences. Also, the library and the Internet have plenty of information on how to develop a business plan."

Nancy continued thinking to herself. "I've learned plenty during the last several weeks, reading and talking with my parents about their flower and gift shop. Working with Mom and Dad on the weekends and working in a catering and event business while in high school also gave me experience. Yet, there's so much I don't know. I've never hired anyone, kept the books, or managed employees. But the idea is so exciting. Will people stop at … Nancy's Parties … for planning fraternity, sorority, and other campus group parties?" Nancy turned back to her computer. "Did I just

name my business?" she asked, smiling to herself.

Many people have dreamed about owning their own businesses. The idea may have crossed your mind, too. These dreams often start as simple ideas. Some dreamers with practical ideas do form businesses. That is how many well-known founders of large businesses got started. Hundreds of young entrepreneurs have started their own firms and managed their own businesses, including Facebook's Mark Zuckerberg, Flickr's Catarina Fake, and Sara Blakely of Spanx.

Most businesses begin with one owner, but some firms start with two or more owners. Sometimes these start-ups grow into large corporations requiring complex management. This chapter will examine the basic elements of managing as an entrepreneur, a proprietor, a partner, or as part of a corporation.

What's Your Reaction? What advice can you give Nancy about the information she should gather for her business plan?

10.1

Entrepreneurs and Proprietorships

Goals

- Describe the characteristics of successful entrepreneurs.
- Evaluate the role of planning in managing your own business.
- Explain the management issues of proprietorships.

Terms

- intrapreneur p. 252
- business plan p. 253
- proprietorship p. 254
- proprietor p. 254
- creditor p. 254

●●● Characteristics of Entrepreneurs

Many businesses start as entrepreneurial ventures. You learned earlier that an entrepreneur is a person who assumes the risk of starting, owning, and operating a business for the purpose of making a profit.

Entrepreneurs must invest months or even years of hard work before they earn a profit. About half of all new businesses end within the first five to six years. Businesses often fail for financial reasons, but many closings of young firms occur because the owners are not well suited to manage an entrepreneurial venture. Some entrepreneurs who are eventually successful previously experienced unsuccessful business start-ups. They learn from their mistakes and start over.

Entrepreneurs must determine if they want to only work for themselves or if they want build a business by working with others. Entrepreneurs who prefer self-employment enjoy the freedom and independence of decision making that comes with being their own boss and making their own management decisions.

Entrepreneurs need a specific set of management skills. They must be self-starters who have plenty of energy and enjoy working on their own. They must be able to take charge of situations and work hard for long periods to meet their goals. Entrepreneurs are also creative thinkers, often coming up with new ideas and new ways to solve management problems. They must be able to create a plan for their business. In addition, most successful entrepreneurs are able to grow their businesses by managing people. As a result, they are often community leaders. You may have met some of these business leaders at school, religious, charitable, or business functions.

INTRAPRENEURS

Entrepreneurship is not just for business start-ups. Many managers in large companies realize that they must be innovative to compete against smaller, more nimble businesses. To keep their businesses on the cutting edge and to encourage their creative employees, some larger employers support intrapreneurs. An **intrapreneur** is an employee who is given funds and freedom to create a special unit or department within a company to develop a new product, process, or service. Although the main company finances the new venture, intrapreneurs enjoy the freedom of running their operations with little or no interference from upper managers.

FACTS & FIGURES

Family Businesses

Family businesses dominate the U.S. economy. According to some estimates, families own about 90 percent of all businesses, including the majority of small- and medium-size companies.

Some of the largest corporations in the United States provide intrapreneurship opportunities. IBM and other major corporations such as 3M and General Electric have also captured the entrepreneurial talents of employees. Employees benefit because they risk neither their salaries nor their savings to launch a new business. Employers benefit by keeping creative employees who might have started successful competing businesses. Furthermore, employers and consumers benefit because new and better products, processes, and services are introduced at a quickened pace.

Intrapreneurs are often given greater freedom to manage than traditional workers or managers. These individuals must be able to drive change forward inside of a business. They must be able to plan and communicate their plan to others. They must organize the resources necessary to champion new ideas. And it is vital that they be able to work with others inside and outside of the business to reach the project goals.

CHECKPOINT

Explain why businesses start-ups often fail.

● ● ● Planning a Business

For business start-ups, the management planning process requires preparing a business plan. A **business plan** is a written document that describes the nature of the business, its goals and objectives, and how they will be achieved. The business plan for a new venture requires a great deal of careful thought.

Investors, such as family, friends, and bankers, evaluate business plans to ensure the entrepreneur is organized well enough to receive start-up funds. Investors will have greater assurance when they see an evaluation of potential problems and solutions. Too many entrepreneurs fail for one of three reasons: (1) they did not prepare a business plan, (2) their plan was unrealistic, or (3) they wrote the plan only because the lender, such as a bank, required it.

By developing a workable business plan, entrepreneurs become aware of their risks. As a result, they may be able to anticipate problems and take preventive action. The business plan also causes the aspiring business owner to become more realistic about the responsibilities of ownership.

FORMS OF OWNERSHIP

Business can have a variety of ownership structures. Each of these structures has implications for both management decisions and management style.

One of the very first management decisions a business owner must make is what legal form of ownership to adopt. The form of ownership selected depends on several considerations, such as the nature and size of the business, the capital needed, the tax laws, and the financial

Management MATTERS

What Are the Chances of Being Successful?

Entrepreneurs are the lifeblood of the U.S. economy. Many of the most successful businesses in the United States started in the most unlikely places, such as college dorm or a home garage. More than two-thirds of businesses start in the founder's homes.

Although there are many success stories, the risk of business start-up failure is high. According to the National Federation of Independent Businesses, about 39 percent of start-ups show a profit, 30 percent break even, and 30 percent lose money. Businesses close because owners don't make enough money, they want to move on to new things, or they get tired. Real failures (loss of money) are most often due to lack of planning. This includes identifying clear business goals and insufficient planning for marketing, management, and financing. Entrepreneurs can lower risk by researching and writing a strong business plan.

Adaptability

Managers often face the need to adapt to varied roles, job responsibilities, and schedules. The ability to adjust to changes in work, technology, people, and the work environment is a key to success. It is particularly important for managers, entrepreneurs, and intrapreneurs.

responsibility the owner is willing to assume. The three legal forms of business ownership are proprietorships, partnerships, and corporations. Proprietorships and partnerships share a common characteristic. They both place owners in the position to receive all of the profits, but at the same time, they take on all of the risks.

CHECKPOINT

Describe two advantages of developing a business plan.

The Nature of Proprietorships

The most common form of business organization is the proprietorship, of which there are over 22 million in the United States. A business owned and managed by one person is known as a **proprietorship**, or **sole proprietorship**, and the owner-manager is the **proprietor**. In addition to owning and managing the business, the proprietor often performs the day-to-day management tasks that make a business successful, with the help of hired employees. Under the proprietorship form of organization, the owner furnishes expertise, money, and management. For assuming these responsibilities, the owner is entitled to all profits earned by the business.

If no debts are owed, a proprietor has full claim to the assets, or property owned by the business. If the proprietor has business debts, however, creditors have first claim against the assets. A **creditor** is person or business to which money is owed. Figure 10-1 shows a simple financial statement of Jennifer York, who is the proprietor of a small retail grocery store and fruit market.

This simple financial statement, known as a statement of financial position or balance sheet, indicates that the assets of the business are valued at $218,400. Because York has liabilities (money owed by a business) amounting to $14,400, the balance sheet shows her capital as $204,000 ($218,400 minus $14,400). In accounting, the terms *capital*, *net worth*, and *equity* are interchangeable and are defined as assets less liabilities. If there are profits, York gets the total amount. She must also absorb losses. Because she owns the land and the building, she does not have to pay rent, although she must pay the cost of maintenance and taxes for the property.

Jennifer York's Balance Sheet					
ASSETS			**CLAIMS AGAINST ASSETS**		
Cash	$	17,760	Accounts Payable	$	14,400
Merchandise		31,680	J. York, Capital		204,000
Equipment		24,960			
Land and Building		144,000			
Total	$	218,400	Total	$	218,400

© Cengage Learning 2013.

Figure 10-1 Jennifer York's balance sheet is a simple financial statement. Her assets appear on the left and claims against assets appear on the right.

MANAGEMENT ISSUES OF PROPRIETORSHIPS

The fact that over 70 percent of businesses are proprietorships indicates that this form of organization has definite advantages. As a potential sole proprietorship manager, you would need to evaluate the advantages and disadvantages below.

SELF MANAGEMENT There can be a great deal of pride and satisfaction in being one's own boss and being responsible only to oneself. The proprietor can be inventive and creative in working out ideas to make the business a success. Proprietors must be able to manage their time and keep driving toward their goals. All of the profits belong to the sole proprietor. As a result, the owner is more likely to work overtime and to think continually of how the business can operate more efficiently. At the same time, proprietors may not have all of the skills or expertise necessary to manage a business. To avoid failure, sole proprietors must also be willing to solicit advice from others.

RELATIONSHIP MANAGEMENT Because most proprietorships are small, the proprietor and the employees know one another personally. This relationship can lead to mutual understanding and a feeling of "family" as employer and employees work side by side in daily business activities. However, this can sometimes lead to difficult management decisions when the proprietor must make decisions such as who should receive raises or be promoted, or who may need to be laid off. Sole proprietors often develop close relationships with their customers as well.

SPEED OF DECISION MAKING Sole proprietors can make rapid decisions without consulting others. If an unusual opportunity to buy merchandise or equipment arises, or if the owner wishes to change the location of the business or to sell on credit terms rather than on a cash basis, there are no dissenting partners to stop such action. Thus, the management of a proprietorship is flexible and can adjust rapidly to changing conditions. Funds, or capital, are needed to both operate and grow a business. Financial assistance on a large scale may be difficult to obtain by a single owner. Therefore, the expansion of the business may be slowed because of the owner's lack of capital.

FREEDOM FROM RED TAPE A sole proprietor can usually begin or end business activities without legal formality. Sole proprietorships can be organized without a lot of legal documents or government red tape. In some types of businesses, however, such as restaurants, it is necessary to obtain a license before operations can begin. The continuing operation of a sole proprietorship depends on the longevity of the proprietor. If the owner becomes unable to work because of illness or dies, the business would have to close.

LIABILITY For most sole proprietorships, the income tax is less than for the corporation form of business, which is explained later in the chapter. While they keep all of the profits after taxes, sole proprietors assume a great deal of risk because they also bear all of the losses if the business fails. If the business fails and the owner is unable to pay the debts of the business, the creditors have a claim against the owner's personal assets, not just the assets of the business. The sole proprietor may therefore lose not only the money invested in the enterprise but also personal possessions, such as a car or home.

Owning your own business and being your own boss has both rewards and challenges. How can sole proprietors increase their chances of success?

© Shutterstock/mangostock

BUSINESSES SUITED TO PROPRIETORSHIP

The kind of business that is primarily concerned with providing personal services is well suited to the proprietorship form of organization. Dentists, accountants, landscape gardeners, carpenters, painters, barbers, beauty salons, website developers, and computer consultants are examples of businesses frequently organized as proprietorships.

Another type of business that seems to be well suited to proprietorship is the type that sells merchandise or services on a small scale. Newspaper and magazine stands, roadside markets, family restaurants, flower shops, gasoline stations, small grocery stores, and many web-based businesses that sell crafts, gourmet foods, or grocery delivery services are examples. In general, the type of business that can be operated suitably as a proprietorship is one that (1) is small enough to be managed by the proprietor or a few people hired by the proprietor and (2) does not require a large amount of capital.

PART-TIME PROPRIETORSHIPS

Not all proprietors run full-time businesses. Many people run part-time businesses out of an office or their home. According to the IRS, more than 6 percent of individual taxpayers file a Schedule C form (tax form for proprietorships) as sole proprietors. Up to a third of all proprietorships are part-time.

CHECKPOINT

List the management issues related to sole proprietorships.

10.1 ASSESSMENT

UNDERSTAND MANAGEMENT CONCEPTS

Determine the best answer for each of the following questions.

1. Which of the following is *not* characteristic of entrepreneurs?
   a. Entrepreneurs are self-starters.
   b. Entrepreneurs like to make sure others do most of the work.
   c. Entrepreneurs enjoy working on their own.
   d. Entrepreneurs usually work hard and for long periods.

2. Which of the following is *not* an advantage of a proprietorship?
   a. The owner is her own boss.
   b. The owner receives all the profits.
   c. The owner deals with limited red tape.
   d. The owner pays more taxes than corporations do.

THINK CRITICALLY

Answer the following questions as completely as possible.

3. Explain why a large business would want to have an employee with entrepreneurial skills.

4. List some of the advantages of having a small business.

Partnerships

Goals

- Discuss the impact of partnerships on managing a business.
- Explain the management issues of partnerships.

Terms

- partnership p. 257
- partnership agreement p. 258
- unlimited financial liability p. 259
- limited partnership p. 260

●●●● The Nature of Partnerships

Jennifer York, who operates the proprietorship mentioned earlier, is faced with the management problem of expanding her business. She has run the business successfully for over 10 years. She sees new opportunities in the community for increasing her business, but she does not wish to assume full responsibility for the undertaking. She realizes that the expansion of the business will entail considerable financial and managerial responsibilities. She also realizes that she needs additional capital to expand, but she does not want to borrow the money. Because of these reasons, she has decided that it would be wise to change her business from a proprietorship to a **partnership**, a business owned by two or more people.

Robert Burton operates an adjoining bakery, where he bakes fresh bread and pastries daily. He has proven to be honest and to have considerable management ability. Combining the two businesses could result in more customers for both groceries and fresh baked goods. Customers who have been coming to the bakery may become grocery customers also. Moreover, those who have been buying at the grocery and fruit market may become customers of bakery products. A discussion between York and Burton leads to a tentative agreement to form a partnership if a third person can be found who will invest enough cash to remodel both stores to form one large store and to purchase additional equipment. The financial statement for Burton's business appears in Figure 10-2.

Robert Burton's Balance Sheet

ASSETS		CLAIMS AGAINST ASSETS	
Cash	$ 10,560	Accounts Payable	$ 7,200
Merchandise	3,600	R. Burton, Capital	153,600
Equipment	26,640		
Land and Building	120,000		
Total	$ 160,800	Total	$ 160,800

© Cengage Learning 2013.

Figure 10-2 When compared to Jennifer York's balance sheet, Robert Burton's balance sheet allows for an analysis of the differences in assets and claims against assets.

Balance Sheet for York, Burton, and Chan at Start-up				
ASSETS			**CLAIMS AGAINST ASSETS**	
Cash	$ 282,720		Accounts Payable	$ 21,600
Merchandise	35,280		J. York, Capital	204,000
Equipment	51,600		R. Burton, Capital	204,000
Land and Building	264,000		L. Chan, Capital	204,000
Total	$ 633,600		Total	$ 633,600

© Cengage Learning 2013.

Figure 10-3 The amounts on this balance sheet reflect the combination of York and Burton's businesses along with Chan's cash investment.

The net worth of Burton's business is $153,600. In other words, after deducting the amount of his liabilities ($7,200) from the total value of his assets ($160,800), his business is worth $153,600. According to Jennifer York's balance, her business is worth $204,000. (See Figure 10-1 on page 254.) In order to have an equal investment in the partnership, Burton must invest an additional $50,400 in cash.

They find Lu Chan, a person with accounting experience, who has $144,000 and is able to borrow the remaining $60,000 to become an equal partner. York, Burton, and Chan draw up and sign a partnership agreement. A **partnership agreement** is a written agreement between two or more people identifying how the partners will add capital, labor, or other assets and divide any profits.

Once the partnership is formed, a statement of financial position (balance sheet) must be prepared. This statement shows the total assets, liabilities, and capital of the owners at the start of the business. The partnership's balance sheet appears in Figure 10-3. Each asset category on the combined balance sheet (merchandise, equipment, and land and buildings) as well as the accounts payable liability category represents the combined totals of these categories from Burton's and York's businesses. The cash category combines the cash from both businesses plus Chan's cash investment of $204,000.

A key factor in the success of a partnership is that the partners must clearly agree upon each person's responsibilities. York, Burton, and Chan divide their duties: York supervises the grocery department, Burton supervises the bakery and meat department, and Chan handles the finances, inventory, and records. During the year, the three partners combine the stores, remodel them, buy new equipment, and open for business.

 **CHECKPOINT**

What are some reasons for considering forming a partnership?

Management Issues of Partnerships

Many businesses are organized as partnerships at the very beginning. There are over 4 million businesses operating as partnerships in the United States, which is a small number in comparison to sole proprietorships. Though most

Manager's Perspective on

SUCCESS

Successful partnerships require a clear understanding of how the partners will share management responsibilities. Partnerships should not only have a written partnership agreement, but partners should communicate often to ensure there is a common understanding for decision making.

partnerships have only two or three partners, there is no limit set on the number of partners. Some businesses have as many as 10 or more partners. Some management issues of partnerships are discussed below.

EXPANDED MANAGEMENT INPUT A partnership is likely to be managed more effectively than a proprietorship, because a partnership can draw on the skills of two or more people instead of just one. One partner may propose a change in the business and another partner may be able to point out disadvantages in the plan and suggest changes that were not initially apparent. Each owner of the business will have a greater interest in the firm as a partner than as an employee. Much of this is due to the greater financial responsibility each person has as a partner.

CAPITAL Often two or more people can supply more capital than one person can. When the business needs to expand, generally several partners can obtain the additional capital needed for the expansion more easily than one person can. The partnership usually has a better credit reputation than the sole proprietorship. This is often true because more than one owner is responsible for the ownership and management of the business.

It may be difficult for a partnership to obtain enough capital to operate a large business unless each member of the partnership is wealthy or unless there are many partners. Too many partners, however, may cause inefficient operations.

EFFICIENCY Two or more proprietors in the same line of business may become one organization by forming a partnership. This move may substantially decrease, or even eliminate, competition. It is often possible to operate more efficiently by combining two or more businesses. In such a case, certain operating expenses—such as advertising, supplies, equipment, fuel, and rent—can be reduced.

TAX ADVANTAGES Partnerships usually have a tax advantage over corporations. Partnerships prepare a federal income tax report but do not pay a tax on their profits, as do corporations. However, partners must pay a personal income tax on their individual share of the profit.

A partnership is a business owned by two or more persons. Why might a partnership be operated more efficiently than a proprietorship?

LIABILITY According to the law, each member of the partnership has an **unlimited financial liability** for all the debts of the business. If some of the partners are unable to pay their share, one partner may have to pay all the debts.

Each partner is bound by the partnership contracts made by any partner if such contracts apply to the ordinary operations of the business. If one partner commits to a contract in the name of the partnership, all partners are legally bound by it, whether they think the contract is good for the business or not. Disagreements can eventually lead to partnership failure.

© Getty Images/Digital Vision

AGREEMENT BETWEEN PARTNERS The decision process between partners must be managed properly or there is the danger of disagreement. The majority of the partners may want to change the nature of the business but are unable to do so because one partner refuses. For example, a partnership may have been formed to conduct a retail business selling audio equipment. After a while, the majority of the partners may think it wise to add cellular phones to their line of merchandise. The change may benefit the business. However, as long as one partner disagrees, the partnership cannot make the change. Furthermore, partners sometimes believe that they are not properly sharing in the management. This situation may cause disagreements that could hurt the business. Such a condition may be avoided if the partnership agreement clearly states the duties of each partner.

UNCERTAIN LIFE The life of a partnership is uncertain. Sometimes when partners draw up a partnership contract, they specify a definite length of time, such as 10 years, for the existence of the business. Should one partner die, however, the partnership ends. The deceased partner may have been the principal manager, and because of his or her death, the business may suffer. The heirs of the deceased partner may demand an unfair price from the surviving partners for the share of the deceased partner. On the other hand, the heirs may insist on ending the partnership quickly to obtain the share belonging to the dead partner. In the latter case, the assets that are sold may not bring a fair price; as a result, all the partners suffer a loss. A partnership can carry insurance on the life of each partner to provide money to purchase the share of a partner who dies. Under the laws of most states, two other causes may bring a sudden end to a partnership. The first is the bankruptcy of any partner; the other is the admission of a new partner.

DIVISION OF PROFITS Sometimes the partnership profits are not divided fairly according to the contributions of the individual partners. Partners should agree up front on how to divide profits according to the amount of labor, expertise, and capital each partner is expected to contribute. The partnership should then specify the agreed-upon division in the partnership agreement, such as 60 percent to one partner and 40 percent to another. If no provision is made in the agreement, the law requires an equal division of the profits. Then if, say, one partner contributes more time, expertise, or labor to the business than do the others, this partner may feel that he or she deserves more than an equal share of the profit.

If a partner wishes to sell his or her interest in the business, it may be difficult to do so. Even if a buyer is found, the buyer may not be acceptable to the other partners.

LIMITED PARTNERSHIPS

In an ordinary (general) partnership, each partner is personally liable for all the debts incurred by the partnership. The laws of some states, however, permit the formation of a limited partnership. A **limited partnership** is a partnership with at least one general partner who has unlimited liability and at least one limited partner whose liability is limited to his or her investment. In many states, the name of a limited partner may not be included in the firm name.

Under the Uniform Limited Partnership Act, the states have created similar regulations for controlling limited partnerships. For example, the law requires that a certificate of limited partnership be filed in a public office of record and that proper notice be given to each creditor with whom the limited partnership does business. If these requirements are not fulfilled, the limited partners have unlimited liability in the same manner as a general partner.

A limited partnership restricts the liability of a partner for the amount of the partner's investment. Why might a limited partnership be a useful form of business organization?

© Getty Images/Photodisc

The limited partnership is a useful form of business organization in situations where one person wishes to invest in a business but does not have the time or interest to participate actively in its management. Any business that is formed as a proprietorship can usually be formed as a limited partnership.

BUSINESSES SUITED TO PARTNERSHIP

The partnership form of organization is common among businesses that furnish more than one kind of product or service. Each partner usually looks after a specialized phase of the business. For example, car dealers often have sales and service departments. One partner may handle the sale of new cars, and another partner may be in charge of servicing and repairing cars. Still another partner could be in charge of used-car sales or of the accounting and financial side of the business. Similarly, if a business operates in more than one location, each partner can be in charge of a specific location. Businesses that operate longer than the usual eight hours a day find the partnership organization desirable. Each partner can be in charge for part of the day.

Partnerships are also common in the same types of businesses that are formed as proprietorships, particularly those that sell goods and services to consumers. It is especially popular among those offering professional services, such as lawyers, doctors, accountants, and financial consultants. Internet businesses have been formed as partnerships as well. Good faith, together with reasonable care in the exercise of management duties, is required of all partners in a business.

CHECKPOINT

What are the disadvantages of being in a partnership?

10.2 ASSESSMENT

UNDERSTAND MANAGEMENT CONCEPTS

Determine the best answer for each of the following questions.

1. Which of the following is *not* an advantage of a partnership?
   a. Partners can pool skills and abilities.
   b. Partners provide greater amounts of capital.
   c. Partners have limited liability.
   d. The business's credit is improved.

2. Which of the following is *not* a disadvantage of a partnership?
   a. Partnerships may reduce competition.
   b. Partners may disagree.
   c. Partners are bound by contracts of others.
   d. Partnerships have an uncertain life.

THINK CRITICALLY

Answer the following questions as completely as possible.

3. Explain the advantages of being a limited partner in a company.

4. Describe the nature of businesses that are suited to being partnerships.

Ben & Jerry's Homemade, Inc.

On May 5, 1978, Ben Cohen and Jerry Greenfield formed an ice cream parlor partnership in a renovated gas station in Burlington, Vermont. The two former seventh-grade buddies used top-quality ingredients and were delighted by their early success.

The business grew rapidly, but they had early concerns about getting too large. When the business was small, they enjoyed working alongside employees while making and experimenting with new products and flavors. As the business expanded, they began to grow apart from their employees and felt as if they were losing the excitement and enjoyment they had experienced during the start-up days. Job fulfillment clearly mattered more than profits.

They tried to resist further expansion but knew the business had to grow or fade away. Jerry retired. Another entrepreneur, however, convinced Ben that he could serve employees and the public while continuing to expand. With a new focus, Jerry rejoined Ben. Together they modified the firm's goals to expand their product line and improve the quality of life for their employees and all of society.

In August 2000, Unilever, an international corporation, purchased Ben & Jerry's. Cohen and Greenfield's partnership continues because they act as spokespersons for the company they started. The principles on which Ben and Jerry founded the company remain relevant today. Ben & Jerry's is still committed to its employees. The company has achieved national recognition for developing a proud and productive workforce.

Ben & Jerry's continues to make, distribute, and sell super-premium ice cream, sorbet, and yogurt to supermarkets, restaurants, and franchised and company outlets in highly populated states and 20 foreign countries.

One important thing has not changed: Ben & Jerry's company is still committed to social responsibility. The Ben & Jerry's foundation gives away over $1.8 million each year to charities and to social and environmental causes. Ben and Jerry—an unusual pair of innovative partners—created a unique style of doing business.

THINK CRITICALLY

1. At the outset, was Ben and Jerry's business typical for a new enterprise? Give reasons for your answer.
2. Why did Ben and Jerry want their company to remain small?
3. If the lowest-paid employee earned $15,000 a year, what would the maximum salary be for the highest-paid manager under the 7-to-1 rule? Why might this manager be unhappy with this rule?
4. Use the Internet to determine what the company is doing today to fulfill its social obligations. Also, find out about its new products, sales, and profits.

Corporate Forms of Business Ownership

Goals

- Explain the basic structure of a corporation.
- Describe how a corporation is formed and organized.
- Explain the management issues of corporations.

Terms

- corporation p. 263
- charter (certificate of incorporation) p. 263
- stockholders p. 264
- board of directors p. 264
- officer p. 264
- close corporation p. 265
- open corporation p. 265
- agency dilemma p. 269

●●●● The Structure of Corporations

Corporations are towers on the business landscape. Although proprietorships are many in number, they are generally small in size. In comparison, corporations are few in number, but generally large in size. Because corporations tend to be large, they play a powerful role in this country and in others. For example, corporations employ millions of people, have many layers of management, and provide consumers with many of the goods and services they use daily. In a recent year, corporate sales of goods and services were more than 20 times greater than sales from proprietorships, and more than six times greater than sales from partnerships in the United States.

Not all corporations are large. Corporations such as Ford, Apple, and Walmart are known to almost everyone, but many small corporations also exist. Small corporations are popular for reasons you will discover later in this lesson.

Because the corporation plays a vital role in business, we need to understand its basic features as well as management implications. To gain knowledge of the basic features of the corporation, we can follow York, Burton, and Chan as they consider incorporating their fast-growing food store partnership, which they launched in this chapter.

BASIC FEATURES

Elena Morales, a lawyer, helped York, Burton, and Chan prepare the partnership agreement under which they now operate. The partners asked Elena to describe a corporation to them. She stated that a **corporation** is a business owned by a group of people and authorized by the state in which it is located to act as though it were a single person, separate from its owners. To get permission to form a corporation, organizers must obtain a **charter**. A charter (often called a *certificate of incorporation*) is the official document through which a state grants the power to operate as a corporation.

A corporation is, in a sense, an artificial person created by the laws of the state. A corporation can make contracts, borrow money, own property, and sue or be sued in its own name. Any act performed for the corporation by an authorized person, such as an employee, is done in the name of the business. For example, the treasurer of a corporation has the power to borrow money for the business. An unauthorized employee, such as a receptionist who was hired to answer the phone and greet visitors, could not borrow money for the corporation.

Morales further explained the important parts played by three key types of people in corporations: (1) stockholders, (2) directors, and (3) officers.

STOCKHOLDERS The owners of a corporation are **stockholders**. Ownership is divided into equal parts called *shares*. A person who buys one share becomes a stockholder, or *shareholder*. Therefore, thousands of people can own a corporation. Each stockholder receives a certificate from the corporation, which shows the number of shares owned. Stockholders have a number of basic rights. Examples include the right to do the following:

- Transfer ownership to others.
- Vote for members of the ruling body of the corporation and on other special matters that may be brought before the stockholders.
- Receive dividends. Dividends are profits that are distributed to stockholders on a per-share basis. The decision to distribute profits is made by the ruling body of the corporation.
- Buy new shares of stock in proportion to one's present investment should the corporation issue more shares.
- Share in the net proceeds (cash received from the sale of all assets less the payment of all debts) should the corporation go out of business.

A stockholder does not have the same financial responsibility as a partner; that is, there is no liability beyond the extent of the stockholder's ownership. If the corporation fails, a stockholder can lose only the money invested. Creditors cannot collect anything further from the stockholder.

DIRECTORS The **board of directors** (often shortened to *directors* or the *board*) is the ruling body of the corporation. The stockholders elect board members. Directors have the management oversight responsibilities to develop plans and policies to guide the corporation as well as appoint officers to carry out the plans. If the corporation is performing successfully, its board is content to deal with policy issues and review the progress of the company. However, if the corporation's profits fall, or if it experiences other serious difficulties, the board often steps in and takes an active role in the operational management of the business.

In large firms, boards generally consist of 10 to 25 directors. A few board members are top executives from within the corporation. The directors often are from outside the corporation and are usually executives from other businesses or people from nonprofit organizations, such as college professors. Often, directors are stockholders who hold many shares, but directors need not be stockholders. Sometimes people who hold few or no shares are elected to the board because they have valuable knowledge needed by the board to make sound decisions. In some countries, such as Sweden, France, and China, one employee of the company is also a board member.

OFFICERS The **officers** of a corporation are the top executives who are hired to manage the business. The board of directors appoints them. The officers of a small corporation often consist of a president, a secretary, and a treasurer. In addition, large corporations may have vice presidents in charge of major areas, such as marketing, finance, and manufacturing. The titles of these officers are often shortened to letters. For example, the top officer is called a CEO (chief executive officer) and the head financial officer is the CFO (chief financial officer).

Which stock would you like to own and why do you want that stock?

© Getty Images/Photodisc

CLOSE AND OPEN CORPORATIONS

A **close corporation** (also called a *closely held corporation*) is one that does not offer its shares of stock for public sale. Just a few stockholders own it; some of them may help run the business in the same manner that partners operate a business. York, Burton, and Chan could form a close corporation. The three former partners would then own all the stock and operate the business as well.

In most states, a close corporation does not need to make its financial activities known to the public. Its stock is not offered for general sale. It must, however, prepare reports for the state from which it obtained its charter. In addition, it must prepare reports for tax purposes for all states in which it operates.

An **open corporation** (also called a *publicly owned corporation*) is one that offers its shares of stock for public sale. One way to announce the sale of common stock to the public is with an ad in the newspaper. The corporation must file a registration statement with the Securities and Exchange Commission (SEC) containing extensive details about the corporation and the proposed issue of stock. A condensed version of this registration statement, called a prospectus, must be furnished to each prospective buyer of newly offered stocks (or bonds). A *prospectus* is a formal summary of the chief features of the business and its stock offering. Prospective buyers can find information in the prospectus that will help them decide if they want to buy stock in the corporation.

The Small Business Administration provides many resources to support small businesses, including information about starting a business.

Access the website for this textbook and choose the link for Chapter 10 Net Bookmark. Explore the SBA website and create a list of the major areas of SBA support. Click on "Starting Your Business." Write a brief summary of the resources available. Explain how this information could help a small business be successful.

www.cengage.com/school/bizmgmt

 CHECKPOINT

List the three key groups of people in corporations.

Formation of Corporations

Over several months, York, Burton, and Chan asked their attorney, Elena Morales, many questions. After careful thought, the partners decided to form a corporation and name it York, Burton, and Chan, Inc. Morales explained that there were three basic steps involved. First, a series of management decisions had to be made about how the corporation would be organized. Second, the proper legal forms had to be prepared and sent to the state office that handled such matters. Third, the state would review the incorporation papers and issue a charter if it approved.

PREPARING THE CERTIFICATE OF INCORPORATION

Each state has its own laws for forming corporations. No federal law exists. To incorporate a business, it is necessary in most states to file a certificate of incorporation with the appropriate state office. The certificate of incorporation calls for basic information about the business. In addition to the firm name, purpose, and capital stock, it requires information about the organizers.

NAMING THE BUSINESS A business is usually required by law to have a name that indicates clearly that a corporation has been formed. Words or abbreviations such as *Corporation, Corp., Incorporated,* or Inc. are used. The organizers have decided to name their corporation York, Burton, and Chan, Inc.

STATING THE PURPOSE OF THE BUSINESS A certificate of incorporation requires a corporation to describe its purpose clearly. In the case of York, Burton, and Chan, Inc., the purpose is simple: to operate a retail food business. It allows the corporation to expand into new food lines, but it does not allow the corporation to start nonfood operations. For major changes in purpose, a new request must be submitted and approved by the state.

INVESTING IN THE BUSINESS The certificate of incorporation could not be completed until York, Burton, and Chan decided how to invest their partnership holdings in the corporation. They agreed that the assets and debts of the partnership should be taken over by the corporation. They further agreed that shares were valued at $100 each at the time of incorporation. There were 10,000 shares in all ($1,000,000 divided by $100 equals 10,000). York, Burton, and Chan each agreed to purchase 2,217 shares. The 3,349 unissued shares (the difference between the 10,000 authorized shares and the 6,651 shares bought by the organizers) can be sold later to raise more funds to expand the business.

PAYING INCORPORATION COSTS Usually a new corporation must pay an organization tax, based on the amount of its capital stock. In addition, a new corporation usually pays a filing fee before the state will issue a charter entitling the business to operate as a corporation. In some states, the existence of the corporation begins when the application or certificate of incorporation has been filed with the appropriate state agency.

OPERATING THE NEW CORPORATION

York, Burton, and Chan, Inc., received approval to operate as a corporation. Then they turned their attention next to getting the business started.

GETTING ORGANIZED One of the first steps in getting the new corporation under way is to prepare a balance sheet or statement of financial position. The new corporation's balance sheet appears in Figure 10-4.

The ownership of the corporation is in the same hands as the ownership of the partnership was. The ownership of the corporation, however, is evidenced

Balance Sheet for York, Burton, and Chan, Inc.			
ASSETS		**CLAIMS AGAINST ASSETS**	
Cash	$ 240,000	Accounts Payable	$ 74,900
Merchandise	60,000	Capital Stock	665,100
Equipment	90,000		
Land and Building	350,000		
Total	$ 740,000	Total	$ 740,000

© Cengage Learning 2013.

Figure 10-4 The balance sheet for the new corporation shows capital stock as a claim against assets.

by the issued capital stock. The former partners each received a stock certificate indicating that each owns 2,217 shares of stock with a value of $100 a share.

The three stockholders own the business and elect themselves directors. The new directors select officers. York is appointed president; Burton, vice president; and Chan, secretary and treasurer. Figure 10-5 illustrates the new corporation.

Organization Chart for a Corporation

Stockholders — Owners who elect board members

Board of Directors — Board selects officers and makes major policy decisions

President
Jennifer L. York — May also be called CEO (Chief Executive Office) and may be elected chair of the board of directors

Vice President
Robert R. Burton

Secretary and Treasurer
Lu Chan

© Cengage Learning 2013.

Figure 10-5 The organization chart formalizes the lines of authority for positions in corporation.

HANDLING VOTING RIGHTS The owners agreed that each owner will have 2,217 votes on matters arising in the meetings of the stockholders. Voting stockholders usually have one vote for each share owned. However, if Chan, for instance, sold 1,200 of his shares to Burton, Burton would own 3,417 shares, or more than 50 percent of the total 6,651 shares of stock that have been issued. Then Burton could control the corporation; that is, York and Chan would lose if Burton voted differently from them on an important issue. Burton would have more votes than York and Chan together.

Their lawyer told the officers of the corporation that they must send each stockholder notices of all stockholders' meetings to be held. Even stockholders with just one share must receive notices of meetings. If stockholders cannot attend the meetings personally, they can be represented through a proxy that can be submitted by Internet, phone, or mail. A proxy is a written authorization for someone to vote on behalf of the person signing the proxy. Corporations often enclose a proxy form with the letter that announces a stockholders' meeting.

CHECKPOINT

List the basic information required in a certificate of incorporation.

●●● Management Issues for Corporations

The corporation can help to solve some of the management issues found with proprietorships and partnerships. At the same time, corporations have their own management issues.

SOURCES OF CAPITAL A corporation can obtain money from several sources. One of those sources is the sale of shares to stockholders. Because corporations are regulated closely, people usually invest more willingly than in proprietorships and partnerships. In addition, corporations usually find borrowing large sums of money less of a problem than do proprietorships or partnerships.

LIMITED LIABILITY Except in a few situations, the owners (stockholders), directors, and managers are not legally liable for the debts of the corporation beyond their investment in the stock shares purchased. Stockholders are more willing to invest in a corporation when there is no possibility of incurring a liability beyond their original investment. At the same time, directors and managers may be more willing to work with a corporation when they cannot be personally liable for debts of the corporation.

PERMANENCY OF EXISTENCE The corporation is a more permanent type of organization than the proprietorship or the partnership. It can continue to operate indefinitely, or only as long as the term stated in the charter. The death or withdrawal of an owner (stockholder) does not affect its life. Directors and managers can change over time without affecting the operation or ownership of a corporation.

EASE IN TRANSFERRING OWNERSHIP It is easy to transfer ownership in a corporation. A stockholder may sell stock to another person and transfer the stock certificate, which represents ownership, to the new owner. When shares are transferred, the transfer of ownership is indicated in the records of the corporation. A new certificate is issued in the name of the new stockholder. Millions of shares are bought and sold every day.

TAXATION The corporation is usually subject to more taxes than are imposed on the proprietorship and the partnership. Some taxes that are unique to the corporation are a filing fee, which is payable on application for a charter; an organization tax, which is based on the amount of authorized capital stock; an annual state tax, based on the profits; and a federal income tax.

Another tax disadvantage for corporations is that profits distributed to stockholders as dividends are taxed twice. This double taxation occurs in two steps. The corporation first pays taxes on its profits as just described. Then it distributes some of these profits to shareholders as dividends, and the shareholders pay taxes on the dividends they receive. (Small close corporations with few stockholders may avoid double taxation by changing their form of ownership, which you will learn about later in this chapter.)

GOVERNMENT REGULATIONS AND REPORTS A corporation cannot do business wherever it pleases. To form a corporation, an application for a charter must be submitted to the appropriate state official, usually the secretary of state. York, Burton, and Chan, Inc., has permission to conduct business only in the state of New York. Should it wish to conduct business in other states, each state will probably require the corporation to obtain a license and pay a fee to do business in that state. State incorporation fees are not very expensive. The attorney's fee accounts for the major costs of incorporating. Each state has different laws that govern the formation of corporations.

Is corporate ownership the best form of ownership for a theme park, given liability and transfer-of-ownership issues?

The regulation of corporations by states and by the federal government is extensive. Managers must ensure that the corporation files special reports with the state from which it received its charter as well as with other states where it conducts business. The federal government requires firms whose stock is publicly traded to publish financial data. As a result, there is a greater need for detailed financial records and reports.

STOCKHOLDERS' RECORDS Corporations that have many stockholders have added problems—and expenses—in communicating with stockholders and in handling stockholders' records. By law, stockholders must be informed of corporate matters, notified of meetings, and given the right to vote on important matters. Letters and reports must be sent to stockholders on a regular basis. In addition, each time a share of stock is bought or sold and whenever a dividend is paid, detailed records must be kept. Keeping records for the thousands of stockholders of Microsoft, for example, is a time-consuming and costly task.

CHARTER RESTRICTIONS A corporation is allowed to engage only in those activities that are stated in its charter. Should York, Burton, and Chan, Inc., wish to sell hardware, the organizers would have to go to the state to obtain a new charter or change the old one. As a partnership, they could have added the other line of merchandise without government approval.

AGENCY DILEMMA An **agency dilemma** can occur when an agent, or someone who works for another, pursues their own interest over their employers. For example, in large corporations where stock ownership is broadly spread over a large number of stockholders, managers may look to their own interests over stockholders by making purchases that benefit only managers. Managers could try to persuade the board of directors to increase management pay, diminishing returns to stockholders. Corporate boards must ensure that managers perform their duties for the benefit of the corporation owners, the stockholders.

Manager's Perspective on
ETHICS

In response to perceived unethical corporate practice, the U.S. government passed the Sarbanes-Oxley Act in 2002. Officers and directors in public (or open) corporations now face much higher levels of responsibility and are held personally responsible for the ethical behavior of their corporations.

CHECKPOINT

What are the disadvantages of the corporate form of ownership?

10.3 ASSESSMENT

UNDERSTAND MANAGEMENT CONCEPTS

Determine the best answer for each of the following questions.

1. A corporation that does *not* offer its stock to the public for sale is called a(n)
   a. close corporation
   b. open corporation
   c. private corporation
   d. none of the above

2. Which of the following is *not* an advantage of a corporate form of ownership?
   a. available sources of capital
   b. double taxation
   c. limited liability
   d. permanency of existence

THINK CRITICALLY

Answer the following questions as completely as possible.

3. List the major advantages of the corporate form of business.

4. List three management issues related to corporations.

10.4

Specialized Types of Organizations

Goals

- Describe organizations that are specialized alliances between companies or individuals.
- Describe specialized forms of corporations formed for tax or nonprofit reasons.

Terms

- limited liability partnership p. 270
- joint venture p. 270
- cooperative p. 271
- limited liability company (LLC) p. 271
- nonprofit corporation p. 272
- quasi-public corporation p. 272

●●● Organizational Alliances

In addition to sole proprietorships, partnerships, and corporations, organizations can be legally formed as limited liability partnerships, joint ventures, cooperatives, limited liability companies, and nonprofit corporations. Limited liability partnerships, joint ventures, virtual corporations, and cooperatives are specialized alliances between companies or individuals.

LIMITED LIABILITY PARTNERSHIPS

A relatively new partnership form is a limited liability partnership or LLP. A **limited liability partnership** is a partnership in which each partner's liability is limited to his or her investment in the partnership. Unlike a limited partnership, each partner can have an active role in the management of the partnership. Like a corporation, these partners are not responsible for the actions of their partners in the management of the business beyond their investment.

Many professional partnerships, such as accounting firms and legal firms, use the LLP business form. Rules governing LLPs can vary depending on the state where they are formed.

JOINT VENTURES

Sometimes businesses want to join forces in order to achieve an important objective. A **joint venture** is an agreement among two or more businesses to work together to provide a good or service. The legal formation of the business is not important. For example, a sole proprietorship and a corporation could agree to work together. Each partner in the joint venture is expected to bring management expertise and/or money to the venture. Many major corporations today have learned that alone they may not have all the expertise or capital they need.

An example of a joint venture is an agreement between two contractors to connect two cities by building a tunnel for a road to go under a river. In this case, neither company has the capital to build the tunnel on its own. In addition, each contractor has special equipment and skills that the other firm lacks. By forming a joint venture, they can acquire the needed capital and expertise. Joint ventures should be managed like partnerships. Clear management roles should be identified and written contracts should be developed. There are thousands

FACTS & FIGURES

Joint Ventures

Joint ventures often include business partners from other countries. Joint ventures help corporations expand into new markets, and companies in developing countries learn about doing business in a free-market economy.

of joint ventures between and among many companies. Many web-based companies rely extensively on joint ventures to build their businesses.

COOPERATIVES

A **cooperative** is a business owned and operated by its user-members for the purpose of supplying themselves with goods and services. The members, who are much like stockholders in a corporation with the protection of limited liability, usually join a cooperative by buying shares of stock. The members elect a board of directors, which appoints officers to run the cooperative. Much like a corporation, a cooperative must also

Farmers can participate in a number of cooperatives to help purchase supplies or sell products. Can you name any farmer cooperatives?

obtain a charter from the state in which it is organized in order to operate. Some types of cooperatives need authorization from the federal government.

The approximately 30,000 cooperatives in the United States represent only a small percentage of all American businesses. This small number, however, does not reduce their importance. A common example of a cooperative is a credit union. Cooperatives are popular in agriculture for buying and selling crops. Many insurance firms are formed as cooperatives. Apartment buildings are often formed as cooperatives as well.

 CHECKPOINT

Describe the differences between the three types of organizational alliances.

 ## Specialized Forms of Corporations

Not all businesses fit easily into proprietorships, partnerships, and corporations. Some business forms allow for reaching special goals. These goals can be to limit liability in small firms or to serve nonprofits or governments.

LIMITED LIABILITY CORPORATIONS

Small, growing partnerships are especially attracted to the limited liability form of corporation. The **limited liability company (LLC)** is a special type of corporation that is taxed as if it were a sole proprietorship or partnership. Two factors make LLCs popular. First, a major disadvantage of a partnership is its unlimited liability, whereas a major advantage of a corporation is its limited liability. Second, a major advantage of a partnership is its lower income tax rate, whereas a disadvantage of a corporation is a higher income tax rate than that paid by partnerships. Stockholders also have to pay personal income taxes on dividends distributed by a corporation (double taxation).

A *Subchapter S* is a popular type of LLC that offers liability protection but allows taxation like a partnership, avoiding double taxation. To qualify, a corporation elects to be taxed under the Subchapter S corporation regulations of the U.S. Internal Revenue Service (IRS). However, not all companies are eligible for Subchapter S status. A few important rules determine eligibility. First, the firm must have no more than 100 stockholders. Second, it must be a domestic corporation and not have any nonresident aliens as stockholders. Third, it must have only one class of stock. Finally, it must meet a list of other specific limitations specified by the IRS, such as not being a bank, insurance company, and so on. Large corporations and multinational firms do not meet these qualifications.

Limited liability corporations provide ideal solutions—lower taxes and limited liability. In addition, the profits from the corporation go directly to the stockholders, who then include the earnings on their individual income tax returns. Double taxation is avoided. York, Burton, and Chan, Inc., would qualify for this special tax advantage.

NONPROFIT CORPORATIONS

Close and open corporations, as discussed earlier, are businesses that operate mainly to make a profit for their owners. A **nonprofit corporation**, on the other hand, is an organization that does not pay taxes and does not exist to make a profit. Organizations that manage cities or operate schools are examples of nonprofit corporations. Because a nonprofit corporation is not established as a profit-making enterprise, it does not pay dividends to shareholders. Otherwise, it operates much like a close or open corporation. The Rotary Club, private schools and universities, the United Way, and most local hospitals are other examples of nonprofit organizations. Even Educational Testing Service, the company that develops the Scholastic Assessment Test (SAT), is a nonprofit organization.

In this country, nonprofit corporations provide nearly one-third of the GDP. However, in most other countries, nonprofit corporations contribute much more to the GDP. The principles of business and management provided in this text apply equally to managers who run profit-making as well as nonprofit corporations.

QUASI-PUBLIC CORPORATIONS

Why would a nonprofit corporation be an appropriate business form for a school?

A business that is important to society but lacks the profit potential to attract private investors is often operated by local, state, or federal government. Government financial support (called a *subsidy*) may also be required. This type of business is usually described as a **quasi-public corporation**. Government imposes regulatory controls over quasi-public corporations.

The Tennessee Valley Authority, a rural electrification program started in the 1930s by the federal government, was one of the first quasi-public corporations. The organizations that run interstate highways, such as the Massachusetts and Pennsylvania turnpike

© Shutterstock/Konstantin L

authorities, are state-owned quasi-public corporations. At the local level, examples of quasi-public organizations include water and sewer systems, parking garages, and civic and cultural facilities. The Los Angeles County Museum of Art is a government-owned cultural organization.

CHECKPOINT

What is the main advantage of choosing an LLC or Subchapter S status?

10.4 ASSESSMENT

UNDERSTAND MANAGEMENT CONCEPTS

Determine the best answer for each of the following questions.

1. Specialized forms of corporations include all of the following except
   a. joint venture
   b. quasi-public
   c. nonprofit
   d. LLC

2. A corporation can have a special tax status by structuring as a(n)
   a. LLC
   b. Subchapter S corporation
   c. nonprofit corporation
   d. all of the above

THINK CRITICALLY

Answer the following questions as completely as possible.

3. Explain the advantages of structuring a joint venture.

4. Explain why a company would elect to have an LLC or Subchapter S status.

CHAPTER 10 Assessment

CHAPTER CONCEPTS

- Most small businesses begin with one or a few owners. Characteristics of successful entrepreneurs include a strong need to be boss, an ability to make decisions, and a willingness to take reasonable risks.

- For business start-ups, the management planning process requires preparing a business plan that describes the nature of the business, its goals and objectives, and how they will be achieved.

- A sole proprietorship is a business owned and operated by one person. A proprietorship is the easiest form of ownership to start. Other advantages include having the power to make all decisions, receiving all profits, paying less in taxes than corporations, and knowing employees and customers personally. Disadvantages include limited ability to perform all key business tasks, limited access to funds for expansion, and inability to survive major financial losses or the illness or death of owner.

- A partnership is a business owned by two or more people. Key advantages include having multiple owners who can contribute skills and capital to start or expand, having more access to credit, and the ability to continue if a partner leaves. Disadvantages include each partner's unlimited financial liability for all business debts and responsibility for contracts made by other partners.

- A corporation is a form of ownership preferred by large and growing firms. Corporations are more difficult to form than sole proprietorships or partnerships. A business must specify its purpose, identify its owners (stockholders), elect a board of directors, select officers, establish operating policies, and prepare a charter for approval by the state.

- The chief advantages of corporations are that liability is limited, more capital can be raised for growth, stock can be bought and sold more easily than ownership shares in partnerships, and the life of the corporation does not end when owners sell their shares. The chief disadvantages of corporations include higher tax rates, double taxation, and more extensive record keeping and government-required paperwork.

- A limited liability partnership limits the liability of each member of the partnership. Joint ventures are alliances formed among companies to produce a product or service that neither alone could provide efficiently. Cooperatives are businesses owned and operated by their user-members for the purpose of supplying themselves with goods and services.

- Limited liability companies (LLC) avoid double taxation and the unlimited-liability disadvantage of partnerships. Nonprofit corporations do not pay taxes and do not exist to make a profit. Quasi-public corporations are important to society but are government-run because they lack the profit potential to attract private investors.

REVIEW BUSINESS MANAGEMENT TERMS

Write the letter of the term that matches each definition.

1. A partnership in which each partner's liability is limited to his or her investment in the partnership.
2. A written agreement between two or more people identifying how the partners will add capital, labor, or other assets and divide any profits.
3. Agreement among two or more businesses to work together to provide a good or service.
4. Business owned and managed by one person.
5. Business owned and operated by its user-members for the purpose of supplying themselves with goods and services.
6. Business owned by a group of people and authorized by the state in which it is located to act as though it were a single person, separate from its owners.
7. Business owned by two or more people.
8. Business that is important to society but lacks the profit potential to attract private investors and is often operated by local, state, or federal government.
9. Corporation that does not offer its shares of stock for public sale.
10. Corporation that offers its shares of stock for public sale.
11. Official document through which a state grants the power to operate as a corporation.
12. Organization that does not pay taxes and does not exist to make a profit.
13. Owners of a corporation.
14. Partnership with at least one general partner who has unlimited liability and at least one limited partner whose liability is limited to his or her investment.
15. An employee who is given funds and freedom to create a special unit or department within a company in order to develop a new product, process, or service.
16. Person who owns and manages a business and often performs the day-to-day tasks with the help of hired employees.
17. Ruling body of a corporation.
18. Situation when an agent, or someone who works for another, pursues their own interest over their employers.
19. Special type of corporation allowed by states that is taxed as if it were a sole proprietorship or partnership.
20. Person or business to whom money is owed.
21. Top executives who are hired to manage the business.
22. When each partner is personally liable for all the debts incurred by the partnership.

a. agency dilemma
b. board of directors
c. charter
d. close corporation
e. cooperative
f. corporation
g. creditor
h. intrapreneur
i. joint venture
j. limited liability company
k. limited liability partnership
l. limited partnership
m. nonprofit corporation
n. officers
o. open corporation
p. partnership
q. partnership agreement
r. proprietor
s. proprietorship
t. quasi-public corporation
u. stockholders
v. unlimited financial liability

Determine the best answer.

23. An intrapreneur's job would include all of the following *except*
    a. funds and freedom to create a special unit
    b. freedom to run their operations
    c. their salaries are at risk
    d. freedom on how to manage

24. Alex wants to be the sole owner of a new landscaping business. The simplest ownership form he could use would be a
    a. proprietorship
    b. joint venture
    c. partnership
    d. corporation

25. To avoid disagreements on the division of profits, partnerships should have
    a. articles of incorporation
    b. a general partner
    c. a partnership agreement
    d. ownership of stock

26. Ownership of a corporation is divided into parts called
    a. shares
    b. corporation parts
    c. memberships
    d. partnerships

27. Stockholders' basic rights include the right to
    a. transfer ownership
    b. vote for members of the board
    c. receive dividends
    d. all of the above

28. A stockholder has all of the following rights *except*
    a. the ability to transfer ownership
    b. vote for members of the ruling body
    c. receive dividends
    d. fire managers who don't perform

29. The United Sates Post Office is most likely to be what type of corporation?
    a. nonprofit corporation
    b. quasi-public corporation
    c. nano-public corporation
    d. Subchapter S corporation

30. If a corporation wants to enter into a different business, it
    a. must close and re-form
    b. can do this at any time
    c. must change its charter or file a new one
    d. must change its name

Answer the following questions.

31. Explain how a good business plan will help someone successfully open a new business.

32. Describe what kinds of businesses are most suited to the proprietorship form of business ownership.

33. Explain the types of situations in which a limited partnership would be most useful.

34. Explain why it is necessary for proprietorships and partnerships to register their company names with local authorities.

35. You have been working part-time and summers at a local service station. You have performed just about every task from pumping gas to repairing cars and even handling some of the bookkeeping. Discuss how your responsibilities as an employee will change if you become the owner of the station.

36. Explain why a corporation can be viewed as an artificial person.

37. Compare the financial responsibility of owners of a corporation with that of owners of a partnership.

38. Discuss whether the Girl Scouts organization meets the qualifications for operating as a nonprofit corporation in light of the fact that it sells a large volume of cookies each year.

MAKE ACADEMIC CONNECTIONS

Complete the following activities.

39. **Research** Assume you are considering forming a small business in your state. Search for information that will help you decide whether to open a sole proprietorship or a partnership. Look for resources aimed at entrepreneurs and small business owners. Make a list of 10 questions you can use to help you decide if a proprietorship or partnership would be best for your new business.

40. **Math** Alvares invested $80,000 and Navarro invested $60,000 in their partnership. They share profits and losses in proportion to their investments. How much should each receive of last year's $33,600 profit?

41. **Technology** George Fernandez purchased stock in the Elite Manufacturing Co., Inc., for $76 a share. Last year he received quarterly dividends of $1, $1, $1, and $0.80 on each share. Use spreadsheet software to answer the following questions.
    a. What were his total dividends for the year as a percentage of the price he paid for each share?
    b. Assume the stock price increases to $100, but the company pays the same dividend. Determine the new percentage return for the year.

42. **Communication** Assume you are in a partnership. Prepare a speech that you will give to your partners to justify changing to a corporate form of ownership. Choose a specific corporate form and link it to your company goals. Justify your choice by addressing its advantages and disadvantages for your company.

CASE 10-1: Partnership Problems

Sharon Gillespie, John Jensen, and Laura Cho have been close friends for years. About two years ago, they formed a partnership to build web pages for small entrepreneurs who want to expand their businesses. Sharon, John, and Laura are experts at what they do. However, their partnership has not been very successful and is not growing. John is in charge of finding and dealing with customers and handling the necessary paperwork. Both Sharon and Laura build the web pages for their customers.

Recently, John confided to Laura that he is getting many complaints about Sharon's treatment of customers. "That may be the major reason we aren't doing that well, but what can we do about it?" He continued, "Her customers don't often come back to us when they need to add new products or offer new services on their web pages. Some have even jotted complaints about her on the bills I send them. Yesterday one customer said he'll take his business elsewhere if we don't replace her." The phone rang, and John excused himself to answer it.

After thinking about this for a while, Laura told John, "We have to get rid of her because she isn't going to change. If we want our business to survive and grow, let's ask her to leave. What else can we do?"

John paused and then said, "She owns one-third of our business. You can't fire a partner."

Laura asked, "Didn't our lawyer provide for this type of problem in our partnership agreement? Or maybe it's in our business plan."

"No, it's not in either place," John responded. "We have to work this out together."

THINK CRITICALLY

Your instructor may wish to place you into groups of three students each to answer the following questions and to your answers to the class.

1. What conditions existed before the partnership was formed that gave rise to this problem?
2. How important are the skills and personalities of the partners to the formation of a successful partnership?
3. Can Sharon's attitude toward customers somehow be changed? If so, how?
4. What is the best solution for this problem? Carefully explain your answer.
5. Do you believe that John and Sharon would be better off trading jobs with each other?
6. How is this partnership situation different from that of student groups that attempt to solve other types of group problems?

CASE 10-2: To Partner or Not to Partner

John Willis, who is 27 and single, had just completed his fifth year of employment as a carpenter for a very small homebuilder. His boss, the sole owner of the company, is Tyrone Young. A few days ago, Tyrone asked John if he would like to become a partner, which he could do by contributing $70,000. In turn, John would receive 40 percent of all profits earned by the business. John had saved $30,000 and could borrow the balance from his grandmother at a low interest rate, but he would have to pay her back within 15 years.

John was undecided about becoming a partner. He liked the idea but he also knew there were risks and concerns. He decided to talk to Tyrone at lunch. Here is how the conversation went.

John: *I've been giving your offer a lot of thought, Tyrone. It's a tough decision, and I don't want to make the wrong one. So I'd like to chat with you about some of the problems involved in running a business.*

Tyrone: *Sure. I struggled with these issues about 15 years ago. When you own your own business, you're the boss. No one can tell you what to do or push you around. You can set up your own hours and make all the decisions. I enjoy the feeling of ownership.*

John: *I don't know if I'm ready to become part owner of a business. I'm still young and single, and I like working for you. I'm not sure I want all those responsibilities—getting customers, paying bills, and buying tools and lumber. You say you set your own hours, but I know you're already working when I arrive each morning, and you're still here when I leave in the evening. I know you spend some nights in the office, because I see the lights on when I drive by.*

Tyrone: *Well, I do put in many hours. That goes with the territory. But, I don't mind all those hours because I like making decisions. And, when you join me as a partner, we'll share the work.*

John: *Then I'll be working longer hours. Both of us could go to work for that big new contracting firm on the other side of town. Let them struggle with all the problems and decisions. Then we could work shorter hours and have more time to relax.*

THINK CRITICALLY

1. Does John have the personality to be a partner?
2. Do you think John is seriously ready to become a partner? Explain your answer.
3. If you were in John's position, how would you decide? Explain.
4. If John decides to accept Tyrone's offer, what action should be taken next?
5. Why would Tyrone offer to make John a partner?
6. Find information from the library or the Internet that might help John make a decision. One possible source is the website of the Small Business Administration.

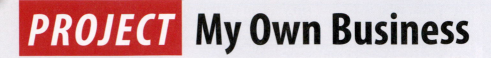

PROJECT My Own Business

Proprietorship or Partnership?

New owners often start a business without carefully considering other possible forms of ownership. In this segment of the project, you will evaluate the advantages and disadvantages of the proprietorship and partnership forms of ownership for your new business.

DATA COLLECTION

1. Review copies of magazines written for entrepreneurs. Identify the current issues and problems faced by individual business owners as well as the successful operating procedures described in the magazines.
2. Identify a person who currently is or has been a partner in a business. Ask the person to describe the advantages and disadvantages of operating a business as a partnership from his or her viewpoint.
3. Go to the U.S. federal government website or your state government website to research the advantages and disadvantages for proprietorships and partnerships in your state. Develop a list of pros and cons for each legal form.
4. Using the Internet, find a sample copy or outline of a business plan. Speak with a banker or your business mentor about the importance of business plans for new businesses. Ask that person to describe the elements he or she believes are most important in a good business plan.

ANALYSIS

1. Develop a chart that compares the proprietorship and partnership forms of ownership for your business. Be certain to consider financial, personal, and management factors. When you have finished the analysis, decide whether you will remain a sole proprietor or form a partnership.
2. Develop an outline for a business plan for your new business. Begin to list the information that will go into each section of the plan. Identify the information you need to complete the business plan and the sources of that information. Continue to develop the business plan during the time you are working on this continuing project.
3. Given the business plan you developed above, outline the specific skills that are needed to make your business successful. Evaluate your skills and resources that you can bring to the business. Identify other skills or resources that a partner will need to bring in.

CHAPTER 11

LEGAL ASPECTS OF BUSINESS

11.1 Regulations Maintaining Competition

11.2 Regulations Protecting Business and the Public

11.3 Business Taxes

© Shutterstock/StockLite

Reality Check

Legal Limits for a Taxi Business

Deion Banks, who owned a small taxi business in his hometown, was meeting for lunch with his lawyer, Laura Maddox. He needed to discuss several matters that had arisen during the past few weeks. While waiting for the server, Laura said, "You seem quite upset."

Deion sat back and replied, "I am, Laura. Here are the new tax forms that need to be filled out. And that's the easy part. Would you check with the town officials to see why they want to review my franchise before I buy another cab? Also, while you're at the Town Hall, see what you can do to prevent those officials from giving another taxi firm a license to operate. This town isn't big enough for two taxi companies. I'll get less business, and it will probably force down my fares. If there is a chance of going bankrupt, I should probably move my business across the river. The income tax rate in that state is much lower."

"Don't do anything drastic," said Laura. "Let me see what I can find out from our government officials. I'll get back to you in a few days with both your tax forms and the answers to your questions."

Deion Banks, like other business owners, must manage his business within the law. Laws that regulate business cover both products and services, and they govern general relationships of businesses with competitors, consumers, employees, and the public. Deion's taxi business is no exception. He currently benefits from being the only taxi company in town, but he now feels threatened. The town may, indeed, allow someone else the right to open a competing firm. So what can Deion do?

What's Your Reaction? What advice would you give Deion about dealing with the possibility of increased competition in his market?

Regulations Maintaining Competition

Goals

- Explain how federal laws help regulate monopolies.
- Explain how federal laws help promote fair competition.

Terms

- monopoly p. 282
- natural monopoly p. 282
- price discrimination p. 284
- false advertising p. 285
- bankruptcy p. 285

●●● Regulating Monopolies

Competition is the rivalry among companies for customers' dollars. Competition, however, does not always operate smoothly by itself. To provide for fair competition, government has passed laws and created regulations to enforce the laws. These laws and regulations grow out of a need to preserve competition, which is done, in part, by controlling monopolies and unfair business practices. Firms that cannot survive in a competitive atmosphere either go out of business or face bankruptcy.

CONTROLLING MONOPOLIES

A **monopoly** exists when only one company provides a product or service without competition from other companies. Without competitors, the one producer can control the supply and price of the product or service. By controlling the supply of an item, a single producer can set a price that will generate the greatest profit. In a monopoly situation, such as Deion Banks's taxi company, the prices are generally very high. Without competitors to lure customers away with lower prices, the monopolistic company can raise its price as high as it wants. If customers want the product or service, they have no choice but to pay the monopolist's price.

In actual practice, however, few monopolies exist, because of the effectiveness of competition. To illustrate, assume a business offers a new product that no other business does. The product suddenly becomes quite popular. The prospect of profits to be made entices other companies to enter the market to help meet the demand. A temporary monopoly will exist until those competitors can produce and sell similar products. Usually, through competitive pricing, the more efficient companies will attract the greatest number of purchasers, whereas the less efficient may struggle for survival or go out of business. Even if some competitors fail, however, a monopoly will not exist as long as there are at least two or more producers.

NATURAL MONOPOLIES

In some situations, a **natural monopoly** may be better for consumers than competition because of the large cost involved in developing or supplying a product or service. These situations usually involve providing public services, such as

Deregulation of the telecommunications industry has helped benefit consumers through lower prices and improved phone services. Are cellular telephone prices deregulated?

© Getty Images/Photodisc

public utilities, which have a fairly stable demand and which are costly to create.

A natural gas company, for example, must build hundreds of miles of pipeline along streets and roads in order to deliver gas to homes and industries to fuel furnaces and stoves. If two or three gas companies incurred these same costs to sell gas to a relatively fixed number of customers, the price of gas would be higher than if only one company existed. Also, installing and maintaining so many pipelines would create nuisance problems along crowded streets and highways. In these types of situations, the government grants a monopoly to one company, regulates the prices that the company can charge, and influences other company policies.

Until recently, the federal government had approved of closely regulated monopolies, such as the postal system, utility companies, railroads, and communication firms. However, the trend has shifted from allowing monopolies to weakening or eliminating them in order to encourage competition. No longer, for example, are passenger fares on commercial airlines regulated. As a result, fares have generally dropped. Even telephone service, the trucking industry, and railroads have been deregulated. Today utilities are undergoing deregulation. Firms such as AT&T and Sprint offer communication services at competitive prices and compete fiercely. The result overall has been that consumers pay lower prices and have more services from which to select.

Management MATTERS

Managing in an Monopoly

Managers in competitive markets must focus on their customers, competitors, and changes in their competitive environment. Managers of regulated natural monopolies, such as publicly regulated utilities, have the same concerns. In addition, they must also be able to operate within the regulations set by the state or local governments. Consider the example of a utility such as a gas and electric company, a waterworks, or a cable television provider. Before a utility can raise prices, the utility managers must present their case to the public utility board, which has the power to grant rate increases.

What Do You Think? Should public utilities be free to raise their prices? What skills would a public utility manager need?

 CHECKPOINT

Describe the reasons that society may want to allow a natural monopoly.

 Promoting Fair Competitions

One way to promote competition is to limit the number of monopolies created and controlled by government. Monopoly conditions can also arise when businesses compete too harshly or unfairly. A large, powerful business can lower its prices deliberately to drive out competitors, thereby discouraging competition. Thus, the federal government supports business practices that encourage competition and discourage monopolies. To achieve this goal, government has passed important laws and created agencies to enforce the laws.

SHERMAN ACT

The first major law promoting competition was the Sherman Antitrust Act of 1890. One of its primary purposes is to discourage monopolies by outlawing business agreements among competitors that might tend to promote monopolies. For example, agreements among competitors to set selling prices on goods are unlawful. If three sellers met and agreed to set the same selling price on the same product each sold, they would all be violating the Sherman Act.

CLAYTON ACT

Like the Sherman Act, the Clayton Act of 1914 was aimed at discouraging monopolies. One part of the law forbids corporations from acquiring ownership rights in other corporations if the purpose is to create a monopoly or to discourage competition. Corporation A cannot, for example, buy more than half the ownership rights of its main competitor, Corporation B, if the aim is to severely reduce or eliminate competition.

Another section of the Clayton Act forbids business contracts that require customers to purchase certain goods in order to get other goods. For example, a business that produces computers cannot require a buyer also to purchase supplies, such as paper and software, in order to get a computer. Microsoft Corporation was once charged with such a violation. Microsoft required computer makers that wanted to buy its dominant Windows operating system to also accept its Internet Explorer browser. The result of this action was to severely damage the sales of Netscape's Navigator browser, which was Microsoft's dominant competitor.

ROBINSON-PATMAN ACT

The Robinson-Patman Act of 1936 amended the portion of the Clayton Act dealing with the pricing of goods. The main purpose of the pricing provisions in both of these laws is to prevent **price discrimination**. For example, a seller cannot offer a price of $5 a unit to Buyer A and sell the same goods to Buyer B at $6 a unit. Different prices can be set, however, if the goods sold are different in

---

Types of Practices Prohibited by the Federal Trade Commission

1. Any act that restrains trade.

2. Any monopolies except those specifically authorized by law, suc as public utilities.

3. Price fixing, such as agreements among competitors.

4. Agreements among competitors to divide territory, earnings, or profits.

5. Gaining control over the supply of any commodity in order to createan artificial scarcity.

6. False or misleading advertising.

7. Imitation of trademark or trade name.

8. Discrimination through prices or special deals.

9. Pretending to sell at a discount when there is no reduction in price.

10. Offering so-called free merchandise with a purchase when the price of the article sold has been raised to compensate for the free merchandise.

11. Misrepresentation about the quality, the composition, or the place of origin of a product.

12. Violation of one's guarantee of privacy of information on the Internet, including e-mail.

© Cengage Learning 2013.

Figure 11-1 Managers are responsible for knowing and abiding by these regulations.

Examples of Federal Regulatory Agencies	
AGENCY	**REGULATION**
Federal Aviation Administration	Safety standards, airplane accidents, and take-offs and landings
Federal Communications Commission	Radio, television, telephone, telegraph, cable, and satellite communications
Food and Drug Administration	Foods, drugs, medical devices, cosmetics, and veterinary products
Nuclear Regulatory Commission	Nuclear power plants
Securities and Exchange Commission	Stocks and bonds

Figure 11-2 Government agencies enforce laws promoting fair practices that benefit businesses and consumers.

quality or quantity. Buyer A is entitled to the $5 price if the quantity purchased is significantly greater or if the quality is lower. The same discounts must then be offered to all buyers purchasing the same quantity or quality as Buyer A.

WHEELER-LEA ACT

In 1938, the Wheeler-Lea Act was passed to strengthen earlier laws outlawing unfair methods of competition. This law made unfair or deceptive acts or practices, including false advertising, unlawful. **False advertising** is advertising that is misleading in some important way, including the failure to reveal facts about possible results from using the advertised products. Under the Wheeler-Lea Act, it is unlawful for an advertiser to circulate false advertising that can lead to the purchase of foods, drugs, medical devices, or cosmetics, or to participate in any other unfair methods of competition.

FEDERAL TRADE COMMISSION

The Federal Trade Commission (FTC) was created as the result of many businesses demanding protection from unfair methods of competition. The FTC administers most of the federal laws dealing with fair competition. Some of the unfair practices that the FTC protects businesses from are shown in Figure 11-1.

OTHER FEDERAL AGENCIES

In addition to the FTC, the federal government has created other agencies to administer laws that regulate specialized areas of business, such as transportation and communication. Figure 11-2 lists some of the more important agencies.

PROVIDING BANKRUPTCY RELIEF

All firms face the risk of failure. The free-enterprise system permits unsuccessful businesses to file for bankruptcy as a means of protecting owners and others. **Bankruptcy** is a legal process that allows the selling of assets to pay off debts. Businesses as well as individuals can file for bankruptcy. If cash is not available to pay the debts after assets are sold, the law excuses the business or individual from paying the remaining unpaid debts. In such a case, all those to whom money is owed would very likely receive less than the full amount.

21st CENTURY SKILLS

Effective Reasoning

Understanding the legal aspects of business requires effective reasoning. Depending on the situation, managers need to use inductive and deductive reasoning. They also need to be able to analyze relationships and make connections. Successful managers understand the need to ask questions and seek advice to help them solve problems and make decisions.

A bankruptcy judge can permit a company to survive bankruptcy proceedings if a survival plan can be developed that might enable the firm to recover. As a result, after starting bankruptcy proceedings, many firms do survive. However, bankruptcy carries serious consequences. The business will have a bad credit rating. A record of the unpaid debts will stay on file for 10 years, and the business may not file for bankruptcy again for eight years. As a result, the business will have difficulty obtaining credit.

 CHECKPOINT

List the four federal acts that are designed to promote fair competition.

11.1 ASSESSMENT

UNDERSTAND MANAGEMENT CONCEPTS

Determine the best answer for each of the following questions.

1. A(n) _____ exists when only one company provides a product or service without competition from other companies.
   a. oligopoly
   b. monopoly
   c. monogamy
   d. none of the above

2. The _____ protects businesses from unfair methods of competition.
   a. Federal Trade Commission (FTC)
   b. Federal Competition Commission (FCC)
   c. Federal Transportation Commission (FTC)
   d. Federal Monopoly Commission (FMC)

THINK CRITICALLY

Answer the following questions as completely as possible.

3. Explain why monopolies are bad for a society.
4. Describe how bankruptcy works for debtors and creditors.

Regulations Protecting Business and the Public

Goals

- Explain how patent, copyright, and trademark protection benefits business.
- Describe the ways in which government regulations protect consumers.
- Describe three methods used by state and local governments to regulate business.

Terms

- patent p. 287
- copyright p. 288
- trademark p. 289
- identity theft p. 290
- information liability p. 290
- cookies p. 290
- interstate commerce p. 290
- intrastate commerce p. 291
- licensing p. 291
- public franchise p. 291
- building codes p. 292
- zoning p. 292

●●● Intellectual Property

The federal government has passed laws to protect the rights of those who create uniquely different products and new ideas. Specifically, it grants intellectual property rights to inventors, authors, and creators of distinct symbols and names for goods and services. Figure 11-3 outlines key information about intellectual property rights in the United States.

PATENTS

A **patent** is an agreement in which the federal government gives an inventor the sole right for 20 years to make, use, and sell an invention or a process. No one is permitted to copy or use the invention without permission. This protection is a reward for the time and money invested to create the new product. An inventor may allow others to make or use a product by giving them a license to do so.

In a sense, through the Patent and Trademark Office, the government gives the inventor a monopoly on newly invented products, designs, and processes. This temporary monopoly provides a profit incentive that encourages manufacturers to spend the huge amounts of money required to research and develop new ideas. Research departments have produced many inventions. For example, Apple, Samsung, and other companies have developed Internet-enabled smart phones that allow users to communicate as well as download digital files and programs. Even synthetic tissue and altered vegetable plants are patentable. For example, insulin that diabetics need and a new rot-resistant tomato are products of biotechnology (biology plus technology) innovations.

New processes as well as new products can be patented, but process patenting can be undesirable at times. For example, Priceline.com, Inc., received a patent for its auction price-bidding system on the Internet. If other companies used this simple process, they would be violating the owner's patent rights. However, the process is so fundamental to many Internet practices that competitors believe the patent is essentially unfair. Should doctors who develop a new

Intellectual Property Protection				
Legal Protection	Copyright	Patent		Trademark
		Design Patent	Utility Patent	
Length of Time	Author's life plus an additional 70 years*	14 years	20 years	Indefinitely†
Examples	• Architectural works • Books • Movies • Music • Photography • Poetry • Software	• Design of beverage container • Design of furniture • Design of jewelry	• Machine • Mousetrap • Pharmaceuticals • Process	• Name • Symbol • Logo • Phrase • Image

© Cengage Learning 2013.

* This applies to works created on or after January 1, 1978.

† Registration renewal is required after the first five years and every ten years thereafter.

Figure 11-3 The federal government grants special property rights.

method for healing people prohibit other doctors from using it or require them to pay a licensing fee? Occasionally, the Patent and Trademark Office revokes or denies patents that discourage desirable competition.

Unfortunately, stealing patents is an acceptable practice in some countries that do not honor the U.S. patent law. As a result, American firms lose millions of dollars. By tightening trade agreements with these countries, this great loss to American firms may begin to decline. On the other hand, patent laws differ worldwide. For example, Japan's patents promote technology sharing, whereas U.S. patents protect inventors.

COPYRIGHTS

A **copyright** is similar to a patent in that the federal government gives an author the sole right to reproduce, publish, and sell literary or artistic work for the life of the author, typically, plus 70 years. No one may publish or reproduce copyrighted work without permission of the copyright owner. However, the law permits occasional copying of copyrighted material for fair use. An important factor in determining fair use is the economic impact of using the copyrighted work. A magazine writer quoting a paragraph from a copyrighted novel would be fair use because it would not reduce the sales of the copyrighted book.

Copyright laws also cover electronic methods for distributing creative work. Copyrights protect creators of video games and music, television shows and movies, and computer software programs, for example. Duplicating video, music files, or software programs for distribution to others is usually illegal. When an employee makes a personal copy of a computer software program for use on a home computer, the employee violates the copyright law. Furthermore, if a warning is not publicized that copying creative work such as a software program is illegal, the employer is also guilty.

Copyrights are regulated by the United States Copyright Office. Like a patent, a copyright is a special type of monopoly granted to authors, publishers, and other creators of original works. An example of a copyright notice appears on the back of the title page in the front of this book.

TRADEMARKS

Trademarks are like patents because they are special types of monopolies. A **trademark** is a distinguishing name, symbol, or special mark placed on a good or service that is legally reserved for the sole use of the owner. Many nationally known products have trademarks that most people recognize. Some trademarks are symbols, such as the Nike swoosh, the Olympic rings, and the Twitter bird. Others are company or product names, such as the Sony PlayStation, Nintendo Wii, and Microsoft Xbox. Trademarks, like patents, are regulated by the Patent and Trademark Office.

 **CHECKPOINT**

Describe the three areas of intellectual property protection.

⬤⬤⬤⬤ Regulations Protecting the Public

The federal government protects the legal rights of not only those who create new products and ideas but also those who consume goods and services. Two major goals of legislation are to ensure safe products for consumers and to prevent the misuse of information.

FOOD AND DRUGS

Products related to the human body are closely regulated. The Food and Drug Administration (FDA) administers the Federal Food, Drug, and Cosmetic Act and related laws. These laws prohibit the sale of impure, improperly labeled, falsely guaranteed, and unhealthful foods, drugs, and cosmetics. Producers of cosmetics, for example, must show that their products will not harm users. Should a product cause harm, the FDA may require the producer to stop its sale or to notify the public of its possible danger.

NONFOOD PRODUCTS

Legislative activity dealing with the safety of nonfood products has increased in recent years. Laws now require labels on many products if possible danger exists from product use. A health warning message, for example, must appear on cigarette packages. The FTC forbids the sale of tobacco and smokeless tobacco to those under 18 because research shows that the majority of those who smoke when young die prematurely of smoking-related diseases. Also, auto and highway safety laws exist to reduce death and injury.

The Consumer Product Safety Act sets safety standards on many items. When products already sold are found to have a dangerous defect, businesses are legally required to recall, repair, or stop selling the products. Dangerous toys, for example, have been removed from the market. And recalls have occurred with such products as cars and sport utility vehicles. A federal Warranty Act requires sellers to specify what they will or will not do if their product is defective. Many product liability laws also exist at the state level.

 **FACTS & FIGURES**

Abandoned Trademarks

Trademark rights may continue indefinitely, as long as the mark is neither abandoned by the trademark owner nor loses its significance in the marketplace as a trademark by becoming a generic term. For example, the generic terms *escalator*, *linoleum*, and *zipper* were once trademarks.

INFORMATION

Businesses need information. This need has resulted in the heavy use of computers to manage data. Vast amounts of information from many sources are collected, processed, stored, and distributed by computer, especially on the Internet. As a result, individuals and businesses need protection from the wrongful use of private information.

Stores check credit card balances, banks check credit ratings, hospitals store patients' health records electronically, and the government collects income tax data on all taxpayers. Incorrect information in any of these sensitive records could be very damaging to the individual. Also, only authorized people should have access to such highly personal information. Unauthorized use of personal information can result in identity theft. According to the Federal Trade Commission, **identity theft** is the unauthorized use of someone's personally identifying information, such as name, Social Security number, or credit card number, to commit fraud or other crimes. In addition to the impact on victims, identity theft creates problems for businesses.

Therefore, businesses that use computer information extensively must handle it carefully to protect the rights of individuals and organizations. Carelessly handled information can lead to **information liability**—the responsibility for physical or economic injury arising from incorrect data or wrongful use of data.

Information liability is similar to product liability. If a defective product injures someone, the injured party can sue the producer of the product. Similarly, if a person's credit rating suffers because an employee keys a Social Security number into a credit record incorrectly, the business is liable for creating the problem. Also, a company not directly involved in collecting or recording incorrect information may be held liable for distributing it. For instance, if a store gives an incorrect credit balance to a bank that results in the refusal for a loan, the bank is as liable as the store that provided the incorrect information.

Occasionally, someone tampers with computerized data. The Electronic Communications Privacy Act and related laws make it a crime for any unauthorized person to access a major computer system and view, use, or change data. The laws deal with the interception and disclosure of electronic communications, including e-mail privacy. Privacy laws help protect the public from the wrongful use or misuse of information.

A debate continues over the electronic collection of information over the Internet. Websites can place small files called "cookies" on the computers of site visitors without their knowledge. **Cookies** are files of information about the user that some Websites create and store on the user's own computer. These cookies can, among other things, track where users go on the Internet to gather information on interests and preferences for marketing purposes. Some people feel that such data gathering is an invasion of privacy. The companies argue that they are simply identifying what consumers want so they can better serve them.

CHECKPOINT

Describe three areas in which government protects consumers.

State and Local Regulations

The federal government regulates interstate commerce, and individual states regulate intrastate commerce. **Interstate commerce** is defined as business operations and transactions that cross state lines, such as products that are produced in one state and sold in other states. **Intrastate commerce**, on the other hand, is defined as business transacted within a state. Most small service firms are involved mainly in intrastate commerce, because they usually sell to customers located within the same state. Because most large companies are likely to be involved in both interstate and intrastate commerce, they are subject to state and federal regulations.

Moreover, each state has a constitution that allows it to create other governing units, such as cities, towns, and counties. These units also regulate business transacted within them. Large businesses especially are subject to local, state, and federal laws.

Many state and local laws are related to federal laws. Most states, for instance, have laws that promote competition, protect consumers and the environment, safeguard the public's health, and improve employment conditions. In addition, however, state and local governments regulate business by issuing licenses, franchises, and building codes, and by passing zoning regulations.

LICENSING

State and local governments have used **licensing** as a way to limit and control those who plan to enter certain types of businesses. To start a business that requires a license, the owner must file an application. If the government believes there is a sufficient number of these kinds of businesses, the application can be refused.

Business is regulated not only by the granting of licenses but also by regular inspections by government officials to see that the company is operated according to the law. If it is not being properly operated, it can lose its license. For example, government agents inspect a licensed restaurant from time to time for cleanliness. If the restaurant fails inspection, the government may withdraw its license, and the restaurant would have to close.

Licensing laws vary from place to place. In some cities, businesses of all types must obtain licenses, whereas in other communities only certain types need licenses. It is particularly common to license restaurants, beauty salons, health and fitness centers, barbershops, and other types of service firms that may affect the health of customers. In most states and in many cities, licensing laws regulate the sale of such items as liquor and tobacco.

Businesses may also license the use of property. For example, a computer software company may give a business a license to use and copy a software program in return for a fee. Likewise, for a fee a business may license another firm to make a product using its patented device. Even firm names can be licensed. For example, Walt Disney Productions licenses its animal characters for use on clothing and other products.

PUBLIC FRANCHISING

Another way for state and local governments to control business is through public franchises. A **public franchise** is a contract that permits a person or

Why would a local government be interested in licensing food vendors?

© Shutterstock/Chuck Wagner

organization to use public property for private profit. No individual member of society, however, has a right to use public property for profit except through a special grant by society. Cities often grant public franchises to companies to operate bus lines, or to install electric power or cable for television. For example, as presented in the story that started this chapter, Deion has a franchise from his community to operate his taxi company.

BUILDING CODES AND ZONING

Local governments regulate business through **building codes**, which control the physical features of structures. Building codes may specify such things as the maximum height, minimum square feet of space, and the types of materials that can be used. Local governments also regulate the types of buildings and where they are built. **Zoning** regulations specify which land areas may be used for homes and which areas may be used for different types of businesses. A business must obey all local regulations relating to zoning and construction.

 CHECKPOINT

List three ways that local governments regulate business.

11.2 ASSESSMENT

UNDERSTAND MANAGEMENT CONCEPTS

Determine the best answer for each of the following questions.

1. A _____ allows an inventor the sole right for 20 years to make, use, and sell an invention or a process.
   a. patent
   b. copyright
   c. trademark
   d. license

2. Business operations and transactions that cross state lines are called
   a. interstate commerce
   b. intrastate commerce
   c. multistate commerce
   d. national commerce

THINK CRITICALLY

Answer the following questions as completely as possible.

3. Describe how the federal government protects consumers of goods and services.

4. Describe how local governments regulate businesses.

F⊕cus On...Ethics

Internet Privacy

Google is the world's largest search provider. It is known for its ability to be intuitive in providing information needed by its users. Google is able to achieve this by tapping into users' personal information. This information can come from numerous sources. When someone registers for a Google service such as Gmail, Buzz, or Google's SMS, data are collected and analyzed. Online browsing behavior is also tracked through "cookies," which are files stored on customers' computers. The cookies collect information on what customers buy and where they go on the web, revealing their preferences and browsing habits.

Many of Google's acquisitions have been companies that can leverage the use of personal information. For example, in 2008 Google purchased DoubleClick, a provider of advertising services to Internet retailers, for $3.1 billion. DoubleClick manages clients' advertising based on the customer information collected online. It then selects the customers that best match a firm's target audience. DoubleClick uses this information to help its clients advertise effectively. Privacy advocacy groups protested Google's acquisition of DoubleClick because of the use of personal information collected by Google.

Google settled a complaint by the Federal Trade Commission over privacy issues related to its Buzz social network. The FTC claimed that Google did not inform its 200 million Gmail users that it would use information in their e-mail accounts to set up the Buzz social network. Users were concerned about the public release of e-mail addresses.

Even Google's cloud computing has received privacy complaints. Cloud computing allows files to be stored at remote servers instead of on a local device, such as a computer or cell phone. Google has stated that information stored in Gmail, Picasa photo storage, and Google Docs would be secure. This may not be the case, however, because individual users do not control access to these remote servers.

Google and other companies are attempting to provide new and more convenient services to individuals around the world. This is possible only by using personal information. Users must understand that there is never a guarantee that online information will remain private.

THINK CRITICALLY

1. Identify three people who have purchased an item on the Internet. Ask these people if they read the privacy policy before purchasing and if they know what a "cookie" is.

2. How do the selling methods of Internet advertisers affect your privacy? How does this compare to companies that mail you advertising or call you at home to try to sell you their products?

3. A very young person is often not concerned about what information he or she provides to others on the Internet. How could an unethical business capture and use this information in a way that could harm the family?

© Shutterstock/Rick Becker-Leckrone

11.3

Business Taxes

Goals

- Discuss the nature of taxes and the fairness of progressive, proportional, and regressive taxes.
- Identify and explain the most common types of taxes that affect business.

Terms

- proportional tax p. 295
- progressive tax p. 295
- regressive tax p. 296
- income tax p. 297
- sales tax p. 297
- excise tax p. 298
- property tax p. 298
- real property tax p. 298
- personal property tax p. 298
- assessed valuation p. 298

●●● General Nature of Taxes

Although government uses many different ways to regulate business, no way is more important than taxes. The types and amounts of taxes influence business decisions that, in turn, can influence the total amount of business activity in a region and in the nation.

Both businesses and individuals pay many kinds of taxes to local, state, and federal governments. Taxes collected by the federal government account for about 56 percent of all taxes collected, while various state and local taxes account for the remaining 44 percent. Most corporations pay nearly one-half of their profits in various kinds of taxes.

Government levies taxes for different reasons. When government decides to levy a particular type of tax, it must consider fairness to taxpayers.

REASONS FOR TAXES

Governments levy taxes mainly to raise revenue (money) to fund new and ongoing programs. Governments also use taxes to regulate business activity.

Governments set revenue goals that must be reached in order to provide the various services desired by the public. Examples of these services range from law enforcement and road building to providing for the military defense of the country. It is costly for government to provide the many services the public wants. To pay for these services, therefore, it must collect taxes.

Governments also use taxes to control business activity. They can speed up economic growth by lowering taxes and slow it by raising taxes. The federal government also taxes certain foreign goods that enter this country in order to encourage consumers to purchase American-made rather than foreign-made products. State and local governments also control business activity through taxation. For example, they often set high taxes on alcoholic beverages and tobacco, in part to discourage customers from purchasing these products.

FAIRNESS OF TAXATION

It is difficult for government to find ways to levy taxes fairly and still raise sufficient amounts of money to meet government expenses. The question of fairness has caused many debates. One problem is determining who will, in fact, pay the tax. For example, a firm may have to pay taxes on the goods it manufactures. But, because the tax is part of the cost of producing the product, this cost may be passed on to the customer. Another problem of fairness is whether those with the most assets or most income should pay at a higher rate than those who own or earn the least. Government tries to solve the fairness problem by adopting a proportional, progressive, or regressive tax policy.

PROPORTIONAL TAXATION

A **proportional tax**—sometimes called a *flat tax*—is one in which the tax rate remains the same regardless of the amount on which the tax is imposed. For example, in a given area the tax rate on real estate per $1,000 of property value is always the same, regardless of the amount of real estate the taxpayer owns. The total dollar amount of the tax paid by someone with a $400,000 home will differ from that paid by the person with a $175,000 home in the same area, but the rate of the tax is the same for both owners. A flat state tax of 6 percent on income is also proportional. Those with higher incomes pay more dollars than those with lower incomes. But the tax rate of 6 percent stays the same.

PROGRESSIVE TAXATION

A **progressive tax** is a tax based on the ability to pay. The policy of progressive taxation is a part of many state and federal income tax systems. As income increases, the tax rate increases. As a result, a lower-income person is taxed at a lower rate than a higher-income person is. In fact, the Tax Foundation found that in a recent year, 5 percent of the taxpayers who pay the most taxes contributed over 58 percent of all the federal individual income taxes collected.

Some local and state governments have combined the policies of proportional and progressive taxes. For example, a state may apply a flat tax of 5 percent to incomes up to $20,000 and 6 percent to all incomes over $20,000.

The current federal tax law is a combination of progressive and proportional taxation policy. Figure 11-4 illustrates the 2010 tax rate schedule used to calculate income tax for single taxpayers. Regardless of total income, everyone

Tax Rate Schedule, Filing Single*				
If your taxable income is over—	But not over—	The tax is—	Plus—	Of the amount over—
$0	$8,375	--------	10%	$0
8,375	34,000	$837.50	15%	8,375
34,000	82,400	4,681.25	25%	34,000
82,400	171,850	16,781.25	28%	82,400
171,850	373,650	41,827.25	33%	171,850
373,650	--------	108,421.25	35%	373,650

* Tax year 2010
Source: Internal Revenue Service

Figure 11-4 The total tax paid is cumulative across the income tax brackets.

Effective Sales Tax Rate as a Percent of Income		
	PERSON A	PERSON B
Take-home pay (after income taxes)	$30,000	$100,000
Take-home pay not spent on sales taxed items	–	20,000
Take-home pay spent on sales taxed items	30,000	80,000
State sales tax rate	6%	6%
Calculation of sales tax	($30,000 × .06)	($80,000 × .06)
Sales taxes paid	1,800	4,800
Calculation of effective sales tax rate on income	($1,800 ÷ $30,000)	($4800 ÷ $100,000)
Effective sales tax rate as a percent of income	6.0%	4.8%

© Cengage Learning 2013.

Figure 11-5 People with very high incomes often prefer regressive taxes.

pays the same rate on taxable income up to $8,375 of income—10 percent. The tax then progresses through the next five brackets. For example, if your taxable income were exactly $8,375, your tax would be $837.50. If your cousin had taxable income of $10,000, her tax would be $1,081.25. Just like you, your cousin pays $837.50 on the first $8,375 of taxable income, plus an additional $243.75. The additional amount is 15 percent on the amount over $8,375 (0.15 × $1,652). Most people consider the tax fair because people with higher incomes pay at a higher rate than those with lower incomes.

REGRESSIVE TAXATION

The third type of tax policy is a **regressive tax**. With this type of tax, the actual tax rate decreases as the taxable amount increases. Although general sales taxes are often thought to be proportional, they are actually regressive, because people with lower incomes pay a larger proportion of their incomes in taxes than those with higher incomes. Suppose, for example, that Person A and Person B live in a state with a 6 percent general sales tax. As shown in Figure 11-5, Person A, with an annual take-home pay of $30,000, pays a 6 percent tax rate, whereas Person B, with an annual take-home pay of $100,000 pays only a 4.8 percent tax rate. Because the sales tax applies to purchases rather than to income, the general sales tax is regressive. For a less regressive sales tax, some states exclude taxes on such purchases as food and clothing. These exclusions are usually items on which low-income families spend a high percentage of their income.

 **CHECKPOINT**

Explain the three types of tax policies.

 **Types of Taxes**

Taxation has become so complicated that the average businessperson spends a great deal of time filling out tax forms, computing taxes, and filing reports. In many businesses, various taxes reduce income by a large percentage. The three most common taxes affecting businesses and individuals are income taxes, sales taxes, and property taxes.

INCOME TAX

The federal government and most state governments use the income tax to raise revenues. An **income tax** is a tax on the profits of businesses and the earnings of individuals. For individuals, the tax is based on salaries and other income earned after certain deductions. For businesses, an income tax usually applies to net profits (receipts less expenses).

The income tax is the largest source of revenue for the federal government. Individuals pay about 80 percent of the total federal income taxes collected, and businesses pay nearly all of the remaining 20 percent. Businesses share the cost of collecting individual income taxes. Every business is required to withhold income taxes from employees' earnings and turn them over to the government. Thus, business performs an important tax service for government. Individuals and businesses pay lower rates in the United States than in most other developed nations, as shown in Figure 11-6.

FICA TAXES

Federal Insurance Contributions Act (FICA) taxes include Social Security and Medicare taxes. Employees and employers share the burden of these taxes and employers withhold the employee portion from wages. For 2010, both employees and employers paid Social Security tax of 6.2 percent and Medicare tax of 1.45 percent. For 2010, only the first $106,800 in income was subject to the Social Security tax. There is no wage base limit for the Medicare tax.

Self-employed workers pay FICA tax at a higher rate than employed workers because they pay both the employer and employee portion. The self-employment tax rate for 2010 was 15.3 percent (12.4 percent for Social Security and 2.9 percent for Medicare.)

SALES TAX

A **sales tax** is a tax levied on the retail price of goods and services at the time they are sold. A general sales tax usually applies to all goods or services sold by

> **Manager's Perspective on**
> ## ETHICS
>
> Managers have a responsibility to pay only the taxes the businesses owes. Legally you can avoid paying taxes by maximizing tax deductions. You cannot evade taxes by not reporting income. This is both unethical and illegal.

Effective Tax Rate as a Percent of Income

Country	Tax Rate*	Country	Tax Rate*	Country	Tax Rate*
Belgium	41.5%	Turkey	27.2%	Australia	22.0%
Germany	41.3%	Luxembourg	26.4%	Switzerland	21.5%
Denmark	39.4%	Sweden	25.3%	Slovak Republic	21.3%
Hungary	38.2%	United Kingdom	25.3%	Ireland	20.9%
Austria	32.7%	Greece	25.1%	Japan	20.1%
Netherlands	31.8%	Poland	24.3%	Spain	19.7%
Italy	29.3%	Canada	22.8%	New Zealand	18.4%
Norway	29.3%	United States	22.4%	Iceland	17.9%
Finland	29.2%	Portugal	22.3%	Korea	11.8%
France	27.7%	Czech Republic	22.2%	Mexico	5.3%

*Single person without dependents
Source: Organisation for Economic Co-operation and Development (OECD)

Figure 11-6 U.S. tax rates are relatively low in comparison to those of other nations.

retailers. However, when a sales tax applies only to selected goods or services, such as cigarettes and gasoline, it is called an **excise tax**.

Sales taxes are the main source of revenue for most states and some cities and counties. Although state governments do not all administer sales taxes in the same way, in most cases the retail business collects the tax from customers and turns this tax over to the state government. A business must be familiar with the sales tax law of the state in which it operates so that it can collect and report the tax properly.

From time to time, federal officials have considered charging a national sales tax. State officials, however, strongly oppose a national sales tax because the state tax is their primary source of revenue. The question as to how and whether to tax Internet sales is also under debate between the states and the federal government. Both see this source of taxes as highly attractive. Traditional retailers who pay sales taxes, however, believe it is unfair for Internet sales not to be taxed.

PROPERTY TAX

A **property tax** is a tax on material goods owned. Whereas the sales tax is the primary source of revenue for most state governments, the property tax is the main source of revenue for most local governments. There may be a real property tax and a personal property tax. A **real property tax** is a tax on real estate, which is land and buildings. A **personal property tax** is a tax on possessions that are movable, such as furniture, machinery, and equipment. Essentially, personal property is anything that is not real estate. In some states, there is a special property tax on raw materials used to make goods and on finished goods available for sale.

A tax on property—whether it is real property or personal property—is stated in terms of dollars per hundred of assessed valuation.

Assessed valuation is the value of property determined by tax officials. Thus, a tax rate of $2.80 per $100 on property with an assessed valuation of $180,000 is $5,040 ($180,000/100 = $1,800; $1,800 × $2.80 = $5,040).

EFFECT OF TAXES ON BUSINESS DECISIONS

Businesses consider taxes in many of their major decisions. Taxes may influence the accounting method a business selects to calculate profits and the method used to pay managers. Often, taxes are used as a basis for deciding where to locate a new business or whether to move a business from one location to another.

For example, assume that a producer of garden tools is trying to decide in which of two cities to build a new factory. City A is located in a state that has a low state income tax and low property taxes. City B is located in a state with no state income tax but high property taxes. After weighing all the factors, the producer decides to locate in City A. City A, which has both an income tax and a property tax, has been selected mainly because the total tax cost each year is less than in City B.

CHECKPOINT

Describe the three most common taxes levied on businesses and individuals.

11.3 ASSESSMENT

UNDERSTAND MANAGEMENT CONCEPTS

Determine the best answer for each of the following questions.

1. A tax based on a person's ability to pay is called a
   a. proportional tax
   b. flat tax
   c. progressive tax
   d. regressive tax

2. The largest source of revenue for the federal government is
   a. sales taxes
   b. income taxes
   c. import taxes
   d. property taxes

THINK CRITICALLY

Answer the following questions as completely as possible.

3. Describe the two ways governments use taxes.
4. Explain how taxes affect business decisions.

CHAPTER CONCEPTS

- Federal, state, and local governments regulate business activities to protect citizens and businesses. The Federal Trade Commission administers federal laws that regulate commerce. Landmark laws such as the Sherman and Clayton Acts helped set the stage for defining fair competition. Other federal agencies regulate basic industries such as aviation, communications, and food and drugs.

- A downside of free enterprise is that some firms go bankrupt, but bankruptcy laws allow businesses to recover or to exit business operations fairly. The federal government protects individuals and firms from the theft or misuse of their inventions, publications, and other intellectual property by granting the owners patents, trademarks, or copyrights. Local and state governments also regulate business through licenses, zoning laws, and franchising regulations.

- Governments obtain revenues through taxes to pay for public services, such as police, schools, and other human services. The most common sources of revenue are income, sales, and property taxes.

- A progressive tax such as an income tax is based on one's ability to pay, and is higher for those who earn more than for those who earn less. A proportional tax such as a county's real estate tax stays the same regardless of a property's current value. A regressive tax, such as a sales tax, requires people who earn less to pay a greater portion of their income than do people who earn more. Arguments can be made for each of the three types of taxes.

REVIEW BUSINESS MANAGEMENT TERMS

Write the letter of the term that matches each definition. Some terms will not be used.

a. assessed valuation
b. bankruptcy
c. excise tax
d. false advertising
e. information liability
f. interstate commerce
g. intrastate commerce
h. personal property tax
i. price discrimination
j. proportional tax (flat tax)
k. public franchise
l. sales tax
m. trademark
n. zoning

1. Setting different prices for different customers
2. Advertising that is misleading in some important way
3. Legal process that allows the selling of assets to pay off debts
4. Distinguishing name, symbol, or special mark placed on a good or service that is legally reserved for the sole use of the owner
5. Responsibility for physical or economic injury arising from incorrect data or wrongful use of data
6. Regulating which land areas may be used for homes and which may be used for different types of businesses
7. Tax rate that remains the same regardless of the income
8. Tax that applies only to selected goods or services, such as cigarettes and gasoline
9. Business transacted within a state
10. Tax levied on retail price of goods and services when they are sold
11. Tax on movable possessions
12. Value of property determined by tax officials

REVIEW BUSINESS MANAGEMENT CONCEPTS

Determine the best answer.

13. A type of tax in which the actual tax rate decreases as the taxable amount increases is the
    a. proportional tax
    b. regressive tax
    c. progressive tax
    d. sales tax

14. An agreement in which the federal government gives an author the sole right to reproduce, publish, and sell literary or artistic work is called a
    a. patent
    b. copyright
    c. trademark
    d. license

15. A contract that permits a person or organization to use public property for private profit is called
    a. public franchise
    b. public license
    c. public patent
    d. none of the above

16. Which of the following are true for computer cookies?
    a. They are stored on the user's own computer.
    b. They can track where users go on the Internet.
    c. They can gather information on user interests and preferences for marketing purposes.
    d. All of the above are true.

17. A tax on real estate is called
    a. excise tax
    b. home tax
    c. property tax
    d. real property tax

18. State and local governments limit and control those who plan to enter certain types of businesses by issuing
    a. patents
    b. copyrights
    c. trademarks
    d. licenses

19. Which of the following are controlled by building codes?
    a. physical features
    b. maximum height
    c. types of materials that can be used
    d. all of the above

APPLY WHAT YOU KNOW

Answer the following questions.

20. Discuss how a business that has a monopoly on a good or service can keep its prices unreasonably high.
21. Explain why it is necessary for the federal government to pass laws promoting fair competition.
22. Explain why state and local governments would want to regulate businesses.
23. Explain how it is possible for a business to continue operating even after it has filed for bankruptcy.
24. Explain how a computer software program might be both copyrighted and licensed.

MAKE ACADEMIC CONNECTIONS

Complete the following activities.

25. **Research** Use the library or the Internet to research the history of the Sherman Antitrust Act. Identify the unethical business practices that led to the passage of this law. Identify the most recent use of this act. Specify how the U.S. economy is stronger because of the Sherman Antitrust Act.
26. **Math** You live in a state that has the following income tax schedule:

Taxable Income	Rate
$0–$6,999	no tax
7,000–14,999	5%
15,000–24,999	6%
25,000 and over	7%

   Your state allows everyone $2,000 of exemptions from total income to arrive at taxable income. Your total income for the year is $22,000. Your friend's total income is $29,000.
   a. What is your tax this year? What is your friend's tax?
   b. What is the actual tax rate you and your friend paid this year based on your total incomes?
27. **Writing** You work for one of three manufacturers that sells nationally. You have heard that your company has discussed prices of a product that all three manufacturers sell but that has become unprofitable to each. These companies believe that it is foolish to sell at a loss. They all agree to raise prices, but they do not agree on how much each will charge. Write a memo outlining your feelings about this action. Refer to specific federal regulations as necessary.

CASE IN POINT

CASE 11: PRICING COMPETITION

Hitesh Nazami owns and operates a hardware store in a community of 50,000 people. The nearest town is at least 25 miles away, but there are two competitors in the area, one of which is a new "big box" home store. All usually run weekly advertisements. Hitesh has noticed that the big-box store is selling many brand-name products at prices lower than he can buy them for from his suppliers. This has hurt Hitesh's overall sales.

Recently a customer Hitesh had never seen before came into the store to replace a broken tool. "I certainly hope you carry Weaver tools," the customer said. "The other stores in town, including that new big-box store, don't carry the Weaver brand."

"Sure, we carry Weaver," answered Hitesh. "It's one of my best lines."

The customer looked happy and relieved, and went to his truck to get the old tool he wanted to replace. While the customer was outside, Hitesh had a chance to think about what the customer had said. Now Hitesh knew why the Weaver brand was so popular in his store. He was happy that the big-box store didn't carry the Weaver brand. As a result, he decided to raise prices on Weaver tools by the next morning. Also, he could promote the fact that he was the only local supplier of Weaver tools in next week's advertisements. A smile crossed Hitesh's face as the customer returned.

"Here's the tool," said the customer. "I hope you can replace it. As you can see, it's quite different from the other brands."

"I can see that it's different," Hitesh responded. "You're lucky to get it at this low price. The price will be going up in the very near future."

THINK CRITICALLY

1. Is the big-box store practicing illegal price competition? Explain your answer. If it is, what federal act is it violating?
2. If the big-box store is not practicing illegal price competition, how can it sell at such low prices?
3. Does Hitesh have a monopoly on Weaver tools in his community?
4. If Hitesh raises his prices by very much, what might happen? What could the big-box store do?
5. Is raising the price suddenly (and for the reason given) an unfair business practice? Discuss your answer.
6. Could Hitesh advertise that he has an exclusive contract with Weaver even though he doesn't?

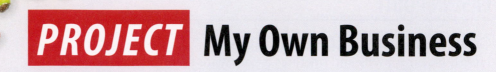

PROJECT My Own Business

Paying Taxes And Meeting Regulations

Regulations and taxes harm businesspeople most often when they are not aware of them or do not understand them. In this segment of the project, you will study the effects of laws on your business.

DATA COLLECTION

1. Identify the city or county office you will need to contact about local zoning regulations, licenses and permits, and taxes and fees.
2. Identify an information source, such as a website, on the legal procedures necessary to start a new business in your city or state.

ANALYSIS

1. Analyze the information you collected. Outline the legal procedures you would have to follow and identify the permits and licenses you would need to start your juice bar. List the problems you might have in adhering to the legal requirements.
2. The legislature in your state has just increased the sales tax from 4 percent to 6 percent of total sales. In order to make prices easier to remember and to simplify making change, you priced your products as shown below to include the 4 percent tax.

Large one-variety juice/yogurt mix	$3.75
Small 3-juice combo	2.50
Vitamin/mineral supplement	.60
Turkey sandwich	5.25
Bagel with cream cheese	1.25
Nutrition bar	1.90

It will be difficult to collect the additional 2 percent for sales tax and keep your pricing method. How will the sales tax increase affect your business? Evaluate several methods for dealing with the tax increase. Define your new pricing structure.

3. To reduce your start-up costs and to find a business location with a large number of potential customers, you have decided to rent a mobile cart in a large local mall in which to start your juice bar. Many fast-food business owners in your city are concerned that if mobile carts are allowed to operate, they will take business away from the other restaurants. They have approached the city council to pass a zoning regulation to prevent food from being sold from mobile carts, suggesting that it might be a health hazard. What actions can you and the owners of other similar businesses take to prevent the zoning law from being adopted by the city council? If the law is passed, how will it affect your business?

CHAPTER 12

TECHNOLOGY AND INFORMATION MANAGEMENT

12.1 Electronic Technology Fundamentals

12.2 Information Management

12.3 Technology and Business Strategy

© Shutterstock/Maridav

Reality Check

Brave New Business World

Mia Herrera started her morning with a stop at her favorite coffee shop. She used the coffee shop's Wi-Fi network to read her latest e-mail on her tablet computer. She then e-mailed several customers who had sent her messages late the previous evening. Mia scheduled a meeting through her company's online calendar with her regional sales manager. Then she used her cell phone to text her assistant about some assignments.

After enjoying a light breakfast and returning to her car, Mia placed her cell phone in its holder and went to the travel map application to check for the most direct but timesaving route to her new client, Egloff and Fox, Inc., in Wichita, Kansas.

She followed the directions and arrived early at E&F. She had time to check a few more e-mails on her cell phone and then used the phone's stock market application to check the stock price for E&F. Before getting out of the car, Mia quickly reviewed E&F's background and database files on her tablet computer and prepared to meet with the purchasing manager.

Mia's company, Tele-Com, provides video conferencing systems for businesses. The system allows for a near face-to-face experience between managers and employees, sales people and customers, and workers within a business. Tele-Com not only offers the video hardware, they also support the technology with high levels of security to ensure company information and communication is protected over both the Internet and company extranets.

As part of Mia's sales presentation today, she plans to demonstrate a mobile version of Tele-Com's system. As Mia walks in the door, she wonders how long it will be before she will be meeting with clients without driving to their offices. She thinks about the convenience of connecting with clients from her office or maybe even her home.

What's Your Reaction? How does technology help Mia do her job?

Electronic Technology Fundamentals

Goals

- Describe the role of information in a modern business.
- Describe how the Internet provides information to users.
- Describe the basic technology infrastructure used by businesses.

Terms

- knowledge workers p. 306
- data p. 306
- information p. 306
- Moore's Law p. 307
- Internet (Net) p. 307
- World Wide Web (WWW, Web) p. 307
- telecommunications p. 308
- local area network (LAN) p. 308
- server p. 308
- wide area network (WAN) p. 308
- cloud p. 308
- intranet p. 308
- extranet p. 309
- search engine p. 309

●●● Managing in a Technology World

Managers have always taken advantage of new technologies to drive their businesses toward greater efficiency and competitiveness. No inventions in recent years have had a greater impact than the computer, the Internet, the World Wide Web, and wireless communication. These tools have profoundly affected the personal and work lives of Mia Herrera and millions of other workers. New technologies have made dramatic changes in the way people live and work, and the pace of change is not likely to slow in the years ahead.

The modern business is an information center operated by people who work with information—**knowledge workers**. Managers, supervisors, and workers at all levels are knowledge workers who handle data and use information to make decisions. **Data**, the original facts and figures that businesses generate, must be collected, processed, stored, and retrieved. Data are turned into **information** when they are processed in a meaningful way. Decision makers can then use the information. The key to effective management is turning vast amounts of data into meaningful information to support the planning, organizing, implementing, and controlling functions.

TECHNOLOGY CHANGE

The technology that has allowed for an information revolution has moved from centralized computing to widely distributed computing. Electronic digital computers were developed in the 1940s during World War II. From the 1950s to the 1980s, a mainframe computer was often the center of a business's computer system. Information processing jobs needed to be run through a central point. In the early 1980s, the personal computer and PC software allowed individuals to enter and process their own data. This helped managers process data into useful information more quickly. In the mid 1990s, the Internet developed into a tool that allowed people and businesses to communicate with each other and gain access to information. Recent changes in technology makes high-speed wireless Internet accessible through a variety of Internet-enabled cell phones and devices. Managers can have access to the entire Internet's resource base—anytime, anywhere. Advances in computer technology occur at an ever-increasing rate. The cofounder of Intel Corporation, Gordon Moore, predicted that the amount of data that a computer chip could process would double about every 18 months. **Moore's Law**, as this prediction is known, has proven to be rather accurate. Figure 12-1 shows the accelerating pace of change over the past three decades. According to Moore's Law, a computer bought only one to two years ago will be obsolete this year. As processing speed increases, high-tech companies are constantly producing new and better software to take advantage of the technology's capabilities.

Moore's Law and Increase Power of Computing			
Microprocessor	**Transistors**	**Top Speed**	**Year**
8086	29,000	10 Megahertz	1978
8036DX	275,000	16 Megahertz	1985
Pentium	1,200,000	25 Megahertz	1993
Pentium III	9,500,000	733 Megahertz	1999
64-Bit Dual Processors	233,000,000	3 Gigahertz	2006
Multi-Core (up to 6-core)	1,170,000,000	3.5 Gigahertz	2011

Figure 12-1 Intel, AMD, and other firms constantly develop microprocessors composed of chips on integrated circuits to process data at faster speeds.

Wireless networks are evolving through a series of generations. The newest is the fourth generation, or 4G. These networks allow 100 megabits per second for high mobility communication such as in cars or trains and up to one gigabit per second for fixed locations. This bandwidth allows for streaming video and video conferencing on a cell phone.

 **CHECKPOINT**

Describe the difference between data and information.

The Internet Platform

The **Internet**, or **Net**, is a worldwide network of linked computers that allows users to transfer data and information from one computer to another anywhere in the world. The Internet includes a technology platform to move electronic information with an open set of standards governing how that information is encoded and used. This allows multiple companies to develop equipment and systems that work on the Internet Protocol (IP) platform. People can use the Net to send e-mail, visit websites, exchange files, and communicate across devices.

The Internet permits businesses to work together electronically and for managers and employees to communicate with co-workers at any distance. Consumers can research products and services and then buy online. They can also sell personal belongings, products, and services through a variety of websites. Other sites allow individuals with common interests to text, chat, join a social network, or compare products. The Internet can transfer any digital information including text, images, audio, video, and computer files. Internet users read magazine articles and newspapers (including photos); make phone calls and listen to music; watch movies, television shows, and YouTube videos; and download files to use and to update computer software. Data transfer over the Internet is virtually unlimited.

WORLD WIDE WEB

The **World Wide Web**, **WWW**, or **Web** consists of a set of standards that have made the Internet accessible to the average person. Early in its history, the Internet was based on mainframe access systems and required sophisticated technical knowledge to use. At first, researchers and the military were the main users. The Web brought graphical user interfaces and browsers to the Internet, allowing individuals with minimal computer skills to use the Internet. Through the Web, the Net grew rapidly during the end of the twentieth century. Currently there is little distinction between the Internet and the World Wide Web in the minds of most people.

 **CHECKPOINT**

Explain the difference between the Internet and the World Wide Web.

●●● Distributing Information

Employees are constantly using computers to record, process, send, store, and retrieve information. **Telecommunications** is the movement of information from one location to another electronically. Information moves electronically through physical lines and broadcast transmission. Physical lines include fixed telephone lines and fiber optic and coaxial cables. Wireless and satellite are examples of broadcast transmission.

A business computer system must be set up to allow workers to share information easily and quickly. These systems are a combination of hardware and software. A **local area network (LAN)** is a network of linked computers that serves users in a single building or building complex. In a LAN, a computer that stores data and application software for all workstations is called a *file server*, or, more commonly, a **server**.

Firms with multiple locations need to allow for communication with employees who are geographically dispersed. A **wide area network (WAN)** is a network of linked computers that covers a wide geographic area, such as a city, state, or country. LANs, WANs, and their servers connect through routers to other systems or to a mainframe computer. The servers are also channels through which individual workers can use their computers to communicate with others inside and outside the organization.

Wireless cellular networks are a form of a wide area network. Wireless cellular networks are so widely dispersed that they are becoming the network of choice for many people. Data storage is also shifting to WANs. Information can be stored on the **cloud**, which is the name given to the data storage systems over widely dispersed Internet networks.

INTRANETS AND EXTRANETS

An **intranet** is a private company network that allows employees to share resources no matter where they are located. An intranet works like the Internet. Users access information through a browser, navigate with hyperlinks, and send e-mail through the intranet. Usually the intranet connects to the Internet, but it is sealed off from the public to protect company information.

Intranets enable employees to accomplish many tasks electronically. Groups of employees working on the same project can discuss, share, plan, and implement ideas without having to leave their desks. These same employees can use company records stored electronically to aid in performing their tasks. Workers may use their computers to check employer-sponsored events, such as training programs, or learn about health care benefits, and see the balance in their retirement account. The easy accessibility of information on an intranet reduces the time spent finding and looking through paper documents.

Another type of network that operates similarly to the Internet is an extranet. An **extranet** is a private network that companies use to share certain information with selected people outside the organization, such as suppliers and major customers. For instance, a merchandise supplier for a national retailer could benefit from tracking the company's daily inventory balance. When inventory gets low, the supplier could deliver its goods just when the company needs them. An extranet enables the supplier to see the company's inventory records without allowing access to other company data.

Internet protocols allow access to information by entering a URL such as www.usps.com to access the website for the United States Postal Service. As an alternative, Internet users can search for information. A **search engine** is a program that helps users locate information on networks. After you type in one or more keywords, the search engine will display a list of sites that contain information matching those keywords. Some of these sites may have the information you want, but others may be way off target. A mouse click will take you to the sites that look promising. Search engines will also look for information over the wider Internet or in a company's internal intranet or extranet.

 **CHECKPOINT**

Describe the difference between a local area network and a wide area network.

12.1 ASSESSMENT

UNDERSTAND MANAGEMENT CONCEPTS

Determine the best answer for each of the following questions.

1. Data storage systems over widely dispersed Internet networks are called
   a. the Web
   b. the Net
   c. a cloud
   d. a WAN

2. The original facts and figures that businesses generate are called
   a. data
   b. information
   c. figures
   d. information points

THINK CRITICALLY

Answer the following questions as completely as possible.

3. Describe the advantages intranets offer to businesses.

4. Explain why Moore's Law is an important idea.

12.2

Information Management

Goals

- Describe the information systems that managers use to aid in their decision making.
- Discuss the advantages and disadvantages of Internet-based communication.
- Describe how information systems can improve business operations.

Terms

- chief information officer (CIO) p. 310
- database p. 310
- information system p. 310
- management information system (MIS) p. 311
- decision support system (DSS) p. 311
- executive information system (EIS) p. 311
- Voice over Internet Protocol (VoIP) p. 311
- firewall p. 313
- digital dashboard p. 314

⬤⬤⬤ Managing Technology

As computers became a dominant force throughout the world, organizations needed to manage the computer systems as well as the computer specialists who operated and manage the systems. In major organizations, the top computer executive is the **chief information officer**, or **CIO**. The CIO reports to the CEO (chief executive officer). The CIO must have extensive knowledge of electronic equipment along with expert management skills.

CIOs must keep up with new technologies and know what types of equipment to purchase to meet an organization's specific needs. Because many workers use computers, keeping them trained and productive is equally important. CIOs make it possible for all managers and workers who need information to get it easily and quickly from anywhere. CIOs also protect information from being used improperly, lost, damaged, or stolen.

ORGANIZING INFORMATION SYSTEMS

Most organizations are experiencing an information explosion. New computerized methods gather information quickly and have huge storage capacity. As a result, many managers suffer from information overload, the existence of more data than anyone can attend to. Information overload leads to needless costs and inefficiencies as managers try to sort through all the available information to find what they really need to make decisions. Thus, organizations need effective means for managing information.

Employees generate business data constantly. They record sales transactions, collect customer data, and track inventory. When employees key such data into their computers, the data become part of the company's database. A **database** is a collection of data organized in a way that makes the data easy to find, update, and manage.

However, a collection of data is not useful until it is processed into a form that decision makers can use. A computer system that processes data into meaningful information is called an **information system**. Three key types of information systems are management information systems, decision support systems, and executive information systems.

MANAGEMENT INFORMATION SYSTEM

A **management information system (MIS)** integrates data from various departments to make the information available to help managers with day-to-day business operations. An MIS deals with specific and highly structured data. Different departments collect and process the data. Employees enter daily transactions into the system as they occur, such as when they prepare purchase orders and record sales. From this gathered and stored information, managers can request reports to help them make daily operating decisions. For example, a sales report can show a manager where sales are slow. From this information, the manager might decide to do a special promotion in areas where sales need to improve.

DECISION SUPPORT SYSTEM

A **decision support system (DSS)** helps managers consider alternatives in making specific decisions. For example, a DSS can help a manager determine the most efficient routes for the company's delivery trucks. The ability to perform what-if analysis is a key capability of a DSS. A manager might ask, What if we continue our current strategy? Would that work? What if we try something else? What are the likely consequences of that action? The company's management information system provides much of the information for its decision support system.

EXECUTIVE INFORMATION SYSTEM

An **executive information system (EIS)** combines and summarizes ongoing transactions within the company to provide top-level executives with information needed to make decisions affecting the goals and direction of an organization. Information used in executive information systems is gathered from the MIS and DSS. An EIS collects data from both internal and external sources to help executives make decisions. For example, executives might use the EIS to collect outside information that affects the company, such as information regarding competitors, the state of the economy, and government policies. With information from inside and outside the organization, top managers make decisions that help a business survive and grow.

 CHECKPOINT

List three types of information systems.

●●● Networked Communication

Businesses use the Internet for communication, both within and outside the company. For businesses, most internal communications use Internet protocols, such as e-mail, file transfers, and data streaming. Using the Internet, a company can post an employee newsletter online. This speeds the information to all employees while reducing mailing and distribution costs. Employees can quickly send reports, memos, and other information to co-workers. However, new tools are available to assist with communications, including **VoIP**, or **Voice over Internet Protocol**

How does the Internet change communication in an office?

(using the Internet for telephone services), videophones, and software that allows several people to share application software and collaborate by using text and graphics tools while sitting at their computers.

Companies use the Internet to communicate with current and potential customers. The Internet has become an important way to provide information about the company and its products to customers. As businesses move to improve communications, they are increasingly turning to the Internet. Search engines are now the primary way that individuals go to a company's website. By using the Internet, a customer can often obtain product descriptions, find out when a business is open, and even print a map showing the location of the business. Today, if a business has not posted information about its location, products, and services on the Internet, it will likely miss customers.

The center of business communication is the Internet. Managers send e-mail messages, exchange documents, and sell their company's products and services to other businesses. Common business-to-business services offered via the Internet include online training, financial planning and accounting, maintaining personnel records, and data processing.

INFORMATION SECURITY

One of the major concerns of chief information officers is information security. The CIO must do whatever is necessary to make certain that hackers cannot steal, destroy, or alter information. The consequence of not controlling information may well be lawsuits by employees, customers, suppliers, and the public, as well as the loss of critical company records.

Information managers must balance the need to collect the information necessary to serve customers with their ethical responsibly when gathering, and sometimes selling, information about people who use the Internet to browse or buy merchandise. Programs launched from websites can track your travels from website to website. Where you go frequently on the Web reveals your general interests and what you buy. After collecting this information, some firms may sell it to businesses that sell goods related to your interests. For example, if you frequently look at websites related to music or games, firms that sell these goods will contact you and try to sell you their products. Information managers should fully inform users on how personal data will be used.

In April 2011, the Sony PlayStation Network was hacked and user information was compromised. Over 100 million users had their personal information stolen, including names, addresses, phone numbers, user names, birth dates, e-mail addresses, and passwords. Sony projected the cost of the data theft at more than $170 million. The amount is based on the costs of a "welcome back" package, customer support, legal costs, and lower future revenue.

When you buy goods on the Net, you must provide basic information, such as name, address, telephone number, and e-mail address. Often

NETBookmark

The World Wide Web is governed by an independent board called the W3C (World Wide Web Consortium).

Access the website for this textbook and choose the link for Chapter 12 Net Bookmark. Visit the W3C site and evaluate its current initiatives. Determine what the W3C is doing to allow the Web to continue to grow and meet people's needs around the world. Determine the background you would need to help the W3C move the Web forward into the future.

www.cengage.com/school/bizmgmt

websites store this information in your computer as a "cookie" file that the sites can retrieve when you visit again. This can be helpful when you buy from the business again. However, the firm can also sell this personal information to other businesses without your knowledge.

Good business practices—as well as the Federal Trade Commission—require businesses to notify buyers of their rights and how personal information will be used. However, some businesses may not properly inform buyers of their rights or may continue to sell confidential information after customers have opted out of information sharing. These actions are unethical and are even illegal in some states. Many computer users would buy on the Internet if they did not fear invasion of their privacy.

How can businesses assure customers that their personal information is safe?

Companies must also take defensive strategies to protect electronic information. Such strategies often include requiring user passwords to access data, saving information as backup files, and scrambling information to make it unreadable to others.

Information managers must ensure that their firms use firewall systems to protect information from outsiders who try to break into their networks. A **firewall** uses special software that screens people who enter a network by requesting specific information such as passwords. Passwords should change frequently. Nevertheless, even firewalls are not completely hacker-proof. Other safety systems are either available or being developed. For example, fingerprint scanning, voice verification, retina scanning, and other methods are being used to safeguard organizational information. Cloud computing developments may provide security because not all data will be stored in one location.

 CHECKPOINT

Describe how businesses can help ensure online security.

Improving Business Operations

The Internet has become an important tool to improve business operations and control costs. Salespeople can log on to the company's website and determine if a certain product is in inventory. When a product is sold, the order can immediately be entered into the computer from anywhere in the world to speed the processing and shipping of the order. A production manager can access the records of a transportation company to see when an expected shipment of raw materials is scheduled for delivery. An accountant in a branch office can download financial statements from the main computer to compare current financial performance with last year's information. Product designers in three different countries can collaborate by examining a three-dimensional drawing online and making changes that each of them can see instantly.

Managers of small businesses can benefit competitively from the use of the Internet. Many small businesses have their own websites to provide information to customers. This is an inexpensive way to provide business information to global markets. Customer databases can be used to send e-mails about products or events to build and maintain relationships with customers. Inventory levels can be linked to suppliers, so products can be shipped from suppliers when needed, lowing inventory carrying costs.

DIGITAL DASHBOARDS

Many companies use their internal extranets to pull multiple sources of information to create digital dashboards. A **digital dashboard** is a management information system that allows multiple sources of information to be displayed graphically on a computer. Like the dashboard in a car, a digital dashboard provides constant real-time information. Managers are able to track company information the way investors are able to track the changing stock market through charts, graphs, and summary spreadsheets. A manager can then "drill down" to other relevant information to help make decisions. For example, if managers see a change in income in a product line, they can call up the records related to these products to see where changes have occurred. In the future, these digital dashboards are expected to be available for mobile Internet devices.

CHECKPOINT

Describe the three ways technology improves business efficiency.

12.2 ASSESSMENT

UNDERSTAND MANAGEMENT CONCEPTS
Determine the best answer for each of the following questions.

1. A company that wants its data to be organized in a way that makes the data easy to find, update, and manage would use a(n)
   a. information system
   b. firewall
   c. DDS
   d. database
2. To prevent unauthorized entry into a computer network, a company should use a(n)
   a. digital dashboard
   b. firewall
   c. network
   d. anti-hacking system

THINK CRITICALLY
Answer the following questions as completely as possible.

3. Describe the role of a CIO in a business.
4. Describe the advantages that information systems offer to businesses.

F⊕cus On...Innovation

The Net's Booster Rocket—The Web

The purpose of the first crude Internet was as an emergency communication system for the military in case an enemy attack knocked out more conventional means of communication. Soon after this important goal was achieved, experts began using the slow, unreliable, and troublesome military Internet to share research findings. Improvements were continually being made, but the system's clumsiness and the need for technical knowledge limited its growth. However, the stage was set for the next breakthrough.

In 1989, Tim Berners-Lee, an English physicist who had been working at the European Particle Physics Laboratory, created the World Wide Web. This relatively unknown Web inventor developed a means for using the Internet to send more than just typed material to any computer in the world. What was needed was a global Internet-based hypermedia means for sharing global information. His new system permitted multimedia—graphics, videos, animations, and sounds—to be sent over the Internet. The Net's popularity grew by leaps and bounds as further refinements were made. The laboratory also created the first web browser, leading to navigation through hyperlinks. The marriage of the Internet and the Web led to rapid global acceptance during the last decade of the twentieth century.

Tim Berners-Lee believes the Web is a powerful force for social and economic change and that it has already modified how we conduct business, entertain ourselves, find information, and swap ideas. His goal is to keep the Web wide open and free to everyone, but he expects the Web will continue to alter our lives. He resisted efforts by major corporations to own and operate parts of the Web, because that would lead to charging user fees, which would not make it free. As the director of the World Wide Web Consortium, Berners-Lee discusses Web refinements with other consortium members worldwide. The group also oversees and recommends solutions to a variety of problems.

Tim Berners-Lee could easily have become very rich if he had personally built his own Web business or worked with a major computer firm to exploit it. He chooses to guide his creation to benefit humankind first and foremost. *Time* magazine named him one of the greatest geniuses of the twentieth century. He is not a household name like Albert Einstein. However, unlike many other famous people before him, he has his own website.

THINK CRITICALLY

1. Why was the first Internet created? Why didn't the early version of the Internet catch on with everyone?

2. How did the addition of the WWW increase use of the Internet?

3. Do you think Tim Berners-Lee would be happier being the CEO of a highly successful firm making millions more than he is making now as an employee in nonprofit organizations?

4. Using a library or the Internet, find out more about Tim Berners-Lee and write a report for the class.

© Shutterstock/Rick Becker-Leckrone

12.3

Technology and Business Strategy

Goals

- Describe technology's impact on strategy.
- Describe the planning process for developing an online business.
- Discuss types of problems that employees face in today's high-technology organizations.

Terms

- data mining p. 316
- social networking p. 317
- e-business p. 318
- web server p. 320
- web-hosting service p. 320
- domain name p. 320
- electronic shopping carts p. 320
- carpal tunnel syndrome (CTS) p. 322
- ergonomics p. 322

●●● Technology's Impact on Strategy

One of the roles of a manager is to develop and implement strategic plans for the company, division, or product. A key component of developing a strategy is to collect information on customers, competition, and the business environment. Information used in strategic planning comes from internal or external sources. Internal information can be pulled from the company's database or digital dashboard. External information can be collected from a variety of online sources.

Just as you use the Internet to gather information for a school project or report, managers use the Internet for research. Much of the information on the Internet is free and is provided by government agencies, colleges and universities, libraries, and even private businesses. Other information that businesses need can be purchased from companies specializing in research, professional associations, trade groups, and publishers. For example, Dun & Bradstreet and Hoovers provide specialized research reports, information, and publications for businesses. They provide both industry and company data.

CUSTOMER DATA

Have you ever had a website suggest products or provide advertisements that seem to be directly related to your interests? This is the result of businesses gathering and analyzing user information. Businesses can serve current and prospective customers better when they can link online activities to individuals. Social networking sites have rich data that can be used to develop user profiles.

Data collected from online behavior are placed into databases where data mining techniques are used to create information. **Data mining** is the process of using data in databases to find relationships between individuals and their behavior or preferences. For example, when an individual purchases a product with a credit card or a debit card, a track is created back to the purchaser. A record of an individual's purchases can be matched to any other information a company has on the individual. Companies use this type of information for a number of decisions. For example, decisions about inventory for a new store can be made based on customer profiles in a region. New products that match customers' needs can be introduced that match customers' needs.

DEVELOPING CUSTOMER PROFILES When companies sell products, they often encourage purchasers to complete a product registration online. Mining the data can identify not only who purchases or is interested in which products, but it can also identify relationships to others who may share the same product interest or purchase intentions.

People who regularly use the Internet are more likely to complete a product registration if it is online than if they have to fill in a registration card by hand and mail it. The registration process allows the company to collect important customer profile information, including address, telephone number, and an e-mail address. Also, the company can gather information on where the product was purchased, the price, reasons for purchasing the product, and other related products the consumer currently owns or plans to purchase. Whenever an individual provides information, a business should include a place where the prospective customer can request information, be placed on an e-mail or mailing list, or obtain answers to specific questions. This allows the company to develop a list of prospective customers and determine their specific interests. The information can be used for future communications and promotions.

A company's database collects data when an individual engages in actual or potential purchase behavior on a website. Websites can track clicks on links to an individual computer or to a registered user. This can show areas of interest to the individual. For example, many retailers use customer searches and purchases to suggest other products or services that match those interests. Registration allows for more in-depth analysis of a customer's preferences because searches or purchases are linked to an individual and not just a computer. The privacy policies of many companies will specifically state how they use customer data.

How can businesses use social networking sites to increase business around the globe?

Product coupons are not just offered through print media. Product coupon websites link registration to product interests. These sites can track customer profiles to requested coupons. Information collected by the coupon companies allow for targeted coupons to customers, and the coupon companies can sell the information they collect to manufacturers. The manufactures can add the customer profile information to their databases to aid in future decision making.

A growing phenomenon on the Internet is the use of social networking sites such as Facebook and LinkedIn. **Social networking** allows users to post information about themselves and share that information with others. These sites are virtual communities. Individuals who use social networks provide personal information about their activities, interests, and opinions. Social networking sites can match advertisements and product offerings to these lifestyle factors. When a user chooses a

relationship status, indicates a like or dislike, selects a group or association, or specifies a hobby or interest, the social networking site captures key terms. These key terms are used to develop customer profiles that allow for targeted advertisements. The advertisements for golf clubs and vacation cruises that a retiree sees when she goes to her social networking site do not appear when a twenty-year-old musician goes to his site. Social network sites were expected to earn more than $6 billion in advertising revenue worldwide in 2011, up from $350 million in 2006.

COMPETITOR DATA

Companies with publicly traded stock will often post their annual reports to stockholders and other information online. Companies that offer products for sales online will post product descriptions, prices, credit terms, distribution policies, and the types of customer services offered. Some websites provide information on product tests, offer reviews of products, and even have places for consumers to discuss their experiences with a company and its products.

Privately held businesses and those that do not sell online will often have less information open to the public. However, the Internet does allow for easy searches on companies by looking at news releases and other sources of industry information.

CHECKPOINT

Describe the data that businesses collect over the Internet.

E-Business Planning

Managers must decide how e-business will fit into their company's strategic planning. **E-business** uses communication technology to support business operations. Many customers use the Internet as the first tool to learn about a business. They visit a company's website to research a company and its products. They might also visit competitors' websites. Large businesses invest millions of dollars in creating and managing their Internet operations. Managers of small businesses can compete by create attractive, professional-looking websites using commercially available Web authoring software. Whether businesses create the websites themselves or hire professional Web designers to do it, managers must still carefully plan the design and content of their site and update it regularly to keep customers coming back.

Managers must evaluate the three major parts of an e-business strategy: business planning, technology development, and site promotion. These strategic issues are important for businesses that sell to individual customers as well as businesses that sell to other businesses.

BUSINESS PLANNING FOR A WEBSITE

The first step in business planning for a website is to determine the purpose. Managers need to decide if the business will operate online only or the website will be just one part of the business. A manager needs to be able to answer the question, what will users be able to do when they visit the site? Some businesses operate only online. Amazon.com is an example. It has no stores; it sells books and other products through its website only. For a company that has its entire business online exclusively, the purpose is clear. The website needs to provide information, allow interaction with customers, and integrate with all aspects of the business.

Some products and services are easier to sell over the Internet than others. A dental practice is an example of a business that cannot operate only online. Patients cannot get their teeth cleaned at the website. Nevertheless, a dental practice can still take advantage of the Internet. A dentist might choose to have an information-only website that provides a list of services, staff bios, office address, and telephone number. Another option is to have a website that is informational and interactive. Interactive components might include allowing users to get driving directions, schedule appointments, pay bills, and search for information about dental health.

Many businesses choose to have a website that is a companion to their more traditional business operations. Many large retail chains have traditional stores as well as websites. This allows customers to interact by using the website, visiting a store, or doing both.

As part of the process of identifying the purpose of the website, managers should study the sites of similar businesses and talk to experts. Some businesses opt to start using the Internet for a limited set of business activities at first and progress toward full integration, while other develop a plan to start with a fully integrated site. Limiting the goals for their site to the informational or interactive stage might be a good option for some businesses.

The second strategic step in business planning for a website is to study the business's customers, their needs, and their online experience. To develop a website that customers will use, managers must identify their customers, know what their customers want, and understand their customers' level of interest for doing business online. Managers need to know whether their customers use the Internet primarily for information gathering or for purchasing products. They need to know which products customers typically buy online, and which ones they are more likely to buy from a bricks-and-mortar business. When managers understand their customers, they can ensure their website is designed to be inviting and give customers confidence in developing a relationship with the business.

The third step is to plan the design aspects of the e-business website. Based on the strategic analysis, the manager will need to determine how the website should be an information-only, interactive, or integrated website. A website can inform customers about a business and its products, close the sale for products, and provide links to service. Good design allows users to easily access all aspects of the business's website goals. This includes deciding on overall design themes, which specific products and services (if any) will be available online, and how users will be able to purchase products and access services. For most businesses that are

Management MATTERS

Managing Tech Employees

Technology companies often top the list of *Fortune Magazine*'s "Top Companies to Work For" ratings. Being paid well and working on exciting new products are among the reasons tech companies make the list, but some of the perks offered by these businesses might have an impact. Google offers perks such as free gourmet cafeterias, a climbing wall, and free laundry. Zappos.com, an online shoe company, offers free lunches, no-charge vending machines, a full-time life coach, and a fun work culture. Although these perks may seem extravagant, they actually benefit both workers and employers. While employees are enjoying the perks, they are likely spending more time working and are less likely to leave to work for a competitor.

What Do You Think? Why are these perks important to tech workers and their companies? Why would a company be concerned about being rated as a top company to work for?

not entirely online, the manager must determine where and how the brick-and-mortar part of the business will fit strategically with the online part of the business.

The fourth step is to decide how the e-business will host its technology. Managers must decide if the business will develop and host the website or outsource some aspect to another company. For example, there are businesses that can facilitate all online processes including hosting a site, managing inventory, handling credit card transactions, and coordinating shipping with companies such as FedEx or UPS. The fees charged by these e-business facilitators depend upon the services used.

TECHNOLOGY DEVELOPMENT

An e-business relies on technology for operations. Information sent over the Internet requires access to a **web server**—a computer that contains the software and stores the data for networks. A web server is the backbone of an e-business. In addition to the server, the website must be easily accessible to a large number of customers at the same time, at any time. If customers cannot access a business's website, they may not return to the business.

Managers of new and small businesses often find that they do not have adequate computer or network technology or the necessary technical skills to build and manage a website. In this case, the managers may decide to use a web-hosting service. A **web-hosting service** is a private business that maintains the websites of individuals and organizations on its computers for a fee. The web-hosting service often provides design services, the hardware and software needed to maintain websites, and the technical personnel to make sure the sites operate effectively.

Web servers are accessed by an IP address, much like a phone number. This is linked to a domain name, such as Cengage.com or USA.gov. A **domain name** is a website owner's unique name that identifies the site. Most business addresses use the format www.businessname.com. Cengage.com is a domain name, but it has multiple Internet domains or server addresses (mirrored sites) to handle high usage. Before a business can use a domain name, it must register with one of several companies that maintain and approve all domain names used throughout the world.

ORDER PROCESSING An e-business that wants to process orders and collect payments online will need special software. **Electronic shopping carts** are programs that keep track of shoppers' selections as they shop, provide an order form for them to complete, and submit the form to the company through the Internet.

A business needs a secure server to accept credit card payments while protecting customers' personal data from theft. In addition, credit card transactions must be processed through a credit card clearinghouse. These companies help to ensure that credit cards and purchases are not fraudulent by checking against credit card company databases. Customers expect online orders to be processed and delivered quickly and accurately. Managers need to make sure customers have a positive shopping experience. This includes the online experience as well as after-purchase services such as accepting returns and replacing damaged products.

WEBSITE DESIGN This step in developing an online business may seem to be out of order. Many managers want to design the website as the first step. However, until the e-business plan is completed, managers will not know what needs to go on the website. To be successful, websites must be attractive and easy to use.

If customers cannot find the information they need, if the site takes a long time to load, or if ordering instructions are confusing, prospective customers will leave and go to a competitor's website. Websites should use a design with easy-to-understand buttons and links. If customers can purchase products through the website, the shopping and ordering procedures should be obvious and simple. Shoppers should be assured of security and customer service.

SITE PROMOTION

Unless managers promote their e-business, prospective customers may not learn about an online business. In addition, current customers can be lost to competitors. Two steps will help managers promote their e-business.

First, the e-business should register with the major search engines, such as Bing, Google, and Yahoo! Each search engine has an electronic means for collecting site addresses and categorizing them by keywords so that searches can find them. However, a manager can make sure search engines include the business's site under appropriate keywords by registering the site with the search engines directly. Registration information is available at each search engine's website.

It is important to place advertising for a business in other online locations where prospective customers are likely to search for information related to the products and services sold. The business may want to sponsor sites that are popular with customers who may have an interest in the business or its products. Managers need to make sure their web address is included in all materials the business distributes and in all advertising.

The second step is to advertise and promote the e-business offline. Although being on a search engine can be useful, it will not necessarily drive viewers to a website. The business may be one of thousands in the search engine database. If the site doesn't make it to the first or second search page, it may never be viewed.

The domain name should be placed on all company materials such as business cards, brochures, and correspondence. Traditional media can create an interest in a site. Then individuals may search for your company's name or go directly to the website.

OPEN FOR BUSINESS

After careful planning and testing, a website is ready to open for business. Once the website is up and running, managers have many responsibilities. Managers are responsible for making sure that the website is maintained properly and updated regularly. They also need to keep in contact with customers to get feedback about the website and purchasing experiences. Visiting other websites allows managers to learn about products and services offered by competitors and to see how other businesses communicate with their customers online. Managers need to keep up with the latest technology and online business procedures to make sure their business continues to be successful.

What are the goals of the USA.gov website?

CHECKPOINT

Describe the three main tasks of e-business planning.

●●●● Technology's Impact on Work and Workers

Computers, the Internet, and other forms of electronic technology affect people's lives as consumers and as workers. The work of employees has changed because of new technological devices and because firms have restructured their operations. Over the last several decades, computers have changed the ways individuals perform work tasks. This has resulted in large gains in work productivity and job flexibility. At the same time, technology change has caused anxieties in people about electronic devices that may affect their health, about job security, and about their ability to cope with new technology.

HEALTH PROBLEMS

Managers need to address health problems faced by employees in modern work environments. In some factory settings, employees face danger because of the work they do or the machinery they use. While jobs that use technology may not use equipment that is inherently dangerous, long hours spent doing repetitive work on a keyboard, looking at a computer screen, or sitting can result in injuries.

Certain complaints arise among workers who spend most of their work time using computers and other automated equipment. Employees may complain about eyestrain, backaches, and hand weakness and pain. Eyestrain is likely to occur when computer operators view computer screens for long periods. To reduce or eliminate eyestrain, managers can suggest adjusting light intensity on screens, shading screens from glare, wearing glare-reducing glasses, and taking breaks every few hours. For some employees, sitting for long periods can cause back and hand problems. Managers can help by making sure that employees have proper workspaces and furniture so that keyboards and chairs are at the proper height for safety and comfort. Proper chair design with good back support can help prevent and alleviate discomfort. Breaks from being seated for long periods are helpful.

Repetitive motion such as using a computer keyboard can lead to a specific type of injury. **Carpal tunnel syndrome (CTS)** occurs when the median nerve, which runs through a tunnel in the wrist, is compressed or irritated. This can result in tingling and numbness in the fingers and hand, pain in the wrist and arm, and weakness that can limit the ability to grasp and hold things. Chances of developing CTS can be reduced by proper posture when using a computer, using a wrist rest or an ergonomic keyboard, and limiting repetitive motion involving the wrist. Treatment for CTS usually starts with rest, icing, medication, and immobilization of the wrist. Surgery is an option in some cases.

To help combat the problems outlined above, managers can adopt a number of strategies. One strategy is to embrace ergonomic designs. **Ergonomics** is the science of adapting equipment to the work and health needs of people. Ergonomic experts study the relationships between people and machines. In recent years, ergonomic experts have focused on making computer hardware, software, furniture, and lights adjustable, practical, and comfortable. For example, they work with industrial designers and engineers to develop chairs that can be adjusted to provide comfort and proper back support. Another strategy for managers is to encourage workers take breaks, exercise, and rotate tasks.

CHANGED JOBS

A major role of today's managers is to manage change. The rapid rate at which changes occur can be disruptive. To survive, businesses must be adaptable and employees must change to meet the needs of employers.

Nearly all jobs have been restructured in recent years and new jobs are evolving. Large numbers of employees use computers to complete tasks that were once done manually. Auto mechanics use computers to diagnose engine trouble, physicians manipulate digital x-ray images to diagnose disease, and lawyers research cases using massive legal databases. In addition to workers learning to use technology for their current jobs, some workers are seeing their jobs, and even their titles, change dramatically. For example, most secretaries have had title changes and seen their jobs grow to include higher-level tasks and more responsibility. As administrative assistants, these workers may take on leadership roles, serve as members of work teams, coordinate projects, and train employees on how to use electronic equipment.

Managers must take advantage of technology changes to reengineer, or redesign, the workflow process. The general result of this has been improved quality with fewer workers, far greater customer satisfaction, higher ranking among competitors, and improved employee morale. Computerization and new technology have reduced the need for some skills and increased the need for others. Today's employees must have technical skills as well as interpersonal skills. For example, employees who work at computer help desks assist workers who have computer problems. Help desk employees must have interpersonal skills, such as a friendly personality and a willingness to help others. They must also have technical knowledge about hardware and software along with problem-solving skills.

In addition to changing the nature of some jobs, technology creates new jobs. Examples include computer programmers, network administrators, systems analysts, software trainers, website designers, and computer repair technicians. Technology is also changing when and where people work. Telecommuting allows employees to work at home using computers, the Internet, and wireless communication to complete their job assignments. Technology even allows individuals to work as entrepreneurs who start and run their own businesses from home. Many popular Internet businesses were started from the homes of entrepreneurs.

THE FUTURE IMPACT OF TECHNOLOGY

Managers must always align their strategic planning to a changing environment. Over the last decade, changes in technology have been a major driver and will continue to force change. Super high-speed networks allow much more information to move even faster around the world. Cellular-based Internet access allows workers and customers access to company and product information. Technology is also allowing information and communication to flow across national borders. The question for managers is, should they take the risk of leading change with technology or should they take the risk of being too late to adapt? Some of the major technological trends facing managers in the next few years are outlined below.

- **Data mining** As more information is collected, data mining will become more valuable in understanding customers' needs and allow for more targeted products and communication. For example, grocery stores use scanner data to determine which product mix is purchased by customers in a market profile.

Technology Literacy

Managers need to understand how employees, customers, and other stakeholders use technology to find, organize, evaluate, and communicate information. It is also important for managers to develop their own technology skills and to be interested in emerging technologies.

- **Social shopping** This emerging trend allows customers to use social networks to shop together or couponing sites such as Groupon and Living Social to gather shoppers together at a business. Businesses use these sites to promote special shopping opportunities in stores and restaurants.
- **Biometric security** To enhance security, biometric systems such as voice recognition and eye scans are being used to identify individuals to allow access to rooms, buildings, computers, and point-of-service terminals.
- **Wireless technology** Wireless systems can communicate not only with computers, but also with almost any other electronic device over an Internet connection. These systems are already being used to control home heating and cooling, lights, and security systems.
- **Cell phone technology** Business applications allow smart phones to act as information hubs, which allow users to input data directly to a central location. For example, nurses in hospitals use cell phones to enter medical reports and receive information to help meet patient's needs.

CHECKPOINT

List five future technology changes managers must consider.

12.3 ASSESSMENT

UNDERSTAND MANAGEMENT CONCEPTS

Determine the best answer for each of the following questions.

1. If a business cannot host its own e-commerce site, it could use a
   a. domain service
   b. web-hosting service
   c. server company
   d. all of the above

2. Which of the following is *not* true about ergonomics?
   a. Ergonomics studies the relationships between people and machines.
   b. Ergonomics engineers design systems that reduce strain.
   c. Ergonomics includes the use of lighting.
   d. All of the above are true.

THINK CRITICALLY

Answer the following questions as completely as possible.

3. Describe how a search engine can help promote a business.
4. Explain why managing change is important for today's managers.

CHAPTER CONCEPTS

- Managers and employees have accepted the Internet and computer technologies as major tools in the operation of their businesses and their jobs.

- The Internet is a worldwide network of linked computers that permits users to share data and information over phone lines or cable. The development of the World Wide Web made the Internet accessible to the public through web browsers and hyperlink navigation.

- The chief information officer is accountable for managing all of an organization's electronic information and supporting systems that help employees make timely and informed decisions.

- Business information systems include management information systems, decision support systems, and executive information systems.

- Technology is having an impact on how businesses undertake strategic planning by allowing for vast amounts of information on competition and customers. E-businesses engage in strategic planning to reach goals, choose the technology needed, and inform the market of the website.

- Technology has affected employees in both positive and negative ways.

REVIEW BUSINESS MANAGEMENT TERMS

Write the letter of the term that matches each definition. Some terms will not be used.

1. Website owner's unique Internet name
2. Prediction that the amount of data that could be processed by a computer chip would double about every 18 months
3. Programs that keep track of shoppers' selections, provide an order form for them to complete, and submit the form to the company over the Internet
4. Network of linked computers that serves users in a single building or building complex
5. Data that have been processed in some meaningful way that is useful to decision makers
6. Virtual community where people share information about themselves
7. Top computer executive in an organization
8. Program that assists in locating information on the Internet
9. Collection of data organized in a way that makes the data easy to find, update, and manage
10. Information system that integrates data from various departments to help managers with day-to-day business operations
11. Information system that helps managers consider alternatives in making specific decisions
12. Using the Internet for telephone services

a. chief information officer (CIO)
b. cloud
c. database
d. decision support system (DSS)
e. domain name
f. electronic shopping carts
g. information
h. local area network (LAN)
i. management information system (MIS)
j. Moore's law
k. search engine
l. social networking
m. Voice over Internet Protocol (VoIP)
n. web-hosting service

Determine the best answer.

13. If a company wanted an Internet based system that would use web pages to allow workers to access company information behind a firewall, it would use a(n)
    a. internet
    b. intranet
    c. extranet
    d. website

14. Knowledge workers are
    a. people who work with information
    b. computer programmers only
    c. college professors only
    d. CIOs only

15. The technique used by companies to look at large amounts of data in databases to identify consumer behaviors and trends is called
    a. data hacking
    b. software mining
    c. computer analysis
    d. data mining

16. If managers want an information system that allows for multiple sources of information to be displayed graphically on a computer, they would use a(n)
    a. application software
    b. decision system
    c. digital dashboard
    d. program software

17. A worldwide network of linked computers that allows users to transfer data and information from one computer to another anywhere in the world is
    a. a wide area network
    b. the Internet
    c. a local area network
    d. all of the above

18. To share certain information with selected people outside a company, such as suppliers and major customers, the company would use a(n)
    a. intranet
    b. extranet
    c. Internet
    d. wide area network

19. An information system that combines and summarizes ongoing transactions within the company to provide top-level executives with information needed to make decisions affecting the present and future goals and direction of an organization is a(n)
    a. information support system (ISS)
    b. decision support system (DSS)
    c. executive information system (EIS)
    d. management information system (MIS)

Answer the following questions.

20. Describe why both managers and employees could be considered knowledge workers.
21. Describe how businesses have benefited from the efficiencies that have resulted from the use of electronic technology.
22. Explain how management information systems use data to help businesses operate.
23. Describe the techniques that are being tried to make sure that the wrong people do not gain access to information on a firm's computer system.
24. On what types of Internet sites would you advertise to make prospective customers aware of a new business?

MAKE ACADEMIC CONNECTIONS

Complete the following activities

25. **Math** The CIO of Smythville, Inc. has proposed spending $20,000 on a new security firewall for the company's network. The company president believes that there is only a 2 percent chance that there could be a security breach and the total loss would be less than $1 million dollars. Should Smythville, Inc. implement the new firewall? At what level of risk or loss would you change your recommendation? If you were CIO, what would you recommend?

26. **Research** Using a library or the Internet, find information about a specific ergonomic problem related to working with electronic equipment, such as one related to radiation from computer equipment, uncomfortable chairs, or poorly designed desks. Prepare a report of your findings.

27. **Technology** Trina Jones is considering purchasing phones with the latest technology for her employees. She wants to determine the yearly cost for each type of phone. Phone 1 costs $300 and has a monthly charge of $65. Phone 2 costs $225 and has a monthly charge of $85. Phone 3 costs $100 and has a monthly charge of $105. Use spreadsheet software to answer the following questions. What would be the total annual cost for each phone? Assume Trina's employees will use the phones for two years at the same monthly cost. Which phone is the least expensive over two years?

28. **Writing** Join other students to write a report about any trouble group members have had with losing data and files from school or home computers. Present the report to your class, specifying the problems and indicating the security steps that could be taken to prevent or reduce these problems.

CASE 12: Technology-driven Job Redesign

Mei Shen and Jack Compton are employed at the Waterside Company, a small life insurance firm. Both Mei and Jack have been with the business for more than 10 years but are now quite upset by recent events. The office manager announced yesterday that all employees must attend several all-day training sessions on two coming changes. A new computer system is replacing the old one, and jobs are being restructured to improve processes that will lead to greater efficiency and productivity.

Unlike past practice, the new plan will have each person in the office doing all of the tasks now done separately. The training will prepare them to do everyone else's work, but all work will be done on the computer. To even the workload, all ten standard insurance policies will be loaded onto each computer, and employees and salespersons will be assigned specific customers on an alphabetic basis. When a salesperson calls with questions, the designated office worker can find the answers immediately. With the old system, answers might take as long as two weeks to get to customers.

The new computerized system has been installed but will not be used until all employees are trained. Mei and Jack have just returned from the first day's training session. The following conversation takes place:

Jack: *I don't know about you, Mei, but this change is just like coming to an entirely new job. I don't know how all of this is going to work out.*

Mei: *We should have at least been told about this in advance, rather than have it come as a complete surprise. We could easily get a job at another insurance company. Maybe we should quit. The company isn't willing to give us more money to learn all the new procedures, new software, and new computers. With our experience, we shouldn't have any trouble finding a new job.*

Jack: *Hold on, Mei. We shouldn't be too hasty. We make good money here, but I agree that they should have told us about this so we could have been doing some reading and getting ourselves ready for the change. If the system works well, our jobs will be more secure. Most other insurance companies already operate the new way.*

Mei: *From what we learned today, we could certainly make the company sorry that they didn't get our opinions before deciding to change computers and our jobs.*

THINK CRITICALLY

1. Describe what mistake the Waterside Company management made in replacing the computer system.
2. In what ways could Mei make the company regret not involving the employees in the decision? Explain.
3. If the new computer system is to be successful, will it be because of restructuring the work, installing a new computer system, or both? Explain your answer.
4. If the new changes are successful, how will the salespeople and customers benefit?

PROJECT My Own Business

Computer Systems Analysis

As the owner of a new business, you will spend a great deal of time dealing with information. Poorly organized business records would make it hard for you to find and use the information you need. Use the following activities to review information management systems for small businesses and make decisions about how technology will benefit your business.

DATA COLLECTION

1. Interview the owner of a small business and discuss the type of information management system used in the business. In your own words, ask the following questions: (a) What type of records and information are maintained? (b) Is the system computer-based? (c) Who is responsible for information management? (d) How could the system be improved?

2. Visit a computer systems retailer and discuss the hardware and software the retailer recommends for new small businesses. Collect information on system prices, capabilities, and ease of operation.

3. Visit an office furniture company in person or online and investigate ways to create an ergonomically healthy work environment for your employees.

4. Use the Internet to identify companies that offer information management services for businesses. Go to the companies' websites to determine the types of services offered and prices charged for those services.

ANALYSIS

1. Create a list of the types of information that your business will need. Identify the hardware and software that you will need to turn data into information useful to management. Describe the types of skills you or your employees will need to use and maintain both the hardware and the software that your company will be using.

2. The Internet can be a very valuable tool for small businesses. Identify and describe five specific types of information accessible through the Internet that can help you develop and manage your business. Then use an Internet search engine to identify one or more sites that supply each type of information you listed.

3. List three ways that e-commerce might have a negative effect on your business and three ways that you might use e-commerce to improve your new business.

CHAPTER 13

ORGANIZATIONAL COMMUNICATIONS

13.1 The Communication Process

13.2 Communication Management

13.3 Organizational Communication

Reality Check

Many Ways to Communicate

Erica Komuro, one of many managers for a multinational corporation, sat at her desk looking at the next day's schedule on her computer. In the morning, she would review the new organization chart for her department that would appear in the employees' manual. Later she would meet with two other managers and her boss to resolve a conflict. She dreaded the shouting match that was sure to occur between two people who never agreed on anything.

The afternoon would include interviewing a candidate for the position of social media specialist and giving her best worker instructions on how to perform a new assignment. Then Erica would write a few business letters and e-mail messages. She also had to finish her monthly report for the division manager. If the morning meeting did not drag on, Erica might also have time to return phone calls that came in while she was dealing with a customer relations problem. Perhaps she could also squeeze in a call to Sabrina in accounting to learn more about a rumor regarding the sudden resignation of the vice president.

After she finished thinking about tomorrow, she scrolled through the next few days of her calendar to see what was coming up. When she saw a teleconference with Mr. Nozaki on her schedule for Friday, she blocked off some time on Thursday to prepare. She was not sure how to deal with the major problems this manager was having running the Tokyo office. At least she could recall a few Japanese words from earlier days when her family lived in Kyoto.

Before she turned off her computer, Erica checked her phone to be sure her e-mail and calendar were linked in and her files were updated. As she closed the office door, she smiled and waved to the workers who were just starting to dust the furniture and vacuum the carpets. On the way to her car she thought, "Tomorrow will be a busy day."

What's Your Reaction? How much of Erica's workday is spent communicating? Do you think this is typical for most managers?

The Communication Process

Goals

- Describe the communication process and barriers to effective communication.
- Describe the various communication channels.

Terms

- communication p. 331
- feedback p. 332
- distraction p. 332
- distortion p. 333
- channel of communication p. 333
- nonverbal communication p. 334
- body language p. 334
- flame p. 335
- spam p. 336
- teleconferencing p. 336

●●● The Communication Model

Erica is a typical manager because much of her time is spent communicating—speaking, listening, writing, and reading. Managers communicate in person, by phone and fax, by e-mail, and by paper documents. They also communicate through other means, such as a smile, a frown, or a wave.

Communication is vital in running organizations. Communication provides a link between employees and customers and between employees and managers. In fact, it has been estimated that managers communicate more than two-thirds of each workday, as shown in Figure 13-1.

Communication is the sharing of information, in which the receiver understands the meaning of the message in the way the sender intended. Communication includes more than passing along factual data. It includes sharing ideas, beliefs, and opinions. It is a *two-way process* between senders and receivers. The

Managers' Communication Activities as a Percent of Time

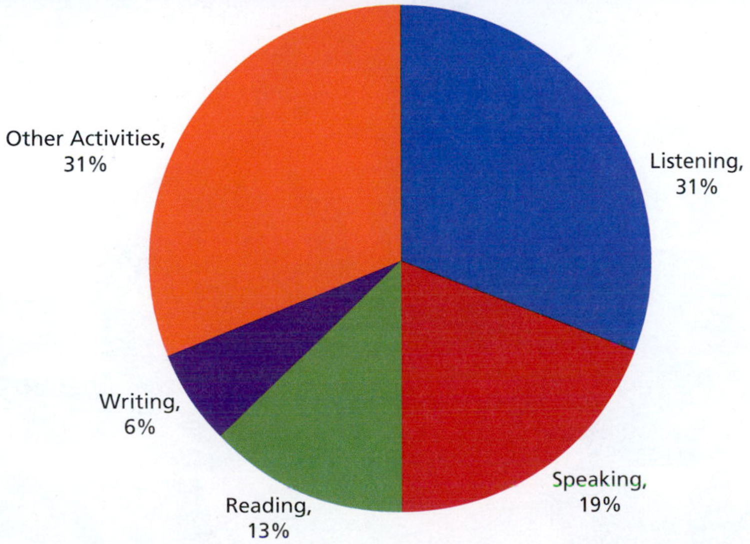

Other Activities, 31%

Listening, 31%

Writing, 6%

Speaking, 19%

Reading, 13%

© Cengage Learning 2013.

Figure 13-1 Managers spend most of their time communicating, especially listening and speaking.

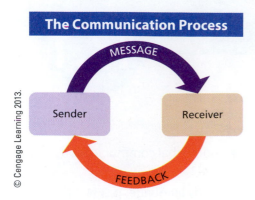

The Communication Process

MESSAGE

Sender → Receiver

FEEDBACK

© Cengage Learning 2013.

Figure 13-2 Feedback helps the sender and receiver make sure that both understand the meaning in the same way.

senders must put the information into clear words, and the receivers must try to understand the message as the senders intended. If the receivers do not fully understand the message or need more information, they should ask for clarification. Thus, feedback is critical to effective communication.

Feedback is a receiver's response to a sender's message. The response may be in the form of asking questions to clarify the meaning of a message. Or, receivers may restate the message in their own words, so that the senders can verify that the receivers understood the meaning as intended. The communication process and the role of feedback are illustrated in Figure 13-2.

Poor communication is one of the biggest problems managers face. Poor communication can lead to disagreements, faulty work, delayed performance, and industrial accidents. Two major barriers that interfere with communication are distractions and distortions.

DISTRACTIONS

Interruptions occur all too often while communicating. Anything that interferes with the sender's creating and delivering a message and the receiver's getting and interpreting a message is a **distraction**. Distractions are potential causes of communication problems. Two workers who whisper to each other during a meeting create a distraction that may cause a nearby worker to miss a point made by the manager. It may also cause the manager to forget to mention a point. Ringing phones, grammar errors in messages, and loud noises are other examples of barriers to communication.

Because distractions affect communication, some managers learn to work with various interruptions, whereas others try to keep interruptions to a minimum. For example, some managers place telephone calls or write messages during specific times of the day when interruptions are less likely to occur.

DISTORTIONS

When senders create messages, they must select the information they want to include. They need not include every bit of data surrounding an idea, event, or

What kinds of distractions can occur during a business meeting? How can these barriers to communication be overcome?

© Getty Images/Stockbyte

situation. Senders select only the information they think the receivers need in order to understand the message. Depending on the information selected, though, the message can become distorted. **Distortion** refers to how people consciously or unconsciously change messages.

Distortion is usually not deliberate. People unconsciously pass along only information they think others need. Often they leave out important data. Distortion may be deliberate, however, for self-enhancement or self-protection. For example, an employee may tell a supervisor about a machine breakdown but not admit that he or she did not oil the machine regularly. Or a manager may give an employee a very good rating because she likes him, even though the worker's performance may be only average.

Distortion can also occur because people often "hear" what they want to. We all bring our own perspectives to any situation. We filter messages we receive through our own system of beliefs and experience. Therefore, sometimes what we understand the sender to say was not at all what the sender meant. Receivers don't necessarily have to agree with the message, but they have a responsibility to use feedback to try to understand it as the sender intended.

CHECKPOINT

Describe the communication model and the factors that lead to poor communication.

Channels of Communication

A **channel of communication** is the means by which a message is conveyed. Channels can carry three types of communication: oral, written, and nonverbal. For example, print on paper channels carry mostly written communication. Radio broadcasts carry oral communication. Video broadcasts can carry oral, written, and nonverbal communication. New cellular systems allow personal digital devices to send and receive oral (voice), written (text), and nonverbal (images) communication.

ORAL COMMUNICATION

In the opening story, we learned that Erica's schedule for the next business day is nearly filled with oral communications. Speaking with employees, attending meetings, and receiving and making phone calls consume a great deal of a manager's time. Day-to-day communications require frequent contact with people on a one-to-one basis. That contact may be formal, as when Erica interviews a potential employee, or it may be informal, as when she chats with another employee about the company picnic. Giving employees oral instructions is an especially common and significant task. How well managers communicate determines in great part how high they rise on the management ladder.

WRITTEN COMMUNICATION

Written business communications take many forms. The most common are e-mails, reports, memos, and letters. Other written communications include

21st CENTURY SKILLS

Responsibility

Often employees receive e-mail messages that are not related to work, such as jokes or product solicitations. These e-mails should not be forwarded to other employees. They are a distraction, and they can be tracked back to the sender.

manuals, invoices, telephone messages, and notes. Written communications sent electronically include e-mails, faxes, and postings to social network sites or blogs.

Figure 13-3 lists some common uses for written business communication. For many businesses, this communication is delivered electronically through e-mail or attachments to e-mail messages. The average manager receives over 100 e-mails a day, with about 15 percent of those e-mails having attachments.

To communicate effectively in writing, senders should compose messages using precise, unambiguous words and proper grammar. The messages should also be concise. Long or unnecessary messages contribute to information overload. In turn, information overload slows decision making and becomes an obstacle to effective use of work time. Written messages may also include the use of psychology. For example, good news should appear early in a message, and bad news should appear later, after the explanation.

NONVERBAL COMMUNICATION

Delivering messages by means other than speaking or writing is called **nonverbal communication**. Flashing lights, stop signs, and sirens are examples of physical ways to communicate. Even colors, such as the green, yellow, and red used for traffic lights, signal messages—go, caution, and stop. Nonverbal communication also appears in written documents in the form of charts, diagrams, and pictures. People also give nonverbal messages through their body movements. Gestures, movements, and mannerism used to communicate are called **body language**. Examples include frowns, smiles, posture, hand or body movements, or the presence or absence of eye contact. Nonverbal messages convey meaning as much as verbal messages do.

Managers should be aware of the nonverbal messages they convey to others and that others convey to them. These messages are often given unconsciously. Sometimes a nonverbal message confirms or contradicts a verbal message. For example, what impression would Erica get if the job applicant said, "I am extremely interested in the position," but came unprepared for the interview and wore jeans and a dirty T-shirt? If you were interviewing this person, which message would you believe—the verbal or nonverbal one? Actions often speak louder than words.

Examples of Written Business Communication	
Acknowledge or Make a Request	**Share an Idea or News**
• Acknowledge request for service	• Announce new product
• Give and refuse credit to customer	• Convince others about an idea
• Request credit from supplier	• Hire or reject job applicant
• Request interviews with job applicant	• Persuade others to take action
Provide or Request Information	**Show Respect or Courtesy**
• List features and benefits of a product	• Congratulate colleague on success
• Request transcript for job applicant	• Honor or commend employee
• Request information from supplier	• Offer sympathy to co-worker
• Sell goods and services	• Thank customer

© Cengage Learning 2013.

Figure 13-3 Written business communications serve many purposes.

Body language may get the message across better than the spoken word. What message is this businesswoman sending?

ELECTRONIC COMMUNICATION

Electronic communication can be verbal, written, or nonverbal. Electronic mail has changed written communication. Each day over 31 billion e-mail messages replace what otherwise would be paper correspondence. Evidence of the growth of e-mail is the decline of first-class mail handles by the U.S. Postal Service. E-mail is popular because it lowers communication costs, minimizes paper handling, speeds communications and decision making, and improves office productivity. Because of its rapid growth and widespread use, businesses have adopted policies and practices that address e-mail use. Managers are responsible for making sure employees understand and abide by these policies and practices.

E-MAIL POLICIES Some businesses establish e-mail policies to protect the organization, business partners, employees, and customers. Typically such policies state that employees should use e-mail only for job-related matters, with occasional exceptions. In fact, businesses can track all inbound and outbound messages and read them if they want. In general, employee communications cannot be considered private, because all employee actions represent the firm. Companies like General Electric remind employees as they log on that most Internet and e-mail use should be solely for business tasks and all activity may be recorded and reviewed.

Also, e-mail should not be considered private, because outsiders can access it. For that reason, some organizations install software programs that automatically self-destruct messages after a designated time, limit the number of times a message can be opened and read, and prevent the forwarding of messages.

Protecting the company from lawsuits is too critical to be left to chance. Jokes, off-color stories, and flame messages reflect negatively on the company image. A **flame** is an electronic message that contains abusive, threatening, or offensive content that may violate company policy or public law. Abusive sexual language, for example, can lead to a sexual harassment lawsuit by offended employees. Abusers are subject to dismissal and firms may be sued for allowing harassment situations to develop.

Cell phones are becoming the hub of electronic communication. What problems can arise from this trend?

E-MAIL PRACTICES Writing and responding to e-mail deserve the same courtesy that other written communication deserves. Good business writing requires that messages have a meaningful subject line as well as a pleasant but businesslike tone that gets to the point quickly and ends graciously. Most messages should be short. If necessary, documents and other files can be sent with the message as attachments.

Every e-mail message should follow good writing guidelines. Writers should construct sentences properly, without spelling errors. Quickly proofreading a message before sending it is worth the time and effort to avoid embarrassing mistakes. Carefully prepared messages reflect on the writer and the organization. In addition to following good writing guidelines, e-mail users should be concerned about the content and tone of their messages. Rumors and gossip should not be shared through e-mail. Managers should keep in mind that e-mail messages can be archived for months or even years. Archived messages can provide valuable documentation in the future. Effective managers set standards for their own e-mail practices and for their employees.

Information overload is a common complaint of managers and workers in information-intensive jobs. High e-mail volume is often part of the problem. Most software programs allow users to sort incoming messages by senders or subject. This can help users prioritize messages and plan how to respond. Setting aside certain times of the day to respond to e-mail can be an effective time-management tool.

Dealing with unwanted e-mail, including spam, can take up valuable time. **Spam** is unsolicited advertising that finds its way into e-mail boxes. Most companies filter e-mail to prevent spam from getting to individual mailboxes. However, individual users must deal with other unwanted e-mail. In some situations, you may need to ask co-workers or subordinates to refrain from sending messages that do not relate to your work. At the same time, you must make sure that you are not creating similar problems for others. Taking a few seconds to consider the needs of others before forwarding a message, copying people on a message, or using the "reply to all" feature can help eliminate reduce unwanted e-mail.

TELECONFERENCING Business communication often takes place during meetings. **Teleconferencing** is an audio or video meeting with participants in two or more locations. Teleconferencing is an increasing part of business communication. It is likely that 75 percent of businesses will use some type of teleconferencing in the next few years.

Teleconferencing allows individuals in multiple locations to meet without the time and expense of traveling across town, across the country, or around the globe. Video teleconferences allow for near face-to-face communication. They also allow presenters to control monitors at remote locations to show videos, slide presentations, and other visuals. Teleconferences can be recorded so participants and others who did not attend a meeting can review communications in the future.

FACTS & FIGURES

Monitoring Employees

A 2008 survey by the American Management Association found that managers monitor employees e-mail, website usage, phone calls, and track employees through GPS. The goal is to monitor behavior in order to manage productivity, minimize litigation, improve security, and reduce other risks.

New cellular systems allow teleconferencing between handsets. This allows an individual to communicate with others face-to-face at remote locations without additional equipment.

WIRELESS The use of cellular phones is growing to dominate electronic verbal communication. New cellular devices allow not only voice communication, but also short message service (SMS) or text messaging, the sending of images, and Internet access. Worldwide, the number of text messages sent per year grew to 6.1 trillion by 2010, or almost 200,000 messages per second. Close to one billion wireless devices are able to access the Internet. Cellular devices allow a businessperson to use verbal, written, and nonverbal communication.

CHECKPOINT

List the three major types of communication.

13.1 ASSESSMENT

UNDERSTAND MANAGEMENT CONCEPTS

Determine the best answer for each of the following questions.

1. The way people consciously or unconsciously change messages is called
   a. feedback
   b. distortion
   c. noise
   d. misunderstanding

2. Approximately what percentage of a manager's time is spent listening?
   a. 10 percent
   b. 20 percent
   c. 30 percent
   d. 40 percent

THINK CRITICALLY

Answer the following questions as completely as possible.

3. Describe how the communication model works.
4. How can electronic communication be verbal, written, and nonverbal?

13.2

Communication Management

Goals

- Explain how organizational culture influences formal and informal communication networks.
- Describe how to manage teams effectively.

Terms

- organizational culture p. 338
- communication network p. 339
- formal communication networks p. 339
- informal communication networks p. 339
- grapevine p. 340
- nominal group technique (NGT) p. 341
- brainstorming p. 342

 **Organizational Culture**

A culture is the shared values, beliefs, and behavior patterns of a group of people. The group may be a corporation, a nation, or any other organized group. An **organizational culture** is the collection of beliefs and patterns of behavior that are shared by people within an organization. Each business has its own internal culture that influences the way formal and informal communications occur. Factors such as the type of business, the personalities of its leaders, and its operating procedures create this organizational culture. An organizational culture often influences the way people interact with each other and with people outside of the organization.

The culture of an organization influences the communication climate. Cultures differ widely among firms. Cultures may be very closed, very open, or somewhere in between. A closed culture is one that relies on top-down decision making and adheres to numerous rules and strict disciplining for violations of established procedures. Rigid rule making and authoritarian leadership can breed distrust and secrecy while discouraging creativity and decision making at lower levels. In such organizations, communications tend to be quite formal. Experts refer to this type of organization as having a closed communication system.

When trust and confidence prevail among employees, an organization is said to have an open communication system. This type of culture encourages creativity and problem solving at all levels and supports communication and information sharing. Trust, supportiveness, risk taking, and decision making influence whether an employee will like or dislike working for a company. In turn, these factors help determine how productive employees will be.

Most organizations have neither a fully open nor fully closed culture. Sometimes a business may change its culture. A comfortable culture for one person, however, may not be comfortable for another. Some employees prefer a culture with primarily an open communication system, whereas others prefer a culture with primarily a closed communication system. Employees often change jobs in search of an organization that has a set of beliefs, values, and practices suited to their needs.

COMMUNICATION NETWORKS

A **communication network** is the structure through which information flows in a business. Communication networks can be formal or informal.

FORMAL NETWORKS

A **formal communication network** is the system of official channels that carry organizationally approved messages. These channels generally follow the reporting relationships in the firm. Formal communication flows upward, downward, and across the organization in a prescribed manner. Typically, certain information, such as budget allocations, flows downward from top-level managers to lower-level managers. Other information, such as requests for budget expenditures, flows from the bottom to the top of the organization.

Upward communication includes oral and written reports from lower-level to upper-level managers. Usually, upper-level managers rely on lower-level managers for information that deals with new or unusual problems, the quality of employee performance, and the way employees feel about their jobs and the company. Supervisors receive upward communication from their subordinates about such things as project status and suggestions for making a task more efficient.

Organizations with closed, rather than open, communications are less likely to benefit from upward communication. Upward communication is subject to distortion, especially in corporate cultures that are relatively closed. Supervisors, for example, might withhold or distort upward-flowing information when problems appear to reflect negatively on their performance. On the other hand, a supervisor might exaggerate information about successes. In a closed culture, employees often fear revealing negative information and avoid making honest criticisms.

Downward communication in organizations occurs mainly by memos, e-mails, reports, and manuals. To be effective, this information should be timely and clear. In organizations with closed communications, there is often no opportunity for feedback, because information does not flow upward easily. However, in open cultures, employees receive downward-flowing information at meetings and their feedback is welcome.

Lateral communication flows horizontally or across the organization. For example, the production manager in one plant might want to know what problems other production managers face. Perhaps common problems could be solved jointly. However, many organizations do not have easy and fast channels for such communications. In a business with an open corporate culture, lateral communications are more likely to exist. One communication expert has estimated that 80 percent of poor management decisions occur because of ineffective communications.

INFORMAL NETWORKS
Like formal communication networks, informal networks exist in all organizations. **Informal communication networks** are the unofficial ways that employees share information in an organization. The most common informal networks include small informal groups and the grapevine. Informal networks rely heavily on interpersonal communications and e-mail.

A great deal of communicating occurs among small informal groups, especially among employees who get along well together. These employees may or may not have the same supervisors, but often they do. They share information about the organization, assist one another in solving work problems, and look after one another. Members may even support one another when conflicts arise with other employees. Most employees belong to a small informal group.

Office grapevines are the most common way employees communicate informally. What types of communication grapevines do you use?

© Getty Images/Photodisc

Managers should be aware of informal groups. Often informal groups have more influence than managers do over the behavior of individual workers. It is extremely important that informal groups support the efforts of the entire business. If they do not, informal groups can interfere with business goals and, in turn, hurt morale and decrease productivity. Managers often work closely with informal group leaders to obtain support and test new ideas.

An extensive amount of organizational communications occurs in an unofficial way through interpersonal relationships. Employees working side by side, for example, generally talk about their jobs and about personal matters. These conversations are normal and usually do not interfere with work. Employees also talk together on breaks, in the hall, or around the drinking fountain.

The informal transmission of information among workers is called the **grapevine**. In a grapevine, one person informally talks to another, and that second person talks to another, and so on. Informal messages travel quickly through the grapevine and can be distorted, because they are often based on unofficial, partial, or incorrect information. That is why grapevine messages are often labeled rumors. Very often, however, grapevines convey accurate messages. For example, when a formal memo announces that a manager has just retired for "personal reasons," the grapevine may provide the actual reason. The manager may have been asked to quit but was given the opportunity to resign voluntarily. When Erica Komuro calls Sabrina in Accounting, she may also learn that the rumor about the vice president's resignation is true.

Generally, managers should not interfere with grapevines. Grapevines often fill the social needs of workers to communicate about their work lives. Only when a grapevine message is inaccurate and negatively affects company business should managers attempt to correct the situation.

 CHECKPOINT

Describe the two types of communication networks.

Managing Teams Effectively

Managing teams is a vital skill for managers. Teams of individuals with different skills and backgrounds often work together on complex projects. To obtain the best results, managers must be able to ensure that all ideas are heard and considered. This helps produce better results and stronger buy-in to the team's recommendations. Managers often prefer team meetings when open communication is needed to encourage discussion and feedback. Team members doing the hands-on work often have good ideas about how to improve their work quality and efficiency. However, team meetings also have disadvantages. The chief disadvantage is the excessive time meetings take. Good managers overcome this weakness by careful planning and by following suggestions such as those shown in Figure 13-4.

A second major problem with team meetings occurs because of differences among those who attend the meetings. For example, an outspoken person may tend to dominate, whereas a quiet person may say nothing. Neither situation is desirable. The person who leads the meeting should encourage but control discussions, so that the team hears and discusses all ideas. Two methods used to encourage group thinking and problem solving are the nominal group technique and brainstorming.

Suggestions for Planning Effective Meetings

1. Have a good reason for calling a meeting.
2. Develop a specific agenda and stick to it.
3. Decide who should and who should not attend.
4. Determine how long the meeting will last.
5. Schedule the meeting at a convenient time and place.
6. Start and stop the meeting on time.
7. Encourage communications by arranging the seating so that participants face one another.
8. Summarize the results at the end of the meeting.

© Cengage Learning 2013.

Figure 13-4 Time spent planning a meeting is often offset by the time saved during the actual meeting.

NOMINAL GROUP TECHNIQUE

The **nominal group technique (NGT)** is a group problem-solving method in which team members write down and evaluate ideas to be shared with the team. For example, assume a manager needs to solve a long-standing problem. The manager begins by stating the problem and then follows the steps described in Figure 13-5.

The NGT encourages each team member to think about the problem, and it gives the quiet person and the outspoken person an equal opportunity to be heard. Private voting encourages employees to choose the best solutions rather than spend time defending their own suggestions. This technique has proven very effective.

BRAINSTORMING

Problems arise in business for which prior solutions do not exist or are no longer acceptable. One technique for handling such situations is brainstorming.

Steps in Using the Nominal Group Technique

1. Present the problem to be resolved to team members.
2. Distribute blank cards and, without discussion, ask members to write possible solutions by using a different card for each solution.
3. Read solutions from the cards and display for all to see.
4. Discuss each solution listed.
5. Distribute blank cards and ask members to write their three best solutions on separate cards.
6. Tabulate and display results.
7. Select the solution receiving the most agreement and present it to the team leader.

© Cengage Learning 2013.

Figure 13-5 NGT encourages each member of the team to participate.

Brainstorming is a team discussion technique used to generate as many ideas as possible for solving a problem. A team leader presents a problem and asks team members to offer any solution that comes to mind. Even wild and imaginative ideas are encouraged. The team should make no attempt to judge any ideas as good or bad while brainstorming is under way. Only after participants have identified all possible solutions should they begin to judge the usefulness of each one. Often, an idea that appeared to be impractical or unusual when first presented may become the best solution to the problem. Brainstorming is frequently used to deal with problems that need especially creative solutions, such as when generating new product ideas and creating advertisements.

CHECKPOINT

Explain the two methods used to encourage communication with teams.

13.2 ASSESSMENT

UNDERSTAND MANAGEMENT CONCEPTS

Determine the best answer for each of the following questions.

1. The system of official channels that carry organizationally approved messages is called a(n)
   a. sanctioned communication network
   b. official communication network
   c. formal communication network
   d. informal communication network

2. A team problem-solving method in which team members write down and evaluate ideas to be shared with the team is the
   a. team idea technique
   b. nominal group technique
   c. brainstorming
   d. none of the above

THINK CRITICALLY

Answer the following questions as completely as possible.

3. Describe how organizational culture influences communication.

4. Explain how managers overcome common problems that occur in team meetings.

Avoiding Disasters

In 1986, the space shuttle Challenger launched with a crew of seven, including a schoolteacher. Seventy-three seconds after launching on a cold January morning, the Challenger exploded. Eventually, the problem was traced to O-rings that should have sealed gaps in the solid fuel booster rockets.

Even though the O-ring failure was a technical problem, communication failure is considered the major cause of the disaster. Engineers of the company that built the boosters knew the O-rings did not perform well at low temperatures. When these engineers communicated their concerns to management, they used engineering terminology. Managers did not understand the importance of the information they received. The O-ring manufacturer told NASA that the cold weather could affect the O-ring, but they didn't stress enough the dangers of launching in cold weather. The information about the O-rings that did get to NASA was not forwarded to decision-makers responsible for final launch control.

NASA is not the only organization that has faced a disaster from lack of or poor communication. The 2010 BP oil spill in the Gulf of Mexico was partly due to lack of communication among the three companies involved in the drilling. There were also communication problems within BP that did not allow information about risks at the Deepwater Horizon well to move to top management.

In 2010, Toyota had to recall a large number of vehicles, eventually costing the company more than $2 billion. The CEO of Toyota Sales USA testified before Congress that complaints and information about defects from the United States, Europe, and China were not shared. As a result, Toyota was not able to spot problems early enough to take preventative actions.

It is difficult to predict catastrophic failures. However, many companies and industries have put strategies in place to reduce risk by improving communication between firms working on projects and improving communication within the business. The communication problems that surrounded these cases are now used as case studies on how to improve communication in an organization.

THINK CRITICALLY

1. What is there in common between the three situations outlined above?
2. How can pressure to perform in a business impact communication in a business?
3. Why would communication between these multiple businesses or multiple divisions be more complicated?
4. What strategies could a business use to ensure that communication failures are less likely to occur? How can an individual ensure that communication problems are less likely to occur?

13.3

Organizational Communication

Goals

- Describe different ways to resolve communication conflicts.
- Describe the problems that can occur with cross-cultural communication.
- Identify ways to improve communication in organizations.

Terms

- conflict p. 344
- avoidance strategy p. 345
- compromise strategy p. 345
- win/lose strategy p. 346

●●● Communication Conflicts

Managers deal with a variety of communication problems. Some problems that challenge the communication skills of managers involve resolving conflicts and handling cross-cultural communication effectively.

At times, people disagree with each other. Most job-related disagreements are likely to be temporary and easy to settle. Disagreements become a concern to a business when they lead to conflict. **Conflict** is interference by one person with the achievement of another person's goals. Conflicts usually occur between two people, but they may also occur between an individual and a group or between groups. Because conflicts are sometimes an obstacle to job performance, managers must deal with conflicts.

DESIRABLE CONFLICT

A small amount of conflict is sometimes beneficial, because it may challenge employees and stimulate new ideas. For example, the advertising manager may decide to budget as little as possible to advertise a particular product, whereas the sales manager may have decided to try to boost sales for that particular product through increased advertising. At this point, conflict exists because the goals set by each manager differ. However, this type of conflict can lead to a healthy discussion of how much to spend on advertising and how best to advertise to produce the highest sales at the lowest advertising cost. The result can lead to the achievement of a goal that is best for the business.

When employees discuss and resolve their conflicting goals, the organization can benefit. However, when conflicting goals are not resolved, long-term problems often result. If the sales and advertising managers went ahead with their individual plans, money would be wasted and sales would be lost.

UNDESIRABLE CONFLICT

Whereas some conflict in organizations may be healthy, too much conflict can be harmful. Undesirable conflict results when the actions of any person or group interfere with the goals of the organization. In the preceding example, if the sales manager became resentful of the advertising manager and undermined the company's budget goals by deliberately spending more than the amount agreed upon for the product, undesirable conflict would result. Employees who dislike others and carry grudges often cause problems for an organization. Therefore, undesirable conflicts should be resolved as soon as possible.

RESOLVING CONFLICT

Conflicts can be resolved in various ways. Because every situation is different, managers must decide which type of strategy will best resolve each conflict.

AVOIDANCE STRATEGY One strategy for resolving conflict is to take a neutral position or to agree with another person's position even though it differs from your personal belief. This approach, known as the **avoidance strategy**, avoids the conflict. One manager may decide to accept the goal of another manager or avoid expressing an opposing opinion about the goal. When a conflict is relatively unimportant, the avoidance strategy may be the best approach. However, if a disagreement involves important issues, avoidance is not a good strategy. It can often lead to resentment.

COMPROMISE STRATEGY A second way to resolve conflict is through a **compromise strategy**. Everyone involved in a conflict agrees to a mutually acceptable solution. Often, a compromise grows out of a thorough discussion of the goals and the best way to achieve those goals. This strategy is better than avoidance because it usually leads to a workable solution, as everyone involved personally contributes to the decision. Also, people are more likely to support a compromise solution that they have helped to develop.

© Getty Images/Photodisc

If handled properly, conflicts can be beneficial and productive. How do you handle conflict with another person?

© Getty Images/Digital Vision

Why is a compromise strategy generally the best solution to a conflict?

WIN/LOSE STRATEGY   The most dangerous approach to resolving conflict is a win/lose strategy. A **win/lose strategy** is one in which no one compromises, thereby resulting in one person winning and one losing. A win/lose strategy is never acceptable to everyone, although people often engage in such a strategy. Win/lose strategies interfere with the achievement of organizational goals because they often (1) take time and energy away from the main problems and issues, (2) delay decisions, (3) arouse anger that hurts human relationships, and (4) cause personal resentment, which can lead to other problems.

Because win/lose situations are destructive, managers should attempt to prevent them. Setting clear objectives that employees understand and agree on, stressing the need for cooperation in reaching objectives, and working for group decisions when special problems or disagreements arise are ways managers can avoid win/lose strategies.

 **CHECKPOINT**

List three ways that managers can resolve conflicts.

●●● Cross-Cultural Communication

A nation's culture sets the broad boundaries of shared values, beliefs, and behavior. Within the nation's culture, there are also subcultures or smaller groups with their own unique values, beliefs, and behavior. Subcultures can reflect regional differences, such as between the northeast and southwest United States. Subcultures also can exist within ethnic groups such as Hispanics, Asian Americans, and Native Americans. Subcultures can even exist between generational groups, based on age. When doing business across cultures and subcultures, companies face communication barriers created by language, customs, and traditions.

What kinds of communication barriers might companies face when doing business abroad?

© Getty Images/Digital Vision

LANGUAGE DIFFERENCES

Few American managers speak a foreign language fluently. However, doing so does not solve all problems when someone is transferred to another country. The people of most nations realize that learning a new language is difficult. But they are more than willing to help foreigners learn. They are especially impressed when someone who does not know their language makes a noble effort to learn. Many corporations now provide intensive language training for managers assigned to foreign branches. Information on the social customs and education, legal, and political systems is included in the training.

Joint ventures between American and foreign firms often reveal language problems. A successful joint venture between Ford Motor Co. and the Japanese Mazda Motors Corp. provides an example of overcoming language difficulties. The president of Mazda estimated that 20 percent of the meaning of a conversation with Ford leaders was lost between him and the interpreters. Another 20 percent was lost between the interpreters and the Ford leaders. Working with only about two-thirds accuracy, the Mazda president tried extra hard to make sure his message was getting through. He strongly believes people should meet face-to-face and talk freely.

CULTURAL DIFFERENCES

People from other cultures often place different values on such things as family, status, and power. In India, for example, providing jobs for male family members in a business is more important than earning a profit. Humor differs worldwide, too. In addition, accepted practices in one country may be impolite elsewhere. For example, American businesspeople generally like to start and end meetings on time. In Japan and certain other countries, this practice would be considered rude rather than businesslike.

NONVERBAL DIFFERENCES

Great differences exist in the area of nonverbal communication, especially body language. For example, how close one stands when talking to someone else differs from culture to culture. For most conversations, Americans stand two to three feet apart, whereas Middle Eastern people stand much closer. Even colors have different meanings. In Western countries, black is often associated with death, but in Latin American cultures, death is represented by white and purple. A handshake also varies from place to place. In Spain, it should last from five to seven shakes, but the French prefer one single shake.

Because differences exist among nations and cultures, executives prefer to conduct extremely important business transactions in a formal manner. Usually, that means greater use of written reports and expert translators. However, for day-to-day international operations, managers must learn to understand the cultural and communication practices of other nations.

Management MATTERS

Managing Nonverbal Communication

There are numerous ways that individuals communicate nonverbally in international settings. Often business meetings are held during a meal. In China, this often will require that a business manager knows meal etiquette. This can include where to sit and how to eat with chopsticks. You should try each type of food. You should know how to make drinking toasts, how to dress for dinner, when to start negotiating, and how to bring a meal to a close. These cultural norms will differ between countries. Before a manager conducts business in a foreign culture, he or she should research that culture's business meal etiquette. Managers should lay out a plan for how to behave during the meal and practice these techniques to be sure they can handle these important cultural norms.

What Do You Think? Why should managers care about meal etiquette in a foreign culture? How can a manager learn a culture's etiquette rules?

New managers often spend time listening to as many employee points of view as possible before making corporate changes. What kinds of questions would you ask employees before making such changes?

© Getty Images/Photodisc

CHECKPOINT

Describe three types of communication barriers managers may encounter doing business abroad.

Improving Organizational Communication

Good managers are usually good communicators. This is often a skill that managers need to learn and practice. Some ways to improve communication are discussed in this section.

ENCOURAGE TWO-WAY COMMUNICATION

Small businesses provide for plenty of two-way communication between owners and employees. As companies get larger, however, a shift to one-way communication often occurs for efficiency purposes. When this happens, problems can arise because valuable feedback from employees and customers is reduced. Good managers develop plans to obtain feedback even when they are extremely busy. Some managers, however, discourage two-way communication because they feel uncomfortable with it and because it is time-consuming. For example, one boss in a firm fired an employee by e-mail, even though the employee's office was right next door. Organizations that encourage managers to consciously engage in two-way communication are often more successful than those that do not.

LISTEN ACTIVELY

Two-way communication assures feedback. Effective listening results in effective feedback. Frequently, employees have questions and encounter problems on the job. They need to talk to someone who listens carefully. Hearing and listening are not the same. Most people can hear when someone speaks, but they may not pay attention to the message. Listening involves hearing and understanding. Good listeners make every effort to practice the rules of good listening shown in Figure 13-6 to make certain that they receive the messages accurately.

FACILITATE UPWARD COMMUNICATION

In large organizations, upward communication is sometimes neglected. Managers may not want to hear complaints or deal with suggestions because they require time. To make certain that upward communications occur, some businesses ask managers to use specific techniques.

One technique is called "management by walking around." Managers leave their offices from time to time and make trips through the working areas. While doing this, they chat with employees about various problems and conditions.

Another practice is for managers to encourage employees to meet with them when they have concerns. To control the time this "open door policy" takes, some managers restrict the practice to one hour per week, when employees can make appointments. Suggestion boxes have been used for many years and have great value in encouraging communication.

No technique is better than regular meetings with employees. Some firms select a certain number of employees from different departments and organizational levels to meet with top managers on a regular basis. The manager informs them about important company matters and invites questions and ideas. Studies have shown that employees who are informed about their companies have stronger positive feelings than those who are not. The top-level managers benefit by getting feedback from people throughout the company.

FACTS & FIGURES

Listening

Listening is considered both a sign of politeness and a valuable skill in business negotiations in Japan. Japanese often think North Americans need to listen more attentively, not talk as much, and certainly not interrupt when someone else is speaking.

Ten Rules for Good Listening	
RULES	**RATIONALE**
1. Stop talking!	You cannot listen if you are talking.
2. Put the talker at ease.	Help a person feel free to talk; create a permissive environment.
3. Show a talker that you want to listen.	Look and act interested; listen to understand, not to oppose.
4. Remove distractions.	Don't doodle, tap, or shuffle papers; shut the door if necessary to achieve quiet.
5. Empathize with talkers.	Try to see the other person's point of view.
6. Be patient.	Allow plenty of time; do not interrupt; do not start for the door or walk away.
7. Hold your temper.	An angry person takes the wrong meaning from words.
8. Go easy on argument and criticism.	These put people on the defensive and may cause them to "clam up" or become angry. Do not argue—even if you win, you lose.
9. Ask questions.	This encourages a talker and shows that you are listening. It helps to develop points further.
10. Stop talking!	This is first and last, because all other guides depend on it. You cannot do an effective listening job while you are talking.

© Cengage Learning 2013.

Figure 13-6 Following these rules helps a listener receive messages accurately.

Communication channels should support communication goals. Why is it good practice to follow an oral communication, such as a commendation for a job well done, with a written one?

© Jupiter Images/Blend Images

SELECT COMMUNICATION CHANNELS CAREFULLY

When managers want to communicate with others, they should carefully select an appropriate communication channel. Generally, when a manager must reprimand an employee or settle a dispute, the oral communication channel is best. The oral channel is most effective for explaining the reason for the reprimand or for working out an acceptable solution to a dispute.

The written communication channel is best when managers want to communicate information requiring future action or information of a more general nature, such as a new policy or a revised operating procedure. Such matters should be put in writing for later reference. Managers should follow up on information provided in writing, because it serves as a reminder that the information is important and it provides an opportunity for the receiver to ask questions. E-mail is a good way to follow up because it is fast, easy, and provides immediate feedback. E-mail is not a good substitute for oral communication in situations that call for face-to-face discussion.

In some situations, two channels of communication work best—first oral and then written. Managers should use both channels when they want to (1) give an immediate order, (2) announce a new policy, (3) contact a supervisor about work problems, or (4) compliment an employee for excellent work. In most of these situations, the information is best delivered orally on a one-to-one basis, which personalizes it and allows for immediate feedback. The written channel then allows for reinforcement and creates a record of the event.

 **CHECKPOINT**

List the three strategies managers can use to improve two-way communication.

UNDERSTAND MANAGEMENT CONCEPTS

Determine the best answer for each of the following questions.

1. The most dangerous approach to conflict resolution is
   a. avoidance
   b. compromise
   c. win/lose
   d. lose/lose

2. The most effective technique a manager can use to improve organizational communication is
   a. regular memos
   b. daily reports
   c. regular meetings with employees
   d. monthly employee evaluations

THINK CRITICALLY

Answer the following questions as completely as possible.

3. Describe how managers can resolve communication conflicts in a company.

4. Explain how a company can overcome cross-cultural communication problems.

CHAPTER CONCEPTS

- Communication is a two-way process that involves creating, sending, receiving, and interpreting messages. The three main channels of communication are oral, written, and nonverbal. Two barriers to effective communication are distractions and distortions.

- Organizational culture involves the shared values, beliefs, and behavior of an organization. Cultures may be (1) entirely open, with extensive interactive communication among all organization members, (2) entirely closed with dominantly downward communication, or (3) a combination of open and closed communication systems.

- Communications in organizations follow both formal and informal networks. Formal communication networks are official company channels, such as between managers and their employees. Informal networks are communications among informal groups.

- Managers must deal with problems that challenge their communication skills, such as conflicts and communication across cultures. They must also learn to run meetings effectively with techniques such as the nominal group technique and brainstorming.

- Good managers are generally good communicators. They listen effectively, facilitate upward communications, and choose the appropriate communication channels for their messages.

REVIEW BUSINESS MANAGEMENT TERMS

Write the letter of the term that matches each definition. Some terms will not be used.

a. channel of communication
b. communication
c. communication network
d. compromise strategy
e. conflict
f. distortion
g. distraction
h. feedback
i. flame
j. formal communication network
k. grapevine
l. informal communication networks
m. nominal group technique (NGT)
n. teleconference

1. Sharing of information in which the receiver understands the message in the way the sender intended
2. A receiver's response to a sender's message
3. The way people consciously or unconsciously change messages
4. The means by which a message is conveyed
5. Electronic message that contains abusive, threatening, or offensive content that may violate company policy or public law
6. Two or more people communicating through audio and video over network connections.
7. Structure through which information flows in a business
8. System of official channels that carry organizationally approved messages
9. Unofficial ways employees share information in an organization
10. Group problem-solving method in which members write down and evaluate ideas to be shared with the group
11. Interference by one person with the achievement of another person's goals
12. Way to resolve conflict in which everyone involved agrees to a mutually acceptable solution

Determine the best answer.

13. Anything that interferes with the sender's creating and delivering a message and the receiver's getting and interpreting a message is
    a. a distraction
    b. a distortion
    c. a barrier
    d. feedback

14. Unsolicited advertising that finds its way into e-mail boxes is called
    a. flame
    b. spam
    c. solicitation
    d. e-mail ad

15. Which of the following is *not* an example of nonverbal communication?
    a. flashing lights, stop signs, and sirens
    b. colors, such as in traffic lights
    c. charts, diagrams, and pictures
    d. All are examples of nonverbal communication.

16. The informal transmission of information among workers can take place via
    a. project status reports
    b. e-mails
    c. memos
    d. none of the above

17. Which of the following statements about conflict are true?
    a. All conflict should be avoided.
    b. A little conflict is sometimes beneficial.
    c. Win/lose strategies are most often used by managers.
    d. Managers should not compromise or they lose authority.

18. A strategy used to resolve conflict in which you take a neutral position or agree with another person's position even though it differs from your personal belief is called
    a. avoidance
    b. compromise
    c. conflict neutral
    d. win/lose

19. A team discussion technique used to generate as many ideas as possible for solving a problem is known as
    a. idea storming
    b. nominal groupthink
    c. creative thinking
    d. brainstorming

Answer the following questions.

20. Explain how a grammar error in a memo might be considered a distraction and thus a barrier to communication.

21. A manager was enjoying giving a talk about business to a group of young people. An audience member asked the manager whether he believed in open communication. The manager looked uncomfortable with the question, snapped a fast "yes," and quickly asked, "Any other questions?" Compare the oral and nonverbal messages the manager was sending.

22. Distortion is not always unconsciously done. Explain why employees may consciously distort information. Do you think such behavior is ethical?

23. Discuss what strategy you would use to help resolve a conflict situation between two employees who always disagree on how a task should be handled.

24. Describe how busy managers can encourage effective listening.

MAKE ACADEMIC CONNECTIONS

Complete the following activities.

25. **Math** LaToya put the following idea in her company's suggestion box: "Rather than hire a new full-time worker at $15 per hour to handle our increased business, hire two half-time workers at $10 per hour. Then, if business slows later, we can cut back to one half-time worker or no workers."

    a. As the manager, write LaToya a note saying that her suggestion has been accepted and she will earn 20 percent of one year's savings for the idea.

    b. Assume one year has gone by and that one half-time employee worked 860 hours and the second worked 600 hours. A full-time employee would have worked 2,000 hours. How much will LaToya receive for her suggestion?

26. **Research** Use your school library or the Internet to research the topic of nonverbal communication. Find pictures in magazines that show examples of nonverbal communication. Show these images to members of your class. See if they can identify the nonverbal message. Ask them to explain why they are making these judgments.

27. **Technology** Keep track of your various types of communication during a school day. Use the charting feature in a software package to develop a pie chart like the one in Figure 13-1. Divide the pie according to the percentage of time you spend each school day (a) listening, (b) speaking, (c) reading, and (d) writing. Compare your communication times to those of a typical manager, as shown in Figure 13-1.

28. **Speaking** Divide into small groups. For this project, you may interact with your group only by e-mail. Brainstorm a list of e-mail do's and don'ts appropriate for a workplace setting. Using your group's ideas, compose an e-mail policy for your workplace. Present your group's policy to your class.

CASE 13-1: Company E-Mail

Lauren Lemaster works at the headquarters of a major Internet corporation that has offices in five countries. The company has a strict set of rules regarding the use of e-mail. Hackers often try to break into the operating system to damage it, and that naturally hurts business.

The CEO sends all newly hired employees the following message: "Be careful what you say to others, especially when sending e-mail to other employees. A year ago a hacker learned that we were planning to buy another business that would increase the value of the company. He took the idea to a competitor, so we lost 'big' on that failed operation. For reasons like this, we require that you sign the attached oath. The oath states that if an employee is responsible in any way for inside information getting to the outside, that employee will be released immediately."

Without further thought, Lauren signed the oath, but that was two years ago. Yesterday on her lunch hour, Lauren sent a secret e-mail message to her best friend, Douglas, who likes to buy stock in Internet companies when they do something new and exciting. Lauren's message said: "Douglas, I learned that my company has its eye on Dawson and Donaldson, Inc. Keep it to yourself. Hopefully this will repay the favor you did to help me get this job. Trash this message after reading it. Lauren."

Douglas bought stock in the company and shared the message with several friends, who also bought stock. Then he deleted the message. Within 24 hours, the stock price for Dawson and Donaldson doubled. However, Lauren's boss called her in and fired her on the spot for violating company policy.

THINK CRITICALLY

1. Was the company's Internet policy too severe? Why or why not? Because Lauren wrote the e-mail on her lunch hour, is she actually in violation of company policy?
2. How did the company find out about Lauren's e-mail message?
3. Does Lauren have any privacy rights that would enable her to sue the company for the loss of her job? Explain.
4. If Douglas e-mailed four friends and they each e-mailed four friends and this happened two more times, how many people heard of the potential purchase as a result of Lauren's action?
5. Was Lauren as unethical as Douglas was? What responsibility does Douglas bear for Lauren's plight?
6. How would the 10 rules for good listening apply when Lauren and Douglas meet to discuss what happened?

CASE 13-2: Changing Corporate Culture

As a former regional manager for Graphix International, Seth McClaren was promoted and transferred to the Philadelphia headquarters several years ago. A close friend, Josh Berry, manages the company's regional office in Atlanta. Seth called Josh and invited him to dinner to discuss concerns about changes going on in the company. After dinner the following conversation occurred:

Seth: *Tomorrow's a big meeting. The new president and the two new vice presidents will be there to explain the new reporting procedures.*

Josh: *Was something wrong with the old method? It worked fine for my office.*

Seth: *The new managers are different. They like meetings and lots of contact with employees. They even stop by my office to chat. They seem friendly . . . even invited me to stop by their offices. Nothing like the former managers! You never saw them and never heard from them unless something went wrong.*

Josh: *Is that why most of the regional managers kept clear of headquarters? The person I replaced warned me not to break any of the rules. "Just keep your nose clean," she said. "If you don't bother them, they won't bother you."*

Seth: *The new managers expect good work, but they also seem to want the employees and managers to discuss problems. They even want us to suggest solutions. Imagine that! Some of us aren't sure whether to trust them yet.*

Josh: *They seem to be practicing what they preach, Seth. The Houston regional manager stuck her neck out and made a suggestion, and a vice president flew down to talk with her. According to the online newsletter, she is going to head up a special team to implement her suggestion.*

Seth: *The way these new people operate . . . it's different. I just want to do my job. I'm not interested in finding problems or offering suggestions.*

Josh: *Let's give them a chance, Seth. At least they're willing to listen, which is more than you could say about the departed managers.*

THINK CRITICALLY

1. Did the corporate culture change between the old and new top management? Explain.
2. What evidence is there that the new top management will encourage or discourage upward communication?
3. Did the new vice president use more than one channel of communication? If so, how?
4. Did the old or the new top managers place more stress on two-way communication? Explain.
5. Will Seth be as comfortable as Josh with the new managers? Explain your answer.

PROJECT My Own Business

Planning Organizational Communication

As a small-business owner, you will be responsible for making sure communications flow smoothly within your business and with others outside your business. Unclear or poor communication can be very damaging to a new business as you work with employees, customers, other businesspeople, and the public. You need to plan communication carefully and use effective communication whenever you interact with others.

DATA COLLECTION

1. Using newspapers, business magazines, and the Internet, identify situations in which businesses faced problems resulting from poor communication. Make a list of the types of communication problems you identify, using the following categories: communication problems with (a) employees, (b) customers, (c) other businesspeople, (d) the public, (e) other.

2. Advertising is one method of communicating with customers. However, advertisements often do not communicate the same message to everyone. Locate three ads for small businesses, preferably businesses similar to your juice bar business. Show each ad to five different people. Record their answers to the following questions for each ad:
   a. What is the most important message you receive from this ad?
   b. In general, do you believe the ad is effective or ineffective?
   c. As a result of the ad, would you be more or less likely to be a customer of the business? Why?

ANALYSIS

1. Compose a letter that you would send to local health clubs and recreation centers. In the letter, request that your juice bar be identified as the "exclusive source for juice drinks" for their facility. Make sure the letter is persuasive and offers some value or benefit to the businesses you will contact.

2. You have been asked by the local organization of retailers to make a brief presentation at their monthly luncheon meeting about your new business. Using presentation software, prepare a five-minute presentation that describes the business, your business plan, and some of the challenges you believe you will face. Give your presentation to the class. Be prepared to defend your business plan. If possible, ask a local retailer to attend and ask questions of the presenters.

CHAPTER 14

DATA ANALYSIS AND DECISION MAKING

14.1 Mathematics and Management

14.2 Basic Math and Measurement Systems

14.3 Understanding and Using Basic Statistics

14.4 Using Data in Decision Making

Reality Check

What's Wrong with This Analysis?

Petra stood up from her desk, stretched, and rubbed her eyes. She was reviewing the quarterly results in preparation for tomorrow's report. After almost two years of losses, preliminary signs indicated sales would be up 6 to 7 percent and costs growing at less than 2 percent.

Petra was studying a complex spreadsheet reporting detailed sales, costs, and inventory data for the company's 16 sales territories. The spreadsheet was so large Petra had to scroll through four screens to review all of the information. But no matter how she studied it, the results were not what she expected. Rather than a sizable increase, overall sales were just barely better than the previous quarter, while costs were up 1.8 percent. Instead of the positive news, it appeared the company would need to find ways to cut costs even further.

She decided to look at the data in a simpler way to try to isolate the problem. She selected only the sales and cost data for each territory and used the charting function on the spreadsheet program to compare those figures with the same information from the previous quarter. As the bar chart appeared on her screen, Petra focused her attention on the top territories. Four of the five were showing no growth in sales, while expenses had climbed in each one.

She quickly texted her assistant, Tim: "Check the current sales figures for territories 4, 8, 11, and 14 to make sure they are accurate."

Five minutes later, Tim called and reported, "The data from each of those territories are incorrect on the spreadsheet. I've entered the new data and you should see an updated spreadsheet in a minute."

As the spreadsheet updated, Petra smiled. Based on the new sales data, the projected performance had been exceeded. It would take her another 30 minutes to create the charts for her presentation, but she no longer felt as tired. She was glad she took the time to check the quarterly results. What might have been a big mistake was now going to be good news for the company.

What's Your Reaction? What possible affects could the type of error Petra identified have on a company?

Mathematics and Management

Goals

- Describe ways that mathematics is used by managers to improve decision making.
- Identify several common and specialized mathematical applications used by business managers.

Terms

- data-based decisions p. 359
- inductive reasoning p. 359
- deductive reasoning p. 359
- statistics p. 359
- raw data p. 360
- processed data p. 360

●●● Mathematics Skills for Managers

Many factors influence decisions, but they do not all carry the same weight. Experience plays a role when managers consider similar situations and what worked and did not worked in the past. Personal beliefs, values, and even intuition can influence a manager's decisions. These factors can shape a manager's approach to a decision and help identify some choices as better than others. However, they should not be the primary basis for making decisions because they do not take into consideration the specific information and conditions surrounding the decision to be made. Today, managers are skilled in data-based decision making.

MATH FOR DECISION MAKING

Data-based decisions use information, facts, and measures, usually in numerical form, as the primary basis for choosing among alternatives. Managers gather and analyze information to keep decisions objective and as free from bias as possible. Because data are collected and analyzed in numerical form, managers rely on mathematics to help them understand and interpret the information and to make effective decisions.

Skill in the understanding and use of mathematics is important for all business people. Many of the applications involve basic arithmetic operations. You will also need to understand and use fractions and decimals as well as basic units of measurement in both U.S. and metric units. Analysis of numerical data typically involves calculating percentages, ratios, and proportions.

The next level of mathematics skills needed in business involves understanding algebra. Algebra moves beyond completing arithmetic operations to the process of thinking logically using numbers, symbols, and equations to solve problems. Algebra requires the use of logic, understanding rules and procedures, and mastery of inductive and deductive reasoning. **Inductive reasoning** uses the analysis of specific data to draw broader conclusions while **deductive reasoning** takes general principles and uses them to make predictions about specific situations or circumstances.

Statistics are used for more advanced numerical analysis in business. **Statistics** are mathematical tools that use carefully selected numerical

Math is used in all businesses and business people must be skilled in basic mathematics applications. How is math used to price and promote products in retail stores?

information to describe the situation being studied and to make predictions about future similar circumstances. For example, the manager of a manufacturing production line may want to know how many defective products to expect in the next six months. Rather than collecting information for the entire month and examining every product produced, the manager samples three percent of the products produced during a two-hour period on five different days. That number is then used to estimate the total number of defective products to expect during the month. In the same way, a development team working on a new product wants to estimate the sales when the product is distributed nationwide. They cannot just guess how many products to manufacture and hope they have enough to meet customer demand without having far more than they can sell. Therefore, they establish three test markets in cities that represent various parts of the country and sell the product for two months. Based on those sales and data from previously introduced new products, they are able to estimate nationwide sales and plan manufacturing based on the estimate.

COMMUNICATING FINDINGS

An additional important mathematical skill needed in business is to be able to organize, analyze, and present data visually. When numerical information is initially collected, it is known as raw data. **Raw data** are the original information that has not been processed for meaningful use. Raw data must be processed and organized to be understandable and useful for decision makers. **Processed data** (also known as *information)* are data that have been checked for accuracy and organized in a way to make them understandable and useable. Processed data can be classified, summarized, and compared in a more easily understood way than if presented as raw data. Well-developed spreadsheets, tables, charts, and graphs are excellent communication tools and make it easier to review and analyze large amounts of numerical information.

CHECKPOINT

Why should managers use data to aid them in decision making?

●●● Business Applications of Mathematics

Some uses of math are common to all managers, while others are specific to the area of management or to unique business operations and activities. An important part of preparing to be a manager is understanding how math is used in business and developing the necessary general and specific skills.

DEVELOPING MATH SKILLS

Using math in business involves much more than being able to make the necessary calculations involved in a numerical problem. In fact, with easy access to calculators, including cell phone apps, there is often little need to be able to complete the full calculation mentally.

In business, electronic database programs and spreadsheets have become the primary tools for analyzing data. Database programs categorize and store detailed information in the form of individual records that can be accessed and reorganized for varied uses. Electronic spreadsheets allow large amounts of data to be analyzed and updated using simple to sophisticated formulas along with charting and graphing tools. Managers should be comfortable using calculators, computers, and common business software.

Even with access to easy-to-use electronic tools, managers need to develop mathematics skills for analyzing situations, determining the data needed to support decision making, organizing the information in the correct way for analysis, and judging the results to make sure the solution is reasonable. Business people need mathematical skills to be able to calculate, compare, plan, analyze, and project. These skills are described in Figure 14-1.

MATH APPLICATIONS IN BUSINESS

All parts of business operations use mathematics. Many common mathematics applications are used throughout a business, while some applications are unique to a specific business function or operation. In addition, each of the four management functions—planning, organizing, implementing, and controlling—requires an understanding of math.

The most widely used mathematical application in business is the budget. A *budget* is a financial tool used to project income and expenditures. Because money is a fundamental resource of businesses, managers must be able to accurately anticipate revenues and other sources of income for their part of the business. They also need to be able to identify and accurately predict all of the expenses. Other common tools used by managers that require mathematics are schedules, standards, business records, and research.

ACCOUNTING AND FINANCE The area of business with the most extensive use of mathematics is accounting and finance. Accounting and finance managers manage the financial resources, maintain all financial records, prepare financial statements and reports, and communicate financial information and performance to owners, other managers, government agencies, and others who need the information.

PRODUCTION AND OPERATIONS Production and operations personnel are responsible for the ongoing operations of a business. They turn the resources of the organization into the products and services that are sold to customers. The major activities of production and operations that require math applications

Common Business Activities that Require Math Skills	
ACTIVITY	**DESCRIPTION**
Calculate	Determine the quantity or value of something
Compare	Determine how two or more values vary from each other
Plan	Use data to set numerical goals or standards
Analyze	Review data to identify relationships, patterns, and explanations
Project	Use past and current information to estimate future performance

© Cengage Learning 2013.

Figure 14-1 Math skills are used by all managers as they complete their day-to-day activities.

are forecasting, resource management, personnel and production planning and scheduling, purchasing, inventory management, and order fulfillment.

MARKETING Marketers complete a variety of activities to identify markets, develop demand, and sell the products and services to maximize profitability. Almost all marketing activities include mathematics applications including budget development and cost controls, pricing, advertising and sales planning, and managing financing and credit services. One of the most important areas of data collection and analysis is marketing research.

HUMAN RESOURCES Human resources management includes the activities involved in acquiring, preparing, and compensating the people who do the company's work. Major areas for human resource personnel that require mathematics skills are planning compensation and benefits programs and managing personnel records including payroll, payroll taxes, and benefits. The human resources department is responsible for planning and documenting employee training and management development and maintains data related to employee performance evaluations.

 **CHECKPOINT**

What are the five common activities managers complete that require mathematics skills?

14.1 ASSESSMENT

UNDERSTAND MANAGEMENT CONCEPTS

Determine the best answer for each of the following questions.

1. Mathematical tools that use numerical information to describe a situation and make predictions are
   a. spreadsheets
   b. algebra
   c. statistics
   d. basic arithmetic operations

2. Which of the following is *not* one of the common activities for which managers need math skills?
   a. delegate
   b. compute
   c. calculate
   d. project

THINK CRITICALLY

Answer the following questions as completely as possible.

3. If a production manager reviews quality data for several months to try to determine which factors seem to result in fewer quality errors, is the manager using inductive or deductive reasoning? Why?

4. Do you believe the increasing availability of electronic tools is increasing or decreasing the importance of mathematics in business? Why?

Basic Math and Measurement Systems

Goals

- Demonstrate understanding of basic mathematical operations.
- Recognize common units of U.S. and metric measurement.

Terms

- fraction p. 365
- ratio p. 365
- percentage p. 365
- metric system p. 366

●●●● Basic Mathematic Operations

Consumers use math every day. A debit card purchase might require a quick calculation to make sure there is enough money in the account to cover the purchase. When a restaurant server presents the bill after a meal, the amount of the tip must be determined. Comparing prices of frozen and fresh-squeezed orange juice requires calculating the cost per serving. A store display announcing 30 percent off the already low price requires the shopper to figure out the price of the merchandise when the discount is taken.

In the same way, business people regularly encounter situations where math skills are needed. A salesperson must quickly recalculate the price of an order after the company approves an additional discount for an important customer. An accountant tries to find an error when two columns in a balance sheet show different totals. When discussing benefits with a new employee, a human resource specialist compares the out-of-pocket costs of two different health care options.

A starting point for effectively using mathematics in business is understanding and applying basic arithmetic operations. Arithmetic involves addition, subtraction, multiplication, and division. In addition, business people need to understand, use, and convert fractions, decimals, and percents. Businesses have two expectations of employees when using math on the job: Calculations must be accurate and they must be completed quickly. Business people need to be comfortable and confident in their use of basic math skills.

ADDING AND SUBTRACTING

The structure and terminology of addition and subtraction equations are shown in Figure 14-2. Many of the numerical situations faced in business that require addition and subtraction involve large numbers in the thousands or even millions and may include decimals or fractions and percentages. Frequently, many numbers need to be added or subtracted in sequence. People who regularly encounter more complex addition and subtraction problems as a part of their jobs typically use spreadsheets or calculators. The use of these electronic tools may speed the process but does not insure accurate results. When encountering a series of small numbers or only a few numbers that need to be added or subtracted, people should be confident they can complete the problem mentally.

Remember the following when adding numbers:

- The order of the addends does not matter. The sum is the total of all addends.
- Check addition answers by adding the numbers again in the reverse order they were added originally.
- Both positive and negative numbers can be added. However, adding a negative number actually reduces the sum.
- A way to simplify the addition of large numbers is to add each column of numbers separately and then add the column sums together.

Remember the following when subtracting numbers:

- Only two numbers can be subtracted at a time. However, a series of numbers can be subtracted one after the other.
- The order of numbers in subtraction is important. The subtrahend must be subtracted from the minuend.
- A larger number can be subtracted from a smaller number. If the subtrahend is larger than the minuend, the difference will be a negative number.
- Check subtraction problems by adding the difference and the subtrahend. The correct answer is the minuend.

MULTIPLYING AND DIVIDING

Multiplication and division are used frequently in business. When multiplication is a regular part of their work, people often use calculators or computers to determine answers quickly and accurately. Figure 14-2 shows the structure and terminology of multiplication and division equations.

Remember the following when multiplying numbers:

- Count the number of decimal places in the multiplicand and the multiplier. The total will be the number of decimal places in the product.
- To check the accuracy of multiplication, divide the product by the multiplier. The correct answer is the multiplicand.

Remember the following when dividing numbers:

- When dividing whole numbers using long division, make sure the decimal in the quotient is aligned with the decimal in the dividend. If the divisor contains a decimal, the decimal in the quotient will be located the number of positions to the right of the decimal in the dividend as it took to make the divisor a whole number.
- To check the accuracy of division, multiply the quotient by the divisor. The correct answer is the dividend.

Structure and Terminology of Basic Math Operations	
ADDITION	**SUBTRACTION**
Addend + Addend + Addend = Sum *Examples* 8 + 16 + 38 = 52 23½ + 86¾ = 110¼	**Minuend − Subtrahend = Difference** *Examples* 52 − 28 = 24 133½ − 62¾ = 70¾
MULTIPLICATION	**DIVISION**
Multiplicand × Multiplier = Product *Examples* 8 × 16 = 128 12½ × 53 = 662½	**Dividend ÷ Divisor = Quotient** *Examples* 150 ÷ 16 = 9.375 ½ ÷ ¼ = 2

Figure 14-2 It is helpful to know the correct terminology when solving problems.

FRACTIONS, RATIOS, DECIMALS, AND PERCENTAGES

Fractions, ratios, decimals, and percentages are frequently used in business. A **fraction** is a part of a whole number expressed as a proportion. For example, the fraction 3/5 represents three parts of five. If $3,000 of a $5,000 weekly advertising budget is spent on radio ads, 3/5 of the total budget is allocated to radio. The top number in the fraction is the *numerator*; the bottom number is the *denominator*.

A **ratio** is the relationship between two quantities. If a department has 4 supervisors and 60 employees, the ratio of supervisors to employees is 1:15. There is one supervisor for every 15 employees in the department. A ratio is similar to a fraction. In the example of employees and supervisors, four of the 64 people in the department are supervisors so 4/64 or 1/16 of the total department workforce are supervisors.

A **percentage** is a part of a whole expressed in hundredths. In the advertising example above, 3/5 of the advertising budget was used to pay for radio ads. When 3 is divided by 5, the percentage of radio advertising is .60 or 60%. A percentage uses a *decimal,* which is a fraction that has a denominator of a power of ten and is expressed with digits and a decimal point rather than as a fraction. For example, the fraction 1/10 is equal to the decimal 0.1 or 10%, and the fraction 238/1,000 is equal to the percentage 23.8% or 0.238. You calculate the percentage represented by a fraction by dividing the numerator by the denominator.

CHECKPOINT

What are the equations for addition, subtraction, multiplication, and division?

●●● Measurement Systems in Business

Precise measurement is critical in business. When a product is assembled, every one of the many parts must fit together perfectly for the product to operate. If a part is damaged and must be replaced, the replacement must be identical to the original part. If a house or factory is being designed, measurements must be exact for walls to meet, floors to be level, and the building to withstand weight, winds, and earthquakes. Customers expect exact measures in products they purchase, whether it is the quantity of cereal in a package or the tons of wheat in a shipment of grain from a farm to a food processor.

With the growth of international business, products move back and forth from country to country. Many manufacturers produce products and parts that will be sold to consumers or other businesses in more than one country. Consumers purchase products for their personal use while seldom considering where they were manufactured. Businesses must be able to develop products that meet the standards and expectations of customers in any country in which they choose to do business. Understanding standards of measurement has become very important for business people. The common measures used in business are length, weight, and volume.

Standard U.S. Measures		
LENGTH	**WEIGHT**	**VOLUME**

inch
foot = 12 inches
yard = 3 feet or 36 inches
mile = 1,760 yards
      or 5,250 feet
	ounce
	pound = 16 ounces
	ton = 2,000 pounds
		pint
		quart = 2 pints
		gallon = 4 quarts
		barrel = 31½ gallons standard;
		          42 gallons petroleum

Figure 14-3 The U.S. system of measures was developed centuries ago and based on the English Imperial system.

TRADITIONAL U.S. MEASURES

Measurement units in the United States are different from most other countries. The U.S. system developed from the traditional English system. The standard units of measurement in the U.S. system appear in Figure 14-3. Several centuries ago, because there was no need for precise measurement, units of measure were based on common, but general, standards. For example, the *foot* was the length of a man's foot and the *inch* the width of his thumb or the first joint of his forefinger. Some believe the mile was the approximate distance a Roman soldier could stride in 1000 paces—*mille* is Latin for thousand.

As the need for precision became greater, governments began to impose specific standards on the traditional measures. The United States federal government first created the Office of Standard Weights and Measures in 1824 to develop standards for commerce. However, it was 1901 before a national research laboratory was created with responsibility for the scientific development of exact measures. Today the National Institute of Standards and Technology, a part of the U.S. Department of Commerce, maintains thousands of standards for precise measurement, quality, safety, and performance.

METRIC MEASURES

For centuries, many different standards and units of measurement were used across the world. The **metric system** is based on the decimal system, meaning that all measures are in common units of ten. It was developed to be a universal system of weights and measures that would be easy to use by average people. Figure 14-4 shows the standard units of measurement in the metric system.

The metric system was first proposed by a French scientist and adopted by the French government in the late 1700s. Over the next century, more and more countries informally and formally adopted versions of the metric system. In 1960, the General Congress of Weights and Measures, representing most of the world's countries, approved the modern form of the metric system called the International System of Units (or SI). The International Bureau of Weights and Measures in Paris, France, is responsible for maintaining the measurement standards.

There have been efforts in the United States as early as the 1800s to make the metric system the official measurement system for the country. However, continued resistance has hindered the conversion. Congress passed the Metric Conversion Act of 1975 to support a ten-year voluntary conversion to the use of metrics. When that effort failed to gain general acceptance, the Omnibus Trade and Competitiveness Act of 1988 designated the metric

Standard Metric Measures		
LENGTH	**WEIGHT**	**VOLUME**

millimeter = 0.001 meter or
              0.1 centimeter
centimeter = 0.01 meter
meter   = 100 centimeters or
           1,000 millimeters
kilometer = 1,000 meters
	milligram = 0.001 grams
	gram = 1,000 milligrams
	kilogram = 1,000 grams
	metric ton = 1,000 kilograms
		milliliter = 0.001 liters
		liter = 1,000 milliliters
		kiloliter = 1,000 liters
		megaliter = 1,000,000 liters

Figure 14-4 The metric measurement system was developed as an international standard and to simplify measurements.

Conversions Between U.S. and Metric Weights and Measures		
LENGTH	**WEIGHT**	**VOLUME**
1 foot = 0.305 meters	1 ounce = 28.35 grams	1 gallon = 3.785 liters
1 meter = 3.28 feet	1 metric ton = 1.103 tons	1 milliliter = 0.034 fluid ounces

© Cengage Learning 2013.

Figure 14-5 Business people need to be prepared to make conversions between U.S. and metric measures.

system as the "preferred system of weights and measures for United States trade and commerce." Since that time, most products produced and sold in the United States carry both metric and U.S. measures. The U.S. now uses metric standards to define the traditional U.S. measures. For example, the yard is 0.914 meter and the pound is 0.454 kilograms. Figure 14-5 shows conversions of common weights and measures between the U.S. and metric systems.

 CHECKPOINT

What is the preferred system of weights and measures for United States trade and commerce?

14.2 ASSESSMENT

UNDERSTAND MANAGEMENT CONCEPTS

Determine the best answer for each of the following questions.

1. Which of the following is an incorrect equation for a basic arithmetic function?
   a. addend + addend = sum
   b. subtrahend − minuend = integer
   c. multiplicand × multiplier = product
   d. dividend ÷ divisor = quotient

2. The metric system
   a. is used only in the United States and a few other countries
   b. was first proposed in the mid-1900s
   c. was developed to be understandable and easy to use by both scientists and average citizens
   d. is based on feet, pounds, and gallons

THINK CRITICALLY

Answer the following questions as completely as possible.

3. Why is it important to double check the answers to simple math calculations?

4. What is the similarity of a fraction, ratio, and percentage?

14.3

Understanding and Using Basic Statistics

Goals

- Explain why statistics is important to managers and identify two types of statistics.
- Recognize important types of statistical information.

Terms

- descriptive statistics p. 369
- inferential statistics p. 369
- data set p. 370
- characteristics p. 370
- range p. 370
- frequency distribution p. 370
- mean p. 371
- median p. 371
- mode p. 371
- population p. 371
- sample p. 371
- probability p. 372
- correlation p. 372

●●● Understanding Numerical Information

Using data in business involves much more than adding, subtracting, multiplying, and dividing. Numerical information provides evidence to help managers understand what works and what does not work. Managers learn from the careful study and interpretation of data. They make better decisions as a result.

THE IMPORTANCE OF STATISTICS

Making decisions may be one of the most challenging responsibilities faced by managers. Decisions involve risks and unknowns. Most decisions have consequences. In some cases, the future success of a company and its employees may depend on a decision. Other decisions may not be as significant, but they still have an impact. The careful and objective use of data is the most effective way to improve management decision making.

Managers frequently use statistics to help them understand, interpret, communicate, and apply numerical information. By using statistics, managers can make decisions more quickly, with greater confidence, and with a higher probability that the best choice has been made.

It would be nice if every decision came down to a correct and an incorrect choice, a simple yes or no. In reality, the decision-making process reveals several options. It is often difficult to evaluate the options to determine the best choice. The effective use of statistics helps the decision maker remain objective. There is no benefit in making a decision and then searching for data to support that decision. Managers must keep an open mind when a problem is identified or a question is asked. Information needs to be collected, organized, studied, and analyzed. The manager examines information carefully and objectively to determine if there is evidence to support one choice or another. Statistics help direct the manager to the best solution or answer.

TYPES OF STATISTICS

Managers face two very different types or situations that call for decisions. The most common is making decisions about current operations. Nancy Denardo is the regional manager for a chain of department stores. She is concerned about the differences in the volume of sales generated from the each of the 24 stores in her region during the most recent quarter. She wants to study information that may help her decide how to divide new inventory among the stores. Nancy gets daily sales reports from each store. Those sales are totaled and summarized each week, month, and quarter. Gathered with her assistant managers, she says, *"We need to know more about the sales results from the stores. What is the greatest percentage of increase and decrease among all the stores? Of the stores that had increased sales, what was the average dollar volume increase?"* Nancy and her assistants will use descriptive statistics to examine the sales information.

Descriptive statistics provide meaningful summaries of data to help managers understand the current situation. The managers want to identify factors that contribute to increases and decreases in sales in order to improve the performance of all stores and to make sure the stores that have increased sales will have enough inventory for the upcoming sales period.

The second situation facing managers is using available information to improve future decisions about similar circumstances. Filipe Herrera is a product manager for a large consumer products company. He and his team are beginning to review all of the data from a three-month introduction of a new sunscreen product that is applied using disposable towelettes. The product was introduced in two markets. The team needs to determine whether to expand sales and which additional markets have the greatest potential. As they start through the data, Filipe asks, *"What percentage of the total market for sunscreen products were we able to capture from our competitors in the three months? How did sales vary based on the age, gender, and income of the customer? What similarities and differences were there between the two markets?"* Most of the questions Filipe is asking will be answered with inferential statistics. **Inferential statistics** use the analysis of information to help managers make predictions about similar circumstances or about the future. Filipe's team wants to use the information gathered during the market test to determine how to expand the sales of the new sunscreen product.

Managers spend much of their time reviewing reports and other information to increase understanding of the operations for which they are responsible. How can managers reduce the amount of time they spend on those activities?

✔ CHECKPOINT

How are descriptive statistics different from inferential statistics?

●●● Statistics Terms and Concepts

Many managers do not actually conduct research or complete the statistical analysis. They receive reports that present the results of data collection and analysis. Managers must be able to read and understand the reports and use the information to make decisions. That understanding starts with recognizing important terms and concepts that are a part of descriptive and inferential statistics.

COMMON DESCRIPTIVE STATISTICS

Descriptive statistics are used when decision makers have a large amount of data and want to understand it better. Organizing the data using descriptive statistics will make it easier to examine important characteristics of the information being studied and to determine if any meaningful relationships exist.

The first step in using descriptive statistics is to identify the important characteristics of the data set. A **data set** is all of the data that have been collected for study. **Characteristics** (also known as *variables*) are the unique, identifiable qualities or features of the people or objects being studied. If a company's customers are being studied, all of the relevant customer information that has been collected is the data set. Important characteristics might be age, gender, income level, number of years as a customer, and types of products purchased. A study of employees might focus on job titles, department, years employed, hours of training received, and job performance rating. Research on a company's products may look at type of product, factory where production occurred, units sold, and dollar sales volume.

When important characteristics have been identified, the data are then classified. Data collected for each characteristic will fall within a range of numbers. A **range** is all of the possible values of a characteristic from lowest to highest. For example, Perlich Industries has 95 employees with work experience ranging from 1–35 years. The complete data set for the years of experience of all 95 employees appears below.

1, 1, 1, 3, 4, 4, 4, 5, 5, 5, 5, 6, 6, 6, 7, 7, 8, 8, 8, 8, 8, 9, 9, 9, 9, 9, 10, 10, 10, 11, 11, 12, 12, 13, 13, 13, 13, 13, 13, 13, 14, 15, 16, 16, 17, 18, 18, 21, 21, 22, 24, 25, 25, 25, 26, 26, 26, 26, 26, 27, 27, 27, 27, 27, 27, 27, 27, 27, 27, 28, 28, 28, 28, 29, 29, 29, 30, 30, 30, 30, 31, 31, 31, 32, 32, 32, 33, 33, 33, 33, 34, 34, 35, 35, 35

When data are *classified*, they are organized within meaningful categories for further analysis. The most common classification of data in research is the frequency distribution. A **frequency distribution** lists each of the values in the range for a characteristic and the number of times that value appears in the data set. For example, the data for Perlich Industries can be classified into categories representing each five years of experience. It is much easier to study the years of experience of the employees when the data are organized in a frequency distribution rather than a list of 95 numbers. The frequency distribution for the Perlich data appears below.

Years of Experience	Frequency
0–5 years	11
6–10 years	18
11–15 years	13
16–20 years	5
21–25 years	7
26–30 years	26
31–35 years	15

In addition to the range and frequency distribution, there are other common ways to summarize data for analysis. The *range* identifies the highest and lowest values and the *frequency* shows how often a particular value or group of values appears. It may be helpful to know what value represents the average, or most common, of all the data. In statistics, an average value is called a *measure of central tendency*. There are actually three different averages used in statistics: the mean, median, and mode. The **mean** is the sum of all values divided by the number of values. The **median** is the middle number in the range of all the values. The **mode** is the value that appears the most frequently in the range. When the three measures of central tendency are calculated on the complete data set for the 95 employees described earlier, the mean is 19.07 years, the median is 21 years, and the mode is 27.

Decision makers may be interested in determining if the values appearing in the range are distributed evenly across the full range or if the values are grouped within parts of the range. To complete this analysis, the range of the data (highest and lowest values) is divided into four groupings representing an equal number of possible values. Then the data set is distributed within the four categories and analyzed to see if the values fall equally into the four groups (*quartiles*) or if they are more heavily represented in one or more. The quartiles of the range for the Perlich data appear below.

1st quartile	1–9 years	26 employees
2nd quartile	10–18 years	21 employees
3rd quartile	19–27 years	22 employees
4th quartile	28–35 years	26 employees

Notice that the employees are not distributed evenly across the 35 years of experience. If they were, one-fourth, or about 24, would have fit into each of the four quartiles.

COMMON INFERENTIAL STATISTICS

Descriptive statistics are used to describe and analyze all of the subjects or objects being studied. Inferential statistics, on the other hand, are a bit more complex. Using inferential statistics, a manager can use a small amount of information to draw conclusions about a larger group, to compare two groups to determine similarities and differences on important characteristics, or to use existing information to make predictions about the future.

To *infer* means to draw a conclusion with only partial information. With inferential statistics, a manager draws a conclusion about a population based on a sample. The **population** is all of the people or objects with a similar characteristic or characteristics being studied. The **sample** is a small, representative part of a population selected for study.

Businesses usually want to serve many more consumers than they can possibly study at one time. What are the advantages and problems of studying a sample rather than all of those consumers?

© Shutterstock/Keith Gentry

When decision makers review data from a sample, there is a chance that the results are not the same as they would have been if the entire population had been studied. They need to know the probability that the results represent the population. A **probability** is the likelihood that a certain outcome will occur. Inferential statistics are also used to identify possible correlations. A **correlation** is a connection or relationship between two things being studied.

Filipe Herrera and his team will use inferential statistics when they evaluate the new sunscreen product and make decisions about its future. Information was gathered from two test markets. All of the customers in those markets make up the population being studied, but information is not needed from every customer. A sample of customers can be used as long as those in the sample have characteristics representative of the population. The new product team will review evidence from the test market to determine the probability that the results obtained in the test market can be obtained in other markets the company enters in the future. They will look for evidence of factors in the test market that appear to be correlated with positive sales results. Those factors should be effective in any new markets that are similar to the test markets.

 CHECKPOINT

Explain the relationship between a sample and a population.

14.3 ASSESSMENT

UNDERSTAND MANAGEMENT CONCEPTS

Determine the best answer for each of the following questions.

1. Which of the following is not a benefit of statistics for managers?
   a. They help the manager remain objective.
   b. They allow decisions to be made more quickly.
   c. They direct the manager toward the best answer or solution.
   d. They help managers build support for decisions they have already made.

2. The sum of all values in a data set divided by the number of values is the
   a. sample
   b. mean
   c. median
   d. probability

THINK CRITICALLY

Answer the following questions as completely as possible.

3. What are two situations in business where a manager would use descriptive statistics to aid in decision making? What are two situations when inferential statistics would be used?

4. What are the advantages of collecting data on a sample rather than a population when attempting to solve a problem?

Moving Into New Markets

On the fiftieth anniversary of Barbie, the iconic fashion doll, Mattel opened its first Barbie store in Shanghai. The move into China was an attempt to expand Mattel's sales in a country with very high potential to counter lagging sales for the doll and her accessories in traditional markets. The store was a six-story, 36,000 square foot gem in the central shopping district. When entering the store, customers were bathed in pink neon lighting as they moved past a large staircase featuring 875 Barbie dolls. Not just a doll showcase, the store featured a spa, cosmetics department, women's fashions, a café, and a fashion runway. Mattel's goal was to attract upscale women in the fast-growing Chinese economy who would make purchases for themselves as well as their daughters. The company even introduced Ling, a Chinese Barbie, before the store opening.

However, the initial excitement failed to translate into sales. Within eight months, the company had to cut sales forecasts drastically. Less than two years later, Barbie's grand entry into China was seen as a failure and the giant store was closed. The lack of success was particularly disappointing given the huge success of the first such international store opened by Mattel in Buenos Aires just one year earlier. How could one good decision be followed so quickly by a bad one?

Upon further analysis, the differences in the two markets were vast. Argentina has a longer history with Barbie with successful sales through other retailers before the Mattel store opened. Young girls and their mothers had recently flocked to a Barbie musical when it toured across the country. In China, where Barbie was previously unknown, Mattel decided to open a store five times as large as the store in Buenos Aires stocked with many unique products targeted at both mothers and their daughters. The company, however, had little experience with or information about the Chinese market. Because of the large store with it high operating costs, Mattel did not have the time or resources to learn from its mistakes before it had to close the store.

Company executives still have their eyes on the Chinese market. But this time, they are moving more slowly and trying to learn more about the market.

THINK CRITICALLY

1. Since there are more potential customers when the Barbie store sells products for both mothers and their daughters, why might that decision cause problems?

2. Why should company executives have been cautious in entering the new market even though they had been successful in Buenos Aires?

3. Despite the failure in China, Mattel is considering entering the large India market. What advice would you give Mattel managers to avoid their recent problems in China?

© Shutterstock/Rick Becker-Leckrone

14.4

Using Data in Decision Making

Goals

- Describe how to identify and communicate the results of data analysis.
- Discuss how data should be used in effective decision making.

Terms

- cause-and-effect p. 375
- executive summary p. 375
- table p. 376
- chart p. 376
- graph p. 377
- trend p. 377
- representative p. 379
- significant p. 379

●●●● Communicating Results of Data Analysis

Managers need information for decision making. However if the information is misinterpreted or misunderstood, poor decisions will result. The time devoted to data collection and analysis will be wasted unless important results are identified, clearly communicated, and used as the basis for answering questions, solving problems, and developing plans. The data analysis procedures are completed by identifying important results and then communicating those results in an understandable way.

COMPLETING DATA ANALYSIS

Having a large amount of data to review can present problems for decision makers. What information is important and what is not important? Are we being objective in reviewing information or are we allowing personal values and biases to influence us? Is our approach to reviewing the information causing us to overlook or misinterpret important information? The following guidelines will help in completing an effective analysis of the data that have been collected.

- *Focus on the problem or question.* Why was the information collected? What decision needs to be made? With a large amount of information, it is easy to lose sight of the reasons the data were collected. Avoid becoming distracted by interesting information that does not directly relate to the decision to be made.
- *Recognize the purpose of the data analysis.* Is the analysis being done to describe, understand, and examine characteristics or is it to make comparisons, examine relationships, or make predictions for the future? Reviewing the purpose will keep the appropriate focus on the correct statistics and data summaries as well as the appropriate uses of the data.
- *Summarize the information accurately.* Going through pages and pages of data or looking at many screens of information on a computer makes it easy to ignore or overlook important information. Prepare effective summaries of the information using appropriate statistical tools. Calculate frequencies, distributions, and averages for all important categories of information. Check the calculations to make sure all of the needed information has been included and the calculations are accurate.

- *Look for changes, differences, and unexpected results.* What information is different from past experience or from what was expected? Are the results from one or more groups quite different from others? Where have the greatest and smallest changes occurred? Are there some variables that seem to be different from most others?
- *Search for patterns or relationships.* Are there characteristics or conditions that seem to be related to particular results? Do changes seem to occur under certain conditions but not others? When patterns and relationships are identified, it is not always a cause-and-effect situation. **Cause-and-effect** is the relationship between two events in which the second event is a consequence of the first. In a cause-and-effect situation, an action or change occurs as a result of something that preceded it. The action or change is the effect and the preceding action or event is the cause. Rain causes grass to grow. Eating too much leads to weight gain. However, in most data analysis, it is difficult to determine with confidence that a change or an action was the result of something else. Typically, decision makers identify *relationships*, meaning two events or actions seem to be related to each other, without judging whether one of the events occurred as a direct result of the other. Only carefully designed and controlled experiments can provide the type of evidence needed to determine cause-and-effect.

SUMMARIZING RESULTS

The reason for information gathering and data analysis is to aid in problem solving and decision making. Almost all employees and managers have more information available to them than they have the time to review and understand. Yet they need information to make good decisions. Information needs to be analyzed, summarized, and communicated to decision makers. Information summaries can also be used to explain how and why decisions were made and to help others understand and support the decisions as they are implemented. In the business environment, information is summarized and communicated in two main ways: in writing and visually using tables, charts, and graphs.

WRITTEN SUMMARIES A complete written report includes a statement of the problem or purpose, a description of the data collection procedure, all important data collected, and the identification and analysis of possible decisions. If a final decision has been made, it will be included in the report along with plans for implementing the decision. People who want to study the information in detail will want to see the full report. However, some people prefer to see the executive summary. An **executive summary** is a written summary of a longer report containing adequate information for the reader to fully understand the information being communicated. It is typically only a few pages long.

Management MATTERS

Data Security

Managers and employees need access to data whenever and wherever they work. Data security becomes an ever more critical issue with many managers traveling, using personal computers and smart phones, and logging in to company databases via public Wi-Fi connections. To protect data from being lost or stolen, security companies recommend:

- Limiting data file access to only essential employees.
- Using strong and secure passwords and data encryption.
- Training employees regularly on security practices for their personal hardware.
- Monitoring networks and data files to determine how and when they are being accessed.
- Using only secure networks for downloading and uploading data.

What Do You Think? How does the loss or theft of sensitive data harm a business? What responsibility do individual managers and employees have for the security of a company's data?

Example of a Table

Regional Sales by Quarter (millions)				
	Q1	Q2	Q3	Q4
Northeast	$33.3	$25.1	$35.2	$22.9
Southeast	25.4	29.1	32.6	34.8
Midwest	30.2	29.9	31.0	30.6
West	34.1	32.8	30.5	27.8

Figure 14-6 Tables organize complex data to make the data more understandable.

TABLES, CHARTS, AND GRAPHS The preferred way of summarizing and communicating numerical information is with tables, charts, and graphs. Many people can more easily study and understand information when it is summarized and presented visually. Well-designed tables, charts, and graphs are more attention getting and memorable than written summaries of the data. In addition to presenting and summarizing data, these visuals can be used to illustrate relationships.

Tables, charts, and graphs have unique characteristics and specific purposes when used to summarize and present data. A **table** is a visual presentation of information organized in rows and columns. When the information in a table is numerical, it is often called a *data table*. Tables are used to summarize data and clearly communicate complicated information to readers. Because information is organized in rows and columns, a table can contain more information than a chart or graph. However, tables need to be well designed and carefully prepared to communicate information clearly and objectively.

The main components of a table are the title, column and row headings, and cell data. The *title* identifies the focus or purpose of the table. It should be concise, specific, and clear. In Figure 14-6, the title indicates the table is presenting information about the company's regional sales for each quarter of the year. The *column and row headings* identify the characteristics or variables from the data set included in the table. In the example table, each of the company's sales regions appears as a row heading and the four quarters of the year appear as column headings. Finally, the *cell data* are presented for each region and quarter. In the table, the data appear as two digit numbers with one decimal place, but the table title indicates the data represent millions of dollars. The table presents an effective summary of the company's yearly sales by region and by quarter.

A **chart** is a type of diagram that organizes and summarizes a set of numerical data. A chart is usually simpler than a table and focuses on summarizing and comparing information for one or two characteristics in a data set. The most common types of charts are the bar chart and pie chart. A *bar chart* presents important characteristics or variables from the data set as bars whose lengths are proportional to their values. A bar chart allows easy comparison of values among characteristics or over periods of time. A *pie chart* represents one or more important characteristics from a data set as a circle divided into sections. Each segment represents a specific part of the characteristic being analyzed. The size of each section represents its proportion of the total value of the characteristic. An example of a chart appears in Figure 14-7.

The main components of a chart are the title, data presentation, data labels, and the legend. As with a table, the chart *title* identifies the focus or purpose of the table. The *data presentation* is the content of the chart. Data in a bar chart show the values of each characteristic as a bar where the length of the bar represents the proportional value. The bars are aligned to provide the clearest comparison of the values related to the problem or issue being studied. In a pie chart, the data are shown as segments of the circle or pie. Comparisons are made based

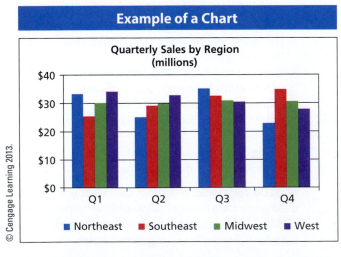

Figure 14-7 Charts provide an effective visual comparison of important characteristics in a data set.

on the relative size of each segment. All characteristics of the data should be summarized and organized into understandable and meaningful categories. The categories should be clearly identified with data labels. Frequently a chart *legend* is included to identify each of the variables in the chart. Legends are usually color coded or shaded to provide a unique identification for each variable.

Review the chart in Figure 14-7. The title states that the company sales are being compared by region and by quarter. The data are grouped by quarter for easier comparison of regional sales in each quarter of the year. Quarters are clearly labeled below each grouping of data. To make it easy to identify the region, a color-coded legend is included in the chart.

A **graph** (also called a *line graph*) is a visual representation of data as they change over time. An example appears in Figure 14-8. Data are shown as one or more lines connecting data points. Each data point identifies the value of the characteristic at a particular time. A line graph may present information on only one or a number of characteristics or categories of the data being studied. The main components of a graph are the same as for charts—title, data presentation, data labels, and legend. The data are presented in graph form with a horizontal axis and a vertical axis.

A graph is an excellent way to study trends. A **trend** is a general direction in which something is developing or changing. The graph in Figure 14-8 compares sales in each region over the entire year. The data presentation makes it easy to observe trends in sales for each region and to compare the full year's sales performance of all regions.

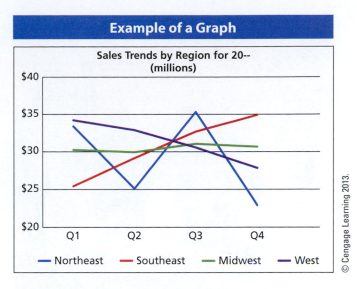

© Cengage Learning 2013.

Figure 14-8 Graphs are an effective way to illustrate trends.

CHECKPOINT

Why should tables, charts, and graphs be used when analyzing and communicating information?

●●● Making Data-Based Decisions

Managers have access to large amounts of data and other information that can be helpful in making decisions. To be successful, managers must become efficient in reading and understanding the information, selecting the information that will be most helpful, and then incorporating their findings into the decision-making process.

READING AND INTERPRETING INFORMATION

In preparing to make a decision, managers should take the time to review written summaries of the information. Most written summaries will include data in the forms of tables, charts, and graphs as well as discussions of procedures and results. For each summary, it is important to determine the source of the data used to prepare the summary and have access to the complete information if needed. Make sure the process used to collect, analyze, and summarize the information

© Shutterstock/Golden Pixels LLC

Often managers want input from others before making important decisions. What benefits can result when several people meet to discuss the results of data analysis?

is clear, objective, and unbiased. In most businesses, people who are skilled in data collection and data analysis are responsible for those procedures and have the expertise and experience needed to prepare reports. If necessary, managers can contact the people responsible for data analysis and ask them to explain any part of the summaries or procedures used to gather, analyze, and summarize the information.

The next step is to study carefully each table, chart, and graph that summarizes the key data needed to make a decision. Because tables, charts, and graphs are summaries, it may be necessary to obtain additional information for complete understanding. However, effective summaries should provide most if not all of the information needed for day-to-day decision making.

The following procedures should be followed when studying tables, charts, and graphs:

1. *Read the title carefully.* The title communicates the specific purpose of the summary. It will identify the type of information that is contained in the graphic and how the data are being presented. Is it a description of information, a comparison of two or more types of information, or a more complex analysis or projection?

2. *Determine what is represented in the data set.* Is it all available data or just a part? If not all of the data are presented, is the information a representative sample or does it reflect a unique portion of the full data?

3. *Review the row and column headings of a table or the data labels and legends on charts and graphs.* What are the characteristics or variables that are examined in the graphic? Is the focus on one characteristic with an analysis of its components (employees by age, gender, years, or experience) or are two or more characteristics being analyzed (sales volume and advertising expenditures)? Determine how information about the characteristics relates to the problem or question being studied. The headings and labels should show the range of possible data being presented. A chart or graph can look very different if a small range of numbers is used for each category compared to one with a very large range.

4. *Examine the type of data being reported in the data cells or data presentation.* The data might be in the form of numbers, percentages, frequency counts, or averages. Each type of data will present a different view of the issue being studied. Make sure of the units being used to report data. Zeros may have been omitted and replaced with decimals to reflect data in thousands or millions. The units being represented should be noted in the title or data labels.

5. *Finally, study all of the data carefully and thoroughly to understand their meaning.* What information stands out? What characteristics or variables seem to be different from others? How do the results compare to what was expected? What are the ranges of data? Are most categories near the top or bottom of the range or are they distributed across the range? Is there evidence of relationships among variables that seems to indicate better or worse performance? Return to the problem or question and analyze how the data offer information that relates to possible solutions or answers.

ANSWERING QUESTIONS AND SOLVING PROBLEMS

Although data are used in decision making, data alone cannot answer a question or solve a problem. Information is incorporated into decision making to make the decision more objective. It helps managers determine possible alternatives and to choose among those alternatives.

Information can be helpful only if the right question is asked or the problem is identified correctly. Reviewing information regularly helps to identify when problems are occurring and what decisions need to be made. When data are not consistent with plans, past performance, or expectations, managers can use that information to begin to identify problems.

Data can also help to identify possible answers to questions or solutions to problems. Looking at differences among groups, results after changes have been made, improvements or declines in performance that appear at various times, and other variations in data can give clues to issues and possible solutions. Managers should seldom rely on information collected from one group or at one time. Monitoring and comparing data from various time periods or several groups gives a much clearer and more objective view.

Finally, data can be misleading and misused if managers do not understand some important characteristics of data. Data need to be **representative**; that is, they need to be consistent with other similar data that could be collected. Results also need to be **significant**, which means they are meaningful and did not occur by chance. In some cases, data may appear to be flawed. For example, the results do not really represent the situation or circumstances in the business, the results do not seem to be important or meaningful in relation to the problem or question, or it seems unlikely that the results could be repeated. It is better to continue to gather and analyze information rather than use the apparently flawed data. Quality information used as a part of an effective decision-making process will result in good decisions.

When using data for decision making, managers should ask the following questions:

1. Do the results point toward one answer or solution or to more than one?
2. Is there other information that could affect the decision that has not been considered?
3. Do differences in the data indicate important differences, or are the differences the result of the type of data collected, the method used to collect data, or the timing of data collection?
4. Does the information appear to present a pattern or trend or does it seem to be a one-time occurrence?
5. Are there multiple factors rather than just one that could be affecting the results?

NETBookmark

One of the most comprehensive data collection and information analysis efforts undertaken is the United States Census. Every household is surveyed and the census attempts to count every person in the country.

Access the website for this textbook and choose the link for Chapter 14 Net Bookmark. Roll your mouse over the interactive map of the United States that illustrates population changes by state from 2000–2010. Compare information from your state with several other states and the national data. Click the link to *Population Distribution and Change: 2000 to 2010* and review several of the tables and charts. What are several ways that businesses can use national, regional, state, and community census information?

www.cengage.com/school/bizmgmt

CHECKPOINT

What are two important characteristics of data?

UNDERSTAND MANAGEMENT CONCEPTS

Determine the best answer for each of the following questions.

1. A type of diagram that organizes and summarizes a set of numerical data is a(n)
   a. table
   b. chart
   c. graph
   d. executive summary

2. The first step a manager should use when studying a table, chart, or graph is
   a. read the title carefully
   b. determine what is represented in the data set
   c. review row and column headings and data labels
   d. study all data carefully and thoroughly

THINK CRITICALLY

Answer the following questions as completely as possible.

3. Why should decision makers be careful not to assign cause-and-effect in a relationship among data?
4. What is the difference between a chart and a graph?

CHAPTER CONCEPTS

1. Data-based decisions use information as the primary basis for choosing among alternatives. Managers gather and analyze information to make objective decisions.

2. Managers use math skills when analyzing situations, determining the numerical data needed to support decision making, organizing the information in the correct way for analysis, and judging the results to make sure the solution is reasonable.

3. A starting point for effectively using mathematics in business is being able to understand and apply basic arithmetic operations as well as the use of fractions, decimals, and percents.

4. The common measures used in business are length, weight, and volume. Understanding both the U.S. and metric standards of measurement is critical in a global economy.

5. By using statistics, managers can make decisions more quickly, with greater confidence, and with a higher probability of making the best choice. Descriptive statistics are used to explain a current situation; inferential statistics are used to make predictions about similar circumstances or about the future.

6. Information summaries are used to make and explain decisions. In the business environment, information is summarized and communicated in two main ways: in writing and visually using tables, charts, and graphs.

REVIEW BUSINESS MANAGEMENT TERMS

Write the letter of the term that matches each definition. Some terms will not be used.

1. The relationship between two quantities
2. Meaningful and not occurring by chance
3. Part of a whole expressed in hundredths
4. The middle number in the range of values
5. The likelihood that a certain outcome will occur
6. Part of a whole number expressed as a proportion
7. Analysis of specific data to draw broader conclusions
8. The sum of all values divided by the number of values
9. A visual representation of data as they change over time
10. Consistent with other similar data that could be collected
11. A small, representative part of a population selected for study
12. A presentation of information organized by rows and columns
13. All of the data that have been collected for study
14. A connection or relationship between two things being studied
15. The value that appears the most frequently in a range of values
16. All the possible values of a characteristic from lowest to highest
17. A general direction in which something is developing or changing
18. Meaningful summaries of data to help explain a current situation

a. chart
b. correlation
c. data set
d. descriptive statistics
e. fraction
f. graph
g. inductive reasoning
h. mean
i. median
j. mode
k. percentage
l. population
m. probability
n. range
o. ratio
p. representative
q. sample
r. significant
s. table
t. trend

Determine the best answer.

19. Which of the following is a basic arithmetic operation?
    a. division
    b. algebra
    c. inductive reasoning
    d. statistics

20. To be understandable and useful for decision makers, raw data must be
    a. presented in tables, charts, or graphs
    b. processed and organized
    c. summarized
    d. simplified

21. The activity managers perform when they review data to identify relationships, patterns, and explanations is
    a. calculate
    b. compare
    c. analyze
    d. project

22. The correct structure and terminology for a division equation is
    a. dividend ÷ product = quotient
    b. divisor ÷ dividend = product
    c. dividend ÷ divisor = quotient
    d. multiplicand ÷ subtrahend = product

23. Which of the following is true about the U.S. measurement system?
    a. It is used by most other countries.
    b. All measures are in common units of ten.
    c. It was first used in the U.S. in 1901.
    d. U.S. measures are now defined using metric standards.

24. In statistics, an average value is also known as a
    a. range
    b. frequency
    c. measure of central tendency
    d. variable

25. A sample is a small representative part of a
    a. population
    b. probability
    c. frequency distribution
    d. census

26. An excellent visual way to study trends is with a(n)
    a. chart
    b. graph
    c. table
    d. executive summary

APPLY WHAT YOU KNOW

Answer the following questions.

27. In the Reality Check at the beginning of the chapter, why do you believe simplifying the data and using a chart to analyze the data helped Petra identify the error?

28. A manager carefully examines the budget figures from the past three years in preparation for developing next year's budget. Is the manager using inductive or deductive reasoning? Why?

29. Why is it a good idea to check your answers when completing addition, subtraction, multiplication, and division by using a different procedure than you used when calculating the first answer?

30. What are advantages and disadvantages of the U.S. continuing to use two different systems of measurement—the traditional U.S. system and the metric system?

31. What do the terms *probability* and *correlation* mean to managers when they are making decisions?

32. Explain why you agree or disagree with the following statement: Information can be helpful only if the right question is asked or the problem is identified correctly.

MAKE ACADEMIC CONNECTIONS

Complete the following activities

33. **Technology** Use the Internet to locate an online calculator that makes conversions between the U.S. and metric measurement systems. Create a chart to record your answers. Convert the following U.S. weights and measures to metric weights and measures: (a) 20 inches, (b) 89 feet, (c) 87 pounds, (d) 2 pints, (e) 103 gallons. Convert the following metric weights and measures to U.S. weights and measures: (f) 1125 kilometers, (g) 1122 grams, (h) 25 metric tons, (i) 135 kiloliters

34. **Math** The human resource manager for the Octold Co. is reviewing employee data in preparation for requesting bids on the company's health insurance plan. The company has 30 employees with the ages shown below. Prepare a frequency distribution of the ages of all employees and determine the range, mean, median, and mode of the employee data.

    38, 59, 59, 36, 37, 30, 44, 42, 37, 46, 47, 46, 28, 42, 27
    59, 59, 25, 43, 30, 59, 32, 30, 48, 39, 28, 27, 30, 52, 63

35. **Research** The U.S. Census Bureau provides an annual report on business activity called County Business Patterns that presents information by state, county, and city. Visit the report website and locate information on your state. Obtain information on the total number of business establishments and total number of employees for the most recent three years of data. Prepare one table, one bar or pie chart, and one graph that present and compare the information you selected. Prepare three one-sentence conclusions about the data you reported.

CASE IN POINT

CASE 14-1: Price Comparisons

Students in a college marketing class decided to undertake research on prices for common food items among grocery stores in their community. They developed a list of ten items that would regularly be purchased by families. Then they shopped at six stores to determine the current prices charged for each item. In each store they compared prices using standard units for each product. If the store offered multiple brands of the same product, students determined the highest and lowest price and then calculated the mean value. After they completed the data collection, they developed a table to present their results.

	Store 1	Store 2	Store 3	Store 4	Store 5	Store 6
Eggs	1.52	1.73	1.69	1.23	1.30	1.42
Spaghetti	1.09	1.17	1.23	1.14	1.25	1.26
Rice	0.75	0.73	0.77	0.71	0.78	0.80
Ground Beef	3.52	3.67	3.85	3.14	3.43	3.53
Chicken	1.26	1.26	1.30	1.29	1.24	1.27
Milk	3.18	3.60	3.65	3.58	3.81	3.85
Apples	1.26	1.35	1.31	1.24	1.35	1.31
Tomatoes	2.42	2.67	2.79	2.32	2.29	2.88
Peanut Butter	2.06	2.02	2.03	1.96	1.83	2.06
Potato Chips	4.59	4.85	4.90	4.52	4.30	4.56

To complete their research they need additional summaries and analysis performed on the raw data.

THINK CRITICALLY

1. Calculate the total cost of the ten products for each of the six stores. Then determine the range and mean of the total product costs for the six stores.
2. If you shopped all of the stores, what is the highest and lowest total price you could pay if you purchased all ten products? What is the percentage savings between the highest and lowest totals?
3. Calculate the mean price for each product using the prices of all six stores.
4. If you were a student in the marketing class, list three conclusions you would draw from the research.
5. If you were a consumer in the town where the research was completed, how would the results affect your decisions about grocery shopping?

CASE 14-2: Analyzing Company Performance Data

Tara Brookings is a consultant for Watr, Inc. a manufacturer of industrial filters used in water treatment plants. Watr had been a leader in the U.S. market for more than 40 years. Ten years ago, due to increasing competition in the U.S. market, the company began selling its filters internationally. These sales have grown steadily but contribute little profit. Watr executives have asked Tara to complete some data analysis to help them as they plan for the next five years. Tara has prepared the following table and is planning to discuss it with the executives.

	Comparison of U.S. and International Market Performance—previous 10 years					
	United States			International (non-U.S.)		
	−10 years	−5 years	Current year	−10 years	−5 years	Current year
Industry Sales	$856 mil.	$1.3 bil.	$1.6 bil.	$2.1 bil.	$3.9 bil.	$4.8 bil.
Watr Sales	$193 mil.	$211 mil.	$220 mil.	$43 mil.	109 mil.	$159 mil.
Watr Cost of Goods Sold	$65 mil.	$71 mil.	$77 mil.	$15 mil.	$38 mil.	$50 mil.
Watr Operating Expenses	$109 mil.	$118 mil.	$124 mil.	$30 mil.	$69 mil.	$105 mil.
Watr Profit	$19 mil.	$22 mil.	$19 mil.	$−2 mil.	$2 mil.	$4 mil.

As Tara reviews the information in the table, she notes the following:

- Industry sales have grown in each of the five-year periods
- Watr sales have grown in each period both in the U.S. and international markets
- Company profits have also grown in each period other when Watr first entered the international market and in the current year for the U.S. market.

Tara believes there is information hidden in the data presented in the table that will be important to the executives as they develop the strategic plan. She decides to do further analysis before she meets with the executives.

THINK CRITICALLY

1. Prepare two line graphs for Ms. Brookings so she has a visual picture of the ten years of data. One graph should present the U.S. data and the other should present the international data.
2. Calculate the shares of the U.S. and international markets for each of the five-year periods. Present the data in a table.
3. Calculate the percentage profit based on sales the company earned in each market for each of the five-year periods. Prepare a table of your results.
4. Based on your additional analysis, prepare three or more statements of facts about the company performance.
5. Prepare two recommendations for Tara to guide Watr's planning. Justify each recommendation with a few sentences.

PROJECT My Own Business

Using Data for Decision Making

As the owner of a new small business, you will be responsible for most if not all of the important decisions. You will want to be certain those decisions are the best possible you can make. That means they should be based on accurate, up-to-date information. Over time, your experience will also become an important part of decision making, but you will always want to remain objective and make decisions only after gathering and studying information related to the problem or question you are facing.

To be an effective manager and decision maker, you will need to be skilled in using data. An important part of using data is being comfortable and accurate with mathematics. The second part is being able to analyze and understand raw and processed data in order to make effective decisions. In the project activities for this chapter, you will review the types of mathematical skills you will need in your business and the important ways you will gather and analyze information to improve your business decisions.

DATA COLLECTION

1. Review news articles and advertisements for community businesses in your local newspaper. Identify 20 examples of ways that basic arithmetic is used regularly in those businesses.
2. Meet with a local small business owner to discuss his or her views of the importance of mathematics skills and using data for decision making in the success of the owner's business.
3. Use the Internet to identify examples of mathematical errors that had a negative effect on business.
4. Contact local government officials, economic development specialists, or the Small Business Administration office. Identify research that has been completed and other data that can help you understand the long-term trends in the economy and retail sales for your community.

ANALYSIS

1. For each of the following areas of your business, identify three or more specific types of numerical information you will need to deal with regularly in managing the business: finance, operations, marketing, and personnel.
2. Choose three different products you plan to sell in your business. Using both U.S. and metric measurements, identify three possible sizes you might use to sell each product and the retail price you would use for each size. Calculate the cost per unit for each product and size for each of the two types of measurement systems (price/ounce or price/milliliter, for example).
3. Identify three local economic and retailing trends that you will want to watch carefully during the first several years of your business as you make plans for your business.

Tax accountants work with businesses and individuals to reduce their taxes by developing strategies that maximize deductions and minimize taxable revenue. They also help develop investment strategies. Tax accountants must understand federal and state tax laws. Some work for federal and state tax agencies.

Employment Outlook

Employment for accountants and auditors is expected to grow by 22 percent between 2008 and 2018. This growth is much faster than the average for all other occupations. This job expansion is linked to changing financial laws and regulations, increased scrutiny of company finances due to accounting scandals, and legislation designed to curb corporate accounting fraud.

Job Titles

Accounting Trainee

Junior Tax Accountant

Tax Accountant

Tax Accounting Manager

Chief Tax Accountant

Needed Skills

- Must possess a bachelor's degree in accounting from an accredited college or university.
- Should have an aptitude for mathematics and be able to analyze, compare, and interpret facts and figures quickly.
- Public accountants must pass the Certified Public Accounting (CPA) exam.
- Forty-six states and the District of Columbia require CPA candidates to have an additional 30 hours of coursework beyond a bachelor's degree. Many colleges and universities now offer five-year combined bachelor's degree and master's degree program to meet these requirements.

Working in an Accounting Firm

Ryan completed his bachelor's degree in accounting. As a student, he worked as a volunteer helping people fill out personal tax forms. After graduating, he started working for a medium-size accounting firm as a trainee. After passing the CPA exam, he worked for three years as a junior tax accountant. He was then promoted to tax accounting, supervising a team of accountants helping businesses develop tax strategies. Ryan hopes to become a tax accounting manager, then a chief tax accountant, and ultimately a partner in the firm.

Career Assessment

Why are tax accountants important to businesses and individuals? Why do they need years of training? What do you like and dislike about this career area?

© Getty Images/Photodisc

Case Study

PAYING CELEBRITIES FOR COMMERCIALS ON MULTIPLE MEDIA

Celebrities have been used in commercials for decades to sell products and services ranging from new automobiles to the latest health care for seniors. Prior to the use of numerous new forms of technology for advertising, the celebrities appeared on television commercials and in print advertisements, receiving a salary or royalty for their work. Most celebrities are paid for the number of times their commercial is aired or the number of times an advertisement that includes their likeness is used in magazines and newspapers.

The digital world of advertising has opened the issue of how celebrities should get compensated for their work. The ad industry and talent representatives agree that the old model formed in the 1950s does not work in today's diversified media landscape. Representatives from the advertising industry and Hollywood are working on a new model for compensation in a digital world. Consultants have been asked by all negotiating parties to submit proposals that will address how actors in commercials will be paid when the spots appear on multiple media.

The ultimate goal of negotiations is to create a system of fair compensation for celebrities who promote products and services through numerous media channels.

THINK CRITICALLY

1. How has the increased use of technology affected the sales potential for products and services?
2. Why should celebrities be eligible for higher compensation when their advertisements are being relayed through many technological avenues?
3. What is your opinion of basing a celebrity's pay on the dollar amount of sales generated through the different avenues of advertisement, including the latest technology?
4. Give five examples of products or services that are promoted by celebrities. Why are these individuals good choices for promoting those particular products and services?

E-Commerce Management Team Decision-Making Event

www.deca.org

For more information about competitive events and performance indicators, go to the DECA website.

PROCEDURE   Your management team will consist of two members. In addition to taking a multiple-choice exam for e-commerce, you must develop a solution for the following case study. You have 30 minutes to prepare your presentation using a laptop computer, if you wish. Your team is allowed 10 minutes to present your information to the judges, who will have five minutes to ask questions.

SCENARIO   The Pottery Stop has successfully operated for five years, selling pottery and garden art along a busy highway in Texas. The mild climate allows the business to remain open the entire year. Customers from all over the United States are pleasantly surprised by the variety and quality of pottery available. The shop customizes orders and will ship merchandise throughout the United States for an additional fee.

YOUR ASSIGNMENT

The Pottery Stop is now ready to expand by selling over the Internet. You must develop a strategy to implement this new source of sales. You must decide what information to include on the website.

PERFORMANCE INDICATORS EVALUATED

- Understand the economics of expanding business through e-commerce.
- Explain the importance of increasing distribution channels.
- Describe the links available on a successful website.
- Describe promotional materials that will be distributed at the store to inform customers about buying merchandise online.

THINK CRITICALLY

1. Why are businesses choosing to sell merchandise online?
2. Why are some consumers hesitant to shop online?
3. Why should the Pottery Stop collect data about customers who purchase online and at the store?

4 UNIT

Financial Management

CHAPTERS

BUSINESS FINANCIAL RECORDS

© Shutterstock/Fotoline

Reality Check

Do I Need to Be an Accountant?

Clark walked into the lobby of his bank carrying two weeks of receipts from his part-time business. He installs audio and video equipment in people's home in the evenings and on weekends. He knew he should make deposits more frequently, especially when he has a large number of checks and some cash. However, he has little time as he tries to balance his full-time work schedule with his own part-time business.

Clark greeted the bank teller, "Good morning, Monica. I've got a stack for you today. Business has been good!"

Monica looked unhappy and said, "Clark, I can process your deposits but I thought you were going to hire a bookkeeping service to help you keep better records for your business. You have all this money you're depositing today but your checking account is overdrawn again."

"I'm thinking about it," Clark replied. "I know I have problems with my records, but my business is growing really fast. If the bank approves my loan application, I'll be able to quit my job and devote full-time to the business."

Monica smiled. "You've been thinking about a bookkeeping service for over a year. How do you know from day to day what's happening with your money? Oh, that reminds me. My boss said if you came in she wanted to see you right away about the loan."

Clark knew he had to keep better records, but he was certain his business was ready to take off once he got the loan approval. However, the bank manager, Jerri Steen, was about to deliver some bad news.

"Either your current assets are too low or your current liabilities are too high," Jerri said. "If you want us to approve a loan for your business, you have to increase your working capital. I realize you are getting more and more customers and your sales are growing, but you're not generating enough profit on your sales."

Clark wasn't really sure what Jerri was saying. The financial terms she was using were almost a foreign language to him.

"Do I need to take an accounting course?" Clark asked. "It's clear I need to understand more about the financial side of my business if I'm going to be successful."

What's Your Reaction? Why is it important for Clark to have a better understanding of accounting and finance before he begins the full-time business?

Types of Financial Records

Goals

- Describe why businesses need to maintain financial records.
- Identify and discuss the purpose of several types of business financial records.

Terms

- financial records p. 392
- record-keeping system p. 392
- accounting p. 393
- data processing p. 393
- cash receipts p. 394
- cash disbursements p. 394
- accounts receivable record p. 395
- accounts payable record p. 395
- asset p. 396
- depreciation p. 396
- fixed assets p. 396
- book value p. 396

●●● Financial Records

All businesses—large and small—must keep records. **Financial records** are organized summaries of a business's financial information and activities. While all businesses are legally required to keep some records, the main purpose of financial records is to determine if the business is profitable. If a business is not making a profit, it will not be able to continue operating for long unless things can be changed. Financial records make it possible for owners and managers to understand a business's financial performance and make the best possible decisions regarding the use of the company's resources.

A very small business could determine how profitable it is by using a business checking account to track all income deposited and by writing checks for all payments. The total deposits (income) less the total of all checks written (expenses) tell the business owner if the business is making money. However, this simple approach does not provide adequate information to fully understand the financial condition of the business.

Businesses need complete and detailed records to satisfy their information needs. All companies must determine what records to keep, how to prepare and maintain them, and who should be responsible for the records. Once a records system is in place, managers can use the information to understand the business's finances, complete financial planning, and establish controls.

RECORD-KEEPING SYSTEMS

A **record-keeping system** is a manual or automated process for collecting, organizing, and maintaining the financial information of a business. There are many options for businesses to organize and maintain their financial records. A small-business owner can keep the records personally or hire a bookkeeper or accountant. Larger businesses have finance and accounting departments with specially trained personnel to maintain financial records, prepare reports, and help with financial planning. Some businesses hire other companies to provide specialized record-keeping services or even to maintain all of the business's financial records.

Whether a record-keeping system is simple or complex, it contains four elements—records, people, procedures, and tools. The system must be accurate, keep information safe and secure, and provide timely and accurate information.

Before computers gained widespread acceptance in businesses, bookkeepers and accountants prepared and maintained all financial records manually. Few businesses rely on manual systems today. Easy-to-use and affordable accounting software has replaced most manual systems. However, standardized accounting forms and records systems for manual recordkeeping are available wherever office supplies are sold.

Some small retail and service businesses use a cash register to gather most of the information needed for their financial records. Cash registers maintain printed tapes showing the details of each sales transaction. This information can be used to enter data into the business's accounting records. However, cash registers record only information on customer sales, which is an incomplete record of the financial transactions of the business. Businesses are replacing cash registers with point-of-sale (POS) terminals. POS terminals include cash register functions but also have credit and debit card processing capabilities, and a scanner that reads product barcodes to update inventory records. The revenues and costs associated with each product can be tracked and analyzed using POS technology. With specially designed software and hardware, the POS terminal can meet unique sales and information gathering requirements of the business.

ACCOUNTING AND DATA PROCESSING

Accounting is the process of recording, analyzing, and interpreting financial activities of a business. Today most firms use accounting software programs to maintain their financial records. Accounting software simplifies and speeds the record-keeping process while reducing errors. A desktop computer is adequate for most electronic record-keeping systems, but large companies need systems that are more complex. They need systems that can quickly and accurately processing huge amounts of data gathered from multiple locations.

Many of the day-to-day data entry and records management activities in large and small businesses are completed by bookkeepers and accounting clerks. Small businesses then hire an accounting firm as needed for specialized activities. Large corporations employ many bookkeepers and accountants, many of whom have specialized skills and knowledge.

Data processing is the set of activities involved in obtaining, recording, organizing, and maintaining the financial information of an organization. A data processing center is the location where data processing activities occur. It contains the computers, software, security systems, and personnel that are needed to complete those activities.

Some businesses have their own data processing centers. However, because data processing can be a highly technical and expensive process, many

Technology allows companies to have their data processing done by companies that may be located in countries thousands of miles away.

© Jupiter Images/Creatas Images

companies now contract with specialized businesses that operate large data processing centers. Some business choose to purchase all their data processing services, while other companies purchase services for selected tasks such as maintaining inventory records or payroll systems. Today, data can be transmitted instantaneously via the Internet from the point of origin to the data processing center and back to the business in the form of records and reports. Therefore, the data processing work for a company can be completed anywhere in the world—across town, across the country, or halfway around the globe.

Large companies require large and complex automated systems for keeping records. The initial recording of financial transactions occurs throughout a company, wherever the transaction occurs. The data processing center receives the transaction data and processes them. The data are then provided to the accounting department, where the financial records and reports of the business are prepared and maintained.

It is common for businesses to divide their accounting department into several sections. Each section is typically responsible for handling one or more specific accounting activities, such as maintaining cash records, receipt and payment records, depreciation records, and tax and payroll records. Accountants prepare financial reports for managers and help them understand the financial condition of the business in order to develop plans based on the financial information.

 **CHECKPOINT**

Identify several reasons businesses need to maintain financial records.

●●● Types of Financial Records

Financial records in all types of businesses have similar characteristics. However, each type of record has a unique purpose and provides specific information for managers.

CASH RECORDS

Money, in the form of cash and checks, is constantly coming into a business from customers and other sources. Money taken in by a business is known as **cash receipts**. Cash goes out to pay for purchases made by a business. Small purchases may be made with actual cash, but most often businesses use checks for purchases. Cash payments made by a business are known as **cash disbursements**. No matter how large or small the cash receipt or payment, a written record of the transaction must be prepared and entered into the business's record-keeping system. Regardless of how financial records are maintained, businesses must develop specific procedures for employees to follow when receiving payments by cash or checks and when using cash for purchases. Figure 15-1 lists several suggestions for the safe handling of money.

CREDIT RECORDS

When a business sells goods and services, customers can make immediate payment with cash or check, or the business may accept credit. With *credit*, goods and services are provided with the expectation of future payment by

Safe and Accurate Handling of Money in a Business

Petty Cash	A *petty cash fund*, a supply of cash maintained in a business for small emergency payments, should be kept in a safe place controlled by a responsible person who follows specific procedures. A written record of all additions and withdrawals to the fund should be maintained.
Cash Withdrawals	A specific policy and procedures should be followed if small cash withdrawals from a cash register drawer are allowed. A written form must be completed, signed by the person making the withdrawal and the immediate supervisor, and placed in the register.
Change	Cash registers should have a daily change fund of a specific amount to start each day's operations. A procedure to collect, count, and verify cash register receipts should be followed on a regular schedule at least daily. Any overages or shortages should be accounted for each time the cash balance is verified. Two or more people should work together to collect and verify cash register receipts.
Bank Deposits	All cash receipts should be counted, recorded, and immediately prepared for deposit. All funds should be maintained in a secure area until transferred to a bank for deposit. Cash transfers or deposit schedules should prevent large amounts of cash from remaining in the business for long periods of time.
Check Endorsement	All checks should be endorsed for deposit when received with either a cash register imprint or a rubber stamp.
Payments	All payments except petty cash amounts should be made by check or credit card so a written record is maintained.
Wage and Salary Payments	Wages and salary payments should be made by check or direct deposit. Use a check rather than cash to pay for any work performed by non-employees so there is a written record for both parties.
Audits	Audit all cash receipts, payments, and deposits regularly and compare them with financial records. Reconcile bank statements as soon as they are received. Business records and bank records must be in balance. Any discrepancies must be resolved immediately.

© Cengage Learning 2013.

Figure 15-1 Every business should develop and follow specific procedures for accurately and safely handling and documenting all types of payments and receipts, including cash.

the customer. The business maintains records of the credit transactions. An **accounts receivable record** shows what each customer purchases, pays, and owes. When a credit sale is made, an electronic or paper record of the transaction is transmitted to the accounting department. The accounting department enters the sale into the accounts receivable record. When the customer makes a payment, the record is updated with the amount of the payment.

Businesses must also keep records showing money they owe and payments they make for all credit purchases. An **accounts payable record** identifies the credit purchases of a business, amounts owed, and payments made. Each time a credit purchase is made, details of the purchase are recorded in the accounts payable record. When payments are made, they are also recorded so the company has an accurate record of what they owe on each account.

DEPRECIATION RECORDS

An **asset** is anything of value owned. Businesses need to have a variety of assets, such as buildings, vehicles, equipment, and inventory, for use in their normal operations. The value of an asset decreases through use over time. This gradual loss of an asset's value due to age and wear is called **depreciation**. For example, an auto repair shop owner buys a computerized diagnostic tool that costs $16,000. The owner knows from experience that at the end of five years the equipment will not be worth any more than $1,000. The owner estimates, therefore, that the equipment will wear out or depreciate at the average rate of $3,000 a year:

$$\$16{,}000 - \$1{,}000 = \$15{,}000 \text{ value lost}$$
$$\$15{,}000/5 \text{ years} = \$3{,}000 \text{ depreciation per year}$$

When the diagnostic equipment loses its usefulness, it must be replaced. Therefore, depreciation represents a cost to the business.

Fixed assets are expensive assets of a business that are expected to last and be used for a long time. Buildings, land, and expensive equipment are common examples of fixed assets. Except for land, fixed assets depreciate over time. The value of each fixed asset is recorded by the company when it is purchased. Fixed assets become part of the property the business owns. As an asset wears out or becomes less valuable, the business is allowed by law to recognize the loss in value each year as an operating expense. The total amount of depreciation is deducted from the asset's original value to determine its **book value**.

Property may also decrease in value because of *obsolescence*. That is, even though the asset is still usable, it becomes out-of-date or inadequate for a particular purpose. An older computer, for example, may not have the processor speed, memory, or storage capacity to run new software or meet the growing information demands of a growing business. Even though the computer still functions, it is no longer as valuable to the business. Therefore, obsolescence is a form of depreciation.

The financial loss due to depreciation is very real, although it is difficult to determine objectively and accurately with great accuracy. Therefore, the Internal Revenue Service (IRS) provides rules and procedures that businesses must follow in calculating depreciation. Businesses need to maintain depreciation records and use them in their planning so they have money available to replace assets as needed.

SPECIAL ASSET RECORDS

Financial statements list assets and their values, but they do not provide detailed information about these assets. As a result, a business must keep special records. For example, a business should maintain a precise record of insurance policies, showing such details as type of policy, the company from which it was purchased, amount, premium, purchase and expiration dates, and the amount to be charged each month as insurance expense. A business

Management MATTERS

Comparing Alternatives

Financial records allow managers to do more than examine revenues and costs to determine profit or loss. Information contained in financial records is useful for comparing alternatives that might improve the financial condition of the company. For example, when faced with a decision to replace an expensive piece of equipment, a manager might consider the impact the purchase might have on the current and future financial condition of the company. Unless the business has adequate cash on hand to purchase the equipment, some type of financing will be needed. An alternative might be to lease rather than buy the new equipment. A review of the company's financial records may help determine which choice is best.

A manager might ask, What would be the total lease costs compared to the purchase price of the equipment over the expected life of the equipment? Is a large down payment required to secure financing if the equipment is purchased? What are the monthly payments required for a loan versus a lease? By reviewing past records of cash, accounts payable, and equipment depreciation costs, and gathering similar information on the cost of leasing, a manager can make an informed decision about the impact of alternatives on the bottom line of the company.

What Do You Think? Why should the manager making a decision about replacing equipment be concerned about the immediate and ongoing monthly costs of alternatives in addition to the total cost?

also maintains detailed special records for all fixed assets, such as trucks and forklifts. These records provide such information as asset description, date of purchase, cost, monthly depreciation expense, and asset book value. *Asset book value* is the original cost less accumulated depreciation. In the auto repair example above, the equipment depreciates at a rate of $3,000 per year. At the end of the second year, the $16,000 equipment will have an asset book value of $10,000:

$3,000 depreciation − 2 years = $6,000 accumulated depreciation
$16,000 − $6,000 = $10,000 asset book value at the end of year 2

TAX AND PAYROLL RECORDS

Federal and state tax laws require every business to keep adequate records in order to report its income and expenses, file required forms, and calculate and pay taxes. Employers must withhold a certain percentage of each employee's wages for federal income tax purposes. It must do the same for Social Security, and Medicare. Other payments that employers must make to federal and state governments are for business taxes and unemployment compensation insurance.

For business planning as well as for tax purposes, businesses must keep detailed payroll records for each employee: hours worked, wage or salary rate, regular and overtime wages paid, and all types of deductions and withholding made from the employee's wages. Companies also record the value of benefits paid for each employee, such as paid vacation, sick days, and employer contributions to health insurance premiums and retirement plans.

For tax purposes, each employee must fill out a W-4 form that provides information on the number of family members and exemptions. Using this information and a table furnished by the Internal Revenue Service, the employer determines the amount to withhold from the employee's paycheck. Employers submit payments of these withholdings to the IRS. Most companies use a computerized payroll system to maintain personnel records, to calculate payroll, and to process payments for each employee. Some companies perform this function internally, but many businesses use payroll service companies.

Many companies no longer issue actual paychecks to employees. The most common alternative to a paycheck is direct deposit. With direct deposit, funds are electronically deposited into employees' bank accounts. Employers usually provide advice of deposit to let employees know that a deposit has been made. They may also provide an earnings report for each employee. This might be a printed statement given to each employee, an attachment emailed to the employee, or a secure page that can be accessed on the company's website. An example of an earnings report appears in Figure 15-2.

PROTECTING BUSINESS RECORDS

All financial records of a business, including personal information about customers and employees, must be maintained and retained for many years. Information must be secure from theft and misuse and also should be protected from hazards of nature such as fire, floods, hurricanes, and earthquakes. Also, the growing threat of terrorism offers a new type of security issue businesses must address. Every business, therefore, should have secure areas such as vaults and safe rooms for records, computer equipment, and data storage. Disaster-proof and secure filing cabinets and other types of storage devices are also needed for maintaining important but frequently used documents. Measures to provide access to authorized people must be developed while keeping the information from those who are not authorized to access it.

21st CENTURY SKILLS

Critical Thinking

Critical thinking involves deciding what to believe and it is a valuable skill for managers. When presented with new information, it is important to be able to compare it with existing knowledge. A critical thinker puts information in context and evaluates the sources.

Employee Earnings Report

Employee Name:	Whitney Bello			Employee Number:		44-9521
Payment Date:	03/24/20--			Net Pay:		$1,276.68

Pay Period:	03/05/20-- to 03/18/20--				Year-to-Date
Earnings	**Hours**	**Rate**	**Amount**		
Regular Pay	80.00	$23.80	$1,904.00		$11,424.00
Overtime Pay	3.50	35.70	124.95		124.95
Other	0.00	0.00	$0.00		0
Earnings Total				$2,028.95	$11,548.95
Pre-Tax Reductions					
401k		5%	−101.45		−577.45
Health Insurance			−35.00		−210.00
Reduction Total				−136.45	
Earnings Subject to Withholding				$1,892.50	$10,761.50
Taxes					
Federal Income Tax Withholding			−303.89		−1674.99
Medicare			−27.44		−156.04
Social Security			−79.49		−451.99
State Income Tax Withholding			−96.00		−541.00
Taxes Total				−506.82	
Other Deductions					
Parking Garage			−100.00		−600.00
Fitness Center			−9.00		−54.00
Other Deductions Total				−109.00	
Net Pay				$1,276.68	$7,283.48

© Cengage Learning 2013.

Figure 15-2 An earnings report provides detailed information on an employee's earnings, tax withholding, and deductions for each pay period.

Important documents such as mortgages, deeds, leases, contracts, and other critical but infrequently used documents may be better placed in bank safe deposit boxes or other secure locations if there is no adequate protection in the business. Companies protect their computer records by using such precautions as firewalls and passwords to keep out intruders. Most large organizations have security personnel or consultants who regularly review computer systems and look for attempts to "hack" or illegally access information from the computer systems. Companies should also store backup copies of electronic records in a secure off-site location. Service companies rent storage space on their computers or in their climate-controlled data warehouses for safe record archiving and protection.

 CHECKPOINT

Describe five types of records a business should maintain.

15.1 ASSESSMENT

UNDERSTAND MANAGEMENT CONCEPTS

Determine the best answer for each of the following questions.

1. Which of the following is *not* a reason businesses need to maintain financial records?
   a. to determine the kinds and values of assets
   b. to track the financial progress of the business
   c. to prepare financial forms and reports required by the government
   d. to provide financial information to competitors

2. Expensive assets of a business that are expected to last and be used for a long time are known as
   a. fixed assets
   b. depreciated assets
   c. obsolete assets
   d. stable assets

THINK CRITICALLY

Answer the following questions as completely as possible.

3. Even if a business owner hires people to maintain financial records, why should he or she understand the procedures they use?

4. Describe several examples of ways that the financial records of a company can be harmed or damaged. For each example, how is the business harmed? How are others harmed? How can the company prevent the harm or damage?

15.2

Budgets and Budgeting

Goals

- Describe the uses of several types of business budgets.
- Discuss the reasons managers prepare more than one budget estimate.

Terms

- budget p. 400
- start-up budget p. 401
- operating budget p. 401
- cash budget p. 401
- capital budget p. 402
- sales budget p. 402

 **Business Budgets**

Budgeting is critical to financial success. Studies of differences between successful and unsuccessful new businesses consistently find that businesses that carefully develop and follow budgets increase their chances of survival and success. The financial practices of successful businesses are (1) maintaining a complete and up-to-date set of financial records, (2) having detailed financial records reviewed regularly by objective professionals, (3) keeping accurate records of business inventory and (4) using financial budgets as planning and management tools.

IMPORTANCE OF BUDGETS

A new company's business plan should include financial budgets for the first year of operations and more general financial projections for two or more additional years. Unfortunately, many small businesses do not update the initial budget even if one was developed as part of the business plan. A large number of business owners and managers report they don't have confidence in their ability to plan and use financial budgets.

A **budget** is a written financial plan for business operations developed for a specific period of time. Budgets are often developed for six months or a year but can cover a longer or shorter time period depending on the type of budget and the nature of the business. Budgets project and offer detail on the business's estimated revenue and expenses over the time period. Based on these estimates, businesses can set financial goals. They then use the budget to develop operating plans for that time period. By comparing actual results with financial goals and budget details throughout the year, managers can control operations and keep expenses in line with income. A realistic budget can prevent overspending and be used to plan for needed income, including the possibility of borrowed funds.

TYPES OF BUDGETS

Actual budgeting procedures depend on the type of business. For a new small business, the process is mostly one of budgeting start-up costs, sales, expenses, purchases, and cash. Large businesses have a number of specialized budgets that predict the financial performance operating areas of the company such as research and development, information technology, human resources, production, marketing, distribution and logistics, and many others.

In large businesses, the final overall budget for a business is made up of several specific budgets, such as the sales, merchandising, advertising, cash, capital, and operating budgets. Most specialized budgets are based on sales and income projections. However, in some types of businesses, either the production capacity or the financial capacity of the business or the unit for which the budget is being prepared must be determined first. Sales and all other estimates are then based on the amount that can be produced or the available financial resources for the time period.

START-UP BUDGET The **start-up budget** projects income and expenses from the beginning of a new business until it is expected to become profitable. A start-up budget is usually prepared in large and established businesses whenever a new venture is being planned, such as the introduction of a new product, expansion into a new market, or the development of a new type of business operation. Business start-ups usually require large expenditures for equipment, inventory, salaries, and operating expenses. Income will not be realized for some time while expenses grow. Even when the new company begins to sell products and services, the income will not be adequate to cover the initial expenses. A start-up budget will identify the start-up costs, initial operating expenses, types and sources of financing, and projected income for the time period of the budget.

OPERATING BUDGET An **operating budget** is a plan showing projected sales, costs, expenses, and profits for the ongoing operations of a business. It projects operating income and expenses for the entire business or for a specific part of the business for an identified time period such as three months, six months, or a year. The operating budget is a particularly useful planning tool because it uses the same financial categories as the company's income statement. By subtracting its total projected costs and expenses from projected income, a business can estimate the profitability of its operations. The projections can then be compared to the actual results achieved when an income statement is prepared at the end of the time period covered by the operating budget.

CASH BUDGET During normal operations, companies receive cash from sales and from borrowing and use cash for purchases and loan payments. The **cash budget** is an estimate of the flow of cash into and out of the business over a specified time period. Companies need a cash budget to make certain that enough cash will be available at the right times to meet payments as they come due. Cash comes into the company from two primary sources: (1) cash receipts and (2) borrowing. When companies borrow money, they must eventually pay it back. Therefore, the cash budget shows borrowed money as cash flowing in and repayments as cash flowing out when each payment is due.

Figure 15-3 shows a cash budget for a small business. Cash budgets are important for all companies, no matter how large or successful they are. A company can be highly profitable yet not have enough cash on hand at the right times to pay its bills. This situation could cause the company to borrow unnecessarily. Cash budgets are also used to prevent the company from holding too much cash when it is not needed. That can result in missing out on profitable uses of the cash during the period when it is not needed.

CAPITAL BUDGET Every business must plan for the costs of buildings, equipment, and other expensive purchases needed for its operations. Over the years, it must also budget to replace worn-out or obsolete fixed assets. For instance,

Manager's Perspective on
TECHNOLOGY

Both large and small companies can now use Internet-based financial programs rather than maintain financial software on a company computer. The use of online programs is called *cloud computing*. With online programs, authorized employees, suppliers, customers, and others needing access to specific financial information from the company can log on anytime from any computer in the world to input, retrieve, or work with company records. Of course the company must ensure that online records are secure and protected.

Cash Budget—for Three Months Ending March 31, 20--			
	January	February	March
Cash On Hand and Receipts			
Beginning cash balance	$33,500	$10,000	$10,000
Receipts from credit sales	70,000	70,000	80,000
Total cash available	$103,500	$80,000	$90,000
Cash Payments			
Accounts to be paid	$45,000	$45,000	$60,000
Wages and contracted labor	9,500	12,000	16,000
Salaries and administrative expense	7,000	7,000	7,000
Sales expense	15,000	15,000	15,000
Other operating expenses	13,000	18,000	24,000
Purchase of fixed assets	0	10,000	10,000
Repayment of bank loan	10,000	0	0
Total cash payments	$99,500	$107,000	$132,000
End of Month Cash Position			
Expected cash shortage	0	$27,000	$45,000
Bank loans needed	6,000	37,000	52,000
Ending cash balance	$10,000	$10,000	$10,000

© Cengage Learning 2013.

Figure 15-3 A cash budget helps a business avoid having too little or too much cash on hand.

if a company owns its own trucks and vans for distributing products, each will need to be replaced after a certain number of miles or years. A growing business plans for expansion by budgeting for the costs of new equipment, additions to buildings, and other major investments.

A **capital budget** is a financial plan for replacing fixed assets or acquiring new ones. Capital budgeting is important because acquiring assets ties up large sums of money for long periods of time. A wrong decision can be costly. For example, a decision to buy three new trucks that have a projected life of eight years involves a large expenditure. The manager must plan well in advance if the money is to be available when the trucks are needed. Assume that the company buys the trucks based on a forecast that future sales will justify their need. However, if sales do not increase as expected, profits will be lower as a result of the added costs related to the purchase.

SALES BUDGET The **sales budget** is a forecast of the sales revenue a company expects to receive in a month, a quarter or a year. Estimated sales are usually projected for sales territories, types of customers (government, industrial, consumer), sales representatives, geographic areas, or product categories. Each of the sales managers responsible for the various categories (territories, customers, products) make estimates for the sales and expenses of their unit. The top sales manager uses those estimates to prepare a final sales budget. Sometimes managers prepare sales estimates with the idea of developing quotas or goals for sales representatives and territories. These estimates provide a goal for the sales department as well as a source of information for preparing related budgets such as production, advertising, or cash and operating budgets.

Figure 15-4 shows sales estimates determined in two different ways for the same company. Because the two sets of estimated figures are not the same, someone must combine them into one satisfactory estimate for the sales department.

Numerous factors influence sales estimates. The specific operating and management factors of each company play an important part. Although one company may enjoy a high sales volume, another—at the same time and under the same conditions—may suffer a decline in sales. Economic conditions are often important in planning sales. If a good harvest and favorable prices for crops are anticipated in a certain area, a company that sells farm machinery should have good sales prospects in that area. A retail store in that same area might not anticipate the same increase in sales if agricultural customers make up a small percentage of their business. A major competitor entering a market for the first time may have a significant effect on established but smaller businesses. These are examples of some of the influences that should guide a manager in making sales estimates.

Two Ways of Forecasting Sales						
Budget Based on Analysis of Sales Representatives				**Budget Based on Analysis of Products**		
Sales Representative	Year 1 Sales (Actual)	Year 2 Sales (Estimate)	Product	Year 1 Sales (Actual)	Year 2 Sales (Estimate)
T. A. Nader	$ 356,720	$ 380,000	Washers	$ 642,840	$ 680,000
H. E. Loch	348,380	360,000	Dryers	202,320	200,000
C. D. Heidel	471,240	440,000	Cooktops and ovens	189,260	180,000
J. H. Sharmon	442,940	440,000	Microwaves	209,360	200,000
C. F. Powell	426,980	440,000	Refrigerators	1,210,840	1,300,000
J. G. Dunbar	408,360	400,000			
Total	$ 2,454,620	$ 2,460,000	Total	$ 2,454,620	$ 2,560,000

Figure 15-4 Sales forecasts can be developed by estimating sales for each salesperson or for each product.

CHECKPOINT

Why is it important for a business to prepare a cash budget and a capital budget?

Administering the Budget

Because a budget is an estimate of what might happen, it usually cannot be followed exactly. Staying close to the amount budgeted is desirable. However, for various reasons often beyond the control of managers, actual income and expenses may vary from the budgeted amounts. For that reason, managers often prepare three budget estimates. The first estimate assumes that sales will be less than expected. The second estimate considers what most likely will occur. And the third estimate assumes sales will be better than expected.

The second estimate is followed unless anticipated conditions change. If sales are less than expected, the business can shift immediately to the first (lower) set of budget figures. Should sales be better than expected, the business can shift to the third (higher) set of budget figures. Having more than one budget estimate allows for realistic flexibility during budget planning. It also forces managers to consider what might happen under favorable and unfavorable conditions and to be better prepared for rapid changes.

Whether a business is large or small or uses one or more budgets, managers must use the budget to monitor ongoing operations and control expenses. That monitoring activity determines whether the business is on, under, or over budget. If expenditures exceed budgeted amounts, managers want to quickly understand why so they can make necessary changes. Some adjustments may be easy, whereas others may not even be possible. For example, labor costs might exceed budget estimates for the planned level of production because a number of new employees have been added who are not as productive as experienced employees. Additional training for those employees might help improve productivity, reducing the labor costs required to meet production goals during the rest of the budget period. However, if labor costs are higher than the budget because of an unanticipated increase in the wage rate needed to hire the new employees, little can be done to lower those costs in the short run.

If a comparison of actual operating performance with the budget estimates reveals that the business will not make the expected profit or will have a loss, the manager must review all expenses to determine what can be done to reduce them. Some expenses may be easier to reduce in the short run than others. However, cutting some expenses may lead to longer-term profitability problems. For example, if a manager tries to reduce costs in the short run by not purchasing new inventory, those costs will need to be increased in the future to replace the inventory or sales will be lost. Cutting the number of employees to save on labor costs may put too much pressure on the remaining employees. Their productivity may go down or some may quit, leading to increased costs to replace them.

The use of budgets and a budgeting system cannot guarantee the success of a business, but these management tools can help reduce losses or increase profits. The entire budgeting process is valuable in planning and controlling activities for managers. But whether a business is a success or not can be determined only after the budget time periods have passed. Comparing budgets with actual operating conditions provides a basis for making timely and knowledgeable management decisions, which, in turn, leads to more accurate budgets and more profitable operations in the future.

 CHECKPOINT

How do managers benefit from developing three different budget estimates for the same time period?

15.2 ASSESSMENT

UNDERSTAND MANAGEMENT CONCEPTS

Determine the best answer for each of the following questions.

1. A financial plan for replacing fixed assets or acquiring new ones is known as a(n)
   a. start-up budget
   b. capital budget
   c. operating budget
   d. cash budget

2. If a manager sees that actual expenses are exceeding budgeted amounts, he or she should immediately
   a. do nothing and see if things change
   b. discard the old budget and develop a new one
   c. review expenses to see what can be done to reduce them
   d. increase the prices of products to improve sales

THINK CRITICALLY

Answer the following questions as completely as possible.

3. How can the owner of a new business develop an accurate start-up budget when the business has not yet begun to operate?

4. Do you believe managers should involve their employees in developing financial budgets? Should they share budget information with employees? Why or why not?

Financial Reports

Goals

- Describe the contents and explain the purpose of a balance sheet.
- Describe the contents and explain the purpose of an income statement.

Terms

- financial statements p. 405
- balance sheet p. 406
- liabilities p. 406
- capital p. 406
- accounting equation p. 406
- accounts receivable p. 407
- accounts payable p. 407
- income statement p. 408
- cost of goods sold p. 408
- gross profit p. 409
- net profit p. 409

Business activity is in large part measured in terms of money. The amount of money a business earns, its level of profitability, and the return received by owners and others who are involved in financing the business are important measures of its success. Because of the importance of the financial performance and financial condition of businesses, every business must (1) keep thorough and accurate records, (2) prepare important financial reports regularly, (3) interpret the financial information in the reports, and (4) make decisions that will have a positive influence on future financial results.

Financial statements are reports that summarize financial data over a period of time, such as a month, three months, half a year, or a full year. The two financial reports businesses use most are the *balance sheet* and the *income statement*. Each provides a specific view of the financial condition and financial performance of a business. Each is necessary to determining whether a business is being well managed or not.

Financial reports have many uses in business. Executives use them as a means to effectively manage a profitable business. Suppliers, lenders, employee unions, government agencies, and owners also use financial reports when making decisions. Figure 15-5 lists some reasons why various users need the financial information available in financial reports.

Example of How Financial Reports Are Used	
User	**Needs financial data to:**
Manager	• make day-to-day decisions • review past results • plan for the future
Owner	• decide to increase or decrease ownership investment • decide whether to continue business operations
Supplier	• decide whether to extend credit to the business • decide how much credit to extend
Lender	• decide whether to lend a business money • decide on the terms of a loan to a business
Union	• determine fair increases in wages, salaries, and benefits
Government	• develop business laws and tax policies • detect fraudulent practices

© Cengage Learning 2013.

Figure 15-5 The financial reports of a business provide information needed by several groups.

● ● ● The Balance Sheet

A **balance sheet**, or *statement of financial position*, is a financial statement that reports a business's assets, liabilities, and capital on a specific date. As you learned in the last lesson, *assets* are anything of value owned, such as cash and buildings. **Liabilities** are claims against assets. In other words, liabilities are the business's debts. And **capital** (also called *net worth, owner's equity, or stockholders' equity*) is the value of the owners' investment in the business after subtracting liabilities from assets.

A balance sheet has two sides. Assets are listed and totaled on the left. Liabilities and capital are listed and totaled on the right. The values of the two sides must always balance—thus the name. That is, the total of all assets must equal the total of all liabilities plus capital. In fact, the basic **accounting equation** is expressed as:

$$\text{Assets} = \text{Liabilities} + \text{Capital}$$

Each balance sheet has a heading that includes the name of the business, the title "Balance Sheet," and the statement date. The information in the balance sheet presents a summary of the business's financial position on the date in the heading. Balance sheets are prepared at least once a year and usually more frequently.

KINDS OF FINANCIAL DATA

An example of a balance sheet for a jewelry store, the Crown Corporation, is shown in Figure 15-6. On December 31, the accountants for the Crown Corporation prepared a balance sheet. The value of every asset the business owns is listed under Assets. As shown in the figure, Crown's total assets are $5,360,000. The company's debts—items purchased on credit and the mortgage still owed on the land and building—are listed under Liabilities, which total $1,360,000. The accountants subtracted total liabilities from total assets to calculate Crown's capital, $4,000,000.

Crown purchases jewelry from a manufacturer and then resells it to customers. Until the jewelry is sold, it is listed as an asset called merchandise inventory. *Merchandise inventory* is the value of goods purchased to sell to customers at a profit.

Crown Corporation
Balance sheet
December 31, 20—

ASSETS		LIABILITIES AND CAPITAL	
Cash	$ 240,000	Liabilities	
Accounts Receivable	80,000	Accounts Payable	$ 320,000
Merchandise Inventory	640,000	Mortgage Payable	1,040,000
Equipment	800,000	Total Liabilities	$1,360,000
Land and Building	3,600,000	Capital	
		Stockholders' Net Worth	4,000,000
Total Assets	$5,360,000	Total Liabilities and Capital	$5,360,000

© Cengage Learning 2013.

Figure 15-6 The balance sheet shows the financial position of a company on a given date.

Crown Corporation sells merchandise on a cash or credit basis. For credit sales, the company allows approved customers to pay over time using the company's credit card. The amount customers owe the business is an asset called **accounts receivable**. It is an asset because the business has a legal right to obtain cash for the goods sold and can sue customers who do not pay. The store will eventually collect cash from the customers.

The **accounts payable** item under Liabilities on the balance sheet is the amount the company owes for purchases it made on credit. In this example, the store bought jewelry worth $320,000 on credit from suppliers. Until the company completes payment on the accounts the amount owed remains on the balance sheet as a liability, or debt.

VALUE OF BALANCE SHEET INFORMATION

The balance sheet for the Crown Corporation provides a great deal of useful data. It lists specific types and amounts of assets and liabilities. The balance sheet also shows that the business owns assets of $5,360,000, owes $1,360,000, and is worth $4,000,000 on December 31. The total figures on the balance sheet agree with the basic accounting formula as follows:

$$\text{Assets} = \text{Liabilities} + \text{Capital}$$
$$\$5,360,000 = \$1,360,000 + \$4,000,000$$

A careful look at the specific items reveals other valuable information. For example, Crown cannot now pay the $320,000 that it owes under accounts payable because it has only $240,000 in cash available. Ideally, the company will make enough cash sales and will collect payments from some of those customers listed under accounts receivable soon enough to pay its bills when due. Even though the money owed under accounts payable is not likely to become due all at once, the company could possibly have trouble meeting other day-to-day expenses. The company would be in trouble if a sudden emergency arose that called for a large amount of cash.

Crown may use its balance sheet to compare financial results with prior time periods or with other companies. Because companies prepare a yearly balance sheet, the business can review its financial progress by comparing this year's results with last year's. It may find, for example, that the amount of capital increased over last year without an increase in liabilities. If Crown wished to do so, it could also compare some information on its balance sheet with that of other businesses of similar size and kind. Published information is available from several sources, such as trade associations. With comparative figures, the business can make judgments about its success and determine ways to improve its financial picture in the future.

CHECKPOINT

How does the term balance sheet reflect the organization of information in the financial statement?

The Income Statement

The **income statement**, or *profit and loss statement*, is a financial statement that reports information about a company's revenues and expenses for a specific period. Income statements are usually prepared monthly, quarterly, or semiannually. An annual income statement is also needed. Income statements have three major parts:

1. Revenue—income earned for the period, such as from the sale of goods and services
2. Expenses—all costs incurred in operating the business, such as the cost of equipment and supplies, inventory, and wages.
3. Profit or loss—the difference between total revenue and total expenses

When revenue is greater than expenses, the company has earned a profit. When expenses are greater than revenue, the company has incurred a loss. The income statement shows the financial performance (profit or loss) that occurs over a specified period of time. The balance sheet, on the other hand, shows the financial condition of a business at a particular point in time. Both types of financial statements serve useful but different purposes. An example of an income statement appears in Figure 15-7. The period covered for the income statement of the Crown Corporation is one year, as shown in the heading.

KINDS OF FINANCIAL DATA

The revenue for the Crown Corporation comes from one source—the sale of jewelry. Total revenue for the year was $1,800,000. If the company earned other income, such as from the repair of jewelry, the income from this source would be listed separately under Revenue.

To earn revenue, a retail business purchases merchandise from suppliers and sells it to customers at a profit. The amount the retailer pays the supplier for the merchandise it buys and sells is called **cost of goods sold**. In a manufacturing

Crown Corporation Income Statement For the Year Ending December 31, 20—		
Revenue from Sales	$1,800,000	
Cost of Goods Sold	630,000	
Gross Profit		$1,170,000
Operating Expenses		
Salaries and Wages	360,000	
Advertising and Promotion	148,000	
Depreciation Expense	132,000	
Utilities	120,000	
Supplies and Materials	112,000	
Miscellaneous Expenses	28,000	
Total Operating Expenses		900,000
Net Profit (before Taxes)		$ 270,000

© Cengage Learning 2013.

Figure 15-7 The income statement describes a business's profit or loss during a specified time period.

business, the cost of goods sold would include the amount the company paid for raw materials and parts to make its products.

Generally, the cost of goods sold is a rather large deduction from revenue. To make the cost of goods sold easy to identify on the income statement, it is listed separately from other deductions. **Gross profit** is the amount remaining after subtracting the cost of goods sold from revenue. **Net profit** is the amount remaining after subtracting all expenses from revenue, except taxes. Gross profit for the Crown Corporation is $1,170,000, which is calculated by subtracting the cost of goods sold ($630,000) from sales revenue ($1,800,000).

Expenses needed to operate the business during the year are listed next on the income statement. *Operating expenses* are all expenses not directly associated with producing or purchasing merchandise the business sells. For example, businesses spend money on advertising, supplies, and maintenance. For Crown Corporation, operating expenses total $900,000. On the income statement, operating expenses are subtracted from gross profit, $1,170,000, to arrive at the net profit or "bottom line," $270,000.

The net result of the business activity reported in the form of revenue, cost of goods sold, expenses, and profit on the income statement appears in one form or another on the balance sheet. For the Crown Corporation, the net profit of $270,000 will be added to its assets (left side of the balance sheet) and capital (right side of the balance sheet). Thus, the two sides of the balance sheet will still balance.

Inventory Management

According to SAS, a leading business software provider, the cost of storing and maintaining inventory for companies averages between 25 and 35 percent of total inventory costs. Reducing that cost requires careful management. Globally, poor inventory management practices cost firms about $300 billion each year.

VALUE OF INCOME STATEMENT INFORMATION

The top management of Crown Corporation, and others who review the income statement, can learn a great deal about the business. Specifically, the total deductions from the $1,800,000 in revenue are $1,530,000, which consists of

Income, Expenses, and Profit	Past 12 Months		Next 12 Months	
	Amounts	Percentage of Sales	Amounts Budgeted	Estimated percentage of sales
Sales	$1,800,000	100.0%	$1,890,000	100.0%
Cost of Goods Sold	630,000	35.0%	655,000	34.7%
Gross Profit	1,170,000	65.0%	1,235,000	65.3%
Operating Expenses				
Salaries and Wages	360,000	20.0%	368,000	19.5%
Advertising/Promotion	148,000	8.2%	150,000	7.9%
Depreciation Expense	132,000	7.3%	125,000	6.6%
Utilities	120,000	6.7%	124,500	6.6%
Supplies and Materials	112,000	6.2%	115,000	6.1%
Miscellaneous Expenses	28,000	1.6%	26,000	1.4%
Total Operating Expenses	900,000	50.0%	908,500	48.1%
Net Profit	$ 270,000	15.0%	$ 326,500	17.3%

Crown Corporation Budgeted Income Statement for 12 Months Ending December 31, 20—

© Cengage Learning 2013.

Figure 15-8 Budgets can be prepared and compared to the actual financial performance shown on the prior period's income statement.

cost of goods sold ($630,000) and operating expenses ($900,000). The manager can also see that the net profit before taxes—$270,000—is a rather small part of the total revenue. Businesses spend a great deal of their revenue to cover the cost to produce or purchase the products they sell and the expenses of operating the business. Losses or very low profits signal possible problems with costs and expenses.

The Crown Corporation management can improve the company's financial controlling and budget planning by doing an item-by-item analysis of the income statement, such as that shown in the first two columns of numbers in Figure 15-8. Each expenditure can be calculated as a percentage of total sales. Managers can then compare the percentages with similar figures from prior months and years to reveal trends.

For instance, the first and largest operating expense is $360,000 for salaries and wages. When $360,000 is divided by total sales, $1,800,000, and the answer is changed to a percentage, the result is 20 percent. If last year the total wages and salaries expense amounted to only 18 percent of sales, the business would know that this expense had increased in relation to total sales. If possible, the company can try to correct this 2 percent increase for the next year by trying to increase sales, raise prices, or get by with fewer employees. The same type of calculation and analysis can be made for each of the remaining expenses on the income statement. In addition, managers can determine the percentages of gross profit and net profit in relation to sales. Based on that analysis, budgets can be prepared for the next 12 months, as shown in the last two columns of Figure 15-8. Managers can compare amounts and percentages for the past 12 months with the budgeted amounts and estimated percentages for the next 12 months.

Managers can also use the information from the budgeted income statement to prepare charts and graphs to illustrate the data. For example, a manager could create a pie chart to show the relationships between sales and gross income, sales and operating expenses, and sales and net profit. Figure 15-9 provides illustrates these relationships for the Crown Corporation based on the budget for the next 12 months.

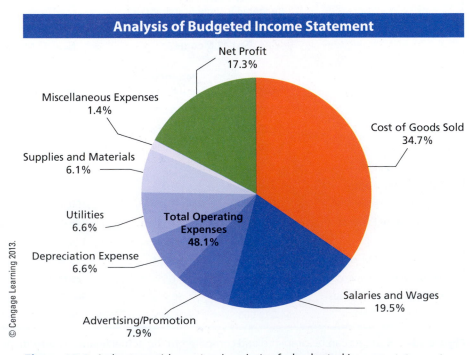

© Cengage Learning 2013.

Figure 15-9 A chart provides a visual analysis of a budgeted income statement.

 **CHECKPOINT**

How are profit and loss calculated on an income statement?

15.3 ASSESSMENT

UNDERSTAND MANAGEMENT CONCEPTS

Determine the best answer for each of the following questions.

1. The basic accounting equation is
   a. income − expenses = profit or loss
   b. liabilities = assets + capital
   c. assets = liabilities + capital
   d. income = profit or loss − expenses

2. The information from the income statement needed to calculate gross profit does not include
   a. revenue
   b. cost of goods sold
   c. operating expenses
   d. assets

THINK CRITICALLY

Answer the following questions as completely as possible.

3. Why is the balance sheet an important financial statement for potential investors in a company to review?

4. Why is it important to study a company's financial performance over a period of time and its financial condition on a specific date?

Cost Cutting at any Cost

The Sunbeam Corporation had been experiencing financial difficulties before the board of directors hired CEO Al Dunlap to fix the company. Sunbeam was a well-known manufacturer of household appliances. Soon after Mr. Dunlap came on board, Sunbeam's stock started to climb. Within seven months, he had saved the company $225 million by such actions as firing 12,000 employees, closing 16 of 26 factories, and disposing of unwanted products and facilities.

Sunbeam's culture changed quickly. Before Dunlap's arrival, the firm was in trouble, with few new products, weakening sales, and declining profits. His arrival seemed to signal a quick turnaround in the company's financial performance. The stockholders and investors were happy.

But soon after the major cost-reduction steps were completed, sales and profits again began to decline. The new CEO required all product managers to show increased sales. He suggested practices, many unethical, that would make it appear as if sales were rising and expenses were falling.

Dunlap pressured employees relentlessly to produce more. Morale dipped. Budget goals were unrealistic. To make it appear as though goals were being met without creating cash flow problems, some managers were forced to postpone paying bills and suppliers were asked to accept only partial payment to keep costs down temporarily. Unrealistic credit terms were extended to large retailers to obtain enough orders to meet sales goals. Large discounts were given to customers to encourage them to buy well in advance so as to make Sunbeam's income statement look good. These undesirable business practices led to high inventory levels, while accounts receivable and payable both rose and cash flow weakened. Sales were recorded for the current year that under accounting rules should have been postponed to the next year. Profit margins got thinner. The firm was in deep trouble.

The board of directors met and agreed it had made a serious error in hiring Al Dunlap. He was fired. The firm reorganized, but it couldn't recover and fell into bankruptcy. Even though Sunbeam eventually emerged from bankruptcy, its image had dropped among investors, suppliers, and customers. It has now become a subsidiary of a large international firm, Jarden Corporation.

THINK CRITICALLY

1. Why do you believe Mr. Dunlap had early success and yet the financial fortunes of the company quickly turned around?

2. Why were Mr. Dunlap and company managers willing to use illegal and unethical practices to try to improve the financial position of Sunbeam?

3. If you were on the board of directors, what questions would you ask Al Dunlap about his beliefs and values before you hired him?

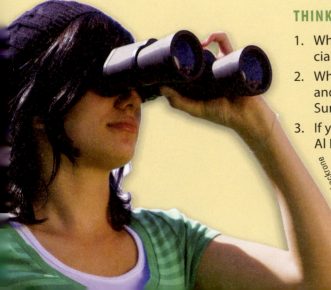

Analyzing Financial Data

Goals

- Describe several types of financial analysis that help in the understanding of a business's financial condition.
- Identify where business owners and managers can turn to get help with understanding and using financial information.

Terms

- cash flow p. 413
- working capital p. 414
- certified public accountant (CPA) p. 416
- audit p. 416
- consultant p. 416
- Small Business Administration (SBA) p. 417

●●● Using Financial Information

Managers use financial statements as well as other financial information to understand the financial health of a business. Others are also concerned about the business's financial health. That includes current and prospective investors; creditors, including banks and suppliers who may make loans and offer credit to the business; government officials involved in taxation and oversight of business practices; and customers. They want to know such things as whether the cash flow and working capital are sufficient to pay the company's bills. They also analyze ratios calculated from financial statements to identify where any financial problems lie.

Financial statements must be prepared in a way that provides a clear and understandable picture of the financial health of an organization. The people who are affected by the financial condition of the business need to have access to the financial information and be able to analyze the information to draw conclusions about its financial health.

CASH FLOW

Cash flow is the movement of cash into and out of a business. Money comes in immediately as a result of the sale of goods and services for cash and later from customers who buy on credit. Money goes out to pay for various costs and operating expenses. Because money does not always flow in at the same rate that it flows out, managers need to carefully plan for the flow of cash.

Regardless of the size of a business, cash is both a short-term and a long-term concern. Businesses must have cash on hand to pay bills when they are due and to plan ahead for large cash payments, such as the purchase of equipment or the launching of a new product.

Figure 15-10 illustrates cash flowing in and out of a retail piano store through the part of the year when cash shortages and overages are likely to occur. The bulk of the company's sales occur during the December holiday season. Although the company sells some pianos for cash, it sells most on credit. That means that even during the month of high sales, not a great deal of cash

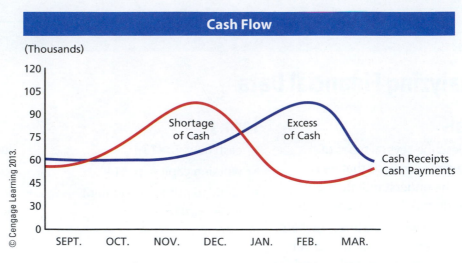

Cash Flow

(Thousands)

Figure 15-10 Cash flow changes in most businesses from month to month. Businesses must plan to deal with cash shortages and excesses.

is generated. The need for cash is greatest during September, October, and November when the company buys its inventory of pianos to sell. It needs large sums of cash to pay for the pianos, for sales promotions such as advertising, and for regular operating expenses. The cash flowing out of the company from October through December is greater than the cash flowing in.

Larger amounts of cash start to flow in during December from customers who pay cash for their purchases. Credit customers who purchased in December, however, will make cash payments in January, February, and March. During these three months, the flow of cash coming into the business will be greater than the cash going out. From this information, managers can plan for short-term borrowing during times of cash shortage. They can also plan when to make any needed large purchases, so that their payments will be due when they have cash available to pay them.

WORKING CAPITAL

Working capital is the difference between current assets and current liabilities. The word *current* refers to assets and liabilities that are expected to be exchanged for cash within one year or less, such as accounts receivable and payable. For example, companies expect most customers to pay for their credit purchases within a year. Therefore, accounts receivable are current assets. Similarly, companies expect to pay for their credit purchases in accounts payable within a year, so accounts payable are current liabilities.

When current assets are much larger than current liabilities, businesses are better able to pay current liabilities. The amount of working capital is one indicator that a business can pay its short-term debts. Businesses with large amounts of working capital usually find it easier to borrow money, because lenders feel assured that these businesses will have the means to repay their loans. The working-capital analysis for the Crown Corporation is shown in Figure 15-11. Notice that the numbers used in the analysis are the current assets and current liabilities drawn from the company's balance sheet shown in Figure 15-6.

FINANCIAL RATIOS

Managers use ratios to examine different areas of the business for possible financial problems. Figure 15-12 describes some important ratios and their uses. The data for these ratios come from Crown Corporation's financial statements: Figure 15-6 (balance sheet), Figure 15-7 (income statement), and Figure 15-11 (working capital). Financial ratios for current financial statements can be compared with the same ratios from prior periods, with ratios from other firms, and with other types of ratios. Organizations such as Dun & Bradstreet publish a standard list of average ratios for various types of businesses. Companies can use those published ratios to compare with their own ratios to get a sense of how they are doing in relation to other companies in their industry.

Lenders use ratios to decide whether a company is a good loan risk. Managers use ratios to identify possible problems needing corrective action. For example, if the company's return on investment is below average for its industry, then managers know that they may have to increase profits to attract new investors. If the company's current ratio keeps decreasing each period, then its liabilities are growing faster than its assets. This indicates that the company may be getting into debt trouble.

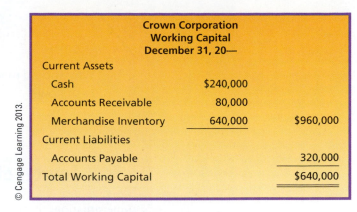

Figure 15-11 Working capital can be calculated using information on current assets and current liabilities from the balance sheet.

Crown Corporation Working Capital December 31, 20—		
Current Assets		
Cash	$240,000	
Accounts Receivable	80,000	
Merchandise Inventory	640,000	$960,000
Current Liabilities		
Accounts Payable		320,000
Total Working Capital		$640,000

© Cengage Learning 2013.

Frequently Used Financial Ratios

Ratio	Calculation	Crown Corporation*	Purpose
Return on Sales	$\dfrac{\text{Net Profit}}{\text{Sales}}$	$\dfrac{270,000}{1,800,000} = 0.15$	Shows how profitable a firm's sales are for a specified period of time.
Inventory Turnover	$\dfrac{\text{Cost of Goods Sold}}{\text{Average Merchandise Inventory}}$	$\dfrac{630,000}{640,000} = .98$	Shows whether the average monthly inventory might be too large or small.
Current Ratio	$\dfrac{\text{Current Assets}}{\text{Current Liabilities}}$	$\dfrac{960,000}{320,000} = 3.0$	Shows whether a firm can meet its current debts comfortably.
Return on Owners' Equity	$\dfrac{\text{Net Profit}}{\text{Owners' Equity}}$	$\dfrac{270,000}{4,000,00} = .0675$	Shows whether the owners are making a fair return on their investment.
Return on Investment	$\dfrac{\text{Net Profit}}{\text{Total Assets}}$	$\dfrac{270,000}{5,360,000} = .0504$	Shows rate of return on the book value of everything owned in the business

© Cengage Learning 2013.

*See fig. 15-6, 15-7, and 15-11 for sources of figures for calculations.

Figure 15-12 Financial ratios are an important tool for management decision making and investment decisions.

✔ CHECKPOINT

Why should managers monitor a business's working capital and cash flow?

●●● Sources of Financial Information

In some situations, businesses may need general advice or special help with a financial problem. Accountants, bankers, and financial consultants can provide expertise beyond what the company's employees and managers can provide. Businesses can also consult specialists from state and federal government agencies.

ACCOUNTANTS

Accountants understand the complex systems used to collect, sort, and summarize financial data. They can analyze and explain the meaning and importance of the details found on financial statements. Accountants also help managers interpret financial data and make suggestions for handling various financial aspects of a business. Large firms have full-time accountants, whereas small firms usually hire accountants on a part-time basis. A firm may hire a **certified public accountant**, or **CPA**, a person who has met a state's education, experience, and examination requirements in accounting. Corporations that sell stock to the public must hire CPAs to audit their financial records annually. An **audit** is an examination of a company's financial records by an expert to verify their accuracy.

The Small Business Administration website is an excellent resource for business information and support for small-business owners and managers, including online education and training.

   Access the website for this textbook and choose the link for Chapter 15 Net Bookmark. When the SBA online accounting training program opens, locate the Course Outline link and select Section 2: Accounting Scorecards—Financial Statements. View the slides to increase your understanding of the three basic financial statements. What other assistance is available from the SBA to help business owners improve financial planning skills? Use the website to locate the nearest SBA office to your community.

www.cengage.com/school/bizmgmt

BANKERS

Bankers also assist businesses with financial decisions. Bankers are well informed about the financial condition of businesses, and they also provide advice on how and where to get loans. Because bankers frequently work with businesses, they are aware of businesses' problems and needs. In the opening story, Clark knew he would need to ask his banker for help and advice to obtain the loan he needed for his business.

CONSULTANTS

A **consultant** is someone who gives professional advice or offers professional services. Businesses hire consultants with specific expertise to help managers solve problems or to provide services that are not available within the business. Consultants are not employees; they are outside experts with specialized knowledge.

   A financial consultant is valuable to people thinking about starting a business and to managers facing financial challenges in existing businesses. Professors of accounting, finance, and management from colleges or universities often serve as consultants. Many large and small consulting firms offer their services to businesses for a fee. Consulting firms employ a variety of experts who have both education and experience in business operations and management. Some specialize in a particular area such as financial services; others offer expertise in a broad set of business issues.

GOVERNMENT

Many state and federal government agencies provide financial information and other resources for businesses. Probably the best known, the **Small Business Administration (SBA)** is an agency of the federal government that provides information, advice, and assistance in obtaining credit and other financial support for small businesses. Regional offices in every state offer expertise and access to a range of technical and managerial information for small-business owners and people considering starting a new business. Other federal agencies offering resources and assistance as well as regulations related to the financial performance of businesses are the Department of Commerce and the Department of the Treasury.

CHECKPOINT

Identify four types of experts who can provide advice and help on businesses' financial problems.

15.4 ASSESSMENT

UNDERSTAND MANAGEMENT CONCEPTS

Determine the best answer for each of the following questions.

1. The amount of working capital available to a business is determined by
   a. subtracting total liabilities from total assets
   b. adding current assets and current liabilities
   c. adding total assets and total liabilities
   d. subtracting current liabilities from current assets

2. An example of an important financial ratio is
   a. current ratio
   b. debt ratio
   c. start-up ratio
   d. profit ratio

THINK CRITICALLY

Answer the following questions as completely as possible.

3. What benefits might managers obtain from comparing the financial performance ratios of their company with the same ratios from competitors' companies? How might the comparisons be misleading?

4. Some businesspeople suggest that consultants should not be used in a business because they aren't familiar with the specific operations of the company. Do you agree or disagree? Justify your opinion.

CHAPTER CONCEPTS

- All businesses, large and small, must keep records to identify sources of income and receipts; identify expenses paid or owed to others; determine the kinds and values of assets; prepare financial statements, forms, and reports; track financial progress; and plan future direction.

- Many financial records are common to all types of businesses. Examples include cash, credit, depreciation, and special asset, tax, and payroll records.

- Actual budgeting procedures depend on the type of business. However, most businesses develop the following types of budgets: operating, cash, capital, sales, and other specialized types of budgets. New businesses develop a start-up budget to help with financial decisions until the business becomes profitable.

- Because of the importance of financial performance and financial condition, every business must keep thorough and accurate records, prepare financial reports, interpret the financial information, and make decisions that will influence future financial results. Two important financial statements are the balance sheet and the income statement.

- Financial statements must provide a clear picture of the financial health of an organization. The people who are affected by the business's financial condition must have access to the financial information and be able to analyze it to draw conclusions about the business's financial health.

REVIEW BUSINESS MANAGEMENT TERMS

a. accounts payable
b. accounts receivable
c. asset
d. audit
e. balance sheet
f. book value
g. capital budget
h. cash disbursement
i. cash flow
j. cash receipts
k. certified public accountant (CPA)
l. consultant
m. depreciation
n. financial statements
o. income statement
p. liabilities
q. sales budget
r. working capital

Write the letter of the term that matches each definition. Some terms will not be used.
1. Money taken in by a business
2. Cash payments made by a business
3. The movement of cash into and out of a business
4. Anything of value owned, such as cash and buildings
5. The amount customers owe the business
6. Gradual loss of an asset's value due to age and wear
7. Claims against assets or things owed—the debts of a business
8. The difference between current assets and current liabilities
9. A financial plan for replacing fixed assets or acquiring new ones
10. The amount the company owes for purchases it made on credit
11. Someone who gives professional advice or offers professional services
12. An examination of a company's financial records by an expert to verify their accuracy
13. An estimate of the flow of cash into and out of the business over a specified time period
14. A financial statement that reports a business's assets, liabilities, and capital on a specific date

REVIEW BUSINESS MANAGEMENT CONCEPTS

Determine the best answer.

15. Manual record-keeping systems have been replaced in most businesses by
    a. accountants
    b. simple checkbook systems
    c. computers running accounting software programs
    d. cash register tapes

16. Studies of differences between successful and unsuccessful new businesses find that successful businesses use
    a. consultants
    b. computers
    c. budgets
    d. business loans

17. The two financial statements most used by businesses are
    a. cash flow and capital assets record
    b. tax and personnel records
    c. income statement and balance sheet
    d. accounts receivable and accounts payable records

18. An agency of the federal government that provides information, advice, and assistance in obtaining credit and other financial support for small businesses is the
    a. SBA
    b. FDA
    c. FCC
    d. EEOC

APPLY WHAT YOU KNOW

Answer the following questions.

19. Based on the Reality Check scenario at the beginning of the chapter, explain the meaning of the following statement by Clark's banker: "Either your current assets are too low or your current liabilities are too high. If you want us to approve your loan, you have to improve your working capital."

20. Can a piece of equipment such as a computer both depreciate and become obsolete? Explain.

21. Why will an operating budget likely be more accurate if the company's sales budget is prepared in advance and used as information for the operating budget?

22. Why is a budget an important tool for managers to use when evaluating current performance?

23. Discuss the accuracy of this statement: "The balance sheet tells you whether you made a profit or a loss for the year."

24. A net loss of $5,000 appears on an income statement. How would this loss affect the capital section of the balance sheet?

25. If the average return on sales for all jewelry stores is 7 percent, how would you judge the success of the Crown Corporation based on the financial information presented in lesson 15.3?

MAKE ACADEMIC CONNECTIONS

Complete the following activities.

26. **Math** As the budget director, you presented the following realistic yearly expense budget to your boss. After studying the figures, she asks you to prepare a flexible set of budget estimates because certain conditions might cause a 15 percent increase in sales, whereas certain other conditions might cause a 5 percent decrease in sales. The amounts budgeted for rent and insurance will not change under any circumstances.

Sales salaries	$300,000
Office salaries	60,000
Supplies	80,000
Advertising	48,000
Rent	36,000
Insurance	8,000

Prepare a new flexible budget showing three columns of figures: 5 percent Decrease, Expected, and 15 percent Increase.

27. **Communications** You have been hired as a financial consultant by the Crown Corporation to analyze the financial statements shown in the chapter. Calculate three financial ratios that you believe offer a realistic picture of the company's financial health. Prepare three computer slides and use them for a three-minute presentation to Crown's managers on what the information means to them.

28. **Technology** Use a computer spreadsheet to prepare an end-of-year balance sheet for the Starboard Corporation, using the following information and the format shown in lesson 15-3.

Cash	$5,000
Accounts receivable	8,000
Merchandise inventory	15,000
Land and buildings	120,000
Accounts payable	12,000
Mortgage payable	90,000
Stockholders' net worth	46,000

29. **Math** Use the following financial information from the Waterwing Company to calculate: (a) inventory turnover, (b) current ratio, (c) return on owners' equity, and (d) return on investment.

Revenue from sales	$600,000
Cost of goods sold	320,000
Net profit	25,000
Current assets	36,000
Total assets	200,000
Current liabilities	15,000
Owners' equity	150,000
Average inventory	20,000

CASE IN POINT

CASE 15-1: The Value of Budgeting

Karen Kline and Joe Kim are both staff accountants in a manufacturing firm. The accounting manager, Brooke Shenker, has asked Karen to prepare the sales budget for next month's annual budget meeting. Brooke asked Joe to construct the cash budget. Both Karen and Joe had prepared similar budgets in the past. They were surprised when the budgets were returned with changes made to their projections. As they started to work on the budgets, Karen expressed her feelings about the process to Joe.

Karen: *We spend weeks developing these budgets and then the budget committee discusses it for two days and changes our estimates. It makes me wonder why they don't trust the figures we submit.*

Joe: *I agree. But no matter where the budgets end up, the actual results never come in on target with the budget. When the collections on customer accounts don't match the budgeted amounts, it throws the cash budget off. Last year they projected sales to be $350,000 for the first quarter, and they were only $335,000.*

Karen: *May be if they would ask us to come to the meeting and explain how we develop the budgets it would save them time and discussion and we would understand how they arrive at the final budget.*

Joe: *Last year they argued for three days and look what happened. With the way the economy changed, we were so far off budget that I heard Brooke say we could have used a dartboard to forecast. Budgeting this way makes it hard to get close to the actual results.*

Karen: *I'll start on the sales budget tomorrow, but I wish the committee would let us come up with a better process to arrive at the final numbers.*

THINK CRITICALLY

1. If Karen and Joe prepared budget figures, why is it necessary for management to discuss them?
2. How serious is the variance between forecasted and actual sales from last year? Do you agree with Joe that it is a problem when budgeted amounts and actual figures do not match? Explain.
3. How do you believe the company's budgeting process could be improved?

CASE 15-2: The Value of a New Business

Anneika Lafferty and her friend Bernie Williams started an Internet business 15 months ago selling affordable musical instruments for beginners. They named it A&B Musical Instruments. Because they live near each other, Bernie keeps the inventory in his garage and Anneika has the computer system, phones, and office space in her home. While the business has done well financially, it requires more time than either expected and affordable instruments for resale are not easy to find. They have decided to try to sell the business and create a different type of online business. A larger Internet music company wants to buy them but the $50,000 offered is not nearly what Anneika and Bernie expected, based on the company's potential. They quickly reject the offer. The offer is based on last year's balance sheet, shown below, and the income statement, which showed $175,000 in sales and $110,000 in expenses. Many of the expenditures were to get the business started.

A & B Musical Instruments
Balance Sheet
December 31, 20—

Assets		Liabilities and Capital	
Cash	$9,000	Liabilities:	
Accounts Receivable	8,000	Accounts Payable	$31,000
Inventory	37,000		
Equipment	25,000	Total Liabilities	31,000
		Capital:	
		A. Lafferty	24,000
		B. Williams	24,000
Total Assets	$79,000	Total Liabilities & Capital	$79,000

THINK CRITICALLY

1. On what basis did the potential buyer probably make the $50,000 offer? What did the buyer learn from the sellers' rejection?
2. How might the working capital, current ratio, and return on sales have affected the offering price? Prepare the necessary calculations before answering.
3. Assume you wish to buy the company. What additional information would you want to gather from the sellers?

CASE 15-3: Can Consultants Help?

For several years, Delia and Lorenzo Garcia have been making leather items such as belts, purses, and wallets in their home as a hobby. They have sold many items to friends and neighbors. Because Lorenzo has just lost his regular job, he and Delia have decided to go into business full-time making leather craft items. The items will be sold at fairs, festivals, and flea markets and hopefully later to retailers. They will need a large amount of money, some of which they have saved, to expand to a full-time business. Both agree that they know a great deal about how to make leather items but very little about financial and other business decisions. Delia believes they should hire a consultant before they do anything else. Lorenzo, on the other hand, believes they should go to a bank to obtain the money they need to start the business. He thinks that they can hire an accountant if they have questions or problems after the business is started. He does not believe the consultant will know enough about the leather business to give advice. "Besides," he adds, "consultants are too expensive. We can use the money to run the business rather than paying someone to learn about it."

THINK CRITICALLY

1. Do you agree with Delia or with Lorenzo about whether they need a consultant? Explain.
2. How could a consultant help them? How might the bank help them?
3. Could the Small Business Administration be of help? How?

PROJECT My Own Business

Completing Initial Financial Planning

As a new business owner, you must be able to assess the financial needs of your business. You will need this information to obtain financing and make operating decisions. Businesspeople need a complete set of financial records to make management decisions. This is very important for new businesses, as financial resources are usually limited. As you complete this part of the project, you will review the financial records needed for your business and the sources of record-keeping assistance available. You will use the information to make initial financial decisions and develop financial statements to serve as initial estimates of the financial condition of your new business.

DATA COLLECTION

1. Interview an accountant or review small-business management materials. Use the interview or materials review to determine the types of financial records you will need for your business. Develop a list of all of the records you believe you will need to maintain as the business owner.
2. Obtain detailed information about small-business financial planning software. Examine each of the forms and records included with the package and determine the type of information the business would need to acquire in order to complete the forms and records.
3. Locate a source of sample financial information for small retail businesses (especially fast-food or specialty-food businesses). You should be able to find average figures for balance sheets and income statements as well as average financial ratios. The Internet and most libraries are good places to begin your search.

ANALYSIS

1. Develop a detailed set of procedures to be followed in your business for the safe handling of cash. Be certain to consider all situations in which cash will be handled.
2. Prepare a sample cash budget for your business. The budget should cover the first three months of business operations.
3. Prepare a beginning estimated balance sheet for your new business. It should show the planned financial position of your business for its first day of operation.
4. Prepare an estimated income statement for the first three months of the operation of your business. Be realistic in your estimates. You may not show a profit.

© Shutterstock/Blaj Gabriel

Reality Check

Show Me the Money!

Diaz DigiPrintz opened for business in a storefront a few years ago. Owner Alana Diaz used her entire savings to launch a drop-in studio where people develop creative paper and fabric prints from the images in their digital cameras and cell phones. The business struggled the first year, but through hard work and creative marketing, Alana has made Diaz DigiPrintz successful.

Cory Wagner, Alana's accountant, was in the store updating financial records. As Cory finished his work, Alana excitedly asked, "Can I open another studio with my current earnings? There's a shopping center opening near the college and I think a Diaz DigiPrintz would be very successful there."

Cory's response came quickly. "No, your earnings are good, but you need more financial muscle before you can expand. You need to build the financial strength of this store before you consider opening another location."

"Cory, my business sense tells me others may jump on this idea if I don't move fast. Don't tell me I can't do it; tell me how. I want to have a chain of Diaz DigiPrintz within the next five years."

Startled by Alana's bold plan, Cory asked, "Have you thought about how you would finance that type of growth?"

"I was hoping that we could work together to come up with some ideas," Alana replied. "For starters, I have an aunt who might be able to lend me some money. And I could get a bank loan based on my success."

Cory interrupted, "Your expansion plans would require big money. Between now and when I return next week, look at the financial statements I prepared today and think about how much money you would need to open a second location. The bank and potential investors, including your aunt, will want to see some numbers."

After Cory left, Alana wondered how she could raise the money to expand her business. "Strike now while the market is hot," she said under her breath as she heard customers walked in.

What's Your Reaction? Do you agree with Alana that she should expand quickly or with Cory that she needs to build a financially strong business before opening a second location? Explain your answer.

Types of Business Capital

Goals

- Explain three methods of financing a business.
- Describe the differences in equity financing based on the ownership structure of a business.

Terms

- capital p. 425
- equity capital p. 425
- retained earnings p. 426
- debt capital p. 426

●●● Methods of Obtaining Capital

Alana faces the same problem most successful business owners face—how to get needed financing. On a balance sheet, *capital* is the value of the owners' investment in the business after subtracting liabilities from assets. **Capital** also refers to the money required to start or expand a business. Businesses need capital to acquire assets. Capital comes from many sources. Owners can provide it from their personal funds or from money they have accumulated in other businesses. They can also raise capital by obtaining loans, by making business purchases on credit, or by leaving earned profits in the business. Business executives and business owners need to be familiar with various methods for raising capital and understand the advantages and disadvantages of sources of capital.

Business owners have several options for obtaining the capital they need to start and operate their business. One way is to contribute their own money to the business. Business owners' personal financial contributions to the business are called **equity capital** or *owner capital*. This capital may come from personal funds, such as from accumulated savings, or from funds the owners borrow using their homes or other personal property as security for the loan. As shown in Figure 16-1, small

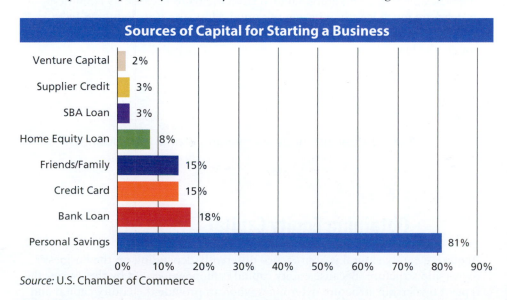

Figure 16-1 Most new business owners use their personal savings to start a business.

McGraw's Pet Shop			
Balance Sheet			
July 31, 20—			
ASSETS		LIABILITIES AND CAPITAL	
Current Assets	$ 65,000	Liabilities	
Cash	25,000	Supplier Credit	$ 60,000
Fixed Assets	310,000	Bank Loan	100,000
		Total Liabilities	$160,000
		Capital	
		Equity Capital	240,000
Total Assets	$400,000	Total Liabilities and Capital	$400,000

Figure 16-2 A balance sheet demonstrates the financial strength of a business.

businesses rely heavily on equity capital. Alana Diaz can consider those sources if she decides to open additional locations for Diaz DigiPrintz. However, because she has already opened one store using all of her savings, it is not likely she has a great deal of money to use as equity capital. If Alana wants to use equity capital to finance expansion, she will likely need to attract other investors willing to use their money in return for partial ownership of the business.

A second way to obtain capital is through retained earnings. **Retained earnings** are the profits that are not taken out of the business but instead are saved for use by the business. Retained earnings are a type of equity capital, because profits belong to the owners of the business. As Alana's business becomes profitable, she may be able to accumulate retained earnings and use them for future business expansion.

A third way of financing a business is through **debt capital**, or *creditor capital*—money that others loan to a business. Banks and other types of lending institutions usually will not lend money to a business unless the equity capital exceeds the debt capital. As a result, businesses in financial difficulty often have trouble getting debt capital. McGraw's Pet Shop, as shown in Figure 16-2 , might be able to get an additional loan from the bank because its liabilities, or debt, are much less than its equity capital. However, if its liabilities were $240,000 and its equity capital were $160,000, the Pet Shop probably would not get the loan.

21st CENTURY SKILLS

Problem Solving

Solving problems often starts with asking questions that help to clarify the situation. Problem solving skills are used by business owners and managers as they look for ways to obtain capital. A manager might start solving the problem by asking the following questions: Why do we need capital? How much do we need? What sources could we tap? What information will potential investors and creditors want?

 **CHECKPOINT**

What are three methods of obtaining capital for a business?

⬤⬤⬤ Obtaining Equity Capital

Acquiring equity capital is approached differently depending on the business's ownership structure. Because equity capital is money invested by the owner, the type of ownership structure determines who can provide the equity capital and how it is obtained and invested in the business.

SOLE PROPRIETORSHIPS

Sole proprietors must rely on their personal assets for capital if they want to retain ownership of the company. If owners are wealthy or the needed amount is small, they can invest more of their own money in the business. If they do not have available cash, they will have to sell personal assets to raise the money. Other options are to mortgage personal property such as a home or obtain a personal loan using the collateral of owned assets such as automobiles, insurance policies, or other property. Of course, funds invested in the business by the sole proprietor are at risk and can be lost if the business is not successful. In addition, other personal assets that were not invested in the business can be lost if the business fails.

If the sole proprietor cannot provide additional financing for the business and chooses to use equity capital, alternative sources will have to be considered. When others provide equity capital, the form of business ownership will need to change. The sole owner of a business can obtain additional funds by (1) forming a partnership and requiring the new partner to invest money in the business or (2) forming a corporation and bringing in additional equity and owners by selling stock.

PARTNERSHIPS

When a business expands by creating a partnership, the new partner is not required to invest money. A partner may be brought into a business because of his or her business expertise rather than the need for additional capital. However, partners usually invest their personal resources in the business to balance the amount of money each owner has in the business and to spread the financial risk among the owners.

When a sole proprietorship is reorganized into a partnership, a formal partnership agreement must be created that identifies the financial contributions of each partner and how business profits will be shared. As with the sole proprietor, a new business partner will need to use personal finances to provide the required equity capital. Those resources can be personal savings, income from the sale of assets, or personal loans and mortgages. And just as in the sole proprietorship, the money invested by each partner as well as any other personal assets that were not invested are at risk if the business fails. If the assets of one partner are not adequate to cover the debts of a business, assets from other partners can be taken.

© Getty Images/Photodisc

When successful entrepreneurs want to expand their businesses, they often face the problem of raising large sums of capital. Other than family and friends, where can a small business obtain money to expand or open additional stores?

NETBookmark

Would you like to ask family members and friends to invest in your business but don't know how to approach them? Do you have a great business idea and believe others might like to contribute to its development? A new strategy for funding business ideas has sprung up called *crowdfunding*. Many people who want to provide support for a new business idea invest small amounts of money. The total contribution may be enough to get the business off the ground.

Peerbackers.com is an example of a crowdfunding organization. Through the Peerbackers website, business ideas are promoted to thousands of people who can invest whatever they can afford to get the idea off the ground. Through a variety of online tools and resources, a description of a business idea can be prepared and then disseminated through simple buttons to Facebook, Twitter, Linkedin, and other social media sites. Investors do not receive equity in the business. Instead, the business owner offers rewards in the form of products and services. Peerbackers encourages projects to be limited to under $25,000 in fund raising.

Access the website for this textbook and choose the link for Chapter 16 Net Bookmark. Review the "how it works" section and then browse several business projects to learn about the business idea. Would you invest a small amount of money to see any of the ideas succeed?

www.cengage.com/school/bizmgmt

When a sole proprietorship expands ownership by forming a partnership, the owner gives up individual control over management and decision-making. If Alana Diaz decides to expand Diaz DigiPrintz by forming a partnership, she will share ownership and management with her new partners.

CORPORATIONS

The third way to raise equity capital is by forming a corporation and bringing in additional owners through the sale of stock. The use of a corporate structure for a small business may be an effective way to raise equity capital because the amount of money that an individual needs to invest is usually much smaller than if a partnership is formed. Also, stockholders are not involved in the day-to-day management of the business. Therefore the person who was the original owner may be able to continue as the primary manager of the business.

Investors in corporations are protected financially; they can lose the money they have invested only if the business fails. This might be viewed as an advantage to Alana Diaz because she will be a stockholder based on her investment in the business, and any losses will be limited to that amount. Currently, as a sole proprietor, all of the money she has invested in the business and all her personal assets are at risk in the event the business fails.

Stockholders who invest in a business expect that the business will use their investment effectively and that they will make money. Stockholders earn money on their investments through dividends paid from profits earned by the business or through the sale of their stock at a profit. Depending on whether a corporation is organized as a public corporation or a close corporation, stockholders have more or less flexibility in the sale of stock and input into the direction of the business. If Alana Diaz decides she wants to expand the number of video stores very rapidly, she may need to choose to reorganize as a corporation. If the prospects for her business are good, she may be able to attract a number of investors who will purchase stock, giving her the needed capital.

There are advantages and disadvantages to each form of ownership in terms of the amount of equity capital that can be raised, the risk to the owners, and the role of investors in managing the business. To raise equity capital, therefore, a business owner must estimate whether it will be more advantageous to remain a sole owner or to form a partnership or a corporation. Alana Diaz must deal with this question if she decides to expand Diaz DigiPrintz.

 **CHECKPOINT**

How is equity capital obtained in each of the three types of business ownership?

UNDERSTAND MANAGEMENT CONCEPTS

Determine the best answer for each of the following questions.

1. Business owners' personal contributions to the business are called
   a. assets
   b. equity capital
   c. debt capital
   d. stock

2. Which form of business ownership provides the greatest protection of the owner's personal assets in case of business failure?
   a. sole proprietorship
   b. partnership
   c. corporation
   d. None of the ownership forms provides protection of an owner's personal assets.

THINK CRITICALLY

Answer the following questions as completely as possible.

3. Why would an owner of a business want to use equity financing rather than debt financing to raise money for a business?

4. What information would you want from a business before you decided to invest your money as a new partner? As a new stockholder?

16.2

Raising Capital Through Stock Sales

Goals

- Differentiate between common and preferred stock.
- Describe factors that affect the value of a company's stock.

Terms

- common stock p. 430
- par value p. 430
- market value p. 430
- preferred stock p. 431
- book value p. 432

 **Types of Stock**

By far the greatest amount of equity investment in U.S. businesses comes from the sale of stock. Dow Jones tracks the total amount invested in the stocks of U.S. corporations. The value in early 2011 was $16.3 trillion. In 2011, 54 percent of all Americans owned stock in some form—individual stocks, stock mutual funds, or stock holdings as a part of a retirement fund. That level of investment is down from 67 percent in 2002. Corporations use several types of equity and debt financing to raise money, but about 44 percent of the total equity in the average corporation is made up of stocks.

Stockholders are the owners of corporations but their ownership rights and responsibilities vary based on the type of stock they hold. Two kinds of stock are issued by corporations, common stock and preferred stock.

COMMON STOCK

Common stock is ownership that gives holders the right to participate in managing the business through voting privileges and the right to share in any profits through dividends. Owners of common stock can vote on basic issues at the corporation's annual meeting and by electing the board or directors. Holders of common stock receive one vote per share of stock owned. As owners they also can share in the corporation's profits. When the corporation makes a profit, some or all of that profit may be paid back to stockholders as dividends. The corporation's board of directors makes the decision about whether holders of common stock will receive a dividend or not and the amount of that dividend per share of stock.

The board of directors decides on the number of shares of common stock that will be issued by the corporation. If they decide to issue new shares, they assign a value to those shares, known as **par value**. The par value is somewhat arbitrary in that it may not be the price that stockholders pay for the shares. If stockholders believe the company is a good investment, they may pay more than par value. The price at which stock is actually bought and sold is its **market value**. The price of stock goes up and down based on the financial performance of the company and general economic conditions. Investors purchase stocks with the expectation that the company's financial performance will be strong, dividends will be paid, and the stock price will increase. They hope to sell the stock in the future for a much greater value than they paid for it.

Common stockholders have the right to purchase any new stock issued before it is offered for sale on the open market. That right protects the interests of the current stockholders. Otherwise it would be possible for management of the corporation to take control away from the current stockholders by issuing and buying a large amount of new stock.

PREFERRED STOCK

Preferred stock is stock that gives holders first claim on corporate dividends if a company earns a profit. In addition, in the event a business fails, preferred stockholders have priority over common stockholders on any remaining assets after creditors have been paid. However, preferred stockholders typically have no voting rights. Preferred stock carries a guaranteed fixed dividend. A corporation must use its earnings first to pay its debts. Then some or all of the remaining profits can be used to pay dividends. Any dividends declared by the board of directors go first to preferred stockholders. If any profits remain, the corporation can then choose to pay dividends to common stockholders.

For example, suppose that a corporation issues $1,000,000 of 7 percent preferred stock and $1,000,000 of common stock. Further assume that dividends for the year are $100,000. The preferred stockholders would receive 7 percent of $1,000,000, or $70,000. The remaining $30,000 would be left for the holders of common stock. Their return on $1,000,000 would yield only 3 percent ($30,000/1,000,000). Even that return is not guaranteed because the board of directors may choose not to declare a dividend for common stockholders.

A special class of preferred stock is *cumulative preferred stock*. If there is no profit in a particular year, the guarantee remains in place for cumulative preferred stockholders, so the dividend will have to be made up in future years when the company is profitable again.

Preferred stockholders have priority over common stockholders for the company's assets as well. If the corporation ceases operations, its assets belong to its owners, the stockholders. The assets are first distributed to preferred stockholders. Any remaining assets go to common stockholders.

What would happen if a corporation with $500,000 of outstanding common stock and $500,000 of outstanding preferred stock ceased operating? Assume that after selling all of the assets and after paying all of its creditors, $800,000 in cash remains. The sum of $500,000 (the par value of the preferred stock) must be paid to the preferred stockholders, because their stock has asset priority. As a result, the common stockholders would receive only $300,000, which is 60 percent of the full value of their stock ($300,000/$500,000). If no stock had been issued as preferred, all stockholders would share equally in the $800,000.

 **CHECKPOINT**

What right do common stockholders have that preferred stockholders do not?

 **The Value of Stock**

The original sale of stock provides the equity that a company needs to operate the business. It is used to finance long- and short-term assets and pay operating expenses. Even though the value of stock may increase or decrease after the original

It used to be difficult to track stock market investments. Investors had to rely on daily newspapers, financial reports on radio and TV, or communications with a stockbroker. Today information on the stock market and individual stocks is available almost instantaneously through financial Internet sites. Investors create their own stock portfolios, which are tracked on their desktops or cell phones along with breaking news that might affect their investments.

sale, that change in value is not directly reflected in the resources the company has available to finance operations. The change in the price of a company's stock is important to stockholders when they buy and sell the stock, so the company's management wants to maximize the value of its stock to make the company attractive to investors. If a corporation wants to increase its capital, it must issue additional stock or keep profits for use in the company rather than using those profits to pay stockholder dividends.

Corporations obtain capital by selling stock. Where would you go to buy a share of stock?

ISSUING STOCK

If an existing corporation needs additional equity and decides to raise it through the sale of stock, that decision will need to be approved by the board of directors. Common stockholders will have the first right to purchase the stock. Stockholders will be concerned about the effect of the sale of new stock on the price of their current shares. Having more shares of a company available usually results in a lower stock price.

Corporations must determine the kind of stock to issue. The certificate of incorporation states whether all authorized stock is common stock or whether part is common and part preferred. Corporations cannot issue other stock unless they receive authorization from the state in which they are chartered.

It is usually a good practice to issue only common stock when starting a business. That provides more flexibility to the board of directors in the way they use any profits earned in the first years of the company. Even if the new corporation earns profits right away, it is often wise to use those profits to improve the financial strength of the business, rather than distribute the profits as dividends. Although a corporation often pays dividends to holders of common stock, it is not required to do so. When the corporation issues preferred stock, however, it is obligated to pay the specified dividend from its profits. If it issues only common stock initially and later wants to expand, it may then issue preferred stock to encourage others to invest in the business. Investors may be attracted to a company whose stock price is not expected to increase if they can be assured of a regular dividend.

VALUING A COMPANY'S STOCK

The par value or market value of stock does not reflect the stockholder's equity in the company. A company's stock shows a par value of $5, for example, but may have a current market value of over $100, depending on how well the company has performed financially. The real value of stock to stockholders is not the par value but the amount buyers are willing to pay for it.

In the same way, the value of a share of stock to the company is not its par value or its market value. The value of stock to the company relates to the financial health of the company, which is measured by the stock's book value. The **book value** of a share of stock is calculated by dividing the corporation's net worth (assets minus liabilities) by the total number of shares outstanding. Thus, if the corporation's net worth is $75,000,000 and the number of shares of stock outstanding is 1,000,000, the book value of each share is $75 ($75,000,000/1,000,000), regardless of the stock's par value or market value. The lower the net worth of a company, the lower the book value of its stock. If the net worth is high, meaning the value of assets is much greater than the value of liabilities, the book value of the stock will also be high. Book value is an important tool when making judgments about the worth of a business. It is used as one measure to determine the value of a business that is about to be sold. It can be useful in a comparison of businesses by potential investors. Book value may also be used, in part, to estimate the amount of money that can be distributed to shareholders when a corporation is dissolved.

RETAINED EARNINGS

Normally, a good policy for a firm is not to distribute all of its profits. A business can hold some of its profits in reserve for use in the business through retained earnings. If the corporation distributes all of its profits as dividends to stockholders, it may later need to borrow money to carry on its operations. As illustrated in Figure 16-3, corporations usually distribute some of their profits as dividends and keep some in the business as retained earnings. In addition, if the corporation earns no profit during a particular period, it can use retained earnings to pay dividends for that period. If the corporation pays out all of its profits to stockholders, it has no retained earnings to fall back on during tough times.

A business that retains some or all of its profits for use in the business is reinvesting its earnings. A business reinvests earnings for some or all of the following reasons:

1. Replacement of buildings and equipment as the result of depreciation
2. Replacement of obsolete equipment
3. Addition of new capital assets for expanding the business
4. The availability of cash to serve as financial protection during periods of low sales and profits, such as recessions and tough competitive times

Even when the business is not making a profit, it should have financial plans to replace assets that decrease in value because of depreciation or obsolescence. For instance, a car rental company starts operations with all new cars. If the owners of the business do not develop an asset replacement fund through retained earnings and instead distribute all profits as dividends, funds will not be available to buy new cars when the present ones need to be replaced with new models.

Retained earnings are not kept in the form of cash only. Retained earnings may be used for current assets such as inventories and accounts receivable, which can be quickly converted to cash if needed. Any unused earnings should be invested in short- or long-term securities that earn interest for the company. Because retained earnings are a part of owner's equity, the earnings can be used for investment purposes and future expansion.

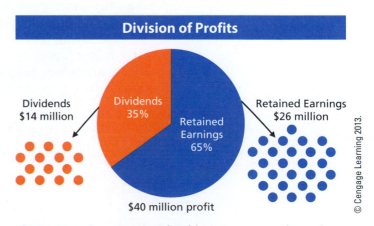

Figure 16-3 A corporation should retain some profits and distribute the rest as stockholder dividends.

© Cengage Learning 2013.

CHECKPOINT

How is the book value of stock determined?

16.2 ASSESSMENT

UNDERSTAND MANAGEMENT CONCEPTS

Determine the best answer for each of the following questions.

1. Which of the following statements about preferred stock ownership is true?
   a. Preferred stock owners are given one vote per share on corporate matters.
   b. Preferred stock owners cannot lose the amount of their investment if the business fails.
   c. Preferred stock owners receive a guaranteed dividend from the company's profits.
   d. Preferred stock owners cannot lose the money they invested if the business fails.

2. The _____ value of a share of stock is calculated by dividing the corporation's net worth by the total number of shares outstanding.
   a. book
   b. par
   c. market
   d. selling

THINK CRITICALLY

Answer the following questions as completely as possible.

3. If you had a choice of becoming a preferred or common stockholder in a new small corporation, which would you choose? Explain your choice.

4. The board of directors of a corporation of which you are a stockholder consistently votes to put 60 percent of profits in retained earnings and distributes only 40 percent to stockholders as dividends. The business is always profitable and you have received a small dividend each year. Do you agree or disagree with the board's policy? Justify your answer.

F⊕cus On... Innovation

Taking UPS Public

For most Americans, the brown UPS vans driven by people in brown uniforms delivering packages to businesses and consumers are a common sight. United Parcel Service also flies brown airplanes to make deliveries in more than 200 countries. Since 1927, much of the company's equity had been held by the original owners and by UPS employees who participated in the firm's popular stock option plan. UPS has been a financially healthy company with plenty of assets and retained earnings. With its sound financial position and growth strategy, it was a formidable competitor to its archrival, Federal Express. So why did it decide to change its ownership strategy and offer stock to the public?

In 1999, UPS launched an IPO (initial public offering) that at the time was the largest in Wall Street history. Its purpose was not the same as that of the typical fast-growing firm that wants additional equity capital to gain money for expansion. The real reason UPS sold the stock was to benefit its current owners, including its current employees and retirees. UPS believed the stock's value would increase with public trading and the cash raised could be used to buy back stock from current owners if they chose to sell. Up to this time, the firm has been a closely held corporation, not a publicly held corporation. A closely held corporation, or close corporation, cannot sell its shares to the public.

The IPO raised what was then a record-setting $5.27 billion through 109.4 million shares of new stock. As a result, the public and UPS employees as well as retirees and other investors can buy and sell UPS stock. Soon after the IPO was completed, the firm offered to buy the stock from its shareholders at a price higher than the market price. All shareholders—insiders and outsiders—were pleased. Since going public, the additional equity has allowed UPS to develop a retail strategy with Mail Boxes, Etc. and to expand its services in China, South America, and Europe.

THINK CRITICALLY

1. Assume you considered buying some of the new UPS stock. Do you think the price would be more than, less than, or the same as the price employees had to pay before the IPO? Why?

2. If you were retired or nearing retirement at UPS, how would you benefit from both the IPO and the firm's offer to buy stock from its shareholders? If you were an investor but not a present or past employee, how would you benefit from UPS's actions?

3. Using your library or the Internet, decide whether today you would prefer to become an owner of stock in UPS or Federal Express.

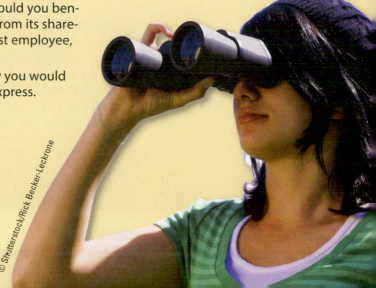

© Shutterstock/Rick Becker-Leckrone

Short- and Long-Term Debt Financing

Goals

- Differentiate between short-term and long-term debt.
- Explain the factors that businesses should consider when choosing debt financing.
- Describe several sources from which businesses can obtain additional capital.

Terms

- short-term debt p. 436
- line of credit p. 436
- promissory note p. 437
- security p. 437
- trade credit p. 437
- factor p. 438
- sales finance company p. 438
- long-term debt p. 438
- term loan p. 438
- lease p. 438
- bond p. 438
- debentures p. 439
- mortgage bond p. 439
- convertible bond p. 439
- investment bank p. 441
- initial public offering (IPO) p. 441
- stock option p. 442
- employee stock ownership plan (ESOP) p. 442
- venture capital p. 442

 Debt Capital

Businesses often borrow capital to expand the business, purchase or build new facilities, purchase equipment, pay operating expenses, or replenish inventory of products for sale. Much of this debt capital is available as a result of the savings of individuals. Millions of people deposit their savings in banks and other financial institutions that then lend the funds to businesses. Because a business can borrow money for just a few days or for many years, debt capital is classified as either short-term or long-term.

SHORT-TERM DEBT CAPITAL

Short-term debt is a loan that must be repaid with interest within a year. The loan period may be as short as 30, 60, or 90 days. Short-term debt capital is usually obtained from a bank or other lending institution but may be obtained from other businesses as well.

OBTAINING FUNDS FROM BANKS Before lending, banks want to be fairly certain that the borrowers will repay their loans. The business will need to supply adequate financial information, and the bank will usually obtain a financial report on the business from a company such as Dun & Bradstreet. If it is satisfied with the information and considers the business a good credit risk, the bank will grant a loan for a specific dollar amount and a set time period. To allow the business flexibility to choose when to use the borrowed money, the bank may approve a line of credit. A **line of credit** is the authorization to borrow up to a maximum amount for a specified period of time. For example, a business may be allowed a line of credit up to $150,000 for a year. Whenever it needs to borrow, it may do so up to the $150,000 limit. Should the business borrow $50,000, it could still borrow an additional $100,000 during the year.

Another form of debt equity similar to an open line of credit is a business credit card, often used by small businesses. The credit card is issued by the bank with a set credit limit. The card can be used to finance purchases as long as the limit is not exceeded. Both the open line of credit and the credit card carry an interest rate that is often lower than similar interest rates charged to consumers for short-term loans and personal credit cards. Normally, businesses have to pay the interest due on the loan monthly and may have a specific payment schedule for the principal as well. Businesses with a good credit history may not have to pay the principal of the loan until the end of the term of the loan.

When a business wants to borrow money from a lending institution, whether the business has a line of credit or not, it must sign a promissory note. A **promissory note** is an unconditional written promise to pay to the lender a certain sum of money at a particular time or on demand.

If the bank has some doubt about the ability of the firm to repay a loan, it may require the business to pledge its accounts receivable, inventory, or some other asset as security for the loan. **Security**, sometimes called *security collateral*, is something of value pledged as assurance of the fulfillment of an obligation. If the loan is not repaid, the bank can claim the property pledged as security and sell it to obtain the value of the unpaid loan.

OBTAINING FUNDS FROM OTHER SOURCES
A business may have access to other sources of short-term capital, depending on the type of business it is. Investment businesses and insurance companies often provide business financing. Federal agencies such as the Small Business Administration (SBA) can assist business owners in locating financing sources and may actually help guarantee repayment of a percentage of the loans to obtain a lower interest rate. Some states, counties, and cities offer loans at favorable rates to encourage businesses to locate in a particular area or to encourage businesses not to leave.

Trade credit is a common form of short-term financing for businesses. **Trade credit** is obtained by buying goods and services that do not require immediate payment. Vendors often provide trade credit as an incentive for a business to purchase their products and services. Trade credit is usually extended for a period of 30 to 60 days and may even be interest free. As an incentive for early payment, the vendor may offer a cash discount of 1 or 2 percent of the total sale if the bill is paid quickly, such as within 10 days. Terms of trade credit are often shown on the invoice in a form such as 2/10, net 30. Those terms mean that the

A business can pledge some of its assets as collateral to obtain short term financing. Why would a bank or vendor be willing to loan money to a company with a large amount current inventory?

Management MATTERS

Interpreting Stock Quotes

Following a stock helps you understand a company's financial picture. Investors use a company's stock performance to decide whether to buy, hold, or sell a stock. That helps managers see how investors view the company.

Stock quotes run continuously on financial websites and cable channels. Daily summaries also appear in the financial sections of newspapers. Here is an example for Target Corporation.

Sym	TGT
52-Week Hi	60.97
52-Week Lo	48.23
M Cap	34.1 bil
Div	.2500
Yld %	2.03
PE	11.0
Vol (mil)	3.1
Ave Vol (mil)	7.2
Hi	49.77
Lo	49.30
Close	49.45
Net Chg	0.07

Sym Symbol, often an abbreviation of the company name, used for the stock

52-week Hi and Lo Highest and lowest price at which the stock was traded over the previous 52-weeks

M Cap Market capitalization, the total dollar value of all outstanding shares of stock

Div Dividend/distribution rate, unless noted in a footnote, reflects the annual dividend

Yld % Dividends paid to stockholders as a percentage of the stock's price

PE Price-to-earnings ratio, the per-share earnings divided by the closing price

Vol (mil) Sales volume, shares traded that day, in millions

Ave Vol (mil) Average sales volume, the average daily sale of shares, in millions

Hi Highest price the stock traded at that day

Lo Lowest price the stock traded at that day

Close Last price the stock traded at that day, which is not necessarily the price the stock will open at the next day

Net Chg Net change in price calculated from the previous day's close

purchaser can receive a 2 percent discount if the bill is paid within 10 days of the invoice date. Otherwise the bill must be paid in full within 30 days.

A **factor** is a firm that specializes in lending money to businesses based on the business's accounts receivable. Rather than lending the business cash, the factor usually purchases the company's accounts receivable at a discount and then collects the full amount when customers pay their bills. In a similar manner, a **sales finance company** provides capital to a business based on installment sales contracts. A sales finance company may lend money to a business and use the business's installment sales contracts as security for the loan. As an alternative, the company purchases installment contracts at a discount from businesses that need cash or that do not care to handle credit and collections.

LONG-TERM DEBT CAPITAL

Long-term debt is capital borrowed for longer than a year. It is usually used when large expenditures are needed for assets that will have a long life, such as land, buildings, and expensive equipment. A business usually obtains this type of debt capital by obtaining term loans or issuing bonds.

TERM LOANS A **term loan** is medium- or long-term financing used for operating funds or the purchase or improvement of fixed assets. Term loans, or *long-term notes*, are written for periods of 1 to 15 years or longer. They are a significant source of capital for most businesses. Because term loans extend for a long period, lending institutions require the principal and interest to be repaid on a regular basis, usually each year, over the life of the note.

As an alternative to borrowing large sums of money, a company may prefer to lease a building or an expensive piece of equipment. A **lease** is a contract that allows the use of an asset for a fee paid on a schedule, such as monthly. The lease may be obtained from the building owner, the equipment manufacturer, a finance company that handles that type of leasing, or a bank. Leasing is a practical substitute for long-term financing, especially if capital is difficult to obtain. The maintenance of the equipment and the costs of insuring it are usually not included in the lease agreement. When businesses lease buildings and equipment, they know exactly what the monthly payment will be and how long the lease will last. They do not have to obtain the large amount of financing that would be needed to purchase the buildings or equipment. The building or equipment is not owned by the business so it cannot be valued as an asset. It is returned to the owner at the end of the lease unless the lease is renewed.

BONDS A **bond** is a long-term debt instrument sold by the business to investors. It contains a written promise by the business to pay the bondholder a definite sum of money at a specified time. The business receives the amount of the bond when it is initially sold. It must then pay the bondholder the amount borrowed—called the *principal* or *par value*—at the bond's maturity or due date. Bonds also include an agreement to pay interest at a specified rate at certain intervals.

Bonds are debt equity and do not represent a share of ownership in a corporation. Rather, they are debts the corporation owes to bondholders. People buy bonds as investments, as they do stocks. But bondholders are creditors, not owners, so they have a priority claim against the earnings of a corporation. Bondholders must be paid before stockholders are paid their share of the earnings. Because bonds are negotiable financial instruments, they can be bought and sold by investors. Based on the interest rate of the bond, economic factors, and the financial health of the company, the value of the bond may increase or decline during the time it is traded.

There are two general types of bonds: debenture and mortgage bonds. **Debentures** are unsecured bonds. No specific assets are pledged as security. Debentures are backed by the financial strength and credit history of the corporation that issues them. Public corporations, such as city, state, and federal governments, usually issue debentures when they need to borrow money. Reputable, successful corporations generally find it relatively easy to sell debentures. However, relatively unknown or financially weak firms usually find it easier to attract investors with secured bonds. **Mortgage bonds** are bonds secured by specific long-term assets of the issuer. Property often used as security includes real estate, equipment, and stocks and bonds held in other companies. If the company does not pay the principal and interest when due, creditors can force the company to sell the pledged property to recover the amount of the outstanding debt. Often, however, property cannot be sold for the amount of the loan. In some cases, a bond contract may have a provision that allows bondholders to claim assets other than the assets originally used as security.

Businesses issue debentures and mortgage bonds when they need funds for an extended period. Special features may be attached to these bonds to attract investors. For example, a mortgage bond may have a convertible feature to make it appealing to bond buyers. A **convertible bond** permits a bondholder to exchange bonds for a prescribed number of shares of common stock.

CHECKPOINT

List several sources of short-term and long-term financing available to businesses.

Obtaining Capital

Companies consider three important factors when deciding how to get the capital they need: (1) the original cost of obtaining the capital, (2) the interest rate, and (3) the power that the contributors of capital will have to influence business operations.

COST OF CAPITAL

It can be costly for a business to obtain capital by selling bonds, long-term notes, and new stock issues. For example, to launch a new bond issue, the business must file forms, obtain approval from government authorities, make agreements, print bonds, find buyers, and keep careful records. These costs are usually so high that only large or highly successful firms even consider obtaining capital by issuing new stocks or bonds. It is far less costly to obtain capital from a simple mortgage or a note.

INTEREST RATES

Interest rates can fluctuate monthly, weekly, or even daily. Borrowing when rates are low costs less than borrowing when rates are high. If a business needs money when interest rates are high, it will usually borrow for a short time with the hope that rates will drop. If rates drop, it can then issue long-term obligations, such as bonds, and use a portion of the capital obtained to pay off short-term obligations. In this way, a company has to pay high interest rates for only a short time. In following this plan, however, a business exposes itself to possible difficulty in obtaining funds when short-term obligations become due, and to the possibility that interest rates may rise even higher.

INFLUENCE OF CAPITAL CONTRIBUTORS

If short-term creditors contribute capital, they usually have no control over the management and operations of the business. If the obligations are not paid, creditors can take legal action to recover the amount due. Otherwise, owners and managers of the business are relatively unrestricted by short-term creditors.

If the company obtains capital from mortgage bonds, however, the holders usually have a lien (claim) on at least part of the assets of the company. This lien may impose limitations on the use of the identified assets, and the agreement under which the mortgage bonds were issued may limit the use of the money the company receives from the bonds.

If new stockholders or new partners contribute equity capital, they gain a voice in the management of the business. In most states, stock can be issued that does not include voting rights, but that stock may be difficult to sell. Of course, if existing stockholders or partners provide the additional funds, the control of the company will not be affected as long as the existing stockholders contribute in proportion to past holdings.

If the company increases the number of shares of stock by selling new shares, it must divide earnings among a greater number of shareholders. For example, when the number of shareholders increases from 2,000 to 2,500, the distribution of $13,000 in dividends changes from $6.50 per share ($13,000/2,000) to $5.20 per share ($13,000/2,500). The original owners may not wish to give up any of their profits or voice in management unless it is profitable to do so. An increase in shareholders would need to be offset by an increase in earnings.

 CHECKPOINT

What can a business do to obtain capital when faced with high interest rates?

●●● Sources of Outside Capital

When a business decides to obtain capital, it must find sources willing to provide the financing. Some common sources of capital are shown in Figure 16-4. The particular source a business selects depends, in part, on such factors as the

FACTS & FIGURES

Buying Bonds

Bonds are usually traded on an agreement between a buyer and seller. Bond trading is usually done through bond dealers who work at the bond trading desks of major investment companies. The major bond investors are financial institutions, pension funds, mutual funds, and governments. For smaller investors, investment brokers organize bond funds that are made up of a portfolio of bonds. Individual investors buy and sell shares of the fund and can make money through dividends and capital appreciation if the fund increases in value.

Sources of Outside Capital	
Banks and similar financial institutions	Make traditional loans and offer lines of credit
Commercial credit companies	Lend money on current assets, such as accounts receivable and notes receivable
Equipment manufacturers	Offer extended-time payment plan for the purchase of equipment
Individual investors and investment groups	Invest their personal funds into businesses, most often in the form of equity capital
Insurance companies	Make business loans and other investments using some of the funds collected from policyholders
Investment banking organizations	Work with businesses to develop security issues and then market them to the public
Pension funds	Make loans to businesses using employee retirement funds
Sales finance companies	Purchase installment sales contracts and provide loans based on the value of the sales contracts held by the business
Small loan companies	Make high risk loans to businesses with less paperwork but higher interest rates than traditional lenders
Venture capital firms	Lend large sums of money to or make investments in promising new or growing businesses

Figure 16-4 There are many sources of capital that should be considered by businesses.

amount of capital needed and the risk involved. Companies with a poor performance record find it hard to sell stocks or bonds to potential investors. A newly formed company has similar difficulties in securing a loan. Many banks avoid doing business with these types of organizations because of the added risk. When they do agree to provide financing, interest rates and other requirements are much higher than for successful, established firms.

UNDERWRITING

Many commercial banks do not generally become involved in helping large corporations raise capital by selling stocks and bonds. For these services, a corporation may turn to an **investment bank**—an organization that helps a business raise large sums of capital through the sales of stocks and bonds. Investment banks are also known as *underwriters*. Investment banks can assist a rapidly growing, privately held company through an initial public offering. An **initial public offering (IPO)** is the first time that a company sells stock to the public. Investment banks provide a variety of financial and investment services for their clients regarding large capital projects.

The process of selling securities is simple but expensive. Assume a corporation wishes to raise $50 million by selling bonds. It first finds a willing investment bank. The bank offers advice, buys the bonds at a price below the expected market value, then sells the bonds to investors through its marketing channels. The bank's profit would be the difference between what it paid the corporation for the bonds and the selling price it receives from the bond purchasers minus the costs incurred in the selling activities.

Venture capitalists provide large sums of money to people who want to start new companies. What do you think would most influence a venture capitalist's loan decision?

STOCK OPTIONS

Some corporations may wish to sell only a small number of additional shares of stock. In that case, a corporation can handle the sale itself. It can make the sale of additional shares attractive to current stockholders by offering stock options. A **stock option** is a right granted by a corporation that allows current stockholders to buy additional shares when issued at a fixed price for a specific period of time. These options give current stockholders the opportunity to buy enough stock to maintain the same percentage of ownership in the company as they had before the new stock was issued. Often the stock option is offered at a lower price to attract more funds to the corporation without the additional expense of selling through an investment bank. If stockholders do not wish to take advantage of their stock rights, they can sell their options to others within a stated period at a small gain. Employers also can offer employees stock options as part of an **employee stock ownership plan (ESOP)**, which is a plan that allows employees to become owners of the company they work for through the purchase of stock.

VENTURE CAPITAL

Venture capital is financing obtained from an investor or investment group that lends large sums of money to promising new or expanding small companies. Venture capitalists often ask for a percentage of ownership rights in the company in return for the investment. These investors expect some of the businesses to fail, but they accept the risks in the expectation that others will be successful enough to more than offset losses. They demand a carefully developed business plan that shows a high potential for success. Venture capitalists, many of whom are former entrepreneurs, have helped many small firms become large successful firms.

CHECKPOINT

Why might a company offer stock options to current stockholders?

16.3 ASSESSMENT

UNDERSTAND MANAGEMENT CONCEPTS

Determine the best answer for each of the following questions.

1. A short-term form of finance obtained by buying goods and services that do not require immediate payment is
   a. a line of credit
   b. trade credit
   c. a term loan
   d. a promissory note

2. An organization that helps a business raise large amounts of capital through the issue of bonds or stocks is a(n)
   a. commercial bank
   b. stock exchange
   c. venture capital firm
   d. investment bank

THINK CRITICALLY

Answer the following questions as completely as possible.

3. Why would a business choose to use a line of credit rather than obtain a loan and receive all of the money at that time?

4. If you were an entrepreneur with a successful new business, would you prefer to obtain financing for expansion from a venture capital firm or from selling stock through an IPO? Explain your choice.

CHAPTER CONCEPTS

- Businesses can obtain capital in three ways: selling ownership shares in the company (equity or owner capital), keeping profits in the company (retained earnings), and borrowing money from others (debt capital). Equity capital is the investment owners have in a business. When equity financing is used to raise capital, owners give up some ownership rights regarding decision making and sharing of profits.

- For corporations, common and preferred stock are shares of ownership. Retained earnings are profits that have not been distributed to stockholders but may be used to help firms through times when profits or cash flow are low and to fund expansion and improvement plans.

- Debt capital consists of either short- or long-term loans, such as notes and bonds, which must be paid back with interest to the lenders. Types of debt financing include loans obtained through banks, business credit cards, open lines of credit, and using factors. Debt financing creates a legal obligation to pay back the lenders, usually on a fixed schedule.

- Large sums of outside capital can be obtained through the sale of bonds, initial public offerings (IPOs) of stock or additional stock issues, and from venture capitalists. Large firms hire investment bankers with special expertise to assist in large stock and bond sales.

REVIEW BUSINESS MANAGEMENT TERMS

Write the letter of the term that matches each definition. Some terms will not be used.

a. bond
b. book value
c. common stock
d. debt capital
e. equity capital
f. investment bank
g. lease
h. line of credit
i. long-term debt
j. market value
k. par value
l. preferred stock
m. promissory note
n. retained earnings
o. short-term debt
p. stock option
q. term loan
r. trade credit
s. venture capital

1. Business owners' personal contributions to the business
2. Price at which stock is actually bought and sold
3. Short-term form of financing obtained by buying goods and services that do not require immediate payment
4. Contract that allows the use of an asset for a fee paid on a schedule, such as monthly
5. Financing obtained from an investor or investment group that lends large sums of money to promising new or expanding small companies
6. Medium-term or long-term financing used for operating funds or the purchase or improvement of fixed assets
7. Stock that gives holders first claim on corporate dividends if a company earns a profit
8. Profits that the owners do not take out of the business but instead save for use by the business
9. Debt that must be repaid with interest within a year
10. Organization that helps a business raise large sums of capital through the sales of stocks and bonds
11. Right granted by a corporation that allows current stockholders to buy additional shares when issued at a fixed price for a specific period of time
12. Figure calculated by dividing the corporation's net worth by the total number of shares outstanding

Determine the best answer.

13. An example of equity capital is
    a. personal savings of a current owner invested in the business
    b. money contributed by a new partner
    c. retained earnings
    d. all of the above

14. An advantage an entrepreneur gains by forming a corporation to raise capital is
    a. the number of owners remains the same
    b. the entrepreneur's personal assets have greater protection
    c. the entrepreneur still retains all profits earned
    d. the corporation has no need for using debt capital

15. The number of shares of stock to be issued by a corporation is determined by
    a. common stockholders
    b. preferred stockholders
    c. company executives
    d. the board of directors

16. The best policy regarding the use of profits for a corporation in most years is to
    a. avoid making a profit so no dividends have to be distributed
    b. distribute all profits as dividends to increase stockholder satisfaction
    c. distribute some profits as dividends and keep some profits as retained earnings
    d. keep all profits as retained earnings to build the value of the company quickly

17. A form of debt equity similar to an open line of credit is
    a. venture capital
    b. a business credit card
    c. trade credit
    d. a lease

18. Another name for *investment bank* is
    a. underwriter
    b. commercial bank
    c. factor
    d. venture capitalist

APPLY WHAT YOU KNOW

Answer the following questions.

19. Based on the Reality Check scenario at the beginning of the chapter, do you believe Alana Diaz should immediately expand her business? Why or why not? If she does expand, what type of financing do you believe would be best for her? Justify your answer.

20. Why might a proprietor with access to personal assets choose debt financing to expand a business rather than putting more personal assets into the business?

21. Why would a corporation's preferred stock probably cost more per share than its common stock?
22. When might a business lease, rather than purchase, equipment? What reasons other than the cost of the lease versus the cost of purchasing the equipment would justify the decision to lease?
23. How can venture capitalists make a profit even when they sometimes invest in firms that eventually fail?

MAKE ACADEMIC CONNECTIONS

Complete the following activities.

24. **Research** The New York Stock Exchange is the largest stock exchange in the world and dates back to the late 1700s. It has been an important part of the economic growth of businesses in the United States and has contributed to the economic success of many individual investors. Use the Internet to study the history and growth of the NYSE. Prepare several computer slides that highlight important events and information in the history of the Exchange.

25. **Technology** Think carefully about the advantages and disadvantages of the three forms of business ownership (sole proprietorship, partnership, corporation) in raising equity capital. Use a word-processing program to prepare a table that summarizes your analysis. Then write a three-paragraph report that describes the circumstances under which each of the forms of ownership would benefit in raising equity capital.

26. **Economics** Use the Internet to gather information on current interest rates. Identify the highest and lowest rates you can find for each of the following:
    a. 30-year fixed rate mortgage
    b. APR for a personal credit card
    c. 6-month certificate of deposit
    d. 48-month new-car loan
    e. a federal student loan for college
    f. the federal prime lending rate
    Prepare a chart to illustrate your findings. Compare your findings with those of other students.

27. **Oral Communication** You are the chairman of the board of directors of a corporation with a long and successful history. Stock prices have been stable and a regular dividend has been paid each year for the past 10 years. The board has decided that the business needs to invest money to upgrade facilities and equipment. They believe the best choice is to retain all profits for the next three years and not pay a dividend. Interest rates are high, so borrowing the money would be expensive. The board does not want to issue new stock and dilute the value of current stock. Prepare a three-minute speech you will deliver to stockholders at the annual meeting justifying the decision. You know many stockholders will be upset that they won't receive the expected dividends.

CASE 16-1: Is Debt The Best Way?

The Kyle Camping Company is located between a major state park and a national park in New York State's Adirondack Mountains. The business sells camping equipment and supplies from May through September to vacationers as well as to local people who enjoy mountain camping and fishing. Kyle Owens, the sole proprietor, started the business five years ago after graduating from college. Kyle is an outdoor enthusiast and the business allows him to work with people and products he enjoys. Kyle was very busy for the first several years, with little personal time to enjoy the outdoors. However, the business has experienced success that has allowed him to add two full-time and five part-time employees. Over the last two years, sales have doubled and profits have increased by 25 percent. He has been able to pay back a loan from his parents that he used to start the business and has saved $75,000 from the business's profits.

Kyle now wants to expand into a year-round business to take advantage of the winter outdoor activities. In addition, he believes he can serve the many local boat owners. To do that he would need to expand the size of his store, add a dock on the lake behind the store, and expand his inventory. He also wants to create an Internet site through which he can sell his merchandise and provide area information that could attract more tourists and visitors to his business.

Kyle is interested only in debt financing because he wants to remain the sole owner and manager of his business. He is willing to consider equity financing only as a last resort. A small community five miles away has a commercial bank with which he has had good relations since starting his business. His credit rating is acceptable but not great; it is marred by several late loan payments during the first two years of business. Kyle does have good relationships with several of his suppliers, who have approved trade credit on some of his purchases.

Kyle has calculated that he will need to find $75,000 to add a dock and additional inventory this year and $30,000 additional capital next year to carry out all of his plans. He does have a concern that sales during the winter season may be slow at the beginning, making it difficult for him to make loan payments during those months.

THINK CRITICALLY

1. If you were the local bank's loan officer, what financial and non-financial information would you request from Kyle in order to make a good decision? Based on the information available in the case, would you recommend financing Kyle's needs through loans? Why or why not?
2. Other than a loan from the local bank, what other types of debt financing might Kyle consider, given his financial situation and his plans?
3. Why might Kyle wish to consider equity financing rather than debt financing? What are two types of equity financing he could use? What would be advantages and disadvantages of each?

CASE 16-2: Taking Stock of Investments

Reika Mori is a member of a four-person carpool. Morning conversations on the way to work often deal with what people did the night before. Reika started the discussion today because she had attended an information session the previous evening on investments. Here is the conversation that occurred among the carpool members.

Lou: *I've always thought about investing but really don't want to get in over my head. I have heard of people who made a fortune but also know that you can easily lose all your money as well. Did you learn anything that can help me, Reika?*

Reika: *I learned that there are all kinds of investments including stocks and bonds. Each has different levels of risk. There seems to be something to meet everyone's needs. But at this point I'm just beginning. I'm going to have to learn a lot more before I would feel comfortable giving you advice.*

Pablo: *My brother is an investment banker, and he told me that bonds might be a good choice to consider when I'm first starting out. He said choosing the right bonds can earn a good return without the risk of stocks. Does that sound right to you, Reika?*

Reika: *We spent most of the evening learning about the stock market. The speaker said that most people want to invest in stocks but they can be risky. We are talking about bonds next week.*

Brenda: *My uncle gave Larry and me some stock for a wedding gift five years ago. We get a regular dividend check every year. It's not a lot of income, but it gives us some spending money. We wonder if we would make more if we sold that stock and invested in an IPO for a new company whose stock value will probably increase rapidly.*

Reika: *Brenda, I did learn a great deal about how to understand a company's financial performance using information from its stock quotes and other public financial information. Meet me at the coffeehouse after work and we'll look at some information on my laptop. IPOs can be risky, but we can compare stocks and see if we can find some companies where the stock is performing better than your current shares.*

THINK CRITICALLY

1. Do you agree with Pablo's brother that bonds are less risky than other investments? Why or why not?
2. What information can Reika obtain from a stock quotes and other financial information available on the Internet that will help Brenda understand what to do with the stock she owns? Do you agree with Reika's advice about IPOs?
3. If you were in the carpool, what would you say to Lou to make him less fearful of investing some of his money?

PROJECT My Own Business

Types and Sources of Capital

A very important step in financial planning for a new business is determining the amount of capital needed and the sources of that capital. Most new businesses fail because they do not have adequate capital to operate the business until it becomes profitable. You have already estimated your business's financial needs in the Chapter 15 activities. Now you need to develop a plan to obtain the capital.

Your plans should consider both immediate and long-term needs, the type of ownership structure you currently have and whether you want to retain or change the form, and whether you believe it will be possible to obtain equity capital, debt capital, or a combination of both. If you choose equity capital, how will it affect your role as owner and manager? Will your business benefit in ways other than having additional capital? If you choose debt capital, how will you be certain your business will be able to repay the debt on schedule? What will happen if you are unable to meet the debt payments? What are other possible consequences of your decision?

DATA COLLECTION

1. Identify three sources of long-term financing for your business. For each source, determine the (a) amount of capital available, (b) interest rate, (c) amount and type of security needed, and (d) procedures for obtaining financing.
2. Identify three sources of short-term financing for your business. For each source, determine (a) what the financing can be used for in your business, (b) what the terms of financing would be, and (c) what information would need to be provided to obtain the financing.
3. Ask several small-business owners how they obtained the initial financing for their businesses. Have them identify problems they have faced in financing continuing operations and any expansions.

ANALYSIS

1. Based on the amount of capital you will need to start your business and operate it for six months, determine:
   a. the amount of money you can personally invest
   b. the capital available from family and friends, and how you can obtain and repay it
   c. sources for the remaining capital needs, interest rates, and procedures for obtaining the capital
2. Develop a written request for funds that can be presented to prospective investors. It must contain enough specific information to encourage them to invest money in your business. Provide supporting data, including the appropriate financial information and graphs or charts showing the source and amount of each type of capital. Prepare a three-minute oral presentation based on the written request you can give to potential investors.

FINANCIAL SERVICES

© Shutterstock/Yuri Arcurs

Reality Check

What Should We Do with the Money?

Andrew Jones was reviewing the monthly financial statements of Kilgore Kitchens, a kitchen design center he owns with his partner, Julie Vernon. Just as he finished, Julie knocked on his door.

"I'm taking a break; do you want to walk to the deli with me?"

"Sure, I could use a break and some coffee," Andrew responded.

As they entered the nearby deli, Julie mentioned the growing cash balance in the company's checking account.

"Andrew, when we started the company, we ran most of the business's financial transactions through the checking account. We kept all our cash in that account because we wanted enough money on hand to pay any unexpected bills. Now we are much bigger and stronger financially. Our cash account continues to grow and I don't think that is the best use of our money," Julie said.

"I agree, we have too much cash that is not doing anything for us. What should we do?" Andrew asked.

"We still need some cash for financial emergencies. We could divide the excess between some good short-term

and long-term investments," Julie suggested.

"Where can we invest the cash? Should we keep all of our resources in our local bank or look at other options? What investment options exist for different periods of time? Can we be sure if we make long-term investments we will always have enough cash to pay our bills?" Andrew asked.

"Let's work together on this," Julie replied. "I'll check with our bank about the options available there. Can you find time to do some online financial shopping"

"Sure, I'll start gathering information on other investment choices," replied Andrew.

Julie nodded her approval. "This could be just what the business needs to move us to the next level."

What's Your Reaction? Should a five-year-old business make different decisions about cash than a new business? What are possible problems with putting cash in long-term investments?

Financial Institutions

Goals

- Identify several types of banks and how they are regulated.
- Discuss the similarities and differences among nonbanking financial institutions and banks.

Terms

- financial institution p. 451
- bank p. 451
- demand deposit p. 451
- time deposits p. 451
- commercial loan p. 451
- consumer loan p. 451
- nonbank p. 452
- Federal Reserve System p. 454
- Federal Deposit Insurance Corporation (FDIC) p. 454

●●● Banks and Banking

Businesses rely on the services of financial institutions. A business like Kilgore Kitchens must deposit cash, make payments, invest excess funds, and borrow money. Knowledge of the types of financial institutions and the services they provide help managers and owners like Andrew and Julie and use their financial resources wisely.

A **financial institution** is an organization that collects money from clients and uses it for investments to benefit both the client and the organization. Banks were probably the best known financial institutions for many years. Other nonbank financial institutions provided specialized services that banks were not legally allowed to offer. However, each year it is getting more and more difficult to distinguish among the services provided by various financial institutions. Nonbank financial institutions have rapidly expanded the services they offer, competing directly with banks in areas such as checking and savings accounts. The deregulation of banking has made it possible for banks to offer a variety of new investment products and other financial services. Computer technology and the Internet allow businesses and consumers to conduct many financial transactions online and have contributed much to changing how financial activities are completed around the world.

BANKS AND NONBANKS

Banks in the United States are financial institutions that historically have been regulated by the government to make sure financial services are widely available and that financial resources of individuals and businesses are protected. In order to operate, a bank must receive a charter. A *bank charter* authorizes the operation of a bank following the regulations established by the state or federal government.

To be recognized as a **bank**, a financial institution must accept demand deposits, make consumer and commercial loans, and buy and sell currency and government securities. A **demand deposit** is money put into a financial institution that the depositors can withdraw at any time without penalty. A checking account is an example of a demand deposit account. **Time deposits** (also known as *certificates of deposit* or *CDs*) are made for a specified period of time and cannot be withdrawn early without some financial penalty. A **commercial loan** is a loan made to a business, whereas a **consumer loan** is a loan made to an individual for personal use.

If the primary purpose of an institution is to offer financial products and services other than deposits and loans, it is classified as a **nonbank** financial institution. Although nonbank financial institutions initially developed to offer financial products such as insurance and investments, they have increasingly begun to offer services traditionally reserved for banks. The distinction between banks and nonbanks is fading fast.

TYPES OF BANKS

Banks are often known as *deposit institutions* because their customers deposit excess funds for the purpose of earning interest on the deposits. Depending on the type of institution, deposits are accepted from individual consumers, businesses, organizations, and government agencies. The banks use those deposits to make loans to customers who need the financial resources for short or long periods of time. Those customers pay interest to the bank for the use of the funds. The bank accepts the risk that the loan may not be repaid. They take steps to reduce the risk by carefully evaluating loan applicants and spreading the risk across a large number of loans.

There are three major types of banks, based on the customers served and the types of deposits and loans offered. The three types are described in Figure 17-1.

COMMERCIAL BANKS Commercial banks as a group are the largest and most important type of deposit institution. Commercial banks offer a broad range of services and they serve many types of customers. More than 6,000 U.S. commercial banks have assets of more than $12 trillion, made up of loans to businesses, government, and consumers, private and public securities, cash, and real estate. They hold deposits from customers of more than $7 trillion. Commercial banks provide most short-term loans to consumers. Nearly 10 percent of their loans are consumer loans. They also make a large number of loans to businesses to finance operations as well as commercial real estate loans. About 50 percent of all loans are made to finance business and individual real estate purchases. Commercial banks provide checking and savings accounts for both consumers and businesses. Ten percent of all deposits are demand deposits, and nearly 85 percent are various types of time deposits.

The number of commercial banks peaked in the mid 1980s at nearly 15,000 banks. Since that time, competition and deregulation reduced that number significantly. The severe economic downturn of the mid to late 2000s led to many bank failures and more consolidations. Figure 17-1 shows that the number of commercial banks had declined by almost 60 percent by 2011. Despite that decline, consumers still have ready access to commercial banks. The total number of branch

Three Major Types of Banks		
Type	**Description**	**Number of U.S. institutions (2011)**
Commercial Banks	Full-service financial institutions that serve all types of customers with a variety of deposit accounts and lending services.	6,453
Savings Institutions	Financial institutions that emphasize loans for residential mortgages; include savings and loan associations and mutual savings banks.	1,114
Credit Unions	Nonprofit associations whose services are restricted to members who generally have a common relationship, such as employees of a large business, members of an employee association such as a union, or employees affiliated with a government unit (state employees, teachers); offer deposit services and loans to members.	7,292

© Cengage Learning 2013.

Figure 17-1 All banks accept deposits from their customers and use those funds to make loans.

offices has doubled in that same time from 41,000 to 82,000. The 10 largest U.S. commercial banks are listed in Figure 17-2.

SAVINGS INSTITUTIONS Savings institutions developed as local or neighborhood locations to promote thrift and savings. They encouraged community members to deposit some of their earnings and other funds and in return offered loans to borrowers needing funds. There are two common types of savings institutions—mutual savings banks and savings and loan associations.

Mutual savings banks began in the early 1800s and are owned by their customers. Rather than buying shares as in a corporation, ownership is based on establishing a relationship with the bank as a depositor or borrower. The profits are divided and distributed in proportion to the amount of deposits of each owner. Customers who borrow funds from mutual savings banks do not have to be depositors or "owners." Both short- and long-term loans are made for a variety of purposes, but a large percentage of the loans are made within the community for long-term needs such as financing home mortgages.

Savings and loan associations served a similar purpose as mutual savings banks. They were often started by pooling the small savings of a large number of people and in turn lending that money back to their members for the purpose of building housing. Often the original savings and loan associations were dissolved when the building needs of members were met. Savings and loans were formed either as closely held corporations where members bought shares or as mutual companies where ownership was based on the value of deposits. Today, most savings and loans have expanded their purpose and no longer require membership to use their services. However, they still emphasize loans for real estate mortgages. Because of their limited size and services compared to many commercial banks, they often pay a slightly higher interest rate on deposits and charge lower mortgage rates.

Together, mutual savings banks and savings and loan associations have assets of about $1.24 trillion, made up mostly of loans and leases. They hold customer deposits of just under $89 billion, over 90 percent of which is in time deposits.

CREDIT UNIONS Credit unions are not-for-profit financial organizations owned and managed by their members. Rather than making a profit, credit unions provide financial benefits to members such as higher interest rates on deposits and lower rates on loans. They also emphasize more personal service than many other financial institutions. Credit unions provide both demand and time deposits and emphasize shorter-term consumer loans such as personal loans, auto loans, and home loans of three to five years. Although there are large credit unions, many credit unions serve a very small number of customers who have a common relationship such as employment, an organizational affiliation, or location. You must be a member to use the services of a credit union. Today nearly 90 million people in the United States are credit union members. Credit unions hold assets of nearly

21st CENTURY SKILLS

Information Literacy

Information literacy is important when choosing and using financial services. Whether you are looking at financial services for a business or for yourself, you need to access information efficiently and effectively. This means acting in a timely manner and seeking information from reliable sources. You also need to evaluate information for completeness and accuracy, as well has how it applies to your situation.

Top 10 U.S. Commercial Banks			
Rank	Institution Name	Bank Location	Total Assets
1	JPMorgan Chase Bank	Columbus, OH	$1,791,060,000
2	Bank of American NA	Charlotte, NC	1,454,051,000
3	Citibank NA	Las Vegas, NV	1,216,291,000
4	Wells Fargo Bank NA	Sioux Falls, SD	1,104,833,000
5	US Bank NA	Cincinnati, OH	310,100,000
6	PNC Bank NA	Wilmington, DE	254,826,000
7	Bank of NY Mellon	New York, NY	236,300,000
8	HSBC Bank USA NA	Mclean, VA	195,100,000
9	FIA Card Service NA	Wilmington, DE	187,296,000
10	State Street Bank & Trust Co.	Boston, MA	141,234,000

Source: Federal Reserve National Information Center, June 30, 2011

Figure 17-2 The size of banks has grown as large banks buy smaller banks.

$920 billion, including loans valued at over $574 billion. Because credit union members are owners, their savings make up most of the owner's equity of the organizations. Total member deposits are just over $791 billion.

REGULATING BANKS

Banks operate in an environment of high risk. Customers who deposit funds with banks risk that the bank will not have adequate funds to pay the interest or return the money when the customer requests its return. When banks make loans to customers, they risk that the customer will be unable to repay the loan with interest according to the terms of the loan. Of course customers should be careful to deposit money with banks that have the financial strength and history to protect deposits. Banks carefully review loan applicants and their applications to determine if they are creditworthy. However, there are many examples of bank failures that resulted in large financial losses to businesses and individuals. The bank failures during the Great Depression in the 1930s were so dramatic in terms of the number of people affected and the size of their financial losses that the federal government increased its regulation of banks and banking. Since that time there have been other economic downturns that have placed severe pressure on financial institutions. Even though banks sometimes fail, federal regulation has reduced the effect of failures on the economy and protected depositors' assets.

THE FEDERAL RESERVE SYSTEM   The **Federal Reserve System (Fed)** is the central bank of the United States. It was developed to regulate banking and manage the economy through control of the money supply. Approved by Congress in 1913, the Fed is made up of a chairman and a board of governors appointed by the president of the United States. The chairman and board members are financial and economic experts who establish the interest rates at which member banks can borrow money. These rates in turn affect the rates on many of the loans and deposits made by consumers and businesses.

Most commercial banks and savings banks are members of the Fed system and must meet its requirements and regulations, which affect the types of loans they can make, the amount of assets that can be loaned, and the security requirements for loans. Banks are required to keep a percentage of their assets in reserve, with some deposited in one of the 12 Federal Reserve district banks.

THE FDIC   In 1933, consumers lost confidence in banks and tried to withdraw all of their money at nearly the same time. Banks had not kept enough money in reserve to cover all of the withdrawals. As a result, more than 4,000 U.S. banks closed, with losses averaging nearly $1,000,000 each. Those losses were actually suffered by the banks' customers, who could not withdraw their deposits. Although many of those funds were eventually recovered and nearly 80 percent was repaid to consumers, Congress wanted to avoid another "rush" on the banks in the future. It established the **Federal Deposit Insurance Corporation (FDIC)**, a federal agency that insures deposits in banks and savings institutions up to $250,000 per depositor in an insured institution. If a depositor has money in several accounts, the total amount insured is typically $250,000 with a few exceptions based on the type of account ownership. Since its creation in 1934, no insured deposits have been lost by customers of failed members of the FDIC.

The FDIC charges member banks premiums for the cost of insurance. The corporation also regularly examines the financial condition and financial statements of member banks to make sure they have adequate capital. If a bank becomes undercapitalized (having a high loan volume in relation to assets), the FDIC can force the bank to take corrective action, including a change in management. It can even force the bank to close if the problems are not corrected. Only bank deposits are insured. Many banks offer a variety of other financial products, but these are not covered by the FDIC insurance.

NCUSIF Credit unions cannot be members of the FDIC. However, credit unions that are members of the National Credit Union Association (NCUA) have a similar federal insurance plan. The National Credit Union Share Insurance Fund (NCUSIF) offers the same $250,000 insurance on member deposits as the FDIC.

 **CHECKPOINT**

Identify and briefly describe the three main types of banks.

 **Nonbank Financial Institutions**

Nonbank financial institutions have grown rapidly because of the many valuable financial services they offer. Many customers value being able to obtain many of their financial services through one organization. The growth of nonbank institutions can be traced to new laws and regulations that reduced restrictions on the traditional banking services they could offer, such as demand and time deposits. At the same time, the banking industry successfully lobbied for other laws that allow traditional banks to offer a broader range of financial services, including investments and insurance, which they previously could not offer. The resulting competition has led to an emerging group of full-service financial institutions, consolidation of businesses in the industry, and many new forms of products and customer services.

TYPES OF NONBANKS

Nonbanks exist in many forms. Stock brokerage firms, for example, not only buy and sell stocks and bonds but also offer checking and even credit card services. Some large brokerage firms also provide mortgages, insurance policies, and credit card services for customers. On the other hand, banks are now allowed to sell stocks and bonds if they wish. Insurance companies and business pension funds are also nonbank financial institutions that offer long-term loans in large amounts to eligible businesses. Nonbanks also include investment companies such as mortgage, insurance, and finance businesses as well as investment firms. Competition to provide banking and other financial services has become fierce. New products and services are regularly developed to attract customers. With the growing number of choices, consumers and business investors must carefully study, understand, and compare companies and products to make the best financial choices and avoid unnecessary risks.

FINANCE COMPANIES A finance company specializes in providing installment loans and leases to consumers and businesses. Unlike banks, it does not accept deposits but obtains funds to make loans by issuing securities. A finance company often works with retailers selling expensive consumer products or manufacturers and vendors selling equipment to business customers. The products are sold on credit and the finance company approves and owns the credit account. Many finance companies such as CIT Group and Springleaf Financial Services are independent companies specializing in consumer and business loans and related financial services. Some large manufacturers have a financial division that operates as a finance company, such as Nissan Motor Acceptance Corporation (NMAC) and John Deere Financial.

INSURANCE COMPANIES Insurance companies collect premiums on insurance products and invest the premiums in securities, real estate, and other low- to moderate-risk investments to earn money. In that role, they provide both business and consumer loans. In addition to selling insurance, most insurance companies offer a number of savings and investment products.

PENSION FUNDS Many companies offer employees retirement benefits. Those benefits are often invested in pension funds. Some pension funds are owned and managed by the employer or by an employee union. However, most are managed by an independent financial services firm. Both employer and employee make regular contributions to the pension fund throughout the employee's working career. Those contributions are invested by the pension fund in stocks, bonds, real estate, and government securities. When the employee retires, money is returned from the fund as a lump-sum payment or as a regular series of payments over a period of years.

MUTUAL FUNDS A mutual fund is a company that pools the resources of a large number of investors to make a variety of investments. Depending on the type of mutual fund, the investments may be in stocks, bonds, government securities, or other financial instruments. Some mutual funds focus their investments in particular industries or types of securities, whereas others look for a more balanced set of investments.

Investors purchase shares in the mutual fund. The price of shares increases or decreases based on the performance of the investments. Many mutual funds charge a small administrative fee for their services. The number of mutual funds and the value of their assets have grown dramatically as people rely on the expertise of fund administrators to increase the value of their investments. In 2010, there were more than 8,000 mutual funds in the United States serving over 90 million investors. The total asset value of those funds was $11.8 trillion.

SECURITIES AND INVESTMENT FIRMS Securities and investment firms provide a variety of professional financial services for clients. Many serve as *brokers,* buying and selling securities, stocks, and bonds for their clients. Another service is underwriting new stock or bond issues. As an *underwriter,* the company purchases new securities from a company and then resells them to investors. It can also be a *dealer*, locating and purchasing securities with the intent of reselling them at a profit.

FINANCIAL SERVICES COMPANIES Large companies that have been a part of the financial services industry have seen the value of offering customers a full range of financial products and services. They often buy companies that offer specialized services such as credit cards, installment credit, or insurance and combine them under the management of one corporation. They serve both business clients and individual consumers with savings and investment plans, loans and credit choices, fund management, and financial counseling. Companies such as American Express, ING, Merrill Lynch, and Barclays operate worldwide and manage trillions of dollars in client assets. Financial services companies have been the leaders in the blending of traditional banking and nonbanking products and services. Large banks now sell insurance, securities, and other investments and provide financial counseling. Nonbank companies accept deposits, make loans, and provide credit card and check-writing services.

 **CHECKPOINT**

Identify several types of nonbank financial institutions and describe the main products and services each offers.

17.1 ASSESSMENT

UNDERSTAND MANAGEMENT CONCEPTS

Determine the best answer for each of the following questions.

1. Which of these types of banks is organized as a nonprofit business?
   a. commercial bank
   b. mutual savings bank
   c. savings and loan organization
   d. credit union

2. A company that pools the resources of a large number of investors and uses that money to make a variety of investments is a(n)
   a. finance company
   b. mutual fund
   c. insurance company
   d. factor

THINK CRITICALLY

Answer the following questions as completely as possible.

3. What are the benefits to a bank of offering a variety of financial services rather than specializing in traditional banking services? What are the problems that might be encountered?

4. Do you think there is still a need for smaller and more specialized financial services businesses? What will they need to do to compete with large, full-service companies?

Common Financial Services

Goals

- Describe the value and uses of checking accounts and loans.
- Discuss the ways in which technology is changing banking services.

Terms

- check p. 458
- endorsement p. 460
- collateral p. 461
- unsecured loan p. 461
- secured loan p. 461
- prime rate p. 462
- fixed interest rate p. 462
- variable interest rate p. 462
- electronic funds transfer (EFT) p. 462
- direct deposit p. 462
- automatic teller machine (ATM) p. 463

●●● Common Banking Services

In spite of the changes that have occurred in the financial world, financial services have improved greatly in recent decades. Today, the majority of banking institutions provide a host of services. Historically, the most complete line of banking services designed for individual consumers and small businesses was offered by commercial banks. Those services included a number of types of savings and checking accounts and various types and lengths of commercial and consumer loans. Many banks offer financial services such as accounting and tax preparation, financial planning, and financial advice, and even rent safe deposit boxes in which customers can store valuables securely.

Now, as specialized banks and nonbanks become more competitive with commercial banks, they are offering the traditional bank services that their customers demand. At the same time, commercial banks are adding more and more nonbank financial services to respond to the competition, attract new customers, and increase their revenues. Two of the most common banking services are checking accounts and loans. Nearly all businesses and many consumers use these services.

CHECKING ACCOUNTS

Checking accounts enable depositors to safely maintain cash in a bank or other financial institution and access it as needed. With most checking accounts, money is deposited in a demand account, meaning that money can be withdrawn at any time. Typically, money is withdrawn by writing a check. A **check** is a written order requiring the financial institution to pay previously deposited money to a third party on demand. Businesses use checks to pay for purchases or to make payments on loans and accounts payable. They also use checks to pay regular expenses such as payroll. Many businesses accept checks from customers as payment for purchases.

Technology has dramatically changed the operations of checking accounts. Rather than making payments using paper checks, businesses and consumers increasingly use debit cards or ATM cards. Many businesses and most banks now offer online bill paying services, which allow customers to move funds electronically from their bank account to the company's bank account. The results are the same as if a paper check was written and processed. However, no paper check is required and the processing of the payment is completed almost instantly.

A typical consumer checking account requires the account holder to pay a monthly fee to cover the bank's costs to administer the account. Banks may charge additional fees for services such as ordering checks. The bank may reduce or eliminate monthly fees if the account holder maintains a minimum average balance. Some banks even pay a very low interest rate on checking accounts with high balances. For those reasons, the costs, requirements, and interest rates should be carefully compared when opening a checking account. If fees must be paid or interest rates are very low, depositors should keep only the amount of money in the checking account needed to be able to pay upcoming bills and keep additional cash in accounts that pay a higher interest rate.

Many part-time or small businesses use consumer checking accounts to handle the cash needs of their businesses. If a consumer checking account is used, the business owner should establish a separate account for the business. This prevents comingling of personal and business funds and provides accurate records for the business.

Banks and other financial institutions offer business checking accounts that are different in some ways from consumer accounts. A checking account is used to handle most of the cash transactions of the business. That means that any cash payments made to the business, whether by cash, check, debit or credit card, or electronic payment will be routed through the business's checking account. Also, most payments made by the company are completed by writing checks or making electronic payments from the checking account.

Banks have established a variety of services that they offer with business checking accounts. The types of services available and the fees charged for those services vary. They are often based on the number and dollar amounts of transactions the bank processes for the business and the average daily or monthly balance the business maintains in the accounts it holds with the bank. Common services associated with business checking accounts include the following:

- Secure and rapid processing of cash, check, debit and credit transactions
- Accepting online customer payments and payments made through neighborhood convenience centers such as supermarkets, convenience stores, and pharmacies
- Online bill paying including sales and payroll tax payments to local, state, and federal governments
- Remote capture deposits allowing businesses to deposit customer checks by scanning both sides of the check and transmitting the scanned images to the banks using an encrypted electronic file
- Print and online account reports and monthly statements documenting all transactions that have been recorded in the account including deposits, receipts, payments, and fees

Businesses with large account balances may be offered a *cash management service* (also known as *treasury service*) as a part of the checking account. With this service, the bank monitors all accounts receivable and payables as well as the cash balance maintained in the business's checking account to minimize expenses and maximize the interest earned. Money is transferred in and out of the checking account daily with the goal of keeping the balance low and maintaining most funds in higher interest paying accounts until needed.

For more than 70 years, it was illegal for banks to pay interest on the money businesses maintained in a checking account. However, with the passage of the Dodd-Frank Wall Street Reform and Consumer Protection Act of 2010, banks and credit unions can now offer interest on all business checking accounts.

FACTS & FIGURES

People Like Electronic Payments

According to the Electronic Payments Association, over 75 of all U.S. employees with access to direct deposit from their employers use it to receive their paychecks with a 97 percent satisfaction rate. Nearly half of all households now use online bill pay services available from their bank or a business so monthly bills are paid directly to a business without writing a check.

Many business checking accounts still do not offer interest and the fees charged may be greater than the interest earned. Therefore, businesses usually have interest-paying savings accounts as well as other investment accounts with financial institutions in addition to a checking account.

ACCEPTING AND PROCESSING CHECKS

Businesses must develop procedures and train employees to accept checks from customers. Accepting a check is the same as receiving cash. However, if the check is not completed properly, if there are not adequate funds in the customer's account to cover the amount of the check, or if fraud is involved in the payment, the business may not receive the funds. A check written to Kilgore Kitchens appears in Figure 17-3. An employee accepting a check for payment must make sure all information is complete and accurate. In addition, the person writing the check must present proper identification to make sure the check is not stolen or forged. When the check is accepted, it should be properly endorsed immediately for bank deposit. An **endorsement** is the payee's signature on the back of the check legally transferring ownership. Businesses often use stamped or printed endorsements on checks rather than a signature. That endorsement lists the name of the bank to which the deposit is to be made, the name of the business, and the checking account number.

Many retail businesses have point-of sale-terminals or cash registers designed to process checks electronically. When a customer presents a check for payment of a purchase, the business employee examines the check and the customer's identification. Then the check is scanned through a check-reading terminal that is connected electronically to a check clearing service. The service either approves or rejects the check based on information about the customer's checking account balance. The terminal prints an endorsement on the back of the check so it is ready to be deposited.

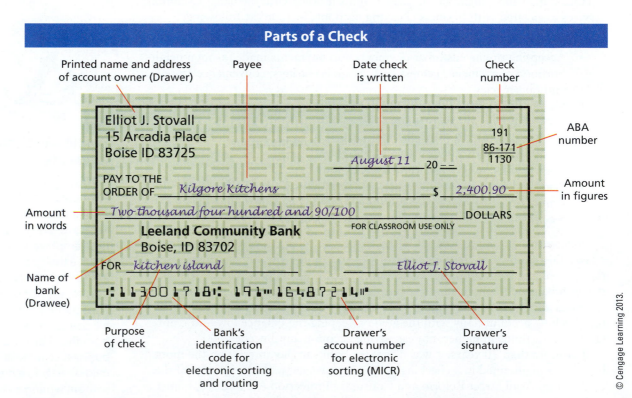

Figure 17-3 All information on a check must be complete and accurate before it is accepted.

In the past, when businesses accepted printed checks, those checks were deposited in the business's bank account. The bank would then route each check through other banks using a process managed by the Federal Reserve. When the check was presented to the check writer's bank, the amount would be deducted from the depositor's account and added to business's account. The process could take several days before it was completed. Today, most checks are processed electronically using procedures established by The Check Clearing for the 21st Century Act (Check 21). Rather than sending paper checks, banks can make "substitute" checks that are exact digital images of the original check. Those images can then be quickly transferred from bank to bank electronically. From its peak in the late 1990s, the number of checks written in the U.S. has declined about 10 percent each year. That decline has resulted from the increased use of debit cards as well as online banking and payment systems. In 2010, the Federal Reserve processed 7.7 billion checks through its system. Today almost 98 percent of all checks are processed electronically.

LOANS

Banks offer loans to both businesses and consumers. Before making a loan, the bank requires the prospective borrower to identify the purpose of the loan and provide financial evidence that the loan can be repaid. Most business loans provided by banks are for short time periods, often a year or less. A business may need funds to cover operating expenses at certain times, such as when it needs new equipment or when sales are temporarily slow. A common loan for reliable business customers is a *line of credit*, which gives the business a maximum amount it can borrow over a specified time period. The business borrows on the line of credit only when the money is needed, but it does not need additional approval as long as the maximum loan amount is not exceeded.

Collateral is property a borrower pledges to assure repayment of a loan. If the borrower does not repay the loan, the lender has the right to use the pledged property for repayment. An **unsecured loan** is a loan that is not backed by collateral. Usually only successful, long-standing business customers can obtain unsecured loans. For new businesses, those without strong financial records, and most consumer loans, banks require a secured loan. A **secured loan**, also called a *collateral loan*, is a loan backed by something of value owned by the borrower. For example, if a business owned a fleet of delivery vans and wanted to borrow $100,000, the fleet could be acceptable collateral. In case of failure to repay the loan, the bank could sell enough of the vehicles in the fleet to collect the money loaned. Businesses may pledge inventory or accounts receivable to secure smaller loans or lines of credit. Typically a secured loan is for an amount substantially less than the actual value of the collateral. The bank does not want to own the collateral. If it must take ownership of the collateral in the event the loan is not repaid, it will want to quickly sell the collateral and recover the money loaned.

Management MATTERS

Rule of 78

When a business gets a short-term loan from a bank or vendor, the loan is typically repaid with monthly payments. The lender calculates the monthly payments by adding the interest to be paid over the term of the loan to the principal amount and then dividing the total by the number of months over which the money will be repaid.

In order to make good decisions, a manager should understand the impact of paying off the loan early. The business will save some of the interest that was originally calculated into the loan, but the manager needs to know how much. A good way to estimate the value of the interest the business will save is known as the "Rule of 78." The percentage is calculated by dividing the sum of the integer numbers (digits) starting from 1 up to the number of payments remaining by the sum of the digits starting from 1 up to the total number of payments specified in the original loan contract. For example, if a five-month loan is paid off by the end of the second month (i.e., there are three payments remaining), the percentage of the interest that the lender would rebate is $(1 + 2 + 3) \div (1 + 2 + 3 + 4 + 5) = (6 \div 15)$, or 40 percent.

The name "Rule of 78" derives from the fact that 78 is the sum of the digits from 1 to 12 and, therefore, is the denominator in calculating interest rebate percentages for all 12-payment (one-year) loans.

What Do You Think? Do you believe it is a good practice for a business to use cash to pay off a loan early? Why or why not?

INTEREST RATES Banks earn income when they loan money by charging interest for the time period of the loan. Interest rates are based on the supply of and demand for money at any given time. As a result, the rate of interest can change daily, based on general business conditions. The lowest rate is the **prime rate**, which is the rate at which large banks lend large sums to the best-qualified borrowers. Small loans and loans to less-qualified customers are made at rates higher than the prime rate. Borrowers and lenders must establish a specific repayment plan so that the deal benefits both parties. Borrowers may be forced into bankruptcy and the lenders may be hurt financially if loans are not repaid. To help prevent losses, repaying a loan at regular intervals is safer than paying one lump sum at the end of the time period. Borrowers can then include the monthly payments in their budget plan and make sure they have adequate cash on hand for the payments.

Rates may be set for the full term of the loan or they may change during the loan period at predetermined times or based on specified conditions. An interest rate that does not change throughout the life of the loan is a **fixed interest rate**. A **variable interest rate** can increase or decline during the life of the loan based on the factors used to adjust the rates. Often variable interest rates are based on changes in the prime rate or in the price of government securities. Variable interest rates are usually lower than fixed rates at the beginning of a loan but may become more expensive over the full term if economic conditions and government policies tighten the money supply.

CHECKPOINT

Why do banks usually require collateral when loaning money to businesses and consumers?

Technology and Financial Services

Remarkable changes are occurring in banking and financial services because of rapid advancement in computers, personal computing devices, and other forms of electronic technology. Much of the work once done by clerks, such as processing checks, recording deposits and withdrawals, and keeping customer accounts up to date, is now done electronically. **Electronic funds transfer (EFT)**, transferring money by computer rather than by check, has enabled financial institutions to provide faster, improved services. For example, EFT transactions reduce the need for checks. Direct deposits, automatic teller machine transactions, and online banking are three common uses of EFTs. The use of debit cards is another form of EFT and will be discussed in the next chapter.

DIRECT DEPOSIT

A **direct deposit** is the electronic transfer of a payment directly into a recipient's bank account. Common uses of direct deposit include paychecks, Social Security benefit payments, and tax refunds. The use of direct-deposit banking has increased in popularity, especially for paychecks. Employees who select this service receive immediate use of their earnings. They no longer have to go to a bank to cash checks or make deposits. For each pay period, the employer must provide the employee with a record listing gross pay and all deductions. The Social Security Administration and the Internal Revenue Service encourage the use of direct deposit for benefit checks and tax refunds. In this way, the funds are immediately available to the recipient and government costs are reduced.

AUTOMATIC TELLER MACHINES

An **automatic teller machine (ATM)** is a computer terminal that enables bank customers to deposit, withdraw, or transfer funds by using a bank-provided plastic card. The card has a magnetic stripe across the back containing account information. After swiping or inserting the card into the ATM, a card user enters a Personal Identification Number (PIN) to access a bank account. ATMs are located at banks and many other convenient places, such as grocery stores, airports, and malls. ATMs are now common throughout the world and can be used to obtain currency quickly and easily.

In addition to making it much more convenient for customers to complete many banking activities, banks lower their operating costs by reducing the need for human tellers and increase income from service fees charged for some ATM transactions. Furthermore, banks use ATMs in many locations to serve their customers rather than opening additional branch offices.

Why have automatic teller machines become so popular with consumers?

ELECTRONIC BANKING

Electronic banking speeds business activities and serves customers more conveniently. Through computers, modems, and the Internet, banking without leaving the office or home has become common. Electronic banking makes it possible to obtain loans, pay bills, and transfer funds from one bank account to another.

The Internet provides opportunities for banks and nonbanks to offer additional products and services and compete for customers. Most have websites publicizing their services. Customers can search the Internet for the best interest rates for loans, best savings account rates, and best checking account terms. Loan and credit card applications can be processed and approved quickly online.

Most traditional financial institutions offer services via the Internet in addition to their on-site services. However, some banks are Internet-only banks and have no buildings customers can visit. Internet-only banks have several advantages over traditional banks. Not only can they perform most of the same services traditional banks offer, but they can also do it at lower cost. An Internet bank does not need large, expensive downtown buildings with numerous branches from which to conduct business. It can operate from a single, low-rent building 24 hours a day, seven days a week, to reach worldwide customers. Banking operations centers may actually be located in other countries. For many customers, online banking can satisfy most day-to-day banking needs.

An AmSouth Bank study found that a face to face banking transaction costs $1.70, and telephone transaction costs $.54, an ATM transaction costs $.27 and an Internet transaction costs $.01. The relatively low-cost of Internet transactions is one reason many banks have developed easy-to-use websites, offer many Internet-based banking services, and encourage their customers to bank online.

CHECKPOINT

How does the use of technology reduce the costs of providing financial services?

UNDERSTAND MANAGEMENT CONCEPTS

Determine the best answer for each of the following questions.

1. Transferring money by computer rather than by check is known as
    a. automated cash transfer (ACT)
    b. computerized money movement (CMM)
    c. electronic funds transfer (EFT)
    d. automated transfer machine (ATM)

2. Internet banks can operate at a lower cost than traditional banks because
    a. they do not have to meet the same government regulations
    b. they serve more customers than even the largest traditional banks
    c. they do not need to hire any employees
    d. they need fewer and less expensive buildings

THINK CRITICALLY

Answer the following questions as completely as possible.

3. Why do some bank customers still refuse to use ATMs and want banks to increase access to bank tellers? If you were a bank executive, how would you respond to those customers?

4. Do you believe that as banks and nonbanks add additional online banking services they should drop the traditional high-cost services that the technology replaces? Why or why not?

Banks Team with Telecoms

Today many banks view the world as their market, and competitive barriers are fast disappearing in the Internet age. Bankers in Europe, for example, are now buying, merging, or partnering with major banks in other countries within the European Union and beyond. Some are also partnering with companies not typically considered a part of banking. For example, Spain's Banco Bilbao Vizcaya Argentaria (BBVA) developed an e-commerce partnership with the giant telecommunication company Telefónica. The stock value of both firms zoomed upward. BBVA is a major financial player in Europe and Latin America. It is now expanding into the United States. In 2005, BBVA acquired Texas-based Laredo National Bank. In 2006, it acquired Texas National Bancshares and State National Bancshares to become the fourth-largest bank in Texas.

Why would a bank and a telephone company team up to play in the world market? Cell phones with Internet access are becoming a primary means for consumers to gain instant access to business information and services. They may also become a primary means of delivering banking services. The phone companies possess both cable lines and excellent computer systems. Banks provide banking services and the telephone companies deliver the services electronically to worldwide customers.

Other banks are seeking telephone company partners. Germany's Deutsche Bank, for example, is becoming an all-Europe e-commerce bank by linking with mobile-telephone provider Mannesmann. The Bank of Scotland and England's Halifax Bank have both teamed with the telecommunications company BT Cellnet. It is expected that the worldwide competition in banking e-commerce will grow more intense, with more and bigger players every year.

THINK CRITICALLY

1. If you owned stock in a large U.S. bank and it signed an agreement with a foreign cell phone company to compete with European banks, would you sell your stock, take a wait-and-see attitude, or buy more stock? Why?

2. What might go wrong with these joint international banking and telephone deals, especially if telephone companies know little about the banking business and banks don't know the telephone business?

© Shutterstock/Rick Becker-Leckrone

Investing and Investments

Goals

- Identify the characteristics of various investment instruments.
- Describe how investment decisions can be made to meet financial goals.

Terms

- investment p. 466
- savings account p. 466
- savings bond p. 467
- certificate of deposit (CD) p. 467
- money market account p. 468
- mutual fund p. 468
- Treasury instruments p. 469
- stock index p. 471

⬤⬤⬤ Investment Instruments

Individuals, families, businesses, and other organizations need adequate financial resources to meet their needs. Money can be obtained in two ways—earnings resulting from the work of individuals or the operation of businesses, and earnings from investments. An **investment** is the use of money to make more money. When individuals or businesses have cash that is not immediately needed, it should be invested.

There are many investment options available, whether the money to be invested is a small or large amount and whether it is available for a short or long time period. Some types of investments carry greater risks than others and some provide greater returns or earnings than others. Interest rates on some options can change rapidly while others remain the same for months or even years. To make wise investment decisions, business managers and individual investors need to know about the types of investment instruments and how to choose among them to meet their investment goals.

Most investments are made using the services of financial institutions. Those institutions are constantly seeking new and better ways to serve customers. They offer a wide variety of financial instruments from which customers can select those that best fit their investment needs.

INTEREST-BEARING CHECKING ACCOUNTS A checking account is a demand deposit through which investors can safely maintain money in a financial institution yet access it at any time through writing a check or making an electronic withdrawal. Many checking accounts pay a very low interest rate if the account balance is kept above a certain minimum amount. If a balance falls below the minimum, the bank may charge a service fee or eliminate the interest. Investors with small sums of money find interest-bearing checking accounts a convenient way to save while having easy access to the funds to pay expenses. Because checking accounts are not primarily designed as savings instruments, however, they serve an investment purpose only to a limited extent. Often the fees associated with a checking account are greater than the interest earned.

SAVINGS ACCOUNTS A **savings account** is also a demand deposit account that allows customers to make deposits, earn interest, and make withdrawals at any time without financial penalties. Investors can deposit small amounts, but the interest rates are usually lower than those on other investment instruments. The bank may charge a service fee if the amount on deposit falls below the minimum balance required. Interest rates may increase slightly if the amount placed in savings is relatively high. However, the interest rate is still quite low compared to rates on other investment choices.

SAVINGS BONDS A **savings bond** is a non-negotiable security sold by the U.S. Treasury. *Non-negotiable* means the bond cannot be sold; it must be held and redeemed by the original registered owner. Savings bonds are especially useful to small investors because they can be purchased frequently in small amounts starting at just $50. However, they can also be owned by companies, estates, and trusts and can be purchased in any amount up to $5,000. The total amount of savings bonds that can be purchased by an investor during any year is $5,000 per series.

Savings bonds offer several advantages to investors. Interest earned is exempt from all state and local income taxes. Federal income tax must be paid but can be deferred until the bonds are redeemed. Savings bonds are one of the safest investments because they are backed by the U.S. government. In addition, they pay competitive interest rates compared to other similar investment choices. Bonds can be used as short- or long-term investments. Savings bonds must be held for a minimum of one year before they can be redeemed. If a bond is redeemed in fewer than five years, a three-month interest penalty will be applied. Savings bonds continue to earn interest for up to 30 years.

In the past, savings bonds were sold in both paper and electronic form, but paper bonds are being phased out. People who own paper bonds can still hold them until they are redeemed. With few exceptions, bonds issued after 2011 are electronic. They can be purchased through an online account opened at TreasuryDirect.gov, the financial services website of the U.S. Department of the Treasury. A one-time purchase can be made or an investor can arrange to make regular purchases by scheduling a recurring deduction from a bank account. Savings bonds can also be redeemed online with appropriate information and authorization. The money is transferred directly into the owner's bank account.

There are currently two series of savings bonds being sold, Series I and Series EE. The primary difference between the two series is the way the interest rate is determined. *Series I bonds* earn interest in two components: a basic fixed-rate and an additional adjustable rate called the *inflation rate*. Both rates are set each May and November. The fixed rate applies to all bonds sold during the six-month period after it is announced. That rate is paid for the life of the bond. The adjustable rate is based on the current consumer price index. That inflation rate is applied to all Series I bonds for the six-month period. During times of inflation, the inflation rate increases the total rate of interest paid on the bonds. If the economy is experiencing deflation, the total rate may actually fall below the fixed rate for the six-month period but can never fall below zero percent.

Series EE bonds earn interest at a fixed rate for the life of the bond. As with Series I bonds, the rates are set each May and November and apply to all bonds sold during that six-month period. Series EE bonds are guaranteed to double in value if held for 20 years. If the fixed interest rate does not result in the bond doubling in value, the U.S. treasury will make a one-time adjustment at the end of 20 years. If the bond is not sold, it will continue to earn the original fixed rate for an additional 10 years.

CERTIFICATES OF DEPOSIT A **certificate of deposit (CD)** is a time deposit account that requires a specified minimum deposit for a fixed period at a fixed interest rate. Banks offer CDs for $500 or more and for periods ranging from three

Manager's Perspective on
ETHICS

Managers do not make decisions based solely on which are the most profitable choices for the company. Ethics and social responsibility guide many investment decisions. This is defined as "putting your money where your morals are," or investing according to your beliefs. Ethical investments tend to avoid companies involved in areas such as environmentally damaging practices or unsafe products and services, and those that operate in countries with poor human rights records.

months to 10 years. Typically, the longer the term of the CD, the higher the interest rate earned. For example, the interest rate on a six-month CD is normally less than on a two-year CD. Although CDs usually pay a higher rate of interest than savings accounts a CD cannot be withdrawn before its stated time without penalty—a substantial loss of earned interest.

Interest is paid regularly on a certificate of deposit, and the interest can be withdrawn as it is earned. If the interest is not withdrawn, it is added to the value of the CD and earns additional interest during the remaining term. CDs are negotiable instruments, so if money is needed the CD can be sold. Usually the bank where the CD was purchased will buy it but at a lower amount than its current value. If the value of the CD is significant, it may be worth the effort to search for other buyers and compare offers. If current interest rates are much higher than the rate being earned by the CD, it may be possible to sell it for more than it has earned. This situation is unusual but can occur with CDs that are purchased for long terms such as five or ten years.

MONEY MARKET ACCOUNTS A **money market account** is a type of savings account in which the deposits are invested by the financial institution in short-term, government-backed securities. The interest rate on the account is not fixed. It goes up and down as interest rates in the economy change. Financial institutions often grant check-writing privileges on money market accounts. The number of checks written during a given time period, such as a month, may be limited and a minimum balance is usually required.

Unlike CDs, there is no minimum time the money must remain in the money market account. Depositors can withdraw their money at any time. Also, initial deposits may be as low as $500. Investors often put funds in money market accounts when they will need the money soon or when they want to earn some interest while waiting for a more profitable investment opportunity. Because government-backed securities are not very risky, the interest paid on money market accounts is generally lower than for other stock or bond investment options. However, money market accounts generally pay slightly higher interest than a typical savings account.

MUTUAL FUNDS A **mutual fund** pools the money of many investors primarily for the purchase of stocks and bonds. Many investors believe they do not have the time or expertise to select individual stocks and bonds and prefer to purchase shares in mutual funds. A mutual fund company develops one or more funds and makes the decisions about the types of investments for each one. Professional fund managers and their staffs carefully evaluate and select a variety of securities in which to invest the fund's money. Fund managers work to select stocks or other securities that will increase in value from the time they are purchased until they are sold. The goal is to earn a high rate of return on investors' money.

Most mutual funds require a larger minimum investment than the investment choices already discussed, often $1,000 or more. Also, investors may need to document that they have adequate financial resources to risk in the mutual fund investment. Investors can easily transfer money from one fund to another, but there may be administrative charges for those changes as well as for general fund management.

Risk is a major consideration in selecting mutual funds. There is no guarantee that the total investment will not be lost if fund managers make poor investment decisions or the economy suffers a serious downturn. Some funds reduce the level of risk by investing in bonds and other relatively safe investments. Those funds aim to generate a steady income for investors who do not expect the rapid growth in their investments that more risky funds might produce.

Whenever sales of stocks and bonds are made by the fund manager that result in profits, or if dividends are paid on the stocks held in the fund, investors must usually pay taxes on their share of those profits. When investors sell their shares in a mutual fund, they will usually have to pay taxes on any increase in the value of the fund during the time they participated.

TREASURY INSTRUMENTS The U.S. government borrows money from investors by selling bills, notes, and bonds backed by the Treasury. **Treasury instruments** are securities issued by the U.S. government. They are used to finance the costs of running the government when income from taxes is not available or when costs exceed the revenues collected. Approximately $8.4 trillion in government securities were issued in 2010. Treasury instruments are considered one of the safest of all short-term investments because they are backed by the U.S. government, which has the resources to meet interest payments on the securities as they become due.

The instruments differ in the term of investment and the interest rates paid. Treasury instruments are sold at auctions where prospective purchasers bid based on the interest rate they are willing to accept. The securities are sold at the lowest available interest rates. Treasury securities are normally purchased from the government by financial institutions and brokers. They then are resold to individual and business investors. Individuals are also able to purchase securities online at TreasuryDirect.gov. Today all Treasury securities are issued in electronic form rather than paper.

Businesses and individual investors with large sums of money frequently invest in Treasury securities because they are practically risk free and are easy to buy and sell. All Treasury securities are very liquid, meaning they are easily traded even though they may not mature for several years. Because the interest rates on securities fluctuate based on demand and economic conditions, investors are willing to purchase securities owned by other investors, usually at a discounted price, with the hope of making a profit.

A *Treasury bill*, or *T-bill*, is a short-term security that pays the lowest interest rates of the various Treasury instruments. T-bills are sold in $100 multiples, but investors can purchase multiple amounts up to a total of $5 million. The bills mature in 4, 13, 26, or 52 weeks. T-bills are purchased at a discount based on the interest rate of the security. For example, a $1,000 bill may cost $960. When it matures in one year, the owner is paid the full $1,000. The $40 difference reflects a 4 percent interest rate.

A *Treasury note* is a medium-length security that is available in $100 multiples and matures in 2, 3, 5, 7, or 10 years. Treasury notes are fixed-rate securities, meaning the interest rate remains the same throughout the term of the note. Interest is paid every six months. When the note is initially purchased, the investor may pay a premium or discount from the face value of the note. That increase or decrease in price reflects the demand for the notes and the value investors believe the note will have at its maturity.

A *Treasury bond* is the longest-term U.S. government security. As with the other securities, the bonds can be purchased in $100 multiples. The bonds mature in 30 years, although they can be bought and sold on bond markets for shorter periods of time. Investors can purchase up to $5 million of bonds at an auction. Treasury bonds are auctioned as needed by the government but not usually as frequently as notes and bills. Sometimes not all of the available bonds are sold at the original auction, and the government may later hold a reissue auction to sell the remaining amount.

Investors concerned about the effects of inflation can purchase TIPS. *Treasury Inflation-Protected Securities (TIPS)* are marketable securities

What kinds of investment instruments are backed by the U.S. Treasury Department?

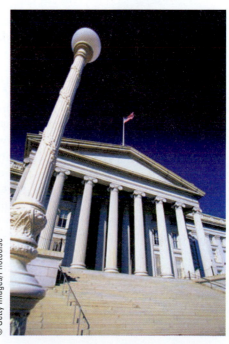

© Getty Images/Photodisc

issued by the U.S. Department of Treasury. Their principal is adjusted based on changes in the Consumer Price Index (CPI). Like other U.S. government securities, TIPS are sold at auction and can be purchased by individual investors or businesses. Purchases can be made directly from the U.S. government or through banks and brokers. They are frequently purchased as a part of a mutual fund so investors can own shares of the fund rather than individual securities. Since TIPS are marketable securities, they can be bought and sold by investors during their term and are traded on securities markets.

TIPS are sold in increments of $100 with a purchase amount ranging from $100 to $5 million. TIPS are issued for 5-, 10-, and 30-year terms. The unique feature of TIPS is how they are adjusted by the Consumer Price Index. The securities are originally sold at auction with a fixed interest rate that is determined by the auction. That interest rate remains the same for the term of the security and is paid on the principal every six months. However, the principal is adjusted to reflect the current Consumer Price Index. Therefore, if the CPI rises, the principal increases; a decline in the CPI reduces the principal. At the end of the term, the owner is paid the adjusted principal or the original principal, whichever is greater. In that way, investors have protection against both inflation with the semiannual CPI adjustment and deflation with the final principal adjustment.

 CHECKPOINT

Describe several low-risk and high-risk investment choices.

⬤⬤⬤ Making Investment Choices

Business managers need to make investment decisions carefully. They need to consider the financial condition of the company, the amount of available cash and cash flow projections, and all available alternatives for investments. To make good choices, business investors must set investment goals based on the amount of liquidity, safety, growth, and diversification that is best for the business.

INVESTMENT GOALS

Liquidity refers to the ease of turning an investment into cash without significant loss. For example, checking accounts are very liquid. Depositors can withdraw their deposit as cash whenever they want without penalty. Certificates of deposit are less liquid. If depositors withdraw their money from a CD before the end of its term, they have to pay a penalty, which may be substantial. If a small company, such as Kilgore Kitchens in the opening scenario, needs cash regularly, it should choose more liquid investments. Kilgore's owners might choose to invest in money market accounts rather than mutual funds so they can get cash when they need it with a low risk of financial loss. On the other hand, an established, profitable firm may have a steady source of cash from its operations. Instead of needing cash soon, it may need to replace costly equipment in five years, so it may choose to invest in less liquid but more profitable investments. Treasury notes and bills might be appropriate choices for this firm. The different objectives of these two firms will determine, in part, the investments they select.

FACTS & FIGURES

International Stock Indexes

In addition to well-known American stock indexes, investors watch indexes around the globe. Examples include Bovespa in Brazil, Hang Seng in Hong Kong, Nikkei 225 in Japan, DAX in Germany, FTSE 100 in the United Kingdom, NSE 20 in Kenya, ISE-100 in Turkey, and TA-100 in Israel.

A second investment goal is the degree of safety desired. In general, riskier investments have higher earning potential than do less risky investments. However, with those choices, investors are more likely to lose all or part of their investment. Some investors want maximum safety—they do not want to risk losing any of their money. To achieve a high degree of safety, they will likely have to accept smaller earnings on the investment. Investment in savings accounts, money market accounts, and government securities should appeal to them because of the low risk. Other investors like to take some risks for the opportunity to earn more money. These investors might prefer to buy stock in a rapidly growing corporation, in international companies operating in countries with strong economies, or in companies developing exciting new technologies.

The third investment goal involves the trade-off between investment growth and a stable income from the investment. Investors who do not need a steady income from their investments and are willing to invest for long periods of time will choose to invest in growth-oriented corporations. They hope to see their investments grow at a faster rate than inflation. Investors who want to count on a regular income might choose to invest in stocks or mutual funds with a history of paying high dividends.

Most experienced investors also suggest another rule that pertains to safety: "Don't put all your eggs in one basket." Investors should *diversify*, that is, spread their risk by placing money in different categories of investments. For example, a diversified investment plan might put one-third of available investment money into bonds, one-third into stocks, and one-third into money market accounts. To follow this rule further, not all investments in bonds should be in one company, nor should all stock investments be in one corporation. Diversification greatly reduces the risk factor.

INVESTMENT TRADING

Buyers and sellers trade all types of securities through special financial markets. The securities are typically bought and sold through the services of securities and investment organizations. For help in making investments, individuals and businesses often consult investment advisers, brokers, or dealers. Investors ask their brokers to buy or sell certain securities. The brokers then process the requests through the appropriate financial market that connects buyers and sellers.

Public corporations that want to sell their stock to investors must be listed on a stock exchange. Although there are a number of such exchanges, the two largest U.S. exchanges are the New York Stock Exchange and the NASDAQ exchange. Technology firms, such as Microsoft, Intel, and Cisco Systems, are listed on NASDAQ, which is the nation's first electronic stock market. The much older New York Stock Exchange (NYSE) trades on Wall Street, with floor traders buying and selling securities face-to-face with other traders on the floor of the exchange. The NYSE attracts more traditional companies. Most stock exchanges handle stocks, bonds, and other types of investments. Mergers and partnerships among stock exchanges continue to evolve as electronic trading grows worldwide. Other U.S. exchanges exist to trade commodities, including the Chicago Board of Trade, Chicago Mercantile Exchange, Memphis Cotton Exchange, and the Minneapolis Grain Exchange.

A **stock index** is a kind of average of the prices of selected stocks considered to be representative of a certain class of stocks or of the economy in general. Investors watch the movement of the indexes to get a sense of stock market trends for those types of

What activities take place in a stock exchange?

© Getty Images/Photodisc

stocks and for the overall growth of the economy. The most well-known indexes in the United States are the Dow Jones Industrial Average Index, the NASDAQ Market Index, and Standard & Poor's 500 Index. When compared over time, each index provides investors with a picture of what is happening in the nation's and the world's financial markets. An index trend of rising share prices may influence investors to buy more shares, and a downward trend may prompt them to sell some shares. Unfortunately, predicting when the market will reach its low and high points is nearly impossible, even for the most skilled investors.

CHECKPOINT

Identify three important goals that can guide investment decisions.

17.3 ASSESSMENT

UNDERSTAND MANAGEMENT CONCEPTS

Determine the best answer for each of the following questions.

1. Treasury instruments are considered low-risk investments because they
   a. are issued in very small denominations
   b. cannot be traded
   c. are backed by the U.S. government
   d. usually pay low rates of interest

2. When money is spread among many types of investments, the investor has
   a. increased the risk
   b. emphasized growth
   c. reduced the initial cost
   d. diversified the investments

THINK CRITICALLY

Answer the following questions as completely as possible.

3. If you had $10,000 to invest, what would you consider the most important factors in choosing among the various investment instruments?

4. Why should investors watch the performance of stock indexes over an extended period of time rather than reacting to daily increases or decreases?

CHAPTER CONCEPTS

- Financial institutions handle transactions that deal primarily with money and securities. Banks traditionally provided savings and loan products while other financial institutions provided investment services that banks did not. Deregulation has made it possible for banks to offer investment products and other financial services.

- Banks accept demand deposits, make loans, and buy and sell currency and government securities. Nonbanks offer financial products and services including those traditionally offered by banks.

- The Federal Reserve System is the central bank of the United States. It regulates banking and controls the money supply. The FDIC is a federal agency that insures deposits in banks and savings institutions.

- Today, most banks provide a variety of financial of services, the most common being checking and savings accounts and business and consumer loans. Many banking transactions can be done electronically through direct deposits, ATMs, and online banking.

- There are many investment options available: savings bonds, certificates of deposit, money market accounts, mutual funds, and U.S. government securities.

- Investors must clarify their investment goals in regard to liquidity, safety, and growth before making investment choices. Investment advice and investment opportunities are available through banks, other financial institutions, and brokers.

REVIEW BUSINESS MANAGEMENT TERMS

Write the letter of the term that matches each definition. Some terms will not be used.

1. The use of money to make more money
2. Federal agency that insures deposits in banks
3. Electronic transfer of a paycheck directly from the employer's bank account into the employee's bank account
4. Non-negotiable securities sold by the U.S. treasury in small denominations to individual investors
5. Loan backed by something of value owned by the borrower
6. Loan made to an individual for personal use
7. Rate at which large banks lend to the best-qualified borrowers
8. Securities issued by the U.S. government
9. Written order requiring the financial institution to pay previously deposited money to a third party on demand
10. Interest rate that can increase or decline during a loan's term.
11. Institution whose primary purpose is to offer financial products and services other than deposits and loans
12. Central bank of the United States

a. check
b. commercial loan
c. consumer loan
d. direct deposit
e. FDIC
f. Federal Reserve System
i. fixed interest rate
j. investment
k. mutual fund
l. nonbank
m. prime rate
n. savings bond
o. secured loan
p. Treasury instruments
q. unsecured loan
r. variable interest rate

Determine the best answer.

13. In order to be considered a bank, a financial institution must do all of the following *except*
    a. accept deposits
    b. make loans
    c. buy and sell currency and government securities
    d. Banks must do all of those things.

14. Which of the following is classified as a bank rather than a nonbank?
    a. securities and investment firm
    b. savings and loan organization
    c. financial services company
    d. bond dealer

15. Before making a loan, banks require that the prospective borrower
    a. make a substantial deposit in the bank
    b. provide collateral even if the loan is very small with low risk
    c. provide financial evidence to show that the loan can be repaid
    d. show that all of the business's cash has been used

16. Which of the following cannot be accomplished through direct deposit?
    a. receiving a Social Security payment
    b. accepting a tax refund from the IRS
    c. providing wage and salary payments to employees in a business
    d. All can be accomplished through direct deposit.

17. Which type of investment instrument would usually pay the lowest interest rate?
    a. checking account
    b. CD
    c. money market account
    d. Treasury bill

18. The savings instrument issued by the federal government that can be purchased in the smallest denominations is the
    a. savings bond
    b. Treasury bill
    c. Treasury note
    d. Treasury bond

19. Of the savings instruments listed, the one with the highest risk is the
    a. savings account
    b. money market fund
    c. mutual fund
    d. Treasury bill

20. "Don't put all your eggs in one basket" is investment advice related most directly to
    a. liquidity
    b. safety
    c. growth
    d. diversification

APPLY WHAT YOU KNOW

Answer the following questions.

21. Based on the Reality Check scenario at the beginning of the chapter, what should be the investment goals of Kilgore Kitchens? What are three investments you would recommend to Andrew and Julie?

22. Why would a business choose to use a bank rather than a nonbank as its primary financial institution? Why might it choose a nonbank?

23. What effects have changes in laws and increases in competition among financial institutions had on consumers?

24. What effect does the prime rate have on those who apply for bank loans?

25. How has the Internet improved banking services? What problems have resulted from its increased use?

26. What are the advantages and disadvantages of certificates of deposit over savings accounts?

27. Why would individuals and businesses want to purchase Treasury securities for terms as long as 30 years? What risks, if any, are they taking when purchasing those very long-term investments?

28. If you had to pick one financial goal today to guide your financial planning, what would it be? Why? How do you think your goals may need to change in 15 years? What will be your top goal at that time?

MAKE ACADEMIC CONNECTIONS

Complete the following activities.

29. **Research** Use the Internet to check the current interest rates offered by (a) a local bank, (b) a credit union, (c) an Internet bank, and (d) a large financial services organization. Determine the rates for a checking account, a 12-month CD of $10,000, a money market account, a 30-year mortgage, and a 48-month auto loan. Prepare a table that compares the interest rates from all of the financial institutions.

30. **Writing** You are an intern for Melinda Jones, a local bank vice president who is concerned about the changing competition the bank is facing. She asks you to use the Internet to investigate the current status of federal banking regulations and their effect on banking. Conduct the research and prepare a one-page memo to Ms. Jones discussing significant developments within the past five years and any proposed changes.

31. **Math** Track the value of the Dow Jones Industrial Average, NASDAQ Market Index, and Standard & Poor's 500 Index for one week. For each index, calculate the actual change and percentage of change for each day and the entire week. Prepare one table and one graph that illustrate and compare the performance of the three indexes.

CASE IN POINT

CASE 17-1: What's Wrong with Savings?

Jun Wang, owner of a delicatessen in a shopping center, often chats outside his business with Cassidy Hall, who owns the bakery next door. One weekday morning just after they opened their businesses, Jun mentioned that he had just returned from his bank to deposit money. He told Cassidy that as a recent immigrant, he was not that familiar with the American financial system. But he had decided it was important to save money from his business and had opened a savings account in the local bank down the street.

Cassidy wanted to help, so she asked Jun if he had a lot of money in the savings account and if he was investing his profits in other ways. Jun said he had a regular practice of putting 10 percent of his profits in the account each month and was getting concerned that perhaps he should start an account with another bank because the balance was getting quite large. The rest of the conversation follows.

Cassidy: *You're losing money you could otherwise be earning, Jun, by putting that much of your savings in a savings account.*

Jun: *What do you mean? I've always believed that a savings account in a bank was the best place to save money. Now you tell me I'm losing money? I've never lost any money, and each month I earn interest.*

Cassidy: *It certainly is a way to save money, but the interest you're making right now is at least 2½ percent less than what you could make by putting that money in other types of accounts. If I were you, I would be looking at CDs and T-bills. At least put some of your money in a money market account. There are several types of businesses in our community other than banks that offer savings opportunities.*

Jun: *Wait. I don't understand all of those options. But I do know that I don't want to lose my hard-earned profits in any risky investments.*

Cassidy: *There is a good financial adviser right here in our shopping center. I meet with her quite frequently, and she has taught me a lot about saving and investments. If you want, I can introduce you to her.*

THINK CRITICALLY

1. Is it likely that Jun could invest his money in other savings instruments at his savings bank? Is it likely that the bank could meet all of his financial needs as his business grows? Why or why not?

2. Are T-bills and CDs considered risky investments? Explain your answer in a way that a new investor like Jun might understand.

3. How much more could Jun earn in one year if he withdrew the $100,000 he has in his savings account and invested it instead in Treasury notes earning 2½ percent more interest? What problems might that create for his finances?

CASE 17-2: Financing Business Expansion

Doria Russell had just sold a half-acre lot on one side of her prosperous home decorating store. She decided to sell it because she needs the money to enlarge the store as part of her business expansion plan. Currently she sells window treatments including shades, curtains, drapes, and other accessories in addition to floor coverings and wallpaper. She wants to add an interior-decorating center with some small model rooms to display her products as they would appear in homes. She needs the remaining empty lot to enlarge her current building and to expand the parking lot.

Doria estimates she will need $500,000 to reach her growth goal, but not all at once. She needs time to find and hire an architect, obtain a building permit, and start construction. Once the building is enlarged, she will then order inventory items, hire a part-time decorator and an additional installer, and plan a promotional campaign. Each step will take time, and overlooked tasks might require additional time and money.

Doria received $200,000 for the half-acre lot she sold and will use this money as the major source of initial financing. Her business currently has $40,000 in a savings account and $80,000 in a mutual fund. She does not want to use any of her personal savings to finance the business's new venture. Because she has some time before she needs money for the project, her plan is to invest her current funds in such a way that cash will be available when needed, but she will also earn as much as possible on the investments until the expansion is completed. Doria believes the total plan will take from 18 to 36 months to complete once it starts six months from now.

Doria is willing to take some financial risk but cannot really afford to lose any of the money she has accumulated to finance the project. She accepts the possibility that she might need a short-term loan once or twice if major costs arise at the same time, but she will resort to loans only if necessary.

THINK CRITICALLY

1. What is the total amount of money Doria has available to invest?
2. As Doria's investment adviser, suggest an overall financial plan that includes a timeline for investing available funds that will enable her to reach her goals. Provide reasons for your investment advice.
3. If Doria needs a short-term loan, what type of loan would you recommend she seek and from what type of financial institution? Justify your recommendation.
4. Assume a year has passed and that Doria's plan is on schedule, but she needs a $75,000 loan. Find out where she can get a six-month loan at the lowest interest rate. Compare your best loan terms with those of others in your class.

PROJECT My Own Business

Selecting Financial Services

A good working relationship with a financial institution is important for a small business. Income received through cash, checks, and credit cards must be invested and protected, because they can be important sources of interest income. You must select the correct types of accounts and manage them carefully, so that your account balance is neither too large nor too small to meet your business's financial needs. You may need short-term loans to solve cash-flow problems. Other banking services may help you make the best financial decisions for your business.

DATA COLLECTION

1. Identify at least two bank and two nonbank financial institutions in your community that offer services for individuals and businesses. Gather information on the types of accounts and services each offers. If possible, identify the interest rates they offer on checking and savings accounts as well as the interest rates they charge for common types of loans. Prepare a chart comparing the information you collected on each of the businesses.
2. Use the Internet to identify:
   a. Financial institutions that offer banking services via the Internet.
   b. Sources of financial information for small-business owners, such as information on loans, interest rates, and investments.

ANALYSIS

1. Assume you will need a four-year loan of $15,000 to start your business. You estimate that you will need a $2,000 line of credit for the first year of operation. Of the financial institutions you studied in Data Collection #1 above, which one would you go to for the necessary financing? Justify your answer. What do you feel the greatest personal obstacles will be in obtaining a line of credit for your new business? Why?
2. Obtain a loan application form from a local bank or an Internet bank and fill in the necessary information as if you were requesting the $2,000 line of credit.
3. Answer the following questions:
   a. What type of financial institution will you use for regular business activities? Why?
   b. What type of checking account will you open?
   c. What minimum and maximum balances will you attempt to maintain in the checking account? What will you do with any excess funds beyond the maximum checking account balance?
   d. What will you do with your deposits of daily receipts? When will you do it?
   e. In what ways can you use technology to access and use financial services? What type of electronic equipment will you need? What risks do you see in using the Internet for financial transactions?

CHAPTER 18

CREDIT AND INSURANCE

18.1 Credit Principles and Practices

18.2 Managing Credit

18.3 Insurance Principles

18.4 Types of Business Insurance

© Shutterstock/Andreas Gradin

Reality Check

Cash or Credit

Ivy Montaigne unlocked the doors and hoped for a good day—nice weather and customers with cash in their wallets. Her handcrafted jewelry boutique had been open for six months, but her sales were not what she had expected.

A little after ten, a woman and her granddaughter entered the shop and started looking around. Ivy looked up, smiled, and watched as her sales associate, Nathan Sohn, approached the shoppers.

Nathan greeted the women and opened the display case. The young woman tried on several bracelets while her grandmother looked on. Ivy was thrilled to see that Nathan was holding a bracelet as he locked the case. It looked like he had made a sale.

A few minutes later she heard the door chimes and saw the women leave the store without one of the shop's signature silver bags embossed with an ivy leaf. As Nathan walked toward her, she saw the disappointment on his face.

"What happened? I thought they were going to buy a bracelet," Ivy said.

"The grandmother didn't bat an eye when I told her it was $800, but she looked stunned when I said we didn't accept credit cards. The two of them talked about going to the ATM and then said they might be back later," Nathan explained.

"You know how that goes—they never come back," Ivy sighed.

"Why don't we take credit cards?" Nathan asked.

"I can't afford it. The credit card charges eat into profits. The credit card companies get a big fee on every transaction plus you have to wait for the credit transaction to be processed to receive the cash," Ivy explained.

"Are you sure you can't afford it? Lots of people want to use plastic. Maybe you can't afford to continue with the cash-only policy if it means customers are walking away empty-handed." Nathan said.

"Well, that's another way to look at it," Ivey responded.

"If you want, I'd be happy to talk to a few other small business owners I know and get some facts and figures," Nathan suggested.

What's Your Reaction? What are some of the questions Nathan needs to ask about the cost of accepting credit cards?

Credit Principles and Practices

Goals

- Describe three types of credit plans used by businesses.
- Identify several types of financial transaction cards and the main uses of each type.

Terms

- merchant account p. 480
- acquiring bank p. 480
- merchant account provider p. 480
- installment credit p. 483
- revolving credit p. 483
- co-branded credit cards p. 484
- affinity credit cards p. 484
- debit card p. 484
- smart card p. 485

●●● Determining Business Credit Needs

Most businesses today must offer credit to their customers. However, many credit choices are available. Credit decisions can have a big impact on business operations and profit. To make the best credit decisions, businesses need to understand the types of credit plans and providers of the plans, the kinds of financial transaction cards, and the guidelines for establishing credit policies. They must also be familiar with sources of credit information, credit laws, and basic practices for managing customers who do not pay on time. Businesses offer credit if they believe it will increase sales and profits while satisfying customer needs. Consumers approach credit from the point of view of convenience and affordability, and they buy from businesses that satisfy those needs.

ACCEPTING MAJOR CREDIT CARDS

Businesses have several choices of credit systems. They can (1) choose to work with a major credit card company, (2) offer their own business credit, or (3) use credit plans managed by a bank or finance company.

ESTABLISHING A CREDIT CARD ACCEPTANCE SYSTEM Starting an operation to accept credit cards begins with the establishment of a relationship with a major credit card company such as Visa, MasterCard, or American Express. However, those companies work directly only with very large businesses. Most businesses need to establish a merchant account in order to be able to accept major credit cards. A **merchant account** is a specialized bank account established by a business in order to process credit card payments from its customers.

Merchant accounts are managed by specialized banks known as **acquiring banks**. Acquiring banks are approved by the credit card company and handle the funds connected to each credit card transaction from the point it is approved until the funds are transferred into the business's regular bank account and payment is collected from the customer.

A merchant account can be obtained from the business's local bank or through an independent merchant account provider. A **merchant account provider** is a private company that acts as an intermediary between businesses and one or more credit card companies to establish and maintain credit services. Using a bank or merchant account provider makes it easier and faster to begin accepting credit cards. It also allows the business to accept several major credit cards while dealing with only one intermediary rather than developing agreements with each of the credit card companies. Merchant account providers can explain the types of services available and their costs, help the business establish a merchant account, recommend and sell the equipment the business will need to process credit sales, and then work with the business to make sure the credit card operations run smoothly.

Why might consumers prefer to pay with a credit card rather than with cash?

To be approved to accept credit cards, a business is evaluated to make sure it is financially strong enough to offer credit and has effective operating procedures in place to process and approve credit purchases. The bank, merchant account provider, or credit card company will request information on the business's operations and history. It will need credit reports and financial statements to determine if the business is a good credit risk. Companies that provide credit card services to businesses must be cautious because too many businesses fail to handle credit operations well. Having a relationship already established with a bank and a good financial record will speed the process of being approved to accept credit cards.

Before beginning to accept credit cards, a business needs credit card-processing equipment. Most businesses use electronic processing and approval systems that are built into point-of-sale terminals or cash registers. A few businesses still rely on a small nonelectronic device, which is used to mechanically imprint the card information on a paper credit sales slip. This process requires the business to process each printed credit slip by hand and deliver it to the bank. It may take a week or more for the transaction to be completely processed and funds transferred to the business. Credit card companies are encouraging businesses to end their use of the older processing systems and new technology is helping ease the transition. Small electronic card readers are now available that can be attached to cell phones so a credit card can be accepted and processed electronically at almost any location.

Computerized credit card systems are now the accepted way to process credit transactions because they are efficient and accurate. The customer's credit card is swiped through an electronic device that records the sale and prints a sales slip for the customer's signature. Some systems record the signature on an electronic pad at the sales terminal. The bank and credit card company receive the credit sales information electronically at the same time. The electronic system also checks to make certain the credit card has not been reported as lost or stolen and the sale is within the customer's credit limit. A quick authorization decision is received on the computer terminal.

Credit card sales can be made over the telephone and via the Internet. Procedures for those sales are developed by each credit card company and must be followed carefully to make sure the information is correct and the purchase is authorized. Internet credit card sales are made on secure websites to protect the customer's personal information, including the credit card account number. Most credit card companies require businesses to establish a separate Internet merchant account because the procedures are different from transactions where the credit card is swiped. In addition, there are additional risks associated with processing credit sales on the Internet.

Once a credit card transaction has been processed and approved by the acquiring bank and the credit card company, the business's bank is notified.

The bank then credits the payment to the business's account. The entire process can actually occur in a day or less. The credit card company collects the payment from the customer through monthly billing. If the customer returns the merchandise, a similar process occurs, and the bank deducts the amount from the business account and returns it to the credit card company.

COMPARING CREDIT CARD PLANS When considering a credit card operation for a business, it pays to shop around. Credit card company and bank agreements are not all the same. Business owners should compare the requirements, services offered, startup costs, and support provided by each company and bank. The business must be able to meet all of the requirements of the credit card plan chosen. Employees will need to be trained to process credit card transactions according to those procedures and requirements.

Equally important are the fees business owners must pay for credit sales. The bank and the credit card company both provide a service for which they receive a fee on each transaction, generally between 2 and 6 percent of credit sales. The rate usually depends on the total monthly credit card sales and the average size of each sale. The greater the volume of credit card sales, the lower the rate will be.

A number of fees are paid on credit card services and individual transactions as the transaction moves from the business through the banks and credit card companies. Fees may be higher for very small transaction amounts, a small number of transactions processed, or for errors made by the business completing the transaction. Businesses also must pay application fees and equipment costs to the credit card company and the merchant account provider when the credit system is first established.

PRIVATE CREDIT CARD SYSTEMS

Some large regional and national businesses, especially retail and service businesses, develop their own private credit card systems using the name of the business—Sears, Target, Home Depot. A few accept only that private card. However, most customers expect them to accept major credit cards as well. Operating its own credit system requires that a business establish a credit department to perform the tasks that a bank and credit card company would do. A credit manager, credit analysts, and clerks will be needed to solicit credit card applications, check applicants' creditworthiness, and issue cards. Then they must manage the credit accounts, including recording credit sales, sending out monthly statements, and collecting unpaid accounts.

Businesses have another alternative to offer a private credit card without the cost and risk of managing a credit department. They work with a bank or other financial services company that actually operates the credit card service under the name of the business. The credit card carries the name of the business but all transactions are processed through the credit services company. Target and Nordstrom are companies that manage their own credit services while Walmart, Lowe's, and Macy's rely on other companies to manage their private label credit.

The major advantage of a store credit card is the opportunity to advertise and offer special promotions available only to the company's cardholders. Customers who regularly use a private card are usually quite loyal to that business. A major disadvantage is the cost and inconvenience of operating a private credit system. Only a very large and efficient system would be less expensive than the fees charged by major credit card companies. Many customers do not want to have to carry a separate credit card for each business where they shop. Some customers sign up for a private credit card to receive a one-time discount or as part of a promotion and then seldom use it after that initial purchase.

CONSUMER CREDIT PLANS

In addition to or instead of accepting credit cards, businesses may offer customers other types of credit plans. For expensive purchases, businesses often offer **installment credit**. Under this plan, customers agree to make a specified number of payments over a fixed period of time at a specified interest rate. Consumers buy cars, furniture, and major home electronics and appliances using installment credit. For example, if you bought a car on an installment plan, you would pay a fixed monthly amount for three to five years until you have paid off the loan and gain full title to the car. Installment credit plans usually have a high interest rate and interest charges are included in each payment made by the customer. For promotional purposes, businesses may offer customers interest-free or low interest payment plans if payments are made on time and all payments are made by a specified date such as six months or one year.

Some businesses operate their own installment credit system. However, unless they are very large and have the financial resources to make multiyear loans to consumers, they offer the credit through a finance company. The business takes the customer application and sends it to the finance company for approval. If the credit is approved, the finance company pays the selling company the selling price of the merchandise less a discount for the cost of the credit service. Then the finance company collects the installment payments from the customer.

A popular type of installment credit is revolving credit, which combines the features of a store credit card and installment credit. With **revolving credit** customers can make credit purchases at any time as long as the credit balance does not exceed a specified dollar limit. Under most revolving credit plans, customers may pay off the full amount by the end of the billing period without a finance charge. Customers who do not choose to pay in full have the option of making partial payments each month. The minimum amount of a partial payment depends on the amount of the unpaid balance in the account. A finance charge, stated as an interest rate, is added each month to the unpaid amount. Usually revolving credit plans carry a high interest rate on unpaid balances. Credit card systems are a type of revolving credit since most credit customers are given a credit limit and are required to make a minimum payment each month if there is an unpaid balance.

CHECKPOINT

Why would a business want to establish its own private credit card system?

Types of Financial Transaction Cards

Consumers often view credit cards as if they are actual money. Over the years, credit purchases have grown steadily. The average consumer has three or four credit cards. The top 15 U.S. credit card companies reported total credit purchases of nearly $2 trillion in 2010. The total unpaid credit card debt by consumers was nearly $1 trillion. The major credit card firms compete intensely in countries around the world. Newer types of credit plans have been developed for financial transactions, and more and more brands of credit cards are offering an increasing number of features to attract customers.

BANK AND NONBANK CREDIT CARDS

Banks and nonbanks provide credit cards. For consumers, bank cards do not differ much from nonbank cards. Visa and MasterCard are bank cards in that their ownership is made up of banks. You can obtain a bank credit card under the MasterCard or Visa brand from many local banks. Examples of nonbank cards are American Express and Discover. American Express is a large financial services company that provides credit through a variety of cards that use the American Express name. Discover was originated by Sears in 1985 and later acquired by Morgan Stanley, a large financial services company. In 2007, Discover Financial Services was formed as an independent company to manage the Discover credit card, Discover Bank, the Pulse interbank electronic funds transfer system, and most recently, the Diners Club credit card.

Consumers obtain nonbank credit cards from the company by filling out and mailing an application, applying online through the company's website, or completing an application at cooperating businesses. Most bank and nonbank credit card companies have different cards for different types of customers. For example, American Express offers cards with a range of services. The blue, green, gold, platinum, and optima cards meet the needs of different consumers. Special cards are offered to business customers with services designed to meet the needs of various types of businesses and occupations. So-called "prestige cards" often charge higher fees for added services but can be free of annual fees for customers with excellent credit who use the card frequently.

Credit cards are often co-branded. **Co-branded credit cards** are cosponsored by two companies and have benefits and rewards designed specifically for their joint customers. For example, the American Express Delta SkyMiles Card is a co-branded credit card for people who travel frequently on Delta Airlines that offers cardholders travel discounts and other travel-related benefits.

Another type of credit card that builds on consumer loyalty is an affinity card. An **affinity credit card** is issued by a financial institution and cosponsored by an organization that receives a small percentage of the sales or profits generated by the card. Affinity cards are offered to people associated with the cosponsoring organizations. The cards often carry the logo of the affiliated charity, club, or school. Many universities offer affinity credit cards to their alumni. People who use affinity credit cards generally do so to help support an organization or cause they care about.

DEBIT CARDS

Debit cards resemble credit cards in appearance but are very different. Using a credit card is like obtaining a short-term loan, while using a debit card is like paying with cash. A **debit card** immediately transfers funds electronically from the cardholder's checking account to the business's account when a purchase is made. With a debit card, customers can also withdraw cash from their checking or savings accounts through ATMs and pay bills by phone or computer. Usually the same system, a card scanner, is used to process debit cards as credit cards. However, with debit cards, customers may have to enter a personal identification number (PIN) before the transaction can be processed.

A debit card transaction assures the business accepting the card that the customer has adequate funds to pay for the purchase. The bank or company that manages the card doesn't have to bill and collect from customers. It does, however, send monthly summaries of transactions to retailers and customers. Fees are charged to both consumers and businesses for debit card services. Those fees and the time needed to process transactions are usually less than with credit cards.

FACTS & FIGURES

Credit Card Fraud

Credit card fraud costs businesses $8.9 billion each year. Companies lose an additional $48 billion annually to uncollectable accounts from credit card holders.

The use of debit cards and credit cards reduces the amount of cash and the number of checks handled in the economy. Customers benefit from debit cards by not having to carry large amounts of cash or a checkbook. People who are not approved for credit cards may be able to obtain a debit card because it reflects money already deposited in a bank. A debit card is riskier than a credit card, however, because the money transfer is immediate. There is less legal protection for consumers using debit cards than for those using credit cards. With credit cards, customers who pay their bill at the end of the month are actually receiving a "free" loan of that money for a short time. Debit card charges are withdrawn immediately from the account, so no money is loaned.

American Express, MasterCard, Visa, and other companies sell prepaid debit cards that can be used as a ready source of funds anywhere major credit cards are accepted. Parents may buy a card with a prepaid amount for their children to use at summer camp, on school trips, or at the mall.

Colleges and universities offer prepaid cards that can be used at campus venues including bookstores, cafeterias, restaurants, and vending machines. The cards can also be used in laundry machines, photocopiers, and parking meters operated by the schools. Students and their families can add funds to the card at regular intervals or as needed. Some high schools, recreation centers, and swim clubs offer similar cards.

Gift cards issued by many businesses are also examples of prepaid debit cards. The cards can be purchased for a specified amount that can be redeemed for merchandise from the retailer. Customers can use gift cards as if they are cash but they have no protection against lost or stolen cards and the value of some prepaid cards expires after a certain date. According to Plastic Jungle, a company that buys and sells unused gift card, 5 to 7 percent of the over $90 billion of gift cards sold each year are never redeemed.

SMART CARDS A **smart card** is a plastic card with an embedded microprocessor that can store and process a large amount of information. The microprocessor has a reader "pad" on the surface that replaces the magnetic strip used on credit and debit cards. Smart cards are used extensively in Europe but are just beginning to be used by consumers in the United States. In Germany, every citizen has a smart card containing his or her health records. Swedish citizens use smart cards to vote. Currently smart cards are used by businesses for computer security, in cable and satellite television receivers, and in cell phones.

The information on smart cards can be tailored to specific purposes, and it can be changed and updated. For example, financial institutions can offer a smart card that serves as a credit, debit, and ATM card. Health care providers can record and update medical information on each patient's smart card. Commuters can use smart cards on city buses, subways, trains, or even to pay tolls on toll roads. University students can use them for student identification, food service, library book checkout, parking meters, copy machines, and campus computer labs.

Smart cards hold several hundred times more data than cards with magnetic strips, and their storage capacity is increasing rapidly. They have the potential to replace debit, credit, and ATM cards for several reasons. First, because a smart card provides up-to-the-minute account balances after every transaction, it can reduce bad debts. Second, because lost or stolen cards cannot be used without personalized verification, the cards can reduce fraud. Uses for smart cards are expected to expand in the future, including online security protection for purchases made on the Internet.

Smart cards have the potential for a wide range of applications. Can you name some ways in which a smart card could be useful to you?

© Shutterstock/nobeastsofierce

A new technology is emerging as a way for consumers to make payments for purchases. With a chip in the customer's smart phone, payments can be made by passing the phone over a business's scanner or reader. The technology also allows customers to access product information, special promotions, maps, and other services from businesses using their cell phones.

CHECKPOINT

How are debit cards and smart cards different from credit cards?

18.1 ASSESSMENT

UNDERSTAND MANAGEMENT CONCEPTS

Determine the best answer for each of the following questions.

1. Which of the following is *not* one of the ways a business can begin accepting major credit cards?
   a. Seek authorization directly from the credit card company.
   b. Work with a merchant account provider to be able to accept several different cards.
   c. Establish a credit account with a bank that represents a major credit card company.
   d. Accept any credit card and bill the customer directly.

2. A credit card associated with a specific organization and offered to people affiliated with that organizations is a(n) _____ card.
   a. co-branded
   b. affinity
   c. private
   d. smart

THINK CRITICALLY

Answer the following questions as completely as possible.

3. Why would a major retailer want to offer its own private credit card, with the additional expense involved and also accept major credit cards?

4. Why will smart cards likely replace other types of financial services cards such as credit and debit cards? What problems, if any, do you see with the widespread use of smart cards?

Managing Credit

Goals

- Identify the information on which decisions about credit applications is based and how that information is obtained.
- Describe procedures for managing and collecting unpaid accounts.

Terms

- creditworthiness p. 487
- character p. 487
- capacity p. 487
- capital p. 487
- conditions p. 488
- credit agency p. 488
- aging of accounts p. 492

●●●● Determining Credit Standing

A business offers credit as a service to customers and as a way of attracting additional sales. If they are not well managed, however, credit sales can result in problems and additional expenses. Every business offering credit should develop policies and procedures for approving customers who will be able to receive credit. **Creditworthiness** is a measure of an individual's or business's ability and willingness to repay a loan. Two methods commonly used to check applicants' creditworthiness are (1) the four Cs of credit and (2) the point system.

THE FOUR CS OF CREDIT

To determine the creditworthiness of people or other companies, businesses gather information as part of the credit application process. They then apply the "four Cs" of credit to analyze the information: character, capacity, capital, and conditions. A review of each factor helps to determine the answers to two important questions about the applicant's creditworthiness: (1) Can the customer pay? and (2) Will the customer pay?

Character is a measure of an applicant's sense of financial responsibility or belief in the obligation to pay debts. It includes honesty, integrity, and attitude toward indebtedness. Credit-granting businesses check an applicant's credit reputation, payment habits, and employment or business stability to judge the person's character. The applicant who is always late in making payments or who frequently changes jobs will not likely be approved for credit.

Capacity is a measure of earning power and reflects the applicant's potential to pay, based on current income and other financial obligations. To judge capacity for consumer credit, businesses look at the person's employment history, income level, and number and amount of debts. For business credit, they carefully examine the business's financial performance and financial statements.

Capital, the third C, is a measure of the credit applicant's current financial worth or ability to pay based on assets. For an individual, "capital" means assets such as savings, a car, or a home. For a business, "capital" means a healthy balance sheet—far more assets than liabilities. Capital is especially important if people lose their jobs or if businesses suffer losses or poor cash flow. With adequate capital, individuals or businesses can still pay for credit purchases. Creditors can also ask that assets be pledged as collateral for loans.

21st CENTURY SKILL

Initiative

When you apply for credit, you need to be aware of the information companies will review to make a decision on your application. Under the Free File Disclosure Rule of the Fair and Accurate Credit Transactions Act (FACT Act), each of the nationwide credit reporting companies—Equifax, Experian, and TransUnion—is required to provide consumers with a free copy of their credit report once every 12 months, upon request.

To ensure the accuracy of your credit history, you need to take the initiative for requesting yearly credit reports. You also need to review each one for accuracy and request corrections for any errors found.

The FACT Act does not apply to businesses. To check its credit history, a business must purchase the credit report from the appropriate credit agencies.

Conditions, the last of the four Cs of credit, is an assessment of the economic environment, such as the economic health of a community or the nation and the extent of business competition. The local economy, for example, may be depressed. As a result, many people would be unemployed. Inflation, and recessions also affect a business's willingness to grant credit.

As part of evaluating the four Cs of credit, businesses often use a point system. They assign points to each of the four C factors. Credit applicants provide information about these factors by answering questions on credit applications. Answers are assigned a specific number of points. To receive credit, an applicant must earn a predetermined score. For consumer credit, factors that are rated and assigned points include the type of job, the length of time the applicant has held the job, and the applicant's income, savings, and total debts. The higher the person's income, for example, the higher the number of points assigned. Having many late payments or a large number of credit cards can reduce the number of points.

The most important factor in a business's credit score is its credit history, whether it has made payments on time to all creditors. Other factors include the number of years the company has operated, and the overall health of its finances.

Credit experts agree that the best single measure of creditworthiness is the applicant's past credit-paying record. For that reason, credit applicants need to build and maintain excellent credit records.

SOURCES OF CREDIT INFORMATION

After selecting a method for making decisions about credit applicants, businesses must collect information about them. They can obtain much of the information directly from the applicants and from credit agencies.

APPLICANTS Banks, credit card companies, consumer credit firms, and businesses that operate their own credit departments obtain information directly from applicants who complete a credit application using a printed form or by entering information online. An application for a consumer requests basic information such as name, address, phone number, date of birth, Social Security number, bank accounts, and employer's name and phone number. The credit application for a business asks for company information, bank references, and trade references. After the business reviews the credit application, it either rejects the application, obtains more information from other sources, or approves the applicant for a limited amount of credit. If the customer demonstrates responsible use of that credit, the business will gradually increase the credit limit.

CREDIT AGENCIES Most businesses want more information than they can gather through a credit application. One of the best sources is a credit agency. A **credit agency** is a clearinghouse for information on the creditworthiness of individuals or businesses. In general, there are two types of credit agencies—those that provide credit information about individual consumers and those that provide credit information about businesses. Private credit agencies, or bureaus, regularly collect data from businesses and publish confidential reports for their subscribers, who are usually retailers or financial institutions. Most credit agencies are associated with the top three national credit reporting firms: Equifax, Experian, and TransUnion. Each national agency maintains vast amounts of computerized data about millions of customers. A business subscriber to one of the agencies can get information almost immediately for making credit decisions, through direct computer or telephone access to credit reports. The credit agency provides a summary report of the individual's credit and financial history and a credit score.

Businesses that sell on credit to other businesses need different types of credit information than retailers that sell to consumers. An important source of information on the credit standing of retailers, wholesalers, and manufacturers is Dun & Bradstreet (D&B). As a service to subscribers, D&B regularly publishes and sells credit ratings and financial analysis reports. Those reports are used to make decisions about prospective business relationships as well as about granting credit. Two of the national consumer credit reporting agencies also have business divisions, Business Equifax and Business Experian.

FEDERAL AND STATE CREDIT LAWS

Credit is governed to a great extent by state and federal laws. Provisions of federal laws that relate directly to credit are summarized in Figure 18-1.

All 50 states have laws that regulate credit transactions. The legal profession created the Uniform Commercial Code and the Uniform Consumer Credit Code to deal with matters not covered by federal legislation. While the Uniform Commercial Code has been adopted in all states, the Uniform Consumer Credit Code has been fully adopted in only a few. However, most states have incorporated important provisions of the Code into their laws. Because of the abundance of laws, businesses hire attorneys who are experts on state and federal credit law to review and approve credit policies, procedures, and forms.

 **CHECKPOINT**

What are the four Cs of credit?

●●● Collections Management

Any business that extends credit to customers is concerned about losses from uncollectible accounts. Some firms have practically no bad-debt losses. Others have very high losses that reduce their financial capabilities in other parts of the business. Surveys show that the losses from uncollected debts can easily run 2 to 4 percent of net sales, even for well-managed businesses. Poor management of credit procedures can increase losses to 7 to 10 percent of sales, which exceeds the profit margins of many businesses. Even with good credit management, if economic conditions are poor, bad-debt losses increase, putting even more pressure on businesses. Effective credit policies and collection procedures can reduce losses and make credit services a valuable element of the business.

COLLECTION PROCEDURES

Once a business establishes a credit system, it must decide how to collect money owed by customers. This is an important function, because it affects the

Federal Laws Regulating Consumer Credit	
Truth-In-Lending Act, 1968	This law requires businesses to reveal on forms and statements the dollar costs of obtaining credit. Businesses must show the finance charge on statements as an annual percentage rate (APR), to make comparing rates easier. If a business advertises credit terms, it must include all information that a buyer might need to compare similar terms with competitors (down payment and number, amounts, and dates of payments).
Fair Credit Reporting Act, 1970	This law is directed at improving the accuracy, fairness, and privacy of information in the files of consumer credit reporting agencies. It regulates how information is collected, disseminated, and used. Consumers have the right to see their credit agency reports and to correct errors.
Equal Credit Opportunity Act, 1974	This law makes it illegal to deny credit because of age, sex, marital status, race, national origin, religion, or public assistance. It requires businesses to notify credit card applicants of their application status within 30 days and give a reason for rejection, if requested.
Fair Credit Billing Act, 1975	This law protects consumers from unfair credit billing practices in credit card accounts and revolving credit accounts. It does not apply to installment sales contracts. Rules and guidelines for resolving credit bill disputes between consumers and businesses are provided in the law.
Electronic Fund Transfer Act, 1978	This law protects consumers who transfer funds electronically though the use of debit cards, automatic teller machines, and automatic withdrawals from bank accounts. It provides a means for correcting errors and limits liability when cards are lost or stolen.
Fair Debt Collection Practices Act, 1996	This law forbids debt collectors from using abusive, deceptive, or unfair collection methods. It describes the required conduct for debt collectors when contacting consumers about a debt as well as specific practices they cannot use, including the times and methods of contact, personal harassment, and misrepresentations.
Fair and Accurate Credit Transactions Act, 2003	This law requires the three major credit reporting agencies to provide consumers with a free copy of their own credit report every 12 months. It also has provisions to reduce identity theft and help victims recover.
Credit Card Accountability, Responsibility, and Disclosure Act, 2009	This law requires that all forms and statements credit card companies send to consumers must use clear and understandable language. It also regulates the type and amounts of fees and rate increases that can be charged.

Figure 18-1 To use credit effectively, both businesses and consumers must understand credit laws.

financial health of the firm. Managers try to meet two objectives when establishing collection procedures: (1) collect the amount due and (2) retain the goodwill of the customer.

Most credit customers pay their bills, but some will often be a few days late. Communicating and enforcing a policy that adds interest when payments are late will encourage prompt payment. The usual collection procedures include sending a statement at the end of the billing period but well before payment is due, followed by reminders at 15-day intervals if the bill is not paid. Businesses often use letters and duplicate copies of invoices to remind customers that their accounts are overdue. Those are followed by telephone calls to discuss the reason for late payment and to negotiate an alternative payment plan. All collection steps should be done professionally, with the goal of retaining the customer if payment is made. After 60 to 90 days, if it appears that the customer is not going to send payment or agree to a payment plan, the final collection step is usually either to turn the account over to a collection agency or to bring legal proceedings against the customer. With installment credit, the business may have to repossess the merchandise that was sold on credit. These actions are a last resort but must be taken unless the amount due is so small it is not worth the cost of those actions.

During the collection process, businesses should try to find out why customers are not paying their overdue accounts. Most people are honest and want help to develop a plan to pay. It is always better for the business to get paid late than not at all. Therefore, it is important to learn why an account is overdue and work out a payment schedule that the customer can meet.

Part of the reason for overdue accounts may be that the business extends too much credit too easily. Overextension of credit is as much the seller's fault as it is the buyer's. Too often, businesses issue credit cards to unqualified applicants who can get carried away by their new purchasing power. When they fall behind in their payments, some get new credit cards to pay off overdue balances on other cards. But more cards only get the customers into further debt trouble. Setting low credit limits to first-time customers until they prove they pay their account on time is a good way to protect against losses. Businesses can encourage customers to pay on time by explaining that an increase in their credit limit is contingent on their payment history.

Collecting unpaid accounts is time-consuming and costly. It is better to spend the time developing effective credit policies and screening credit applicants before credit is extended than having to work to collect accounts that are not paid.

ANALYZING CREDIT SALES

It is important for every business to watch its accounts receivable (money customers owe to the business), so that the total does not grow out of proportion to the amount of credit sales. For example, if credit sales are not increasing but accounts receivable are gradually growing larger each month, then the company

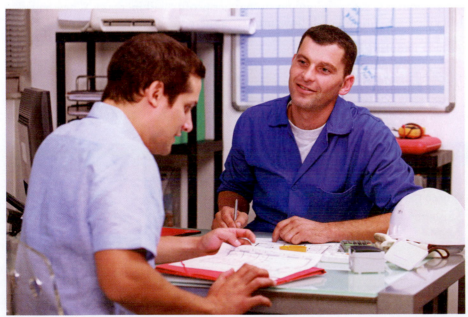

© Shutterstock/auremar

is not collecting payments from customers quickly enough. Soon, the company may not have enough cash to pay its own bills. Before accounts receivable get too large, the company must take action to collect accounts more efficiently.

The total accounts receivable may not show the true picture. For instance, an analysis may show that most of the overdue accounts are only 30 or 60 days overdue, with only a few 90 days or more overdue. In this situation, the problem lies with just a few customers. The company can take aggressive action with those customers and may not have to change overall collection policies. On the other hand, if an analysis of the accounts receivable record shows that most of the late accounts are 90 days or more overdue, the collection problem is much greater. In this case, the company may have to take stronger action to secure payments and to discourage other customers from falling behind on their accounts.

One common method of studying accounts receivable is **aging of accounts**, a process in which customers' account balances are analyzed in categories based on the number of days each customer's balance has remained unpaid. An example of the first few lines of a report showing the aging of accounts for a business appears in Figure 18-2.

In the example, the amounts owed by the Adams-Jones Company and the Artwell Company are not overdue. However, Brown and Brown owes $82.23, which has been due for more than 60 days but less than 90 days; $120, which has been due for more than 30 days but less than 60 days; and $157.50, which has been due less than 30 days. The $228.18 owed by Custer Stores has been due more than 60 days but less than 90 days. And the amount due from A. Davis, Inc., has been due more than 90 days. The report enables the manager to see clearly the status of all accounts receivable and to plan corrective actions.

Another method of measuring the efficiency of collections is to compute the percentage of delinquent accounts in relation to the total unpaid credit sales. For example, if 10 percent of the accounts in January are delinquent, 15 percent are delinquent in February, and 20 percent are delinquent in March, this indicates an unfavorable trend. One study revealed that if accounts are not paid within three months, the chance of collecting is nearly 70 percent; after 12 months, it is less than 30 percent.

By carefully analyzing credit sales, a business can learn which policies and procedures are most effective for increasing total sales while keeping uncollectible account losses to a minimum so that net profits will increase. When bad debts increase, a firm's cash flow, profits, and credit reputation decline.

 CHECKPOINT

How do businesses benefit from aging of accounts?

Aging of Accounts Receivable

Date	January 2, 20—					
Name	1 to 30 Days	31 to 60 Days	61 to 90 Days	Over 90 Days	Total	Comments
Adams-Jones Co.	$ 705.00	$ -	$ -	$ -	$ 705.00	
Artwell Company	1,279.53				1,279.53	
Brown & Brown	157.50	120.00	82.23		359.73	Established payment plan
Custer Stores	-		228.18		228.18	Cash only
A. Davis, Inc.	-			525.00	525.00	Turned over to attorney

Figure 18-2 The status of each account is apparent through aging of accounts.

18.2 ASSESSMENT

UNDERSTAND MANAGEMENT CONCEPTS

Determine the best answer for each of the following questions.

1. A measure of earning power that reflects the person's potential to pay, based on current income and other financial obligations, is
   a. character
   b. capacity
   c. capital
   d. conditions

2. Which of the following should *not* be an objective of a company's collection procedure?
   a. converting credit customers to cash customers
   b. collecting the amount due
   c. maintaining the goodwill of customers
   d. resolving collection problems as quickly as possible

THINK CRITICALLY

Answer the following questions as completely as possible.

3. What do you believe is evidence of a person's character that would make him or her a good credit customer? A poor credit customer?

4. What can a business do before a customer's account becomes overdue to encourage timely payments?

Competition in Credit Ratings

Jonathan Allan worked as a computer specialist. He and his wife, Anita, used the same national credit card. For five years, they always paid the balance of their monthly credit statements on time and paid all of their other household expenses on schedule. But six months ago, Jonathan lost his job when a larger firm purchased his employer's firm. While Anita still had her job, she did not earn nearly enough to pay the household expenses.

To get by, Jonathan and Anita used the credit card to purchase necessities but were often not able to pay on time and finally missed payments for two consecutive months. The credit card firm reported their recent poor credit record to the national credit agencies. As a result, Jonathan and Anita now have a low credit score.

Jonathan finally found another job that paid almost as well as his previous one. He and Anita wanted to restore their credit record, so they worked hard to save money. By the end of the year they were up-to-date on their household expenses and had paid off their credit card debts. But unknown to Jonathan and Anita, the credit card firm deliberately did not report this positive information to the credit agencies. Six months later, Anita decided she wanted to obtain a new credit card being offered through one of her favorite stores, now that the family financial picture was much better. She was shocked when the credit application was rejected.

Jonathan and Anita are not alone in facing this dilemma. A study reported by Experian, one of the three largest credit bureaus, found that one in four credit consumers do not always get as good a credit rating as they actually deserve. Some of the largest credit-issuing firms have withheld information about customers who improve their credit performance. They don't want that information to reach their competitors. As competitors search for new customers, they tend to avoid people like Jonathan and Anita with poor credit histories to focus on people with good credit ratings. In Anita's case, the lack of updated information from her current credit card firm is preventing her from qualifying for credit with a competitor. If competitors had the updated information showing the higher credit score, they would likely issue a credit card and the original company could lose a current customer.

THINK CRITICALLY

1. Why should consumers regularly ask for copies of their credit reports especially before a major credit transaction or after resolving a credit problem?
2. Assume you are the CEO of a credit card company that reports both positive and negative information. How would your action help and hurt your company?
3. Do you believe the credit card companies will stop their unethical practice voluntarily? Explain why or why not. If they don't, how should the practice be changed?

Insurance Principles

Goals

- Discuss several ways that businesses can attempt to reduce risks.
- Define important insurance terms.
- Describe several noninsurable risks facing businesses and how managers can respond to each.

Terms

- insurance p. 495
- reinsurance p. 497
- insurance rate p. 497
- actuaries p. 497
- insurable interest p. 498
- deductible p. 499

 Insurance and Risk Reduction

If you have $5 in your pocket, there is a risk that you might lose it. Although you might not want to lose the money, its loss would not be a serious problem. However, if you own a $600 bicycle, you may not be able to afford to replace it if it is stolen. You may choose to buy insurance to protect against the larger loss.

WHEN BUSINESSES NEED INSURANCE

If you own a business, you face uncontrollable events that could result in financial loss. A fire could destroy your building. Someone might steal your property or cash. A customer or employee could get hurt at the business and sue you. Or an important employee could quit or even die, leaving a gap in the skills needed to run the business. Some events could be minor (like a broken window) and so have little effect on the business. However, a major loss could result in the failure of the business. Consider the problem Ivy Montaigne would face if a fire destroyed her jewelry store. Without proper insurance, she would have no way to replace her losses and reopen the business. Without insurance, most businesses do not have the resources to survive a loss of that size.

Businesses face risks every day. Managers must determine the types of risk the business is likely to face and find ways to reduce or eliminate the risk. If an important risk cannot be eliminated or reduced, the business may purchase insurance to protect against a loss that would result in its failure. **Insurance** is a risk management tool that exchanges the uncertainty of a possible large financial loss for a certain smaller payment.

MANAGING TO REDUCE RISK

Just as you would not buy insurance to protect against the loss of a $5 bill, businesses do not insure against every possible financial loss. As a normal part of operations, businesses experience losses due to operational problems. Planning can anticipate those problems and prevent them from harming the business so much that it cannot continue to operate. Most businesses expect a certain amount of shoplifting and employee theft. Rather than insuring against that loss, they take steps to improve security. For example, if Ivy Montaigne loses one inexpensive piece of jewelry, she might be able to make up for the loss

through additional sales. However, she would not be able to handle the financial loss associate with the theft of many expensive pieces as the result of a burglary. She needs to manage risk by making sure theft protection equipment and procedures are in place and having insurance.

Businesses can also lose money if employees do not show up for work. An absent employee's work will not be completed unless the company takes some action to get the work done. Because large businesses expect a number of employees to be absent on any given day, they may have part-time workers available on short notice or have a contract with a temporary employment agency to provide replacements. Some businesses may actually employ more people than necessary because of the expected absentee rates. Managers should watch absentee rates carefully and keep them as low as possible through policies, incentives, and penalties.

In most manufacturing processes, small amounts of materials are wasted or damaged. To make sure that losses do not interfere with production, a company should keep a larger quantity of those materials on hand to ensure an adequate supply to complete production. Planning, training, and controls for production processes should also reduce the amount of material loss in the manufacturing process.

Many businesses, such as banks, investment firms, and insurance companies, base their operations on records. The records are so valuable that the businesses could not operate if the records were damaged or destroyed. In this case, insurance is not adequate protection. The businesses must rely on the safety and security of their records. They store them in well-protected, secure areas. They also keep duplicate records in a separate location, often in another city.

Another way businesses attempt to protect their vital operations is with a disaster plan. Businesses anticipate the types of disasters that could occur, the protection required, and ways to respond. Each department in the company regularly practices the disaster plan. For example, a manager may be asked without warning to assume that an electrical problem has shut down all computers in a department. The department must recover and operate again as quickly as possible by following the procedures developed in the disaster plan.

In each of the cases described, the company is gathering information, making plans, and in some cases spending a small amount of money to prevent large losses. This may be a better strategy for the company than purchasing insurance for those losses, but it does not replace the need for insurance.

CHECKPOINT

In what ways can managers anticipate and reduce the effects of risks to their business without insurance?

●●● Basic Insurance Concepts

Even with effective management, companies cannot reduce or eliminate all risks. They will need to purchase insurance to cover the possibility of large financial losses that they might suffer from many types of risks Figure 18-3 defines some basic terms related to the purchase of insurance.

It is difficult for one business to predict specific losses or the amount of those losses. However, many businesses face the same types of perils. Based on records kept over many years, insurance companies can estimate that a certain number of businesses will have fires each year and a percentage of merchandise will be shoplifted from retail businesses. By grouping the loss records of a very large number of businesses, insurance companies can estimate the probability of a certain type of loss and the amount of the loss that a business might suffer. For example, using historical records of fire losses over many years, insurance companies estimate the probable amount of fire damage that 10,000 businesses will suffer during a year. The actual amount of loss in a specific year might be different from the estimate, but over a number of years the estimates prove to be very accurate.

Insurance companies insure only against losses that are reasonably predictable. Because they cannot know which specific business will suffer a loss, they spread the cost of the predicted losses across many businesses by selling many policies. Each policyholder pays a regular premium to the insurance company to insure against a specific type of loss. A premium is a small amount of money that pays for protection against a larger possible loss.

Insurance companies use the funds collected from policyholders in somewhat the same way that banks use deposits: They make investments that earn an income. They then use the income to cover losses suffered by insured companies. To make a profit, the insurance company must earn more from premiums and investments than it pays out in claims to policyholders.

Sometimes insurance companies lose money because they do not make wise investments or because policyholders have many more losses than the company anticipated. For example, in a recent year, several large natural disasters (hurricanes, floods, and fires) occurred in several parts of the United States at about the same time. Because of the number of disasters and the large amount of property in each area that was damaged or destroyed, insurance companies had to pay out a much higher amount than they expected. Some small insurance companies failed, and larger companies raised their rates to recover their losses. To protect themselves from greater than expected losses, insurance companies often share the risks they have assumed with other companies through reinsurance. With **reinsurance**, another insurance company charges a premium to cover some of the risk facing the original insurer.

INSURANCE RATES

An **insurance rate** is the amount an insurance company charges a policyholder for a certain amount of insurance. For example, a business may pay $60 a year for each $10,000 of property insured against fire loss. Rates vary according to the risk involved. For instance, if a particular type of business, such as convenience stores, experiences a large number of robberies, theft insurance rates are likely to be higher for that type of business than for dry cleaners, which have a lower rate of robberies. If fire protection is poor in a particular city or the building codes do not require fire walls or sprinkler systems in buildings, the fire insurance rates will be high in that city.

Calculating insurance rates is a very scientific process performed by people known as actuaries. **Actuaries** review records of losses, determine the number of people or organizations to be insured, then use statistics to calculate the rates insurance companies must charge

Common Insurance Terms	
Term	**Definition**
Insured	Persons or organizations covered by the insurance policy.
Insurer	Company that sells insurance.
Peril	Cause of a loss for a person or organization. Common perils are fire, accidents, sickness, death, and theft.
Policy	Written agreement, or contract, between the insurer and the policyholder.
Policyholder	Person or business purchasing insurance.
Premium	Payment by a policyholder to the insurer for protection against risk.
Risk	Uncertainty that a loss may occur.

© Cengage Learning 2013.

Figure 18-3 Knowing the meaning of common terms helps in understanding insurance.

Management
MATTERS

The Right Amount

Determining the right amount of insurance to carry is a difficult task. Managers must carefully assess each possible risk in terms of damage to the firm if the greatest possible loss occurs as well as the likelihood of such a loss. A financial analysis is needed to determine the cost of insurance to cover each risk and the effect of those premiums on cash flow and profits. Additional analysis attempts to determine the financial impact on the business if the uninsured risk occurs. Finally, all possible risks, premium costs, and potential losses are combined and compared. While it is not likely that multiple losses would be suffered at the same time, the effect on the business in a "worst case" scenario must be considered. The wrong decision either way could result in business failure.

What Do You Think? How does the task facing managers in choosing the right amount of insurance coverage compare to the work of actuaries in an insurance company?

to be able to cover the cost of losses and make a reasonable profit. Insurance companies compete with each other for business, so they must set their rates carefully. If rates are set too high, potential customers will purchase from a company with lower rates. However, if rates are set too low, the insurance company may sell many policies but be unable to pay for the losses that occur among its policyholders. Insurance companies are very careful in setting insurance rates and rely on skilled and experienced professionals to determine possible losses, total amounts of premiums to be collected, and returns on investments. In many cases, state governments have departments that review rates charged by insurance companies to make sure those rates are fair to the purchasers and insurance companies.

Regardless of the basic rates set by an insurance company, the rate for a specific policyholder may be lower or higher than the basic rate, depending on circumstances. For example, a new building that has an automatic sprinkler system and is located where there is good fire protection can be insured at a lower rate than an older building that does not have a sprinkler system and is located where there is poor fire protection. In many states, automobile rates vary from the basic rate depending on the driver's age and accident record and the brand, model, and age of the car.

CANCELLATION OF INSURANCE

An insurance policy contains information about how the contract may be terminated. Most property or liability insurance contracts may be canceled by the insurer or may not be renewed when they expire if the insurer believes the risk has increased. If the insurer cancels the insurance, it must give enough notice to policyholders to allow them to find another insurer. Most states have passed laws that do not allow companies to arbitrarily cancel insurance without a good reason. Many states allow companies and individuals whose insurance has been canceled to purchase insurance from a special state-sponsored fund, although often at a much higher rate.

INSURABLE INTEREST IN PROPERTY

To insure any kind of property, the policyholder must have an insurable interest in it. An **insurable interest** is generally defined as the possible financial loss that the policyholder will suffer if the property is damaged or destroyed. For example, if a business owns a van, it has an insurable interest in that van. If the van were stolen or destroyed in an accident, the business would suffer a financial loss. People who use a building for storage have an insurable interest in the property they house in the building, even though they do not own the building. A fire could destroy their property in the building, causing financial loss. Even if their property is not damaged they could suffer a loss by having to relocate to another building as a result of the fire. The amount of a policyholder's insurable interest in the property to be insured is usually specifically indicated in the policy and forms the basis for the insurance rate.

DEDUCTIBLES

Many insurance contracts include deductibles. A **deductible** is the amount the insured pays for a loss before the insurance company pays anything. A deductible makes the insured responsible for part of the loss in return for a lower premium. For example, if a vehicle insurance policy has a $500 deductible and a $3,500 loss occurs, the insurer pays $3,000 and the insured is responsible for $500 (the amount of the deductible). If the loss is only $400, the insured would bear the entire loss, and the insurer would pay nothing.

To reduce their premiums, policyholders often choose to include a higher deductible in their policy if they can afford to pay the amount of the deductible in case of a loss. For example, the premium for an auto insurance policy with a $250 deductible may be $1,850 a year. The premium for a $500 deductible policy may be $1,600. Having the $500 deductible policy saves the policyholder $250 a year. Of course, if there is a loss, the policyholder must pay $500 rather than $250.

CHECKPOINT

What do insurance companies do with the premiums they collect?

Noninsurable Risks

Businesses are also concerned with risks for which there is no insurance. It is particularly important for businesses to recognize and plan for noninsurable risks since it won't be possible to receive payments from an insurer if a loss occurs. Examples of noninsurable risks faced by businesses are described below.

- Fashion, styles, and product features constantly change. If consumer tastes change, a business may suffer a loss if it can't sell its products or it must drastically reduce prices.
- A business that is new or has well maintained equipment and uses the latest technology may attract customers away from a business that appears outdated or run down.
- Improved methods of order processing, product handling, delivery, or customer service may give one business an advantage over its competitors.
- The owners and managers of a business are counted on to make effective decisions. But decision making is risky. The wrong decisions or unethical or illegal actions by managers or employees can result in financial loss or even failure of the business.
- Changes in economic conditions present another serious risk. Rising unemployment rates cause people to be more careful when spending their money. Higher gasoline prices add to business costs and may cause customers to spend less on travel or other purchases.
- Within any business community, there are numerous local risks. For example, extensive road maintenance or infrastructure repairs on a major street may cause customers to change their shopping behavior. Zoning changes made by a local government may have a negative effect on certain types of businesses. A major plant closing may result in the inability of surrounding businesses to survive.

Manager's Perspective on
TECHNOLOGY

A major risk to companies conducting business on the Internet is information security. One of the ways transactions are protected as they are transmitted over the Internet is Secure Sockets Layer. SSL "encrypts" confidential data (converts it into an unreadable form) to ensure that it cannot be viewed or modified as it moves between the customer and the business's website. The online order form is secured with a "digital certificate." Customers see a closed lock at the bottom of the web page and *https://* in the address bar when the transaction is secure.

Insurance cannot protect businesses from these and similar risks. Unless managers anticipate these risks and trends and take action, they may find their businesses in danger of failing. Noninsurable risks pose a great challenge to managers.

CHECKPOINT

List several noninsurable risks that businesses should anticipate and prepare for.

18.3 ASSESSMENT

UNDERSTAND MANAGEMENT CONCEPTS

Determine the best answer for each of the following questions.

1. The possible financial loss that a policyholder will suffer if property is damaged or destroyed is
   a. a risk
   b. an insurable interest
   c. an insurance policy
   d. a deductible

2. Which of the following would not be an example of a noninsurable risk?
   a. a poor investment choice by a financial manager
   b. a road closure that makes it difficult for customers to get to a business
   c. the theft of expensive jewelry from a jewelry store
   d. old buildings, equipment, and technology that make a business appear out-of-date to customers

THINK CRITICALLY

Answer the following questions as completely as possible.

3. What could happen to a business if the owners decide to put money into a savings account to pay for possible losses rather than purchase insurance?

4. What changes are occurring in your community that may have a negative effect on businesses but are not insurable? What actions could businesses take to reduce the impact of the changes?

Types of Business Insurance

Goals

- Describe how insurance is purchased and several types of business property and vehicle insurance
- Identify the types of business insurance for people associated with the business.
- Describe additional business insurance that covers special types of risks.

Terms

- insurance agents p. 501
- no-fault insurance p. 503
- health insurance p. 503
- disability insurance p. 504
- life insurance p. 504
- beneficiaries p. 505
- liability insurance p. 505
- malpractice insurance p. 505
- bonding p. 505

●●● Selecting and Buying Insurance

Most insurance contracts are purchased from insurance agents. **Insurance agents** represent insurance companies and sell insurance to individuals and businesses. Some agents represent several different insurance companies and can provide many types of insurance for a business. Other agents represent only one company and sell only the policies offered by that company.

Most communities have reputable agents offering all types of insurance. However, there may be differences in the policies and services offered by different insurance companies and agents. A businessperson should discuss insurance needs with two or three agents before selecting a company and the type and amount of insurance. It is usually not the best business practice to select an agent just because he or she is able to offer the lowest rates. The service another agent and company provide if a loss occurs may more than make up for slightly higher insurance premiums Figure 18-4. describes important factors to consider when choosing an insurance company and an agent.

The primary objectives when purchasing insurance are to get the proper coverage of risks at a reasonable cost and to make certain that the insurance company will pay the claim and provide needed services in the event of loss. For example, a business that needs fire insurance wants to be sure that the insurance company that issues the policy will pay a claim promptly so that business activities will not be interrupted. A business that buys liability insurance wants to be sure that if a person is injured, the insurance company will help determine the business's responsibility and make a fair settlement with the injured person. Business owners should consider the areas where major losses could occur when planning the purchase of insurance.

PROPERTY INSURANCE

A business may obtain various types of insurance to fit its needs in protecting its property. The major types of property insurance that a business might have are (1) fire insurance, (2) burglary and robbery insurance, (3) business income insurance, (4) transportation insurance, and (5) vehicle insurance.

Fire insurance provides funds to replace such items as buildings, furniture, machinery, raw materials, and inventory damaged or destroyed by fire. Fire insurance on a building may not cover the equipment, machinery, and materials

Selecting an Insurance Company and Agent

1. Can the company that the insurance agent represents furnish the right kind of insurance?

2. Does the insurance agent have a thorough knowledge of each type of insurance?

3. Are the policies understandable and well explained by the agent?

4. Are the company's rates reasonable and comparable to other companies' rates?

5. What kind of service does the agent and the insurance company furnish? Is it easy to contact the agent and company when information is needed or a loss occurs?

6. What kind of reputation does the agent and company have for helping when losses occur?

7. What reputation does the company have for settling claims?

8. Does the company offer help in identifying and reducing risks?

Figure 18-4 Several factors should be considered when choosing an insurance company and agent.

FACTS & FIGURES

The Cost of Disasters

Of the top four most expensive catastrophes for the insurance industry in the United States, three were natural events and one was the result of terrorism. The most expensive was Hurricane Katrina in 2005. The estimated total of insured property losses was $40.6 billion. The next three most expensive disasters were Hurricane Andrew in 1992 ($21.6 billion), the World Trade Center and Pentagon terrorist attacks in 2001 ($20.7 billion), and the Northridge, California, earthquake in 1994 ($16.5 billion).

in the building. Separate policies may be required to protect the contents as well as the building itself from fire loss. The owners of a building should obtain insurance to protect their investment. The occupants of a rented building should look into insurance to protect their property inside the building. You should know exactly what the policy covers when buying fire insurance.

Some basic fire insurance policies may be extended to cover additional risks, such as wind, hail, and hurricanes. Additional protection beyond the primary peril is called *extended coverage*. It is obtained by paying an additional premium and adding a special clause to the insurance contract. Because extended coverage costs more, businesses generally buy it only if the additional perils are fairly common in their area. For example, West Coast businesses may buy earthquake insurance because earthquakes occur there, but Midwest businesses usually do not need this coverage. In some areas of the country, insurance companies will not sell extended coverage for some perils because the chance of loss is too high. For example, insurance companies are not willing to sell flood insurance to cover homes built in an area close to rivers or along the coast where flooding regularly occurs. Because of that, the federal government manages the National Flood Insurance Program. The flood insurance program follows strict regulations and provides standard policies through approved insurance companies.

Burglary and robbery insurance provides protection from loss resulting from the theft of money, inventory, and other business assets. Because of the differences in types of businesses and operating methods, the risks vary considerably, as do premium rates. Burglary and robbery insurance does not cover the loss of products and equipment taken by employees or shoplifted merchandise. Separate insurance is available to cover these losses, but it is often very expensive. Businesses usually spend a great deal on security equipment and training to prevent these types of losses. However, they may purchase insurance as well to protect against unusually large losses.

Business income insurance (also known as *business interruption insurance*) is designed to compensate firms for loss of income during the time required to restore damaged property. For instance, after a hurricane, a damaged store suffers an additional loss because it cannot earn an income until its facilities are restored and it can start selling merchandise again. Some of its expenses continue even though the business cannot operate, such as interest on loans, taxes, rent, insurance payments, advertising, and salaries.

Transportation insurance protects against damage, theft, or complete loss of goods while they are being shipped. Although the transportation company may be responsible for many losses during shipment, some losses may be the responsibility of the seller or buyer. The seller can purchase insurance, or the transportation company may provide insurance as part of the cost of transportation. Anytime businesses ship products, they should find out if the goods are insured and who is paying the cost of the insurance.

VEHICLE INSURANCE

Many businesses own a large number of vehicles, including cars, trucks, and specialty vehicles. Several different kinds of vehicle insurance are needed for protection against theft, property damage, and personal injury.

Collision insurance provides protection against damage to the insured's own vehicle when it is in a collision with another car or object.

Comprehensive insurance, included in most basic vehicle policies, covers loss caused by something other than collisions, such as rocks hitting a windshield, fire, theft, storm damage, and vandalism.

Vehicle liability insurance provides protection against damage caused by the insured's vehicle to other people or their property. Most states require all vehicle owners to carry a minimum amount of liability insurance.

Medical payments insurance covers medical, hospital, and related expenses caused by injuries to any occupant of the vehicle. These payments are made regardless of the legal liability of the policyholder.

Normally, the insurance company of the person responsible for an accident must pay the costs of damages. However, some states have passed no-fault insurance laws. Under **no-fault insurance**, each insurance company is required to pay the losses of its insured when an accident occurs, regardless of who was responsible for the accident. The intent of no-fault insurance is to reduce automobile insurance costs that result from legal actions taken to determine fault and obtain payment for losses.

© Getty Images/ Photodisc.

What is the intent of no-fault insurance?

CHECKPOINT

What are the major types of property insurance that businesses need?

●●● Insuring People

People are important to the success of all businesses. Owners and managers, employees, people working for suppliers or other businesses, and customers influence the financial success of the business. There are economic risks that involve all those people. Insurance is available to protect businesses from those risks. The primary types of insurance related to employees are health, disability, life, and liability insurance as well as employee bonding.

HEALTH AND DISABILITY INSURANCE

Health insurance provides protection against the expenses of individual health care. Typically, businesses offer three categories of coverage to their employees: (1) medical payments, (2) major medical, and (3) disability. *Medical payments insurance* covers normal health care and treatment costs. *Major medical insurance* provides additional coverage for more critical illnesses or treatments that are particularly extensive and expensive.

Disability insurance offers payments to employees who are not able to work because of accidents or illnesses. Insurance companies typically do not pay disability claims unless the injured employee is unable to perform any work for the company. Then it usually pays a portion of the salary the employee was earning before the disability.

Because the health and wellness of employees are important to both the business and the employee, both often share the cost of health insurance. Most medium and large businesses offer a group insurance policy. Under this type of plan, all employees can obtain insurance, regardless of their health, and the cost is typically lower than if they purchased coverage individually.

Health insurance has become an important concern for American businesses, individuals, and government. Because of the high costs of medical care, insurance costs have increased to the point that many people and even companies cannot afford them. Businesses, insurance companies, the health care industry, and government continue to study alternatives that can control costs while providing basic coverage to as many people as possible.

An alternative health insurance plan for employees is a health maintenance organization (HMO). An HMO is a cooperative agreement between a business and a group of physicians and other medical professionals to provide for the health care needs of the business's employees. The HMO receives a regular payment for each employee that covers an agreed-upon set of medical services. To control services and costs, employees obtain treatment from the health care providers in the HMO. The goal of the HMO is to keep people healthy rather than waiting until they become sick and only then seeking treatment.

Some people prefer to receive health care services from a physician and hospital they select rather than from the assigned health care practitioners in an HMO. To fill this need, insurance companies offer another alternative: the preferred provider organization (PPO). A PPO is an agreement among insurers, health care providers, and businesses that allows employees to choose from a list of physicians and health care facilities. The insurance company negotiates with a number of physicians and hospitals for a full range of health care services. The contracts establish the costs that the insurer will pay for those services to control costs while still offering consumers a choice of providers.

Health care and health insurance costs are two of the most rapidly growing expenses of many businesses today. Most are looking for alternatives, and many are shifting more and more of the cost to employees or are reducing benefits. Recognizing the problems of rapidly rising health care costs and the increasing numbers of uninsured and underinsured, the U.S. Congress passed the Affordable Care Act of 2010. Many provisions do not go into effect until 2014 so the impact on coverage and costs is not yet known. The costs and methods of health insurance are one of the areas of employee benefits that both businesses and the federal government are studying closely.

LIFE INSURANCE

Another common form of insurance on people is life insurance. **Life insurance** pays money upon the death of the insured. The person or persons identified in the insurance policy to whom the

NETBookmark

Floods are one of the major risks many businesses and homeowners fail to insure. Flood insurance is usually not offered as part of home and business policies but is sold through a cooperative agreement between the federal government and private insurance companies and agents.

Access the website for this textbook and choose the link for Chapter 18 Net Bookmark. Play the flood-risk scenarios that demonstrate how flooding can affect people in various parts of the country. Decide which of the scenarios could affect people in your community. You may also want to review The Cost of Flooding Link on the same page.

www.cengage.com/school/bizmgmt

payment is made upon the death of the insured are **beneficiaries**. With life insurance, individuals can provide some financial protection for their families in the event of their death. Some companies provide a specific amount of life insurance as a standard part of employee benefits. Others offer the opportunity for employees to purchase life insurance at a favorable rate but the employees must pay most or all of the cost.

Many businesses insure the lives of owners and top managers because of their importance to the financial success of the business. In the case of sole proprietorships, owners usually find it easier to borrow money if they carry adequate life insurance on themselves. Life insurance has an especially important place in partnerships. Generally, a partnership is dissolved upon the death of one partner. Each partner usually carries life insurance on the other partner, so that if one dies, the other will receive, as beneficiary of the insurance policy, sufficient money to buy the other's share of the business. Life insurance on the owners, top managers, or employees with skills that would be difficult to replace is known as *key person life insurance*.

 **CHECKPOINT**

What is the difference between health insurance and disability insurance?

Other Business Insurance Needs

In addition to insuring business operations and people, businesses often buy insurance to cover special types of risk. Two special areas of concern are the risks of business operations and international business activities.

BUSINESS OPERATIONS

Businesses face many risks that result from the operation of the business. People may get hurt while on the job, products may cause damage or injury, and employees may do things that damage people or their property. **Liability insurance** protects against losses from injury to people or their property that result from the products, services, or operations of the business. For example, if a toy injures a child, the child's family may sue the toy manufacturer. Liability insurance would protect the company in such circumstances.

Clients sometimes sue professionals, such as lawyers and physicians, who provide personal services. **Malpractice insurance** is a type of liability insurance that protects against financial loss arising from suits for negligence in providing professional services. Malpractice claims are a major cost to many professionals. Even if the businessperson is not proven guilty of malpractice, the legal fees can be very high.

Some businesses need a special type of insurance protection called bonding. **Bonding** pays damages to people whose losses are caused by the negligence or dishonesty of an employee or by the failure of a business to complete a contract. Bonding is often required for contractors hired to construct buildings, highways, or bridges, and for companies such as Brink's and Loomis that transport large sums of money between businesses and financial institutions.

FACTS & FIGURES

Liability Claims

On average, businesses spend $5.50 of every $1,000 of revenue to pay liability claims. Small businesses spend $20 of each $1,000 earned.

INSURANCE FOR INTERNATIONAL OPERATIONS

Many businesses operate or sell products in other countries. Insurance policies typically do not cover losses or liability resulting from international operations. Special coverage may be available at additional cost within existing insurance policies. Businesspeople should keep in mind that the insurance laws of the country in which the business is operating apply to loss situations. To encourage international business with developing countries, the U.S. government formed the *Overseas Private Investment Corporation*. The corporation provides insurance coverage for businesses that suffer losses or damage to foreign investments as the result of political risks. Although coverage is expensive, companies can even purchase insurance that covers losses suffered if the purchasers of exports do not pay for their purchases. Companies that are just beginning to engage in international trade or have not worked with a specific international company before may want to consider such insurance. Businesses shipping products to other countries should also obtain special transportation insurance, because several different companies and transportation methods may be involved as the products move from country to country.

 **CHECKPOINT**

What types of businesses require malpractice insurance?

18.4 ASSESSMENT

UNDERSTAND MANAGEMENT CONCEPTS

Determine the best answer for each of the following questions.

1. Payments to employees who cannot work because of accidents or illnesses are offered through _____ insurance.
   a. health
   b. malpractice
   c. disability
   d. liability

2. A special type of insurance that pays damages to people whose losses are caused by the negligence or dishonesty of an employee or by the failure of the business to complete a contract is
   a. bonding
   b. beneficiary
   c. agent
   d. preferred provider

THINK CRITICALLY

Answer the following questions as completely as possible.

3. If you are choosing among employers for a full-time job and one offers health insurance and the other does not, how important would that be in deciding which job to choose? Why?

4. How does having life insurance policies on the owners of a partnership help protect the business in case of the death of one of the partners?

CHAPTER CONCEPTS

- To accept credit cards, a business must establish a relationship with a bank and a credit card company. Some firms both offer their own store credit card and accept other credit cards. Installment plans are another common form of consumer credit.

- Debit cards make electronic payments by immediately withdrawing cash from the cardholder's bank account and crediting the payment to the seller's account. They can be used to make purchases and withdraw cash from ATMs. Smart cards can perform all the functions of credit and debit cards while electronically storing a great deal of personal data.

- Businesses obtain information on customers' creditworthiness from credit applications and credit bureau ratings. Ratings are based on the four Cs: character, capacity, capital, and conditions.

- Effective collection procedures and aging of accounts receivable are two ways to manage credit sales. When accounts remain unpaid, businesses may work out alternative payment plans, use a collection agency, or take legal action.

- Managers must identify and reduce business risks. To protect against major losses, businesses purchase property insurance, vehicle insurance, insurance on people, liability insurance, and other insurance for unique risks.

- Many risks, such as changing technology and economic conditions, cannot be insured. Managers must be prepared to respond to noninsurable risks.

REVIEW BUSINESS MANAGEMENT TERMS

Write the letter of the term that matches each definition. Some terms will not be used.

1. Measure of a credit applicant's current financial worth or ability to pay based on assets
2. Credit plan in which customer agrees to make a stated number of payments over a fixed period of time at a specified interest rate
3. Persons who represent the insurance company and sell insurance to individuals and businesses
4. Possible financial loss that a policyholder will suffer if the property is damaged or destroyed
5. Insurance that protects against losses from injury to people or their property that result from a business's products, services, or operations
6. Private company that acts as an intermediary between a business and credit card companies to establish and maintain credit services
7. Risk management tool that limits financial loss from uncontrollable events in exchange for regular payments

a. affinity credit cards
b. aging of accounts
c. bonding
d. capacity
e. capital
f. character
g. co-branded credit cards
h. credit agency
i. debit card
j. disability insurance
k. installment credit
l. insurable interest
m. insurance
n. insurance agents
o. liability insurance
p. malpractice insurance
q. merchant account provider
r. no-fault insurance
s. smart card

REVIEW BUSINESS MANAGEMENT CONCEPTS

Determine the best answer.

8. Which of the following would *not* be an efficient way for a business to accept customer credit
   a. Work with each major credit card company to establish a credit account.
   b. Seek a merchant account provider.
   c. Establish a private credit card system while also accepting other cards.
   d. Obtain a line of credit from the company's local bank.

9. A person using revolving credit can do all of the following except
   a. make a credit purchase at any time
   b. charge less than the approved amount
   c. pay off the full amount by the end of the billing period without a finance charge
   d. charge any amount as long as the total is paid on schedule

10. _____ cards are used by businesses for computer security, in cable and satellite television receivers, and in cell phones.
    a. Credit
    b. Debit
    c. Affinity
    d. Smart

11. To determine the creditworthiness of people or organizations, businesses apply the
    a. four Cs of credit
    b. 80/20 rule
    c. "keep it simple" policy
    d. minimum approval rate standard

12. Which of the following is an objective managers try to meet when establishing credit procedures?
    a. Give customers extra time to pay if they request it.
    b. Immediately drop customers who cannot meet payment deadlines.
    c. Use procedures that retain the goodwill of the customer.
    d. Encourage credit sales when customers do not have the financial means to pay.

13. Businesses use aging of accounts to
    a. study the effectiveness of accounts receivable collection
    b. determine which accounts payable to pay first
    c. decide when equipment needs to be replaced
    d. increase the credit limit for customers who have difficulty paying their accounts

14. Which of the following is *not* a fact on which the concept of insurance is based?
    a. It is difficult for a business to predict whether it will have specific losses or the amount of those losses.
    b. Many businesses face the same type of perils.
    c. Insurance companies can accurately estimate the probability of certain types of losses.
    d. Insurance companies insure against both predictable and unpredictable losses.

Answer the following questions.

15. Using the information in the Reality Check scenario at the beginning of the chapter, what types of business insurance would you recommend Ivy Montaigne should consider? Divide your recommendations into three categories: (a) must have, (b) should have, (c) probably doesn't need. Justify your decisions.

16. Identify several possible future uses for smart cards: (a) for financial transactions, (b) for other personal uses, (c) for other business uses. What problems do you anticipate might result for the widespread use of smart cards carrying a large amount of personal information?

17. Although the use of credit usually leads to increased sales for businesses, when could credit sales actually lead to decreased profits? What can business owners and managers do to reduce that possibility?

18. If you owned a restaurant in your community how would you try to identify noninsurable risks that might have a negative effect on the business? Identify several things that are more likely to have a negative effect on a restaurant than on other types of businesses.

MAKE ACADEMIC CONNECTIONS

Complete the following activities.

19. **Writing** Assume you are the credit manager of a retail store. A customer of several years, who has an excellent credit background, now has a $4,600 unpaid balance. The customer has made no payments in several months. You learn from your credit bureau that she is making minimum monthly payments on all other accounts but the credit balances on each of the accounts is increasing. Write a realistic one-paragraph proposal for how you might handle this customer.

20. **Math** Use a computer spreadsheet program and the following information on unpaid purchases to prepare a credit report dated November 30 on the accounts receivable for a business that offers 30-day credit terms. The report should contain an aging of accounts receivable, similar to the one shown in Figure 18-2, and the percentage of delinquent accounts in relation to the total accounts receivable.
    - Sykes purchased $600 on November 15.
    - Sanford purchased $1,500 on November 19 and $750 on September 15. A payment of $750 was received on October 14.
    - Jenkins purchased $2,100 on November 12.
    - Sanchez purchased $900 on October 17 and $400 on September 20. A payment of $300 was received on October 14.
    - Godowski purchased $600 on October 10.
    - Yamamoto purchased $300 November 28 and $550 on September 25.

CASE IN POINT

CASE 18-1: Is Credit for Everyone?

Alissa has just accepted a job in the credit department of Kriall's, a fashion-oriented clothing store with an exclusive image. Alissa feels that even though most customers can pay for their merchandise with cash, check, or debit card, credit is very convenient. Alissa met Tay-Von at employee orientation when they both started working for Kriall's. Tay-Von is in the management training program. He worked in the collections department of a discount store while in college and formed some strong opinions about the use of credit by consumers.

Over lunch one day, Alissa and Tay-Von discussed their views on credit. Tay-Von started the conversation. "I can't understand why a store like Kriall's, which attracts exclusive, well-to-do customers, has to offer credit. The customers certainly have enough money to pay cash, and the cost of the credit operations reduced the business's profits. With the availability of debit cards, customers don't even have to carry cash to make a purchase."

Tay-Von continued, "I just reviewed the aging-of-accounts report for our store. I'm amazed at how many customers are always late paying their bills. Yet even when they're late with their payments, we continue to accept their credit card just to keep them from getting upset with our store. Why, one of our customers, who is the CEO of a large company, is now over 60 days late paying for two very expensive suits he purchased."

"I'm sure it was just an oversight," Alissa said. "I expect he is busy and just hasn't remembered to pay the bill. I'm sure he can make the payments and we wouldn't want to lose him as a customer."

"It's more complicated than that," said Tay-Von. "We've sent him two notices 30 days apart and he hasn't responded. It's no oversight. He just knows he can pay whenever he wants and he doesn't seem to mind paying the interest we charge." Tay-Von could not resist adding, "Do you really believe credit is so great for everyone? If people with plenty of money can't pay on time, what about the people who don't have that much money? How do they pay their bills? Credit encourages people to buy more than they can afford. Without easy credit, everyone would be better off. Stores wouldn't lose money on uncollected accounts and customers would be able to buy only what they can afford."

"And you and I wouldn't have jobs," Alissa retorted. "People shop in this store because we offer credit. And we charge interest if they don't pay on time, so when they do pay we cover our costs. Credit is good for business and good for consumers. With experience, everyone can learn to use credit wisely."

THINK CRITICALLY

1. Do you agree more with Tay-Von or Alissa? Justify your choice.
2. Do you feel that people tend to take advantage of the credit offered by businesses even when they have the money to pay?
3. Do businesses have a responsibility to help their customers use credit wisely? Why or why not?

CASE 18-2: Costs versus Risk

Xavier and Olivia Abrego are making final plans to open the small antiques shop they have been planning for several years. They have bought and sold antiques as a hobby for many years. They would purchase one or two pieces, clean and repair them as needed, then display them at local flea markets and crafts fairs. They have many customers who know them very well and who regularly call them for help in locating specific pieces they are looking for. They are viewed by many as real experts in the antiques business.

In the beginning, buying and selling antiques was just a hobby the Abregos enjoyed. Gradually they decided to turn their hobby into a full-time business. They have taken several steps to realize their dream. They rented an older building in the downtown area, spent the last six months going to auctions and making some very good purchases, and worked with their banker to develop a business plan for their shop. With the help of the SBA, they obtained a three-year loan to pay the initial costs they cannot cover from their personal savings.

Now they are ready to open the business. They have little money left other than the money they have put aside for their living expenses until the business starts to make a profit. All the money they borrowed is tied up in inventory, display equipment, advertising, and a reserve for operating expenses, including the first six months of rent. They are running the shop themselves so will have no employee expenses. They are confident they can get by on the money they have saved. They expect that their location and advertising will bring many customers into the store.

As they review their budget and bank account balances one last time, Olivia reminds Xavier that they have not purchased any business insurance as their banker recommended. She is worried that they face several risks that could result in serious financial problems for them and their business. However, Xavier believes that because the money from their loan is already committed and the money in their personal savings is very limited, they will have to do without insurance until the business starts making a profit. "After all," he reasons, "we're renting the building, so we don't need fire insurance. If there is a fire, the landlord's policy will cover us. And we don't have any employees, so we don't need health or life insurance. Why should we waste money right now on unnecessary insurance?"

THINK CRITICALLY

1. Do you agree that if the owner of the building has a fire insurance policy, the Abregos will not need to purchase their own fire insurance for their inventory? Why or why not?
2. What types of insurable risks in addition to those identified by Xavier should the Abregos consider when deciding whether to purchase insurance?
3. What noninsurable risks might the Abregos face? What do you recommend they do to reduce the impact of those risks?

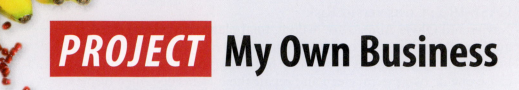

PROJECT My Own Business

Making Credit and Insurance Decisions

Credit and insurance decisions are important for every business. New businesses in particular should consider whether to accept credit and which credit system to use. They should also study the types of insurable and noninsurable risks the business will likely face. In this project segment, you will study and determine credit policies and insurance needs for your company.

DATA COLLECTION

1. Visit a bank and determine the differences between the credit and debit cards that the bank offers. Identify the cost to a business to accept each type of card from customers. Determine what information the bank will need from a new business to decide whether it will give the business approval to accept credit and debit cards.

2. Obtain a credit application from a business. Review it and determine what information the business collects from the form. Categorize the information according to the four Cs of credit.

3. Interview an insurance agent to determine the types of insurance coverage available for small businesses, the protection provided, and the cost of each type of insurance.

4. Review newspapers for several days and identify the types of risks and reported losses suffered by businesses. Identify which companies appeared to be insured and which were not.

ANALYSIS

1. Many small businesses accept debit cards in the same way they accept cash but do not accept credit cards. Decide whether you will accept debit or credit cards for purchases in your business or operate on a cash-only basis. Develop a written justification for your decision, then develop one or more policy statements for the business based on your decision.

2. Assume as your business grows you decide to provide beverage and food services to local businesses and allow them to purchase on credit. Consider the procedures you will follow to collect receivables from customers who do not pay their accounts on time. List the steps you will follow to attempt to collect. Write two collection letters you would send to customers at the end of 30 days and at the end of 60 days if the account is unpaid.

3. Make a list of each type of insurance you believe you will need to carry on your business. Identify the amount of insurance you will carry, the estimated annual cost of each policy, and the company or insurance agent you plan to use to purchase the insurance.

Financial Manager

Managing finances and making financial decisions affect every part of a business. Financial managers develop budgets, manage investments, monitor financial resources, prepare and file government reports, and analyze the effects of business activities on the business's financial condition. The goal is to support top executives and other managers in using financial resources effectively and increasing the company's profits. Most financial managers work in private industry, insurance, banking, and financial services with opportunities in government and other public organizations.

Employment Outlook

Financial management jobs will grow as fast as most jobs over the next decade. The number of financial jobs is closely tied to changes in the economy. However, the increasing importance of financial information as well as increasing financial regulation affecting businesses will result in a higher demand for people skilled in financial management.

Job Titles

Controller
Treasurer
Finance officer
Financial planner
Risk manager

Needed Skills

- Must have a bachelor's degree in finance, accounting, or a related field at a minimum; master's degree in business administration, economics, or finance required in many positions.

- Courses in business law, economics, accounting, finance, mathematics, and statistics desirable.
- Must be analytical, pay attention to detail, be able to work under pressure, manage time effectively.

Working in Financial Services

As the cash manager for a large service business, Emily monitors cash receipts and disbursements in the day-to-day operations. She ensures that adequate cash is available to fund short-term operations and excess cash is invested. She makes cash flow projections and tracks the use of cash against projections to improve the company's cash management decisions.

Career Assessment

Check your library or the Internet for information about financial managers to identify the many diverse roles they play in business. Describe what you like and don't like about financial management careers.

© Shutterstock/Alliance

Case Study

AGING OF "BOOMERS" LEADS TO POTENTIAL BUSINESS INVESTMENT OPPORTUNITIES

Baby boomers, people born between 1946 and 1964, are already beginning to have a strong impact on the health care and retirement planning systems. This group will make up 20 percent of the population by 2030. The wants and needs of aging baby boomers provide a wide range of business investment opportunities.

Industries producing boomer-friendly products and services offer attractive investment opportunities. Top boomer industries include travel, leisure, and recreation; senior living; health care services companies; chronic disease management; generic pharmaceuticals; "vanity" products and services; and financial services.

The money that baby boomers spend on travel, leisure, and recreation will help the industries related to cruises, motor homes, high-end hotels, at-home entertainment systems, health clubs, and golf.

Companies that provide senior housing services will benefit as boomers enter retirement. Home improvement businesses will profit as boomers retrofit their homes to accommodate their changing needs. Assisted living and continuing care facilities could see a dramatic increase in demand as people live longer.

Boomers' consumption of health care products and services is rising. Specialty pharmaceutical and biotechnology companies that develop drugs for diabetes, arthritis, osteoporosis, cancer, heart disease, and Alzheimer's will experience greater demand from an aging population. Higher demand for pharmaceuticals will increase the need for benefit service managers.

Baby boomers have the highest rate of cosmetic procedures of all age groups, according to the American Society for Aesthetic Plastic Surgery. Industries linked to cosmetic procedures and personal-care products will benefit from boomers' attention to their appearance.

Advice and guidance in the areas of wealth management and trust services are increasingly important to boomers as they move into their golden years. The aging of the baby boom generation could provide investors with a variety of attractive investment opportunities.

THINK CRITICALLY

1. What investment opportunities arise from the needs of an aging population?
2. Why are baby boomers an attractive customer base for many businesses?
3. Give an example of how aging baby boomers affect the housing industry.
4. How can traditional financial services offered by banks be adjusted to the needs of individuals in assisted care centers?

Banking and Financial Systems Event

PROCEDURE   The FBLA Banking and Financial Systems Event consists of two parts: an objective test and a performance component. The performance component is a case study consisting of a problem or scenario encountered in the banking or financial business community. Twenty minutes before the performance, each team will receive the case study and two note cards. Participants may write on both sides of the note cards during the prep time and they many use the cards during the performance of the event. Note cards will be collected after the performance. No reference materials, visual aids, or electronic devices are allowed during the preparation or performance. The team will have seven minutes to interact with a panel of judges and present the solution to the case.

SCENARIO   A bank has asked your team to make a presentation to a group of young entrepreneurs who will likely need loans or lines of credit to start or grow their businesses. The bank wants you to include information about the C's of credit and the steps individuals must take to be worthy of credit.

YOUR ASSIGNMENT

Your assignment is to prepare a presentation that gives entrepreneurs guidelines they can follow to help them qualify for credit needed to start or grow a business.

PERFORMANCE COMPETENCIES

- Demonstrate understanding of the case.
- Explain, discuss, and describe recommendations.
- Demonstrate critical thinking/reasoning skills.
- Use correct grammar, tone, and style.
- Demonstrate professional presentation skills.

THINK CRITICALLY

1. What are the C's of credit?
2. Why must entrepreneurs prepare a plan before applying for credit?
3. Why is a presentation about credit important for people who aspire to be successful entrepreneurs?

5 UNIT

Production and Marketing Management

CHAPTERS

© Shutterstock/Yuri Arcurs

CHAPTER 19

MANAGING PRODUCTION AND OPERATIONS

19.1 Developing New Products

19.2 Planning a Manufacturing Business

19.3 Service Businesses

© Shutterstock/Andresr

Reality Check

Adventures in Shopping

Laresa walked through the door of her home and collapsed on the couch. She and her friend, Desiree, had just returned from a shopping trip to a new store called Millennium. It was promoted as "the shopping experience for the twenty-first century," and "the alternative to the American mall." Although she was tired, she couldn't wait to tell her mother about the experience.

"It's the biggest store I've ever seen—bigger than the discount warehouses. The store seemed to have every product you could want and a lot of products I've never seen before."

Noticing how tired Laresa appeared, her mother asked, "With such a big store and so many products, do people really enjoy shopping there? I would think it would be confusing and exhausting."

Laresa replied, "It's really easy and fun. You don't have to walk. Instead, you can stand on slowly moving walkways,

like the ones you see in airports, that move you up and down the aisles. There are huge video displays that identify the types of products in each area of the store as well as smaller computer screens you touch to find the products you want, see demonstrations of the products, and get answers to your questions. You don't have to carry any packages. If you see something you want to buy, you enter the information in the computer. They guarantee that if the product isn't in stock, it will be delivered to your home within 24 hours. All of your purchases are packaged and waiting for you when you're ready to leave. At the checkout, the clerk reviews your order, processes your payment, and even has the packages delivered to the curb so you can drive up with your car."

What's Your Reaction? What are the advantages and disadvantages of the Millennium business concept?

19.1

Developing New Products

Goals

- Describe the steps in new-product development.
- Describe the differences between alternative manufacturing processes.

Terms

- product development p. 518
- consumer panel p. 520
- pure research p. 520
- applied research p. 521
- manufacturing p. 522
- mass production p. 523
- continuous processing p. 523
- repetitive production p. 523
- intermittent processing p. 524
- custom manufacturing p. 524

 Product Development

Laresa's experience demonstrates that businesses are constantly trying to find better ways to please customers. As consumers, we are offered a growing number of choices of products and services to satisfy our wants and needs. Businesses compete to develop and sell the products that consumers want. If consumers in Laresa's city decide that the new business offers them a better shopping experience, other stores will have to change in order to compete. Before a business can offer new products to consumers, it must complete three steps.

1. Develop an idea for a new product that consumers want to buy.
2. Turn the idea into a workable product design.
3. Produce the product and make it available to consumers at a price they are willing to pay.

If any one of the steps cannot be completed successfully, the product will fail. Figure 19-1 outlines some of the activities associated with the three steps.

Developing new products for sale is a very difficult and expensive task. For example, a national fast-food restaurant spent over a million dollars on research to develop a new sandwich for its menu. Then it spent additional millions of dollars developing a production process that would maintain a consistent taste and quality for the sandwich, no matter where the customer purchased it. In this case, the sandwich was popular with consumers as soon as it was introduced, so the company was able to recover all of its costs and make a profit. However, companies sometimes spend that much money and more, only to find that not enough customers want the product. Their new product fails, and they lose all of the money they spent to develop it.

Only a small number of new product ideas ever reach the market. Even for those that do, over half do not survive in the market for five years. Therefore, producers risk large amounts of money in buildings, equipment, materials, and personnel to provide the products that we consume.

Product development is the process of creating or improving a product or service. As a result of many factors, products are continuously changing—old

The Steps in Product Development

1. Develop an idea for a new product that customers want to buy.
   • Conduct consumer research.
   • Conduct product research.

2. Turn the idea into a workable product design.
   • Build and test models of the product.
   • Determine what resources will be needed to produce large quantities of the product.
   • Determine the costs of producing the product and compare them to the product's price.

3. Be able to produce the product and make it available to consumers at a price they are willing to pay.
   • Build or remodel manufacturing facilities, if necessary.
   • Purchase raw materials.
   • Train employees.
   • Promote, distribute, and sell the product.

Figure 19-1 Developing a successful product requires the completion of all three steps.

products go out of use or are improved, and new products appear. Most of the products you will be using in 10 years are not available today. For a company to survive, it must continually search for ways to improve even its most successful products and regularly develop new products. Product development drives other business activities. Before a company can market, advertise, distribute, and sell a product, it must create and produce it. Think of the millions of dollars that were invested to develop the new store, Millennium, described at the beginning of the chapter. The investors in that business are excited by the new business idea, but to earn a return on their investment, the product must succeed.

CREATING PRODUCT IDEAS

The first step in product development is to come up with a good new product idea. You have probably seen a new product and said to yourself, "I could have thought of that." But developing successful product ideas is not easy. The process for coming up with product ideas is both creative and scientific.

Ideas for new products can come from many sources. People inside and outside the company may suggest new product ideas. A company may get ideas from salespeople and production personnel, from other businesspeople, and from research projects. Many companies employ people whose primary responsibility is to create and test new products.

CONSUMER RESEARCH Many companies gather information to help in product development by contacting the people who are likely to purchase the product. One of the best sources of ideas for product improvements or new products is a company's customers. They have used the company's products and know what they like and don't like, and what new products they would like to have. Companies can get this information from customers in many ways. Some companies send questionnaires to people who recently bought a product, asking for their opinions. Others have telephone numbers that customers can call or e-mail addresses they can use when they have questions or problems.

Salespeople can also gather information from customers. Because salespeople regularly talk to customers, they collect valuable information that can help the company improve its products. Managers should encourage salespeople to learn

FACTS & FIGURES

Consumer Satisfaction

J. D. Power and Associates is an internationally recognized marketing information firm. Automotive studies are the product for which the company is best known. These consumer opinion studies measure customer satisfaction from vehicle purchase through five years of ownership. Automobile manufacturers are provided with information that helps them anticipate and respond to changes in the time-sensitive automobile industry.

Why might a company use its customers' shopping behavior to help in the process of product development?

© Shutterstock/bikeriderlondon

as much as they can about customer likes and dislikes. Many companies have specific procedures and forms for salespeople to use when they gather important information from customers. The procedures ensure that the information is communicated to the people responsible for product development.

If a company wants to get a great deal of information from consumers about possible new products, it might form a **consumer panel**—a group of people who offer opinions about a product or service. The panel consists of several people who have bought or are likely to buy the company's products. Panel members meet with trained interviewers to discuss their feelings about new products and what they think the company can do to improve its current products.

Have you ever been shopping in a mall when someone asked you to participate in a short interview or product review? Companies often conduct research in places where customers shop. The research may involve asking customers a short series of questions about their experiences with products or a more complicated process in which consumers are shown samples of new products and asked detailed questions about them. The developers of Millennium, the large store described earlier that was so exciting to Laresa, likely used a great deal of consumer research to design the best combination of products, services, and store layout to meet customer needs.

PRODUCT RESEARCH Product research is performed by engineers and other scientists to develop new products or to discover improvements for existing products. There are two types of product research—pure research and applied research. **Pure research** is done without a specific product in mind. Researchers in many companies are continually searching for new processes, materials, or ideas. They are experts in specific areas, such as biology, chemistry, robotics, electronics, or energy sources. They conduct experiments and tests in order to make discoveries that might lead to new products.

Many products we use today have been developed as a result of such research. The latest computer technology, life-saving drugs, energy-efficient appliances and homes, and improved food products have resulted from pure research projects. Many of the products we consume have been changed and improved through chemical research. Some examples are low-calorie sweeteners, meat substitutes made from soybean products, and vitamin-enhanced soft drinks. Insulation used in beverage coolers and nonstick surfaces on cooking utensils and razor blades are products that have been developed through research conducted by scientists involved in the space program.

Universities, medical research facilities, and government-sponsored research programs are heavily involved in pure research. Because of those efforts, we will likely see products in the near future that use energy more efficiently, apply laser technology, provide more effective treatments for diseases, and result in improved prediction and control of the weather.

Applied research is research that studies existing product problems or possible design improvements for current products. Improvements in electric battery storage and the mechanics of engines were critical in the development of a new type of fuel-efficient automobile that combines a small combustion engine with a battery that can recharge while you drive. Fiber-optics research continues to increase the amount of voice and data communications that can move on the same transmission line while maintaining security and quality. Innovations in cell phone technology allow users to send and receive live video. Phones that support high-speed Internet connection and a wide variety of applications are redefining the way people communicate and access information.

To be successful for a long time, products must be constantly changed and improved. Many types of improvements result from product research. Changes can be made in the physical product, or new features can be added to existing products. Researchers may discover new uses for the product or ways to make the product easier to use. Sometimes changes in the package itself—without actual product changes—can improve a product.

DESIGNING NEW PRODUCTS

In planning and producing a new product, businesses should involve all major departments, including production, finance, human resources, and marketing. The product should be designed to meet customer needs. Customers should be able to identify features of the new product that are different from and better than those of competing products. Also, products must be safe and easy to use. They must meet all state and federal laws for product quality and environmental and consumer safety.

If research results in a new product idea that has a good chance for consumer acceptance, the company begins to design the product. In this step, engineers and researchers build models of the product and test them to be sure that the company can produce a quality product. The design process should include factors such as durability, ease of use, and a pleasing appearance. Usually a great deal of testing is conducted to ensure that the product meets all requirements for success before the company makes the large investment needed to produce it.

Once a model has been built and tested, the company must determine what resources it will need to produce the product in large quantities. It may have to buy production facilities and equipment or modify those it is currently using to produce other products. If the company can use existing facilities and equipment, it must develop a production schedule that shows how it can produce the new products without disrupting the production of current products.

The company will have to determine the costs of producing the product and compare those costs to the price it will charge for the product. It is possible that the product cannot be sold at a price that will cover all the research, design, and production costs. In this case, the company will decide not to produce the product. If the company makes the decision to halt development at this point, it will incur less financial loss than if it produces a large quantity that goes unsold or must be sold at a loss.

 CHECKPOINT

List the three steps a business must take in order to offer new products to consumers.

●●●● Producing the Product

If the new product has survived the research and design process, the company can begin producing for sale. This is an expensive step. The company may have to build or remodel its manufacturing facilities. It must purchase raw materials and hire and train enough employees to produce the product. Then it must promote, distribute, and sell the product. However, if the company has carefully planned and produced the product, the product has a better chance of succeeding and earning a profit for the company when customers purchase it.

Production is making a product or providing a service. **Manufacturing** is a form of production in which raw and semifinished materials are processed, assembled, or converted into finished products.

Manufacturing is a complex process, even when only one product is produced. Examine any product you purchased recently. Very likely, it is made of several parts. The company must either manufacture those parts or purchase them from other companies. The manufacturer must store the parts until it needs them. Then people and machinery must assemble the parts. Once assembled, the product must be packaged. Many products are packed together for shipping and then stored in a warehouse for delivery to the businesses that will sell them.

In addition to the activities just described, the manufacturing process involves many other tasks. The manufacturer must maintain equipment, purchase supplies, and train people to operate the equipment. And often, manufacturers produce many products at the same time.

DIFFERENT TYPES OF MANUFACTURING PROCESSES

When you think of a manufacturing business, you may have an image of a large factory with a long assembly line. Workers perform specific activities on the assembly line as the product moves past. Many products, all looking exactly alike, are produced on assembly lines each day. But assembly lines are only one of several ways to manufacture products. Brief descriptions and examples of five different types of manufacturing appear in Figure 19-2.

Different Types of Manufacturing

Type	Process	Examples
Mass Production	An assembly process produces a large number of identical products.	• Automobiles • Home appliances • Personal computers
Continuous Processing	Raw material moves through special equipment that changes its form to make it more usable for consumption or further manufacturing.	• Milling grain • Producing steel • Refining oil
Repetitive Production	The same thing is done over and over to produce a product. The products are often sub-units to larger mass produced items.	• Circuit boards • Motor units • Plywood
Intermittent Processing	Short production runs are used to make predetermined quantities of different products.	• Commercial baking • Magazine printing • Furniture
Custom Manufacturing	A unique product is designed and built to meet the purchaser's specific needs.	• Bridges • Buildings • Computer programs

© Cengage Learning 2013.

Figure 19-2 Manufacturers use the most efficient means of production for their customers.

MASS PRODUCTION **Mass production** is an assembly process that produces a large number of identical products. It usually involves an assembly line in which employees at each workstation continuously perform the same task to assemble the product. Many products you use are assembled through mass production. Automobiles, cameras, home appliances, and many brands of computers are mass-produced.

Mass production enables companies to manufacture products at a low cost and in large quantities. But many changes have occurred in mass production since Henry Ford first used assembly lines to produce cars in the early 1900s. Now manufacturers often train assembly line workers to perform several different activities. Workers can then switch tasks periodically to make the job more interesting. Teams of workers and supervisors meet regularly to identify problems and develop solutions. Computers monitor the assembly process to ensure that needed parts and materials are available at the right time and the right place. Robots stationed at many places along assembly lines complete tasks such as painting, welding, and quality-control testing.

© Getty Images/Photodisc

How has mass production changed since its first use in the early 1900s?

CONTINUOUS PROCESSING Raw materials usually need to be processed before they can be consumed. With **continuous processing**, raw materials constantly move through specially designed equipment that changes their form to make them more usable for consumption or further manufacturing. Steel mills, for example, convert iron ore into steel to be used by other manufacturers. Oil refineries change crude oil into a variety of petroleum products, including gasoline and heating oil. Cereal manufacturers process many different kinds of grain into the cereals you eat for breakfast. Production runs may last days, weeks, or months without equipment shutdowns.

REPETITIVE PRODUCTION **Repetitive production** is a type of mass production where the same thing is done over and over to produce a product. The activity is usually rather simple and can be completed in a short time. Repetitive production often uses modules (preassembled parts or units) in the mass production assembly process. For example, the repetitive process is used to produce washing machine parts. First, the motor is assembled as a separate module. Then it is installed in the frame, which has been assembled separately. Controls, hoses, and other features may be added in yet another process. Mobile homes and recreational vehicles are often assembled using repetitive production. Individual sections are constructed and then brought together for final assembly on the frame or chassis.

NETBookmark

The International Organization for Standardization (ISO) has done a remarkable job of ensuring that companies around the world meet quality standards across a number of products. Their latest standards are helping to ensure that companies meet environmental standards as well.

Access the website for this textbook and choose the link for Chapter 19 Net Bookmark. Read the overview of the ISO system and the ISP 9000 and 14000 standard. Explain how these standards are helping companies, customers, and the general public worldwide. Would a company want to compete in the world market without meeting these standards?

www.cengage.com/school/bizmgmt

INTERMITTENT PROCESSING **Intermittent processing** uses short production runs to make predetermined quantities of different products. The most common form of intermittent processing is the manufacturing or assembly of a specific product to meet a customer's order or specifications. An example of a business using intermittent manufacturing is a printing company. Each printing job varies in quantity, type of printing process, binding, color of ink, and type of paper. When the company receives an order, the printer assigned to the job assembles the necessary materials, selects the correct printing equipment, and completes the printing. A bakery uses intermittent processing, as does a company that roasts, blends, and grinds many varieties of coffee beans to order.

CUSTOM MANUFACTURING Often there is a need to build only one unit or a very limited number of units of a product. The product may be very large or complex and take a long time to build. **Custom manufacturing** is the process used to design and build a unique product to meet the specific needs of the purchaser. Buildings, bridges, and computer programs are all examples of custom manufacturing. If a company needs a special piece of equipment built, it hires a custom manufacturer.

A custom manufacturer must be able to work with a customer to develop a unique product. The company must be flexible enough to build a different product each time, and it may need to build part of a product or the entire product at a new location each time.

CHECKPOINT

Describe five alternative ways a product can be manufactured.

19.1 ASSESSMENT

UNDERSTAND MANAGEMENT CONCEPTS

Determine the best answer for each of the following questions.

1. Research done without a specific product in mind is called
   a. applied research
   b. product research
   c. pure research
   d. scientific research

2. An assembly process that produces a large number of identical products is called
   a. continuous processing
   b. intermittent processing
   c. mass production
   d. repetitive production

THINK CRITICALLY

Answer the following questions as completely as possible.

3. Describe where new product ideas come from.
4. Explain the differences between the alternative ways of manufacturing.

Planning a Manufacturing Business

Goals

- Discuss the important considerations in locating a manufacturing business.
- Describe the factors that influence the organizing and production process.

Terms

- inventory management p. 528
- human resource planning p. 528
- production scheduling p. 528
- quality management p. 529
- computer-aided design (CAD) p. 529
- computer-integrated manufacturing p. 529

●●●● Locating the Business

Establishing a manufacturing business requires a company's management team to make a number of important strategic decisions. They must evaluate the company's ability to get the materials it needs to build products. They must have buildings designed and built. The company must purchase specialized machinery and equipment and arrange it in the buildings so that it can produce quality products rapidly and at a low cost. The company must hire people with the skills to perform the many activities needed to produce the products. If it cannot find people with the needed skills, it must train others. Finally, after manufacturing the products, the company must store them until it can sell and distribute them to customers.

One of the first decisions a manufacturing company must make is where to locate the business. Although it might seem that a business could locate anywhere it wants to, finding the best location is a very complicated procedure. Several factors influence the decision of where to locate a manufacturing business.

AVAILABILITY OF RAW MATERIALS

If a manufacturer must process raw materials as part of the production process, it must have a reliable supply of those materials. Also, the cost of the raw materials must be as low as possible. The manufacturer may therefore choose to locate close to the source of the raw materials to keep the cost of transporting them as low as possible. Furniture and textile manufacturers, steel mills, and food-processing companies are examples of industries that locate close to the source of needed raw materials. Consider what the most important raw materials are for each of these manufacturers and where the manufacturers are likely to locate because of the need for these materials.

TRANSPORTATION METHODS

The company must decide how to obtain the materials needed to manufacture the products and how it will ship the products to customers. The choice of transportation method can determine whether the company will receive

Manager's Perspective on
TECHNOLOGY

Just-in-time inventory (JIT) systems use computer communication to connect manufacturers' inventory levels to suppliers. Suppliers are notified to deliver inventory just in time for its use in manufacturing. This reduces the cost to manufacturers because they don't need to carry large amounts of inventory.

materials and deliver products on time. The major transportation methods include air, rail, truck, water, and pipeline. Each has specific advantages based on time, cost, and convenience. Very bulky, fragile, or perishable products need special transportation. Companies may decide to locate close to a railroad, an interstate highway system, or a major airport to be able to conveniently access the type of transportation needed. If the company is involved in international business, it may need to locate near a variety of transportation sources.

SUPPLY AND COST OF ENERGY AND WATER

The costs and supply of energy that manufacturers use is an important consideration in production planning. The company must have an uninterrupted supply of energy (such as electricity, gasoline, or coal) at a reasonable cost. There have been times in recent years when several types of energy, including electricity and gasoline, have been in short supply. Energy prices can change dramatically in a short time, making it difficult to control costs. As a result, companies had to switch to other forms of energy or reduce operations.

Water supplies are limited in many parts of the United States as well as in other countries. Governments tightly control access to water as well as the requirements for treatment and discharge of wastewater. Cities and states have passed environmental laws that regulate access to water and energy resources and where specific types of businesses can and cannot locate. A company must be sure to locate where it will have enough energy and water to be able to operate for many years.

LAND AND BUILDING COSTS

Some companies can operate in small buildings, but others may need several hundred acres of land. Companies can purchase or lease land and buildings. Constructing a large manufacturing building costs many millions of dollars. A company will need a source of financing for the construction and will normally pay the cost of the building over many years.

As a business grows, it must plan for possible future expansion. Many companies have had to expand several times since they started business. Expansion is easier if enough land is available close to the existing buildings and buildings are designed to be flexible and allow for expansion.

Companies must carefully consider how the manufacturing process will affect other people and organizations in the same area. Businesses with production processes that create odors or high noise levels may be severely restricted in where they can locate or may face lawsuits from adjoining neighborhoods.

LABOR SUPPLY

Well-trained employees are an important part of most manufacturing operations. Few businesses can operate effectively today without well-educated employees. In selecting a location, a company should look at the available supply of workers, the training they might need, and the cost of the labor. The choice of location depends on whether the company needs highly skilled employees or unskilled labor. The days of easily available and inexpensive labor providing the skills a company needs are over. Businesses are working with government agencies, colleges, and universities to design training programs to ensure a competitive workforce.

FACTS & FIGURES

Lean Manufacturing

E-commerce is creating new pressures on manufacturers for quicker response and shorter cycle times. "Lean manufacturing" is aimed at the elimination of waste in customer relations, product design, supplier networks, and factory management. Its goal is to reduce human effort, inventory, and time to develop products—while producing top-quality products in the most efficient and economical manner possible.

LOCATION OF CUSTOMERS

Just as some companies need to locate near the source of raw materials, others may consider the location of their customers. This is an important factor when most of the customers can be found in one part of the country, when they need the products regularly and rapidly, or when transportation costs of the finished products will be very high.

Manufacturers that supply parts for the auto industry usually locate near the automobile production facilities. Some companies locate near seaports if they have important markets in other countries. Because soft drink companies must provide a regular, fresh supply of their product to many stores and businesses, they have bottling plants and distribution centers in most cities to reduce transportation costs.

Today some states are developing large air freight centers. These are airports that are surrounded by efficient distribution centers and have easy access to interstate highways and rail lines. Air freight centers are being created to attract manufacturing businesses that need to ship products quickly by air.

© Shutterstock/Semen Lixodeev

What factors influence the location of a manufacturing business?

ECONOMIC AND LEGAL FACTORS

A company also considers the type and amount of taxes it must pay in the location of its manufacturing facilities. Some cities offer reduced tax rates or may even waive some taxes for several years to encourage new businesses to locate there. Others have taxes on inventory and equipment that increase the costs of business operations. Most towns and cities use zoning laws to restrict where businesses can locate and how they can operate. Environmental regulations control the use of water and energy as well as require businesses to avoid polluting the water, air, and land.

 CHECKPOINT

List five factors a company's manager must consider when planning for production.

●●● Production Planning

Developing a production plan can be compared to planning a meal. All the ingredients must be available in the right quantities and at the right time. Cooking utensils need to be assembled. Some foods require longer cooking times than others, so preparation of each item must begin at the correct time. If scheduled and completed correctly, all the dishes can be served at the same time.

When planning production, the company identifies all the resources required to produce the product and estimates when each will be needed and in what quantity. Because production occurs over a period of time and in a sequence, the company will not need all resources at once. If the company receives the materials before it needs them, it will have to use both space and money for storage. On the other hand, if the company can't get the resources when it needs them, it will have to delay production and spend money on nonproductive employee time until the necessary materials arrive.

Three important activities are part of production planning. **Inventory management** is planning the quantities of materials and supplies needed for production and the number of finished products required to fill customer orders. **Human resource planning** is determining the types of jobs required for each part of production, the number of people needed for each job, and the skills each person will need in order to do the job. **Production scheduling** is identifying the steps required in a manufacturing process, the time required to complete each step, and the sequence of the steps. Managers use sophisticated planning systems to develop production schedules. Computers are very useful in scheduling production and monitoring progress toward meeting production schedules.

BUILDING LAYOUT

A manufacturer must organize its facilities, equipment, and materials to produce products efficiently. Products have to move through the building, parts must be added, and employees must be able to work on the product easily and safely. The manufacturer must have cost-effective methods for receiving and storing raw materials, parts, and supplies. Once products are finished, the manufacturer must store them or load them for shipment.

The type of layout a manufacturer uses depends on the product and the assembly process. For example, one company that builds tractors has a continuous assembly line that is nearly a mile long. Many of the parts have to be stored long distances from the place they are needed. The parts are delivered to the assembly line with overhead conveyor belts and chains.

A small company that builds electric motors delivers all needed parts to each assembler's work area. The assembler puts the parts together to finish the motor. The motor then moves to the shipping area for packaging and storing for delivery.

A company that manufactures desktop computers organizes its manufacturing employees in teams with their own work areas. Each team orders the parts it needs and keeps them in easy-to-reach bins around its workspace. The entire team works on the assembly, tests each computer to make sure it works, and packages it for delivery. This procedure allows the company to quickly build a customized computer for each customer's order.

In addition to the type of product and the assembly process used, other factors influence the layout of the business. The layout should be designed to make product assembly easy and safe. Employees may need areas to test and repair products. Products and people must be able to move around the building. Employees need food services and break areas. Other activities that support the manufacturing process, such as purchasing, information management, training, and administrative services, require space as well.

For most companies, the layout should be flexible so they can add new machinery and equipment. Also, companies may need to expand the layout as the company grows or change it to produce new products.

IMPROVING PRODUCTION PROCESSES

Improving quality and productivity has been one of the most important challenges facing businesses in the last decade. Increasing global competition has resulted in a larger number of products from which customers can choose. Businesses have found that customers buy the best product available for the price they can afford, resulting in increased pressure to improve quality while holding down costs and prices.

For many years companies were more interested in production efficiency than in quality. As early as the 1950s, W. Edwards Deming was encouraging businesses to focus on quality as the most important company goal, but his ideas were largely ignored in the United States. Today, however, because of the success of companies that have adopted Deming's ideas, most manufacturers use principles of quality management. **Quality management** is the process of assuring product quality by developing standards for all operations and products and measuring results against those standards. For quality management to succeed, the company must believe that no defects are acceptable and that all employees are responsible for quality. Everyone must be able to identify problems and take responsibility for correcting them. Rewards must be based on achieving the quality standards rather than meeting a certain level of production.

To encourage American companies to improve quality, Congress created the Malcolm Baldrige National Quality Award in 1987. To win the award, a company must demonstrate that it has implemented a program to develop and maintain quality in all of its products and activities. Companies compete for the award because customers are more likely to buy from companies that can prove their commitment to quality by winning this honor.

Technology has contributed to the improvement of manufacturing for many years. Computers have dramatically improved the quality and speed of production and have reduced costs. Robots now perform many of the routine and repetitive tasks previously done by low-skilled employees. Fewer people are now needed to accomplish the same level of production. However, those people must be skilled in computer operations and modern production processes.

In addition to routine tasks, computer technology can also accomplish more difficult and challenging tasks. Using a computer application known as **computer-aided design (CAD)**, engineers can design and test products before they are even built. They can view a design from various angles, study possible modifications, and test the products for strength and durability.

The most extensive use of computers in manufacturing is a system known as **computer-integrated manufacturing**. In this process, all manufacturing systems are designed and managed with computers. Design work, planning and scheduling, resource management, and control are all tied together through computers. When someone makes a change in one area, computers determine the impact of the change on other areas and communicate that information to the affected work units.

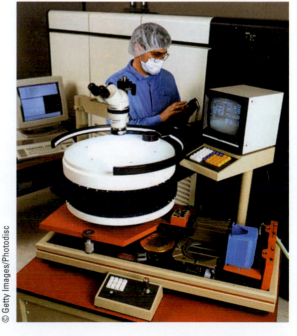

Technology has greatly contributed to the improvement of manufacturing. What effect have computers had on the employees of such companies?

© Getty Images/Photodisc

The Internet has become a powerful resource in improving the speed and quality of manufacturing. Some of the uses of the Internet are very basic but have an amazing impact on how a business operates. As an example, it used to be a very expensive and time-consuming process for companies to get approval from the Food and Drug Administration when they wanted to produce a new food product or drug. They had already spent months and often years developing and testing the product. Then they had to prepare, print, and ship volumes of reports to the FDA for approval. Today that entire process can be managed on the web. Companies can transmit reports instantly, research questions online, send answers to the FDA by e-mail, and conduct meetings on computer screens. The approval process time has been cut in half, and the cost of approval has gone down substantially.

An automobile manufacturer with plants in many countries around the world is improving the automobile design process using the Internet. Product designers come together in cyberspace to share ideas and plan new products. If one factory identifies design or manufacturing problems, it can immediately share information about the problems with every other facility and cooperatively develop a solution. The system is resulting in cost savings because there are fewer design problems and good designs are now being used over and over in many locations. Also, the manufacturer benefits from greater creativity in developing new automobile models as people from around the world share their ideas.

 CHECKPOINT

Describe the factors companies consider when they plan production.

19.2 ASSESSMENT

UNDERSTAND MANAGEMENT CONCEPTS

Determine the best answer for each of the following questions.

1. All of the following should be considered when deciding where to locate a manufacturing company *except*
   a. availability of raw materials
   b. transportation methods
   c. supply and cost of energy and water
   d. international competition

2. Production planning includes all of the following *except*
   a. building planning
   b. human resource planning
   c. inventory management
   d. production scheduling

THINK CRITICALLY

Answer the following questions as completely as possible.

3. Explain why a company would need to consider the supply and cost of energy and water.

4. Explain why quality standards are important for manufacturing businesses.

F⊕cus On...Quality

ISO Standards

Global trade has created a variety of problems for companies, along with opportunities to reach new customers with their products and services. One of the greatest challenges has been the lack of standardization among the products produced by different companies. Consider the problems that a company creates when it produces machinery that cannot be sold in another country because it is not compatible with the machinery that customers in that country already use. What if a company needs to make repairs and the available parts don't match the broken parts?

The International Organization for Standardization (ISO) was organized to deal with the standardization issue, which is a barrier to international trade. The two primary goals of this international organization are:

- to develop agreements on production designs to increase compatibility among products that are used with each other, and
- to establish standards to ensure quality and reliability when one company purchases the products of another company.

Over 130 countries participate in the voluntary organization. Because of the agreements developed by the ISO, products such as credit cards can be used in cash machines in any country and batteries produced in one country will work in a CD player produced in another country. If an airline needs to replace a bolt in an engine mount while the plane is in another country, it can be assured that the bolt produced in that country will fit.

Standards known as ISO 9000 establish very specific requirements for manufacturing processes and product specifications. Any business that works with another ISO-certified business can trust that the requirements have been met. A newer set of standards, ISO 14000, describes specific requirements for environmental management. A company that agrees to these standards assures that it will follow rigorous guidelines in the use of resources and protection of the environment.

Many government agencies and individual companies do not purchase products from a company that is not ISO certified. Companies spend a great deal of time and undertake expensive training programs to make sure that their products and processes meet ISO requirements. The result is much more efficient trade among businesses and countries, plus a higher quality of products and operations in thousands of companies.

THINK CRITICALLY

1. What are some examples of products that are not standardized, resulting in problems using one brand with another?

2. Why would a company refuse to work with other companies that are not ISO certified?

3. Why might a company decide not to meet the standards established by ISO?

19.3

Service Businesses

Goals

- Identify the characteristics of services that make them different from products.
- Describe the ways businesses maintain product and service quality.

Terms

- intangible p. 533
- tangibles p. 534
- reliability p. 534
- responsiveness p. 534
- assurance p. 535
- empathy p. 535

●●● The Nature of Services

Service businesses are the fastest-growing segment of our society. More than three-fourths of the U.S. labor force is now employed in service-producing businesses or service jobs. Over 70 percent of economic activity in the United States is service related. Therefore, the United States is changing from the world's leading manufacturing economy into its leading service economy. Many service businesses are quite small and employ only a few people, and others have total sales of millions of dollars each year and employ thousands of people.

Figure 19-3 shows how pure services are different from tangible products. Services are activities of value that do not result in the ownership of anything tangible. Traditional service businesses include theaters, travel agencies, hair salons, barbershops, lawn care businesses, and insurance agencies. New types of services are emerging as well, such as online music and video download services, comprehensive financial services, information management, and human resource management.

HOW SERVICES DIFFER FROM PRODUCTS

Services have important characteristics that make them different from other products. These differences in form, availability, quality, and timing require unique operating procedures for service businesses.

Differences Between Services and Products		
	Services	**Products**
Form	Tangible	Intangible
Availability	Available only from the person providing them	Available whenever the purchaser wants them
Quality	Quality depends on the skill of the provider and may vary from provider to provider	Quality depends on the manufacturing process but should not vary significantly among batches of the same product
Timing	Cannot be stored	Can be stored for later use

© Cengage Learning 2013.

Figure 19-3 The U.S. economy is based primarily on providing services.

FORM Services are **intangible**. Intangible services do not have a physical product, they cannot be seen or examined before purchase, and they do not exist after the consumer uses them. When you go to a theater to see a play, you rely on a review in the newspaper or what you have heard from others to decide if it is something you want to attend. If a company hires a carpet-cleaning business for its offices, it will need to bring them back when the carpets must be cleaned again.

AVAILABILITY A service cannot be separated from the person or business supplying it. Dental care requires a dentist, a concert requires an orchestra, and tax preparation requires an accountant. People who purchase services are also purchasing the availability and the skill of the person performing the service. If a business or individual is unable to deliver a service, customers must go without. Trading in the stock market using the Internet has become popular as investors bypass traditional stockbrokers. However, in several instances, a business offering Internet stock trading had serious hardware or software problems that prevented customers from accessing accounts to buy and sell stocks.

QUALITY The quality of the service depends on who provides it as well as where and when that service is provided. Removing 10 inches of snow from a parking lot may be more effective with a tractor and a dump truck than with a small snow blower. A hairstylist who has not completed training recently may not be able to offer the latest hair designs. A service provider who is tired, untrained, or unconcerned about the customer may not provide the same quality of service each time. Understanding these factors makes it easier for a business to control the quality of services and ensure that customers get the same quality time after time.

TIMING A service cannot be stored or held until needed. After a movie starts, it is no longer available in its complete form until it is replayed. If the courts in a tennis club are full, no one else can play tennis at that time. Likewise, the owner of a taxi company must have cars and drivers available at all times, even if no one is using a taxi at a specific time.

MANAGING A SERVICE BUSINESS

By understanding the unique characteristics of services, managers in charge of planning services can do a better job of meeting customer needs. Consider the planning that must be done by the managers of Millennium, the new store described at the beginning of the chapter. They must make sure the business offers the best level of customer service possible to the thousands of people who shop there.

Because a service is intangible, service providers must find ways to describe their service to prospective customers. They may have to demonstrate how they will provide the service and the benefits the customers will receive. To help overcome this problem, service businesses sometimes provide a product to customers as part of the service. Insurance companies provide policy documents and leather cases to hold the documents, tour services provide travel bags, and hotels provide small gifts in their rooms to remind their guests of the service and the service provider.

FACTS & FIGURES

Quality Standards

The Baldrige program has quality criteria for educational institutions. These service businesses must evaluate their leadership, their management governance process and societal responsibility strategies, their strategic planning process, how they include the voice of their customers, how they measure performance, how the workforce is treated, the work process, and results of measuring outcomes. Past winners include K-12 public schools and colleges.

How can managers make sure the employees of service businesses do a good job of meeting customer expectations?

The service must be provided in an acceptable way to the customer. A client visiting a barbershop may want the services of a specific barber. A person completing a bank transaction may want to talk with a teller rather than use an ATM. Airline travelers may prefer not to stand in long lines to check their luggage and get a boarding pass for their flight.

The people providing the service must be well trained. They must be able to work with customers, identify needs, and provide the appropriate service. They must recognize that customer satisfaction is directly related to how well they perform. In turn, customers will expect the same quality of service each time they purchase it.

The supply of a service must be matched to the demand. If a bus company expects a large number of customers to ride its buses on the Saturday of a home football game, it may have to schedule more buses. If a snowstorm is anticipated, companies that clear parking lots and driveways may need to find additional equipment and operators. During a particularly cool and rainy summer, the operator of a swimming pool will probably need to schedule fewer lifeguards and pool attendants.

© Getty Images/Photodisc

 **CHECKPOINT**

Describe the four basic characteristics of a service business.

Ensuring Service Quality

Just as manufacturers are constantly improving their products and processes to better satisfy customers, service businesses also look for better ways to provide services. Some of those ways include hiring and training employees more carefully, thoroughly planning how to maintain service quality standards, and using technology to improve the availability and delivery of services. The Internet is providing both opportunities and challenges for service businesses. For example, landscaping services can advertise and demonstrate services online. At the same time, individuals who may have at one time hired a landscaping business to provide landscaping advice can now look online for designs and plans.

SERVQUAL

Business researchers have developed a means of measuring service quality, the SERVQUAL survey. This survey measures five dimensions that customers consistently rank as important to service quality:

- **Tangibles:** the appearance of physical facilities, equipment, personnel, and promotional material
- **Reliability:** the ability to perform the promised service dependably and accurately
- **Responsiveness:** the willingness to help customers and provide prompt service

With so much online competition today, how can video game stores improve service and maintain a loyal customer base?

- **Assurance:** the knowledge and courtesy of employees and their ability to convey trust and confidence
- **Empathy:** the caring and individualized attention the business provides its customers

The SERVQUAL survey measures service quality perceptions of customers, service providers (individuals who deal directly with customers), and managers. Researchers look at the differences, or gaps, between these groups to identify differences in expectations and service quality perceptions.

STANDARDIZING SERVICES

Franchises for service businesses are becoming quite common. Franchising allows a service to be provided in a variety of locations while maintaining a consistent image and level of quality. Examples of franchised service businesses include car repair, restaurants, tax preparation and legal services, and house-cleaning businesses.

Service businesses are responding to the specific needs of customers. Extended hours, more service locations, a greater variety of services, and follow-up activities with customers to ensure satisfaction are all ways that businesses are attempting to meet customer needs. Managers of service businesses are learning that they must plan their service processes as carefully as manufacturers plan their production processes. In both cases, customers expect a quality product or service delivered in a timely fashion at a fair price.

 **CHECKPOINT**

Explain how a business can ensure service quality.

21st CENTURY SKILLS

Social Skills

Well-developed social skills can help you be successful in all aspects of your life. They are particularly important when working in a service business.

Look at the five dimensions of the SERVQUAL survey shown on this page. Notice that three of them can also be described as social skills. Reliability, responsiveness, and empathy are social skills you can learn and develop. With practice, these skills will become second nature.

19.3 ASSESSMENT

UNDERSTAND MANAGEMENT CONCEPTS

Determine the best answer for each of the following questions.

1. Which of the following describes a service business accurately?
   a. Services are tangible.
   b. A service is separate from the person or business.
   c. Service businesses do not need to worry about quality.
   d. A service cannot be stored or held.

2. The SERVQUAL survey measures all of the following *except*:
   a. intangibles
   b. reliability
   c. responsiveness
   d. assurance

THINK CRITICALLY

Answer the following questions as completely as possible.

3. Explain how services are different from tangible products.

4. Explain why the SERVQUAL survey collects data from customers, service providers, and managers.

CHAPTER CONCEPTS

- Businesses are continually looking for new product ideas that meet consumer needs and ways to improve their current products. Product development is based on consumer and product research.

- During product design, models are tested to make sure they meet consumer needs and will be safe and durable. The company then determines the resources and facilities needed and if a product will be profitable.

- Products are manufactured in several different ways: mass production, continuous processing, repetitive production, intermittent processing, and custom manufacturing.

- Decisions about where to locate a business are based on the location and availability of raw materials, transportation methods, supplies of energy and water, the costs of land and buildings, the labor supply, the location of customers, and any economic and legal factors that may affect the business.

- Production planning involves inventory management, human resource planning, and production scheduling. Quality management sets standards for products and operations and ways to measure results.

- Service businesses are the fastest-growing segment of the U.S. economy. Services are different from products in form, availability, quality, and timing.

REVIEW BUSINESS MANAGEMENT TERMS

Write the letter of the term that matches each definition. Some terms will not be used.

1. Process of creating or improving a product or service
2. Research that studies existing product problems or possible design improvements for current products
3. Planning the quantities of materials, supplies, and finished products required to meet customer orders
4. Computer application engineers use to design and test products before they are built
5. Group of people who offer opinions about a product or service
6. Form of production in which raw and semifinished materials are processed, assembled, or converted into finished products
7. Process in which all manufacturing systems are designed and managed using computers
8. Assuring product quality by developing standards and measuring results against those standards
9. Identifying the steps required in a manufacturing process, the time required to complete each step, and the sequence of the steps
10. Manufacturing process that uses short production runs to make predetermined quantities of different products
11. Research done without a specific product in mind
12. Process used to design and build a unique product to meet the specific needs of the purchaser

a. applied research
b. computer-aided design (CAD)
c. computer-integrated manufacturing
d. consumer panel
e. continuous processing
f. custom manufacturing
g. intermittent processing
h. inventory management
i. manufacturing
j. product development
k. production scheduling
l. pure research
m. quality management
n. repetitive production

Determine the best answer.

13. Human resource planning determines all of the following *except*
    a. the types of jobs required for each part of production
    b. the number of people needed for each job
    c. the salaries of each worker
    d. the skills each person will need in order to do the job

14. Companies use this process do the same thing over and over to produce a product.
    a. customer manufacturing
    b. intermittent processing
    c. mass production
    d. repetitive production

15. Buildings, bridges, and computer programs are all examples of
    a. custom manufacturing
    b. intermittent processing
    c. mass production
    d. repetitive production

16. To encourage American companies to improve quality, Congress in 1987 created the
    a. American National Quality Award
    b. ISO National Award
    c. Malcolm Baldrige National Quality Award
    d. Total Quality Management Award

17. The major transportation methods include
    a. rail, truck, and water
    b. air, rail, truck, and water
    c. air, rail, truck, water, and freight
    d. air, rail, truck, water, and pipeline

18. The International Organization for Standardization (ISO) was organized to
    a. deal with global standardization issues
    b. develop agreements on production designs and compatibility
    c. establish standards to ensure quality and reliability
    d. all of the above

19. The manufacturing process that produces a large number of identical products and usually involves an assembly line where employees at workstations continuously perform the same task to assemble the product is called
    a. custom manufacturing
    b. intermittent processing
    c. mass production
    d. repetitive production

APPLY WHAT YOU KNOW

Answer the following questions.

20. Explain why a company would use both consumer research and product research when developing new product ideas.
21. Describe the methods used by product developers to collect data for research. Explain how technology can be used in research.
22. Describe the circumstances in which a company might decide to go ahead with the production of a new product rather than spend time developing and testing a model.
23. Explain why companies would compete for the Malcolm Baldrige Award.
24. Describe the economic and legal factors that might affect the location of a manufacturing business.

MAKE ACADEMIC CONNECTIONS

Complete the following activities.

25. **Math** The Neveau Corporation spent $8,937,250 on research last year. It spent 30 percent on consumer research, 25 percent on pure research, and the remainder on applied research. The company's annual sales for the last year were $297,550,000.
    a. What percentage of sales did the company spend on research?
    b. How much did the company spend on each of the three types of research?
26. **Research** Join a team with several other students in your class. Your teacher may assign you to a specific group and topic. Use the Internet or your library to gather information on one of the following topics: W. Edwards Deming, the Malcolm Baldrige National Quality Award, the ISO, Total Quality Management, or Continuous Quality Improvement. Prepare an oral report. Include slides developed with computer presentation software. Provide at least three Internet addresses (URLs) where you found useful information on the topic.
27. **Writing** Place yourself in the role of your city's economic development director. Evaluate your city against the criteria that manufacturers consider in locating their facilities. Write a letter that you would use to convince a manufacturer to locate in your city.
28. **Speaking** Participate in a debate with other students in your class. Your teacher will provide instructions on how the debate will be organized. Do research to gather information in support of your position. The two positions to be debated are:
    a. Cities and states should encourage economic development and provide better jobs for their citizens by reducing the amount of regulation on where manufacturing businesses can locate.
    b. Cities and states should increase the regulation on where businesses can locate to protect the environment and its citizens.

CASE 19-1: Maintaining Quality in a Competitive Market

TaeMark, a major software development company, is facing increasing competition from many new businesses. It prides itself on staying in touch with its customers and carefully testing all new software products and upgrades to ensure that they are easy to use and free of "bugs" before distributing them for sale. That process is both time-consuming and expensive. It often takes more than a year to get a new type of software on the market. The cost of the research and testing makes the company's software among the most expensive on the market.

TaeMark has noticed a new trend in software development in the past several years. Small and large competitors are flooding the market with new software. Many of the new products never achieve a high level of sales and often are removed from the market after a few months. However, it appears the competitors are willing to develop many products that don't sell with the hope that a few will be very successful and profitable. Also, most of the new software products are introduced without much testing to ensure quality. The new software developers believe that customers will put up with problems as long as the company quickly puts out a new edition of the software that corrects the problem. Competitors may put out two or three editions of a product in the time it takes TaeMark to develop and test one product. Because of the way the new software developers operate, they can price their software much lower than TaeMark can. TaeMark is also finding a change in customer attitudes about software developers. Customers express growing dissatisfaction with quality and say they are not willing to pay high prices for software when they know they will have to upgrade the software frequently.

THINK CRITICALLY

1. Why do you believe some companies are willing to forgo the time and cost of research and testing in order to get products on the market faster?
2. Why do you believe customers appear to have negative attitudes toward software developers yet are still willing to purchase their products?
3. The new competitors are allowing customers to identify problems with their software. Then they develop new editions that correct the problems. Is this really a form of research? Why or why not?
4. Would you advise TaeMark to change its product development process to be more like that of new competitors, or to continue the process it has used in the past? What are the advantages and disadvantages of each choice?
5. Explain how TaeMark could use the SERVQUAL survey to improve the quality of its software. Would ISO certification help TaeMark sell its software?

CASE 19-2: Delivering a Quality Vacation Experience

Rebecca and Jacob DeNucci vacation with their family each summer on an island just off the coast of North Carolina. The island is a popular tourist area, with several large hotels and a ferry boat that brings people from the mainland to the island for day-long visits. Rebecca and Jacob began to think about ways they could use their time to make money during the summer. They considered the needs of the tourists visiting the island and decided to begin a guide service for people who wanted to explore the hills and forests of the island.

They spent some time planning two different tours. The short tour would last one hour. It would be for people who wanted to see some of the beautiful spots on the island but were not prepared for extensive hiking. The long tour would take half a day and would include hiking over five miles. It was designed for more experienced outdoors people who wanted to study the plants, trees, and wildlife unique to the island. Rebecca and Jacob would provide the short tour to groups of 10 to 15 people at a rate of $2 per person. The long tour would serve four to eight people and would cost $10 per person.

After planning, Rebecca and Jacob developed small posters and some business cards that described their guide service, listed the days and hours the tours were available, and gave their home phone number. They distributed their materials to the hotels and restaurants on the island and the mainland.

THINK CRITICALLY

1. Do you think Rebecca and Jacob have done effective planning for their service business? What are some additional things they may want to consider before beginning the business?
2. Suggest ways that the DeNuccis can (a) help prospective customers understand the type and quality of their service, (b) ensure that customers get a high-quality service each time, and (c) provide the service to customers at an appropriate time and location.
3. Explain how Rebecca and Jacob can ensure they are providing quality service.
4. During the second summer, the DeNuccis' business became extremely successful, and more tours were requested than they could personally lead. Now they are considering hiring other teenagers who also vacation on the island to lead the tours. What recommendations would you make concerning the qualifications and training of the new employees?
5. Describe what the DeNuccis can include in their advertising to convince potential customers that they are offering a quality experience.

PROJECT My Own Business

New Product Planning

Two important elements of product planning for a new retail business are (1) gathering information from potential customers about their attitudes toward the product, and (2) scheduling the activities to be completed in organizing the business. You will complete those two activities in this section of the project.

DATA COLLECTION

1. Identify five people who represent potential customers for your business. They are your consumer panel, so select people who represent different ages, income levels, occupations, and interests. If possible, meet with them as a group. If that is not possible, then meet with them individually. During the meeting, describe your business idea and provide them with a survey that asks for their reactions. Have them recommend what they would like to see in the products, prices, and location. They might also recommend some effective ways to promote the business. After you have met with the panel, write a report that summarizes its recommendations.

2. Identify and complete a detailed analysis of as many different juice drinks and related products as you can find in the town or city in which you live. For those that seem to be most popular, try to identify what product features (including factors such as the package) make them successful. Also identify any product features that you believe should be improved. Prepare a survey questionnaire to test your analysis of the product features. Your goal is to find out what features your customers really want. Ask at least 10 people (who are not classmates) to complete your survey.

ANALYSIS

1. Prepare a written analysis of the recommendations you collected from your consumer panel. Select the recommendations that you would implement and give your reasons.

2. Prepare a written analysis of the data you collected from your product survey. Summarize your conclusions about what product features your customers want.

3. Search the Internet to find a list of the recommended steps for opening a new business. Then develop a schedule that lists the activities in the order you would complete them for your business. Prepare a timetable for the completion of each activity, making certain you allow enough time for each one. Project the date you will be able to open your business.

4. Because your juice business relies on effective service, prepare a list of services you will provide to customers. Then prepare a step-by-step procedure for each service to ensure high-quality delivery each time.

CHAPTER 20

NATURE AND SCOPE OF MARKETING

20.1 Nature of Marketing

20.2 Elements of Marketing

20.3 Marketing Plan

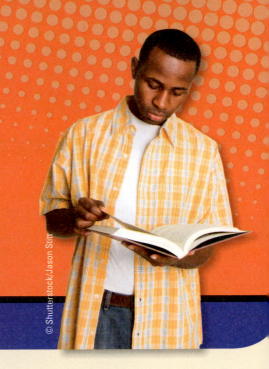

© Shutterstock/Jason Stitt

Reality Check

Supply and Demand

Tony Taylor looked back on the previous week with amazement. He remembered that on Monday he sat through his economics class learning about the concept of supply and demand. As he listened, he thought, "This doesn't apply to me. At most, it might affect some very large businesses. I wonder why we're studying it." But what a week!

He and three friends had wanted to see a certain movie for several weeks but could not find a time when they could all go together. Finally, everyone was available after school on Tuesday to catch the four o'clock showing. Tony rushed out of school and down to the ATM at his bank to withdraw some money for the movie and snacks. A computer problem had shut down all the ATMs, so everyone had to do their banking in person. When he entered the bank, he encountered a long line of customers waiting for the bank tellers.

By the time Tony got his cash, he was already late for the movie. As he dashed up to the theater, he saw his friends standing outside. Attendance for the movie they wanted to see had recently fallen off, so the theater was no longer showing that movie.

Then, on Wednesday, Tony heard that his favorite music group would be performing locally and tickets would go on sale this weekend. Promoters announced that due to the expected high demand for tickets, a $15 surcharge was being added to the price of each ticket. Tony thought the tickets were already expensive and didn't see why he should have to pay more when several other, less popular groups had played with no surcharge added.

But today had been the most frustrating day. Tony's parents own a small landscaping business, and Tony helps them find high school students to work during the summer. Last year he had problems getting enough applicants for the available jobs. However, a number of people he talked with today were interested. They told him that they were shut out of many jobs. Other jobs that pay more and don't require physical labor are not available to high school students because unemployment is so high.

Now Tony thought back through his week's experiences and remembered Monday's economics discussion. "Maybe supply and demand affect my life more than I realize," he reflected as he picked up his textbook.

What's Your Reaction? How has Tony's life been affected by supply and demand?

20.1

Nature of Marketing

Goals

- Discuss the importance of marketing and its role in the economy.
- Describe the factors that are part of the nature of marketing.

Terms

- marketing p. 544
- retailers p. 545
- wholesalers p. 545
- marketing managers p. 545
- buying p. 545
- selling p. 545
- transporting p. 545
- storing p. 545
- financing p. 545
- researching p. 546
- risk taking p. 546
- grading and valuing p. 546
- production-oriented p. 546
- sales-oriented p. 547
- customer-oriented p. 547
- marketing concept p. 547

 Importance Of Marketing

In our private enterprise economy, it is not always easy to match production and consumption. Individual managers make decisions about what they will produce, and individual consumers make decisions about what they want to purchase. For the economy to work well, producers and consumers need information to help them make their decisions, so that producers can provide the types and amounts of products and services that consumers are willing and able to buy. Marketing activities, when performed well, help to match production and consumption. **Marketing** is a set of activities that gets products from producers to consumers. From this basic definition, you may think that marketing is simply transporting products. However, it is much more than that. It includes packaging, developing brand names, and determining prices. Marketing even involves financing and storing products until customers purchase them. Also, most products require some type of promotion. Marketing is involved in all of these activities and many more.

A more detailed definition will provide a better description of modern marketing. The American Marketing Association defines *marketing* as the activity, set of institutions, and processes for creating, communicating, delivering, and exchanging offerings that have value for customers, clients, partners, and society at large. Because marketing is the key tool in matching supply and demand, it can be viewed in another way as well. If marketing is successful, businesses can sell their products and services and consumers can purchase the things they want. Therefore, the goal of effective marketing is to create and maintain satisfying exchange relationships between buyers and sellers.

Every consumer comes into daily contact with marketing in one form or another. Whenever you see an advertisement on television or on the Internet, notice a truck being unloaded at a warehouse, or use a credit card to purchase a product, you are seeing marketing at work. Each retail store location, each form of advertising, each salesperson, and even each package in which a product is sold is a part of marketing. A great deal of business activity centers on marketing.

Millions of businesses worldwide engage in marketing as their primary business activity. Those organizations include **retailers**—businesses that sell directly to final consumers—and **wholesalers**—businesses that buy products from businesses and sell them to other businesses. The thousands of businesses that sell services, rather than products, are also included. In addition, advertising agencies provide promotional services, finance companies offer loans and other financial services, and transportation companies handle and move products. All of these types of business as well as many others that support the marketing efforts of other businesses are directly involved in marketing.

THE ROLE OF THE MARKETING MANAGER

Many businesses have marketing departments run by marketing managers. **Marketing managers** are responsible for coordinating marketing functions across departments to meet customer needs. For example, a marketing manager must ensure that market research, product design, and sales functions are all coordinated to reach company goals. There are a number of other marketing jobs in advertising and sales promotion, customer service, credit, and insurance. Well over one-third of all people employed in the United States work in a marketing job or a marketing business.

 **CHECKPOINT**

List the three primary business organizations that engage in marketing.

● ● ● **Nature of Marketing**

When many people think of marketing, they think only of advertising and selling. However, many marketing activities must occur before a product can be advertised and sold. To better understand marketing, we will examine the major marketing activities, the cost of marketing activities, and the role of marketing in business.

MARKETING ACTIVITIES

The following are the most common marketing activities:

- **Buying** Obtaining a product to be resold. Buying involves finding suppliers that can provide the right products in the right quality and quantity at a fair price.
- **Selling** Providing personalized and persuasive information to customers to help them buy the products and services they need.
- **Transporting** Moving products from where they were made to where consumers can buy them.
- **Storing** Holding products until customers need them. Products are stored in locations such as on shelves, in storage rooms, and in warehouses.
- **Financing** Providing money to pay for the various marketing activities. Financing includes obtaining credit when buying and extending credit when selling.

FACTS & FIGURES

Value

Consumers see a relationship between product benefits and the product price. This is called value. There is a mathematical formula for this relationship: Product Benefits ÷ Price = Value. A product is seen as having greater value if it offers more benefits for the same price or the same benefits at a lower price. One product may have more features or a better brand image but a higher price. Another product may be less expensive but have fewer benefits. Marketers often try to persuade consumers that a product has many benefits in order to justify a higher price. Often those benefits are intangible, such as high social value or status. Consumers may be willing to pay a higher price to fit in.

Storing is a common marketing activity. What are some others?

- **Researching** Studying buyer interests and needs, testing products, and gathering facts needed to make good marketing decisions.
- **Risk taking** Assuming the risk of losses that may occur from fire, theft, damage, or other circumstances.
- **Grading and valuing** Grouping goods according to size, quality, or other characteristics, and determining an appropriate price for products and services.

COST OF MARKETING

Whether the product is paper clips for offices or huge generators for utility companies, businesses must perform all eight marketing activities just described as the product moves from producer to customer. Because performing these activities requires many people and special equipment, the cost of marketing a product is sometimes higher than the cost of making that product. Therefore, perhaps half or more of the price you pay for a product may result from marketing expenses. Although this amount may appear high, the well-spent marketing dollar contributes much to the success of products and businesses as well as to the satisfaction of customers. Good marketing makes the product or service available to customers when and where they want it.

ROLE OF MARKETING

Marketing's role changes as environmental conditions change. Marketing has not always been an important part of business. In the early 1900s, business conditions were much different than they are now. Customers had only a few products to choose from and a limited amount of money to spend. Usually only a few producers manufactured a product, and the manufacturing process was not very efficient. Demand for most products was greater than the supply. As a result, most producers concentrated on making more kinds of products in greater quantities. Under these conditions, firms were **production-oriented**; that is, decisions about what and how to produce received the most attention. Businesses did not have to worry a great deal about marketing.

When production becomes efficient and more businesses offer similar products, competition among businesses increases. Each business has to work harder to sell its products to customers when customers see they have many choices. Companies must emphasize distribution to get their products to more customers. In addition, advertising and selling become important marketing tools as businesses try to convince customers that their products are the best. Production may be considered the most important activity, but it is not enough for a business to be successful. Under these conditions, businesses may become **sales-oriented**; that is, they emphasize widespread distribution and promotion to sell their products.

Figure 20-1 A marketing executive plays a key role in the strategic planning of a business.

In many product categories today, consumers realize they can choose from a wide range of goods and services. Many businesses are competing with one another to sell the same product. But companies realize that it is not enough just to produce a variety of products; they must produce the *right* products. Companies that produce what customers want and make buying easy for customers will be more successful than those that do not.

Today, more and more businesses are focusing on customer needs. They have become **customer-oriented**; that is they direct the activities of the company toward satisfying customers. Keeping the needs of the consumer uppermost in mind during the design, production, and distribution of a product is called the **marketing concept**.

A company that has adopted the marketing concept has a marketing executive who is part of top management and is involved in all major decisions, as illustrated in Figure 20-1. Marketing personnel work closely with the other people in the business to make sure the company keeps the needs of customers in mind in all operations. The company's success is determined by more than current profits. Profit is important, but long-term success depends on satisfying customers so that they will continue to buy from the company.

 **CHECKPOINT**

List the eight most common marketing activities.

20.1 ASSESSMENT

UNDERSTAND MANAGEMENT CONCEPTS
Determine the best answer for each of the following questions.

1. Marketing department employees do which of the following?
   a. market research
   b. product design
   c. product sales
   d. all of the above

2. A business that focuses on widespread distribution and promotion is
   a. production-oriented
   b. sales-oriented
   c. customer-oriented
   d. market-oriented

THINK CRITICALLY
Answer the following questions as completely as possible.

3. Explain why marketing is an important activity in an economy.

4. Explain why the costs of marketing a product are justified.

Elements of Marketing

Goals

- Describe the role that market determination plays in marketing.
- Define basic marketing concepts and the four elements of the marketing mix.

Terms

- market p. 548
- market research p. 549
- target markets p. 549
- positioning chart p. 549
- marketing mix p. 549
- product p. 550
- price p. 550
- distribution (place) p. 551
- promotion p. 551

●●● Market Identification

Before a company decides to make and distribute a product, marketing managers must identify the market to be served. Here, **market** refers to the types of buyers a business wishes to attract and where those buyers are located. All companies need to clearly identify their markets.

WHOM TO SERVE

There are many potential customers for a product. Some people may be searching for the product, whereas others do not currently want the product and will have to be convinced to buy it. Some people are very easy to reach, but others are more difficult. For cost reasons, it is usually unwise to try to reach all potential customers. Therefore, a business identifies several groups of potential customers and then decides which group or groups will be the best markets for its product.

Marketing managers often develop customer profiles based on population characteristics, such as age, gender, family status, education, income, and occupation, in which to group consumers. A clothing manufacturer, for example, could handle women's or men's clothing, clothing for children or adults, casual clothing or the latest high fashion, and so on. The producer of cellular telephones may want to attract families, people concerned about their safety, or businesspeople. A business can decide to serve one or more markets. Companies choose a market based on the opportunities for success that the market presents. For example, an attractive market may have few existing competitors, a large number of customers with a need for the product, and customers with sufficient money to spend on such a product. If the business has the ability to produce a product that will satisfy the needs of that market, then it is a good market for the business to serve.

WHERE TO SERVE

Producers often limit the scope of their business operations to certain geographic areas. Marketing managers study sections of a city, state, country, or continent to determine whether their product might sell more successfully in one area than another. Climate, for example, may cause a small producer of air conditioners to concentrate its marketing efforts on countries with hot and humid climates, whereas the maker of snow skis may concentrate on areas with cold winters and mountains. Some products may sell better on the coasts than in the middle of the country, or in rural areas better than in cities. Finding the best marketing locations enables a business to achieve the most sales for its marketing dollar.

IDENTIFYING TARGET MARKETS

Companies can produce goods and services that meet consumers' needs better if they know who their customers are, where they are located, and what they want and need. Many companies spend a great deal of money on market research before they begin to develop products. **Market research** is the study of a company's current and prospective customers.

Companies use market research to identify their target markets. **Target markets** are groups of customers with very similar needs to whom the company plans to sell its product. If the company can find a group of people with very similar needs, it can more easily produce a product that will satisfy everyone in the group. On the other hand, if people in the group have needs that are quite different, it will be almost impossible to develop a product that will satisfy each of them.

Imagine developing a product like a bicycle. It can be made in a variety of sizes and shapes with a number of special features. No one bicycle will satisfy everyone's needs. Long-distance racers want something very different from what the weekend rider desires. However, if you could find a group of people with very similar needs, you could successfully design a bicycle for that group. A **positioning chart** can identify alternate market segments with unique needs based on major choice criteria. In the positioning chart in Figure 20-2, the choice criteria would be price and performance.

Positioning Chart for Target Market for Bicycles

High / Low — PERFOMANCE

Low — PRICE — High

Mountain Biking

Competitive Biking

Lightweight Touring

Leisure Biking

Age 6–10 (First Bike)

© Cengage Learning 2013.

Figure 20-2 A positioning chart can show the relative market shares for alternative markets.

CHECKPOINT

List six customer profile characteristics that can be used to identify markets.

The Marketing Mix

Marketing managers have many decisions to make. These decisions center on four elements of marketing: (1) the *product*, (2) its *price*, (3) *distribution* (sometimes referred to as *place*), and (4) *promotion*. Planning each element involves answering some important questions. For example, assume that you want to market a new product. You must answer the following questions related to the four elements of marketing: (1) Will you make the product in one size and color, or in several? (2) Will you price the product high, medium, or low? (3) Will you sell the product in retail stores or over the Internet? (4) Will you use newspaper, radio, television, or Internet advertising?

The blend of all decisions related to the four elements of marketing—product, price, distribution, and promotion—is called the **marketing mix**. The marketing mix

Coffeehouses are a popular place for people to meet and socialize. Which elements of the marketing mix should a new competitor focus on to attract customers?

for a new product may be to design the item for young adults, give it a low price, sell it through retail stores, and advertise it on the radio. Or it could be to produce a medium-priced item to be advertised on television and sold door-to-door to senior citizens. Can you identify the marketing mix for one of the businesses that Tony Taylor thought about in the chapter-opening scenario?

Several companies marketing the same product may use very different marketing mixes, because they made different decisions. Furthermore, they must review their decisions frequently, because conditions change constantly. Changes in general economic conditions, changes in consumer needs, and the development of new or improved products by competitors are factors that may require a change in the marketing mix. Next, you will learn about the decisions involved in each marketing mix element.

PRODUCT

The first marketing mix element is the product. **Product** can be defined as all attributes, both tangible and intangible, that customers receive in exchange for the purchase price. For example, when consumers buy a computer, they are also buying the company's customer service and technical support as well as other intangibles, such as the prestige of the brand name. All of these attributes are part of the product. Products include services as well as physical goods. A critical question relating to the product is: What do customers want? Product planning and development deal with finding answers to that question.

By identifying the target market for a product and knowing what customers in that market want, the company can design a product to fit those customers. Market information can help marketing managers develop a product strategy that includes decisions such as:

1. The *number* of items to produce.
2. The *physical features* the product should possess, such as size, shape, color, and weight.
3. The *quality* preferred by the target market.
4. The *number of different models* and the *features* of each model needed to serve the various markets the company wants to attract.
5. The *packaging features* of the item, such as the color and the shape of the package, as well as the information printed on it.
6. The brand name.
7. Product *guarantees* and *services* the customers would like.
8. The *image* to be communicated to customers by the product's features, packaging, and brand name.

PRICE

The second mix element around which marketing decisions are made is price. **Price** is the amount of money given to acquire a product. The many decisions a company makes during product development influence the price. First, the price

21st CENTURY SKILLS

Accountability

Marketing may have one of the worst ethical reputations in business, often because marketing is seen as pushing products on people who may not need them, promoting products with half-truths, and pricing products unfairly. Today marketing managers need to be concerned about maintaining long-term relationships and being accountable for their actions.

must be high enough to cover the costs of producing and marketing the product. If the company decides to manufacture a high-quality product, it would likely have to set a higher price to cover its costs than it would for a low-quality product. The number of competing products and their prices, the demand for the product, and whether the product will be sold for cash or credit are some of the many other factors that influence price decisions.

When making price decisions, a company must do more than just set a price that customers will pay for the product. It must decide what price to charge other companies that buy and resell the product. Will the company offer coupons, discounts, or other promotional bonuses to attract customers? Will it allow customers to bargain for a lower price or trade in a used product for a new one? As you can see, pricing is not an easy marketing decision.

DISTRIBUTION

The third element around which marketing decisions are made is distribution. Distribution decisions relate to the economic concept of place utility. *Place utility* means that the product must be in a place where customers need or want it. **Distribution** (or **place**), therefore, is the set of activities required to transport and store products and make them available to customers.

Marketing managers must select businesses to handle products as they move from the producer to the consumer. Many manufacturers prefer to use other businesses to sell their products rather than try to reach consumers directly. Therefore, they may sell their products to retailers or to wholesalers, which then sell to retailers. Choosing the various routes that products will follow as they are distributed and the businesses that will sell them to consumers are important marketing decisions.

Planning distribution also includes the actual physical handling of the products and the customer service provided when orders are processed. Have you ever opened a product you purchased, only to find it damaged or missing pieces? Have you ordered something from a catalog or the Internet and received the wrong merchandise or no merchandise at all? Each of these examples describes a problem with a company's distribution system and will result in dissatisfied customers as well as a loss of sales and profits for the company.

PROMOTION

The fourth marketing mix element for which decisions must be made is promotion. **Promotion** means providing information to consumers that will assist them in making a decision and persuade them to purchase a product or service. The major methods of promotion are advertising and personal selling. You will learn about other types of promotion in a later chapter.

Promotional decisions for a digital camera might involve selecting advertising as the main vehicle and deciding whether to advertise in magazines or by direct mail to prospective customers. Marketing managers decide when and how frequently to advertise. Then they must decide whether to stage product demonstrations in stores or at

Management MATTERS

Managing Marketing Management

Marketing managers must be able to work with professionals in a wide variety of business disciplines to develop marketing plans. For example, developing a new product or entering a new market requires working with researchers, designers, manufacturers, and shippers. At the same time, finance and accounting professionals must evaluate the profitability of any proposed expansion. This process is even more complicated when entering international markets or dealing with global competitors. Marketing managers need strong communication skills. They also need cross-functional knowledge in order to understand the perspectives of everyone involved in getting products to markets.

What Do You Think? What skills would you need to have to be a marketing manager? Why would having cross-functional knowledge be important for a marketing manager?

consumer electronics shows. Managers must also decide the type of information to communicate to consumers and whether to try to communicate directly with each customer or use more impersonal messages that can reach a larger audience at a time.

The type of product and its price influence promotional decisions. The strategy for promoting an expensive piece of jewelry will be much different from that for promoting tennis shoes.

Although the product and its price provide general guides for promotion, marketing managers must consider many other factors before developing the actual promotions. For example, the company will budget only a certain amount of money for promotion. Managers must decide when to spend the money and how much to spend on advertising, displays, and other types of promotion. They must consider what promotions competitors are using and what information consumers need in order to decide to buy.

CHECKPOINT

List the elements of a marketing mix.

20.2 ASSESSMENT

UNDERSTAND MANAGEMENT CONCEPTS

Determine the best answer for each of the following questions.

1. Groups of customers with very similar needs to whom the company plans to sell its product are called the
   a. target customers
   b. target consumers
   c. target market
   d. target groups

2. The four elements of the marketing mix include all of the following except
   a. product
   b. price
   c. customer
   d. promotion

THINK CRITICALLY

Answer the following questions as completely as possible.

3. Explain how companies identify their markets.

4. Describe what a customer receives in exchange for a purchase price.

Marketing Plan

Goals

- Describe the role of a marketing plan.
- Explain the four stages of the product life cycle.
- Identify the consumer goods classifications.

Terms

- marketing plan p. 553
- product life cycle p. 554
- introduction stage p. 554
- growth stage p. 554
- maturity stage p. 554
- decline stage p. 555

- industrial goods p. 555
- consumer goods p. 556
- convenience goods p. 556
- shopping goods p. 556
- specialty goods p. 556
- unsought goods p. 557

●●● Developing a Marketing Plan

All the marketing decisions for a particular product must work together for the product to succeed. For example, advertising may be timed to coincide with a product's introduction. To help coordinate marketing activities, businesses develop marketing plans. The **marketing plan** is a detailed written description of all marketing activities that a business must accomplish in order to sell its products. It describes the goals the business wants to accomplish, the target markets it wants to serve, the marketing mixes it will use for each product, and the tactics that make up the marketing strategy. It identifies the ways in which the business will evaluate its marketing to determine if the activities were successful and the goals were accomplished. The marketing plan is written for a specific time period (often one year).

The marketing managers develop the marketing plan, based on information from many other people. Market research is very important in developing a marketing plan. Once a written plan is completed, all of the people involved in marketing activities can use it to guide their decisions about each marketing mix element and to coordinate their efforts as they complete the planned activities.

SUCCESSFUL MARKETING STRATEGIES

Marketing managers cannot afford to guess about which types of marketing mixes to use. Marketing is too expensive and customers have too many choices for businesses to risk making mistakes. Marketers use concepts such as the product life cycle and consumer goods categories to plan effective marketing mixes. For example, if a product is in the growth stage, the mix will be quite different than if it is in the maturity stage. If consumers view a product as a specialty good, marketers will emphasize different mix elements than if it is a convenience good. Marketers study markets and competition and use their knowledge of marketing to make decisions that will satisfy customer needs and result in a profit for the company.

 CHECKPOINT

List the marketing activities that should be included in a marketing plan.

●●● The Product Life Cycle

Successful products move through fairly predictable stages throughout their product lives. They are introduced, and then their sales and profits increase rapidly to a point at which they level off. Eventually, both profits and sales decline as newer products replace the old ones. The **product life cycle** consists of the four stages of sales and profit performance through which all brands of a product progress: introduction, growth, maturity, and decline. The product life cycle usually describes an industry's progression. Figure 20-3 is a graphical depiction of sales and profits at different stages of the product life cycle.

INTRODUCTION

In the **introduction stage**, a brand-new product enters the market. Initially, there is only one brand of the product available for consumers to purchase. The new product is quite different from, and expected to be better than, products customers are currently using. Examples of products that were recently in the introduction stage include video conferencing cellular telephones, 3-D televisions, and small portable tablet computers.

When a company introduces a product, it is concerned about successfully producing and distributing it. The company needs to inform prospective customers about the brand-new product and its uses, because people will be unfamiliar with it. There is no competition from the same type of product, but customers are probably using other, older products. The company must show customers how the new product is better than the products they are currently using. Initially, only a few customers will buy the product, but their experience will often determine whether other people will want to buy it as well.

The costs of producing and marketing a new product are usually very high, resulting in a loss or very low profits for the firm initially. The company is counting on future sales to make a profit. If a product is successfully introduced, an increasing number of consumers will accept it, sales will rise rapidly, and profits will grow.

GROWTH

When competitors see the success of the new product, they will want to get into that market as well. When several brands of the new product are available, the market moves into the **growth stage** of the life cycle. If customers like the new product, they will begin buying it regularly and telling others about it, so more and more customers become regular purchasers.

In the growth stage, each company tries to attract customers to its own brand. Companies attempt to improve their brands by adding features that they hope will satisfy customers. They also add to their distribution to make the product more readily available to the growing market. Most companies make a profit in this stage. Profits are likely to increase as companies sell enough of the product to cover the research and development costs. Examples of products that have been in the growth stage recently are digital video cameras, smartphones, and wireless computers.

MATURITY

A product in the maturity stage has been purchased by large numbers of customers and has become quite profitable. In the **maturity stage**, the product is competing with

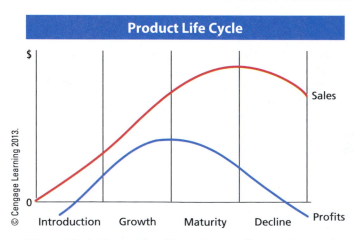

Figure 20-3 The product life cycle typically describes the change in sales of product categories over time.

many other brands with very similar features. Customers have a hard time identifying differences among the brands but may have developed a loyalty to one or a very few brands.

In this stage, companies emphasize the promotion of their brand name, packaging, a specific image, and often the price of the product. Because there are so many customers, each business has to distribute the product widely, adding to their costs. Competition becomes intense. Companies must spend a lot on promotion and reduce prices, because customers have many brands from which to choose. Profits usually fall even though sales may still rise. Products in the maturity stage include automobiles, desktop computers, personal-care products such as toothpaste and deodorant, and many other products that you use regularly and purchase without a great deal of thought.

One way that businesses respond to the maturity stage of the life cycle is to look for new markets. Businesses often move into international markets as competition increases in their home countries. As several fast-food companies found fewer and fewer attractive locations for new stores in the United States, they began to open outlets in Canada, Europe, and Mexico. Now they are expanding into South America and even into Russia and China.

How might a fast-food company respond to the maturity stage of the product life cycle?

DECLINE

Many products stay in the maturity stage of the life cycle for a long time. However, sooner or later products move into a decline stage. The **decline stage** occurs when a new product is introduced that is much better or easier to use and customers begin to switch from the old product to the new product. As more and more customers are attracted to the new product, the companies selling the old product see declines in profits and sales. The companies may not be able to improve the older products enough to compete with the new products, so they drop them from the market when declining profits no longer support their existence.

Some companies have been able to move old products out of the decline stage by finding new uses for them. For example, petroleum vapor rubs are being used for fungus infections, and baking soda is used to remove odors from refrigerators and cat litter boxes. If companies cannot save a product from the decline stage, they attempt to sell their remaining inventory to the customers who still prefer it. However, they spend as little money as possible on marketing the product and do not produce any more.

 **CHECKPOINT**

Identify the stages of a product life cycle.

●●● Product Categories

When making marketing decisions, marketing managers need to understand how customers shop for and use products. Products can be classified as either industrial goods or consumer goods. **Industrial goods** are products designed for use by another business. Frequently, industrial goods are purchased in large quantities, are made to special order for a specific customer, or are sold to a selected group of buyers within a limited geographic area. Examples of industrial goods include bricks purchased by a building contractor, aluminum purchased by an aircraft manufacturer, and computers and computer supplies purchased by accounting firms. Many, but not all, industrial goods are used to produce other products or are incorporated into the products being produced. Some are used in the operation of the business.

Consumer goods are products designed for personal or home use. Jewelry, furniture, magazines, soft drinks, and computer games are some of the many products used by consumers. Consumer goods require careful marketing attention, because there are so many products and brands available and so many possible customers throughout the world.

Depending on who is making the purchase and how they will use it, a product may be both a consumer good and an industrial good. Gasoline and laptop computers, for instance, may be purchased by consumers in small quantities or by businesses in large quantities.

TYPES OF CONSUMER PRODUCTS

To look at the attributes of consumer goods more specifically, marketers group them into four categories: convenience goods, shopping goods, specialty goods, and unsought goods. The categories are based on (1) how important the product is to the customer and (2) whether the customer is willing to spend time to compare products and brands before making a decision to buy. Companies make different marketing decisions, depending on which category of consumer goods they are selling.

CONVENIENCE GOODS **Convenience goods** are inexpensive items that consumers purchase regularly without a great deal of thought. Consumers are not willing to shop around for these products because they purchase them often, the many competing products do not differ much from each other, and they don't cost much money. Therefore, marketers must sell their convenience goods through many retail outlets that are conveniently located close to where people work and live. Products that are usually treated as convenience goods are candy, milk, soft drinks, pencils, soap, and many other inexpensive household items.

How are specialty goods different from other types of goods?

© Getty Images/Digital Vision

SHOPPING GOODS Products that consumers purchase less frequently than convenience goods, usually have a higher price, and require some buying thought are called **shopping goods**. Customers see important differences between brands in terms of price and features. Therefore, they are willing to shop at several businesses and compare products and brands before they make a purchase. Shopping goods do not have to be sold in as many places as convenience goods. They need effective promotion so customers can make informed decisions. Cars, furniture, large appliances, and houses are all examples of shopping goods for most people.

SPECIALTY GOODS **Specialty goods** are products that customers insist on having and are willing to search for until they find them. Customers who decide that only one product or brand will satisfy them will shop until they locate and buy that brand. Marketers place their specialty goods in fewer businesses within a shopping area, price them higher than competing products and brands, and need not promote them as much as other types of consumer products. Examples of specialty goods are designer clothing, expensive jewelry, and certain brands of cameras, computers, and automobiles.

UNSOUGHT GOODS Customers do not shop for some products because they do not have a strong need for them. Such products are known as **unsought goods**, and they present a difficult marketing problem. Life insurance, cemetery plots, and funeral services are unsought by most consumers. A company marketing unsought goods usually has to go to the customer and use personal selling to discuss the need for the product. Unless the customer recognizes a need that the product can satisfy, the product will remain unsold.

Many consumer complaints today involve marketing activities. Misleading advertisements, poor customer service, high prices, and poor delivery are all marketing problems. Managers must be as careful in making marketing decisions as they need to be in producing a quality product.

 **CHECKPOINT**

List the four different categories of consumer goods.

20.3 ASSESSMENT

UNDERSTAND MANAGEMENT CONCEPTS

Determine the best answer for each of the following questions.

1. The product life cycle stage in which there is only one brand of a product available for consumers to purchase is the
   a. introduction stage
   b. growth stage
   c. maturity stage
   d. decline stage

2. Products that customers insist on having and are willing to search for until they find them are called
   a. convenience goods
   b. shopping goods
   c. specialty goods
   d. unsought goods

THINK CRITICALLY

Answer the following questions as completely as possible.

3. Explain why a product's life cycle stage influences marketing strategy.

4. Describe the factors that influence consumer goods classification.

Marketing to Children

Marketing to children continues to be a controversial issue. The Federal Trade Commission's Children's Online Privacy Protection Act requires publishers of children's websites to post comprehensive privacy policies on their sites. In addition, the sites must notify parents about their information practices and obtain parental consent before collecting any personal information from children under age 13.

Retailers that Changed Business

Most manufacturers of consumer goods rely on retailers to provide the connection with the customers who will purchase their products. The retailers purchase the products from the manufacturer, stock them in stores that are close to where customers live, advertise and sell the products, and often offer delivery of the products and many customer services. Retailers provide these important marketing functions for manufacturers.

A few retailers have changed the way business is done. Because of their ideas, they forced their competitors to respond or risk going out of business.

One of the first was Sears Roebuck. In the late 1800s and early 1900s, some of the largest retailers reached their customers by mail. They sent catalogs to people all over the country and filled customer orders by mail or by shipping in trucks and trains. Sears decided customers wanted faster service and the opportunity to examine merchandise before making a purchase. The company began building large stores filled with a wide variety of products. Customers flocked to the stores, and Sears became the largest retailer in the world.

Sears stores were located in large and mid-size cities. Sam Walton saw opportunities in the thousands of small communities around the country. Walmart grew because of its emphasis on carefully chosen locations, working with manufacturers to buy at the lowest prices, developing an efficient product distribution system, and creating a friendly shopping experience. Because of those efforts, Walmart could offer lower prices than most other retailers. With this new philosophy of retailing, Walmart replaced Sears as the world's largest retailer.

Today, a new form of retailing is advancing, led by Jeff Bezos, who recognized the potential of Internet commerce. By developing an easy-to-use website and offering customers secure online transactions, rapid product delivery, and effective customer service, Amazon.com developed into the largest e-retailer, with revenues approaching $35 billion.

In each example, the success of the companies resulted from finding new ways to offer products and services to consumers. By performing marketing activities more effectively than its competitors, each company has become a leading retailer.

THINK CRITICALLY

1. Why were major retailers using catalogs and mail order in the late 1800s and early 1900s to sell products to their customers? What changes were occurring in the United States that provided the opportunity for Sears Roebuck to change the way products were sold?

2. Review the eight marketing activities described in the chapter and suggest which of the activities were most important to the success of Walmart. Why were many of Walmart's competitors not able to offer the same low prices to customers?

© Shutterstock/Rick Becker-Leckrone

CHAPTER CONCEPTS

- Marketing helps to balance the supply of products with the demand for those products. The goal of effective marketing is to create and maintain satisfying exchanges between buyers and sellers. Every business is involved in marketing.

- Marketing involves eight activities: buying, selling, transporting, storing, financing, researching, risk taking, and grading and valuing.

- A business may be production-oriented, sales-oriented, or customer-oriented. The marketing concept focuses on the needs of consumers during the design, production, and distribution of a product.

- Businesses use marketing research to identify target markets—customers with very similar needs that the business wants to serve.

- Marketing decisions center on the four elements of the marketing mix: product, price, distribution, and promotion. A marketing plan describes the goals the business wants to accomplish, the target markets it wants to serve, the marketing mixes it will use for each product, and the tactics that make up the marketing strategy.

- The product life cycle consists of four stages: introduction, growth, maturity, and decline.

- Consumer goods can be classified as convenience, shopping, specialty, or unsought goods, based on their importance to consumers and how much time they are willing to spend making buying decisions.

REVIEW BUSINESS MANAGEMENT TERMS

Write the letter of the term that matches each definition. Some terms will not be used.

1. Businesses that sell directly to final consumers
2. Keeping the needs of the consumer uppermost in mind during the design, production, and distribution of a product
3. Emphasizing widespread distribution and promotion to sell products
4. Types of buyers a business wishes to attract and where those buyers are located
5. The study of a company's current and prospective customers
6. Groups of customers with very similar needs to whom the company plans to sell its product
7. All attributes, both tangible and intangible, that customers receive in exchange for the purchase price
8. Detailed written description of all marketing activities that a business must accomplish to sell its products
9. Set of activities required to transport and store products and make them available to customers
10. Blend of all decisions related to the four elements of marketing—product, price, distribution, and promotion
11. Amount of money given to acquire a product
12. Product life cycle stage in which several brands of the new product are available

a. customer-oriented firm
b. distribution (place)
c. growth stage
d. market
e. market research
f. marketing concept
g. marketing mix
h. marketing plan
i. maturity stage
j. price
k. product
l. retailers
m. sales-oriented firm
n. target markets

Determine the best answer.

13. Businesses that buy products from businesses and sell them to other businesses are called
   a. industrial companies
   b. marketer retailers
   c. wholesalers
   d. retailers

14. A _____ producer concentrates on making more kinds of products in greater quantities.
   a. production-oriented
   b. sales-oriented
   c. market-oriented
   d. product-oriented

15. The four stages of sales and profit performance through which a product progresses are called the
   a. product categories
   b. marketing mix
   c. product life cycle
   d. product evolutionary cycle

16. In the _____ stage, a brand-new product enters the market and there is only one brand of the product available for consumers to purchase.
   a. introduction
   b. growth
   c. maturity
   d. decline

17. In the _____ stage, there are many competing brands with very similar features and customers have a hard time identifying differences among the brands.
   a. introduction
   b. growth
   c. maturity
   d. decline

18. Inexpensive items that consumers purchase regularly without a great deal of thought are called
   a. convenience goods
   b. consumer goods
   c. shopping goods
   d. specialty goods

19. Providing money for various marketing activities, such as by obtaining credit when buying and extending credit when selling, is called
   a. granting credit
   b. setting price
   c. financing
   d. risk taking

APPLY WHAT YOU KNOW

Answer the following questions.

20. Describe the ways that trucking companies, banks, and warehouses are marketing businesses.
21. Explain why it is important to conduct market research to determine the markets to be served before deciding what to produce and sell.
22. Describe how customers might know if a company has a customer orientation rather than a sales orientation.
23. What are some examples of goods or services that would sell well only in specific geographic locations?
24. Describe how the price is influenced by the other three elements of the marketing mix. What could a marketing manager do with other mix elements to increase or decrease a product's price?

MAKE ACADEMIC CONNECTIONS

Complete the following activities.

25. **Math** Complete the following table for the four products listed by determining the total cost of each product and the percentage of the final product price that was spent on marketing.

	Product 1	Product 2	Product 3	Product 4
Retail Price	$45.20	$576.00	$32,750.00	$4.80
Raw Materials	6.20	28.00	12,650.00	.78
Other Product Costs	3.80	56.50	2,500.00	.14
Operating Expenses	4.30	74.00	4,825.00	.32
Marketing Expenses	14.90	96.50	3,500.00	2.50

26. **Research** Interview 10 people to determine how they purchase jeans. Ask each of them the following questions: Where do you usually buy your jeans? What product features are important to you? How important is price in your decision to purchase jeans? Do you usually buy one brand? Do you usually look in several stores before you buy a pair of jeans?

    Based on each person's answers, determine whether he or she is treating jeans as a convenience, shopping, specialty, or unsought good. Write a short report discussing your findings and your conclusions. Include a chart or graph illustrating your findings.
27. **Speaking** Participate in a debate with other class members. Your teacher will assign you to one side of the issue or the other and will give you specific instructions and guidelines. The issue is: Marketing causes people to spend money for things they otherwise would not buy and do not need.
28. **Technology** Use the Internet to find examples that illustrate each of the four elements of the marketing mix—product, price, distribution, and promotion. Use presentation software such as PowerPoint to link to examples and to the concept of a marketing mix.

CASE IN POINT

CASE 20-1: Computer Life Cycle

The personal computer market has evolved over time. Sales of desktop models to home users have become extremely competitive, and it is increasingly difficult for manufacturers to make a profit from desktop computers. In addition, technology changes rapidly. If a company has not sold its inventory of one desktop model when a competitor introduces a newer, faster, more powerful model, it often must sell its older model at a loss. Many computer purchasers are not loyal to a particular brand. They look for low price or expect the manufacturer to include related products, such as a monitor, printer, scanner, or software with the new computer. Portable personal laptop models have increased in sales as prices have dropped.

Online computer sellers have created considerable competition for traditional store outlets. Many consumers today do not believe they need much technical advice when they buy computers. Businesses are also buying online because they can configure computers to meet their own needs.

The newest categories of portable personal computers include wireless tablets and netbook computers. In 2010, netbooks accounted for more than 20 percent of laptop sales. However, some people are not thinking about tablets or netbooks. They are ready to move their Internet access to their cell phones and digital TVs. These customers may not buy any personal computers at all.

THINK CRITICALLY

1. Which stage of the product life cycle do you believe desktop computers are in, based on the case information? Why?
2. Explain how this stage affects the price of computers.
3. Are computers industrial or consumer products? Explain your answer.
4. In which consumer product category do you believe consumers classify computers, based on the case information? Why?
5. How does your product category choice in question 4 fit with companies' ability to sell computers on the Internet? Explain your answer.
6. At what stage of the product life cycle do you believe tablet computers and netbooks fit? Explain your answer.
7. How likely are all variations of personal computers to move through the product life cycle into the decline stage?

CASE 20-2: Appliance Marketing Mix

The Willomette Company manufactures small household appliances, such as toasters, blenders, and food processors. Ron Willomette started the company 20 years ago as a sole proprietorship. Initially, Mr. Willomette reconditioned and resold used appliances that other companies had manufactured. Now he has incorporated the business and has two manufacturing plants that produce his own brand of appliances. The Willomette Company has a full line of over 50 models of products that are sold throughout the United States.

Willomette appliances are higher priced than many other national brands and imported products. They are usually sold through smaller non-chain-store outlets. Willomette usually advertises in kitchen design magazines and other media that cater to higher-income consumers.

In the past five years, competition from foreign companies in the small-appliance market has increased. The competition hasn't hurt Willomette yet, but company executives don't want to wait until sales and profits start to decline before acting. One vice president recommended that Willomette begin a program of international marketing. Based on the traveling she has done, she believes that the demand for Willomette's appliances would be very strong in Europe and several countries in Africa and South America. Because there has been strong customer acceptance of the company's products in the United States, she believes Willomette should have no trouble selling the same products in other countries.

THINK CRITICALLY

1. Which stage of the product life cycle do you believe Willomette is in, based on the case information? Why?
2. In which consumer product category do you believe consumers would classify Willomette's products, based on the case information? Why?
3. Describe the elements of Willomette's marketing mix.
4. Describe the target market that you believe might be attracted to Willomette appliances.
5. Which of the major marketing activities would Willomette have to perform to sell its products in international markets?
6. How does the marketing concept relate to the decision Willomette must make about entering international markets?
7. Do you agree that products that are successful in the United States will also be successful in other countries? Explain.
8. What would Willomette have to do if it wanted to increase the demand for its products in the United States by selling industrial products?

© Shutterstock/Dudarev Mikhail

PROJECT My Own Business

Market Planning

To market your products effectively, you will need to identify the target market for your business. Then you must determine how customers will view your product as they make decisions to buy. The activities in this section of the project will help you understand your customers so you can develop an effective marketing mix.

DATA COLLECTION

1. Locate books, newspaper and magazine articles, Internet resources, and other information sources that describe people who are interested in healthy lifestyles and nutrition. Make a list of the sources of information that will help you describe possible target markets for your juice bar and provide brief descriptions of the information in each of the sources you list.

2. Review advertisements from other businesses that might compete with your juice bar. For each business, prepare a description of the target market it appears to be appealing to and the key part of its marketing mix that it is advertising.

3. Using library or Internet resources, locate several marketing-oriented magazines or trade journals that you could consult for information. Also identify some marketing-related professional organizations or trade associations that might be helpful to you.

ANALYSIS

1. Using the categories of consumer goods listed in the chapter, determine if customers will treat your product as a convenience, shopping, specialty, or unsought good. Describe how that decision will influence the way you market your products.

2. Markets are made up of many segments of people with one or more similar characteristics. Segments of a market can be identified that have one or more strong needs or wants in common. What market segment(s) can you identify for your product?

3. Develop a detailed customer profile of one or more target markets that you can serve successfully. Make sure that your profile description includes both an identification of the target market and the important needs of the market that are related to your product.

4. Develop a set of questions that you would use to collect information from your target market so that you can be market-oriented in your marketing offerings.

5. Prepare a general description of the marketing mix you believe would satisfy the consumers in your target market. Develop a marketing plan that describes the goals your business should accomplish, the target market you want to serve, the marketing mix you will use, and the tactics that make up your marketing strategy.

CHAPTER 21

PRODUCT DEVELOPMENT AND DISTRIBUTION

21.1 Product Management

21.2 Distribution Management

21.3 Channel Design

© Shutterstock/Radu Razvan

Reality Check

Decisions, Decisions

Alexis Converse sat at her computer in the purchasing manager's office late into the night. She was challenged by a crisis facing her company. A major piece of manufacturing equipment had failed today and could not be repaired. Each day that the equipment was not operational would cost the company several thousand dollars in lost production and sales.

The machine was over 10 years old, and it had worked well for most of the time the company owned it. In discussing its replacement with the production manager, Alexis agreed that they should replace the machine with the same brand. However, there were now two new models to consider. Alexis could purchase the equipment directly from the manufacturer in Italy or from an equipment distributor located two states away. It would take the manufacturer eight days to deliver, whereas the distributor could have one model available in two days and the other in four.

Alexis was concerned about installation and maintenance. She wanted to make sure the new machine would not break down. The manufacturer had a specialist who would travel to the plant to install the equipment and make sure it was working. The manufacturer also included a five-year warranty with on-site service, but the warranty added 25 percent to the cost of the equipment. Alexis had heard that the distributor could help with the installation but did not provide an additional warranty or service. Delays or problems in installation would only add to the company's losses.

All Alexis wanted to do was to get the equipment replaced and the company back into production. Why did these decisions have to be so difficult?

What's Your Reaction? What factors will Alexis need to consider in order to make a high-quality management decision?

Product Management

Goals

- Explain how products, product lines, and product assortments are developed.
- Discuss how product selection, packaging, and branding improve product sales and customer satisfaction.

Terms

- basic product p. 567
- enhanced product p. 567
- extended product p. 567
- product line p. 568
- product assortment p. 568
- brand p. 569

Product Development

Companies develop a marketing mix to satisfy customers and make a profit. The marketing mix is made up of the product, distribution, price, and promotion plans. Offering products that meet the needs of customers would seem to be a company's most important responsibility. The product is important, but it must be carefully coordinated with each of the other mix elements. In this chapter, we will examine how companies manage their products and make distribution decisions.

A *product* consists of all attributes, both tangible and intangible, that customers receive in exchange for the purchase price. It includes both physical goods and services. Some products are very simple and easy for the customer to understand and use, and others are very complex. Because of the variety of customer needs, the uses for products, and the number of competing companies producing and selling products, product development decisions must be made carefully. If companies produce the wrong products in the wrong quantities without the features and services customers need, they will have invested a great deal of time and money with no chance to sell the products at a profit. They will quickly lose out to competitors who make better product decisions.

Product managers need to ensure that the company's products satisfy customer needs. They need to ensure that the right products are designed, that the products are at the right location when needed by customers, and that the proper service, packaging, and branding enhance the product's value. The company that manufactures the machine Alexis needed to purchase at the beginning of the chapter designed a product to perform a specific production function. The company is expert in the technology of equipment design, so it builds what it believes to be a good product that customers will prefer over the alternatives. Alexis wants a good piece of equipment but is also very concerned about delivery, installation services, maintenance, and cost. If the equipment manufacturer does not carefully consider all of Alexis's needs, it probably won't make the sale.

Even the simplest products are made up of several components. An inexpensive handheld calculator consists of the operating unit to make the calculations, a case, display, and keys. It may be battery operated or use solar power or electricity. It could have a backlight to illuminate the display in the dark. It could be pocket- or desk-sized and be capable of special mathematical functions. Also, it might come in a variety of colors and include a protective case and an instruction manual. Given the combination of features, the price of the calculator could range from a few dollars to as much as $50 or more. If you were the person responsible for designing a calculator to sell, what combination of design features would you include? This example shows that product planning can be very complex. Businesses have many choices in designing products. In developing their product strategy, marketers pay close attention to their customers' needs and wishes.

PRODUCT DESIGN LEVELS

There are three levels of product design—a basic product, an enhanced product, and an extended product. The **basic product** is the physical product in its simplest form. It should be easy for consumers to understand and see how it can meet a need. The basic product of one company is usually similar to that of its competitors.

© Getty Images/Digital Vision

Why should a company make product development decisions very carefully?

The basic product will meet an important consumer need. However, most consumers are attempting to satisfy several needs at one time with a purchase, or they have very specific needs different from those of other consumers. In that case, the basic product will not be satisfactory. Therefore, a business develops an **enhanced product**. An enhanced product offers different features and options for the consumer. For example, a basic computer can be produced in desktop or laptop form. Other choices might include the size of the screen, the speed of the processor, and the memory capacity. If you visit the website of an online computer manufacturer, you can see the many options available to prospective purchasers. Choices are grouped by categories of customers, such as education, home, small business, and large enterprises, making it easier for customers to design the computer system they need.

The third level of product development is to plan extended products. An **extended product** includes additional features that are not part of the physical product but increase its usability. Examples are customer service, information on effective use of the products, and even additional products that improve the use of the original purchase. If you purchase a new tablet computer, you may want to purchase a service contract in case there is a problem. In addition, accessories such as an external keyboard could make keying easier. Some tablet computers require a wireless connection for printing. The right combination of choices allows customers to get just the right product to meet very specialized needs.

Companies may offer a warranty (a statement from the seller about the product's qualities or performance) or a guarantee (an assurance from the seller that a product will perform to your satisfaction for a certain period of time). This can help reassure the customer about the product.

 CHECKPOINT

List and define the three levels of product design.

Product Selection

After designing the product, product managers must make another set of decisions to plan the product mix element. The first decision is whether to offer a product line. A **product line** is a group of similar products with obvious variations in the design and quality to meet the needs of distinct customer groups. New and small companies may begin by offering only one category of product to its customers. That product may have choices of features, options, and enhancements, but the basic product is the same for all customers. With more experience and resources, the company may decide to expand its product line.

One of the obvious ways to expand a product line is to offer different sizes of the product. That can be done with the serving sizes of food items, as well as with the sizes of automobiles. As an example, when sports utility vehicles (SUVs) were first introduced, most manufacturers produced one midsize model, such as the Chevy Blazer or Ford Explorer. As the popularity of SUVs grew, manufacturers began to appeal to other market segments with smaller models, such as the Toyota RAV4, and then very large models, including the Mercury Mountaineer and Cadillac Escalade. Rising gas prices opened a market for fuel-efficient SUVs, such as Honda's CR-V. Some companies offer only one model size, but others have a model in each size category for a full product line.

Another way to develop a product line is to offer variations in quality and price. If you visit an appliance store, you will usually find low-, mid-, and high-priced choices for each type of appliance, such as refrigerators, dishwashers, and microwaves. The price differences are based on the construction, quality of materials, and available features and options. A person buying a microwave for a college dorm room probably does not want the most expensive, full-featured choice, and so will be drawn to the lower-priced end of the product line. On the other hand, a gourmet chef making a purchase for a new kitchen may want only the highest quality and latest features.

Once a company has made decisions about a product line, it continues planning by determining the product assortment. A **product assortment** is the complete set of all products a business offers to a market. A product assortment can have depth, breadth, or both. A company offering a deep product assortment carries a large number of choices of features for each product category it handles. Walk into a Bath and Body Works store and look at the variety of fragrances, colors, bottle sizes, and packages for any of the major products sold there. That is an example of a deep assortment. Compare that to the choices of bath lotions that you might find in a small drugstore, where the assortment would be limited.

With a broad product assortment, a business offers a large number of different but often related products to its customers. If you visit a garden center, you may find many different types of products for lawns and gardens, ranging from plants, shrubs, and trees to lawn mowers, hoses, and patio furniture. There may not be a wide range of choices within every product category, but customers

NETBookmark

It is often difficult to identify the total number of product lines a store carries by walking through the store. But product lines are often used to organize a customer's online shopping experience.

Access the website for this textbook and choose the link for Chapter 21 Net Bookmark. Look at the department drop down menu in the website. How do these indicate product lines? Click on one of the department links. Describe how this shows Walmart's online product assortment. Based on your research, how does the online site differ from Walmart stores you have visited?

www.cengage.com/school/bizmgmt

should be able to satisfy most of their outdoor home needs at one location. As shown in Figure 21-1, businesses can choose any combination of depth and breadth for their product assortment. Some will be very small and specialized, and others will offer a wide variety of many different products.

PACKAGING

Two important product mix decisions are packaging and branding. Neither decision is directly related to the actual physical product itself, but each can be an important influence on purchase decisions.

Most companies package their products before selling them. The package can serve four different purposes. First, it protects the product while it is being shipped and stored. Products can easily be damaged when they are grouped together for shipment from the factory to the retail store. Boxes and containers are needed for protection. The actual container or wrapping in which the individual product is packaged also offers protection on the store shelf and may provide security to keep the product from being lost or stolen.

Second, the package can provide important information to customers on product composition, special features, and proper use. Boxes and containers also provide information to shippers on appropriate handling, storage, and delivery.

A package can be designed to make the product easier to use. A plastic bottle of soda is less likely to be broken if dropped. An easy-opening lid or a container that fits the hands of the consumer makes product handling easier. Window cleaner that is premixed in a spray bottle is much more convenient than one that must be poured into a bucket and applied with a sponge.

Finally, especially for consumer products, the package is often an important promotional tool. A well-designed, attractive package calls attention to itself on the store shelf, helps the customer recall previously seen advertising, and provides a reminder of the needs that the product will satisfy if purchased.

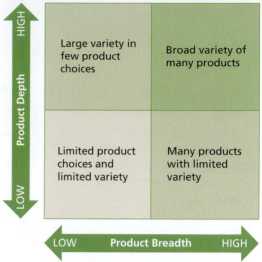

Product Assortment Matrix

	LOW **Product Breadth** HIGH
HIGH Product Depth	Large variety in few product choices / Broad variety of many products
LOW	Limited product choices and limited variety / Many products with limited variety

© Cengage Learning 2013.

Figure 21-1 Businesses build product assortment to meet their customers' needs.

BRANDING

Can you name the brands of clothing, pizza, and toothpaste you prefer? Do you and your friends regularly shop at certain stores but not others? Product and store brands play a major role in buying decisions. A **brand** is a name, symbol, word, or design that identifies a product, service, or company.

Why are brands so important to consumers? Have you ever shopped in a store that had generic (nonbranded) products or that sold only unfamiliar brands? With no information to guide you, it is difficult to make a product selection with which you are comfortable. You and people you trust have had experiences with various brands. If a particular company's products consistently meet your needs, you will likely buy from that company again. If you have a negative experience, however, you are likely to avoid similar purchases in the future. If you are satisfied with one product from a company, you are likely to have confidence in a different product sold under the same brand. Businesses understand that brand recognition is an important influence in increasing sales. The levels of consumer brand awareness are shown in Figure 21-2 (see p. 570).

What different purposes could the packaging of this product serve?

© Comstock

The Five Levels of Consumer Brand Awareness

- Consumers are unable to identify the brand.
- Consumers can identify the brand but it has little influence on their purchase decision.
- Consumers can identify the brand but will not purchase it because of its brand.
- Consumers easily recognize the brand and will choose it if it is available.
- Consumers view the brand as the most satisfying and will not purchase a different brand.

© Cengage Learning 2013.

Figure 21-2 Brand awareness does not always lead to a purchase decision.

✓ CHECKPOINT

Name four purposes of packaging.

21.1 ASSESSMENT

UNDERSTAND MANAGEMENT CONCEPTS

Determine the best answer for each of the following questions.

1. A(n) _____ product offers different features and options for the consumer.
   a. augmented
   b. basic
   c. enhanced
   d. extended

2. A group of similar products with obvious variations in design and quality to meet the needs of distinct customer groups is called a
   a. product assortment
   b. product mix
   c. product line
   d. product design

THINK CRITICALLY

Answer the following questions as completely as possible.

3. Describe the different perceptions of a product that are usually held by businesspeople and consumers.

4. Explain how a business can expand its product line.

Distribution Management

Goals

- Discuss the important factors to be considered when selecting channels of distribution.
- Describe the different channels of distribution.

Terms

- economic discrepancies p. 571
- economic utility p. 571
- channels of distribution p. 572
- channel members p. 572
- direct distribution p. 572
- indirect distribution p. 572
- direct marketing p. 573
- administered channel p. 575
- channel integration p. 575

● ● ● Purposes of Distribution

Our economic system relies on the successful exchange of products and services between businesses and consumers. But no matter how good a product is, this exchange will not occur successfully unless the company fills orders correctly and delivers the product undamaged and on time to the correct locations. These functions are all part of effective distribution management. Successful exchanges are not easy. In fact, most of the problems consumers and businesses face in our economy occur during the exchange process.

Economic discrepancies are the differences between the business's offerings and the consumer's requirements. Marketing managers are concerned about four important economic discrepancies:

1. Differences between the *types* of products produced and the *types* consumers want.
2. Differences between the *time* of production and the *time* consumers want the products.
3. Differences between the *location* where products are produced and the *location* where consumers want them.
4. Differences between the *quantities* produced and the *quantities* consumers want.

Producers manufacture large quantities of one or a very few products; consumers want small quantities of a variety of products. Producers manufacture products at a specific time and in a particular location; that time and location do not typically match the time and place consumers need the product. Distribution systems are designed to get the types and quantities of products customers want to the locations where and when they want them.

ECONOMIC UTILITY

Businesses create customer satisfaction by providing economic utility. **Economic utility** is the amount of satisfaction received from using a product or service. Businesses create economic utility and customer satisfaction by designing the form, time, place, and possession of a product.

Businesses create *form utility* by designing a product that is better or easier to use. Creating a product that is durable, has important features, or is sold in the size or quantity desired enhances form utility.

Distribution creates both time and place utility. *Time utility* is created when consumers are able to purchase a product when they need it. Time utility is enhanced when a customer can obtain a product at a convenient time and does not have to wait for delivery. Distribution creates *place utility* by having products and services available at a convenient location so customers do not have to drive a long distance to find them or are unable to purchase several related items at the same location.

Possession utility is created by developing a product that consumers can afford to purchase. Businesses can increase possession utility by extending credit, allowing the customer to make several payments for the purchase over a period of time.

CHECKPOINT

Describe the four types of economic discrepancies.

●●● Channels of Distribution

The routes products follow while moving from producer to consumer, including all related activities and participating organizations, are called **channels of distribution**. Businesses that participate in activities that transfer goods and services from the producer to the user are called **channel members**.

Channel members are generally retailers and wholesalers. A retailer sells directly to the consumer. A wholesaler, on the other hand, buys from and sells to other businesses or organizations rather than to final consumers. Wholesalers, retailers, and other channel members serve important and specific roles in the exchange process.

Determining the number and type of businesses and the activities they will perform in a channel of distribution is an important decision. Adding businesses to the channel makes the channel more complex and difficult to control. However, using businesses that have particular expertise in transportation, product handling, or other distribution activities may result in improved distribution or actual cost savings. The activities that need to be performed as a product moves from producer to consumer help to determine the number and types of businesses in the channel.

Customers influence the development of a distribution channel. When developing a channel, businesses must consider the location of customers, the number of customers wanting the product, and the ways in which customers prefer to purchase and consume the product.

Producers need distribution channels whether they make products for consumers or for other businesses. The channels that products follow may be quite simple and short or long and complex. The shortest path is for the producer to sell directly to the user; the longest path can include a retailer, a wholesaler, and even other businesses.

When producers sell directly to the ultimate consumer, it is called **direct distribution**. When distribution takes place through channel members, it is called **indirect distribution**. Figure 21-3 illustrates different types of distribution channels.

Management MATTERS

Distribution Management

Distribution managers take a systems perspective when they design channels of distribution. They look at how all parts of a distribution system work together to meet customer needs at the lowest possible cost. Businesses use their distribution systems to gain competitive advantages.

In some industries, such as retailing, distribution is so important that top managers specialize in this field. The last three chief executive officers of Walmart, David Glass, Lee Scott, and Mike Duke, all had expertise in distribution.

What Do You Think? Why would the retail industry consider channels of distribution a top priority? Why would Walmart hire CEOs with a background in distribution?

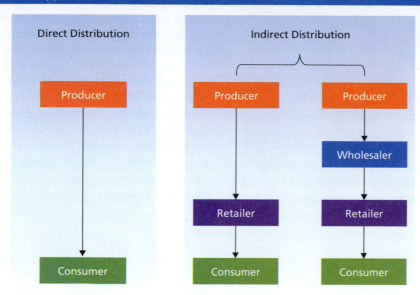

Figure 21-3 E-commerce is shortening channels by eliminating middlemen.

DIRECT DISTRIBUTION

Direct distributors do not use a wholesaler or another type of channel member, such as a retailer, to reach customers. However, direct distributors do need a means of communicating and selling to customers. Industrial sales, such as General Electric, often occur directly from a manufacturer to another business through a sales force. Avon, Amway, and Mary Kay are multi-billion dollar companies that sell products directly to consumers through personal sales.

In addition to a sales force, direct distributors often use direct marketing to communicate to customers. **Direct marketing** offers products to customers through media such as catalogs, direct mail, telemarketing, e-mail marketing and websites. One of the most popular methods of facilitating direct marketing sales is through e-commerce. By allowing customers to purchase online, manufacturers can sell directly to customers without a sales force. Dell Computer started by placing direct marketing print advertisements and grew over time to become the largest online computer sales company.

Direct distributors don't always rely solely upon one direct channel. Dell not only sells online, you can also find their computers in many retail outlets. Avon, which primarily sells through a direct sales force, also sells to consumers through its website. Both of these businesses follow a *multi-channel strategy*, selling through direct and indirect channels.

Direct distributors do not have other channel members to provide service or help solve customer problems. Many firms employ *call centers* to provide telephone support. Call centers take incoming calls to fulfill sales orders and to handle customer problems. Call centers can also be involved with outgoing sales calls, a process called *telemarketing*. Telemarketing is the marketing of goods and services by telephone. Call center operators use computer technology to look up customer records and record sales information.

INDIRECT DISTRIBUTION

When producers cannot or choose not to perform all marketing activities, they need an indirect channel of distribution. Manufacturers can simplify many of

What are some of the positive and negative aspects of call centers?

their marketing operations by selling to retailers. They will need fewer salespeople, because they sell to a small number of retail customers rather than to a very large number of final consumers. They can share advertising with the retailers, and the retailers will be responsible for much of the product storage, consumer credit management, and other activities. Retailers specialize in marketing activities, and this allows producers to specialize in manufacturing activities. Specialization leads to improved efficiency, which benefits consumers through lower prices and added or improved services.

Retailers benefit consumers in several ways. Unlike producers, retailers can be conveniently located near consumers and can provide the products of many manufacturers in one place, thereby permitting consumers to make comparisons among a variety of types and brands of products. Furthermore, retailers can offer several kinds of products that consumers may need, making it possible for consumers to do all their shopping at one or a few locations. Retailers offer convenient shopping hours, credit terms, merchandise exchanges, and other special services to encourage customers to shop in their businesses.

Retail businesses range from large department stores that stock a broad variety of merchandise to small retailers specializing in a limited variety. Also, there are a number of nonstore retailers. They sell products to customers in a number of ways that do not require a shopping trip to a store. Those ways include vending machines; direct marketing by retailers through telephone, catalog, or online ordering services; in-home parties and sales presentations; and shopping channels on cable television.

Producers prefer to sell products to retailers that buy in large quantities, such as department and discount stores and supermarkets. Smaller retailers are usually not able to deal directly with the manufacturer, so they must buy from other channel members. They turn to wholesalers, who consolidate the orders of a number of smaller businesses and then place the larger orders with manufacturers. Also, many wholesalers offer credit terms to retailers and provide help in planning promotions and sales strategies.

Wholesalers sell business products as well as consumer products. Many small businesses cannot purchase in the quantities required by large manufacturers or meet their terms of sale. They seek the service of a wholesaler, often called an industrial distributor, to purchase the products they need.

Wholesalers are an important part of international marketing today. Those that have developed international customers and distribution systems offer an effective way for companies to enter those markets. International wholesalers can also import products from other countries to sell to their customers.

Wholesalers provide valuable services that producers may not provide. They sell to retailers in small quantities and can usually deliver goods quickly.

INTEGRATED MARKETING CHANNELS

Usually the businesses involved in a channel of distribution are independent businesses. They make their own decisions and provide the activities they believe their customers want. It is not unusual for businesses in a distribution channel to have conflicts with each other. One way for channels to work together more effectively is for a large business in the channel to take responsibility for planning, coordination, and communication. The business organizes the channel so that each participant benefits and helps the other businesses perform their functions successfully. An **administered channel** is one in which one organization takes a leadership position to benefit all channel members.

Cooperation is difficult among businesses that operate at different levels of a channel and have very different responsibilities. Some very large businesses attempt to solve that problem through channel integration. **Channel integration** occurs when one business owns the organizations at other levels of the channel. A manufacturer may purchase the businesses that provide wholesaling or retailing functions. A large retailer may decide to buy a wholesaler or even several small manufacturing businesses. Each business can still perform the specific functions needed for a successful channel, but having one owner for all businesses avoids the conflicts that occur in other channels.

CHECKPOINT

List three factors businesses must consider when developing a channel of distribution.

21.2 ASSESSMENT

UNDERSTAND MANAGEMENT CONCEPTS

Determine the best answer for each of the following questions.

1. The routes products follow while moving from producer to consumer, including all related activities and participating organizations, are called
   a. routes of distribution
   b. methods of distribution
   c. channels of distribution
   d. the marketing route

2. When producers sell directly to the ultimate consumer they are using
   a. direct distribution
   b. indirect distribution
   c. indirect marketing
   d. Internet marketing

THINK CRITICALLY

Answer the following questions as completely as possible.

3. Explain how economic discrepancies are related to economic utility.
4. Describe the differences between direct and indirect channels.

F⊕cus On...Technology

Direct Marketing Challenges

Direct marketing is a time-honored strategy. What changes over time are the tools that allow it to thrive. In the 1880s, Sears started as a direct mail catalog company that took advantage of expanded rail lines to ship products directly to customers. By the beginning of the 1900s, wealthy people had telephones in their homes; this led marketers to call customers and take orders. Ninety years later, the Internet has allowed e-mail marketing to reach just about everyone on the planet.

For as long as direct marketing techniques have been used, customers have complained about them. When customers received advertisements they didn't request, postal direct marketing gained the reputation of junk mail. Many people throw it away without even looking at it.

More annoying than junk mail are unsolicited telephone calls. Telemarketers call when they expect people to be home; dinnertime is often a prime calling time and particularly annoying to consumers. In addition, some telemarketers are rude or unprepared. Others mislead customers into thinking they are participating in a survey. Complaints about telemarketing from consumers across the country lead to *no call lists* enforced by state governments and the Federal Trade Commission. Once consumers register on a no call list, they should not receive telemarketing calls unless they have a pre-established relationship with the marketing company.

As much as people use and like e-mail, establishing it as direct marketing medium has not been easy. Unethical spammers use the Internet to flood mailboxes with unwanted ads. As a result, customers and businesses now use spam filters to block most of the 200 billion spam e-mails sent around the world each day. E-mail marketing can work well when an individual has opted-in to receive e-mail communication. Many businesses allow customers to limit the number of e-mail communications they receive.

Cell phones are the most recent direct marketing opportunity. Short message services (SMS), or text messages, are also subject to spam. Over 40 percent of cell phone users have received spam text messages attempting to sell unwanted products services.

THINK CRITICALLY

1. Why do consumers continue to complain about direct marketing?
2. Explain how your reaction to direct marketing differs when the contact is unsolicited compared to when you have opted in.
3. What responsibilities do consumers have in dealing with unethical situations they encounter with direct marketing?
4. Prepare several statements of ethical practices that should apply to direct marketing.

Channel Design

Goals

- Discuss the factors that affect a producer's choice of distribution channel.
- Describe the characteristics of major forms of transportation used to distribute products.
- Give examples of product-handling procedures that improve product distribution.

Terms

- piggyback service p. 579
- containerization p. 580
- bar codes p. 581
- warehouses p. 581
- distribution center p. 581

●●● Selecting a Channel of Distribution

From the available channels of distribution, ranging from direct and simple to indirect and complex, distribution managers must decide which channel or channels will best fit their needs. Companies generally prefer to use as few channels and channel members as possible. Sometimes companies need to use more than one channel to get the widest distribution for their product. Products such as books, candy, pens, and soap are purchased by many people in a variety of locations. Such items require several channels to reach all of the possible consumers. The manufacturers may sell directly to national discount stores that can sell large quantities of the product. To reach other markets, the manufacturers may sell to large wholesalers that, in turn, sell to supermarkets, convenience stores, vendors, or other types of businesses.

Selling to different types of customers requires different channels of distribution. For example, a computer game producer may sell games through retail stores, game rental companies, as well as directly downloaded through the Internet. Figure 21-4 illustrates these different channels.

Distribution managers must consider many factors when deciding which channel or channels to select for distributing their products. Some of the main factors are:

- *Perishability of the product.* Highly perishable articles, such as bread, fresh flowers, and ice cream, require rapid and careful handling. Those products are usually marketed directly to the consumer or through very few channel members.
- *Geographic distance between producer and consumer.* Many products are now sold internationally as well as throughout the country in which they are produced. If the market is very close to the point of production, there is less need for channel members. Generally, more businesses participate in handling a product as the distance from producer to consumer increases.
- *Need for special handling of the product.* If the product requires costly procedures or equipment for handling, it is likely to pass through as few channel members as possible. Gasoline, which requires pipelines, special tanks, and trucks for handling, is moved from the refiner to the retailer

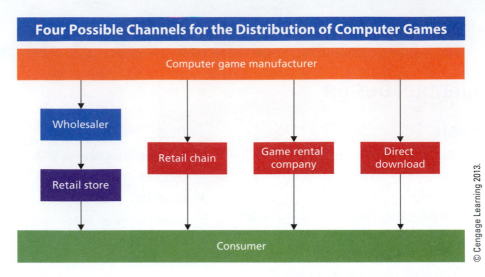

Four Possible Channels for the Distribution of Computer Games

Computer game manufacturer

Wholesaler

Retail store

Retail chain

Game rental company

Direct download

Consumer

© Cengage Learning 2013.

Figure 21-4 Direct downloads are a shorter channel of distribution to the consumer than through a wholesaler and retail stores.

as directly as possible. Refiners own some gasoline retail outlets. Products that are highly complex and need experts to install and repair also require short channels. Manufacturers of large computer systems, for example, sell directly to users.

- *Number of users.* The greater the number of users of a product, the more channel members there probably are. For instance, a manufacturer of steel is likely to sell directly to a few large users, whereas a shoe manufacturer may sell to wholesalers that then distribute to a variety of retail businesses.

- *Number of types of products manufactured.* A producer with only one product, such as pottery, will probably sell to a wholesaler. It is too expensive to maintain a sales force large enough to contact all retailers in the country. But if a producer manufactures a large number of electrical products, such as coffeemakers, clocks, heaters, and toasters, it might sell directly to large retailers that handle all of these products. The marketing costs can be distributed over many products.

- *Financial strength and interests of the producer.* Large companies that are strong financially are better able to perform the marketing activities required to move goods from producer to consumer through the least number of channel members. They may find it more profitable to handle the marketing activities within the company rather than using other businesses. They also have more control over the channel rather than relying on others to perform many of the activities.

Channel decisions, like other marketing decisions, require careful study and are subject to change. With all the recent advances in technology, transportation and storage facilities, and retail methods, producers are constantly looking for more efficient ways to market their goods.

21st CENTURY SKILLS

Flexibility

In today's fast-paced business environment, being flexible is a valuable skill. Managers need to be flexible in the way they work and in the way that they lead businesses. Successful managers effectively incorporate feedback from customers, vendors, employees, and other managers. They also know how to offer and accept praise and criticism. Being flexible allows managers and workers to understand and appreciate diverse views and beliefs in a multicultural environment.

 CHECKPOINT

List six factors that producers consider when deciding which channel or channels to select for distributing their products.

●●●● Transportation Decisions

Selecting the channel members that will help sell the product to the consumer is only one of the decisions a distribution manager must make. Another important decision is how to physically transport the products from producer to consumer.

Buyers and sellers face several common problems related to transportation. One problem deals with the types of products to be shipped. Factors to consider in shipping include the size, shape, and weight of the goods. Also, certain goods are fragile and may need special care in handling. Transporting 100 tons of steel, for example, requires very different treatment from that required to move a carton of glassware.

Another transportation problem is the time needed for delivery. Some buyers expect or need shipment within a matter of hours, and others may not need or expect delivery for several weeks. Still another shipping problem is cost. In addition to the basic transportation charges, there are the costs of packaging products for shipment, insurance, and often storing products before, during, and after delivery to the buyer. Producers that do not perform their own shipping activities must first decide on their products' distribution requirements, then select the transportation method and companies that meet these requirements.

Both consumers and businesses are concerned about the quality of products at the time of purchase. They also want products available where and when they need them and at a reasonable cost. Because distribution activities affect all of these concerns, businesses plan them carefully.

COMMON TRANSPORTATION METHODS

The most commonly used methods of transporting goods are by railroad, truck, and airplane. A business may use more than one type of transportation, depending on the requirements for the shipment.

Railway transportation is one of the most common forms of shipping in the United States. Over a third of the volume of products shipped in the United States goes by rail car. The principal advantage of rail transportation is the low cost of moving heavy and bulky items long distances. However, products move slowly on long train routes as cars are added or dropped off. For bulky products or large quantities, the cost of shipping by rail is usually lower than by other methods.

Trucks are frequently used for short-distance shipping. Trucks are essential to smaller communities and rural areas that other transportation methods do not serve. Industries such as agriculture, mining, and lumber depend on trucks to move products from the source of production to the processing location.

Much long-distance shipping is also done by truck. For products that need to be moved rapidly, in smaller quantities than can be economically shipped by rail, or where rail is not accessible, trucks are the typical transportation choice. Some transportation companies load truck trailers and place them on railroad cars to be shipped close to the final destination. This service is called **piggyback service**. Many trucking companies now use computer systems to track customer orders and reroute trucks for rapid pickup and delivery. This flexibility is important for businesses that are trying to keep inventories low while maintaining high service levels.

Airplanes provide the most rapid form of transportation, but their rates are much higher than those for other methods. Airplanes can move products quickly over long distances. Items can move across a country in a few hours and around the world in a day, if necessary. The majority of air shipments involve items of relatively small bulk, high value, or quick perishability. Packages and mail are

FACTS & FIGURES

UPS by the Numbers

United Parcel Service is the world's largest package distribution company. It transports almost 4 billion parcels and documents annually. The company uses more than 218 aircraft, 93,000 vehicles, and over 20,000 service locations including UPS Stores, Mail Boxes Etc. and other authorized centers to provide service in more than 220 countries and territories.

How does containerization improve shipping services?

moved regularly on passenger airlines as well as by air parcel companies. Airlines are also used for shipping cut flowers, high-fashion clothing, seafood, vegetables, and jewelry. Air shipments are very important for items needed in emergencies, such as medicine and blood, parts for machines needing quick repairs, or important documents.

Increasingly, businesses are shipping large and bulky items on special cargo planes designed for easy loading and unloading. Regional air freight terminals are being constructed so products can be moved rapidly into and out of airports without interfering with passenger travel. As rapid and efficient transportation becomes more important to businesses and consumers, more products are being shipped by air, even though the cost is higher. People pay more for the transportation that meets their requirements.

OTHER TRANSPORTATION METHODS

Water transportation (ocean, lake, and river) is the slowest method of transporting goods. However, it is also the cheapest for bulky goods, such as coal, iron ore, oil, lumber, grain, and cotton. Those are the principal items transported by water. Many products that are produced in large volume for international markets, such as automobiles and large pieces of equipment, are shipped across the oceans. At any large harbor on a coast you can see hundreds of types of products being loaded and unloaded from ships.

In the United States, as well as in many other countries, networks of thousands of miles of pipelines have been built. Pipelines mostly transport petroleum and natural gas. In many countries, however, pipelines are important methods of moving water for irrigation and human consumption.

One way to improve shipping services is through **containerization**. Products are packed in large shipping containers at the factory and are then shipped by a number of transportation methods before being unpacked. The containers can easily be loaded and unloaded from trucks to rail cars, ships, and cargo planes, and back to trucks. This method reduces the amount of product handling and product damage.

 **CHECKPOINT**

Compare the three principal methods of transporting products.

●●● Product Handling

Lost, late, or damaged products are of little value to customers. Product handling is an important part of the distribution process. Most products are handled several times on their way from producer to consumer. Each time a product is handled adds to the cost of distribution, increases delivery time, and increases the chances that damage will occur. Businesses evaluate their product-handling procedures to find ways to improve the process. Improvements may include more secure packaging, more efficient procedures for packing and unpacking, and better equipment for handling and storing products.

TRACKING PRODUCTS

An important part of product handling is keeping track of the products. Businesses and customers want to know where products are in the distribution channel and when they will be delivered. The record keeping required is often a very time-consuming task. Businesses now use bar coding to track products during distribution. **Bar codes** are product identification labels containing a unique set of vertical bars that computer scanning equipment can read. Each product or container has a bar code. The scanning equipment can read the code at any time during distribution to track the product's progress.

How are bar codes used in product handling?

PRODUCT STORAGE

Manufacturers or channel members often must store products at points along the way from producer to consumer. Usually, consumers do not buy products as soon as they are produced. Producers and channel members may want to accumulate a large quantity of products to make shipping more efficient. Also, consumers buy some products more during one time of the year than another. Lawn mowers, air conditioners, snowmobiles, and skis are examples of such products. Most companies produce those products throughout the year to make production more efficient. They then store the products until they are ready to distribute them for sale.

Warehouses are buildings used to store large quantities of products until they can be sold. They are usually large buildings with racks, shelves, or bins for storing products. Warehouse operators may control temperature or humidity if the stored products need special protection. They must carefully handle and store the products to prevent damage. Warehouse personnel keep computerized records of where each product is stored in the warehouse. When they receive an order, the computer displays the quantity of the product available and its location in the warehouse.

Handling products and storing them for a long time is expensive. Also, moving them around increases the chances for damage. For more efficient handling with less risk of damage, many companies use mechanical equipment and robots to handle the products in their warehouses. Computers control both the equipment and the robots as products are moved into storage and subsequently removed for shipment.

Large wholesalers and retailers that handle a variety of products and sell them through a number of outlets have replaced traditional warehouses with distribution centers. A **distribution center** is a large building designed to accumulate and redistribute products efficiently. A wholesaler or retailer usually buys products from a number of manufacturers. Each manufacturer ships these products to the distribution center in large quantities. Center workers

Manager's Perspective on
TECHNOLOGY

A new technology based on tiny radio frequency identification (RFID) tags allows businesses to track products without bar codes. These small chips can be placed in or on product packaging and emit a radio code when scanned. They are used to track inventory in warehouses and allow for scanless purchasing.

then repackage the products into smaller quantities, combine them with products from other manufacturers, and ship them to stores that sell that bundle of products to consumers. Distribution centers can save businesses a great deal of money. They reduce transportation and storage costs and provide individual stores with the products they need quickly. Individual stores can order smaller quantities than if they had to order merchandise from each manufacturer, so products will not become outdated as easily.

ORDER PROCESSING

Customers place orders in person or by mail, telephone, computer, or fax. When an order reaches the business, employees must process the paperwork to fill the order and bill the customer. If customers have questions or problems with the order, employees must handle them in a friendly and courteous fashion. Some employees are responsible for tracking orders until they reach the customers to make sure the customers receive what they expect.

Most companies have automated some or all of the order-processing system. Orders entered into a computer system can be easily tracked. Some companies make computer records available to channel members and customers so they can also track orders at any time from their own computers.

 **CHECKPOINT**

Describe how manufacturers or channel members store products at points along the way from producer to consumer.

21.3 ASSESSMENT

UNDERSTAND MANAGEMENT CONCEPTS

Determine the best answer for each of the following questions.

1. The transportation method in which truck trailers are placed on railroad cars is called
   a. railback
   b. piggyback
   c. truck to rail
   d. trainback

2. Buildings used to store large quantities of products until they can be sold are called
   a. distribution centers
   b. storage houses
   c. warehouses
   d. wholesalers

THINK CRITICALLY

Answer the following questions as completely as possible.

3. Describe some of the common problems related to transportation.
4. Why is product handling an important part of the distribution process?

CHAPTER CONCEPTS

- Companies develop a marketing mix to satisfy customers and make a profit. The marketing mix is made up of the product, distribution, price, and promotion plans.

- Businesses develop products on three levels: basic product, enhanced product, and extended product. Also, businesses must decide whether to offer product lines and product assortments.

- Packaging adds value by protecting the product during shipping and storage; providing information about product composition, features, use, and proper handling; making the product easier to use; and promoting the product.

- Branding gives customers confidence in making a purchase. If they recognize a brand name and have had good experiences with that brand, they will be more likely to buy the brand again.

- Effective distribution gets the correct products to customers at the right place and time and in the correct form.

- Channels of distribution can be either direct (from manufacturer directly to purchaser) or indirect (using retailers and sometimes wholesalers to handle some of the marketing activities).

- Distribution activities include product handling and storing, transporting and tracking the product, order processing, and customer service.

REVIEW BUSINESS MANAGEMENT TERMS

Write the letter of the term that matches each definition. Some terms will not be used.

1. Physical product in its simplest form
2. Product that includes additional features that are not part of the physical product but increase its usability
3. Group of similar products with obvious variations in the design and quality to meet the needs of distinct customer groups
4. Routes products follow while moving from producer to consumer, including all related activities and participating organizations
5. Complete set of all products a business offers to a market
6. Differences between a business's offerings and the consumer's requirements
7. Businesses that participate in activities that transfer goods and services from the producer to the user
8. Distribution in which producers sell directly to the ultimate consumer
9. Distribution that takes place through channel members
10. Channel in which one organization takes a leadership position to benefit all channel members

a. administered channel
b. bar codes
c. basic product
d. brand
e. channel integration
f. channel members
g. channels of distribution
h. direct distribution
i. distribution centers
j. economic discrepancies
k. extended product
l. indirect distribution
m. product assortment
n. product line

Determine the best answer.

11. A product that offers different features and options for the consumer is a(n)
    a. augmented product
    b. branded product
    c. enhanced product
    d. total product

12. All of the following are forms of direct marketing *except*
    a. catalogs
    b. e-mail marketing
    c. retail store marketing
    d. telemarketing

13. A distribution channel in which one business owns organizations at other levels of the channel is a(n)
    a. administered channel
    b. channel integration
    c. channel captain
    d. channel linkage

14. Packing products in large shipping containers at the factory and shipping them by a variety of transportation methods is
    a. multishipping
    b. containerization
    c. factory shipping
    d. piggybacking

15. Which of the following are functions of packaging?
    a. protecting products
    b. providing information to customers
    c. making the product easier to use
    d. All of the above are functions of packaging.

16. The type of distribution that does not use a wholesaler or another type of channel member, such as a retailer, to reach customers is called
    a. direct distribution
    b. indirect marketing
    c. telemarketing
    d. database marketing

17. The preferred low-cost transportation system used to move heavy and bulky items is
    a. air freight
    b. ocean freight
    c. rail
    d. trucks

Answer the following questions.

18. Identify a company with a product that has an extensive product line. Identify specific products that are part of the product line. Then describe the differences among those products and why they meet different customers' needs.

19. For a product with which you are familiar, describe ways that the packaging improves sales and usability. Now identify examples of packaging that interferes with sales and usability.

20. Make a list of products you have purchased that were probably stored for a length of time before you purchased them. Then make a similar list of products that were not stored or were stored only a short time before you purchased them. Discuss the differences among the products.

21. Provide examples showing that the ways in which consumers purchase a product influence the type of distribution channel used.

22. Discuss the problems businesses and consumers might encounter with product distribution and order processing when the Internet is used for selling and buying.

MAKE ACADEMIC CONNECTIONS

Complete the following activities.

23. **Math** An appliance store can purchase a certain brand of electric heater for $45.00 from a firm in City A or for $48.50 from another firm in City B. The transportation cost from City A is $3.88 per heater. From City B, the transportation cost is $2.77 per heater. What is the difference in cost between the two firms if the appliance store buys 500 heaters? What factors other than cost should the appliance store consider when deciding from which firm to make the purchase?

24. **Technology** A student organization to which you belong has decided to sell containers of bottled water at after-school activities, athletic events, and other functions as a fund-raiser. Your organization made an agreement with the supplier that allows you to design a unique package for the water bottle. Use a computer graphics program, like Microsoft's Paint, to design a package that will meet the four different purposes of packaging described in the chapter.

25. **Writing** Assume you work for a company located in Utah that manufactures children's toys and games. Your potential customers are located throughout the world. Write a one-page report stating the ways in which you can use each of the following methods to improve customer service or profitability: (a) Internet sales, (b) containerization, and (c) bar coding.

26. **Research** Use the Internet to identify two companies that specialize in shipping products. List the services they offer and describe how they specialize. Compare your answers to those of other students.

CASE IN POINT

CASE 21-1: A Photographic Assortment

Aisha Muran has been a part-time photographer for many years. She uses high quality digital cameras and professional printers for her work. She has specialized in individual family portraits and children portraits for most of her business. Her customers learn of her primarily via word of mouth or when they see her portraits in other people's homes. She enjoys the work but doesn't make enough money to do it full-time.

Part of Aisha's problem involves the lowering costs of technology. Many people are now buying inexpensive digital cameras and printers. This equipment allows individuals to take their own pictures, send copies over the Internet or by disk, and print high-quality images.

She has discussed the issue with several business advisers, who suggested she consider expanding beyond portrait photography. They recommended expanding into weddings and special events; taking photos of landscapes, buildings, animals, and other subjects that would meet the needs of a broader audience; or purchasing and reselling home accessories that would complement the purchase of pictures and portraits. They have also mentioned that she could learn to enhance and improve the quality of digital photos taken by her clients and then print them using a professional-quality printer.

Aisha is unsure of what direction to take with her business. She has considered spending money to advertise. She is also not sure that she wants to get involved with editing other peoples' work.

THINK CRITICALLY

1. Describe a basic product, enhanced product, and extended product that you would recommend to Aisha for expanding her business.
2. List the elements in Aisha's current product assortment. Develop a new product assortment that she could offer. Identify which of these two assortments would be most appealing to potential customers.
3. If Aisha decided to purchase and resell home accessories, how could she use the concept of a product line to effectively market those products?
4. Describe how the Internet has made possible a new distribution system for photographic images. Explain how editing other's digital photography would enhance Aisha's product offerings.
5. Construct a grid like the one shown in Figure 21-1 for Aisha, illustrating how she could develop a business that would fit into each of the four quadrants. Describe the types of products she could offer for each of the four positions on the grid.
6. Should Aisha spend any money on advertising before she has made her product decisions? Explain your answer.

CASE 21-2: A Direct-Marketing Dilemma

The Elegant Affair is a specialty retail shop. It sells assorted gift boxes of various meats, cheeses, nuts, jams, and jellies. The business is located in a midwestern city and is facing declining sales due to the city's economic difficulties. One major manufacturing plant has closed, and layoffs from other businesses have caused many people to move from the area in search of new jobs.

The president of the company has been studying a number of alternative distribution methods. She has considered moving her retail business to another city. This would require a large investment and hiring and retraining a new set of employees. She has also considered closing the retail shop and finding other stores to carry her products. This would lower her profit per box but could increase the total number of boxes sold. She has also considered direct marketing as a way to increase sales without having to move the store or build a new store in an area with a more attractive economic climate.

Direct-marketing alternatives she has considered include using the Internet and telemarketing. She believes that by using salespeople and a computerized telemarketing system, the company can sell gift boxes to people throughout the United States. She also believes that the cost of those sales will actually be lower than the cost of selling the products to people who come into the store. However, she is concerned about the increasing use of no-call lists. The Internet could open sales across the country, but will require an investment in technology and new personnel.

THINK CRITICALLY

1. List each of the alternative distribution systems that The Elegant Affair is considering. List the advantages and disadvantages of each of these alternatives.
2. What types of activities would The Elegant Affair have to do to start a telemarketing system?
3. How can the company identify prospective customers for its telemarketing salespeople to call?
4. What types of activities would The Elegant Affair have to do to start an Internet-based marketing system?
5. Identify two distribution methods that The Elegant Affair might use for the products it sells through telemarketing or the Internet. What are the advantages and disadvantages of each?
6. Develop a brief script for the telemarketing salespeople to use to introduce the company and its products to prospective customers.
7. How could the increasing use of no-call lists impact the telemarketing strategy? What types of customers are likely to be on a no-call list?
8. Do you believe an online system for customer ordering might be a better method for the company than telemarketing? Why or why not?

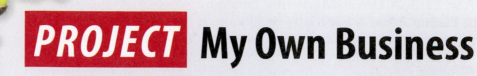

PROJECT My Own Business

Developing Your Product and Distribution Strategy

Two important marketing decisions for your new business are the type and assortment of products you will offer and how to distribute them. Some new businesses have very limited product choices, and others offer an extensive set of enhanced and extended products. Most retail businesses purchase products and supplies from other channel members, so they are part of an indirect channel of distribution. An important part of distribution is to select a good location for the business that makes it convenient for customers to find the business and purchase your product. In this project segment, you will study product development and distribution decisions for your new juice business.

DATA COLLECTION

1. Identify your basic physical product. It will be very similar to that offered by many competitors. Study as many competitors as you can and identify the possible extended and enhanced product choices for this type of business.
2. Study competitors and collect additional information about this type of business from magazines and the Internet. List possible product lines and product assortments that seem appropriate for the juice products.
3. Collect examples of the packages and brand names used by the primary competitors selling these products in your community.
4. Develop a simple map of the area of your town or city where you might locate your new business. Mark on the map the locations of the businesses that offer the same types of products you are considering.

ANALYSIS

1. Develop a product strategy that identifies the products, product lines, and product assortments you plan to offer during your first six months in operation. Justify your choices.
2. Review a business directory from your community or on the Internet. Identify at least four manufacturers or suppliers from whom you might purchase the products and supplies you will need for your business.
3. Design the basic juice cup or container you will use to package your product. If possible, contact a supplier and determine the cost of various sizes of cup or container. Identify any other packaging you will need.
4. Once your facility has been determined, analyze any immediate and long-term improvements needed for the facility. Develop a sales presentation on your products. Videotape it or present it to your class.
5. Develop a distribution plan. Include the methods you plan to use to store products and supplies and transport them to your stores. Also list other possible channels for distributing your products.

CHAPTER 22

PRICING AND PROMOTION

22.1 The Business Buying Decision

22.2 Pricing & Costs

22.3 Promotion

© Shutterstock/Mark Ross

Reality Check

Why Pay More?

Michi and Arturo walked out of Windzors, a sporting goods store that had just opened in the new Regency Park shopping plaza. "I can't believe that store will be successful," said Michi. "I've never seen sports equipment priced that high!"

"The products really were expensive," agreed Arturo. "But it certainly isn't a normal sporting goods store. The salesperson said they would help design your own set of personalized golf clubs and that you would get five hours of lessons with the golf pro at the Regency Sports Center if you purchased a set of clubs."

"Did you see the area where they sold downhill skis?" asked Michi. "They had a moving slide like an escalator where you could actually ski. They also had a machine that formed molds around your feet for custom-fitting ski boots. They sponsor a ski club and organize vacations to the mountains in the United States and even to other countries. I've never seen that in a sporting goods store."

"Why would people want to pay that much?" Arturo wondered. "Sure, they have the top brand names and unique services. But you can get the same type of products for 40 to 50 percent less at other stores."

"I don't know," said Michi. "They certainly have effective advertising, sales brochures, and customer service. And the store was filled with people. Maybe the owners are on to something."

A business is successful when it brings buyers and sellers together and they are both satisfied with the exchange. To be successful, marketing managers must offer the type and quality of products and services that meet the needs of customers. The products must be priced so that buyers consider them a good value for the money.

Whether the buyers are businesses purchasing raw materials to use in manufacturing, equipment to operate the business, or products for resale, or consumers buying products for their own use, they must have information to make their decisions. Buyers must be aware of the products, how the products will meet their needs, and where they can buy them. Then buyers and sellers must agree on a price and method of payment.

What's Your Reaction? Why might customers be willing to pay high prices for products at Windzors?

22.1

The Business Buying Decision

Goals

- Discuss how businesses make their buying decisions.
- Describe the steps in the business buying process.

Terms

- business buying process p. 592
- new task purchase p. 592
- modified rebuy p. 593
- straight rebuy p. 593

●●● Planning a Business Purchase

Marketing managers are responsible for ensuring that their companies are able to develop long-term relationships with business customers. To achieve this, marketing managers must understand how business customers make decisions.

When planning a purchase, business buyers make several specific decisions. They must decide what to purchase, when to purchase, from whom to purchase, and how much to purchase.

WHAT TO PURCHASE

To be successful, a business must keep the right kind of products in stock. Manufacturers buy products to use in producing products to sell to their customers. Wholesale or retail businesses purchase products for resale or for use in the operation of their businesses. In all cases, the most important consideration in making purchases is the customers' needs. Businesses that do not satisfy customers will not thrive. Businesses must consider both quality and assortment of products in deciding what to purchase.

Some buyers try to sell more products than their competitors do by offering low-quality products at a low price. They believe that price is so important to customers that they will accept lower quality to save money. This strategy can backfire. Customers compare price and quality to make the best possible decision. They usually do not select the absolute cheapest product if it is of inferior quality, nor do they always pay the highest price even if quality is superior.

Two factors influence a business's selection of product assortment. The first is competition. A new store will have a hard time attracting customers if it carries only the same products or brands that are carried by local businesses that are already successful. A business needs to emphasize the products customers want but offer some differences from competitors' products.

The second factor in choosing a product assortment is the financial strength of the business. It costs a great deal to keep a wide selection of products available. Businesses can stock a limited variety of products while still offering customers a good selection. Product variety is a difficult decision. Businesses need to stock items that customers want, but their budget has limits.

Businesses have several resources for helping to determine what to purchase. Websites, catalogs, and salespeople are valuable tools. Trade associations and their publications can also help. Businesses should listen carefully to their customers in determining what to purchase to meet customer needs. They should also review company sales records and regularly study what products sell well for competitors.

When planning a purchase, what decisions does a business typically make?

© Shutterstock/Michal Kowalski

WHEN TO PURCHASE

The types of products, the types and locations of suppliers, and other factors such as style and price trends influence the decision about when to purchase. For a manufacturer, raw materials and component parts must be available when needed for production, or the business will not be able to maintain its production schedule. Wholesalers and retailers need an adequate supply of products when customers want to buy. Businesses often must place orders well in advance for products to be available when their customers need them. For example, retail clothing stores often order summer fashions in January or earlier. Whether a buyer believes the prices of products will fall or rise also influences when product orders are placed.

FROM WHOM TO PURCHASE

Part of the purchasing decision is to choose the right suppliers. Businesses consider the reputation of each supplier in such areas as dealing with customers, filling orders rapidly and exactly as requested, and providing necessary services. Other considerations are the supplier's price and credit terms.

Businesses must decide whether to make purchases from only one supplier or to spread the orders among several suppliers. Most businesses concentrate their buying among a few suppliers. This practice usually develops better relationships between the suppliers and the purchaser. Better prices, credit terms, and service are also likely to result. However, relying on one supplier leaves the purchaser vulnerable when that business experiences problems.

HOW MUCH TO PURCHASE

A business should have sufficient products available to meet customer demand. If customers cannot purchase the products they want when they want, they will go

Management MATTERS

Marketing Science

The field of marketing is a science with its own researchers, scientific journals, and theories. Marketing managers must be able to understand and use these theories and concepts to understand customers' buying motives and perceptions. Marketing theories are based on research from a number of fields. These include psychology, sociology, social psychology, and economic psychology. These fields help marketers understand both individual and business buying processes and motives.

What Do You Think? How can these "ologies" help marketers understand the needs of their customers? What classes could you take that would help improve the selling process?

elsewhere. If a manufacturing business runs out of the necessary raw materials and parts, they must delay production.

On the other hand, if businesses have a much larger inventory than they need, they are tying up large amounts of money in inventory that they could use in other ways to make a profit. The large inventory also requires extra storage space. If businesses keep only small quantities in stock, they reduce the risk of loss from spoilage, changes in design, or changes in demand. Many suppliers are now able to fill orders quickly, making it easier for companies to carry lower quantities of many of the products they sell.

 CHECKPOINT

List the specific decisions businesses must make when planning a purchase.

● ● ● ● Business Buying Process

Businesses typically follow a set of formal procedures when they decide to purchase a product. This process is called the **business buying process**, as outlined in Figure 22-1. Businesses do not always go through every step of this process. There are three different types of buying processes.

Businesses must conduct a **new task purchase** process when they are purchasing a product, inventory item, or supply for the first time. Businesses typically purchase a large quantity of products and face larger risks than consumers making purchases. For example, if a supplier is unable to supply inventory items, a business could lose sales or have idle workers, resulting in higher

Business Buying Process		
Step	**Explanation**	**Example**
1. Problem Recognition	A business buying need is recognized.	Business inventory is low or it receives an order from customers.
2. Product Specification	Specific details about the product needs are developed.	Ideal inventory level determines ordering or a product design is specified.
3. Supplier Search	Suppliers are requested to submit bids showing how specifications are met and at what price.	A supplier sends a bid with information on product prices, shipping dates, and support details.
4. Supplier Selection	Suppliers are evaluated to determine if they are able to meet needs.	Buyer may check with trade organization or other buyers as reference.
5. Order Submission	Order is placed with quantity needs, delivery date, return policies, warranties, and other pertinent information.	Order may be placed as need is recognized; if relationships are developed, orders could be automated.
6. Review Performance	The suppliers are reviewed on an ongoing basis.	Buyers will evaluate timely delivery and request new bids to evaluate newest pricing.

© Cengage Learning 2013.

Figure 22-1 The stronger the relationship between the buyer and seller, the less often the buyer needs to go through the stages of the buying process.

costs. To lower these risks, businesses conduct careful searches for suppliers, following all the steps in Figure 22-1. Depending on the purchase, new task purchases can take over a year to complete.

In a **modified rebuy**, a business purchases a new or modified product from established suppliers. In this case, a business may submit new specifications or ask for bids from new suppliers to ensure they are getting the best price for their needs.

Many purchase decisions are low risk and can be made without modifications. This is often the case when a business is engaged in a **straight rebuy**. For example, when a business needs more paper for copiers or printers, it often repurchases from suppliers it has used before.

 CHECKPOINT

List the three levels of the business buying process.

22.1 ASSESSMENT

UNDERSTAND MANAGEMENT CONCEPTS

Determine the best answer for each of the following questions.

1. Businesses use which of the following sources of assistance in determining what to purchase?
   a. company records
   b. salespeople
   c. trade associations
   d. all of the above

2. When a business is purchasing a new or modified product from established suppliers, it is engaging in
   a. a new task purchase
   b. a modified rebuy
   c. a straight rebuy
   d. an established purchase

THINK CRITICALLY

Answer the following questions as completely as possible.

3. Describe the factors that influence a business's decision about when to purchase.

4. Explain the differences between the three purchase processes used by businesses.

22.2

Pricing & Costs

Goals

- Distinguish between various types of discounts and price components.
- Describe factors involved in establishing product prices and common pricing strategies.
- Discuss ways that companies try to control costs that can lead to higher prices.

Terms

- list price p. 594
- discounts p. 594
- trade discount p. 595
- quantity discount p. 595
- seasonal discount p. 595
- cash discount p. 595
- selling price p. 595
- cost of goods sold p. 596
- operating expenses p. 596
- margin (gross profit) p. 596
- net profit p. 596
- markup p. 596
- markdown p. 597

●●● Payment Terms and Discounts

Marketing managers help a business maximize profits by developing pricing strategies. This requires that a marketing manager understands pricing principles and the mathematical relationships between a product's price and business expenses. Marketing managers establish a price at which they would like to sell a product. The initial price that the seller posts on a product is its **list price**. Often, however, customers do not pay the list price. The terms of sale offered by the seller or requested by the buyer affect the actual price paid. The terms of sale identify delivery conditions, when invoices must be paid, and whether the buyer can receive credit or discounts.

The buyer may specify requirements the seller must meet. The buyer and seller discuss those requirements and then negotiate any changes before a final decision is made. The buyer and seller discuss price, quantity, and delivery, and agree on the terms of the sale. The supplier then receives the buyer's purchase order or contract, which details the form, quantity, and price of the products to be supplied.

PAYMENT TERMS

Companies that sell to other businesses often extend credit to their customers. They list their credit terms on the invoice. Invoices often state credit terms in a form such as *net 30 days*, which means that the buyer must pay in full within 30 days from the date on the invoice. Some businesses offer longer payment terms, such as net 60 days. The longer the term, the better for the buyer, who then has a chance to sell the goods by the time payment is due or earn interest on the money that otherwise would be paid to the supplier.

DISCOUNTS

Suppliers may offer discounts on products that their business customers purchase. **Discounts** are reductions from a product's list price designed to encourage customers to buy. Common types of discounts are trade, quantity, seasonal, and cash discounts.

A **trade discount** is a price reduction that manufacturers give to their channel partners, such as wholesalers or retailers, in exchange for additional services. For example, a manufacturer may give retailers a 30 percent discount but may give wholesalers a 45 percent discount from the list price (or 15 percent more than retailers). In this case, the manufacturer expects the wholesalers to perform additional marketing activities beyond those expected from retailers.

A **quantity discount** is a price reduction offered to customers that buy in quantities larger than a specified minimum. For example, a retail paint store that orders

Why might a business offer a seasonal discount for its products?

200 gallons of paint from a wholesaler pays a certain price per gallon. However, the wholesaler may lower the price per gallon if the store orders at least 1,000 gallons at one time. The purpose of the discount is to encourage customers to buy in large quantities. The manufacturer can afford to sell the larger quantity for a lower price because that sale reduces the cost of inventory, the amount of storage space needed, the insurance costs, and the administrative costs of product handling. Quantity discounts may be based on the number of units purchased or on the dollar value of the order.

A **seasonal discount** is a price reduction offered for ordering or taking delivery of products in advance of the normal buying period. It encourages the buyer to purchase earlier than necessary or at a time when orders are normally low. An example is a discount on snowmobiles purchased in the summer. The seasonal discount is a way the manufacturer attempts to balance production and inventory levels throughout the year for products that are normally purchased at a few specific times during the year.

To encourage early payment, many businesses offer a cash discount. A **cash discount** is a price reduction given for paying by a certain date. A cash discount is usually stated as a percentage of the purchase price (for example, 2 percent). Businesses offer cash discounts with various dating and credit terms. For example, the terms of a purchase may be net 30 days with a 2 percent discount for payment within 10 days. If the invoice is dated May 1, the buyer can deduct 2 percent from the total price when paying on or before May 11. Otherwise, the buyer must pay the full amount by May 31. Businesses express terms like these in this form: 2/10, n/30.

COMPONENTS OF PRICE

The prices businesses charge can make the difference between the success and failure of their products. Customers must view the product as a good value for the price. The price must be competitive with prices of competitors' products, yet high enough for the business to make a profit on the sale.

The **selling price** is the actual price customers pay for the product. The selling price is determined by subtracting any discounts from the list price. Businesses often set list prices higher than the price at which they end up selling the products. To make a profit, businesses must plan for discounts when setting their list prices.

Figure 22-2 illustrates the components that marketing managers consider when setting prices. To make a profit, marketers must set prices high enough to

Manager's Perspective on CAREER

Everyone in business must understand accounting and costs related to products. Salespeople cannot sell products if they do not know these costs. Buyers must know their costs before they buy inventory, raw material, or supplies. The more you know about accounting, the better you will understand your business career field.

more than cover all costs. The income remaining after deducting costs from the selling price is the net profit for that sale.

The largest cost that the price must cover is the cost of goods sold. The **cost of goods sold** is the cost to produce the product or buy it for resale. For manufacturers, the cost of goods sold is the total cost of the materials, operations, and personnel used to make the product. For wholesalers and retailers, it is the price they pay their supplier to buy the product plus the cost of transporting it to their location for resale to their customers. For example, if the invoice price of an item is $55 and the transportation charge is $5, the cost of goods sold is $60.

Operating expenses are the costs of operating a business. They do not include costs involved in the actual production or purchase of merchandise, which would be part of the cost of goods sold. Most costs involved in the day-to-day running of a business fall into this category. Figure 22-3 lists some common operating expenses.

The **margin** or **gross profit** is the difference between the selling price and the cost of goods sold. In Figure 22-2, the margin is 40 cents. Marketers think of the margin as the percentage of sales available to cover operating expenses and provide a profit. For example, a business may operate on a 25 percent margin. If operating expenses are more than 25 percent of sales, the company will lose money.

Net profit is the difference between the selling price and all costs and expenses of the business. Net profit can be calculated using the following formula:

Net profit = selling price − cost of goods sold − operating expenses.

Markup is the amount added to the cost of goods sold to determine the selling price. It is similar to margin. When stated in dollars and cents, markup and margin are identical. For example, in Figure 22-2, the markup is also 40 cents. Often businesses express the markup as a percentage of the cost of goods sold or as a percentage of the selling price. Thus, the markup in Figure 22-2 is 66 2/3 percent of cost (40 cents/60 cents). Expressed as a percentage of the selling price, it is 40 percent (40 cents/100 cents).

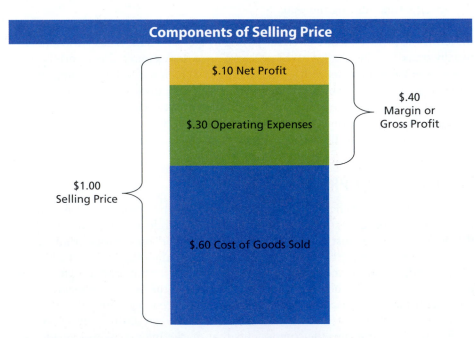

Figure 22-2 The ratios between price and expenses allow marketing managers to analyze profitability.

Some consumers confuse the markup percentage with profit. They believe that if a business has a 50 percent markup, it is making a profit of 50 percent of the selling price. However, markup must cover operating expenses. If the business with a 50 percent average markup on its products has operating expenses of 45 percent of sales, it will have a profit of 5 percent of total sales.

Markdown is any amount by which the original selling price is reduced before the item is sold. Companies use markdowns when their inventory is not selling at a satisfactory rate. Because the costs associated with the products remain the same, markdowns reduce profits, so companies want to avoid them.

Common Operating Expenses	
• Advertising	• Rent
• Cost of business services	• Repairs and maintenance
• Customer service expenses	• Salaries, wages, and benefits
• Delivery costs	• Supplies
• Depreciation expense	• Taxes
• Donations	• Telephone service
• Furniture, fixtures, and equipment	• Uncollected accounts and collection expense
• Insurance	• Utilities
• Interest paid on borrowed money	
• Inventory losses	

© Cengage Learning 2013.

Figure 22-3 Businesses consider operating expenses such as these when setting a product's price.

CHECKPOINT

Explain how net profit is calculated.

Pricing Strategies

Because businesses operate for profit, they must set prices that will entice customers to buy the products yet will make a profit after costs are deducted. Businesses can use different strategies to achieve this goal. For example, a business can establish a high price. Fewer customers will buy at a high price than a low price, but the company will make a greater gross profit per item sold. On the other hand, a business can choose to set a low price. More customers will buy at a low price than a high price, but the company will make less gross profit per item sold. In this case, the company hopes to make a satisfactory profit by selling a large number of items.

No one strategy is best in all cases. Either of these strategies can result in a satisfactory profit for the company. Consider the following example:

Business A buys a product for $500 and offers it for sale at $1,000. It sells four of these in a month, making a gross profit of $2,000:

$1,000 × 4 items = $4,000 revenue from sales
$500 × 4 items = $2,000 cost of goods sold
$4,000 revenue − $2,000 cost of goods sold = $2,000 gross profit

Business B, selling the same product, thinks it can make a better profit by setting a lower price and selling a greater quantity. It offers the item for $800. In one month it sells six items, for a gross profit of $1,800:

$800 × 6 items = $4,800 revenue from sales
$500 × 6 items = $3,000 cost of goods sold
$4,800 revenue − $3,000 cost of goods sold = $1,800 gross profit

In this case, Business A's strategy made the higher profit. However, either strategy could result in the higher profit. The challenge is to choose the strategy that works best for the situation.

Both of these companies made a gross profit, but they must deduct operating expenses to arrive at their net profit. If Business A's operating expenses are much greater than Business B's, then Business B might make the greater net profit, even though its gross profit was lower.

Businesses must be careful about setting extremely high or extremely low prices. With extremely high prices, the business may not sell a sufficient quantity to yield a net profit. With extremely low prices, the business may not be able to cover its costs no matter how many products it sells. Between these two extremes is a reasonable price that satisfies customers and allows a reasonable profit. Next you will learn about some of the strategies marketing managers use to set a reasonable price.

PRICING TO MEET COMPETITION

The amount of competition among companies handling similar products or services is an important factor in establishing prices. If one company has much higher prices than its competitors for the same products, some of the company's customers are likely to buy from the competitors. Even similar businesses in separate locations may compete for the same customers. If prices are too high in one area, many people will travel elsewhere to purchase goods or services. For example, if a service station in one neighborhood is selling a certain brand of gasoline for $2.39 a gallon and a station two miles away is selling the same brand for $1.99, customers may be willing to travel to buy where the price is lower.

The Internet has had a major impact on pricing, because it makes price comparison easy for customers. Some websites search for the lowest prices for specific products. Customers who value low prices over service may buy from the lowest-priced competitor.

A business may need to offer some of its merchandise at a price that does not allow a profit because a competitor has established an even lower price. However, it is not always necessary to have a lower selling price than competitors. If a company has a loyal group of customers and offers a product with some distinct advantages, or provides services that customers want and other companies do not offer, the company may be able to charge a higher price without losing

Why has the Internet had a major effect on pricing?

customers. Remember that the cost of providing higher-quality products or more services may be expensive, so profits may not be higher just because prices are higher. Windzors, the exclusive sporting goods store in the chapter-opening case, was relying on unique products, exclusive services, and an interesting shopping experience to justify much higher product prices.

When competition is intense, some companies may have to set some of their prices at or below the actual costs of doing business. In such a competitive situation, only the most efficient businesses make a net profit. Even when competition is not strong, if a company sets its prices too high, people will try to do without its products or find substitutes rather than pay prices that seem to give that company an unduly large profit.

PRICING TO EARN A SPECIFIC PROFIT

When introducing a new product, many businesses base their selling price on a specific profit they want to make. The business first determines the costs of producing and marketing the product, as well as all related operating expenses. It then sets the price by adding the amount necessary to make the target profit. But even setting prices based on a target profit won't guarantee that the company will make that profit. Customers must like the product well enough to buy it at that price. Also, competitors selling the same product might sell for less, luring away customers. In either case, the company may have to mark down its price to attract more buyers, reducing profit below its target.

PRICING BASED ON CONSUMER DEMAND

The marketing managers of a fashion merchandise business know that at certain times the products will be in great demand, and at other times the demand will be very low. Swimsuits sell quickly early in the season but slowly late in the season, unless the retailer greatly reduces the prices. Because a retailer cannot accurately predict the exact number of suits it will sell, it will set a selling price at the beginning of the season that should ensure a net profit on the entire inventory of swimsuits, even though it may have to drastically reduce prices later in the season.

A manufacturer of a product that suddenly becomes popular may want to sell at a high price while the demand is great. When new competitors enter the market or customers tire of the product and demand begins to decline, the manufacturer will need to sell the product at a much lower price.

The introduction of new products in the market presents an interesting study in price decisions. When high-definition televisions (HDTVs) were introduced in the market, a few brands were priced extremely high—several thousand dollars—compared to older style televisions. As customer demand increased, many more competitors entered the market, and prices began to drop to between $1,000 and $2,000. Eventually prices dropped even lower.

PRICING TO SELL MORE PRODUCTS

Products that are priced higher usually sell more slowly than those that cost the same but are priced lower. For example, a product that cost $40 may be priced at $60 but may not sell for two months. A similar product that also cost $40 may be priced at $48 and sell in two weeks. If the second product continues to sell at that pace, the business will sell more of it and achieve a larger net profit over the course of the year. The business must be careful that the lower price is high enough to cover operating costs and still contribute to profit. Otherwise, using the lower price is a poor decision. For example, if the product priced at $48 had a cost of goods sold of $40 and must cover $10 worth of operating expenses, then the business will never make a net profit on the product no matter how many it sells.

If a business has a low rate of inventory turnover, it must charge higher prices to cover the cost of the inventory and the operating expenses of the business. For instance, many items in an exclusive jewelry store may be sold and replenished at the rate of once a year or less. The jeweler, therefore, must mark the retail price of the products very high in relation to their cost to make a reasonable profit.

PRICING TO PROVIDE CUSTOMER SERVICES

A business that offers credit, free delivery, or 24-hour emergency service will have higher operating expenses than one that offers no services. Higher operating expenses require a higher selling price to yield the same

How do extra customer services affect pricing?

net profit as that earned by a business with lower expenses. If a business's customers expect a high level of service, or if the business is using the extra service to appear different from competitors, it will have to set prices higher to achieve a profit.

✓ CHECKPOINT

List five different pricing strategies that businesses use.

●●●● Controlling Costs

Marketing managers are not always able to increase prices just because they are not making a profit. The costs of merchandise and operating expenses often increase, but prices charged to customers cannot be raised due to competition. Businesses have to make careful purchasing and operating decisions to avoid unnecessary expenses. Three important areas that can affect costs are (1) markdowns, (2) damaged or stolen merchandise, and (3) merchandise returns.

MARKDOWNS

In many cases, businesses are forced to sell some products at lower prices than they had planned. This can happen because they purchase products that customers do not want or that go out of style. Businesses must also sell products at lower prices when they overestimated demand and bought too many products, when competition increases, or when competitors lower prices.

Businesses cannot always avoid markdowns, but they can usually control them. Careful purchasing can eliminate many markdowns. Proper product handling and marketing practices can also reduce the number of markdowns.

DAMAGED OR STOLEN MERCHANDISE

Some products may be damaged so much that they cannot be sold. Other products may be stolen by shoplifters or employees. These situations have a serious effect on profits.

Assume that a product with a selling price of $5.00 is damaged or stolen. The product cost the business $4.00, and operating expenses amounted to $.75 for each product. Expected net profit was $.25. In order to recover the cost of that one damaged or stolen product, the business will have to sell 16 more products than originally planned (16 products × $.25 = $4.00). It will have to sell another three products to cover operating expenses. The business will not earn a profit on the sale of the 19 products if just one product out of 20 is damaged or stolen. To reduce the amount of damaged and stolen merchandise, companies may take actions such as employing security guards or installing surveillance cameras and training employees to handle merchandise carefully.

The Internet is gaining in popularity with advertisers. This medium facilitates the targeting of individuals with customized ads. But companies must learn how to use this medium. The Interactive Advertising Bureau provides information to help companies develop e-mail, wireless, and interactive television strategies.

Access the website for this textbook and choose the link for Chapter 22 Net Bookmark. Identify the benefits of membership in the IAB. Evaluate the information provided on the IAB site. How does the IAB help companies?

www.cengage.com/school/bizmgmt

RETURNED MERCHANDISE

If customers are not satisfied with their purchases, they may return the products for a refund. This adds to expenses in two ways. If the business can resell the merchandise, it will have to sell it at a reduced price. Also, many expenses are involved in handling and reselling the returned merchandise, which increases operating expenses. Some returned merchandise cannot be resold.

To make a profit, businesses must consider their record of returned merchandise when buying and pricing merchandise. They must try to buy just the type and quality of merchandise that customers prefer in order to help reduce returns. Salespeople should be trained to sell products that customers need rather than attempting to convince customers to buy things they do not need. Offering customer service and support to help customers use the products properly and resolve their problems also reduces the amount of merchandise returned.

When managers give close attention to the three problem areas of markdowns, damaged or stolen merchandise, and returns, they can keep operating expenses to a minimum. As a result, they can maintain profits while lowering the markup percentage. In that way, both the businesses and their customers benefit.

 CHECKPOINT

List three purchasing and operating areas in which a business can control costs.

22.2 ASSESSMENT

UNDERSTAND MANAGEMENT CONCEPTS

Determine the best answer for each of the following questions.

1. A purchase that is net 60 days with a 3 percent discount for payment within 30 days would be indicated by
   a. 3/60, n/30
   b. 30/60, n/3
   c. 30/3, n/60
   d. 3/30, n/60

2. What is it called when a business sells a product at a price lower than planned?
   a. markup
   b. markup on price
   c. markdown
   d. price discount

THINK CRITICALLY

Answer the following questions as completely as possible.

3. Explain how competition influences pricing strategy.

4. Explain why stolen merchandise can have a strong impact on a company's profits.

F⊕cus On...Feature

Yahoo for Yahoo!

Yahoo! is an iconic Internet brand with one of the most recognized dot com names. In 1994, David Filo and Jerry Yang were doctoral candidates at Stanford University when they began developing a list of their favorite websites. David and Jerry realized they had a business when friends wanted to search their list to find websites. They started their business in 1995 under the name Yahoo!

Yahoo! rapidly grew to be a world leader in providing search results. By 2011, over 500 million users used Yahoo! every month. Yahoo!'s strategy was to grow into a media business by purchasing a number of companies that would allow Yahoo! to add services for email, webhosting, e-commerce, Internet radio and television, sports, and news. At the height of the dot com bubble, Yahoo!'s stock price was over $100. After the dot-com bubble burst, the stock price dropped to close to $4 in 2001.

In 2000, Yahoo! began using a search engine from a company called Google to provide search results. By 2004, Yahoo! had its own search technology. In 2008, Microsoft offered $44.6 billion to purchase Yahoo!, but the company refused the offer.

In 2010, Yahoo! earned almost $2 billion in advertising revenue from rich media and video ads on its sites. By 2011, Yahoo!'s advertising revenue had started to slow. Yahoo! had moved to a distant second behind Google in providing search results. The Yahoo! board of directors fired their CEO and the marketing vice president left the company.

The value of Yahoo! had dropped to below $20 billion and the board needed to figure out what to do with the company. One option was to break up the media conglomerate into smaller companies. The smaller divisions might be more innovative and devise new means of marketing and creating advertising revenue. Another option would be to hire a new CEO and new marketing team to attempt to turn the company around. Either strategy would require Yahoo! to find a way to contend in a competitive environment with diminishing advertising revenue.

THINK CRITICALLY

1. Why would Yahoo! purchase so many different types of online media companies? How would this help in selling marketing services?
2. What could account for Yahoo!'s problems in generating advertising revenue and loss of market value?
3. If you were on the board of Yahoo!, what would you recommend: breaking up the company or hiring a new CEO? Justify your answer.
4. Use the Internet to find out what happened to Yahoo!.

Promotion

Goals

- Discuss the purpose of promotion in meeting business and consumer needs.
- Discuss how businesses use advertising to promote their products.
- Explain the parts of the selling process and how each is used to help customers make buying decisions that meet their needs.
- Describe the different types of sales promotions.

Terms

- advertising p. 604
- advertising media p. 604
- full disclosure p. 607
- substantiation p. 607
- cease-and-desist order p. 607
- corrective advertising p. 607
- personal selling p. 607
- buying motives p. 607
- objections p. 609
- sales promotions p. 610
- self-service merchandising p. 611

●●● Promotion as Marketing Communication

Marketing managers use communication strategies to create customer interest in products and services. Consumers need to know about a product before they can buy it. They need to know a product is available and where they can purchase it. They must be able to easily see the differences among brands and determine which brand will best meet their needs.

Promotion is the primary way that businesses communicate with prospective customers. Businesses use a promotional mix to inform consumers about the features and benefits of products and services and to encourage them to buy.

The model for effective communication is the basis for successful promotion. The company that develops the promotion is the sender. The information in the promotion is the message, and the method of promotion determines the communication medium. The prospective consumer is the receiver. Feedback from the receiver helps the sender determine if the promotion was successful and decide if the message needs adjustment.

Marketing managers use a promotional mix to move customers from recognizing a need to purchasing a product. A promotional mix that businesses commonly use to communicate with customers includes advertising, personal selling, and sales promotions, such as coupons, sampling, and in-store displays.

Consumers generally follow five steps in progressing toward a purchase decision. Figure 22-4 summarizes the steps in the consumer decision-making process. Although the five steps are common to all consumers, each consumer has different needs and gathers information in different ways to satisfy those needs. Some customers spend a great deal of time and consult many information sources before deciding to buy or not to buy. Other consumers might not be as careful or use the same methods. Therefore, businesses must provide appropriate information to help consumers move through the decision-making process to select the product that meets their needs.

Consumer Decision-Making Process		
Step	**Explanation**	**Example**
1. Problem Recognition	The consumer identifies a need to satisfy or a problem to solve.	Consumer runs out of a product or finds a new product he or she wants.
2. Information Search	The consumer gathers information about alternative solutions for the need or problem.	Consumer can ask friends' advice, search the Internet, or visit multiple stores.
3. Alternative Evaluation	The consumer weighs the options to determine which will best satisfy the need or solve the problem.	Consumer can compare multiple products from past experience, use online evaluations, or consumer magazines.
4. Purchase	If the consumer identifies a suitable and affordable choice, he or she makes the purchase.	Consumer can make the purchase in a store or online.
5. Post-Purchase Evaluation	The consumer uses the product or service and evaluates how well it met the need or solved the problem.	Consumer reflects on what he or she expected to receive and what was actually received.

© Cengage Learning 2013.

Figure 22-4 If consumers receive more than expected, they will be satisfied. If they receive less than expected, they will be unsatisfied.

CHECKPOINT

List the three different methods of promoting a product.

Advertising

Advertising is any form of paid promotion that delivers a message to many people at the same time. Because the message is designed to appeal to many people, it is rather impersonal. However, because the message reaches thousands of people, the cost of communicating with each person is very low.

Organizations spend more money each year in the United States on advertising than on any other type of promotion. The average business spends less than 3 percent of total sales annually on advertising, but some businesses spend over 20 percent. Companies in industries such as beverages, cosmetics, and electronics rely heavily on advertising and spend a significant amount throughout the year to keep their brand names in front of consumers.

ADVERTISING PURPOSES AND MEDIA CHOICES

Advertising is a powerful tool because it can help a business accomplish a variety of objectives. Companies must consider carefully what they want to communicate to consumers and plan specific advertising to accomplish that communication goal. The major purposes of advertising are shown in Figure 22-5.

Most businesses use some form of advertising to attract prospective customers. However, the methods of reaching consumers—the advertising media—vary a great deal. **Advertising media** are the methods of delivering the promotional message to the intended audience. The most widely used forms of advertising media are classified by categories in Figure 22-6.

FACTS & FIGURES

Ad Dollars

In 2010, Procter & Gamble was the U.S. corporation that spent the most dollars on advertising. P&G spent more than $3.1 billion to advertise Pampers, Tide, Old Spice, Ivory, and other brands.

PLANNING AND MANAGING ADVERTISING

Businesses have many choices of media to use to communicate information to customers. However, planning an advertising program involves more than selecting the media. Advertising should be planned to support other promotion and marketing decisions. Most businesses that spend a significant amount of money for advertising throughout the year develop an advertising plan. The plan outlines communication goals and specifies an advertising budget, a calendar of advertising activities, and how the advertising will be evaluated.

Small businesses often need help in developing their advertising plans and writing their advertisements. A printing company may have specialists who can write the copy and design the advertisement for a direct-mail piece. The people who sell advertising space may offer suggestions for preparing newspaper ads. Radio and television station marketing people may also help plan advertising.

As the business grows, the owner has the option of hiring someone to handle the advertising or of placing all of the company's advertising planning in the hands of an advertising agency. Full-service agencies provide all the services related to planning and producing advertisements for all media and buying the space or time for the ads in the media. Most agencies also offer research services to determine customers' product and information needs. For their services, advertising agencies usually charge a percentage of the total amount spent for the advertising, but some may charge for the actual costs of developing and placing the ads.

Some very large companies have a complete advertising department that performs all the functions of an ad agency. Because of the amount of advertising large companies do and its cost, it is more efficient for those companies to have their own advertising personnel than to pay an ad agency.

THE ADVERTISING BUDGET Companies allot an amount for advertising when they develop their overall company budget. Most businesses plan the advertising program for one year or less. Of course, emergencies may arise that require a quick decision, but planning helps avoid budget misuse. If the company is developing a new product, it will usually prepare an advertising budget to support the new product's introduction into the market.

Large businesses often develop separate advertising budgets for new products, product lines, customer groups, or market regions. Separate budgets make it easier to determine the effects of specific advertising on sales and profits.

The amount a business spends on advertising depends more on the characteristics of the product and target market than on the competition. A business with a loyal group of customers and a product that has been in the market for a long time may need to spend less than a business with a new or very complex product or one positioned in an extremely competitive market. A business that relies on advertising for the majority of its promotion will, of course, spend a larger percentage of sales on advertising than a business that has a balanced promotional program of advertising, personal selling, and sales promotion.

TIMING OF ADVERTISING Advertising is more effective at some times than others. Companies determine the times when potential customers are most willing and able to buy the products or services advertised. Many products and services are

Advertising Purposes

1. To inform and educate consumers.
2. To introduce a new product or business.
3. To announce an improvement or product change.
4. To reinforce important product features and benefits.
5. To increase the frequency of use of a product.
6. To increase the variety of uses of a product.
7. To convince people to enter a store.
8. To develop a list of prospects.
9. To make a brand, trademark, or slogan familiar.
10. To improve the image of a company or product.
11. To gain support for ideas or causes.

© Cengage Learning 2013.

Figure 22-5 Advertising can accomplish many purposes. Businesses carefully plan each ad to focus on a specific purpose.

Types of Advertising Media by Categories	
Publication Advertising	Newspapers, general and special interest magazines, business and professional journals, and directories
Mass Media Advertising	Radio, network and local television, cable television
Outdoor Advertising	Billboards, signs, posters, vehicle signage, and electronic displays
Direct Advertising	Sales letters, catalogs, brochures, inserts, telemarketing, and fax messages
Display Advertising	Window, counter, and aisle displays; special signage; self-service merchandising; trade show displays
Internet Advertising	Banners, buttons, pop-up, podcasts, e-mail marketing, interstitial ads, rich media

© Cengage Learning 2013.

Figure 22-6 Marketing managers use a combination of advertising media to reach their communication goals.

seasonal, with the majority of sales concentrated in a few months of the year. Companies spend more advertising dollars during those times when consumers are considering the purchase of the product than during times when customers are less likely to buy. For example, advertising for ski resorts or ocean cruises increases during the winter months, and advertising for air conditioners and lawn mowers appears mostly in the spring and summer.

Occasionally, companies advertise to increase purchases at times customers do not traditionally consider buying the product. By emphasizing new product development and advertising, turkey producers and processors have increased the sale of turkey products throughout the year. Those businesses had previously sold almost all of their products near the Thanksgiving holiday and one or two other holiday times during the year.

A single advertisement may produce temporary results, but regular advertising is important in building a steady stream of customers. If advertising does not appear often enough, customers tend to forget about the business or product. To keep their name and brands fresh in consumers' minds, businesses often spread their advertising over the entire year. Only when the company wants an immediate impact, such as for a new-product introduction or for a special event, would it consider a large, one-time expenditure.

ADVERTISING EVALUATION Advertising effectiveness is evaluated in a number of ways. Researchers measure which advertisements a market sees, what they remember from the ads, and whether or not the ads have influenced their attitudes or feelings about a product.

A number of companies specialize in advertising evaluations. The A. C. Nielsen Company measures advertising performance for broadcast media, online media, and mobile media. The Arbitron Company has people record in a diary which radio programs they listen to throughout a day.

TRUTH IN ADVERTISING AND SELLING

Laws and regulations protect consumers from unfair promotional practices. Nationally, the Federal Trade Commission (FTC) and the Federal Communications Commission (FCC) are responsible for regulating promotion. False advertising is a violation of the law. *False advertising* is defined by federal law as "misleading in a material respect" or in any way that could influence the customer's purchase or use of the product.

To protect consumers, advertisers are required to make **full disclosure**, providing all information necessary for consumers to make an informed decision. They must also provide **substantiation**—that is, be able to prove all claims they make about their products and services in promotions.

If a business violates laws and regulations in its advertising, it may face three types of penalties from the regulating agencies: (1) The agency may impose a **cease-and-desist order**, which requires the company to stop using specific advertisements. (2) If the advertising has harmed consumers, the company may be required to spend a specified amount of its advertising budget to run corrective advertising. **Corrective advertising** is new advertising designed to change the false impression left by the misleading information. (3) In unusual situations, the company may have to pay a fine to the government or to the consumers harmed by its illegal advertising.

Long-term business success is built on honesty and fair practices. A businessperson may occasionally be tempted to exaggerate or to imitate a competitor who seems to be stretching the truth. In the long run, however, it does not pay to destroy customers' confidence. If customers do not get what they believed was promised to them in advertisements or by salespeople, they will likely not return to the business. On the other hand, a satisfied customer is often an important source of promotion for a business.

CHECKPOINT

List the components of an advertising plan.

Personal Selling

Personal selling is promotion through direct, personal contact with a customer. The salesperson usually makes direct contact with the customer through a face-to-face meeting. There are many types of customers, and a salesperson must be able to adjust to each type. Some customers know exactly what they want, but others are in the early stages of decision making. A critical sales skill is understanding the customer's motivations.

STUDYING THE WANTS OF CUSTOMERS

Individuals are motivated to buy for different reasons. **Buying motives** are the reasons people buy. Some common consumer buying motives are listed in Figure 22-7. To be successful, the salesperson must determine a particular customer's buying motive and then tailor the sales presentation to appeal to that motive. In many cases, the salesperson can appeal to more than one buying motive. For instance, a laundry company representative attempting to sell laundry services to a working couple with three children may talk about the comfort and convenience of having the laundry done outside the home rather than doing it themselves. The salesperson may also explain that it is less expensive to send the laundry to a professional service because of all the expenses involved in doing laundry at home.

Suppose this same salesperson calls on the owner of a barbershop or beauty salon. The salesperson can emphasize the special sterilizing treatment

Common Consumer Buying Motives		
Status	Ease of use	Affection
Appetite	Love of beauty	Wealth
Comfort	Amusement	Enjoyment
Desire for bargains	Desire for good health	Pride of ownership
Recognition	Friendship	Fear

© Cengage Learning 2013.

Figure 22-7 Understanding common buying motives of consumers is an important selling skill.

given to towels, capes, and uniforms and the speedy delivery of the laundered items. Both the family and the business owner might find individually scheduled pickup and delivery services attractive. Providing customer satisfaction through a sale is the ultimate goal of a salesperson. This method of selling does not require high-pressure selling; it requires intelligent customer-oriented selling.

PRESENTING AND DEMONSTRATING THE PRODUCT

Customers are interested in what the product will do for them and how they can use it. Salespeople must have a thorough knowledge of the product so they can provide accurate information and answer questions. For example, customers might ask: "How much paint will I need for a bathroom 12 feet by 8 feet?" "Which vinyl is best for a concrete basement floor?" "Why is this pair of shoes $68 and that pair $55?" Different customers value different types of information about the same product. Salespeople should study the products they sell as well as the competition's products, so they can be prepared to answer any questions customers might ask. Nothing is more frustrating than to listen to a salesperson talk at length about product information that is of no interest to the customer.

In addition to giving customers information, salespeople should be able to demonstrate the use of the product so that customers can determine whether or not the product will meet their needs. It is usually a good idea for salespeople to show the product and its uses at the same time that they provide information about it. The salesperson can then focus the customer's attention on the product while explaining its features and advantages. Whenever possible, salespeople should encourage the customer to participate. When a customer is directly involved and becomes comfortable using the product, initial interest can change to desire to own the product.

In certain selling situations, such as selling very large or bulky products or selling services, salespeople demonstrate without having the actual product. They use items such as photographs, charts, catalogs, videotapes, or computer displays. Such situations make it more difficult for the customer to get a true feeling for the use of a product, so the salesperson must rely on effective communication to increase understanding and desire to purchase the product.

ANSWERING CUSTOMER QUESTIONS

A customer usually has many questions during the salesperson's presentation and demonstration. The salesperson should not be concerned by the questions

21st CENTURY SKILLS

Media Literacy

Knowing how to use media to communicate your thoughts, ideas, and questions with others is an important life skill. Equally important is knowing how to use and evaluate media to gather information and draw conclusions. As a consumer, you need to understand the motives behind promotion and advertising.

but should view them as an opportunity to better understand the customer's needs and help the customer make the best decision.

When customers are not certain the product is suitable for them, they may raise objections. **Objections** are concerns or complaints expressed by the customer. Objections may represent genuine concerns, or they may simply be an effort to avoid making a decision to purchase. It is difficult to second-guess a customer to determine if the objection is real or not. The salesperson should listen carefully to the objection, then help the customer make the best decision.

CLOSING THE SALE

For many salespeople, the most difficult part of the selling process is asking the customer to buy. As you saw in Figure 22-4, a decision to purchase involves several steps, and each customer moves through those steps in a different way and at a different speed.

If the salesperson has involved the customer in the sales presentation and has listened carefully to the customer's needs, the customer's interest in buying should be rather apparent. Typically, effective salespeople give the customer the opportunity to buy several times during the sales presentation by asking for a decision on a specific model, color, price, or type of payment. If the customer continues to ask questions, the salesperson answers the questions and continues the discussion until the customer appears satisfied. Then the salesperson attempts to close the sale again.

Many sales, particularly for expensive products, take several meetings between the salesperson and the customer. In business-to-business selling, teams of salespeople and company specialists may meet several times with teams of buyers from the customer's company. Several people will likely make the final decision. Salespeople should continue to work with the customers until it is clear that they do not want the product or until the sale is made.

FOLLOW-UP

The selling process is not complete just because the customer agrees to purchase a product. Selling is successful only when the customer is satisfied. Satisfied customers lead to repeat sales that help the company remain profitable in the future.

A plan for retaining customers includes several follow-up activities after the sale. The salesperson should check with the customer to make sure that the order is correct, that the customer knows how to use the product, and that the product meets the customer's needs. If there are problems, they should be corrected immediately. If following up with each customer is impractical, the business could periodically conduct a customer satisfaction survey. This could be done with an in-store, mailed, or e-mailed questionnaire or through phone calls to random customers. The follow-up contact will remind satisfied customers where they made their purchases, so they may choose to buy from the business again.

 CHECKPOINT

Name the five areas that salespeople must master to be successful.

● ● ● ● **Sales Promotions**

Sales promotions are any promotional activities other than advertising and personal selling intended to motivate customers to buy. Some sales promotions are designed to encourage customers to buy immediately. Others are designed to display the products in an attention-getting or attractive way to encourage customers to examine the products.

Coupons are a type of sales promotion used extensively to promote consumer products. Coupons are an effective method of increasing sales of a product for a short time. They are used principally to introduce a new product or to maintain and increase a company's share of the market for established brands. Coupons usually appear in newspaper and magazine advertisements, but they are also distributed by direct mail and are now even available on the Internet. A coupon packaged with a product the customer just purchased may encourage the customer to buy the same brand the next time. Or the enclosed coupon may be for another product from the same company, to encourage the customer to try it.

Manufacturers often cooperate with wholesalers and retailers by providing promotional materials. Some of these materials, commonly furnished without cost or at a low price, include window displays, layouts and illustrations for newspaper ads, direct-mail inserts, display materials, and sales presentation aids.

When producers are introducing a new product, they may distribute samples through the mail. The purpose of this activity is to familiarize people with the products to create a demand for them in local businesses. Coupons often accompany the samples to encourage consumers to go to a local store and buy the product.

Producers and distributors also cooperate with retailers by arranging special displays and demonstrations within stores. For example, demonstrators may cook and distribute samples of a new brand of hot dog to customers in a grocery store. This practice usually helps the retailers sell the new product. The retailer, of course, gives this merchandise preference over other competing products because of this special promotion. Sometimes distributors pay merchants for the privilege of giving demonstrations or offer special prices for the opportunity.

Today, store designs, displays, labels, and packaging promote products so well that many stores let these promotions alone sell the products, rather than employ

How do businesses use coupons as a sales promotion tool?

© Getty Images/Photodisc

many salespeople. In **self-service merchandising**, customers select the products they want to purchase, take them to the checkout counter, and pay for them, without much help from salespeople. The display of merchandise in self-service stores attracts attention and makes it convenient for the shopper to examine the merchandise. The labels on the merchandise provide adequate information about the merchandise for the shopper to make a decision.

 **CHECKPOINT**

Name at least five different types of sales promotion.

22.3 ASSESSMENT

UNDERSTAND MANAGEMENT CONCEPTS

Determine the best answer for each of the following questions.

1. Any form of paid promotion that delivers a message to many people at the same time is called
   a. advertising
   b. promotion
   c. sales
   d. sales promotion

2. Customer objections in a sales situation are typically the result of
   a. real customer concerns
   b. avoiding decisions
   c. neither a nor b
   d. both a and b

THINK CRITICALLY

Answer the following questions as completely as possible.

3. Explain why a good salesperson studies a customer's buying motive.
4. Describe the major goals of sales promotion.

CHAPTER CONCEPTS

- Businesses must decide what to buy, when to buy, from whom to buy, and how much to buy. Mistakes result in unsold products, dissatisfied customers, and losses rather than profits.

- When setting a product's price, businesspeople consider payment terms, discounts, and the elements that make up a product's price. Pricing strategies include pricing to meet the competition, to earn a specific profit, to sell more products, and to provide customer services.

- Businesses attempt to control costs by establishing practices that help reduce markdowns, damaged or stolen merchandise, and customer returns.

- The most common methods of promotion are advertising, personal selling, and sales promotion.

- Advertising is paid promotion directed at a large number of people at the same time. An advertising plan outlines communication goals, timing, budget, and evaluation criteria. The FTC and the FCC protect consumers from unfair and illegal promotion. Companies must be able to prove all claims made in ads and can be asked to stop using illegal ads, run corrective advertising, or pay a fine.

- Personal selling is selling through direct personal contact. Salespeople study buying motives, demonstrate the product, answer customer questions, and close the sale when customers are prepared to make a purchase decision. The sale is complete when the salesperson follows up with the customer to determine if he or she is satisfied with the purchase.

REVIEW BUSINESS MANAGEMENT TERMS

Write the letter of the term that matches each definition. Some terms will not be used.

1. Initial price that the seller posts on a product
2. Price reduction given for paying by a certain date
3. Cost to produce a product or buy it for resale
4. Difference between the selling price and the cost of goods sold
5. Promotion through direct, personal contact with a customer
6. Methods of delivering a promotional message to the audience
7. The reasons people buy
8. Any promotional activities other than advertising and personal selling intended to motivate customers to buy
9. Difference between the selling price and all costs and expenses of the business
10. Providing all information necessary for consumers to make an informed decision
11. Ability to prove all claims made about a product or service in promotions
12. Requiring a company to stop using specific advertisements

a. advertising media
b. buying motives
c. cash discount
d. cease-and desist-order
e. cost of goods sold
f. discounts
g. full disclosure
h. list price
i. margin (gross profit)
j. markdown
k. net profit
l. personal selling
m. sales promotions
n. substantiation

Determine the best answer.

13. A price reduction that manufacturers give to their channel partners, such as wholesalers or retailers, in exchange for additional services is a
    a. manufacturer's discount
    b. trade discount
    c. sales promotion
    d. wholesale discount

14. Reductions taken from the price of a product to encourage customers to buy is known as a
    a. selling price
    b. markdown
    c. markup
    d. trade discount

15. A price reduction offered for ordering or taking delivery of products in advance of the normal buying period to encourage buyers to purchase earlier than necessary or at a time when orders are normally low is called a(n)
    a. quantity discount
    b. seasonal discount
    c. annual discount
    d. special discount

16. The costs of operating a business, not including costs involved in the actual production or purchase of merchandise, are the
    a. cost of goods sold
    b. normal expenses
    c. operating expenses
    d. operating costs

17. If a company violates federal law by "misleading in a material respect" or in any way that could influence the customer's purchase or use of the product, it could be forced to
    a. cease and desist
    b. use corrective advertising
    c. pay a fine
    d. all of the above

18. Subtracting any discounts from a product's list price yields the actual price customers pay for the product, or its
    a. actual price
    b. sale price
    c. selling price
    d. trade price

19. Advertising designed to change false impressions left by misleading information is called
    a. corrective advertising
    b. false advertising
    c. normal advertising
    d. misleading advertising

APPLY WHAT YOU KNOW

Answer the following questions.

20. Explain why it is important for businesses to consider both the customer and the business when planning the sale of products.

21. Using the formula for calculating net profit, suggest several ways that a business can increase the net profit from the sale of a product.

22. Which advertising media do you believe are most effective for the products you purchase? Why? Would the same media be most effective for advertising the products your parents buy? Why or why not?

23. Explain why high-technology products are often sold initially at very high prices but later at prices that have dropped dramatically.

24. Why do you believe that closing the sale is the most difficult step of the selling process for many salespeople? As a customer, what would you recommend to salespeople to make that step easier and more successful?

MAKE ACADEMIC CONNECTIONS

Complete the following activities.

25. **Math** A book and gift store with average annual sales of $700,000 spends 3 percent of its sales for advertising. The store's advertising budget is divided as follows: catalogs, 30 percent; calendars and other sales promotions, 7 percent; window displays, 15 percent; newspaper advertising, 15 percent; direct mail, 20 percent; and miscellaneous, 13 percent.
    a. How much is the average annual advertising budget?
    b. What is the amount spent on each type of advertising?

26. **Research** Use the Internet to identify the cost of ad placement in a number of media. Identify the cost per thousand (cost/1,000 people reached) for each medium. Identify which media have a higher cost. Specify why these media are able to charge a higher price.

27. **Technology** Use the Internet to find online examples of each of the following types of advertising: static banner, interactive banner, button, sponsored site, and affiliate listing with another Internet site. Using a screen capture, take an example of each online advertisement you find and prepare a slide show of the various types of Internet advertising.

28. **Speaking** Assume that you are a salesperson in a furniture store. Develop a list of the buying motives you believe might be prompting each of the following types of customers to consider buying a sofa sleeper: (a) a college student who is buying furniture for a one-bedroom apartment, (b) a family that is outfitting a family room they are remodeling, and (c) a motel owner who is deciding between a less expensive sofa and the sofa sleeper for 50 rooms. Prepare and present a sales presentation to the class that you would use for each of these customers.

CASE IN POINT

CASE 22-1: Advertising: The Root of All Evil?

Peter and Torrie were watching television. During a commercial they discussed how companies use advertising.

Peter: *Companies spend too much money on advertising. If they would spend less, the prices of products would be a lot lower. I heard that companies that advertise on the Super Bowl program spend more than $1 million for one ad.*

Torrie: *Companies are not only placing ads in the middle of shows, they're also putting them into movies and television shows. I think they should remove ads from television and radio. I usually switch between channels during commercials anyway.*

Peter: *It seems like advertising is everywhere. No matter where you go or what you do, you see products promoted. We record our shows on our DVR, so I don't even see commercials on our system.*

Torrie: *It seems that companies advertise to get people to buy products they don't want. I've bought some things just because of the ad and regretted it later. Companies with good products shouldn't have to advertise. People will find out about them from others who try the products and like them.*

Peter: *The worst thing about advertising is that businesses can say anything they want to about products, even if the statements are untrue. They often criticize their competitors, making you think there's something wrong with the other product. After watching or listening to an ad, you're more confused than ever about what to buy.*

THINK CRITICALLY

1. Do you believe product prices would decrease if companies did not advertise? Explain.
2. Explain why some companies would pay $3 million to advertise during the Super Bowl.
3. What would happen to television and radio if advertising support was dropped?
4. Do good products need to be advertised? Why or why not?
5. What types of controls are there on what a business can say in its advertising? What can consumers do if they believe they have been misled by advertising?
6. Do you believe advertising results in more confusion than help for consumers? Justify your answer.
7. Do you think that the high level of advertising creates needs rather than simply informing the customer of product benefits? Explain your answer.
8. How do channel surfing and DVRs affect the effectiveness of advertising? How are companies shifting strategy in this new environment?
9. Develop an argument to convince Peter and Torrie that advertising is a vital part of a marketing strategy.

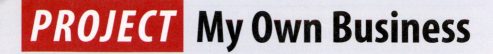

PROJECT My Own Business

Developing A Pricing and Advertising Strategy

A businessperson must set prices on products that will provide a reasonable net profit. In addition, a new business needs to plan promotion to introduce people to the business and its products and to encourage customers to try the products.

DATA COLLECTION

1. Locate information on start-up expenses for small businesses and develop a list of the common types of expenses and the range of costs you might expect when you begin your business.
2. Interview two small-business owners. Ask them to explain the terms and policies of some of the vendors they deal with.
3. Ask two small-business owners to explain the types of promotion they use, what assistance they get with promotional planning, and how they estimate the amount of money they can spend on promotional activities.
4. Collect samples of advertising and promotion that local small businesses are using. Analyze their effectiveness in communicating with prospective customers. Analyze the publicity's potential impact. Prepare possible strategies for dealing with it.
5. Check with several media that offer advertising in your community. Obtain a price list that indicates the costs of advertising in each medium, based on the size, type, and frequency.

ANALYSIS

1. Assume that, in an average month, your sales will include 700 small drinks, 800 large drinks, 900 supplement additions to the drinks (beyond any free supplements), and 2,000 high-energy snack bars. First, determine the price you will charge for each product, being realistic about what you believe customers are willing to pay. Then estimate your monthly expenses. Have several people review your estimates to determine if they are realistic. Then calculate your estimated monthly profit or loss.
2. Is your estimated monthly net profit adequate? If not, consider what changes you could make to improve it. (Don't make any price changes at this time.) Which of the possible changes are most likely to be successful? Which are least likely to be implemented?
3. Being as creative as possible, list several ways of promoting your new business that would be (a) informative, (b) unique, and (c) affordable. Consider methods in addition to advertising.
4. Develop a three-month promotional plan for your new business. Include methods, media to be used, time schedule, budget, and samples of the promotions.

Marketing Manager

The objective of any business is to market its products or services profitably. Marketing managers develop the business's detailed marketing strategy. They determine the demand for products and services, identify potential consumers, develop a pricing strategy, monitor trends in new products and services, and oversee product development and promotion.

Employment Outlook

Marketing manager jobs will grow at an average rate over the next 10 years. The greatest demand will be for sales managers, marketing managers, advertising and promotions managers, and public relations managers.

Job Titles

Director of Marketing
Marketing Assistant
Marketing Manager
Marketing Vice President

Needed Skills

- College or graduate degree in business administration with an emphasis in marketing preferable.
- Courses in business law, economics, accounting, finance, mathematics, and statistics desirable.
- Must be creative, motivated, able to handle stress, able to communicate persuasively (both orally and in writing).
- Must have computer skills to conduct advertising, marketing, promotion, public relations, and sales activities on the Internet.

Working in Marketing

John works as a marketing assistant to a marketing-division vice president. He must act as a jack-of-all-trades in marketing. He has been assigned jobs that include creating marketing presentations, conducting research, working with sales teams, developing promotional material, and helping to develop strategies for product lines. His boss is being considered for a corporate vice president's role. This would allow John to move to a marketing manager's position, where he would be in charge of a variety of marketing projects.

Career Assessment

Check your library or the Internet for resources about marketing managers. Identify the roles that marketing managers play in a business. Specify what you like and dislike about this career area.

© Corbis

Case Study

NEW PRODUCTS AND INCENTIVES COUNTER RISING GAS PRICES

Rising gas prices have spurred the production of hybrid and electric vehicles and the use of ethanol, a plant-based alcohol fuel that may help reduce U.S. dependence on foreign oil. In 2005, President Bush signed an energy bill that encourages greater use of ethanol as an ecologically sound fuel additive. Government incentives along with high gas prices have led to a mini-boom in ethanol plant construction in major corn-growing states like Iowa and Nebraska. By 2010, almost 33 billion gallons of ethanol were produced worldwide, with over 13 billion gallons produced in the United States.

Ethanol makers received a boost not only from the energy bill but from Detroit automakers who are promoting vehicles that can burn E85, a blend of 85 percent ethanol and 15 percent gasoline. The more common gasohol consists of 10 percent ethanol.

Electric and hybrid vehicles have been increasing their market share. Some hybrids charge their batteries from a gas or flex fuel engine; others can be plugged into an electrical outlet. The U.S. federal and some state governments put in place tax credits for plug-in hybrids and electric vehicles. Federal credits allow up to $7,500 for the vehicle plus $2,000 for charging equipment. State credits are in addition to federal credits.

Even with these incentives, electric and hybrid vehicles account for only 3 percent of the U.S. automotive market. Although drivers can save money on gasoline, consumers find electric vehicles to be more expensive to purchase and possibly more expensive to repair. As the price of carbon-based fuels increases and the price of electric vehicles decreases, the number of electric vehicles should increase.

THINK CRITICALLY

1. What are the cost factors that customers are likely to consider when purchasing a vehicle?
2. What products have benefited from higher fuel costs?
3. Why would farmers be interested in the trends covered in this article?
4. Why is it wise for automakers in Detroit to get involved in this special project?

Marketing Management Series Event

www.deca.org

For more information about competitive events and performance indicators, go to the DECA website.

PROCEDURE The DECA series event consists of a written comprehensive exam and a role-play that challenges students to develop solutions for business scenarios. You will have 10 minutes to review the situation and develop a professional approach to solving the problem. The judge has five minutes to ask questions. You are not allowed to give any materials to the judge.

SCENARIO The manager of a busy hotel has hired you to develop a strategy to improve the performance of weekend desk clerks. Full-time employees work at the hotel desk during the week. Guests frequently compliment the hotel staff during the week for their extra attention to detail. For weekend shifts, the hotel hires part-time college students as desk clerks. Hotel guests complain about slow service, no follow-up on guest concerns, unprofessional attitude, and desk clerks working on schoolwork.

YOUR ASSIGNMENT

Your assignment is to develop a training plan and incentives to raise the level of weekend performance. You also have been asked to improve the selection process for part-time weekend employees.

PERFORMANCE INDICATORS EVALUATED

- Explain the importance of professional development for all hotel employees.
- Communicate a strategy to improve the performance of weekend hotel desk clerks, including a training plan.
- Describe a way to monitor the performance of weekend desk clerks.
- Explain the financial value of raising the performance bar for weekend hotel desk clerks.

THINK CRITICALLY

1. Why is consistent performance by both weekday and weekend desk clerks important?
2. How can the full-time desk clerks help improve the performance of weekend employees?
3. How could a customer survey card be used to monitor the performance of hotel desk clerks?

6 UNIT

Human Resources Management

CHAPTERS

© Shutterstock/Yuri Arcurs

MANAGING HUMAN RESOURCES

23.1 Human Resources in Business

23.2 The Employment Process

23.3 Employment Law

© Shutterstock/Yuri Arcurs

Reality Check

Which Job to Choose?

Patrick Szabo and his parents were discussing two job offers he had received. One job was with a consumer research organization, and the second was in the marketing department of an international manufacturer. He thought he would enjoy working for either company.

The major difference between the job offers was the rate of pay and the benefits. In the first job, Patrick would be considered a contract employee. He would receive $20 per hour. He would work a minimum of 35 hours per week and most weeks would work a full 40 hours. However, there were no benefits such as insurance or paid holidays.

The second job paid an annual salary of $29,000. Patrick would work a minimum of 40 hours per week, with occasional weekend work during busy times. He would receive two weeks' paid vacation. The company would contribute $150 per month and Patrick would pay $55 per month for health insurance. He would also have a company-paid life insurance policy worth twice his annual salary. The company would contribute an amount equal to 5 percent of Patrick's salary to a retirement plan. If Patrick stayed with the company for five years, he would become part of the retirement plan and would be entitled to the money upon retirement.

As Patrick considered the choices, he was impressed with the possibility of earning over $40,000 per year at the first company if he worked 40 hours per week for the entire year. He had a number of school loans to pay off, and the extra money would come in handy.

However, his parents reminded him that he was not guaranteed all of those hours and could take no vacations if he expected to earn that much money. While he was healthy, unforeseen medical expenses would be covered by the health insurance of the second company but not by the first. Even though Patrick was only 26 years old, it was not too early to begin retirement savings. Patrick faced a difficult decision. He had never considered how salary and benefits could affect a job decision.

What's Your Reaction? How should Patrick compare the differences in salary and benefits the jobs offer?

Human Resources in Business

Goals

- Identify the reasons human resources management is important to businesses and employees.
- Identify and describe each of the major human resources activities.

Terms

- human resources management (HRM) p. 622
- 360-degree feedback p. 626
- employee assistance programs p. 627

⬤⬤⬤ The Need for Human Resources

Of all the resources used by a business, probably the most important to its success is people. People are responsible for the effective use of all other resources in the business. People make decisions, operate equipment, maintain records, and deal with customers. Because of their value to the business, managing people is a critical function.

All managers work with people. However, **human resources management (HRM)** consists of all activities involved with acquiring, developing, and compensating the people who do the company's work. HRM is sometimes called *personnel management*. Employees' pay, training, benefits, work environment, and many other factors contribute to their productivity, performance quality, and satisfaction with the company. The people who work in human resources management perform the tasks that help the business keep the skilled and productive employees it needs to accomplish its goals.

To begin human resources planning, companies must determine the number of people they will need in order to perform all tasks as well as the skills those people will need. Then they must recruit, hire, and train those employees. Once on the job, the employees will need equipment and other resources to accomplish their jobs. Directions provided through descriptions of job duties, policies, and procedures help the organization operate effectively. Human resources employees take part in all of these activities.

Businesses must be sure that employees are satisfied with their jobs and motivated to perform well. They need to be concerned about employee safety and health, working conditions, wages, and benefits. Employees who are doing a good job need to be recognized and rewarded, and those who are not must be given training and support to improve their performance. In some cases, employees must be removed from their jobs if their performance does not improve or if there are major changes in company operations. As you can see, working with people involves many responsibilities.

Most companies have a department that is responsible for human resources management. Large companies may have several specialized divisions within the department, each of which deals with a specific area in human resources. Some human resources activities may be performed in other departments across the organization but are planned and coordinated through the human resources department, sometimes called the *HR department* or just *HR*. Most managers regularly use the services of the human resources department as they work with their employees. Employees also receive a variety of services from the people who work in human resources.

 **CHECKPOINT**

What do the people who are involved in human resources management do?

●●● Human Resources Activities

Human resources activities support the overall goals of the organization. Although the size of the business, the number of employees, and other factors may influence how human resources activities are carried out, a number of activities are completed in all organizations. The important human resources activities common to many businesses are listed in Figure 23-1 and are described next.

EMPLOYMENT

Employment is the one area most people associate with human resources management. The employment function of human resources involves all activities required to maintain an adequate number of qualified employees in the company. Employment activities include determining the need to hire employees, recruiting applicants, determining the qualifications of applicants, and hiring the most qualified applicants to fill the available jobs. In addition, transfers, promotions, retirements, dismissals, and other job changes are part of the employment function.

Human Resources Activities	
Activity	**Focus**
Employment	Maintaining an adequate number of qualified employees in the company
Wages and Benefits	Planning and managing the financial and nonfinancial rewards available to employees
Performance Improvement	Training and educating employees to ensure high quality and efficient work
Employee Relations	Ensuring effective communication and cooperation between management and employees
Health and Safety	Working with managers to establish and monitor safe work procedures, maintain safe work areas, and enforce laws and regulations related to health and safety
Performance Management	Developing procedures and materials and educating managers and employees on the proper methods for evaluating and improving performance
Employee Assistance	Helping employees balance their work and personal lives
Employment Planning and Research	Researching and maintaining the information that managers need to determine personnel needs and manage the workforce

© Cengage Learning 2013.

Figure 23-1 Human resources personnel complete many activities to keep employees well prepared, productive, and satisfied with their jobs.

Why is it important for businesses to carefully plan the package of wages and benefits offered to employees?

WAGES AND BENEFITS

The amount a company pays employees directly and spends to provide employee benefits such as insurance and vacation time is a major part of its operating budget. The level of wages and benefits, especially when compared to that of competitors, helps to determine who will apply for job openings and whether they are likely to make a long-term commitment to the company or will be looking for higher-paying jobs. When performing the wages-and-benefits function, human resources employees plan and manage the financial and nonfinancial rewards available to employees.

Wages and benefits must be carefully controlled. Employee productivity (the amount of work accomplished) compared to the pay and benefits will determine whether the company can be profitable or not. It is important that employees view the system for determining pay as fair and that there is a reasonable relationship between the amount paid to an employee and the value of that employee's work to the company. Human resources is typically responsible for developing a pay system that classifies jobs according to levels and pay ranges. When a person is hired, promoted, or given a pay increase, human resources manages the procedures to ensure that the employee gets paid the correct amount.

Companies offer benefits to their employees in addition to wages. Some benefits, such as Social Security and Medicare, are required by law. Others, such as insurance and vacations, are not legally required, but many companies provide them. Often benefit plans are different for full-time than for part-time employees or are based on the length of time the employee has worked for the company. People who work in human resources study what benefits can be offered, determine the current and future costs of each type of benefit, and help management develop the benefits plan. They also provide information to employees about each type of benefit and make sure that employees recognize the value of the benefits to them.

Some companies offer employees choices of benefits, so helping employees make the best decisions and keeping track of each person's choices can be quite complicated. Once employees make their decisions, human resources personnel help them complete the necessary paperwork or enter the data into the company's computer system. Each benefit program must be monitored to control costs and to make sure employees receive the benefits to which they are entitled.

PERFORMANCE IMPROVEMENT

Companies cannot continue to compete effectively if employees' skills are the same today as they were the day they were hired. Employees must improve their skills and learn new ones on the job. The role of human resources in performance improvement involves training and educating employees to ensure high quality and efficient work. Often the human resources department plans and manages performance improvement programs in cooperation with managers and employees.

Most businesses conduct several types of training and education programs. Once hired, employees receive an orientation to the company and initial training to make sure they are successful in the new job. Then, as equipment or procedures change, the company must prepare employees for those changes. Finally, when evaluations indicate that an employee is not performing as well as expected, the company provides support to improve the employee's performance so that it does not result in poor-quality products or customer service.

Employees may be promoted or transferred to a new job in the company. Part of the process of preparing employees for possible promotions or moving current employees to new jobs is a continuing education and training program. Many companies also allow employees to participate in education programs for their own personal development, believing that such programs increase employee motivation and productivity. Companies sometimes reimburse employees for some or all of the costs of education as an employee benefit.

Finally, if the company cuts back on the number of employees, eliminates a department, or undergoes a major change in its business activities, it may help the employees who will be terminated prepare for new jobs. Some of those jobs may be in other parts of the company that are adding employees, but the education and training may be for jobs in other companies. It may seem strange that companies would spend money to educate employees to work for other companies. However, progressive employers view these programs as a responsibility to employees who have contributed to the company's past success. They also believe that people are more likely to work for a company that demonstrates this level of commitment to its employees.

EMPLOYEE RELATIONS

Human resources plays a major role in employee relations by ensuring effective communication and cooperation between management and employees. If a labor union is organized within a company, a very formal set of relationships exists between employees and management. The human resources personnel responsible for employee relations assist in negotiating labor contracts with the union and deal with employee activities and issues that relate to the contract. If employees are not represented by a union, human resources still performs the same types of activities, but will follow company policies and procedures rather than a negotiated labor contract.

The flattened organizations of today mean fewer managers. Businesses expect employees to take more responsibility for their own work. Work teams made up of employees and managers take responsibility for many decisions once made only by managers. These decisions may include hiring, determining how work will be performed, and improving work procedures. Human resources personnel help to prepare people for their new responsibilities and develop supporting materials, training, and computerized forms and procedures to help the teams successfully perform their new tasks.

Another important area of employee relations is assuring that the company complies with all laws related to equal employment and affirmative action. In addition, human resources personnel work with employees and managers to prepare people for future job openings and promotions, as well as help them work cooperatively. Companies are most successful when all employees have access to any job for which they are qualified and when there is no discrimination in employment decisions or in any part of the work environment.

HEALTH AND SAFETY

Employee illnesses and injuries are expensive. When employees are unhealthy or injured, they may not be able to work. Other employees will have to complete their co-workers' assignments, or the company must hire temporary employees. The cost of insurance and health care rises as the number of employee illnesses and injuries increases. The company and its employees usually share those increasing costs.

Manager's Perspective On
TEAMWORK

As HR managers plan the work of their department, they must look at the needs of all employees. A diverse workforce requires a broad range of services to meet individual needs. A recently promoted manager will have different needs than an experienced one. A recent college graduate and someone nearing retirement will likely view HR services differently. A successful HR manager knows that each executive, manager, and worker needs to be treated as an individual client. HR must work as a team to provide the range of specialized services required by everyone in the business.

Why might a company provide a benefit such as fitness programs for employees?

Substance abuse leads to a number of job problems. Workers under the influence of illegal drugs or alcohol have reduced dexterity and impaired judgment. As a result, they may ignore safety procedures or be unable to perform their work properly. Substance abuse also lowers worker productivity and increases absenteeism.

Along with company managers, the human resources department is responsible for establishing and monitoring safe work procedures and maintaining safe work areas. They are also responsible for enforcing laws and regulations related to safety and health.

Most human resources departments plan and provide regular safety training, place posters and materials in the workplace to remind workers to follow safety procedures, and monitor work to identify and correct possible safety problems. They also collect and report data on work-related injuries and illnesses to meet legal requirements and to be sure the company and employees are well informed about the level of safety in the company and in each department. Companies often reward work units that operate for a specific amount of time without a job-related injury.

Companies promote good health by maintaining a smoke-free environment and offering help for employees to stop smoking through education programs, support groups, and even financial bonuses. To reduce employee absences and control insurance costs, companies organize wellness and fitness programs, build and staff fitness centers, and encourage employees to enroll in health education classes.

PERFORMANCE MANAGEMENT

Managers regularly evaluate their employees' performance. They identify employees' strengths and reward them for superior performance. If they discover performance problems, they provide advice and training to help the employee improve.

Individual managers are responsible for evaluating the employees they supervise and using the results of the evaluation to improve performance. The role of human resources in performance management is to develop the evaluation system and materials and to educate managers and employees on the proper methods for evaluating and improving performance. Human resources personnel work with managers and experienced employees to design the performance management system and then prepare the forms and materials needed. They then train the managers to evaluate employees objectively, complete the evaluation forms, and conduct follow-up evaluation conferences with the employees. They also help employees understand their role in the evaluation process. The human resources department usually maintains the results of the evaluations in each employee's personnel file.

A newer method of performance evaluation, **360-degree feedback**, uses performance feedback gathered from a broad range of people with whom the employee works. Supervisors, co-workers, and subordinates all contribute performance feedback. For example, a manager receives feedback from his or her boss, from other managers who work at the same level, and from the employees the manager supervises; employees receive feedback from their manager and from co-workers. Sometimes even suppliers and customers are asked for feedback on the performance of a person with whom they have a working relationship.

In the 360-degree feedback system, people completing the reviews fill out a detailed questionnaire about the person's performance. The responses are anonymous, so the person evaluated does not know who specifically provided the information. The information is summarized, a report is prepared, and a performance improvement conference is held with an evaluation expert to ensure that the employee and the manager interpret the information correctly and know how to use it to improve performance.

EMPLOYEE ASSISTANCE

Today, businesses recognize that employees have many important responsibilities in addition to their jobs. Personal and family concerns may interfere with an employee's work. Issues ranging from financial problems to family issues to alcohol or drug abuse are increasingly common among employees.

Employee assistance programs provide confidential personal problem-solving, counseling, and support services for employees. For the most part, participating in the services is voluntary, and employees can choose to receive assistance whenever they need the help and support. For serious problems that are interfering with work, managers can refer employees to specific assistance services, but, again, employee participation is confidential. For these types of employee assistance programs, the company hires specialists such as counselors, psychologists, and medical personnel to provide the services.

Some employee assistance programs have expanded to provide services needed by single-parent or two-working-parent families, or by employees in transition because of job changes or moving to a new location. Even special financial services such as short-term loans or financial assistance for education may be offered. Human resources personnel involved in employee assistance programs may arrange day care for children or elderly parents, help with short-term housing needs, plan carpooling or other transportation services, and facilitate many other activities that help employees balance their work and personal lives.

EMPLOYMENT PLANNING AND RESEARCH

You can see from the human resources services described above that maintaining an effective workforce is very complex. Companies change rapidly, but it may take weeks and months to hire new people, design training programs, or complete performance reviews. Federal and state employment laws as well as company policies and procedures require a great deal of information about each employee to be collected and maintained.

Management MATTERS

Safety First

Every business is responsible for the health and safety of its employees. According to the Insurance Information Institute, the costs of workplace injuries now exceed $50 billion per year. The most common causes of injury are improper lifting, pushing, pulling, or carrying and accidental tripping or falling.

Human resources has an important role in reducing workplace accidents and injuries. The first responsibility is to design safe work areas and plan safe work procedures. Work areas should be well lighted, have no slippery surfaces, and be free of clutter. Tools, equipment, and storage areas that reduce the need for heavy or awkward lifting and carrying should be available. All equipment should be in good repair with all safety shields in place.

A second responsibility is employee training. Employees should complete training for the safe handling of products, tools, and equipment. They also need to learn to lift, move, and carry materials correctly. Successful training should result in employees being committed to following safe procedures and taking responsibility for the safety of others.

What Do You Think? Should HR managers and employees be held responsible if a company has an increase in the number of accidents and injuries? Explain your answer.

A major human resources function involves researching and maintaining the information that managers need to determine personnel needs and manage the workforce. The people working in this area of human resources gather data, use computer programs to analyze that information, and maintain and review employee records as well as company and competitive employment information. They then distribute this information to managers to alert them to problems, the need for changes, and ways to improve employee productivity.

CHECKPOINT

What are the major human resources activities performed by most companies?

23.1 ASSESSMENT

UNDERSTAND MANAGEMENT CONCEPTS

Determine the best answer for each of the following questions.

1. Another name for human resources management is
   a. operations management
   b. supervision
   c. personnel management
   d. training

2. Providing confidential personal problem-solving, counseling, and support services for employees is called
   a. performance management
   b. employee assistance
   c. employee relations
   d. performance improvement

THINK CRITICALLY

Answer the following questions as completely as possible.

3. Why are benefits considered to be as important as the amount of wages or salary to many employees?

4. What are some possible advantages and disadvantages of using a 360-degree system for performance evaluation?

The Employment Process

Goals

- Describe procedures a business should follow to hire an employee.
- Discuss effective procedures for promoting, transferring, and releasing employees.

Terms

- job description p. 629
- job specification p. 629
- promotion p. 632
- transfer p. 633
- discharge p. 633
- layoff p. 633
- employee turnover p. 633
- exit interview p. 634

●●● Selecting Personnel

Hiring employees is an important activity for every business. Effective selection means hiring people with the right skills for the right job. The process can be expensive and time consuming, but hiring people who do not meet specific job qualifications results in high training costs, poor performance, and dissatisfied employees and customers.

Some businesses occasionally need to hire employees, but for many companies, recruiting and hiring new employees is an ongoing process. This section discusses procedures for selecting personnel in a company with a human resources department.

ESTABLISHING A NEED

As a first step in the process of hiring an employee, managers must establish the actual need for a new employee. Businesses often need to replace an employee who has left the company, been promoted, or retired. If the company or department is growing, new employees are needed to handle the additional work. Changes in the operations of a department or the use of new procedures or equipment may require that employees be hired to perform those duties. After identifying a need, the department manager works with human resources specialists to complete the hiring process.

The human resources department must have detailed and accurate information about the position in order to screen applicants and choose only the most qualified people to consider. A **job description** is a list of the duties and responsibilities that make up a job. It defines the job, where it fits within the organization, and what the jobholder is expected to do. A **job specification** is a list of the qualifications and skills a worker needs to do the job. With a job description and job specification, people responsible for filling the job will know what to look for in an applicant. At the same time, applicants will understand what the job entails and if they have the necessary qualifications.

Human resources employees work with managers and employees who are currently doing each job to prepare job descriptions and specifications. This information is maintained in the human resources department and is updated regularly as job requirements and activities change. The data are used in a variety of ways, but in the selection process, the information is used to recruit a pool of qualified applicants and to help determine the best candidate for the job.

Why is it important to hire employees with the right skills for each job?

RECRUITING APPLICANTS

After the human resources department has received a request to fill a position and has reviewed the job description and specifications, it begins to recruit applicants. An effective recruitment process results in a number of appropriately qualified applicants. If the pool of applicants is too small, the chances of finding someone who is well qualified decreases. If the pool is too large, the process of selecting the most qualified applicant takes longer and adds to the company's costs.

Internal recruitment is the process of looking within the organization for employees to fill open positions. Companies should make information about all job vacancies available to everyone in the company and give current employees the first opportunity to apply. *External recruitment* seeks new employees from outside of the organization. Human resources personnel should consider all possible external recruitment resources and select those most likely to reach qualified people who have an interest in working for the company. Some common resources include current employees, on site applications, the Internet, private and public employment agencies, and advertising.

CURRENT EMPLOYEES When current employees are happy with their work, they can become an effective recruiting resource. Companies need to inform employees about open positions and ask for their help in recruiting candidates. Many companies offer incentives to employees who are a part of successfully recruiting an external candidate.

ON SITE APPLICATIONS Many large companies accept applications on site because they have a continuing need to hire new employees. While some companies provide printed application forms, others ask applicants to enter their information electronically. Companies may restrict the applications to jobs that are currently open. However, some companies accept applications even when there are no openings. After applications are screened, they are kept for six months to a year to be reviewed when openings occur.

THE INTERNET The Internet has become a popular resource for recruiting personnel. Employment websites (sometimes called *job boards*) such as Monster and CareerBuilder provide thousands of job listings that job seekers can search by job category, location, company, or salary expectations. Most major Internet employment sites make it possible for applicants to submit their resumes to prospective employers online. They also allow job seekers to post their resumes so that recruiters can find them. In addition to posting job openings on these sites, some businesses pay for special services such as resume screening and applicant testing. Companies that regularly hire employees place a link to employment opportunities on their home page.

Social and professional networking offers additional recruitment opportunities. Facebook and Twitter can be used to send job announcements to people with special interest in the company. Managers and employees can use networking sites such as LinkedIn and Plaxo to encourage applications from among their professional contacts.

EMPLOYMENT AGENCIES Employment agencies are organizations that actively recruit, evaluate, and help people prepare for and locate jobs. Private agencies provide a broad range of services and receive a fee from the applicant or from the employer for the services used. Services for job seekers include job matching, resume preparation, skills analysis, and interview coaching. Services for employers include resume screening, active recruiting, initial interviewing, and testing. Clients choose the service they need.

Manager's Perspective on
TECHNOLOGY

With online recruiting providing wide access to candidates, companies often receive hundreds of resumes for a single position. Human resources departments frequently use technology that scans resumes for key information. As a result of the scanning, resumes are prioritizes and only a limited number are reviewed by human resources personnel. Businesses must make sure that technology doesn't result in missing the top candidates.

All states maintain a *public employment service* supported by state and federal taxes. The goal of public employment agencies is to help employers find qualified applicants and to help job seekers find employment. In addition, many agencies are involved in workforce development to help people qualify for available jobs.

ADVERTISING Advertising is a commonly used method of attracting job applicants. Companies frequently advertise in local media, including newspapers, television, and radio, when they need a large number of employees or they must fill an opening quickly. For longer-term needs or specialized jobs, companies may place advertising in industry magazines or other specialized publications.

OTHER SOURCES Colleges and universities, career and technical schools, and some high schools have placement offices to assist graduates looking for jobs. Businesses can use the placement offices to obtain lists of potential employees and, in some cases, to obtain resumes and other information about graduates. The offices may provide assistance in scheduling interviews with a number of applicants to help the recruiting business.

Job fairs are becoming an increasingly popular way to reach a large number of potential applicants at one time. The goal is to attract hundreds of job seekers at one time to learn about job opportunities with one or more prospective employers. Job fairs are commonly organized by communities, educational institutions, professional associations, and employers. Some employers use job fairs as forums for exchanging information, while others accept applications and conduct preliminary interviews.

●●●● Processing Applications

Most job seekers fill out an application form. The form asks for the information necessary to identify applicants who meet the employment criteria established by the business and who are qualified for a specific job. It must be carefully developed to solicit needed information but not ask for inappropriate, illegal, or discriminatory information. Once the application is received, human resources and the hiring department complete additional procedures to process the applications and choose the best candidate for the job. The specific process varies, but most companies complete a series of similar activities.

APPLICATION REVIEW Each application is reviewed to eliminate applicants who do not meet minimum qualifications. Those qualifications are determined from the job description and job specification and typically include level of education, previous employment experience, specific training, certifications, or licenses.

SCREENING Critical applicant information such as education and employment history is checked for accuracy. This may be done by contacting schools attended, previous employers, and agencies and organizations that issue licenses and certifications. In some cases, an initial interview may be conducted to gather additional information and to determine oral communications skills. That interview is often conducted via telephone.

TESTING For some jobs, employees need an appropriate level of knowledge or specific skills. If so, the top applicants may be tested as a part of the application process. To be legal, the tests must measure only characteristics that can be linked directly to successful job performance.

FACTS & FIGURES

Screening Job Applicants

The Small Business Administration reports that for every $1 an employer invests in screening new employees, the business saves $5 to $16 in reduced absenteeism, turnover, insurance, and employer liability.

21st CENTURY SKILLS

Innovation

Managers need to be proactive in integrating innovation into their work. They also need to lead companies in the effort to take advantage of innovation throughout the organization. In addition to developing innovative products, it is important to be informed about new and innovative work processes.

INTERVIEWING A face-to-face interview presents an excellent opportunity to learn more about an applicant than can be determined by looking at a resume or application. Human relations and oral communications skills, as well as the decision-making ability of the applicant, will become evident during the interview. The manager of the hiring department usually conducts the interview. The manager asks specific questions related to the applicant's qualifications and potential. The interview also provides an opportunity for the manager to share details about the job and answer questions from the applicant.

SELECTION AND BACKGROUND CHECK The final hiring decision is made by comparing information gathered through the selection process with the job requirements. Once the best candidate is identified, the business may choose to complete a background check before making an offer. Some companies require a drug screening before finalizing an offer. When an offer is made, the prospective employee will have the opportunity to accept or decline the offer or possibly negotiate different employment terms.

JOB INTRODUCTION AND ORIENTATION Once a person is hired, members of the HR department help the new employee understand and complete the necessary paperwork, such as tax forms and insurance enrollment forms, and review all employment requirements and benefits. Many business help new employees get off to a good start with an orientation program and initial training. After the new employee has been at work for some time, human resources should follow up with the hiring manager and the employee to see whether the right person was selected and to continue to improve the company's employment procedures.

 CHECKPOINT

What are some commonly used effective sources of prospective employees?

● ● ● Promoting, Transferring, and Releasing Employees

The amount of time and money invested in recruiting, hiring, and training a new employee is very high. Because of the expense, once the company finds a good employee, it should attempt to keep that person as long as possible. Offering opportunities for promotion and transfer can help retain good employees. The company also needs a procedure for dealing with employees who are not performing satisfactorily and for reducing the number of employees if changing economic conditions require downsizing.

CHANGES IN EMPLOYMENT STATUS

A **promotion** is the advancement of an employee within a company to a position with more authority and responsibility. Usually, a promotion includes an increase in pay and may include greater prestige and additional benefits. Promotion opportunities occur when another person vacates a job (through promotion or retirement, for example) or when the company creates a new position.

Whenever possible, a business should fill vacancies by promotion. If the company has an effective selection procedure, it should have well-qualified employees who, with training and experience, could be promoted. All employees should have an equal opportunity to receive promotions for which they are qualified. Employees should be informed about jobs to which they can advance and the factors considered in promotion. Many companies now provide career counseling services for employees. Through career counseling, employees can plan career paths, determine the education and training required for the jobs in the career path, and develop plans to prepare for the jobs they want.

A **transfer** is the assignment of an employee to another job in the company that, in general, involves the same level of responsibility and authority as the person's current work. A transfer is sometimes called a *lateral move*. There are many reasons for transfers. Examples appear in Figure 23-2.

Some situations require employees to leave the company. Some employee separations are permanent, and others are temporary. They may result from a downturn in the economy or from a change in the company's plans or profitability. Employees may also be released because they have violated company policies or have not met job performance standards. A **discharge** is the release of an employee from the company due to inappropriate work behavior. In ordinary language, this means that the employee is fired. Careful procedures must be followed to make sure the reasons for the discharge are a clear violation of company rules and policies and have been communicated to the employee. A **layoff** is a temporary or permanent reduction in the number of employees because of a change in business conditions. After a layoff, employees may be called back to work when jobs become available again. When a company plans a large number of layoffs, the human resources department should help employees plan for them. HR may help locate other jobs, offer personal and career counseling, or provide retraining for other jobs within the company.

EMPLOYEE TURNOVER

Employee turnover is the rate at which people enter and leave employment in a business during a year. The rate of turnover is important to a business because the loss of experienced employees means that new employees have to be hired and trained. New employees will not be as productive as experienced ones for some time. Between the time an experienced employee leaves and a new employee is hired, the remaining employees are often called on to get the work done. Most companies watch their employee turnover rate carefully and make every effort to keep it low.

Two common formulas for computing the rate of employee turnover are shown in Figure 23-3. An example will illustrate the difference between the two methods. Suppose that over the last year 150 employees left their jobs in a company. The company hired 120 new employees to replace those who had left. The average number of employees during the year was 1,000. According to the termination method, the employee turnover was 15 percent (150/1,000). According to the replacement method, it was 12 percent (120/1,000). The termination method reflects only the employees who have terminated during the year. Consequently, it does not reflect major changes in the growth or reduction of the company's labor force. The replacement method calculates employee turnover based on the current size of the company's labor force. A company in which the size of the workforce is stable from year to year may prefer the termination method, while one in which the size of the workforce is changing dramatically may believe the replacement method more accurately reflects the turnover of existing employees. To make it easier to study employee turnover trends, the company should use the same formula from year to year.

Reasons for Transfers

- **Development** Employees being trained for management positions may be transferred among several positions to gain experience.

- **Opportunity** Employees may be transferred to give them a better opportunity for promotion.

- **Necessity** Employees may be transferred to new departments or new company locations due to growth or reduction of the size of departments.

- **Interest** Employees may choose to transfer to jobs that better meet their current interests and needs.

- **Performance** Employees may be transferred to overcome difficulties resulting from poor performance or conflicts with other people on the job.

© Cengage Learning 2013.

Figure 23-2 Some transfers benefit the worker, others benefit the business, and many are mutually beneficial.

Calculating the Rate of Employee Turnover				
Method	**Formula**			**Example**
Termination Method	$\dfrac{\text{Number of employees terminated}}{\text{Average number of employees}}$	$=$	Turnover Rate	$150 \div 1000 = 15\%$
Replacement Method	$\dfrac{\text{Number of replacement employees hired}}{\text{Average number of employees}}$	$=$	Turnover Rate	$120 \div 1000 = 12\%$

Figure 23-3 Companies carefully track the rate of employee turnover and attempt to keep it as low as possible.

EXIT INTERVIEWS

Whenever an employee leaves a company, managers should be interested in the reasons. An **exit interview** is a formal interview with an employee who is leaving the company to determine the employee's attitudes about the company and seek suggestions for improvement. The exit interview provides insight into the causes of employee turnover and feedback about the company's policies and procedures, management, and operations. The interview procedure should be carefully planned to get important information in a way that is comfortable for the person being interviewed and to accurately record the information so it can be used to improve operations and employment procedures.

 **CHECKPOINT**

What is the difference between layoff and discharge?

23.2 ASSESSMENT

UNDERSTAND MANAGEMENT CONCEPTS

Determine the best answer for each of the following questions.

1. Which of the following steps comes first in the employment process?
   a. preparing a job description and job specification
   b. recruiting a pool of applicants
   c. completing a background check on applicants
   d. reviewing applications that are on file

2. The rate at which people enter and leave employment in a business during a year is the
   a. transfer rate
   b. unemployment rate
   c. employee turnover rate
   d. employee discharge rate

THINK CRITICALLY

Answer the following questions as completely as possible.

3. Why should HR take most of the responsibility for the application process rather than the employing department?

4. What are the disadvantages of having managers identify employees for promotions rather than opening up the process to all employees?

Increasing Employment Opportunities through the ADA

Many companies search to fill increasingly technical and complex jobs with qualified applicants. Some employment divisions report screening hundreds of applications to find one person who meets the necessary job requirements. At the same time, businesses have overlooked millions of Americans who have the necessary job qualifications for many jobs. Why? They have disabilities that many employers mistakenly believe will prevent them from performing job duties effectively.

Because of the widespread misunderstanding, stereotypes, and discrimination faced by disabled Americans in the workplace, a law to correct the discrimination was enacted in 1990 and amended in 2008. The Americans with Disabilities Act (ADA) prohibits employment discrimination against individuals with physical and mental handicaps or chronic illnesses if they are able to perform the basic functions of the job. Under ADA, employers must provide the opportunity for all disabled applicants who are otherwise qualified to compete for available jobs. A qualified applicant is a person who has the required education and experience and can perform the work if the employer provides "reasonable accommodation."

Providing reasonable accommodation means making facilities, equipment, procedures, and activities accessible and usable; restructuring jobs and work tasks when possible; and providing access to the same benefits and privileges available to other employees. The word *reasonable* is used to ensure that employers do not have to make changes that result in a severe financial hardship for the business or that alter the job so that required work cannot be completed. With careful planning, many accommodations for disabled employees can be accomplished at no additional cost. Other changes can be made at relatively low cost by implementing creative solutions. Although some organizations continue to be concerned about the impact and cost of complying with the Americans with Disabilities Act, many now believe they are better prepared to access a group of potential employees they had previously ignored.

THINK CRITICALLY

1. Why do you believe it was necessary for the federal government to pass the ADA legislation?

2. If you were a businessperson, how would you respond to the ADA requirements?

3. Using your school as an example, in what ways have the facilities, equipment, and materials been modified to meet the needs of disabled students, faculty, and staff? Are there areas in the school where you believe additional reasonable accommodations can be made?

Employment Law

Goals

- Describe several ways that employees are protected through federal and state employment legislation.
- Discuss the steps that government and businesses have taken to eliminate discrimination in employment opportunities.

Terms

- Fair Labor Standards Act (FLSA) p. 636
- Occupational Safety and Health Act p. 636
- Social Security p. 637
- Medicare p. 637
- Family Medical Leave Act (FMLA) p. 637
- workers' compensation p. 637
- unemployment insurance p. 637

●●●● Regulating Employment Conditions and Benefits

State and federal governments have passed many laws to protect employees, improve their health and safety, and provide minimum employee benefits. At the federal level, the Department of Labor (DOL) is responsible for administering and enforcing nearly 200 laws and hundreds of related regulations. These laws affect more than 10 million businesses and close to 125 million workers. HR departments are responsible for understanding the laws and ensuring that businesses comply with their requirements. The major categories in which laws regulate employment relationships are wages and work hours, health and safety, retirement and employee benefits, and workers' compensation and unemployment.

WAGES AND WORK HOURS

The primary federal law regulating wages paid and hours worked by employees is the Fair Labor Standards Act. The **Fair Labor Standards Act (FLSA)** prescribes standards for wages and overtime pay. FLSA affects most private and some public employers. It requires employers to pay covered employees at least the federal minimum wage and overtime pay of one-and-one-half times the regular rate of pay. Most managers and other salaried employees are exempt from FLSA regulations. Also, businesses that are not involved in interstate commerce but conduct all their activities within one state may not be covered. However, most states have their own minimum-wage laws. The FLSA also regulates the employment of young people. For regulated businesses, restrictions apply to the occupations and hours worked for anyone under age 18.

WORKER SAFETY AND HEALTH

The **Occupational Safety and Health Act** created the Occupational Safety and Health Administration (OSHA) to ensure safe and healthful working conditions for working men and women by setting and enforcing standards and by providing training, outreach, education, and assistance. OSHA, part of the Department of Labor, regulates safety and health conditions in most businesses. Employers have a duty to provide their employees with a workplace free from unsafe working conditions and other hazards. The act allows the government to set specific health and safety standards for businesses. Workplace inspections and investigations are key to enforcement.

RETIREMENT AND EMPLOYEE BENEFITS

Social Security is a social insurance program funded through payroll contributions. The formal title of the program is the Federal Old-Age and Survivors Insurance Trust Fund and the Federal Disability Insurance Trust Fund (OASDI). The largest component of OASDI is the payment of retirement benefits. Throughout a person's life, contributions are made by both the employer and employee. The Social Security Administration keeps track of the contributions. Upon retirement, the person can begin to receive payments from the account. The amount of the monthly benefit depends on the earnings record and the age at which benefits begin. A worker who becomes totally disabled, regardless of his or her age, can also receive benefits under the Social Security law. There are also provisions for payments to survivors after the death of a person who has made contributions.

Even when established in 1935, Social Security was not planned to provide the entire income for retirees. However, according to the Social Security Administration it is the primary source of income for most retired Americans. As of 2010, the average annual social security payment to an individual retiree was slightly less than $14,000.

Medicare is health insurance for people 65 or older and for people under 65 with certain disabilities. There are three parts to Medicare coverage—hospital insurance, medical insurance, and prescription drug coverage. As with Social Security, the costs of Medicare are covered by payroll taxes. Employers and employees share those costs at rates established by Congress. Self-employed people pay the entire amount of the payroll tax.

The **Family and Medical Leave Act (FMLA)** entitles eligible employees to take unpaid leave for specified family and medical reasons. The law requires that employers covered by the law must allow an eligible employee up to a total of 12 weeks of leave during a year for one of the following reasons:

- the birth, adoption, or foster-care placement of a child of the employee
- caring for an immediate family member (spouse, child, or parent) with a serious health condition
- medical leave for a serious health condition

WORKERS' COMPENSATION AND UNEMPLOYMENT

All states have workers' compensation laws. **Workers' compensation** requires employers to provide insurance for the death, injury, or illness of employees that result from their work. Some states maintain the insurance programs, but many offer coverage through private insurance companies. **Unemployment insurance**

NET Bookmark

The Social Security Administration has developed a simple calculator that anyone can use to estimate the amount of benefits they will receive based on the wages they earn, the number of years they plan to work, and the age at which they plan to retire.

Access the website for this textbook and choose the link for Chapter 23 Net Bookmark. Open the Quick Calculator and experiment by putting in different estimates of income and retirement options to see the impact on potential retirement payments.

www.cengage.com/school/bizmgmt

Fair Wages

Supply and demand cause the compensation for some jobs to be higher than for others even when the jobs are of similar difficulty and responsibility. The level of compensation is also influenced by what competing firms pay for similar jobs. However, laws and regulations can affect the level of compensation by requiring there is no discrimination based solely on gender, age, or disability.

is a state-managed program that provides temporary income to individuals who have been laid off from their jobs. Specific requirements must be met in terms of the length of employment and steps taken to regain employment. Employers make contributions to the state unemployment fund based on the number of employees and their employment history.

CHECKPOINT

What employment laws are administered by states rather than the federal government?

Equal Opportunity in Employment

Reducing discrimination and increasing employment opportunities is good for business and good for society as a whole. Government plays a role in equal opportunity for employment by passing laws that protect workers and guide employers. Significant laws related to equal employment are listed and described in Figure 23-4.

In recent years, many businesses have taken positive steps to correct discrimination in employment. Those steps include the development of written plans for fair employment practices, a review of recruitment and selection procedures, improved access to job training to qualify employees for promotion who may have been excluded in the past, diversity training for all managers and employees, and improved performance evaluation procedures that reduce bias. Companies that have taken a sincere and active interest in improving the diversity of their workforce and eliminating discrimination have found that diversity improves decision making by bringing a rich array of ideas and perspectives to company planning and problem solving.

Laws that Expand Employment Opportunities	
The Civil Rights Act	This act prohibits discrimination in hiring, training, and promotion on the basis of race, ethnicity, gender, religion, or national origin.
Equal Pay Act	This act prohibits unequal pay for men and women who are doing substantially the same work.
Age Discrimination in Employment Act	This act prohibits discrimination in conditions of employment or job opportunities for persons over 40 years old.
Immigration Reform and Control Act	This act requires employers to verify that potential employees are not aliens unauthorized to work in the United States and prohibits employment discrimination because of national origin or citizenship status.
Americans with Disabilities Act	This act prohibits discrimination against qualified people with disabilities in employment, public services, transportation, public accommodations, and telecommunications. It requires employers to make reasonable accommodations to support the employment of disabled employees.

© Cengage Learning 2013.

Figure 23-4 Businesses have made progress in increasing employment opportunities and reducing discrimination in employment and promotions.

Two of the most effective strategies for reducing discrimination and increasing opportunities for promotion and advancement in an organization are the use of self-directed work teams and cross-training. When diverse work teams are formed, each team member has the opportunity to develop personal skills, interact with others, and assume leadership positions. Cross training allows each person to broaden his or her skills and demonstrate increased value to the organization. In each case, employees gets opportunities to work with others, develop new skills, and demonstrate their abilities to co-workers and managers.

CHECKPOINT

List the important laws that regulate employment discrimination and equal employment.

23.3 ASSESSMENT

UNDERSTAND MANAGEMENT CONCEPTS

Determine the best answer for each of the following questions.

1. The federal law that prescribes standards for wages and overtime pay is the
   a. Fair Labor Standards Act
   b. Occupational Safety and Health Act
   c. Federal Old-Age and Survivors Insurance Trust Fund
   d. Medicare Act

2. Which of the following is *not* provided protection from employment discrimination by federal law?
   a. age
   b. income
   c. gender
   d. citizenship status

THINK CRITICALLY

Answer the following questions as completely as possible.

3. Why do you believe federal and state governments have taken a specific interest in wages, working conditions, and the health and safety of employees?

4. What are some ways a prospective employee can determine if an employer provides equal employment opportunity or continues practices that discriminate in hiring and promotions?

CHAPTER CONCEPTS

- Human resources personnel perform the tasks that help a business keep the skilled, productive, and satisfied employees it needs to succeed.

- The HR employment function involves all activities required to maintain an adequate number of qualified employees in the company. HR is also responsible for wages and benefits, performance improvement, employee relations, health and safety, performance management, employee assistance programs, and employment planning and research.

- Effective selection means hiring people with the right skills for each job. Hiring people who do not meet specific job qualifications results in high training costs, dissatisfied employees and customers, and poor performance.

- Companies can retain good employees by offering opportunities for promotion and transfer. Procedures are also needed to deal with employee discharges and layoffs.

- HR departments are responsible for understanding federal and state employment laws and ensuring that the business complies with them.

- Employee diversity improves organizations by bringing a rich array of ideas and perspectives to a company. Companies must be aware of and follow laws related to equal opportunity and discrimination.

REVIEW BUSINESS MANAGEMENT TERMS

Write the letter of the term that matches each definition. Some terms will not be used.

a. 360-degree feedback
b. employee assistance programs
c. employee turnover
d. exit interview
e. Fair Labor Standards Act
f. human resources management
g. job description
h. job specification
i. layoff
j. Medicare
k. Occupational Safety and Health Act
l. promotion
m. Social Security
n. transfer
o. unemployment insurance
p. workers' compensation

1. Confidential personal problem-solving, counseling, and support services for employees
2. State-managed program that provides temporary income to individuals who have been laid off from their jobs
3. Advancement of an employee within a company to a position with more authority and responsibility
4. Employer-provided insurance for the death, injury, or illness of employees that result from their work
5. Temporary or permanent reduction in the number of employees because of a change in business conditions
6. Performance feedback gathered from a broad range of people with whom an employee works rather than from just the employee's manager
7. Federal law that prescribes standards for wages and overtime pay
8. Rate at which people enter and leave employment in a business during a year
9. List of the qualifications a worker needs to do a specific job
10. All activities involved with acquiring, developing, and compensating the people who do the company's work
11. Supplemental health insurance for retirement-age people and others with specified disabilities
12. Social insurance program funded through payroll contributions

Determine the best answer.

13. Of all the resources used by a business, probably the most important to its success is its
    a. technology
    b. capital
    c. people
    d. raw materials

14. Which of the following is *not* a situation in which HR should provide training in an organization?
    a. when an employee is first hired
    b. when an employee is promoted or transferred
    c. when layoffs occur, to help employees prepare for new jobs
    d. All are situations in which HR should provide training.

15. Job descriptions and job specifications are used in the employment process to
    a. get the largest pool of applicants possible
    b. provide information to applicants so they can understand the job for which they are applying
    c. allow managers to describe jobs in a way that fits the qualifications of the person they prefer to hire
    d. provide justification for a wage rate increase for the job.

16. Which of the following is not an appropriate use of job transfers?
    a. Employees may transfer to new departments or new company locations due to growth or reduction in the size of departments.
    b. Employees may transfer to jobs that better meet their current interests and needs.
    c. Employees may be transferred to overcome difficulties resulting from poor performance or conflicts with other people on the job.
    d. Employees may be transferred after a clear violation of company rules or inappropriate work behavior.

17. Medicare provides retirees with which of the following benefits?
    a. monthly retirement income
    b. dental insurance
    c. prescription drug coverage
    d. free medical care

18. Employers are expected to make reasonable accommodations in work procedures, facilities, and equipment as part of the
    a. Americans with Disabilities Act
    b. Age Discrimination in Employment Act
    c. Civil Rights Act
    d. Social Security Act

Answer the following questions.

19. Based on the Reality Check scenario at the beginning of the chapter, what additional factors other than salary and benefits do you believe Patrick should consider when deciding on the job? How could Patrick use the employment process and job interview to gather additional information that will help him make the best decision?

20. Businesses must be sure employees are satisfied with their jobs and motivated to perform well. What are the most important activities that human resources departments perform that you believe support that goal? Justify your choices.

21. What would you like and dislike about the 360-degree feedback system if your employer used it to evaluate your work performance?

22. Why should a company eliminate applicants who are careless and make errors in completing an application even if they are otherwise well qualified for a job?

23. In some businesses, experienced employees have a higher accident rate than new employees. What actions would you recommend to increase safety and accident prevention for those employees?

24. If you were a manager, what steps would you take to create a work environment that is diverse, expands employment opportunities, and does not discriminate?

MAKE ACADEMIC CONNECTIONS

Complete the following activities.

25. **Writing** Think of a job that interests you and would fit your current skills and education. Prepare a job description for the ideal job. Then write an advertisement that a company could place online or in a newspaper to recruit applicants for the job. Share your finished products with a classmate and ask for feedback on whether the job description and ad provide clear and adequate information for an applicant.

26. **Communication** You are a manager meeting with a new employee who is at the mid-point of the six-week probationary period. The employee has missed work one day and been tardy two other times. Several work assignments have been submitted late. Ask another student to play the role of the employee. Your goal is to have a positive meeting to present the facts and to encourage the person to recognize the seriousness of the problems and to correct the weaknesses in the next three weeks.

27. **Math** Use the Internet to locate information from the U.S. Bureau of Labor Statistics on workplace injuries for a recent year. Create at least three tables that present important findings about the number and type of injuries in several occupations and industries.

28. **Visual Arts** Identify a safety concern in your school that might result in an accident that injures people or damages property. Prepare a poster that encourages people to follow safe procedures related to the safety concern.

CASE IN POINT

CASE 23-1: Did Charles Have a Chance?

Charles Morgan was hired five weeks ago to work in the mailroom of the Teletron Trading Corporation. His job was to collect mail twice daily from each office in the building, sort and process outgoing mail, deliver outgoing mail to the post office, and pick up incoming mail from the post office. He learned the job in one day by working with the outgoing employee, Tomika Williams. Tomika was retiring and had only one day left with the company by the time Charles was hired.

After one month, Charles thought that he was doing well. Some of the first few days had been rather rough, but things seemed to be going more smoothly now. He rarely saw his supervisor, but when he did the supervisor always greeted him pleasantly.

A week later he received notice that he was being discharged at the end of his probationary period. There was no explanation for the discharge, and Charles had not even been aware of the probationary period. He went to the human resources office immediately. The employment manager pulled out a folder and began reading notes that had been placed there during the past month. Charles responded truthfully to each item.

a. An hour late to work on May 15: "My car wouldn't start, but I called to say that I would be in as soon as possible. I worked an extra hour at the end of the day to finish my duties."

b. Two offices complained that the mail had not been picked up on the second of the month: "It was my second day on the job, and I couldn't remember all of the stops. After the second day, I made a schedule and I haven't missed an office since."

c. The Research Department complained that an important document was sent by regular mail when it should have been sent by express mail: "I didn't know the policy for deciding when and how to send items until I was told I had done it wrong. After explaining the situation to my supervisor, I received a procedures manual to study. Tomika didn't give me the manual or tell me that one existed."

Several other similar complaints were included in the file. Charles readily admitted to but explained each one. According to the employment manager, Charles was being discharged in keeping with company policy. The policy stated that any employee who received five or more confirmed complaints about work procedures during the probationary period was automatically discharged.

THINK CRITICALLY

1. What is your opinion of what happened to Charles? What responsibility should he take for what happened? Justify your opinion.

2. Develop several reasons to justify the probationary and discharge policy of the company. Describe what you believe the company should do to improve the policy.

3. Why do you believe Charles was prepared for his job in the way he was? What role should the human resources department play when employees receive that type of training? What recommendations can you make to improve the company's training procedures?

CASE 23-2: What Can We Cut?

The executive team of the Drindel Corporation was facing a crisis. International competition was putting tremendous pressure on the company. Several longtime competitors in the United States had already either been purchased by foreign companies or had moved most of their production operations to other countries to take advantage of lower wage rates and production costs. Drindel had operated in the United States for more than 80 years. Managers wanted to keep their U.S. operations and continue to provide jobs for their current employees. However, they also knew they had to find ways to reduce costs to be able to remain competitive and profitable. They had already cut all the costs they could in production and operations and now were turning to a major cost area—personnel. Drindel had always prided itself on paying competitive wages and offering a comprehensive set of benefits, including insurance, vacations, employee assistance programs, and ongoing training. As a result, Drindel employees were very loyal and the company had one of the lowest turnover rates in the industry. However, the cost of wages, benefits, and human resources services was the one remaining area that Drindel executives felt they had to examine carefully. These were the choices they considered:

a. Ask all employees, including managers, to take a 10 percent reduction in wages and salaries to bring those costs near the industry average.

b. Ask employees to pay the full cost of health insurance. Currently the company paid 80 percent and employees 20 percent. The total monthly cost of health insurance through the company would still be lower than what employees would have to pay if they purchased it individually.

c. Offer each Drindel employee a credit of $400 to spend on any of the benefits the company offers. That would reduce the company's cost of benefits by nearly half and allow employees to pick those most important to them. If employees chose no benefits, they would be paid the $400.

d. Reduce the size and cost of the human resources department by eliminating all employee assistance programs and the personnel who provided them and by cutting the amount of training by 50 percent.

THINK CRITICALLY

1. Why do you believe Drindel executives were attempting to protect their company by cutting personnel costs rather than choosing their competitors' strategy—moving operations to another country?

2. Evaluate each of the choices in terms of its possible effect on the company and its immediate and long-term cost savings.

3. If you were a Drindel employee, which option would you prefer? Why? If you were an executive, which option would you choose? Why?

PROJECT My Own Business

Planning and Managing the Employment Process

Because a small business has only a few employees, each employee is very important to the success of the company. When you begin to hire employees for your business, you will need procedures designed to hire excellent employees. You will also need to develop effective human resources policies and procedures that will encourage employees to be productive and help you keep them working for you.

DATA COLLECTION

1. Review several employment ads for small service businesses. Study the qualifications required and descriptions of duties listed.
2. Interview the owner of a small business. Discuss each of the human resources activities described in lesson 23-1. Identify challenges the business faces in managing human resources. Ask the owner how he or she deals with the challenges.
3. Investigate Internet resources for completing background checks of job applicants. Identify the benefits and problems of completing employee background checks for your business.
4. Obtain and study the health and safety policies of two local businesses. Then outline your concerns regarding health and safety that could affect your business for your employees.
5. Search the Internet to identify recommendations on offering employee benefits in small businesses. Sites such as the Small Business Administration and the Department of Labor are excellent starting points for your research.

ANALYSIS

1. Develop a job description and job specifications for an important employee position you will need to fill in the next three months. Then write the copy for a newspaper or Internet advertisement you would use to recruit potential employees.
2. Develop a specific set of procedures for hiring and orienting new employees. Include a policy statement about diversity and equal opportunity in employment and promotion that can guide your company.
3. Develop a list of benefits you would like to provide to part-time and full-time employees. Identify those that could be offered immediately at no or very low cost and alternatives for offering more expensive benefits (cost sharing with employees, for example).

© Shutterstock/Jason Stitt

CHAPTER 24

REWARDING AND DEVELOPING EMPLOYEES

24.1 Compensation Planning

24.2 Employee Benefits

24.3 Improving Employee Performance

Reality Check

Changing an Employee Reward System

The human resources leadership team for Petro Services, Inc. was meeting to review a proposed change in the company's compensation plan. For 25 years, the company had a bonus system. The board of directors approved a specific amount of money to be used at the end of the year for employee bonuses. Division managers determined the amount of each bonus based on their review of each employee's performance. Bonus amounts varied considerably across the business. Some managers awarded large bonuses—several thousand dollars—to only a few employees. Other managers awarded smaller bonuses—up to a few hundred dollars—to most employees. Complaints from employees had been growing about the seeming unfairness of the bonus system. In addition to concerns about employee dissatisfaction, the board wasn't sure the system contributed to improving company-wide performance.

The new plan under consideration took a different approach. Money to reward employees at the end of the year would be allocated by the board of directors as a percentage of Petro's annual profits. If the company was not profitable, money would not be available for the program. If there was a profit, every employee would receive a monetary reward in the form of profit sharing. The amount of the reward would be based on employees' job classifications and the number of years they had worked for the company. It was expected that in a year when the company made a small profit, the reward for each employee would range between $250 and $750. In more profitable years, those amounts could triple.

The goal of the program was to develop a fair system and to encourage all employees to take responsibility for the profitability of the company. The more profitable the company, the higher the end-of-year reward for everyone. The HR leadership team expected most employees to welcome the change. However, people who had earned large bonuses in the past might be upset, and all employees would be unhappy if there was no profit.

What's Your Reaction? What do you see as the advantages and disadvantages of the new plan? Do you believe it will contribute to better company-wide performance than the old bonus system?

Compensation Planning

Goals

- Describe several types of compensation systems and the reasons each is used.
- Discuss important factors that affect pay levels in a business.

Terms

- compensation p. 647
- wage p. 647
- salary p. 647
- compensation plan p. 647
- time plan p. 647
- commission plan p. 648
- piece-rate plan p 648
- combination plan p. 649
- bonus p. 649
- minimum wage law p. 650

●●● Compensation Plans

One of the important reasons people work is to earn money. But money is just one valuable benefit that employees receive for their labor. Other benefits include such things as paid vacations, company-sponsored insurance, health and wellness programs, on-site day care, and employee assistance programs. The pay and other benefits employees receive in exchange for their labor are called **compensation**.

The method used to determine pay can be an important factor in attracting employees to the company, motivating them to give their best efforts, and retaining good employees. Therefore, the compensation system must pay employees fairly, in a way that encourages them to work effectively for the company while using the company's resources efficiently.

Many factors affect the amount of pay an employee receives. These include the skill required for the job, the work conditions, the amount of education and experience the person has, the supply and demand for that type of work, and economic conditions.

A **wage** is pay based on an hourly rate or for the completion of a specified amount of work. **Salary** is a fixed amount of pay made on a regular schedule such as weekly or monthly. Salaries are most often paid to executives, supervisors, professionals, and others who do not work on a fixed schedule of hours each day or week. Companies develop compensation plans to specify how employees will be paid. A **compensation plan** is a system of policies and procedures for calculating the wages and salaries in an organization.

Because businesses vary a great deal in terms of the type of work completed and the qualifications of their employees, different methods are used to determine how employees are paid. Under some plans, employees with the same qualifications and experience are paid the same no matter what job they do or whether one is more productive than another. Other systems determine pay levels by the type of work, the amount produced, or the quality of the work. Commonly used compensation plans are based on time, performance, or a combination.

TIME PLANS

The most common payment method is a **time plan**, which pays a certain amount for a specified period of time worked. Wages are typically a time-based plan. For example, an employee might earn $12.50 per hour. A salary is also based on time worked. For example, a company may pay an employee a salary of $3,800 per month, whereas another company may set an employee's salary at $43,800 per year. In either case, the employee receives a regular paycheck, often on a semiweekly or monthly basis, with the payment based on the time worked and the wage or salary rate established for that person or job.

Time plans are easy to administer because pay is based directly on the amount of time worked. However, time plans do not financially reward employees who provide extra effort or do outstanding work. Changes in the total compensation paid by the business can be made by scheduling employees for fewer or more hours and by adjusting wage and salary rates. Employees are neither rewarded nor penalized with compensation based on their efforts. The only way to earn more money is to work additional time periods if available. If the hours of work are reduced through no fault of the employee, compensation is reduced as well.

PERFORMANCE PLANS

Two types of plans pay employees for the amount of work they produce. A **commission plan** pays employees a percentage of the volume of sales for which they are responsible. For example, a salesperson may earn a commission of 5 percent on total sales. If the salesperson makes sales worth $25,000 during one week, he or she would earn $1,250 that week. The commission system provides a direct incentive to employees because their efforts directly determine their pay. Also, the business can control the relationship between compensation and costs because pay relates directly to the amount of sales. A negative result of the commission plan is that it encourages the salesperson to concentrate on activities that lead to the largest commissions. A salesperson may try to sell products a customer doesn't need, may concentrate on larger customers while ignoring smaller but important customers, and may not attend to other responsibilities that detract from selling time.

A similar type of performance pay system is the piece-rate plan. The **piece-rate plan** pays the employee a fixed rate for each unit produced. An individual employee's pay is based directly on the amount of work the employee produces. For example, if an employee earns 30 cents for each unit and produces 500 units in a day, the employee earns $150 for the day.

Although piece-rate plans were first used in factories to encourage employees to increase production, companies also pay other types of employees on the basis of units of work completed. They may pay billing clerks based on the number of invoices processed, data-entry personnel according to the number of lines of copy entered, order pickers based on the number of items they pull from inventory to fill orders, and market researchers based on the number of phone interviews they complete.

How might receiving a salary versus a commission affect the way a salesperson works with customers?

© iStockphoto/Duygu Ozen

Well-designed pay plans based on productivity usually result in increased performance, at least in the short run. However, performance plans can make it difficult for new employees to earn a reasonable amount because they are inexperienced and cannot work as efficiently as experienced workers. Performance plans may also encourage experienced employees to find shortcuts to increase their production, resulting in quality or safety problems.

Performance plans are a bit more difficult to control than other compensation plans.

It is difficult to predict the quantity of work that one employee or a group of employees can actually complete when their goal is to increase the amount of pay they will earn. Production may increase to a much higher level than expected, resulting in more products than can be sold. Costs are then higher than budgeted and profits are reduced. But if a company tries to limit the level of production or cut the piece rate to hold down costs, employees will be upset.

Some companies are developing innovative ways to compensate performance on specific, short-term projects that motivate employees while not adding greatly to the organization's costs. The reward is often in the form of a product or service the employee values rather than a direct wage or salary payment. Under one such plan, managers reward employees who have performed well or have accomplished a specific, challenging goal. When an individual or a work team achieves the established goal, the manager provides rewards such as event tickets, gift certificates, or some other reward that is meaningful to the employees in recognition of their efforts.

COMBINATION PLANS

To get the advantages of various types of pay systems, some companies use combination plans. A **combination plan** is a pay plan that provides each employee a base wage or salary and adds incentive pay based on performance. Such a plan assures the employee a specified amount of money but allows the person to earn an additional amount based on work results. It is particularly effective for jobs that require a number of activities that do not directly result in increased production or sales. Some companies provide the incentive based on the performance of a work team or group rather than on the individual's performance, in order to encourage cooperation and group effort.

A variation of the combination plan is the use of bonuses. A **bonus** is money paid at the end of a specific but long period of time (3, 6, or 12 months) for performance that exceeds the expected standard for that period. Bonuses relate employee rewards to achievement of important department or company goals or to the overall organizational performance for the time period. If the work unit or company does well, employees share in the financial success. The bonus system is used to encourage employees to focus on long-term performance rather than on day-to-day efforts only. It also encourages them to consider the overall success of the business and how their individual job and the work of their department contribute to that success. To receive a bonus, each person in the department and organization must do well.

Comparing the Cost of Living

The cost of living is a major factor in determining the real value of your total compensation. For example, a person who earns $50,000 in Anchorage, Alaska, would need to earn only $37,500 in Little Rock, Arkansas, to maintain the same standard of living. A $55,000 salary in Raleigh, North Carolina, is equal to $74,000 in San Diego, California.

CHECKPOINT

Describe the differences in the three major types of compensation plans.

●●● Factors Affecting Pay Levels

Determining the compensation plan and the total amount of wages and salaries to be paid is an important business decision. In addition to the type of pay plan, companies consider other factors when determining wages and salaries. For example, employees who bring more skills to the job may be more valuable to the company and therefore receive greater pay than other employees in the same job. Also, some jobs may be more important to the company than others, justifying greater pay. The company may pay more for greater experience or more years worked for the company. The supply and demand for that type of labor, current economic conditions, and the prevailing wage rates in the community and the industry also affect the rate of pay. Companies may choose to provide a range of employee benefits as an alternative to high wages. Finally, federal and state labor laws affect employee pay.

THE IMPORTANCE OF COMPENSATION PLANNING

Human resources departments are usually charged with developing and maintaining a company's compensation system. Because compensation is often one of the largest expenses of a company, it is important that the total compensation paid is consistent with the sales and other income earned by the business. If compensation costs are too high, the company will be unable to earn a profit. On the other hand, if wages and salaries are too low, the company will be unable to attract employees with the skills required to perform the company's work. In either case, the company will be at a competitive disadvantage.

Usually human resources departments of large companies employ economists and other specialists to develop pay plans and to help determine the total amount of money that should be spent on employee compensation, including benefits. Smaller companies usually attempt to compare the wages and salaries they offer to those offered by competitors so as not to lose valuable employees to other companies as a result of low wages. Compensation plans are reviewed frequently to make sure they are accomplishing the goals for which they were established, to make sure that they are fair to various categories of employees, and to evaluate the total amount of compensation in relation to the company's financial performance.

Changing a total compensation plan or even parts of the plan is a very difficult task but must be done from time to time. Before changing the plan, human resources needs the approval of executives and should involve employee groups in reviewing proposed changes and determining the effects of the changes on employees. The actual changes, the reasons for the changes, and the effects of the changes on compensation should be carefully explained to employees. Employees should be given time to adjust to the changes, especially if the changes may result in a lower level of pay or fluctuations in the amount the employee earns from pay period to pay period.

MEETING LEGAL REQUIREMENTS

Employers must be sure that compensation plans meet all federal and state laws. For the most part, laws do not identify the amount that must be paid to any employee. One exception is minimum wage laws. However, they do mandate that employers do not discriminate in the way compensation is determined.

MINIMUM WAGE   A **minimum wage law** specifies that it is illegal for employers to pay less than an identified wage rate to any employee. Minimum wage laws have been developed as both social and economic policies in many countries. They suggest that workers should not be exploited by employers and that the country wants its citizens to receive at least a minimum level of financial resources for their work. Most businesses and jobs are covered by minimum wage laws, but there are some exceptions.

The Unites States first established a federal minimum wage in the 1930s. At that time, the minimum hourly rate was set at $.25. It has been increased from time to time, usually after significant political debate. In 2009, the federal minimum wage rate was raised to $7.25. Most states have established minimum wage rates that apply to businesses in those states not covered by the federal minimum wage. Only five states do not have their own minimum wage. Most states have established a higher minimum wage than the federal level. Ten states link their minimum wage rates to a consumer price index, resulting in small increases in most years. Figure 24-1 shows the minimum wage for states and other jurisdictions.

COMPENSATION DISCRIMINATION Employers must also follow laws establishing fair levels of compensation. One category of compensation law deals with equal compensation. Under these laws, employers must pay equal wages to workers who perform jobs that require substantially equal skill, effort, and responsibility and are performed under similar working conditions within the same business. It is legal to have compensation differences based on seniority, merit, or the quantity or quality of production. More broadly, it is illegal to use compensation plans that result in unfair differences in compensation levels based on race, ethnicity, religion, gender, national origin, age, marital status, or disability.

COMPETITIVE PRESSURES

Businesses are affected by their competitors when establishing pay rates. Prospective employees will often consider several businesses when deciding on a job and will be attracted to those that offer the best combination of compensation, benefits, working conditions, and possibilities for advancement. Therefore, businesses must offer compensation that is competitive with businesses offering similar jobs. Some employers have shown that by offering higher wages and

Minimum Wage Rates for States and Jurisdictions, 2011		
Higher than Federal		
Washington $8.67	Vermont, $8.15	Michigan, $7.40
Oregon, $8.50	California, $8.00	Ohio, $7.40
Connecticut, $8.25	Massachusetts, $8.00	Rhode Island, $7.40
District of Columbia, $8.25	Alaska, $7.75	Colorado, $7.36
Illinois, $8.25	Maine, $7.50	Arizona, $7.35
Nevada, $8.25	New Mexico, $7.50	Montana, $7.35
Same as Federal		
Delaware	Maryland	Pennsylvania
Florida	Missouri	South Dakota
Guam	Nebraska	Texas
Hawaii	New Hampshire	U.S. Virgin Islands
Idaho	New Jersey	Utah
Indiana	New York	Virginia
Iowa	North Carolina	West Virginia
Kansas	North Dakota	Wisconsin
Kentucky	Oklahoma	
Lower than Federal		
Arkansas, $6.25	Georgia, $5.15	Puerto Rico, $4.10
Minnesota, $6.15	Wyoming, $5.15	
None		
Alabama	Mississippi	Tennessee
Louisiana	South Carolina	

Source: U.S. Department of Labor

Figure 24-1 Most states have minimum wages at the same level or higher than the federal rate.

benefits, they can attract employees who are more productive and loyal. If compensation levels are much higher than those of competitors, it may be difficult for a company to maintain profitability.

As businesses respond to more and more international competition, it is no longer possible to compare compensation levels only with those of competitors in the same state or country. U.S. businesses now compete with companies in countries that have much lower wage rates. As a result, some companies have relocated operations to those lower-wage countries. For example, a 2009 comparison of wage rates of several countries by the U.S. Bureau of Labor Statistics reported the average hourly wage for U.S. manufacturing employees was $23.03. The average rate was $26.90 in Germany, $11.68 in Korea, $3.93 in Mexico, and $1.36 in China. There are also differences in the productivity of and training costs for workers from various countries. Some companies that moved operations to other countries expecting great savings in labor costs have found that other costs are higher than expected.

CHECKPOINT

List several factors that should be considered by a company when establishing a compensation plan.

24.1 ASSESSMENT

UNDERSTAND MANAGEMENT CONCEPTS

Determine the best answer for each of the following questions.

1. Which performance plan pays employees a percentage of the volume of sales for which they are responsible?
   a. wage plan
   b. bonus plan
   c. commission plan
   d. piece-rate plan

2. Which of the following is *not* a factor that can be used to determine discrimination in equal compensation laws?
   a. skill level
   b. quantity of work
   c. effort required
   d. responsibility

THINK CRITICALLY

Answer the following questions as completely as possible.

3. Why do you believe most jobs are paid on a time plan rather than a performance plan? Which type of compensation plan would you prefer as an employee and as a manager and why?

4. Why would some states choose to have a higher minimum wage rate than the one established by the federal government? What effect might the higher rate have on businesses that operate in several states?

Employee Benefits

Goals

- Recognize how employee benefits add to the total compensation received.
- Describe several ways companies can improve HR services while controlling costs.

Terms

- employee benefits p. 653
- defined benefit plan p. 654
- defined contribution plan p. 654
- tax-deferred p. 654
- profit-sharing plan p. 654
- flex-time p. 655
- job sharing p. 655
- cafeteria plan p. 655
- outsourcing p. 656

Customary Employee Benefits

In addition to pay, employees often receive other valuable benefits from their employer as part of their total compensation. When employees make decisions about which employer to work for or whether to accept a promotion, the wage or salary level is often considered the most important factor in the decision. However, the total compensation package is probably more important. One job may pay significantly more than another, but if the second job provides a number of benefits and the company pays most or all of the cost of those benefits, the total compensation may be higher for the second job. Having insurance, paid vacations, medical leave, and contributions to a retirement plan can make an otherwise lower-paying job more attractive.

Employee benefits are all forms of compensation and services that a company provides to employees in addition to salaries and wages. Employee benefits can significantly increase the total compensation an employee receives. It can also increase the costs to the employer. On average, companies spend an additional 20 to 40 percent of employee wages and salaries on benefits. Assume that a company employs 300 people at an average salary of $30,000. In addition to the $9,000,000 in salaries, the cost of benefits may be as much as $3,600,000. In the same way, rather than earning $30,000, the average employee receives as much as $42,000 in total compensation. If the employer did not pay for those benefits employees would have to pay the costs from their wages and salaries to obtain insurance, establish a retirement fund, or take a day off for vacation or illness.

CUSTOMARY EMPLOYEE BENEFITS

INSURANCE Many businesses make it possible for their employees to obtain insurance at lower costs through group insurance policies. Health, vision, dental, life, and disability insurance are common types of coverage provided. The company may pay part or all of the employee's insurance costs. Most business insurance plans offer coverage for the employee's family members. Although employees usually must pay the additional cost for family coverage, they pay a much lower rate than if they purchased the same insurance privately.

RETIREMENT PLANS As employees get older and begin to consider retirement, they become increasingly concerned about the income they will need once they stop working. Retirement plans are designed to meet that need. There are two major categories of retirement plans available to employees. A **defined benefit plan** provides a specific monthly benefit to retired employees determined by their years of employment and amount of earnings while employed. A **defined contribution plan** requires regular payments to an employee retirement account but does not guarantee a specific monthly benefit to be paid on retirement. The amount of retirement income depends on the value of the earnings from the investments. Defined benefit plans are usually funded entirely by the employer who manages the investments in order to pay the retirement benefits. Defined contribution plans may be funded by the employer, the employee, or by contributions from each and are managed by an investment company. Figure 24-2 compares several types of defined contribution plans.

Employee contributions to most retirement plans are **tax-deferred**, meaning the contribution is made before taxes are calculated on the employee's income. Tax deferment reduces the amount of income taxes to be paid. When the employee retires, benefits received are taxed, but usually at a lower rate than when the contribution was made. In addition to the common retirement plans, some companies provide special funds to reward employees. A **profit-sharing plan** makes contributions to employee retirement funds based on the profits earned by the company during the year. The amount varies from year to year and there are no contributions when the company does not make a profit. Profit sharing encourages employees to do things that increase company profits in order to obtain the benefit. *Stock-bonus plans* are similar to profit-sharing plans but contributions to employee retirement are made in the form of company stock. The value of the employee's retirement funds rises and falls with the value of the stock.

VACATIONS AND TIME OFF After employees have worked for a company for a specified time, often one year, they may begin to earn vacation days. Most companies pay employees their regular wage or salary during vacations. In addition to earned vacations, some companies are closed for holidays and may pay their employees for those days. Other common benefits are paid or unpaid days for absences due to illness or to attend to personal business, the illness or death of family members, and the birth or adoption of a child.

Common Types of Defined Contribution Retirement Plans	
TYPE OF PLAN	**DESCRIPTION**
401k Plan	A 401k plan (named for the section of the IRS code) is a company-sponsored retirement plan in which employees may choose to have a percentage of their pay contributed to one of several alternative investment plans selected by the employer. The contributions may be entirely from the employee's wages or the employer may choose to contribute a percentage of each employee's earnings to the plan. Employees rather than the employer own their retirement accounts and the funds are managed by an investment company. A 403b plan is a similar retirement pan for employees in public education and some nonprofit organizations.
IRA Plan	An Individual Retirement Account (IRA) plan is used by employees who are not covered by an employer plan or who want to contribute more than allowed in a company plan. The employee makes all contributions to the IRA plan. The amount of an employee's income that can be invested in an IRA each year is regulated by law.
SEP Plan	A Simplified Employee Pension (SEP) retirement plan is most often used by individuals in business for themselves or small business owners with a few employees. Contributions are made by the business to an IRA held in the name of the employee. Limits on contribution amounts are usually higher than for traditional IRAs.

Figure 24-2 An employee's retirement income from defined contribution plans depends on the earnings from the plan's investments.

REQUIRED BENEFITS Federal and state laws require companies to offer a number of benefits to employees, including Social Security and Medicare contributions, workers' compensation, and unemployment insurance. Companies employing 50 or more people must offer unpaid family and medical leave.

HOURS OF WORK

To respond to the changing lifestyles and the operating needs of businesses, some companies are moving away from the standard 40-hour, five-day workweek. One alternative involves scheduling employees to work 10 hours a day for four days per week. Another variation, **flex-time**, lets employees choose their own work hours within specified limits. **Job sharing** allows two people to share one full-time job. Each person works half the time, either half days or alternate days of the week.

Companies may also stagger the workweek by having some employees start their week on days other than Monday. In this way, the business can operate seven days a week without having employees work more than five days, thereby obtaining maximum use of facilities and equipment while controlling labor costs. It is also a way to reduce traffic congestion or demands on employee services, such as parking and food services, at peak times.

© Getty Images/Photodisc

Some companies include a generous retirement plan in their benefits package while others offer no retirement plan at all. How might these differences affect a company's ability to attract and retain employees?

OTHER BENEFITS

Increasingly, businesses are providing other types of benefits for employees. Many companies provide free or low-cost parking, food services and cafeterias, and discounts on the purchase of products produced or sold by the company. Many businesses contribute to the cost of college classes or other educational programs completed by employees. More and more companies are allowing employees to take time off to participate in school and community programs including volunteer opportunities. Some companies today even offer unique services, such as hiring someone to do gift shopping or take clothing to a dry cleaner for busy employees and offering transportation to employees who carpool but need to go home due to an emergency.

Free or low-cost professional services for employees, including the services of financial and investment advisers, lawyers, accountants, and counselors, are offered by many benefit plans today. Other increasingly important benefits are programs that help employees locate and pay for convenient care for children or other family members including elderly parents.

Companies offer new benefits as employee needs change and as companies compete to attract and keep good employees. Because individual needs can be quite different, businesses have a difficult time providing the right set of benefits for every employee. Some companies have attempted to solve that problem by letting employees choose from among a number of available benefits. A program in which employees can select the benefits that meet their personal needs is known as a **cafeteria plan**. In this program, each employee can choose among benefits with equal value or give up certain benefits and receive their cost as additional compensation. Under IRS regulations, some benefits are taxable while others are not. Employers must carefully construct the cafeteria plan options to meet legal requirements and assist employees in making appropriate choices.

21st CENTURY SKILLS

Cross-Cultural Skills

Managers are in a unique position to leverage cultural differences that result in benefits to the company, its employees, and customers. Successful managers respect cultural differences and understand the advantages of working with people from different social and cultural backgrounds. A key to developing cross-cultural skills is keeping an open mind to different ideas and values.

✓ CHECKPOINT

On average, what percentage of employee wages and salaries do companies spend on benefits?

●●●● Improving Human Resources Services

Companies are looking at ways to improve human resources services while controlling the costs of providing those services. They are finding many ways to use technology to reduce paperwork and streamline the process of maintaining and distributing information to employees. Some companies use other businesses that specialize in managing human resources activities to perform some or all of the tasks.

USE OF TECHNOLOGY

Managing human resources requires a great deal of information pertaining to every employee in the organization. Much of the cost of managing human resources goes into the efforts needed to gather and update this information. Employees must fill out a number of forms when they join the company. Then HR employees must make copies, store them, and retrieve them when needed. Whenever a change occurs, the process must be repeated.

Computers have greatly improved the way companies gather and store employment information. Some companies use computerized forms to collect information and store it electronically. This makes entering, retrieving, and updating personnel information much more efficient. When an employee gets a raise or promotion, HR employees can easily make changes in the computer system. Some companies allow employees to access the system to update personal information such as their address or phone number. To keep records confidential, companies take security precautions, such as limiting access and requiring a password to access employees' files.

The Internet has also made HR activities more efficient. The Internet provides a way for employers and job seekers to exchange information. Companies can use the Internet to communicate new policies or new benefit options to employees throughout the company and the world. Companies may even set up information kiosks in cafeterias and break rooms, so employees can easily check on benefits and other employment information. People participating in employee evaluation, such as the 360-degree feedback process, can complete their evaluation forms online.

OUTSOURCING SERVICES

Some companies are now outsourcing some or all of their HR services. **Outsourcing** is hiring an outside firm to perform specialized tasks.

NETBookmark

The Bureau of Labor Statistics conducts annual surveys of the compensation and benefits offered by U.S. employers and posts summaries at an easy-to-use website.

Access the website for this textbook and choose the link for Chapter 24 Net Bookmark. Choose several categories of data and click on the links to review the data table for each category. After reviewing the information, suggest how it would be helpful to employers, HR personnel, and employees.

www.cengage.com/school/bizmgmt

For example, a company may hire an outside employment agency to perform all of its employment activities, including recruiting, selecting, and even training. A second common use of outsourcing in human resources is to contract with an information systems company to manage all the personnel data required to manage human resources.

CHECKPOINT

Identify ways that companies are controlling the costs of human resources management.

24.2 ASSESSMENT

UNDERSTAND MANAGEMENT CONCEPTS

Determine the best answer for each of the following questions.

1. On average, companies spend an additional _____ percent of employee wages and salaries on benefits.
   a. 0 to 10
   b. 10 to 20
   c. 20 to 40
   d. 40 to 60

2. Which of the following is *not* one of the ways most companies are attempting to control the rising costs of benefits?
   a. outsourcing HR services to other companies
   b. using technology such as the Internet
   c. having employees share more of the costs of some benefits
   d. eliminating all employee benefits

THINK CRITICALLY

Answer the following questions as completely as possible.

3. How can cafeteria plans actually reduce the total cost of benefit plans for employers?

4. What types of problems might companies that outsource many of their HR activities encounter? As an employee, how would you feel about other companies having access to your personal information?

Focus On...Ethics

Employees Lose Jobs and Retirement

When Enron declared bankruptcy in 2002, it was the largest corporate failure in U.S. history. Its estimated 21,000 employees were hurt in two ways. Not only did most lose their jobs, but a large percentage also lost all of their retirement savings. They had invested in 401k retirement plans offered by the company. Enron's contributions to the retirement plans consisted entirely of company stock. Employees were encouraged by executives to purchase Enron stock with their individual contributions to their retirement plans. Because the stock was regularly increasing in value, often at a rate much higher than that of most other investment choices, it seemed to be a good decision, especially with the endorsement of executives. The value of many employees' retirement accounts was nearing or surpassing $1 million, and employees were looking forward to a very comfortable retirement. Then reality hit.

When executives were accused of gross mismanagement and illegal activities that manipulated the stock price, Enron stock dropped quickly from $90 to $9 per share, then to $.30. The retirement plan did not allow employees to sell the stock the company had invested until they reached retirement age, so they were forced to hold on to their shares as the price plummeted. At the same time, Enron executives changed the company that administered the retirement funds and employees were prevented from accessing or changing any of their investments. In the end, employees who had hoped to retire as millionaires were left with a retirement fund worth almost nothing. Lawsuits were filed to recover the money lost as a result of the illegal activities of Enron executives. However, with most company assets lost through bankruptcy, and with the losses in value of the retirement funds estimated at $2.1 billion, few recovered anything of value.

Traditional pension funds of corporations that pay a specified monthly amount to retirees are insured by the Pension Benefit Guaranty Corporation. This federal agency was created in 1974 to provide protection to employees if their company's pension fund or the company itself failed. It currently pays benefits to about 1.5 million retirees in 4,200 pension plans. However, the protection does not extend to retirement plans that are investment based without guaranteed benefits, such as 401k plans. So employees such as those of Enron, who thought they were building good retirement "nest eggs," now find themselves with limited resources in their retirement accounts.

THINK CRITICALLY

1. Even though the Enron executives acted unethically and illegally, do Enron employees share any responsibility for their losses? Why or why not?

2. Could a similar situation occur in another company today? What can employers and employees do to protect retirement funds? Should the government have any role in protecting these types of retirement plans? Justify your answer.

24.3

Improving Employee Performance

Goals

- Describe the procedures for reviewing employee performance.
- Discuss several important training needs of businesses.

Terms

- performance review p. 659
- formal training p. 661
- informal training p. 661

● ● ● Employee Performance Review

Companies depend on effective and satisfied employees. Just as a company cannot operate if equipment is outdated or regularly needs repair, it must have employees with up-to-date skills who perform their jobs accurately and efficiently. Two requirements for maintaining a high-quality workforce are an effective system for performance review and well-designed training and development programs.

Companies must make sure employees are performing as well as they possibly can. The process of assessing how well employees are doing their jobs is called **performance review**. The information obtained from performance reviews is then used for career planning, determining increases in wages and salaries, and planning training programs. Continuing poor performance reviews may lead to employee transfer, demotion, or even discharge.

CONDUCTING A PERFORMANCE REVIEW

The first step in developing a performance review process is to determine what to evaluate. Each job should have a complete description of duties and performance expectations, which should be the primary focus of the review. Next, the human resources department prepares forms and procedures for performance reviews. Those materials should be designed to make the review process as easy and objective as possible.

Managers conduct formal performance reviews of all employees usually once or twice a year. The formal review is based on regular observations of the employee's performance throughout the year, checking the quality and quantity of the work the employee has produced, and gathering information on the effectiveness of the employee's interactions and relationships with co-workers and others. Some managers fail to conduct regular objective reviews of each employee's work and instead base their evaluation on the most recent work, general observations, or even biases. This procedure is unfair to the employee and does not result in an accurate evaluation or provide the chance to recognize positive performance or improve employee performance in weaker areas.

To be most objective, managers should use observation forms and record information on the employee's performance. Those forms and records should be specific to each employee's job and based on the employee's job description and job responsibilities. They should also take into account the employee's experience and training. If observations are too general or do not consider any unique

Management MATTERS

Don't Ignore Praise

In a recent Gallup poll, 80 percent of surveyed employees said that praise and recognition motivate them. Yet 79 percent of people who left an organization said that lack of recognition and appreciation was the number one reason for leaving. Here are some tips for offering praise to others.

- Recognize a specific action and identify its importance.
- Recognize people's efforts and contributions by saying "thank you."
- Recognize the things people do that make improvements.
- Recognize the small things as well as the big ones. Praise steps in the right direction rather than waiting for the final results.
- Personalize the praise when possible.
- Spread praise around. Find everyone doing something well and recognize it.

What Do You Think? Why are many managers reluctant to praise people for their efforts?

requirements or expectations, they will not be fair, can be legally challenged, and will not contribute to specific performance improvement.

Based on the information collected, the manager fills out an evaluation form about the employee's performance. The process in many companies also requires the employee to complete a self-evaluation using the same form. Some companies use 360-degree feedback, or similar methods, to obtain feedback from other people.

Employees should be just as careful and objective in completing their self-evaluation as they expect their supervisor to be. Some employees find it difficult to specifically identify their strengths and the things they do well. But being specific and honest in the self-assessment is important if the goal is to be recognized for positive efforts and results as well as to identify ways to improve performance. In the same way, the employee should not cover up skills or work that have not been up to standard. If the supervisor believes the employee is not being honest, it will be difficult for him or her to recognize the positive parts of the self-evaluation.

PERFORMANCE REVIEW CONFERENCE

After the manager and employee have completed the performance evaluation forms, they should discuss the information in a performance review conference. The conference is scheduled soon after the performance review. The goals of the meeting are to review all evaluation information, discuss the employee's performance and the reasons for the ratings, recognize areas of strengths as well as those needing improvement, and agree on a plan for performance improvement, including support the manager will provide.

An upcoming performance review conference may be a source of anxiety for both managers and employees. However, if carefully planned, the evaluation meeting should be a positive experience. The following guidelines for managers can help in achieving that goal:

1. Schedule enough time for the discussion and plan for it by reviewing the employee's job requirements, previous evaluations, and career plans. Inform the employee well in advance and provide copies of the information that will be reviewed.
2. Focus on the employee's performance, not on the employee. Feedback should be based on objective information, not opinions.
3. Allow the employee to discuss his or her performance, the job, working conditions, and available support. Encourage the employee to be objective and focus on the job, not on other individuals.
4. Discuss strengths and areas needing improvement. Identify how the strengths can contribute to the employee's career goals and specific ways the employee can develop needed skills and improve performance.
5. Agree on a specific development plan for the next work period. The plan should detail how the employee can improve, what rewards he or she will receive for meeting goals, and the support that will be provided.

If performance is so far below standard that the employee will be penalized or even terminated, the manager should plan particularly carefully for that conference. The employee should not be surprised by the negative information. The decision should be based on previous evaluations as well as personal discussions the manager has held with the employee. Specific and objective reasons based on company policies and job requirements should be presented and discussed. The employee should have the opportunity to offer information but the discussion must remain positive rather than turn into an argument. The manager should give the employee specific information on the penalties or termination procedures and arrange a meeting for the employee with the appropriate human resources personnel. Although the conference will not be easy, the manager should maintain a positive tone and thank the employee for the contributions made to the department and the company.

INFORMAL REVIEWS

In addition to the formal performance review procedures, managers should regularly provide informal feedback, support, and encouragement to every employee. Employees also can conduct regular self-assessments or ask managers, co-workers, or others who know them well for feedback. These informal reviews can be very helpful to employees in understanding how well they are performing their jobs and what needs to be done to improve performance or to prepare for promotions and career advancement.

CHECKPOINT

Describe the steps that should be taken to conduct a positive performance review conference.

● ● ● Planning Training and Development

Businesses spend a great deal of money on training activities designed to improve the productivity of their employees. Training is divided into two categories, based on how it is organized and delivered. **Formal training** is carefully planned instruction with a specific curriculum and instructor. It may be conducted by supervisors, experienced employees, or professional trainers. Formal training may be offered by the company, professional and trade associations, schools and colleges, or private companies. Formal training can be delivered in traditional classrooms, training centers, laboratories, or organized areas in the workplace. It is increasingly delivered using such technology as computers, the Internet, and training simulators.

Informal training is unstructured instruction developed for specific situations or individuals. Informal training is often delivered by a supervisor, co-worker, or mentor in one-on-one situations with an individual employee or a small group of employees. For example, a co-worker might show a new employee how to perform a specific job, or a vendor might demonstrate a new piece of equipment to employees who will use it. Informal training also includes self-study by individual employees and coaching provided by a supervisor or mentor.

Studies estimate that U.S. companies spend $50–60 billion each year on formal training programs. Informal training may cost businesses as much as an additional

Should we play games at work? Companies find that playing games as a part of new employee orientation or built into training programs is an effective and enjoyable way for new teams to get to know each other and builds friendship, respect, and trust. Simple board games, puzzles, scavenger hunts, or problem-solving challenges offer learning experiences as well as fun. Outdoor team activities such as miniature golf or navigating a maze can quickly develop camaraderie that can transfer back to the workplace.

Characteristics of Effective Training Programs

TO BE EFFECTIVE, TRAINING SHOULD:

1. Be interesting to the trainee.

2. Be related to knowledge the trainee already has developed.

3. Explain why as well as how something is done.

4. Progress from simple to more difficult steps.

5. Let the trainee learn complicated procedures in small steps.

6. Allow plenty of practice time.

7. Let the trainee concentrate on becoming comfortable with a new procedure before worrying about accuracy.

8. Provide regular and positive feedback to the trainee on progress being made.

9. Be done in short time blocks using a variety of activities.

10. Involve the learner in training activities as much as possible.

Figure 24-3 Effective training programs are carefully designed to improve employee performance.

$200 billion each year. Beyond the costs of training, many companies pay some or all of the costs of college courses that employees take as part of preparing for promotions and career advancement or as an employee benefit. The large allocation of money for training and development can be justified if the result is employees who are able to perform more and higher-quality work.

EFFECTIVE TRAINING

As companies recognize the value of training, they are working to develop more effective training procedures. On the average, companies spend nearly $1,000 on every employee each year for training. Therefore, they want to be sure the training is effective at improving employees' performance. Effective training is designed to help people learn. It follows important principles of teaching and learning that are highlighted in Figure 24-3.

IDENTIFYING TRAINING NEEDS

An important activity for all companies is determining the need for employee training. Some training needs are obvious. When the company buys new equipment, begins new operations, or introduces new procedures, employees must be trained for the changes. Also, when new employees are hired or experienced employees are promoted to new jobs, they do not have all the skills they need to begin work immediately. In these cases, companies should offer the needed training.

Other training needs are not as obvious. In some instances, poor work performance can be a symptom of insufficient training. Conflicts among employees, areas of customer dissatisfaction, or work hazards and employee injuries often signal the need for training. Unless companies are aware of problems and try to determine whether training can help solve them, the problems likely will not disappear.

In some companies, each department forms a problem-solving group made up of managers and employees. Those groups can identify training needs in addition to their other responsibilities. Because they work regularly with the equipment and the procedures of the department, the groups are in a good position to identify performance problems and help design training programs.

How does employee training benefit both the employee and the business?

TYPES OF TRAINING

The Bureau of Labor Statistics reports on the common types of training provided by U.S. employers. They are:

- Basic-skills training: training in reading, writing, arithmetic, and language skills, including English as a second language
- Occupational-safety training: information on safety hazards, regulations, and safe working procedures

- Employee health and wellness training: information and guidance on issues such as stress reduction, nutrition, and smoking cessation
- New-employee orientation training: introduction to the organization, co-workers, personnel, and workplace rules and procedures
- Awareness training: information and guidelines on policies and practices that affect employee relations or the work environment, including affirmative action, workplace diversity, and sexual harassment
- Communication, employee development, and quality training: training in public speaking, conducting meetings, writing, time management, leadership, working in groups or teams, employee involvement, total quality management, change management, and job reengineering
- Job skills training: training in specific skills for different types of jobs in the organization.

 **CHECKPOINT**

What is the difference between formal and informal training?

24.3 ASSESSMENT

UNDERSTAND MANAGEMENT CONCEPTS

Determine the best answer for each of the following questions.

1. The process of assessing how well employees are doing their jobs is
   a. a career plan
   b. a performance review
   c. a training plan
   d. an employee evaluation

2. Which of the following is *not* a characteristic of formal training?
   a. based on a specific curriculum
   b. taught by an instructor
   c. planned
   d. unstructured

THINK CRITICALLY

Answer the following questions as completely as possible.

3. Why are managers and employees often anxious before a performance review? What would you do as a manager to help reduce anxiety?

4. Why do you believe companies deliver more informal training than formal training? Is one more effective than the other? Why?

CHAPTER CONCEPTS

- Factors that affect the amount of pay an employee receives include the skill required for the job, working conditions, education and experience, supply and demand for that type of worker, and economic conditions.

- Companies develop compensation plans to determine how employees will be paid. Common compensation plans are time plans, performance plans, and combination plans.

- Companies may choose to provide a range of employee benefits in addition to wages. Employers must be sure that compensation plans meet all federal and state laws.

- On average, companies spend between 20 and 40 percent of employee wages and salaries for benefits. Customary benefits include insurance, retirement plans, paid time off, as well as benefits required by law.

- Performance reviews assess how well employees are doing their jobs. Specific procedures and forms should be developed and followed for completing the review process as well as for follow-up actions to be taken after the review.

- The money companies spend on training can be justified if the result is more effective and productive employees. Careful planning should be used to identify training needs and to design and carry out effective training.

REVIEW BUSINESS MANAGEMENT TERMS

Write the letter of the term that matches each definition. Some terms will not be used.

a. bonus
b. cafeteria plan
c. combination plan
d. commission plan
e. compensation
f. compensation plan
g. employee benefits
h. flex-time
i. formal training
j. informal training
k. job sharing
l. minimum wage law
m. performance review
n. pension plan
o. piece-rate plan
p. profit-sharing plan
q. salary
r. tax deferred
s. time plan
t. wage

1. Process of assessing how well employees are doing their jobs
2. All forms of compensation and services a company provides to employees in addition to salaries and wages
3. Payment method that pays a certain amount for a specified period of time worked
4. Carefully planned instruction with a specific curriculum and instructor
5. Payment method that pays the employee a fixed rate for each unit produced
6. Arrangement in which employees choose their own work hours within specified limits
7. Law that specifies it is illegal for employers to pay less than an identified wage rate to any employee
8. Pay based on an hourly rate
9. Program in which employees can select the benefits that meet their personal needs
10. Company-sponsored retirement plan that makes regular payments to employees after retirement
11. Pay and other benefits employees receive in exchange for their labor
12. Pay based on a time frame other than hourly, such as weekly or monthly

REVIEW BUSINESS MANAGEMENT CONCEPTS

Determine the best answer.

13. Which of the following is *not* a factor companies should use to determine the amount of pay an employee receives?
    a. the skill required for the job
    b. the age and gender of the employee
    c. the work conditions
    d. economic conditions

14. Which of the following is *not* a benefit that companies are required to offer based on federal laws?
    a. a minimum wage
    b. Social Security
    c. Medicare
    d. paid family and medical leave

15. At the end of a performance review conference, the manager and employee should agree on
    a. an increase in salary
    b. each of the ratings of employee performance
    c. a specific development plan for the next work period
    d. changes to be made in the performance evaluation forms and procedures

16. Which of the following statements is true about employee training?
    a. Businesses spend more money on informal training than on formal training.
    b. An example of formal training is a co-worker showing a new employee how to perform a specific procedure.
    c. If new employees are well trained, they will seldom need additional training.
    d. Employees should always identify their own training needs.

APPLY WHAT YOU KNOW

Answer the following questions.

17. What are the advantages and disadvantages of time and performance pay plans? How do combination plans emphasize the advantages and reduce the disadvantages of each plan?

18. Offer some examples of jobs for which salaries have recently been affected by supply and demand. How should a company respond when it finds that employees are leaving to obtain higher wages and salaries at other companies?

19. What do you believe would be the most important employee benefits to a young, beginning employee? To an experienced, married employee with children? To an older employee nearing retirement? Are there any benefits you believe all three types of employees would value?

20. How can the way employee performance reviews and conferences are conducted affect employee morale? What are reasons both managers and employees have negative feelings about performance

reviews and conferences? How can human resources managers work to change those feelings?

21. Some of the best-performing companies also spend the most on employee training. Why would a successful company want to devote more time and money to training? Why do you believe low training budgets can negatively affect a company's sales and profitability?

MAKE ACADEMIC CONNECTIONS

Complete the following activities.

22. **Writing** Use the library and the Internet to research the history of minimum wage legislation in the United States or in your state. Prepare a report including the reasons some people support regular increases in the minimum wage and others oppose them.

23. **Mathematics** A telemarketing firm has a complex pay structure for its sales associates. Each person is given a base salary and a quota (minimum expected sales). In addition to the base salary, the company pays the following commissions on sales:

4 percent for all sales up to $75,000
5 percent for sales of $75,001 to $150,000
6 percent for any sales above $150,000

Any salesperson who exceeds the assigned quota is paid a bonus of $5,000. Complete the following table using the information given.

Salesperson	Base Salary	Commission	Bonus	Total Salary
Egan	_____	_____	_____	_____
Ranelle	_____	_____	_____	_____
Chen	_____	_____	_____	_____

Egan has a base salary of $20,000, sales of $80,000, and a quota of $75,000.
Ranelle has a base salary of $28,000, sales of $140,000, and a quota of $150,000.
Chen has a base salary of $31,000, sales of $220,000, and a quota of $200,000.

24. **Data Analysis** Using the data below, calculate (a) the average hours of training per employee, (b) the average amount spent on training for each employee, (c) the percentage of payroll spent on training, and (d) the percentage of net sales spent on training. Develop a table and at least two charts or graphs to present your results.

Company A: 585 employees, 23,985 hours of training, $497,250 training budget, $18.19 million payroll, $28.87 million net sales
Company B: 1926 employees, 55,854 hours of training, $1,136,340 training budget, $54.7 million payroll, $75.97 million net sales
Company C: 244 employees, 8,540 hours of training, $268,400 training budget, $9.61 million payroll, $16.57 million net sales
Company D: 969 employees, 63,954 hours of training, $494,190 training budget, $48.20 million payroll, $77.7 million net sales

CASE IN POINT

CASE 24-1: The Benefit of Benefits

Joanne Wilkens and Teresa Soto were exercising on stationary bicycles in the health and fitness center of the Wainwright Company. The company added the fitness center a year ago and both employees have used it extensively ever since. They use the equipment and take several fitness classes taught by on-site fitness personnel. In addition, they have completed a number of health-and-wellness programs the company has started offering. Joanne and Teresa are both pleased with the effects on their overall health and fitness levels. Today, however, as they exercised, they discussed an article in the company's online newsletter.

Joanne: *The article said that the average employee in the company receives total compensation of $36,500 a year. I can't believe that. I think I'm close to the average in salary, and I'll only take home a little more than $28,000 this year.*

Teresa: *That's right. What they don't say is that we have a lot of money deducted from our checks each month for taxes, insurance, and the retirement plan.*

Joanne: *As a matter of fact, the article says the company contributes an additional $9,000 on average for each employee to pay for benefits. That makes over $17,000 difference between what I take home and what the company says I receive in compensation and benefits. I can't imagine what benefits we get that cost that much money. There must be a mistake in those figures.*

Teresa: *Let's stop in at the human resources office when we're finished here. Maybe they can explain the difference.*

THINK CRITICALLY

1. If the newsletter information is accurate and if Joanne is paid about the average amount for all employees, can you explain the difference between the compensation figures?
2. Should employees consider the amount that is taken out of their paychecks each month for taxes, insurance, and pensions as part of their compensation? Why or why not?
3. If you worked in the human resources department, how would you explain the difference between the salary and benefits the company says it pays and the amount of money Joanne and Teresa take home in their paychecks?
4. Although the company's fitness facility and programs are a benefit for employees, should they be considered part of the employees' benefits costs? Why or why not? How do employees and the company benefit from the addition of a fitness center and health-and-wellness programs?
5. Why do you believe that many employees are like Joanne and Teresa and don't recognize the total cost of employee benefits? What should a company do to avoid that problem?

CASE 24-2: Changing a Business Image

Fred Anderson and Julia Parente own and operate a pre-owned-auto business. They recognize that many people are wary of used car dealers, believing the dealership and salespeople may not always be truthful and will do almost anything to make a sale. Consumers may view used cars as risky because they don't know the vehicle's history and the dealership may not disclose defects or problems. They believe many used car customers end up stuck with a vehicle that brings nothing but headaches and repair expenses.

Fred and Julia are determined to have a very different image for their business. They want customers to feel good about their experience with the business and the car they purchase. They want customers to return for service and future purchases. They have developed an operating plan that is more like the new car dealerships customers are used to. They have a modern facility with a large showroom and a well-lighted lot to display their cars. They carefully inspect and service every car before it is sold. They have established an up-to-date service center with highly qualified technicians using the latest technology.

Another important difference is the sales process. They know most auto dealerships pay salespeople commissions on sales. Fred and Julia believe commission sales can result in high-pressure tactics to make a sale. Fred and Julia do not want customers dissatisfied because of the actions of their salespeople. However, they also know that they need sales to make a profit, so the salespeople must be able to convince prospective customers to buy the used cars. They are willing to hire the best people and offer them the necessary training. But they also believe the compensation system may be part of the solution.

The partners are considering several compensation options: (a) an attractive hourly wage, with hours assigned to each salesperson based on his or her sales history; (b) a small weekly salary and a reasonable commission based on the number of cars sold; (c) an attractive salary that is not tied to sales but a careful, regular performance review by the sales manager to determine the effectiveness of the sales and customer service skills of the salesperson; or (d) a combination plan of a reasonable monthly salary, a small commission on each car sold, and a bonus based on the satisfaction level of customers after they have purchased a car.

THINK CRITICALLY

1. Do you believe the changes the partners have already implemented for their dealership will result in a different image for their business? Why or why not?
2. What are the advantages and disadvantages of each compensation option in meeting the partners' goals for a different image for the business and for a profitable business?
3. How do you believe each option will be viewed by prospective salespeople?
4. Which compensation plan would you recommend the partners adopt to achieve their goals? Why?

PROJECT My Own Business

Compensating and Preparing Employees

Small businesses are usually at a disadvantage compared to larger businesses when developing pay and benefit plans for employees. They usually cannot compete in terms of wages or salaries and benefits. Owners and managers of small businesses must be creative in developing ways to attract and retain employees.

DATA COLLECTION

1. Use the Internet to find data on the average wages and benefits paid to employees in service industries related to your business. Also determine whether your state and city have a higher or lower cost of living than average.
2. Contact two business owners in your area and discuss the types of benefits they offer to employees, why they decided to offer or not offer benefits, and how they believe the wages and benefits they offer affect their ability to attract and retain employees.
3. Search the Internet for recommendations on benefit plans for small businesses. Sites such as the Small Business Administration and the Department of Labor are excellent starting points for your research.
4. Talk with several of your classmates, friends, and family members who work for small businesses. Discuss why they chose to work for a small business, whether they believe their wages and benefits are competitive with those of larger businesses, and how important benefits are to them currently and in the future when deciding which jobs to accept.
5. Use a telephone directory, business directory, local newspapers, and the Internet to identify schools, colleges, government agencies, and other public and private organizations that are sources of employee training and training resources for small businesses in your area.

ANALYSIS

1. Identify the advantages and disadvantages of two pay plans you would consider using for employees. Then select the plan you would use and establish the wage or salary rate for full- and part-time employees.
2. Identify the benefits you will provide for employees, including those required by federal and state law. Prepare an estimate of the cost of each benefit for one employee. Document the basis for your estimate.
3. Make a list of the types and number of employees you will employ in the first six months of your business operations. Expand the list to the types and numbers of employees you believe you will employ by the end of the second year. Develop a budget of salary and benefits costs for each time period.

DEVELOPING AN EFFECTIVE ORGANIZATION

Reality Check

Facing a Career Change

James Lane has a good life. Since graduating from high school, he has worked for Alliance Industries, one of the largest employers in Fenton. For the last 15 years, he has enjoyed his work and earned a comfortable living. Ten years ago, he and his wife, Bethany, purchased an old farmhouse and spent several years rehabbing it. Now they spend their free time gardening and biking. James is also an avid runner.

Like many companies, Alliance Industries is being challenged by competition and changes in technology. Those changes require major investments in new equipment. At the same time, competition is forcing cost cutting. Alliance has decided to close the facility in Fenton and consolidate operations at a new facility 600 miles away.

James is proud of his accomplishments at Alliance. After starting in an entry-level position, he progressed to machine operator, and then five years ago to team leader for his work group. James now faces an important decision. The company has offered James the opportunity to transfer to the new location. He would initially have to accept a machinist position at a slightly lower salary and complete an training program to qualify to operate the new equipment. If he chooses not to accept the job change, Alliance will provide a severance package of six months pay as well as career counseling to help him find another job. However, there is no guarantee that there will be a job for which he is qualified in or near Fenton.

James was thinking about his situation this morning as he headed out the door in his running gear. Bethany stopped him.

"Are you running by yourself?" Bethany asked.

"I've got a lot on my mind. I think running alone is a good idea this morning. We probably need to talk when I get back," James said as he hugged Bethany.

After stretching a little bit, James started his run and started thinking. He and Bethany have spent their entire lives in Fenton. Could they really leave and start a new life 600 miles away?

What's Your Reaction? What advice would you offer James as he considers the job transfer? What other options are possible for James and Bethany?

The Changing Organizational Environment

Goals

- Describe challenges facing businesses that require major organizational changes.
- Discuss the two important components of an organizational development program.

Terms

- job security p. 671
- free-trade agreements p. 672
- organizational development p. 672
- career development p. 672
- business environment p. 674

●●●● The New Employment Environment

As the twentieth century came to an end, many companies faced global competitive pressures unlike those they had seen before. That competition forced companies to reconsider their organizational size, structure, and operations. Many were forced to downsize their operations by cutting the number of employees, reducing product offerings, or cutting costs in other ways. Other companies restructured their operations to work and use resources more efficiently. Many large companies reduced employment by thousands of people. Like James Lane with Alliance Industries, employees who had spent many years with the same company (some nearing retirement) suddenly found themselves without a job.

Many employees who lost their jobs when businesses cut back have been unable to find satisfying employment. Some have had to accept lower-level jobs or jobs that pay less or offer fewer benefits. Those who were able to keep their jobs are not certain of their **job security**, the likelihood of being employed by the same company in the future. They may distrust their employer, believing that the actions of businesses today demonstrate a lack of commitment to employees.

ECONOMIC AND POLITICAL CHANGES

Now, in the second decade of the twenty-first century, the focus is on developing a whole new generation of businesses. The Internet has led to the creation of many new organizations that look quite different from traditional businesses. They may have only a few employees, and the employees may not work in the same building or even in the same city. Internet companies may rely on other businesses to perform many of the traditional business functions, and the owners may have more skill and experience with technology than with organizing and managing a business. As traditional businesses observed the impact of the Internet, most began to integrate Internet services and resources into their own companies. Faced with that competition, new Internet businesses had to become more effective in both business operations and management, or they were forced out of business. Today, few businesses rely on the Internet only, but most have incorporated extensive Internet-based operations within their more traditional operations.

Human resources personnel help employees prepare for changes in the organization and changes in their own careers. Why is it important for employees to focus on the future of the company as well as on their personal plans?

International competition has grown dramatically as large firms expand into new markets, develop cooperative agreements with foreign firms, or purchase competing businesses that allow them to expand their operations for greater influence and control in the marketplace. Governments as well as businesses and economic associations are attempting to reduce barriers to international trade by reorganizing relationships among countries and negotiating free-trade agreements. **Free-trade agreements** are treaties between two or more countries that eliminate almost all trade restrictions and subsidies between the countries. In 2011, the United States had free trade agreements with 20 countries, including Australia, Canada, Chile, Mexico, Peru, and South Korea.

Probably the most significant change in political structure affecting international business competition and trade was the development of the European Union (EU) in 1967. The European Union was the first and most important international market system in the world. It was formed to increase the economic and political power of the countries of Western Europe in the face of growing global competition. The EU agreements support the free movement of goods, services, capital, and labor across all member countries. The EU parliament also develops and coordinates economic, social, and environmental policies among members. By 2007, the European Union had expanded from the original nine countries to 27, including countries in Eastern Europe.

ADAPTING TO CHANGE

Today, almost all business are facing dramatic changes. Dealing with those changes presents challenges to both employees and managers. Much of the pressure to help organizations adapt to change falls on the human resources department. Whether it is a traditional business that has gone through a major restructuring or a new business attempting to build a unique type of organization, human resources personnel help all parts of the organization be effective and successful.

Organizational development and career development are two major responsibilities that have emerged for the human resources department in today's organizations. **Organizational development** refers to carefully planned changes in the structure and operation of a business to adjust to a competitive business environment. Human resources managers help companies make changes in the way they are organized while maintaining positive management/employee relations. **Career development** is an effort to match employees' career plans with the changing employment needs of the business. Human resources managers work with individual employees and managers to prepare them to take responsibility for their own career development through effective career planning.

CHECKPOINT

What are the two major responsibilities that have emerged for human resources departments in today's organizations?

●●●● The Role of Human Resources in Change

Consider all the ways that employees can contribute to the success or failure of a business. Employees play a major role in product quality, customer satisfaction, equipment maintenance, and efficient use of materials to limit waste. You can probably think of many other ways that employees can help or hurt the business for which they work.

The ways businesses organize work and resources also affect their success. Inefficient work processes, delays in receiving needed materials, and problems within channels of distribution all hinder a business's ability to meet customer needs. In order to maintain their competitiveness, companies are now paying a great deal of attention to the way in which they structure their organization, how work flows through the business, and how employees work together and with their managers. Today, businesses are making important changes in their organizations to make sure they can remain competitive and profitable.

Two important ways that businesses are using organizational development to make changes are making improvements in work processes and building effective working relationships. Improving work processes means improving the way work is accomplished. The goals of work process improvement are to eliminate errors, improve quality, and reduce costs.

The focus of the second element of organizational development is on the people who complete the work. Studies have shown that employees who believe they are an important part of the organization will be committed to its success and will work to achieve the company's goals. Several important relationships contribute to an effective organization: relationships among a company's personnel including management-employee relationships, relationships with people in other organizations with whom the company works, and relationships with the company's customers.

IMPROVING WORK PROCESSES

One of the purposes of organizational development is to improve the way work is accomplished. This includes the materials and resources used, the organizational structure and relationships among work units, the job duties assigned to individuals and groups, and work procedures and operations. Most of the emphasis on improving work processes is directed inside the company. But improving work processes also involves the way businesses work with each other as part of product development, production, distribution, sales, and customer service.

Improving the way work is accomplished may require using new technologies, rearranging work areas, changing relationships between departments and work groups, and modifying procedures for completing tasks. Remember the concerns James Lane had about the changes Alliance Industries was planning. The company was undergoing

Management MATTERS

Doing Business in 2020

In research conducted by *The Economist*, 500 senior executives predicted the most important changes that will occur in international companies by 2020:

- Companies will enter into more foreign markets where they will face their strongest competition. They will hire more foreign workers than workers in their home country.
- Companies will use more temporary and outsourced rather than permanent workers and more jobs will be automated.
- The workforce will grow and be spread across many countries, requiring effective cross-cultural communication.
- There will be greater flexibility in where and when people work, many choosing to work from home. More workers will choose freelance work.
- Both employees and managers will be more diverse and international, requiring a global perspective and an understanding of local cultures and customs.
- Smaller companies will have an advantage over large companies in building a sense of community among far-flung employees.
- Companies and managers will need to respond even more quickly to new opportunities, sometimes at the risk of making wrong decisions.

What Do You Think? How will the changes described affect you?

changes that would affect all of its operations and employees. The company had to find ways to reduce costs while keeping quality high.

It is not easy for any company to make these types of changes. People may be reluctant to use new technologies or change the way they have been doing things for many years. It may be difficult to identify new ways to organize and accomplish work, because people in the company are familiar only with the way things have been done in the past. Often organizational development programs bring in experts from outside the company to help identify new work processes and to work with employees and managers to help them accept and respond positively to the changes.

IDENTIFYING THE NEED FOR CHANGE

The history of business is filled with stories of organizations that experienced years of success, only to fall on hard times and ultimately fail. The causes of a business failure may be that competitors were able to improve their products and services, customers did not receive the service they expected, costs were not controlled, or the organizational structure did not adjust to new conditions. No matter what the specific cause, the reason for the failure of a previously successful business is most likely the inability to change. It may be that the executives of the company did not recognize the need for change, believed the company did not need to change, or were unable to plan and manage the needed change.

The factors and conditions within which a business operates and that can affects its success are known as the **business environment**. Factors and conditions outside the business are the *external environment*; those occurring inside the business are the *internal environment*. Today, the external factors most likely to result in problems for an organization involve changes in workforce demographics, competition, consumer expectations, technology, and the global economy. Several important internal factors that affect a company's success are quite similar. They include changes in the makeup of the company's workforce, employer-employee relationships outdated work processes and technology, ineffective organizational structure, and poor management practices.

Figure 25-1 shows several key indicators that an organization may be experiencing problems requiring major change. Every organization should pay careful attention to its external and internal environment to monitor those indicators. Companies that do not pay attention often recognize problems too late to take the necessary action. When sales and profits decline and the business has not recognized the need for change or invested in new technology and procedures, it is often too late.

When a business tries to solve a problem, it often discovers that the problem results from a fundamental flaw in operations. Effective organizational development programs identify and resolve the underlying operational flaw in order to fix the original problem. For example, one company found that production levels had declined significantly during June, July, and August. When company managers studied the problem, they discovered that employee absences were almost double on Mondays and Fridays what they were on the other days of the week. Production was frequently delayed on both of those days because work teams were not full or

Important Indicators That an Organization Needs to Make Changes

- New competitors entering the market
- Introduction of new technologies by other businesses
- Changes in laws and regulations affecting the business
- Major changes in products and services offered in markets served
- Rapid growth
- Loss of market share
- Increasing customer complaints
- Poor relationships with business partners
- Increasing operating costs
- Decreasing revenues or profits
- Decline in employee morale and increasing employee turnover
- Conflicts among departments or other work units
- Participation in a merger or acquisition

Figure 25-1 Companies must constantly look for indications that changes need to be made.

temporary employees brought in on those days were not as efficient. To solve the production problem, the employee absence issue had to be resolved. Working with employees, the managers learned that the way vacation days were scheduled encouraged employees to take off Mondays and Fridays to create short summer vacations. A revised policy allowed employees to schedule two- or three-day vacations in the middle of the week. This change reduced Monday and Friday absences and solved the production problem.

Another company experienced an increasing number of customer complaints regarding late deliveries of products. The company had used the same parcel delivery service to make deliveries to customers for more than 20 years. A study of the problem revealed that the delivery company had changed its distribution procedures. It was using larger trucks and making fewer trips to many cities to cut its costs. To improve customer service, the company stopped using that parcel service and contracted with a new, smaller delivery company that used a computerized delivery scheduling system. This change allowed the company to schedule product delivery with customers at the time of purchase and reduced late deliveries by more than 80 percent. Fixing the underlying delivery service flaw resolved the issue of customer complaints.

CHECKPOINT

Identify the two important ways businesses are using organizational development to make changes?

25.1 ASSESSMENT

UNDERSTAND MANAGEMENT CONCEPTS

Determine the best answer for each of the following questions.

1. Which of the following is one of the major responsibilities of a human resources department in responding to organizational change?
   a. restructuring company finances
   b. leading organizational development
   c. making personnel cutbacks
   d. outsourcing more business activities

2. The goals of work process improvement include all of the following *except*
   a. eliminating errors
   b. improving quality
   c. reducing costs
   d. terminating employees

THINK CRITICALLY

Answer the following questions as completely as possible.

3. How has the formation and expansion of the European Union benefitted companies in those countries? Do you see any negative effects on those companies?

4. Why do you believe that many managers and employees have a difficult time adjusting to the changes businesses are making?

25.2

Managing Organizational Change

Goals

- Summarize the major steps in planning and implementing an organizational development program.
- Discuss three job design strategies that can increase employee satisfaction.

Terms

- customer service standards p. 676
- performance standards p. 677
- job design p. 678
- job enlargement p. 678
- cross training p. 678
- job enrichment p. 679

 Planning Organizational Development Programs

As soon as the company identifies a problem or a need for change, it should plan and implement an organizational development program. Because almost all important changes in a business involve or affect employees, the human resources department should have an important role in the program. The changes may involve developing new employee skills or increasing or decreasing the size of the workforce. A major reorganization may affect management-employee relationships. The company may decide to change the pay or benefits plans to reduce costs.

Planning and implementing an organizational development program involves six major steps.

STEP 1. AFFIRM MISSION AND GOALS Affirmation of the mission and goals of the organization is critical. There must be agreement within the company about the purpose of the business and the criteria used to determine if the company is successful. A company should not easily change its mission or goals but may need to change them in response to the external and internal environment if it otherwise would mean failure.

STEP 2. IDENTIFY IMPORTANT MARKETS AND PRODUCTS The organization needs to identify the important markets that will be the company's primary focus and the products and services needed to serve those markets. This step will require establishing customer service standards. **Customer service standards** are measures against which the company judges its performance in meeting customer expectations. Those standards may include the minimum acceptable levels of product quality, delivery speed, order-fulfillment accuracy, and customer support and follow-up.

STEP 3. DETERMINE NEEDED CHANGES The business must determine the organizational changes required to achieve the company's mission, goals, and customer service standards, and prepare a plan for implementing the changes. These will usually involve one or more of the following factors: work processes,

Competition requires that businesses constantly look for ways to change and improve. How have changes in manufacturing procedures affected the jobs of factory workers?

© Getty Images/Photodisc

the organizational structure, work relationships, and employee skills. Also, the plan should include **performance standards**, which are specific statements of the expected results from critical business activities. These types of changes will not occur immediately. Implementation may take many months, and the company may not see results for a year or more.

STEP 4. BUILD COMMITMENT

It is necessary to build commitment within the organization for the changes. Successful organizational change requires the understanding and support of managers and employees. That is most likely if all employees are fully informed of (a) the change, (b) the reasons change is necessary, (c) the likely results if the change is not made, (d) how employees will be affected by the change, and (e) how the organization and its employees will benefit if the change is successful. Successful organizational development usually results when company personnel are involved early in the process and when they have a role in designing the plan.

STEP 5. FOLLOW THROUGH

Every successful organizational development plan requires follow through. Employees will support the plan if they see that the organization is committed to it and that change is occurring. Managers should keep employees informed of results of the changes even if they are not always positive at the beginning. Unless something occurs that makes it clear that the plan will not work, the organizational development plan should continue until it achieves the stated goals.

STEP 6. INCORPORATE THE CHANGE

Making the new process part of the organization's culture is the final critical step. If people believe the change is not important or is only temporary, they will not commit to its success. When the new process is implemented and supported, the organization has changed, and the old procedures are no longer appropriate, the organizational development program is complete.

Alliance Industries, discussed in the opening scenario, needed to implement an organizational development program for the major changes it was planning. Can you find evidence that Alliance used any of the six steps you just studied?

 **CHECKPOINT**

What is the evidence that an organizational development program is complete?

Improving the Work Environment

The needs and expectations of workers today are very different from those of workers in the past. Work is just one part of an employee's life. Of course, employees want jobs that provide a reasonable wage or salary. But the amount of money earned is not always the most important thing. Today, employees are concerned about a variety of factors related to their work, including the work schedule and working conditions. Vacations, insurance, pensions, and other benefits are also important to most people. They also want an interesting and challenging job as well as recognition for their work. Both personal and financial needs are important to employees, and managers must recognize those needs in order to maintain an effective workforce.

Satisfied employees are more productive, have fewer absences, and are more likely to want to stay with the company. Therefore, managers spend considerable time working with employees to make the work environment as satisfying as possible. Studies have found that employees are most satisfied with their work when they (1) perform interesting work, (2) feel responsible for the work, (3) receive recognition for good work, and (4) have a feeling of achievement.

It is surprising to many managers that although the amount of compensation is important to employees, it is not necessarily more important than other factors related to the job. Because of these studies, companies are directing their organizational development efforts toward the design of the work environment and jobs to better meet employee needs. **Job design** refers to the kinds of tasks that make up a job and the way workers perform these tasks in doing their jobs.

JOB ENLARGEMENT

Organizations try to make work more meaningful and motivating for employees. One way to do this is through **job enlargement**, or making a job more interesting by adding variety to the tasks. For example, three workers on an assembly line might be responsible for three separate tasks, each one performing one task over and over. With job enlargement, each worker is given responsibility to complete all three tasks. In this way they can perform a greater variety of tasks, making the work less monotonous and boring. Also, the company now has three people who can perform all of the work rather than three specialized employees who can perform only one part of a complex job.

Employees should be involved in making the decision to change the job and in redesigning the job. Employees also need training and adequate time and practice to develop the new skills. Companies should not enlarge jobs just to reduce the number of employees or to get employees to do more work. If employees believe that these are the real reasons for enlarging their jobs, they will not accept the changes willingly.

CROSS TRAINING

Another use of job design to increase employee effectiveness and motivation is cross training. With **cross training**, employees are trained to perform more than one job in the company, even though they typically perform only one.

Employees can be rotated to other jobs when an absence or illness occurs, while a replacement employee is being trained, when a significant increase or decrease in the amount of work occurs for a specific job, or simply to provide change and variety for employees. Cross training makes an employee more valuable to the company because that person can perform a broader set of work tasks. Employees learn more about the work performed in the organization as they learn multiple jobs and increase their skills.

JOB ENRICHMENT

Another way to use job design to improve employee satisfaction is to involve employees in decision making. **Job enrichment** gives employees the authority to make meaningful decisions about their work. For example, managers may allow workers to make choices about how to do their jobs. Managers may ask employees for advice on how to improve performance or reduce errors. Job responsibilities may be changed so employees can solve problems themselves without checking with their supervisor. For example, in one major hotel chain, employees are authorized to immediately take the necessary steps to resolve a customer problem or complaint at a cost of up to $200 without consulting a manager.

Some companies have given work teams responsibility for the entire assembly of a product, performance of a service, or operation of a small unit in the business. The team helps with goal setting, shares all tasks, and is responsible for the results. Companies using this system have found that team members develop a strong loyalty to the other members and take personal responsibility for the effective operation of the team and the quality of its work.

Some companies expand the duties and responsibilities of employees for the wrong reasons. To save money, the companies cut the number of personnel and divide the additional work among the remaining employees. Sometimes that is done without providing additional training or any recognition or rewards for employees who are required to take on the additional work. Employees are already upset about losing co-workers and concerned that they might also lose their jobs. If they feel forced to take on additional responsibilities that may require longer work hours and greater job pressure, they will not have positive feelings about the changes.

An improved work environment and worker involvement are important goals of organizational development. Improving management and employee relationships, making work more meaningful, and developing effective work teams are all important organizational development programs. They affect the internal environment of the business. In addition, some organizational development programs work to improve relationships in the external environment, including the way employees interact with other businesses in the distribution channel and with customers. Many businesses involve personnel from cooperating businesses in solving problems and developing new procedures. They frequently gather information from customers in order to consider their needs and perceptions in planning organizational changes.

© Shutterstock/Alberto Zornetta

What effects does the termination of some employees have on those who remain?

 **CHECKPOINT**

What is the difference between job enlargement and job enrichment?

UNDERSTAND MANAGEMENT CONCEPTS

Determine the best answer for each of the following questions.

1. The first step in planning and implementing an organizational development program is
   a. affirm the mission and goals of the organization
   b. identify important markets, products, and services for the company
   c. determine the organizational changes required to meet the company goals
   d. brainstorm solutions to important problems

2. Giving employees the authority to make meaningful decisions about their work is known as
   a. job design
   b. job enlargement
   c. job enrichment
   d. cross training

THINK CRITICALLY

Answer the following questions as completely as possible.

3. If you were an employee in a company undergoing change, would you want to be informed of and involved in the planning even if it requires additional work time and responsibilities? Why or why not?

4. If you were a manager, would you be in favor of the increased use of work teams among your employees? How would your job change as a result? What new problems do you believe you would encounter?

Career Development

Goals

- Describe the requirements for a career development program.
- Identify the specific career development responsibilities of various groups in a business.

Terms

- career development program p. 682
- career path p. 682
- individual career plan p. 683
- career centers p. 683

●●● The Importance of Career Development

In the past, many companies were shortsighted when they planned for their employment needs. When a position was vacant, they would begin the recruitment and selection process. If they no longer needed certain employees, they might terminate those employees without considering future employment needs. Those procedures were based on the belief that companies could easily find the employees they needed. Those companies did not view employees as a particularly valuable resource.

CHANGING VIEWS OF EMPLOYEES

Successful businesses view their relationships with employees very differently today. They realize that it is not easy to find employees with the required qualifications. It is also very expensive to hire and train a new employee. Companies invest in employees and want to get the greatest value from them. That occurs when companies hire employees with skills that closely match the needs of the job, train them, and then keep them happy, so they will want to contribute to achieving the company's goals. Companies following this new philosophy recognize that the knowledge and performance of their employees are major factors in their success.

Changing technology requires employees to regularly update their skills. For example, not many years ago, businesses processed most information manually, using typewriters and calculators. Today, companies process information with computers. Auto mechanics used to rely on hand tools and their own knowledge and observational skills to repair automobiles. Now they have access to a variety of electronic tools, machines, and computerized diagnostic equipment. Every business has similar examples of new skills that are required of employees. It is not possible to be successful with the old equipment and old skills. To get the needed skills, businesses offer training to current employees when new technology requires it and search for new employees with up-to-date skills to fill vacancies.

In the scenario at the beginning of the chapter, James Lane had been a very valuable employee to Alliance Industries for many years. Even though the company was undergoing major changes, it was attempting to include James in its plans by offering him another job and the needed training to prepare for that job.

CAREER DEVELOPMENT PLANNING

A **career development program** is a plan for meeting the company's future employment needs by systematically preparing current employees for future positions in the company. Human resources personnel are responsible for implementing the career development program, but they need the support of all parts of the company for the program to be successful. A career development program requires a long-term organizational plan, career paths, effective employee performance reviews, career counseling, and training and development for employees.

LONG-TERM PLANS Career development starts with the job opportunities in a company. Companies must determine what jobs will be available in the future, how many people will be needed in each job, and the knowledge and skills those employees will require. In the previous section, you learned that companies study their external and internal environments to identify business opportunities and needed changes in the organization. One part of that study includes employment needs. The HR department works with that information to project specific job opportunities in each part of the company and the requirements employees must meet for each job.

CAREER PATHS A **career path** is a progression of related jobs with increasing skill requirements and responsibility. Career paths provide opportunities for employees to advance within the company, make additional contributions, and receive greater satisfaction from their work.

Traditionally, a career path moved an employee from an entry-level position into management. However, companies also offer career paths that allow employees to advance into nonmanagement positions. Some people do not want to be managers, and companies have relatively few management positions. Therefore, companies need to make other opportunities available so that employees are not locked into one job if they choose not to become managers or are unable to qualify for management positions. Examples of a management career path and a nonmanagement path are shown in Figure 25-2. Companies should identify a variety of career paths. Each job in the company should be part of a career path, and employees should be aware of the paths available to them.

PERFORMANCE REVIEWS Employees need accurate information on their skills and abilities to make good career decisions. When employees know how well they are performing, they can determine what skills they need to improve to meet current job requirements or to qualify for another job in a career path. In an effective career development program, the manager carefully evaluates an employee's performance and regularly reviews the information with the employee. Together, the manager and employee determine whether the employee needs additional training to improve performance and to advance in the organization. The results of performance reviews should be compared to new job requirements as the company makes changes, so that employees know what is expected of them.

CAREER COUNSELING For career development to be effective, employees must be aware of opportunities and plan their career paths. The human resources department offers career information and counseling services as part of the career development program. Many companies have made career counseling part of every employee's performance review conference. Managers are often trained to provide career information to the employees they supervise.

Manager's Perspective on
SUCCESS

Employees need to be encouraged and prepared to take responsibility for their own performance improvement. They should (1) commit to achieving performance goals, (2) solicit performance feedback and coaching, (3) communicate openly and regularly with the manager, (4) collect and review performance data, and (5) prepare for and participate effectively in performance review conferences. Managers should support each employee's efforts by providing feedback and assistance with performance improvement efforts.

Examples of Management and Nonmanagement Career Paths

A MANAGEMENT CAREER PATH IN RETAILING	A NONMANAGEMENT CAREER PATH IN RESEARCH
Regional Manager	Senior Strategic Consultant
↑	↑
Store Manager	Strategic Planning Consultant
↑	↑
Merchandise Manager	Research Design Specialist
↑	↑
Shift Leader	Statistician
↑	↑
Customer Experience Specialist	Data Analyst
↑	↑
Sales Associate	Focus Group Leader
↑	↑
Clerk	Telephone Interviewer

© Cengage Learning 2013.

Figure 25-2 Businesses should provide both management and nonmanagement career paths for employees.

Career counseling may result in an **individual career plan**, which identifies the jobs that are part of the employee's career path, the training needed to advance along the career path, and a tentative schedule for the plan's activities. The plan is jointly developed by the employee, a human resources specialist, and usually the employee's manager.

Some companies have **career centers**, facilities where human resources employees manage career development activities. Employees visit the center to obtain career information (computer programs, Internet sites, books, pamphlets, DVDs, and so on), consult career counselors, and schedule career-planning workshops or testing.

TRAINING AND DEVELOPMENT The final part of a career development program is helping employees obtain the training and education they need for changing job requirements and new jobs. With careful planning, companies can develop training programs and other educational opportunities to prepare employees for new job requirements before the need arises. In that way, the business can be assured that it will have well-trained employees to fill job needs and employees will be trained for job changes.

 **CHECKPOINT**

What is an individual career plan and how is it developed?

Implementing a Career Development Program

Career planning does not just happen. It also cannot be considered the responsibility of employees alone. Businesses that want to match employees and jobs successfully must do several things to ensure that the career development program works well. Everyone in the company has specific responsibilities for career development.

21st CENTURY SKILLS

Initiative

Taking initiative can be a key skill in developing a rewarding career. For example, employees should take the initiative to learn about education and training offered through their employer. In addition they should look beyond what the company offers to find opportunities to make sure they gain the knowledge and learn the skills needed to achieve their career goals.

CAREER DEVELOPMENT RESPONSIBILITIES

Responsibility for organizing and managing the career development program is usually assigned to the human resources department. The department does much of the initial planning and puts together the people, resources, and procedures needed for the program.

Everyone in the business must be educated about the career development program and his or her role in career planning. Managers need to identify career opportunities in their departments and work with human resources personnel when changes are planned in their departments that will affect the career plans of employees. Managers also have specific responsibilities in a career development program. They evaluate employee performance and include career planning in follow-up conferences. They help identify employees who are ready for career advancement. They serve as coaches and mentors to help each worker make effective career choices.

Employees should be aware of career development resources and how the career-planning process works. They are responsible for much of their individual career planning and development but must know where to get help when they need it. Employees use performance reviews and evaluation conferences to gather information to make career plans. They can then schedule assessments, counseling, and training to prepare for career advancement.

The human resources department manages the career development program. Specialists provide career counseling, training, and help in understanding the performance review process. They continually remind managers and employees of the importance of supporting career planning and development, evaluate the effectiveness of the company's program, and make sure the career development program is aligned with the company's mission and goals.

SPECIAL CAREER DEVELOPMENT PROGRAMS

Companies that offer career development programs should make the services available to all employees, from the newest to the most experienced. However, there are situations in which specific individuals or groups of employees participate in programs designed to meet specific needs in the company. Those programs may not be available to all employees.

Most large businesses offer career planning, training, and counseling to employees selected to be managers. These employees receive testing services, obtain experience in all parts of the business, and often are assigned to an experienced manager who serves as a role model and mentor.

Nonmanagement jobs can be targeted for specific career development programs as well. For example, many jobs are more frequently held by men than women or women than men. Companies may make extra efforts to encourage and prepare people from the underrepresented gender for those jobs.

Some companies may have difficulty finding qualified candidates for certain jobs. Those positions may be targeted for career development attention. Employees who are interested in or have the skills to qualify for hard-to-fill jobs are encouraged to participate in the special programs. For example, if a company is having difficulty recruiting data analysts or customer support specialists, it may undertake a career development program to encourage current employees to complete the necessary training for those jobs. These efforts demonstrate the company's commitment to its current employees. They provide opportunities for promotion and advancement that serve as a strong motivator for employees and encourage them to make a career with the business rather than look for opportunities outside the company. Finally,

FACTS & FIGURES

Please Don't Leave

Some managers are afraid to encourage their top employees to participate in training or continue their education. The managers fear employees will be more likely to leave after broadening and enhancing their skills. In fact, research reported in the *Harvard Business Review* reveals that the opposite is true. Making people more employable increases the chances they will stay with the business.

developing current employees who have already selected the company and have demonstrated their abilities is usually less expensive and more reliable than recruiting outside the company.

 **CHECKPOINT**

In what situations might a company offer special career development programs that are not open to all employees?

25.3 ASSESSMENT

UNDERSTAND MANAGEMENT CONCEPTS

Determine the best answer for each of the following questions.

1. A progression of related jobs with increasing skill requirements and responsibility is a career
   a. goal
   b. review
   c. plan
   d. path

2. Career development programs are managed by
   a. the human resources department
   b. each employee
   c. company executives
   d. specially trained consultants hired by the company

THINK CRITICALLY

Answer the following questions as completely as possible.

3. What evidence would you look for in a business that would demonstrate it believes in the importance of career development?

4. How can a business believe in equal opportunity for all employees and still have special career development programs that are not open to all employees?

Ideas for Sale

Most businesses are faced with the need to change, so it is not surprising that people are starting new businesses to help other businesses manage change. One of the most unusual new business concepts is selling ideas. The BrainStore in Biel, Switzerland, offers just such a service. Its owners refer to their business as an "idea factory." In fact, they believe companies cannot rely on the typical way that new ideas are generated. Using a brainstorming session or just thinking about a problem will not achieve the needed results when businesses are faced daily with problems and challenges. The BrainStore has broken down the process of idea generation into a specific sequence of activities.

The process starts in the *creativity lab*. The lab is an open room with pens, paper, scissors, crayons, beads, and other "toys." These are the tools that support creativity. The room looks more like an elementary school classroom than a place where businesspeople meet. The atmosphere encourages play, experiments, and "completely unrealistic thoughts." The result is usually a large number of creative ideas that can then be processed through the idea factory. The next step in the idea sequence is *compression*, where ideas are sorted, compared, and narrowed to the few judged as best. Then the idea moves through *testing*, where research is done to determine if the idea will work and can be implemented. Often models or prototypes of solutions are built for review and further testing. The final step is called *finishing*. Here the idea that has been successfully tested is prepared for implementation. This step may include developing marketing and communications strategies or the actual development of products, services, or processes that will support the needed change or solve the problem.

Initially the BrainStore worked with large businesses to create new products, develop marketing programs, or solve challenging problems. However, the owners now believe their ideas can help individual consumers as well, so they have opened a retail version of the business. For about $20, they will provide ideas for home decorating, improving a personal relationship, or writing an important speech.

THINK CRITICALLY

1. Do you believe ideas can actually be developed in the same way that a company might manufacture a product? Why or why not?

2. What are the advantages of creating a room that looks like an elementary school classroom for the first step in idea generation? How do you think the results would be different if the company used a typical business office for that activity?

3. After working with the BrainStore, what other activities should an organization perform to implement the ideas that were developed?

© Shutterstock/Rick Becker-Leckrone

Personal Career Planning

Goals

- Describe the variety of career opportunities in business, including international business careers.
- Outline the steps in preparing an individual career plan.

Terms

- entry-level occupations p. 688
- career-level occupations p. 688
- specialist occupations p. 688
- supervisor/management occupations p. 688
- executive/entrepreneur occupations p. 688
- career portfolio p. 691

●●● Business Careers

Business careers are appealing because of the number and variety of jobs available and the opportunities for advancement. No matter what your interests, skills, or level of education and experience might be, there is a job in business that matches them. Once you have obtained your first job and gained both experience and knowledge of business procedures, many opportunities open up. You can advance with additional education or with continuing experience and training on the job.

You can identify career paths in almost any business. If you begin work in a clerical position, you may progress to more specialized jobs in information management or office administration. You can then advance from assistant manager to department manager or to a highly specialized position in either area. Some people progress to the very top of the company as executives. Similar career paths are available to people who begin as counter workers in fast-food restaurants, supply clerks in factories, or bell staff in hotels.

Because common areas of knowledge and skills are important to many types of businesses, you are not limited to one career path, one type of business, or one geographic area. People who begin in banking may change to an insurance career. Someone who is a salesperson for a computer products company may decide to move to a pharmaceutical company for a higher salary or more responsibilities. If job prospects are not particularly good in one part of the country, a skilled businessperson can probably find employment in another part of the country or even another part of the world. Career paths in business are usually very flexible.

LEVELS OF EMPLOYMENT

When you first enter the workforce, you will most likely begin in an entry-level position. Many people get their first job in business while still in high school, with little prior work experience and only a beginning understanding of business principles and operations. The top positions in large corporations are held by people with many years of experience. Executives usually have worked in several areas of the business and often have experience in several businesses. Most business executives today have a college degree and, increasingly, graduate degrees.

Businesses have several levels of employment, based on the amount of education and experience required. Common levels are entry, career, specialist, management, and executive/entrepreneur.

Entry-level occupations usually involve routine activities and require little training. These jobs are open to people with little or no previous business education or experience. If you have not worked in business before, this is where you might begin. People hold entry-level jobs for only a short time until they have developed enough experience and skill for promotion. Examples of entry-level jobs are cashier, counter person, clerk, receptionist, and operator.

Career-level jobs require more complex duties. People in **career-level occupations** have the authority to control some of their work and make some decisions. To be successful, they should have a basic understanding of business and skills in the areas in which they are working. They usually view their work as more than a job and have an interest in the area of business as a potential career. Career-level jobs include sales associate, manufacturing technician, telephone research surveyor, bank teller, and customer account representative.

Specialist occupations require a variety of skills in one or more business functions and extensive understanding of the operations of a specific company or industry. Specialists are the people considered the most skilled or expert in the activities they perform on the job. Specialists in businesses include buyers, researchers, website designers, programmers, analysts, professional salespeople, technicians, machine operators, and people in similar technical or skilled positions.

Supervisors/managers hold the first levels of management positions. They must have a high level of knowledge in the parts of the organization that they supervise. They also must be effective decision makers and have strong leadership ability. People in **supervisor/management occupations** are responsible for specific units in a business and must make decisions about operations and personnel. The job titles associated with this level of employment are supervisor, assistant manager, and manager. The people who perform management tasks within work teams are often called *team leaders*.

Executives/entrepreneurs perform all the management tasks associated with owning a business or managing a major function, a large unit in a company, or the entire company. People who work in **executive/entrepreneur occupations** are fully responsible for the success or failure of the company. They must possess a comprehensive understanding of business and management. They spend most of their time planning and evaluating the work of the organization. The positions held by executives/entrepreneurs are vice president, president, chief executive, and owner.

CAREERS IN INTERNATIONAL BUSINESS

The growth of trade between countries and increasing global competition provide continuing evidence of the importance of international business. It has never been easier to travel to other countries, communicate with people around the world, buy products produced in other places, and sell products and services abroad. The Internet makes access to almost any business and millions of customers only a mouse-click away. We are members of a global community generally, and a global business community specifically. As businesses expand into international markets, so do the opportunities for international business careers.

International business careers have all the advantages of a career in one country plus more. In addition to the excitement and challenges that accompany any business career, international careers usually offer additional job choices and the chance to develop new skills, travel, and interact with a wide variety of people from different cultures.

What are some advantages of international business careers?

© iStockphoto/AIMSTOCK

The international businessperson must be familiar with the cultures of the countries in which the business will operate or to which the company's products and service are directed. The economic and political environments of countries is another important area of study. Currently, English is the international language of business. However, there is no substitute for understanding the language of the country in which you will work. People are favorably impressed when you take the trouble to learn their language. It is difficult to predict which languages will be the most important in your future. Your commitment to study and learn a second language will impress employers as well as your international contacts. You will also find it easier to learn an additional language if needed later. Your selection of international courses in high school and college, travel opportunities, and interactions with people from other countries and cultures are all valuable experiences if you would like to work in international business.

 CHECKPOINT

List the levels of business employment in order of least experience and education to most.

●●● Preparing for a Business Career

Preparing for a career in business may seem like trying to negotiate a maze. People who are not familiar with business may have difficulty determining what preparation they need and how to obtain the job they want. If you talk to people who have worked in business for many years, you will find that some did not plan or prepare for the job they currently hold. They often ended up there after starting in another part of the business or in an entirely different occupation.

Today, a person is less likely to enter a business career without specific preparation. In your study of business, you have seen that a business career requires a great deal of knowledge and skill in a number of areas. People who understand the requirements and carefully plan to develop the necessary skills are more likely to succeed in business. In some ways, preparing for a business career is complicated, but in other ways, it is really quite simple. It is often a matter of matching your personal qualities, education, and experience with a career path in business.

Good business education programs are offered in high schools as well as in community and junior colleges and career and technical schools. Business is usually one of the largest degree programs in colleges and universities. You can complete a general business preparation or specialize in a specific area, such as accounting, computer science, marketing, or even e-commerce. Many businesses offer education and training programs for their employees or pay for some or all of the costs of college coursework. You can also attend conferences and seminars sponsored by businesses and professional associations.

Experience in business is always an advantage. Experience in working with people in any way can give you confidence and develop important communication and interpersonal skills. Even if you have not worked part-time or full-time in a business, other types of experiences are useful. Working on projects in an organization, writing for the yearbook or school newspaper, forming a Junior Achievement company, or helping in a parent's business are all examples of experiences that can develop skills important in business.

Most employers value experience when they hire employees. It is relatively easy to find an entry-level job if you are not particularly concerned about the type of work or working conditions. These entry-level jobs provide the work experience that will qualify you for the jobs you prefer. Even though the pay may not be as high as you would like and work schedules are sometimes difficult to manage with school and extracurricular activities, it is important to have a good work record at your first jobs.

Beginning employees who stay with one employer for a length of time and receive favorable evaluations will find it easier to receive promotions or be hired by an employer offering a better job. Employees who take advantage of training, opportunities for leadership, or the chance to supervise other employees or contribute to team activities will have an excellent employment record to use when applying for promotions or advanced jobs in other companies.

DEVELOPING AN INDIVIDUAL CAREER PLAN

Many people do little planning, even for the things that are most important to them. You know from your study of business that planning is an important skill. Businesses that plan are much more successful than those that do not. Likewise, people who plan their careers are more likely to achieve their career goals than those who do not plan. By developing a career plan, you will be able to practice an important business skill. In addition, you can show your plan to potential employers to demonstrate your understanding of business as well as your planning and communication skills.

The following steps provide an outline for developing your own career plan.

1. *Develop an understanding of business concepts and the different types of business careers.* Study careers in depth to determine the industries, businesses, and jobs that most interest you and the types of career paths related to those jobs.
2. *Complete a self-assessment of your knowledge, skills, and attitudes that are related to those needed in business careers.* Ask a counselor to assist you with appropriate interest and aptitude tests that can help you with your assessment. Get feedback from people who know you well (family, friends, teachers, and employers) about their perceptions of the important skills, knowledge, and attitudes you have identified.

Manager's Perspective on
TECHNOLOGY

If you are interested in a technology career in business, either as a manager or nonmanager, the top four skills business recruiters look for in information technology applicants are applications development, information security, project management, and customer support skills. A big problem faced by recruiters is finding people with the right skills in the right locations. Well-qualified applicants willing to relocate will continue to have many choices of information technology jobs. The ability to lead technology employees as a manager or team leader will continue to be in high demand.

3. *Identify the education and experience requirements for business careers that interest you.* Compare those career requirements with your current preparation, and determine the additional education and experience you will need to qualify for those careers.

4. *Discuss the education and experience you will need with people (counselors or businesspeople) who are familiar with education programs and employment opportunities.* Ask them to help you select those that fit your career plans and qualifications.

5. *Develop a career plan that identifies the knowledge and skills needed for the career you have chosen and how you will develop them through a combination of education and experience.* The plan can identify the jobs in a career ladder, the schools or educational programs you plan to attend, the length of time you anticipate you will spend on each step of the career ladder, and the ultimate career goal you would like to achieve.

PREPARING A CAREER PORTFOLIO

Artists, models, and advertising people have used portfolios for many years to demonstrate their abilities and present examples of their work. You may already have been asked to develop an education portfolio to document your work in several of your classes. A **career portfolio** is an organized collection of information and materials you develop to represent yourself, your preparation, and your accomplishments. You might want to create a portfolio to help with career planning and to represent yourself when you apply for jobs or for admission to an educational institution.

Your portfolio should provide clear descriptions of your preparation, skills, and experience. Those descriptions can include examples of projects you have completed in school and on the job or for organizations to which you belong. They can even be work you have done as a hobby that demonstrates an important business skill. You can include evaluations of your skills and work evidenced through tests, checklists of competencies you have mastered, and performance reviews from employers. Also, you might ask people who know you well to write recommendations that relate to your skills and abilities or critiques of your projects or work.

You can develop your portfolio over a long period of time. You might start it now and continue to add to it as you complete high school, go on for additional education, or move through jobs in your career ladder. You should prepare a portfolio that allows you to add and remove items. Put your materials in a binder or other protective covering to keep them in good condition. As you become increasingly skilled with computer technology, you might want to develop a digital version of your portfolio. You can scan printed materials, photograph objects, and add video and audio files to your digital portfolio. Whether in digital or print form, make and keep backup copies of your important materials in a secure place.

The portfolio should include your best and most recent materials. Many people develop a personal website that includes a summary of their career portfolio and some examples of recent

NETBookmark

ACT is an independent, not-for-profit organization that provides a variety of career assessment, research, and information resources. An interesting tool for matching personal interests with jobs is ACT's World of Work Map.

Access the website for this textbook and choose the link for Chapter 25 Net Bookmark. Use the tool to see what types of careers match your personal interests. Did you identify careers that you had not considered in the past? Talk with your teacher or guidance counselor about career interest and aptitude instruments and other resources available in your school to help you with your career planning.

www.cengage.com/school/bizmgmt

accomplishments. It provides an efficient way to share information with a prospective employer or mentor. It can also be used when apply for admission to an educational institution. If you decide to use the Internet for this purpose, be careful to protect personal and confidential information.

A portfolio is a good way to identify important materials that will help you with your self-assessment. It also keeps materials organized so you can show them to others to demonstrate achievement, or as you apply for educational programs and jobs. Because it must communicate your preparation and skills effectively, it should be well organized, professional, and easy for others to review and understand. Two essential items for every career portfolio are an up-to-date resume and a sample application letter. With these items, you are ready to apply for any job that fits into your career plan. By maintaining up-to-date copies of the resume and sample letter, you can quickly tailor them to a specific employer when you are ready to complete an application.

CHECKPOINT

How can a career portfolio help you in career planning?

25.4 ASSESSMENT

UNDERSTAND MANAGEMENT CONCEPTS

Determine the best answer for each of the following questions.

1. People in _____ occupations are responsible for specific units in a business and must make decisions about operations and personnel.
   a. entry-level
   b. career-level
   c. supervisor/management
   d. specialist

2. An organized collection of information and materials developed to represent yourself, your preparation, and your accomplishments is a
   a. resume
   b. career portfolio
   c. job application
   d. career plan

THINK CRITICALLY

Answer the following questions as completely as possible.

3. Why is it fairly easy for businesspeople who work in one company or industry to move to a job in a different company, industry, or country?

4. How can a well-developed career portfolio provide an advantage for an applicant for a new job?

CHAPTER CONCEPTS

- The dramatic changes facing both traditional and new businesses present challenges to both employees and managers. Human resources personnel can help businesses respond to those changes by establishing organizational development programs.

- Two important elements of an effective organizational development program are improving work processes and building effective working relationships. The goals of the program are to eliminate errors, improve quality, and reduce costs in an organization.

- Successful businesses value their employees. They use job enlargement, cross training, and job enrichment to improve employee satisfaction.

- Career development programs meet a company's future employment needs by systematically preparing current employees for future positions in the company. A successful career development program requires a long-term organizational plan, career paths, employee performance reviews, career counseling, and training and development.

- Common levels of business employment are entry, career, specialist, supervisor/management, and executive/entrepreneur. Career paths exist in all types of businesses. Developing and implementing a career plan will help you obtain a job that is both satisfying and rewarding.

REVIEW BUSINESS MANAGEMENT TERMS

Write the letter of the term that matches each definition. Some terms will not be used.

1. Training employees to perform more than one job in the company, even though they typically perform only one
2. Occupations in which employees have the authority to control some of their work and make some decisions
3. Likelihood of being employed by the same company in the future
4. Facilities where human resources employees manage career development activities
5. Progression of related jobs with increasing skill requirements and responsibility
6. Program that matches the career plans of employees with the employment needs of the business
7. Making a job more interesting by adding variety to the tasks
8. Measures against which the company judges its performance in meeting customer expectations
9. Occupations that involve routine activities and require little training
10. Carefully planned changes in the structure and operation of a business to adjust to a competitive business environment
11. The kinds of tasks that make up a job and the way workers perform these tasks in doing their jobs
12. Occupations fully responsible for the success or failure of a company

a. career centers
b. career development
c. career-level occupations
d. career path
e. cross training
f. customer service standards
g. entry-level occupations
h. executive/entrepreneur occupations
i. individual career plan
j. job design
k. job enlargement
l. job enrichment
m. job security
n. organizational development
o. performance standards
p. specialist occupations
q. supervisor/management occupations

Determine the best answer.

13. The responsibility for planning and managing organizational development and career development programs is usually given to
    a. managers
    b. individual employees
    c. consultants
    d. the human resources department

14. Studies have found that employees are most satisfied with their work based on all of the following factors *except*
    a. performing interesting work
    b. being paid more than their co-workers
    c. receiving recognition for good work
    d. having a feeling of achievement from their work.

15. Which of the following is *not* a requirement of an effective career development program?
    a. long-term company plans to determine job opportunities
    b. career paths leading to both management and nonmanagement positions
    c. regular employee performance reviews
    d. the opportunity for all employees to advance to a management job

16. Web designers, programmers, analysts, professional salespeople, technicians, machine operators, and similar technical or skilled positions are all examples of _____ occupations.
    a. entry-level
    b. career-level
    c. specialist
    d. supervisor/management

APPLY WHAT YOU KNOW

Answer the following questions.

17. Based on the Reality Check scenario at the beginning of the chapter, how can James Lane use career planning to help make the best decision for his future? What kinds of help and assistance should Alliance Industries provide to James and other employees to help them prepare for the upcoming changes?

18. In what ways is the employment environment today different from the environment 10 years ago, and in what ways is it similar? What changes do you predict will occur in the employment environment over the next 10 years?

19. How can work processes be improved without changing the technology or equipment used to complete the work?

20. What are some valuable sources of information that managers can use to identify possible changes in the external environment?

21. Using jobs with which you are familiar, suggest some ways organizations could use job enlargement and job enrichment to increase employee satisfaction and motivation.

22. Some companies believe that each employee should be totally responsible for his or her career development. Why is it likely that career development will not be successful in those companies?

23. In what ways would planning for a career in international business be similar to or different from planning for a career in one's home country?

MAKE ACADEMIC CONNECTIONS

Complete the following activities.

24. **Problem Solving** Form a team with several classmates. Identify one problem related to the "work" environment or "work" relationships of your school. Identify why the problem exists and how the school would be better if the problem were solved. Then propose several solutions and analyze each to determine its advantages and disadvantages. Select the one solution your group believes could be implemented and would be acceptable to administrators, teachers, and students. Prepare a written report from your group that identifies the problem, the proposed solution, and the key steps to successfully implementing the solution.

25. **Math** Yarcho and Slayton, Inc. has been training employees to prepare them for a changeover in computer technology. A report on the training program reveals the following data:

Date of Training	Number of Participants	Cost of Training	Department
2-04	45	$ 900	Marketing
1-13	11	495	Information
4-05	58	870	Management
7-26	26	3,120	
5-30	65	3,250	Operations
9-29	32	960	
3-19	12	900	Accounting
7-12	38	760	and Finance
11-08	29	435	
12-01	19	855	

a. Calculate the cost per participant of each training session.
b. Determine the average cost of training per participant for the entire company.
c. If the company has a total of 206 employees with 45 in Marketing, 58 in Information Management, 65 in Operations, and 38 in Accounting and Finance, determine the average amount spent on each employee for training for each department and for the entire company.

CASE 25-1: Encouraging Employee Involvement

The Orion Corporation recently implemented employee involvement teams as part of an organizational development program. The employees in the customer support department of the engineering division were excited about the chance to participate in solving a problem they had been facing for some time. Fourteen of the 20 employees had school-age children. Several times during the year, the employees needed time off from work to attend parent-teacher conferences, help with projects in their child's school, or attend an important school activity involving their children. Orion had no policy that allowed employees time away from work. The employees either had to miss the school activities or call in sick. Most of the employees felt uncomfortable about taking a "sick day" when they really were not sick.

The employee team worked carefully and developed the following plan: Each employee could have up to two half-day absences for school-related activities during the year. The absence would have to be scheduled at least one week in advance and only one employee could be absent at a time. The other employees would complete the work of the absent employee before they left for the day without additional pay. The department manager could cancel the absence with one day's notice if the department had special assignments or extra work.

The employee team submitted its plan to the department manager. The manager rejected the employee recommendation. She identified two reasons for rejecting the plan: (1) The company could not have different policies concerning employee absences for each department. (2) Not all employees in the department had school-age children, so the policy would be unfair to those employees who did not.

THINK CRITICALLY

1. Do you believe the manager made the right decision about the team's recommendation? Why or why not? What should the manager do now, based on her decision not to accept the team's recommendation? If you were the manager, how would you respond to the team's recommendation?
2. How do you believe the employees will feel about the organization, based on the manager's response to their proposal? What would you recommend the employees do, based on the responses of the manager?
3. How can the Orion Corporation improve the way it organizes and uses teams in the future? Should the manager's role change now that employee involvement teams are being formed?

CASE 25-1: Getting Serious about Career Planning

Felicia Bendine is starting her senior year of high school. She wants her last year in school to be enjoyable, but she also knows she has to get serious about her future. Many of her friends have already submitted applications for admission to colleges and universities, and a few have decided on military careers. Some intend to obtain full-time jobs right after high school, and others are going on to a community college for specialized technical training. Felicia is open to all those ideas but hasn't really decided on any particular one.

Felicia has always wanted to own a business, preferably a collectibles shop that relates to her hobby. Felicia has collected rare dolls since she was a little girl. She has more than 200 dolls in her collection, a few of which are worth several hundred dollars. She has them displayed in their original boxes in her bedroom and frequently attends collectible shows in the area. She has made both sales and purchases to add to her collection.

For the past three years, Felicia has worked for Mr. and Mrs. Abbott in their antique shop in her neighborhood. She had visited the Abbotts' store one day, and when they found out about her doll collection, they gave her a 1930s doll from their inventory. She volunteered to help out in the store, and it turned into a part-time job. She has given them several ideas about business operations from the courses she has taken in school and even set up a simple website where they can advertise their business. It has brought many out-of-town visitors to the store.

The Abbotts have suggested to Felicia that someday, when they decide to retire, they would love to see her take over the business. Felicia expects that their retirement is many years away but is intrigued by the idea. However, she doesn't know if she wants to wait that long to own her own business or what she should do after graduating from high school to prepare for that opportunity or another route to her goal of being an entrepreneur. She does know that she has to do some serious planning in the next few months.

THINK CRITICALLY

1. What education beyond high school do you believe Felicia will need to be a successful small-business owner? What types of business experience would help her prepare to own and operate a business?

2. What are the advantages and disadvantages to Felicia of waiting for the Abbotts' retirement and then buying their business? What information about the business and the Abbotts' plans does Felicia need to help her with that decision?

3. If you were Felicia's friend, what would you recommend she do during her senior year to plan for her future? Justify your recommendations.

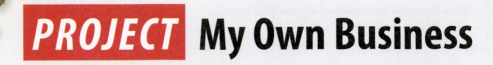

PROJECT My Own Business

Developing An Effective Organization

Even new businesses must be concerned about change and maintaining an effective work environment and work processes. One of the serious problems faced by small businesses is how to provide a motivating and rewarding experience for employees so they will continue to work for the business even though wages and benefits may be less than they can obtain in larger businesses. The following activities will help you consider how to maintain an effective organization and prepare for your role as a small-business owner.

DATA COLLECTION

1. Review magazine and newspaper articles and Internet information about small-business operations. Identify issues small businesses face that often lead to major problems or failure.
2. Identify a small number of people who have worked in a small business for a short time and then changed jobs due to dissatisfaction with the job. Also identify a small number who have worked in a small business and are satisfied with their jobs. Ask each group the reasons for their satisfaction or dissatisfaction. Ask them to identify which of the reasons are directly related to the size of the business.
3. Review information on innovative small businesses and analyze how they are responding to local and global competition, changes in technology, and improvements in work procedures.
4. Identify the business operations, management, and interpersonal skills you will need to develop as the manager of a small business. Gather information from the library or the Internet about opportunities for formal education, professional self-improvement, and life-long learning that could help you improve your skills as a business owner.

ANALYSIS

1. Compile a list of things you could do as the owner of a new small business to develop a work environment that would motivate employees while encouraging effective performance. Try to list things that would not be particularly expensive to implement.
2. Assume that your business has been receiving an increased number of customer complaints. When you question your employees, they tell you that they are unsure of how to deal with difficult customers. Identify employee attitudes that result in customer satisfaction. Develop a procedure your employees could use in complex situations, including follow-up techniques.
3. List the jobs in a career path you can follow to develop the experience and skills you will need to own and operate your own business. Describe the formal education and informal education you will need to achieve that goal.

Human resources specialists provide a link between management and employees. They recruit and interview prospective employees and advise on hiring decisions in accordance with policies and requirements that are consistent with employment laws. They also help prepare employees for their jobs, provide training, and prepare both managers and employees for performance review procedures. They are involved in career planning and efforts to improve the work environment.

Employment Outlook

Human resources specialists are employed in virtually every industry. Some are self-employed consultants to public and private employers. The private sector accounts for about 80 percent of salaried HR jobs. The growing importance of occupational safety and health, equal employment opportunity, wages, health care, pensions, and organizational change will increase the demand for many types of human resources specialists.

Job Titles

Employment Manager

Manager of Diversity

Training and Development Specialist

Compensation and Benefits Specialist

Needed Skills

- Must have a college degree, generally with a major in human resources, personnel, or industrial and labor relations.
- Advanced education and training in areas such as law, counseling, education, or change management preferred.
- Must have excellent communication and human relations skills.

Working in Human Resources

Evelyn is an instructional designer in the training department. She works with managers and experienced employees to determine training needs for a department or job area. Expert employees help her identify the correct procedures for completing job tasks and operating any special equipment. Working with other specialists, she develops instruction that can be delivered in a laboratory, classroom, or over the Internet. Her training programs are carefully tested and improved before they are used by the company.

Career Assessment

Check your library or the Internet for information on HR careers and career paths. Which HR jobs might you consider, and why?

© Getty Images/Photodisc

Case Study

DO NICE EMPLOYEES FINISH LAST?

Business is not an easy game to play. Individuals are sometimes tempted to put their interests above those of others. The *Harvard Business Review* found that personal feelings toward an individual are more significant in the formation of productive work relationships than the person's competence. The ability to connect with others is increasingly important, as the global business environment requires individuals who can collaborate with diverse teams of employees and outside contacts. Companies expect employees to work on project-based teams more frequently in the next 10 to 15 years. Individuals who are pleasant and personable will have the greatest success in forming productive professional partnerships.

A positive, friendly disposition can be a valuable career asset. There is a difference between being nice and being a pushover, however. People who try too hard to be liked may seem disingenuous or out of touch with reality. Some professional situations simply require individuals to take a stand, even when it would be easier to ignore the circumstances. Being overly accommodating can result in shouldering a disproportionate amount of work, losing out on promotion opportunities, and suffering from burnout. For example, offering to stay late to help a colleague finish a project before she leaves on vacation is a gesture that may build goodwill and increase the likelihood that the co-workers will lend you a hand when you need it. Being too nice, on the other hand, occurs when you stay late every night because you have a hard time telling colleagues that your plate is full. The result is burnout from not being able to balance work and leisure.

Another example of being nice is receiving kudos from a satisfied client for a job well done and forwarding the message to those who worked on the project with you to let them know that everyone's effort was appreciated. The entire team receives a morale boost. Receiving praise from a satisfied customer and giving all the credit to everyone else on your team because you don't want to seem self-serving is an example of being too nice. Your accomplishments go unnoticed and your superiors do not realize the true value you bring to the firm.

THINK CRITICALLY

1. What is the fine line between being nice and too nice at work?
2. Why is it important to give colleagues the credit they deserve?
3. What is the danger faced by efficient employees who frequently take on extra responsibilities and regularly help others complete their tasks on time?
4. How would an unethical employee handle praise for a task successfully completed by a team?

Human Resources Management Event

PROCEDURE   You have 30 minutes to prepare a speech for the employees of a store called Latest Edition. Your speech will be seven minutes long followed by three minutes for questions.

SCENARIO   Full-time employees are paid on commission and earn 14 percent of all sales during the year. It is not unusual for the top sales associates to sell $10,000 worth of merchandise on a weekend shift during the busy holiday season. On a summer weekday, however, sales can be slow. Full-time employees receive four weeks of paid vacation and the company pays 80 percent of the cost of health insurance. Part-time employees earn $8.50 an hour and no commission or fringe benefits.

Latest Edition must carefully control its total budget to compete with national department stores. Therefore, it plans to change the way employees are compensated. Full-time employees will now be paid a base salary of $20,000 and 10 percent commission on all sales. They will still have four weeks of paid vacation, and the company will cover 90 percent of their health insurance. Part-time employees will earn $7.00 per hour plus 8 percent commission on sales, with no benefits. All employees will receive a 40 percent discount on clothing they purchase for themselves.

YOUR ASSIGNMENT

You must explain the pay and benefits package in a positive way to help calm employee concerns about changes.

PERFORMANCE INDICATORS EVALUATED

- Apply critical-thinking skills to interpret personnel policies.
- Demonstrate effective persuasive and informative communication and presentation skills.
- Discuss compensation, benefits, and incentive programs.

THINK CRITICALLY

1. Why are changes in compensation and benefits difficult topics to present to employees?
2. Name advantages and disadvantages of paying commission on sales.
3. How do you think the change of compensation for part-time employees will affect their sales performance?

Glossary

A

accountability The obligation to accept responsibility for the outcomes of assigned tasks.

accounting The process of recording, analyzing, and interpreting financial activities of a business.

accounting equation Assets = Liabilities + Capital

accounts payable The amount the company owes for purchases it made on credit.

accounts payable record A record showing purchases of a business, money owed and payments made by the business.

accounts receivable The amount customers owe the business.

accounts receivable record A record showing what each customer purchases, owes and pays.

achievement need In McClelland's theory, the need to take personal responsibility for work, set personal goals, and have immediate feedback on work.

acquiring banks Specialized banks that manage merchant accounts.

actuaries Persons who calculate insurance rates.

administered channel A channel in which one organization takes a leadership position to benefit all channel members.

administrative management Management theory that identifies the most effective practices for organizing and managing a business.

advertising Any form of paid promotion that deliver a message to many people at the same time.

advertising media The methods of delivering the promotional message to the intended audience.

affiliation need In McClelland's theory, motivation related to relationships with others and fitting in with a group.

affinity credit cards Credit cards issued by a financial institution and cosponsored by an organization that receives a small percentage of the sales or profits generated by the card.

agency dilemma Situation when an agent, or someone who works for another, pursues their own interest over their employers.

aging of accounts Analyzing customers' account balances within categories based upon the number of days each customer's balance has remained unpaid.

applied research Research that studies existing product problems or possible design improvements for current products.

assessed valuation The value of property determined by tax officials.

asset Anything of value owned, such as cash and buildings.

asset book value The original cost less accumulated depreciation.

assurance SERVQUAL dimension; the knowledge and courtesy of employees and their ability to convey trust and confidence.

audit An examination of a company's financial records by an expert to verify their accuracy.

authority The right to make decisions about work assignments and to require other employees to perform assigned tasks.

autocratic leader One who gives direct, clear, and precise orders with detailed instructions as to what, when, and how work is to be done.

automatic teller machine (ATM) A computer terminal that enables bank customers to deposit, withdraw, or transfer funds by using a bank-provided plastic card.

avoidance strategy A strategy for resolving conflict that takes a neutral position or agrees with another person's position even though it differs from your personal belief.

B

baby boom The high birth rate period from 1945 to 1965.

baby bust The low birth rate period following the baby boom period.

balance of payments Accounting statement in which all international transactions are recorded; consists of current account and capital account.

balance sheet (statement of financial position) A financial statement that reports a business's assets, liabilities, and capital on a specific date.

bank A financial institution that accepts demand deposits, makes consumer and commercial loans, and buys and sells currency and government securities.

bank charter Authorization for the operation of a bank following the regulations established by the state or federal government.

bankruptcy A legal process that allows selling assets to pay off debts.

bar codes Product identification labels containing a unique set of vertical bars that computer scanning equipment can read.

basic product The physical product in its simplest form.

behavioral management Management theory directed at organizational improvement through understanding employee motivation and behavior. Behavioral management is sometimes called *human relations management*.

beneficiaries Persons who receive a life insurance payment on the death of an insured person.

board of directors Ruling body of a corporation.

body language Gestures, movements, and mannerism used to communicate.

bond A long-term debt instrument sold by the business to investors that contains a written promise to pay a definite sum of money at a specified time.

bonding Insurance protection which provides payment of damages to people who have losses resulting from the negligence or dishonesty of an employee or from the failure of the business to complete a contract.

bonus Money paid at the end of a specified but long period of time for performance that exceeds the expected standard for that period.

book value (1) The value of a share of stock that is found by dividing the net worth (assets minus liabilities) of the corporation by the total number of shares outstanding. (2) The total amount of depreciation is deducted from the asset's original value.

brainstorming A team discussion technique that is used to generate as many ideas as possible for solving a problem.

brand A name, symbol, word, or design that identifies a product, service, or company.

budget A written financial plan for business operations developed for a specific period of time.

building codes Codes that control physical features of structures.

business An organization that produces or distributes a good or service for profit.

business buying process A set of formal procedures followed by a business when it decides to purchase a product.

business competition The rivalry among companies for customers.

business cycles A pattern of irregular but repeated expansion and contraction of the GDP.

business environment The factors and conditions within which a business operates and that can affects its success.

business ethics A collection of principles and rules that define right and wrong conduct for an organization.

business plan A written document that describes the nature of the business, its goals and objectives, and how they will be achieved.

buying Obtaining goods to be resold.

buying motives The reasons people buy.

C

cafeteria plan A benefit program in which employees can select the benefits that meet their personal needs.

capacity A measure of earning power and a reflection of a loan applicant's potential to pay based on current income and other financial obligations.

capital (1) The money required to start or expand a business. (2) A measure of the credit applicant's current financial worth or ability to pay based on assets.

capital (net worth, owner's equity, stockholders' equity) The value of the owners' investment in the business after subtracting liabilities from assets.

capital account An account that records investment funds coming into and going out of a country.

capital budget A financial plan for replacing fixed assets or acquiring new ones.

capital formation The production of capital goods.

capital goods Buildings, tools, machines, and other equipment that are used to produce other goods but do not directly satisfy human wants.

capitalism A political-economy system in which private citizens are free to go into business for themselves, to produce whatever they choose to produce, and to distribute what they produce.

career centers Facilities where human resource employees manage career development activities.

career development An effort to match employees' career plans with the changing employment needs of the business.

career development program A plan for meeting the company's future employment needs by systematically preparing current employees for future positions in the company.

career-level occupations An occupation in which the employee has the authority to control some of their work and make some decisions.

career path A progression of related jobs with increasing skill requirements and responsibility that provide opportunities for employees to advance within a company.

career portfolio An organized collection of information and materials you develop to represent yourself, your preparation, and your accomplishments.

carpal tunnel syndrome (CTS) A medical condition that occurs when the median nerve, which runs through a tunnel in the wrist, is compressed or irritated.

cash budget An estimate of the flow of cash into and out of the business over a specified time period.

cash disbursement Cash payments made by a business.

cash discount A price reduction given for paying by a certain date.

cash flow The movement of cash into and out of a business.

cash receipts Money taken in by a business.

cause and effect The relationship between two events in which the second event is a consequence of the first.

cease-and-desist order Legal penalty requiring that a company stop using specific advertisements.

centralized organization Business structure in which a few top managers do all the major planning and decision making.

certificate of deposit (CD) A time deposit account that requires specified minimum deposit for a fixed period at a fixed interest rate.

certified public accountant (CPA) A person who has met a state's education, experience, and examination requirements in accounting.

channel integration When one business owns the organizations at other levels of the channel.

channel members Businesses that participate in activities transferring goods and services from the producer to the user.

channel of communication The means by which a message is conveyed.

channels of distribution (marketing channels) The routes products and services follow while moving from the producer to the consumer, including the activities and participating organizations.

character A measure of a person's or business's sense of financial responsibility or belief in the obligation to pay debts.

characteristics The unique, identifiable qualities or features of the people or objects being studied.

chart A type of diagram that organizes and summarizes a set of numerical data.

charter Official document through which a state grants the power to operate as a corporation.

check A written order requiring the financial institution to pay previously deposited money to a third party on demand.

chief information officer (CIO) The top computer executive.

classical management Management theory that studies the way work is organized and the procedures used to complete a job in order to increase worker productivity.

close corporation Corporation that does not offer its shares of stock for public sale.

cloud Data storage systems over widely dispersed Internet networks.

co-branded credit cards Credit cards cosponsored by two companies which have benefits and rewards designed specifically for their joint customers.

code of ethics A formal, published collection of values and rules that reflect the firm's philosophy and goals.

collateral Property a borrower pledges to assure repayment of a loan.

combination plan A plan that provides each employee a small wage or salary and adds incentive pay based on the person's performance.

command economy An economic system in which a central planning authority, under the control of the country's government, owns most of the factors of production and determines what, how, and for whom goods and services will be produced.

commercial loan A loan made to a business.

commission plan A compensation plan in which employees are paid a percentage of the volume of business for which they are responsible.

common stock Ownership that gives holders the right to participate in managing the business through voting privileges and the right to share in any profits through dividends.

communication The sharing of information, in which the receiver understands the meaning of the message in the way the sender intended.

communication network The structure through which information flows in a business.

communism Extreme socialism, in which all or almost all of a nation's factors of production are owned by the government.

comparable worth Paying workers equally for jobs with similar but not identical job requirements.

comparative advantage theory A theory suggesting that a country should specialize in products or services that it can provide more efficiently than other countries in order to gain a trade advantage.

compensation The pay and other benefits employees receive in exchange for their labor.

compensation plan A system of policies and procedures for calculating the wages and salaries in an organization.

competition Rivalry among sellers for consumers' dollars.

compromise strategy A strategy in which everyone involved in a conflict agrees to a mutually acceptable solution.

computer-aided design (CAD) Computer application that allows engineers to design and test products before they are even built.

computer-integrated manufacturing Process in which all manufacturing systems are designed and managed with computers.

conditions An assessment of the economic environment that affect credit decisions.

conflict Interference by one person with the achievement of another person's goals.

consultant Someone who gives professional advice or offers professional services.

consumer goods Products designed for personal or home use.

consumer goods and services Goods and services that satisfy people's economic wants directly.

consumer loan A loan made to an individual for personal use.

consumer panel A group of people who offer opinions about a product or service.

consumer price index (CPI) A measure of the average change in prices of consumer goods and services typically purchased by people living in urban areas.

containerization A process in which products are packed in large shipping containers at the factory and then shipped using a number of transportation methods before being unpacked.

continuous processing Manufacturing process in which raw materials constantly move through specially designed equipment that changes their form to make them more usable for consumption or further manufacturing.

controlling Evaluating results to determine if the company's objectives have been accomplished as planned.

convenience goods Inexpensive items that consumers purchase regularly without a great deal of thought.

convertible bond A bond that allows a bondholder to exchange bonds for a prescribed number of shares of common stock.

cookies Files of information about a user that some websites create and store on the user's own computer.

cooperative Business owned and operated by its user-members for the purpose of supplying themselves with goods and services.

copyright Sole right given to an author by the federal government to reproduce, publish, and sell literary or artistic work for the life of the author plus 70 years.

corporate branding A business process that is planned, strategically focused, and integrated throughout the organization.

corporate identity A company's name or logo; its visual expression or its "look."

corporate image The public's perception of a company.

corporation Business owned by a group of people and authorized by the state in which it is located to act as though it were a single person, separate from its owners.

corrective advertising New advertising designed to change the false impression left by misleading information.

correlation A connection or relationship between two things being studied.

cost of goods sold The amount a retailer pays a supplier for the merchandise it buys and sells or the amount a manufacturer pays for raw materials and parts to make its products.

cost standard The predetermined cost of performing an operation or producing a good or service.

credit (1) The provision of goods or services to a customer with an agreement for future payment. (2) Purchase arrangement in which goods and services are provided with the expectation of future payment by the customer.

credit agency A clearinghouse for information on the creditworthiness of individuals or businesses.

creditor Person or business to whom money is owed.

creditworthiness A measure of an individual's or business's ability and willingness to repay a loan.

cross training A process in which employees are trained to perform more than one job in the company even though they typically perform only one.

crowdfunding A strategy for funding a business idea with small amounts of money from many people.

culture The customs, beliefs, values, and patterns of behavior of the people of a country or group.

cumulative preferred stock A special class of preferred stock that pays the dividend in future years if there is no profit in a particular year.

current account An account that records the value of goods and services exported and those imported from foreigners, as well as other income and payments.

customer-oriented firm Focused activities toward satisfying customers.

customer service standards Measures against which a company judges its performance in meeting customer expectations.

custom manufacturing Process used to design and build a unique product to meet the specific needs of the purchaser.

D

data Original facts and figures that businesses generate.

database A collection of data organized in a way that makes the data easy to find, update, and manage.

data-based decision Result of using facts and measures as the primary basis for choosing among alternatives.

data mining The process of using data in databases to find relationships between individuals and their behavior or preferences.

data set All of the facts and figures that have been collected for study.

data processing The set of activities involved in obtaining, recording, organizing, and maintaining the financial information of an organization.

debentures Bonds that are not secured by assets but based upon the faith and credit of the corporation that issues them.

debit card A card used to transfers funds electronically from the cardholder's checking account to a business's account when a purchase is made.

debt capital (creditor capital) Money that others loan to a business.

decentralized organization A business which is divided into smaller operating units, and managers who head the units have almost total responsibility and authority for operations.

decision support system (DSS) A system that helps managers consider alternatives in making specific decisions.

decline stage Stage of the product life cycle when a new product is introduced that is much better or easier to use and customers begin to switch from the old product to the new product.

deductible The amount the insured pays for a loss before the insurance company pays anything.

deductive reasoning Use of general principles to make predictions about specific situations or circumstances.

defined benefit plan A retirement plan that provides a specific monthly benefit to retired employees determined by their years of employment and amount of earnings while employed.

defined contribution plan A retirement plan that requires regular payments to an employee retirement account but does not guarantee a specific monthly benefit to be paid on retirement.

demand The number of products that will be bought at a given time at a given price.

demand deposit Money put into a financial institution by depositors which can be withdrawn at any time without penalty.

democratic leader One who encourages workers to share in making decisions about their work and work-related problems.

depreciation Gradual loss of an asset's value due to age and wear.

depression A long and severe drop in the GDP.

descriptive statistics Meaningful summaries of data to help explain a current situation.

digital dashboard A management information system that allows multiple sources of information to be displayed graphically on a computer.

direct deposit The electronic transfer of a payment directly into a recipient's bank account.

direct distribution When producers sell directly to the ultimate consumer.

direct marketing Offering products to customers through media such as catalogs, direct mail, telemarketing, e-mail marketing, and websites.

disability insurance Insurance which offers payments to employees who are no longer able to work because of accidents or illnesses.

discharge The release of an employee from the company due to inappropriate work behavior.

discounts Reductions from the product's list price designed to encourage customers to buy.

distortion The conscious or unconscious way people change messages.

distraction Anything that interferes with the sender's creating and delivering a message and the receiver's getting and interpreting a message.

distribution (place) The set of activities required to transport and store products and make them available to customers.

distribution center A large building designed to accumulate and redistribute products efficiently.

diversify To spread investment risk by placing money in different categories of investments.

domain name A website owner's unique name that identifies the website.

domestic goods Products made by firms in the United States.

downsize Reduce the amount and variety of goods and services produced and the number of employees needed to produce them.

dumping The practice of selling goods in a foreign market at a price that is below cost or below what the business charges in its own home country.

E

e-business The use of communication technology to support business operations.

economic discrepancies Differences between the offerings of a business and the requirements of a consumer.

economic growth Situation in which a country's output exceeds its population growth.

economics The body of knowledge that relates to producing and using goods and services that satisfy human wants.

economic system An organized way for a country to decide how to use its productive resources; that is, to decide what, how, and for whom goods and services will be produced.

economic utility The amount of satisfaction received from using a product or service.

economic wants The desire for scarce material goods and services.

effectiveness Making the right decisions about what products or services to offer customers and the best ways to produce and deliver them.

efficiency Producing products and services quickly, at low cost, without wasting time and materials.

electronic funds transfer (EFT) Transferring money by computer.

electronic shopping carts Programs that keep track of shoppers' selections as they shop, provide an order form for them to complete, and submit the form to the company through the Internet.

embargo A process in which the government bars companies from doing business with particular countries.

empathy SERVQUAL dimension; the caring and individualized attention the business provides its customers.

employee assistance program Employer programs that provides confidential individual assistance including counseling and support services for employees experiencing serious personal or family issues.

employee benefits All forms of compensation and services the company provides to employees in addition to salaries and wages.

employee stock ownership plan (ESOP) A plan that allows employees to become owners of the company they work for through the purchase of stock.

employee turnover The rate at which people enter and leave employment in a business during a year.

empowerment (1) Authority given to individual employees to make decisions and solve problems they encounter on their jobs with the resources available to them. (2) Letting workers decide how to perform their work tasks and offer ideas on how to improve the work process.

endorsement The payee's signature on the back of the check legally transferring ownership.

enhanced product A product that offers different features and options for the consumer.

entrepreneur A person who starts, manages, and owns a business.

entry-level occupations Occupations which usually involve routine activities and require little training.

equity capital (owner capital) Business owners' personal financial contributions to the business.

ergonomics The science of adapting equipment to the work and health needs of people.

ethics Standards of moral conduct that individuals and groups set for themselves, defining what behavior they value as right or wrong.

euro The currency of the European Union.

European Union (EU) A trading bloc of European countries.

exchange rate The value of one country's currency expressed in the currency of another.

excise tax Sales tax that applies only to selected goods and services, such as gasoline.

executive information system (EIS) Information system that combines and summarizes ongoing transactions within the company to provide top-level executives with information needed to make decisions affecting the goals and direction of an organization.

executive summary A written summary of a longer report including concise analysis, recommendations, and conclusions.

executive A top-level manager who spends almost all of his or her time on management functions and decisions that affect the entire company.

executive/entrepreneur occupations Occupations in which the people are fully responsible for the success or failure of the company.

exit interview A formal interview with an employee who is leaving a company to determine the person's attitudes and feelings about the company and seek suggestions for improving the company.

expert power Power given to people because of their superior knowledge about the work.

exporting When a company sells its goods and services to buyers in a foreign country.

extended product A product that includes additional features that are not part of the physical product but increase its usability.

extranet A private network that companies use to share certain information with selected people outside the organization, such as suppliers and major customers.

F

factor A firm that specializes in lending money to businesses based on the business's accounts receivable.

factors of production Land, labor, capital goods, and management—the four basic resources that are combined to create useful goods and services.

Fair Labor Standards Act (FLSA) Federal law that prescribes standards for wages and overtime pay.

false advertising Advertising that is misleading in some important way, including the failure to reveal facts about possible results from using the advertised products.

Family Medical Leave Act (FMLA) Federal law that entitles eligible employees to take unpaid leave for specified family and medical reasons.

Federal Deposit Insurance Corporation (FDIC) A federal agency that insures deposits in banks and savings institutions.

Federal Reserve System (Fed) The central bank of the United States.

feedback A receiver's response to a sender's message.

finance Business activity that deals with all money matters related to running a business.

financial institution An organization that collects money from clients and uses it for investments to benefit both the client and the organization.

financial records Organized summaries of a business's financial information and activities.

financial statements Reports that summarize financial data over a period of time.

financing Providing money that is needed to perform various marketing activities.

firewall Special software that screens people who enter a network by requesting specific information such as passwords.

fixed assets Expensive assets of a business that are expected to last and be used for a long time.

fixed interest rate An interest rate that does not change throughout the life of the loan.

flame An electronic message that contains abusive, threatening, or offensive content that may violate company policy or public law.

flattened organization An organization with fewer levels of management than traditional structures.

flex-time A plan that lets employees choose their own work hours, within specified limits.

foreign goods Products made by firms in other countries.

formal communication network System of official channels that carry organizationally approved messages; flows upward, downward, and across the organization in a prescribed manner.

formal training Carefully planned instruction with a specific curriculum and instructor.

fraction Part of a whole number expressed as a proportion.

franchise A legal agreement in which an individual or small group of investors purchases the right to sell a company's product or service under the company's name and trademark.

franchisee The distributor of a franchised product or service.

franchisor The parent company of a franchise agreement that provides the product or service.

free-trade agreements Treaties between two or more countries that eliminate almost all trade restrictions and subsidies between the countries.

frequency distribution List of the values in the range for a characteristic and the number of times each value appears in the data set.

Frost Belt The colder states in the north and northeast of the United States.

full disclosure Providing all information necessary for consumers to make an informed decision.

G

Generation X People born in the low birth-rate period between 1960 and 1980.

Generation Z People born between 1991 and the end of the millennium; also called millennials.

glass ceiling An invisible barrier to job advancement.

global competition The ability of businesses from one country to compete with similar businesses in other countries.

goal A specific statement of a result the business expects to achieve.

goods-producing businesses firms produce goods used by other businesses, organizations, or consumers.

grading and valuing Grouping goods according to size, quality, or other characteristics, and determining an appropriate price for products and services.

grapevine The informal transmission of information among workers.

graph A visual representation of data as it changes over time.

gross domestic product (GDP) The total market value of all goods produced and services provided in a country in a year.

gross profit The amount remaining after subtracting the cost of goods sold from revenue.

growth stage Stage of the product life cycle when several brands of the new product are available.

H

health insurance Insurance which provides protection against the expenses of health care.

high-context culture A culture in which communication occurs through non-verbal signs and indirect suggestions.

home country The country in which a multinational corporation has its headquarters.

host country The foreign country where a multinational firm has production and service facilities.

human capital Accumulated knowledge and skills of human beings; the total value of each person's education and acquired skills.

human relations How well people get along with each other when working together.

human resources management (HRM) All activities involved with acquiring, developing, and compensating the people who do the company's work.

human resources planning Determining the types of jobs that are required for each part of the production process, the number of people needed for each job, and the skills each person will need in order to do the job.

hygiene factors Job factors that dissatisfy when absent but do not contribute to satisfaction when they are present.

I

identity power Power given to people because others identify with and want to be accepted by them.

identity theft The unauthorized use of someone's personally identifying information, such as name, Social Security number, or credit card number, to commit fraud or other crimes. In addition to the impact on victims, identity theft creates problems for businesses.

implementing Carrying out plans and helping employees to work effectively.

importing Buying goods or services made in a foreign country.

income statement (profit and loss statement) A financial statement that reports information about a company's revenues and expenses for a specific period.

income tax Tax on the profits of businesses and the earnings of individuals.

indirect distribution Distribution that takes place through channel members.

individual career plan A strategy which identifies the jobs that are part of the employee's career path, the training needed to advance along the career path, and a tentative schedule for the plan's activities.

inductive reasoning Analysis of specific data to draw broader conclusions.

industrial goods Products designed for use by another business.

Industrial Revolution The era of the eighteenth and nineteenth centuries in which machine power replaced human and animal power in the production process leading to major business and social changes.

industry Term often used to refer to all businesses within a category doing similar work.

inferential statistics Analysis of information used to make predictions about similar circumstances or the future.

inflation A rapid rise in prices caused by an inadequate supply of goods and services.

informal communication network Unofficial way of sharing information in an organization.

informal training Unstructured training and instruction developed for specific situations or individuals.

information Data processed in a meaningful way.

information liability Responsibility for physical or economic injury arising from incorrect data or wrongful use of data.

information system A computer system that processes data into meaningful information.

initial public offering (IPO) The first time that a company sells stock to the public.

innovation Something entirely new.

installment credit Credit used when a customer makes an expensive purchase and agrees to make payments over an extended but fixed period of time.

insurable interest The possible financial loss that the policyholder will suffer if the property is damaged or destroyed.

insurance A risk management tool that exchanges the uncertainty of a possible large financial loss for a certain smaller payment.

insurance agents People who represent the insurance company and sell insurance to individuals and businesses.

insurance rate The amount an insurance company charges a policyholder for a certain amount of insurance.

insured Persons or organizations covered by the insurance policy.

insurer Company that sells insurance.

intangible When applied to services, having no physical form, visibility, or existence after consumer has used the service.

intermittent processing Manufacturing process that uses short production runs to make predetermined quantities of different products.

international business Business activities that occur between two or more countries.

international licensing Arrangement in which one company allows a different company in another country to make and sell its products according to certain specifications.

International Monetary Fund (IMF) International institution that helps countries that are facing serious financial difficulties in paying for their imports or repaying loans.

Internet (Net) Worldwide network of linked computers that allows users to transfer data and information from one computer to another anywhere in the world.

interstate commerce Business operations and transactions that cross over state lines.

intranet A private company network that allows employees to share resources no matter where they are located.

intrapreneur An employee who is given funds and freedom to create a special unit or department within a company in order to develop a new product, process, or service.

intrastate commerce Business transacted within a state.

introduction stage Stage of the product life cycle when a brand-new product enters the market.

inventory All the materials and products a business has on hand for use in production and available for sale.

inventory management Planning the quantities of materials and supplies needed for production and the number of finished products required to fill customer orders.

investment The use of money to make more money.

investment bank An organization that helps businesses raise capital through the sale of stocks and bonds.

J

job description A list of the duties and responsibilities that that make up a job.

job design The kinds of tasks that make up a job and the way workers perform these tasks in doing their jobs.

job enlargement Making a job more interesting by adding variety to the tasks.

job enrichment Encouraging employee participation in decision making.

job security The likelihood of being employed by the same company in the future.

job sharing An employment plan that allows two people to share one full-time job.

job specification A list of the qualifications and skills a worker needs to do a job.

joint venture Two or more businesses that agree to provide a good or service, sharing the costs of doing business and also the profits.

just-in-time (JIT) inventory controls A method in which the company maintains very small inventories and obtains materials just in time for use.

K

knowledge workers People who work with information.

L

labor The human effort, either physical or mental, that goes into the production of goods and services.

labor agreement Contract between management and the union identifying rights and responsibilities of the business and its employees.

labor force Most people aged 16 or over who are available for work, whether employed or unemployed.

labor participation rate The percentage of the adult population that is in the labor force.

labor union Organization of workers formed to represent their common interests in improving wages, benefits, and working conditions.

layoff A temporary or permanent reduction in the number of employees resulting from a change in business conditions.

leader Manager who earns the respect and cooperation of employees to effectively accomplish the work of the organization.

leadership The ability to influence individuals and groups to cooperatively achieve common goals.

leadership style The general way a manager treats and supervises employees.

lease A contract that allows the use of an asset for a fee paid on a schedule.

liabilities Claims against assets or things owed—the debts of a business.

liability insurance Insurance which provides protection against losses from injury to people or their property that result from the products, services, or operations of the business.

licensing A way to limit and control those who plan to enter certain types of businesses.

life insurance Insurance that pays money on the death of the insured to a person or people identified in the insurance policy.

limited liability company (LLC) Special type of corporation allowed by states that is taxed as if it were a sole proprietorship or partnership.

limited liability partnership A partnership in which each partner's liability is limited to his or her investment in the partnership.

limited partnership Partnership with at least one general partner who has unlimited liability and at least one limited partner whose liability is limited to his or her investment.

line-and-staff organization The addition of staff specialists to a line organization.

line of credit The authorization to borrow up to a maximum amount for a specified period of time.

line organization Business structure in which all authority and responsibility can be traced in a direct line from the top executive down to the lowest employee level.

liquidity The ease of turning an investment into cash without significant loss.

list price The initial price that the seller posts on the product.

local area network (LAN) Network of linked computers that serves users in a single building or building complex.

long-term debt Capital that is borrowed for longer than a year.

low-context culture A culture in which people communicate directly and explicitly.

M

malpractice insurance A type of liability insurance that protects against financial loss arising from suits for negligence in providing professional services.

management The process of accomplishing the goals of an organization through the effective use of people and other resources.

management information system (MIS) (1) A computer-based system that stores, organizes, and provides information about a business. (2) A system that integrates data from various departments to make it available to help managers with day-to-day business operations.

management principles The fundamental guidelines for the decisions and actions of managers.

management role A common set of activities that make up an important part of a manager's job.

management science The careful, objective study of management decisions and procedures in order to improve the operation of businesses and organizations.

management strategy A carefully developed overall approach to leading an organization.

manager Person who completes all four management functions on a regular basis and has authority over other jobs and people.

manufacturing Form of production in which raw and semifinished materials are processed, assembled, or converted into finished products.

margin (gross profit) The difference between the selling price and the cost of goods sold.

markdown Any amount by which the original selling price is reduced before an item is sold.

market The types of buyers a business wishes to attract and where such buyers are located.

market economy An economic system in which individual buying decisions in the marketplace together determine what, how, and for whom goods and services will be produced.

marketing (1) The activities between business and customers involved in buying and selling goods and services. (2) A set of activities that gets products from producers to consumers.

marketing concept Keeping the needs of the consumer uppermost in mind during the design, production, and distribution of a product.

marketing managers Managers responsible for coordinating marketing functions across departments to meet customer needs.

marketing mix The blend of all decisions that are related to the four elements of marketing.

marketing plan A detailed written description of all marketing activities that a business must accomplish in order to sell a product.

market research The study of a company's current and prospective customers.

market value The price at which stock is bought and sold on any given day.

markup The amount added to the cost of goods sold to determine the selling price.

mass production Assembly process that produces a large number of identical products; usually involves an assembly line.

matrix organization An organization which combines workers into temporary work teams to complete specific projects.

maturity stage Stage of the product life cycle when there are many competing brands with very similar features.

mean The sum of all values divided by the number of values.

median The middle number in the range of values.

Medicare Health insurance for people 65 or older and for people under 65 with certain disabilities.

merchandise inventory The value of goods purchased to sell to customers at a profit.

merchant account A specialized bank account established by a business in order to process credit card payments from its customers.

merchant account provider A private company that acts as an intermediary between businesses and one or more credit card companies to establish and maintain credit services.

metric system Measuring method based on the decimal system in which all measures are in common units of ten.

middle manager A manager who completes all of the management functions, but spends most of the time completing specialized work in one management function or is responsible for a specific part of the company's operations.

minimum wage law A law that specifies that it is illegal for employers to pay less than an identified wage rate to any employee.

mission A short, specific statement of the business's purpose and direction.

mixed economy An economic system that uses aspects of a market and a command economy to make decisions about what, how, and for whom goods and services are produced.

mode The value that appears the most frequently in a range of values.

modified rebuy A purchase of a new or modified product from established suppliers.

money market account A type of savings account in which the deposits are invested by the financial institution in short-term, government-backed securities.

monopoly Situation created when only one company provides a product or service without competition from other companies.

Moore's Law The prediction that the amount of data that a computer chip could process would double about every 18 months.

mortgage bond A bond secured by specific long-term assests of the issuer.

motivation The set of factors that cause a person to act in a certain way.

motivators Job factors that increase job satisfaction.

multinational firm A business that owns or controls production or service facilities outside the country in which it is based.

mutual fund Company that pools the money of many small investors for the purchase of stocks and bonds.

N

natural monopoly Type of monopoly that usually involves providing public services, such as public utilities, which have a fairly stable demand and are costly to create.

natural resources Anything provided by nature that affects the productive ability of a country.

need for esteem In Maslow's hierarchy of needs, the need for recognition and respect from others.

net profit (1) The amount remaining after subtracting all expenses from revenue, except taxes. (2) The difference between the selling price and all costs and expenses of the business.

new task purchase Process when a business is purchasing a product, inventory item, or supply for the first time.

no-fault insurance Insurance that requires each insurance company to pay the losses of its insured when an accident occurs,

regardless of who might have been responsible for the loss.

nominal group technique (NGT) Group problem-solving method in which team members write down and evaluate ideas to be shared with the team.

nonbank Financial institution whose primary purpose is to offer financial products and services other than deposits and loans.

noneconomic wants Desires for nonmaterial things that are not scarce.

nongovernmental organizations (NGOs) Independent groups which influence businesses through lobbying, publicity, and pressure tactics to alter their activities.

nonprofit corporation Organization that does not pay taxes and does not exist to make a profit.

nontariff barriers Barriers other than tariffs that restrict imports.

nonverbal communication Delivering messages by means other than speaking or writing.

North American Free Trade Agreement (NAFTA) A trading bloc consisting of the United States, Canada, and Mexico.

O

objections Concerns or complaints expressed by the customer.

obsolescence The condition of being out-of-date or inadequate for a particular purpose.

Occupational Safety and Health Act Federal law that regulates safety and health conditions in most businesses.

officer Top executive who is hired to manage a business.

open corporation Corporation that offers its shares of stock for public sale.

open leader Manager who gives little or no direction to employees.

operating budget A budget showing projected sales, costs, expenses, and profits for the ongoing operations of a business.

operating expenses (1) All expenses not directly associated with producing or purchasing merchandise the business sells. (2) The costs of operating a business.

operational planning Short-term planning that identifies specific activities for each area of the business.

operations The major ongoing activities of a business.

operations management Effectively directing the major activities of a business to achieve its goals.

organizational culture The collection of beliefs and patterns of behavior that are shared by people within an organization.

organizational development Carefully planned changes in the structure and operation of a business to adjust to a competitive business environment.

organization chart An illustration of the structure of an organization, major job classifications, and the reporting relationships among the organization's personnel.

organizing Determining how plans can be accomplished most effectively and arranging resources to complete work.

output The quantity, or amount, produced within a given time.

outsourcing Hiring an outside firm to perform specialized tasks.

P

par value (stated value) A dollar value shown on a share of stock, which is an arbitrarily assigned amount that is used for bookkeeping purposes.

parent firm A company that controls another company.

partnership Business owned by two or more people.

partnership agreement A written agreement between two or more people identifying how the partners will add capital, labor, or other assets and divide any profits.

patent An agreement in which the federal government gives an inventor the sole right for 20 years to make, use, and sell an invention.

pension plan A company-sponsored retirement plan that makes regular payments to employees after retirement.

percentage Part of a whole expressed in hundredths.

performance review (1) A procedure that evaluates the work and accomplishment of an employee and provides feedback on performance. (2) The process of assessing how well employees are doing their jobs.

performance standards Specific statements of the expected results from critical business activities.

peril Cause of a loss for a person or organization. Common perils are fire, accidents, sickness, death, and theft.

personal property tax Tax on possessions that are movable, such as furniture, machinery, and equipment.

personal selling Promotion through direct, personal contact with a customer.

physiological needs In Maslow's hierarchy of needs, things required to sustain life, such as food and shelter.

piece-rate plan A compensation plan that pays the employee a fixed rate for each unit produced.

piggyback service A distribution method where truck trailers are loaded and placed on railroad cars to be shipped close to their final destination.

place utility Means that the usefulness of a product being in a place where customers need or want it.

planning Analyzing information and making decisions about what needs to be done.

policies Guidelines used in making decisions regarding specific, recurring situations.

policy Written agreement, or contract, between the insurer and the policyholder.

policyholder Person or business purchasing insurance.

population All the people or objects with a similar characteristic or characteristics being studied.

positioning chart Chart used to identify alternate market segments with unique needs based on major choice criteria.

position power Power that comes from the position the manager holds in the organization.

power The ability to control behavior.

power need In McClelland's theory, desire to influence and control others and to be responsible for a group's activities.

preferred stock Ownership that gives holders preference over the common stockholders when distributing dividends or assets.

premium Payment by a policyholder to the insurer for protection against risk.

price The amount of money given to acquire a product.

price discrimination Setting different prices for different customers.

prime rate The rate at which large banks loan large sums to the best-qualified borrowers.

principal (par value) Amount the company borrows when it issues a bond.

private property Items of value that individuals can own, use, and sell.

privatization Transfer of authority to provide a good or service from a government to individuals or privately owned businesses.

probability The likelihood that a certain outcome will occur.

problem A difficult situation requiring a solution.

procedure A sequence of steps to be followed for performing specific task.

processed data Data that have been checked for accuracy and organized in a way to make it understandable and useable.

process improvement Efforts to increase the effectiveness and efficiency of specific business operations.

producer Anyone who creates utility.

product All attributes, both tangible and intangible, that customers receive in exchange for the purchase price.

product assortment The complete set of all products a business offers to a market.

product development Process of creating or improving a product or service.

production Making a product or providing a service.

production-oriented firm Focused on what and how to produce.

production scheduling Identifying the steps required in a manufacturing process, the time required to complete each step, and the sequence of the steps.

productivity Producing the largest quantity in the least time by using efficient methods and modern equipment.

product life cycle The four stages of sales and profit performance through which all brands of a product progress.

product life cycle theory Theory stating that companies look for new markets when products are in the maturity and decline stages of the product life cycle.

product line A group of similar products with obvious variations in the design and quality to meet the needs of distinct customer groups.

profit (1) Income minus costs. (2) The incentive, as well as the reward, for producing goods and services.

profit-sharing plan A benefit plan that pays employees a small percentage of the company's profits at the end of the year.

progressive tax Tax based on the ability to pay.

promissory note An unconditional written promise to pay to the lender a certain sum of money at a particular time or on demand.

promotion (1) Providing information to consumers that will assist them in making a decision to purchase a product or service. (2) The advancement of an employee within a company to a position with more authority and responsibility.

property tax Tax on material goods owned.

proportional tax (flat tax) Tax rate that remains the same regardless of the amount on which the tax is imposed.

proprietor Person who owns and manages a business and often performs the day-to-day tasks, with the help of hired employees.

proprietorship Business owned and managed by one person.

public franchise A contract that permits a person or organization to use public property for private profit.

pure research Research done without a specific product in mind.

Q

quality control The process of making sure work meets acceptable standards.

quality management (1) The process of assuring product quality by developing standards for all operations and products and measuring results against those standards. (2) A total commitment by everyone in an organization to improve the quality of procedures and products by reducing waste, errors, and defects.

quality standard A specific measure that describes expected consistency in production or performance.

quantity discount A price reduction offered to customers that buy quantities larger than a specified minimum.

quantity standard A specific measure that establishes the expected amount of work to be completed.

quasi-public corporation Business that is important to society but lacks the profit potential to attract private investors and is often operated by local, state, or federal government.

quotas Limits placed on the quantity or value of units permitted to enter a country.

R

range All the possible values of a characteristic from lowest to highest.

ratio The relationship between two quantities.

raw data Original facts or figures that have not been processed for meaningful use.

real property tax Tax real estate, which is land and buildings.

recession A decline in the GDP that continues for six months or more.

record-keeping system A manual or automated process for collecting, organizing, and maintaining the financial information of a business.

recycling Reusing products or product packaging.

regressive tax Taxation wherein the actual tax rate decreases as the taxable amount increases.

reinsurance Another insurance company charges a premium to cover some of the risk facing the original insurer.

reliability SERVQUAL dimension; the ability to perform the promised service dependably and accurately.

repetitive production Type of mass production where the same thing is done over and over to produce a product.

representative Consistent with other similar data that could be collected.

researching Studying buyer interests and needs, testing products, and gathering facts needed to make good marketing decisions.

responsibility The obligation to do an assigned task.

responsiveness SERVQUAL dimension; the willingness to help customers and provide prompt service.

retailers Businesses that sell directly to final consumers.

retained earnings Profits that are not taken out of the business but instead are saved for use by the business.

revolving credit A credit plan that allows customers to make credit purchase at any time as long as the balance does not exceed a specified dollar limit.

reward power Power based on the ability to control rewards and punishments.

risk Uncertainty that a loss may occur.

risk taking Assuming the risk of losses that may occur from fire, theft, damage, or other circumstances.

rules Prescribed guides for actions and conduct.

Rust Belt The north central and northeastern states where major manufacturing centers were once dominant.

S

salary A fixed amount of pay made on a regular schedule such as weekly or monthly.

sales budget A forecast of the sales revenue a company expects to receive in a month, a quarter, or a year.

sales finance company Firm that provides capital to a business based on installment sales contracts.

sales-oriented firm Focused on widespread distribution and promotion.

sales promotions Any promotional activities other than advertising and personal selling intended to motivate customers to buy.

sales tax Tax levied on the retail price of goods and services at the time they are sold.

sample A small, representative part of a population selected for study.

sanctions A milder form of embargo that bans specific business ties with a foreign country.

savings account A demand deposit account that allows the customer to make deposits, earn interest, and make withdrawals at any time without financial penalties.

savings bonds Non-negotiable securities sold by the U.S. Treasury.

schedule A time plan for reaching objectives.

search engine A program that assists in locating information on networks.

seasonal discount A price reduction offered for ordering or taking delivery of goods in advance of the normal buying period.

secured loan (collateral loan) A loan backed by something of value owned by the borrower.

security (security collateral) Something of value pledged as assurance of the fulfillment of an obligation.

security needs In Maslow's hierarchy of needs, things required to make sure you and those you care about are safe and free from harm.

self-actualization In Maslow's hierarchy of needs, the need to grow emotionally and intellectually, to be creative, and to achieve your full potential.

self-directed work team A team in which members together are responsible for the work assigned to the team.

self-service merchandising Customers select the products they wish, take them to a cashier or checkout counter, and pay for them without much help form a salesperson.

self-understanding An awareness of your attitudes and opinions, your leadership style, your decision-making style, and your relationships with other people.

selling Providing personalized and persuasive information to customers to help them buy the products and services they need.

selling price The actual price customers pay for the product.

server A computer in a LAN that stores data and application software for all workstations.

service businesses Businesses that use mostly labor to offer mostly intangible products to satisfy consumer needs.

shopping goods Goods that are bought less frequently than convenience goods, usually have a higher price, and require some buying thought.

short-term debt A loan that must be repaid within a year.

significant Meaningful and not occurring by chance.

situational leader One who understands employees and job requirements and matches actions and decisions to the circumstances.

small business Company operated by one or a few individuals.

Small Business Administration (SBA) An agency of the federal government that provides information, advice, and assistance in obtaining credit and other financial support for small businesses.

smart card Plastic card with an embedded microprocessor that can store and process a large amount of information that can be read by computers.

socialism An political-economy system in which the government controls the use of the country's factors of production.

social needs In Maslow's hierarchy of needs, the need to belong, to interact with others, to have friends, and to love and be loved.

social networking Virtual communities that allows users to post information about themselves and share that information with others.

social responsibility The duty of a business to contribute to the well-being of society.

Social Security A social insurance program funded through payroll contributions.

sole proprietorship Business owned and managed by one person.

spam Unsolicited advertising via e-mail.

span of control The number of employees that any one manager supervises directly.

specialist occupations Occupations that require a variety of skills in one or more business functions and extensive understanding of the operations of a specific company or industry.

specialty goods Products that customers insist upon having and are willing to search for until they find them.

stakeholders The owners, customers, suppliers, employees, creditors, government, general public, and other groups who are affected by a firm's action.

standard A specific measure by which something is judged.

start-up budget A budget that projects income and expenses from the beginning of a new business until it is expected to become profitable.

statistics Mathematical tools that use carefully selected numerical information to describe the situation being studied or to make predictions about future similar circumstances.

sticky floor syndrome The inability of workers to move up from low-paying jobs that require little skill and education.

stockholders Owners of a corporation.

stock index An average of the prices of selected stocks considered to be representative of a certain class of stocks or of the economy in general.

stock option A right granted by a corporation that allows current stockholders to buy additional shares when issued at a fixed price for a specific period of time.

storing Holding products until consumers need them.

straight rebuy A repurchase from previously used suppliers.

strategic alliances Arrangements in which firms agree to cooperate on certain aspects of business while remaining competitors on other aspects.

strategic planning Long-term planning that provides broad goals and directions for the entire business.

subordinate Someone who is subject to the authority and control of another person.

subsidiaries Foreign branches of a business, registered as independent legal entities.

substantiation Proof of all claims made about products and services in promotions.

Sun Belt The warmer states in the south and southwest of the United States.

supervisor A manager whose main job is to direct the work of employees.

supervisor/management occupations Occupations involving responsibility for specific units in a business and for decisions about operations and personnel.

supply The number of like products that will be offered for sale at a particular time and at a particular price.

sustainability Considering the needs of the environment, society, and the economy to meet present needs without compromising the ability of future generations to meet their needs.

SWOT analysis An examination of an organization's internal strengths and weaknesses as well as external opportunities and threats.

symptom A sign or indication of something that appears to be the problem.

T

360-degree feedback A method of performance evaluation that uses performance feedback gathered from a broad range of people with whom the employee works, both inside and outside the organization.

table A presentation of information organized by rows and columns.

tally Any kind of mark used as a memory device.

tangibles SERVQUAL dimension; the appearance of physical facilities, equipment, personnel, and promotional material.

target markets Groups of customers with very similar needs to whom the company plans to sell its product.

tariff A tax on foreign goods to protect domestic industries and earn revenue.

tax-deferred Term referring to retirement plan contributions made before taxes are calculated on the employee's income.

team building Getting people to support the same goals and work well together to accomplish them.

team organization Business structure that divides employees into permanent work teams.

telecommunications The movement of information from one location to another electronically.

telecommute Staying in contact with the employer electronically while working from home or on the road.

teleconferencing An audio or video meeting with participants in two or more locations.

telemarketing The marketing of goods and services by telephone.

term loan Medium or long-term financing used for operating funds or the purchase or improvement of fixed assets.

time deposits (certificates of deposit or CDs) Deposits made for a specified period of time that cannot be withdrawn early without some financial penalty.

time management Managing work schedules to achieve maximum productivity.

time plan A compensation plan which pays a certain amount for a specified period of time worked.

time standard A specific measure that establishes the amount of time needed to complete an activity.

total quality management *A commitment to excellence that is accomplished by teamwork and continual improvement of work procedures and products.*

trade credit Short-term financing obtained by buying goods and services that do not require immediate payment.

trade discount A price reduction that manufactures give to their channel partners, such as wholesalers or retailers, in exchange for additional services.

trademark A distinguishing name, symbol, or special mark placed on a good or service that is legally reserved for the sole use of the owner.

trading bloc Group of two or more countries that agree to remove all restrictions on the sale of goods and services among them, while imposing barriers to trade and investment from countries that are not part of the bloc.

transfer The assignment of an employee to another job in the company that involves the same level of responsibility and authority as the person's current work.

transporting Moving goods from where they were made to where consumers can buy them.

Treasury instruments Securities issued by the U.S. government.

trend A general direction in which something is developing or changing.

U

underground economy Income that is not recorded in the GDP.

unemployment insurance A state-managed program that provides temporary income to individuals who have been laid off from their jobs.

unity of command Principle which states that no employee has more than one supervisor at a time.

unlimited financial liability When each partner is personally liable for all the debts incurred by the partnership.

unsecured loan A loan that is not backed by collateral.

unsought goods Products that many customers will not shop for because they do not have a strong need for the product.

utility The ability of a good or service to satisfy a want.

V

values Underlying beliefs and attitudes.

variable interest rate An interest rate that can increase or decline based on the factors used to adjust the rate.

variance The difference between current performance and the standard.

venture capital Financing obtained from an investor or investment group that lends large sums of money to promising new or expanding small companies.

vision A broad, lasting, and often inspirational view of a company's reason for existing.

Voice over Internet Protocol (VoIP) Using the Internet for telephone services.

W

wage Pay based on an hourly rate or the completion of a specified amount of work.

warehouses Buildings used to store large quantities of products until they can be sold.

web server A computer that contains the software and stores the data for networks.

web-hosting service A private business that maintains the websites of individuals and organizations on its computers for a fee.

what-if analysis A systematic way to explore the consequences of specific choices using computer software.

wholesalers Businesses that buy products from businesses and sell them to retailers or other businesses.

wholly owned subsidiary When a firm sets up a business abroad on its own without any partners.

wide area network (WAN) A network of linked computers that covers a wide geographic area.

win/lose strategy A strategy in which no one compromises, thereby resulting in one person winning and one losing.

work coach An experienced manager who meets regularly with a new manager to provide feedback and advice.

work rules Regulations created to maintain an effective working environment in a business.

work schedules Schedules identifying the tasks to be done, employees assigned to the work, and the time frame for completion of each task.

work team A group of individuals who cooperate to achieve a common goal.

workers' compensation Insurance provided by employers for the death, injury, or illness of employees that result from their work.

working capital The difference between current assets and current liabilities.

World Bank International institution that provides low-cost, long-term loans to less-developed countries to develop basic industries and facilities.

World Trade Organization (WTO) International organization that creates and enforces rules governing trade among countries.

World Wide Web (WWW, Web) A set of standards that makes the Internet accessible to the average person.

Z

zoning Regulations that specify which land areas may be used for homes and which areas may be used for different types of businesses.

Glossary/Glosario

A

accountability *responsabilidad* La obligación de aceptar responsabilidad por los resultados de las tareas asignadas.

accounting *contabilidad* El proceso de registrar, analizar e interpretar las actividades financieras de un negocio.

accounting equation *ecuación de la contabilidad* Activos = Adeudos + Capital

accounts payable *cuentas por pagar* La cantidad que debe la compañía por las compras que realizó a crédito.

accounts payable record *registro de cuentas por pagar* Un registro que muestra las compras de un negocio, el dinero que se debe y los pagos hechos por el negocio.

accounts receivable *cuentas por cobrar* La cantidad que le deben los clientes al negocio.

accounts receivable record *registro de cuentas por cobrar* Un registro que muestra lo que cada cliente compra, debe y paga.

achievement need *necesidad de logro* En la teoría de McClelland, la necesidad de tomar responsabilidad personal por el trabajo, establecer metas personales, y tener información retroactiva inmediata sobre el trabajo.

acquiring banks *bancos compradores* Bancos especializados que administran cuentas mercantiles.

actuaries *actuarios* Personas que calculan cuotas de seguros.

administered channel *medio administrado* Un medio por el cual una organización toma una posición de liderazgo para beneficiar a todos los miembros de ese canal.

administrative management *gerencia administrativa* Teoría de la administración que identifica las practicas más efectivas para organizar y administrar un negocio.

advertising *publicación* Cualquier método de promociones pagadas que transmite un mensaje a muchas personas a la vez.

advertising media *medios publicitarios* Los métodos de divulgación del mensaje promocional al público deseado.

affiliation need *afiliación necesaria* En la teoría de McClelland, la motivación relacionada sobre las relaciones con otros, de llevarse bien con todos y encajar en el grupo.

affinity credit cards *tarjetas de crédito de afinidad* Tarjetas de crédito expedidas por una institución financiera y copatrocinadas por una organización que recibe un pequeño porcentaje de las ventas o ganancias generadas por la tarjeta.

agency dilemma *conflicto de agencia* Una situación en la cual un agente, o alguien que trabaja para otro, da preferencia a sus intereses encima de los de su empleador.

aging of accounts *antigüedad de cuentas* El analizar los balances de cuentas de los clientes dentro de categorías basadas en el número de días que el balance de cada cliente ha permanecido sin pagar.

applied research *investigación aplicada* El estudio de problemas con productos en existencia o posibles mejoras en el diseño para productos de actualidad.

assessed valuation *valuación fiscal* El valor de la propiedad determinada por agentes de impuestos.

asset *activo* Cualquier cosa de valor que se poseen como dinero en efectivo y edificios.

asset book value *valor contable del activo* El costo original menos la depreciación acumulada.

assurance *confianza* Dimensión de *SERVQUAL* (también RATER o evaluador de servicio y calidad); el conocimiento y cortesía de los empleados y su habilidad de demostrar fe y confianza.

audit *auditoria* Una revisión de los archivos financieros de una compañía por un experto para verificar su exactitud.

authority *autoridad* El derecho a tomar decisiones sobre la distribución de trabajo y a requerir que otros empleados desempeñen el trabajo asignado.

autocratic leader *líder autocrático* Es quien da órdenes directas, claras y precisas con instrucciones detalladas como qué, cuándo y cómo el trabajo se debe hacer.

automatic teller machine (ATM) *cajero automático* Una terminal de computadora que permite a los clientes de bancos depositar, retirar o transferir fondos usando una tarjeta plástica que el banco provee.

avoidance strategy *estrategia evasiva* Una estrategia para resolver conflictos la cual toma una posición neutral o apoya a la posición de otra persona aun cuando sea diferente a su creencia personal.

B

baby boom *baby boom (generación de posguerra)* Se refiere al alto nivel de nacimientos durante el período de 1945 a 1965.

baby bust *disminución súbita de la natalidad* Se refiere al período de bajo nivel de nacimientos que siguió al período del *baby boom*.

balance of payments *balance de pagos* Un estado de contabilidad en la cual se registran todas las transacciones internacionales; consiste de cuenta corriente y cuenta de capital.

balance sheet (statement of financial position) *balance general (estado financiero)* Un estado financiero que informa sobre todos los activos, las obligaciones y el capital de un negocio en una fecha específica.

bank *banco* Una institución que acepta depósitos a la vista, concede préstamos comerciales y para consumidores, y también compra y vende moneda extranjera así como valores bursátiles del gobierno.

bank charter *estatuto bancario* La autorización para operar un banco siguiendo las normas establecidas por el gobierno federal o estatal.

bankruptcy *bancarrota* Un proceso legal que permite vender los activos para pagar las deudas.

bar codes *códigos de barras* Etiquetas de identificación de productos que contienen un conjunto de barras verticales únicas las cuales puede leer un escáner computarizado.

basic product *producto básico* El producto físico en su forma más simple.

behavioral management *control del comportamiento* La teoría de administración orientada a las mejoras organizacionales al comprender las motivaciones y conducta de los empleados. El control del comportamiento a veces es llamado administración de relaciones humanas.

beneficiaries *beneficiarios* Las personas que reciben un pago de seguro de vida tras la muerte de una persona asegurada.

board of directors *consejo directivo* El cuerpo directivo de una corporación.

body language *expresión corporal* Gestos, movimientos, y peculiaridades que se utilizan para comunicarse.

bond *bono* Un instrumento de deuda a plazo largo que el negocio le vende a los inversionistas que contiene una promesa por escrito de pagar una suma determinada de dinero en un tiempo específico.

bonding *garantías* Protección asegurada que provee pagos por daños a personas que han sufrido pérdidas por negligencia o deshonestidad de un empleado o por el fracaso de un negocio para cumplir un contrato.

bonus *bonificación* Dinero que se paga al vencimiento de un plazo largo y específico de tiempo por el desempeño que excede los estándares anticipados por ese plazo.

book value *valor contable* (1) El valor de una acción que se basa al dividir el valor neto (activos menos las deudas) de la corporación entre el número total de acciones pendientes. (2) El valor total de la depreciación se le resta al valor original del activo.

brainstorming *aportación masiva de ideas* Una técnica de discusión en grupo que se usa para generar cuantas ideas sea posible para resolver un problema.

brand *marca* Un nombre, símbolo, palabra o diseño que identifica un producto, servicio o compañía.

budget *presupuesto* Un plan financiero por escrito para la operación de negocios desarrollado para un plazo específico de tiempo.

building codes *códigos de la construcción* Códigos que controlan las características físicas de las estructuras.

business *negocio* Una organización que produce o distribuye un bien o servicio con intención de beneficiarse.

business buying process *proceso de compras de un negocio* Un conjunto de procedimientos formales que sigue un negocio cuando decide comprar un producto.

business competition *competencia mercantil* La rivalidad entre negocios para obtener clientes.

business cycles *ciclos mercantiles* Un modelo irregular, pero repetitivo de la expansión y contracción del producto doméstico bruto (GDP).

business environment *ambiente empresarial o de negocios* Los factores y condiciones dentro de las que funciona un negocio las cuales pueden afectar su éxito.

business ethics *ética mercantil* Conjunto de principios y normas que define lo que es la conducta correcta e incorrecta para una organización.

business plan *plan de negocio* Un documento por escrito que describe el tipo de negocio, sus metas y objetivos, y cómo serán alcanzadas.

buying *comprar* Obtener bienes para revender.

buying motives *motivos de compra* Las razones por las que la gente compra.

C

cafeteria plan *plan selectivo* Un programa de beneficios en el cual los empleados pueden escoger los beneficios de acuerdo a sus necesidades personales.

capacity *capacidad* Una medida de la capacidad de ganancia y una imagen del potencial de un solicitante de un préstamo de pagarlo basado en los ingresos actuales y otras obligaciones económicas.

capital *capital* (1) El dinero requerido para comenzar o expandir un negocio. (2) Una medida del valor financiero del solicitante de crédito o su habilidad de pagar basado en sus activos.

capital (net worth, owner's equity, stockholders' equity) *capital (valor neto, patrimonio, inversión de los accionistas)* El valor de la inversión del titular en el negocio después de restar las obligaciones de los activos.

capital account *cuenta de capital* Una cuenta que registra los fondos de inversión que entran y salen de un país.

capital budget *presupuesto de capital* Un plan financiero para reemplazar los activos fijos o de adquirir nuevos.

capital formation *formación de capital* La producción de los bienes de capital.

capital goods *bienes de capital* Edificios, herramientas, maquinaria y otros equipos que se usan para producir otros bienes, pero que no satisfacen directamente las necesidades humanas.

capitalism *capitalismo* Un sistema político-económico en el cual los ciudadanos están libres de establecer negocios para producir lo que deseen y distribuir lo que producen.

career centers *centros profesionales* Instalaciones en donde empleados en recursos humanos administran actividades para el desarrollo profesional.

career development *desarrollo profesional* Un esfuerzo de igualar los planes de carrera de los empleados con las necesidades de empleo del negocio.

career development program *programa de desarrollo profesional* Un plan para cumplir con las necesidades de empleo en el futuro al sistemáticamente capacitar a los empleados de hoy para futuros puestos en la compañía.

career-level occupations *ocupaciones a nivel profesional* Una ocupación en la cual el empleado tiene la autoridad de controlar partes de su trabajo y la toma de algunas decisiones.

career path *trayectoria profesional* Una progresión de empleos relacionados con mayor nivel en los requisitos de habilidades y responsabilidades que provee a los empleados oportunidades para avanzar dentro de la compañía.

career portfolio *portafolio de carrera* Una colección organizada con información y materiales que has desarrollado para representarte, tu capacitación, y tus logros.

carpal tunnel syndrome (CTS) *síndrome de túnel de carpiano* Una condición médica que se da cuando el nervio mediano, la cual corre por un túnel en la muñeca, se encuentra comprimido o irritado.

cash budget *presupuesto de efectivo* Un cálculo del flujo del efectivo que entra y sale del negocio durante un plazo de tiempo específico.

cash disbursement *desembolso en efectivo* Pagos en efectivo hechos por un negocio.

cash discount *descuento en efectivo* Una reducción en el precio que se da por pagar en una fecha determinada.

cash flow *flujo de efectivo* El movimiento de efectivo que entra y sale de un negocio.

cash receipts *recibos de efectivo* El dinero que recibe un negocio.

cause and effect *causa y efecto* La relación entre dos eventos dentro de la cual el segundo evento es la consecuencia del primero.

cease-and-desist order *orden de cesar y desistir* Penalidad legal que requiere que una compañía deje de utilizar publicidad específica.

centralized organization *organización centralizada* Una estructura del negocio en la cual algunos de los ejecutivos más altos se hacen cargo de los planes mayores y la toma de decisiones.

certificate of deposit (CD) *certificado de depósito (CD)* Una cuenta de depósito a plazo la cual requiere un depósito mínimo por un plazo específico a un interés fijo.

certified public accountant (CPA) *contador público* Una persona que ha cumplido con la educación, experiencia y exámenes de contabilidad requeridos por el estado.

channel integration *medio de integración* Cuando un negocio es propietario de las organizaciones en otros niveles del medio.

channel members *miembros del canal (de distribución)* Negocios que participan en actividades que transfieren bienes y servicios del fabricante al consumidor.

channel of communication *medio de comunicación* Maneras mediante las cuales se comunica un mensaje.

channels of distribution (marketing channels) *canales de distribución (canales de mercadeo)* Las rutas que siguen los productos y servicios mientras se mueven del fabricante al consumidor, que incluyen las actividades y organizaciones participantes.

character *carácter* Una medida del sentido de responsabilidad financiera de un negocio o persona o creencia en la obligación de pagar deudas.

characteristics *características* Las cualidades exclusivas e identificables o características de las personas u objetos siendo estudiados.

chart *gráfica* Un tipo de diagrama que organiza y resume un conjunto de datos numéricos.

charter *acta constitutiva* Documento oficial mediante el cual el estado le otorga el poder de funcionar como una corporación.

check *cheque* Una orden por escrito la cual requiere que pague la institución financiera dinero previamente depositado a un tercer partido cuando éste lo requiera.

chief information officer (CIO) *director de informática* El ejecutivo más alto en computación.

classical management *administración clásica* Teoría de administración que estudia cómo es organizado el trabajo y los procedimientos a seguir para completar un trabajo para poder incrementar la productividad de un trabajador.

close corporation *corporación cerrada* Una corporación que no ofrece sus acciones a la venta pública.

cloud *computación en nube* Sistemas de almacenar datos a través de redes de Internet extensamente dispersadas.

co-branded credit cards *tarjetas de crédito de marcas compartidas* Tarjetas de crédito copatrocinadas por dos compañías las cuales tienen beneficios y recompensas diseñadas específicamente para sus clientes en común.

code of ethics *código de ética* Una colección formal, publicada de los valores y reglas que reflejan las metas y filosofías de la empresa.

collateral *garantía* Propiedad que ofrece un prestatario como garantía para asegurar el pago de un préstamo.

combination plan *plan combinado* Un plan que provee a cada empleado un pago o salario bajo y añade incentivo de pago basado en el desempeño del empleo.

command economy *economía planificada* Un sistema económico en el cual una autoridad central de planificación, bajo el control del gobierno del país, es propietario de la mayoría de los factores de producción y determina qué, cómo y para quién serán producidos los bienes y servicios.

commercial loan *préstamo comercial* Un préstamo que se hace a un negocio.

commission plan *plan de comisión* Un plan de compensación dentro del cual a los empleados se les paga un porcentaje del volumen del negocio por el cual son responsables.

common stock *acción común* Titularidad que le da a los dueños el derecho a participar en la administración del negocio mediante el privilegio de votación y el derecho de compartir en las ganancias por los dividendos.

communication *comunicación* El compartir información, en la cual el receptor entiende el significado del mensaje tal como el emisor pretendía.

communication network *red de comunicaciones* La estructura mediante la cual fluye la información en un negocio.

communism *comunismo* Socialismo extremo, en el cual todos o casi todos los factores de producción de una nación pertenecen al gobierno.

comparable worth *valor equivalente* Pago igual a empleados por trabajos similares, pero no con los requisitos idénticos.

comparative advantage theory *teoría de ventaja comparativa* Una teoría, que sugiere que un país debe especializarse en productos o servicios que pueda proveer de manera más eficaz que otros países, para poder tomar una ventaja de comercio.

compensation *compensación* El pago y otros beneficios que los empleados reciben a cambio de su trabajo.

compensation plan *plan de compensación* Un sistema de procedimientos y políticas para calcular los sueldos y salarios en una organización.

competition *competencia* Rivalidad entre vendedores por los dólares del consumidor.

compromise strategy *estrategia de acuerdo intermedio* Una estrategia en la cual todos los involucrados en un conflicto acuerdan en una solución mutuamente aceptable.

computer aided design (CAD) *diseño asistido por computadora* Una aplicación de computadora que le permite a los ingenieros diseñar y probar productos antes de que sean construidos.

computer integrated manufacturing *fabricación integrada por computadora* Proceso en el cual todos los sistemas de fabricación en un negocio están diseñados y administrados por medio de computadoras.

conditions *condiciones* Una evaluación del ambiente económico que afecta decisiones de crédito.

conflict *conflicto* La intervención de una persona en el logro de las metas de otra persona.

consultant *asesor* Alguien que da consejo profesional u ofrece servicios profesionales.

consumer goods *bienes de consumo* Productos diseñados para uso personal o doméstico.

consumer goods and services *bienes y servicios de consumo* Bienes y servicios que satisfacen directamente los deseos económicos de las personas.

consumer loan *préstamo al consumidor* Un préstamo hecho a un individuo para uso personal.

consumer panel *panel de consumidores* Un grupo de personas que ofrece opiniones sobre un producto o servicio.

consumer price index (CPI) *Índice de precio al consumidor* Una medida del cambio en el precio promedio de bienes y servicios de consumo que típicamente compran las personas que viven en áreas urbanas.

containerization *carga contenerizada* Un proceso en el cual los productos se empacan en las fábricas en contenedores grandes para transporte y luego son enviados por distintos medios de transportación antes de ser desempacados.

continuous processing *proceso continuo* Proceso de fabricación por el cual los materiales brutos se mueven a través de equipos especiales que cambian su forma para hacerlos más útiles para el consumo o fabricación adicional.

controlling *regulando* Evaluación de resultados para determinar si los objetivos de la compañía se han cumplido según la planificación.

convenience goods *bienes de uso común* Artículos económicos que compran los consumidores con regularidad sin pensarlo mucho.

convertible bond *bono convertible* Un bono que le permiten al titular intercambiarlo por un número establecido de acciones comunes.

cookies *cookies* Archivos de información acerca de usuarios de algunos sitios Web que se generan y almacenan en la computadora del usuario.

cooperative *cooperativa* Un negocio que pertenece y es operado por sus miembros usuarios con el propósito de auto suministrarse de bienes y servicios.

copyright *derecho de autor* Derecho exclusivo otorgado a una autoridad por parte del gobierno federal que le da a un autor el derecho exclusivo para reproducir, publicar y vender el trabajo literario o artístico durante la vida del autor y 70 años más.

corporate branding *marca corporativa* Un proceso de negocio que es planificado, estratégicamente enfocado, e integrado en toda la organización.

corporate identity *identidad corporativa* El nombre o logotipo de una compañía; su expresión visual o su "look."

corporate image *imagen corporativa* La percepción pública de la compañía.

corporation *corporación* Negocio poseído por un grupo de personas y autorizado por el estado en el cual radica para actuar como si fuera una sola persona, independiente de sus dueños.

corrective advertising *publicidad correctiva* Publicidad nueva diseñada para cambiar la impresión falsa que queda de una información engañosa.

correlation *correlación* Una conexión o relación entre dos cosas siendo analizadas.

cost of goods sold *costo de bienes vendidos* La cantidad que un minorista le paga a un distribuidor por la mercancía que compra y vende o la cantidad que un fabricante paga por materia prima y partes para hacer sus productos.

cost standard *costo estándar* El costo predeterminado de desempeñar una labor o para producir un bien o servicio.

credit *crédito* (1) El proveer bienes o servicios a un cliente con el acuerdo de pagar en el futuro. (2) Acuerdo de compra en el cual los bienes y servicios son proveídos con la expectativa de un pago futuro por parte del cliente.

credit agency *agencia de crédito* Un centro de distribución de información sobre la capacidad crediticia de individuos o negocios.

creditor *acreedor* Persona o negocio a quien se le debe dinero.

creditworthiness *capacidad crediticia* Una medida de la habilidad y la voluntad de una persona o negocio para pagar un préstamo.

cross training *capacitación diversificada* Un proceso en el cual los empleados son capacitados para desempeñar más de un trabajo en la compañía aun cuando generalmente desempeñen uno solo.

crowdfunding *financiación colectiva* Una estrategia para financiar una idea para negocios con cantidades pequeñas de varias personas.

culture *cultura* Las costumbres, creencias, valores y patrones de comportamiento de las personas de un país o grupo.

cumulative preferred stock *acciones preferentes acumulativas* Una clase especial de acciones preferidas que paga los dividendos en años futuros si no hay ganancias en un año en particular.

current account *cuenta actual* Una cuenta que registra el valor de bienes y servicios que se exportan y los que se importan del extranjero así como otros ingresos y pagos.

customer-oriented firm *empresa orientada hacia el cliente* Empresa que realiza actividades enfocadas en la satisfacción de clientes.

customer service standards *estándares para el servicio al cliente* Medidas por las cuales una compañía mide su desempeño de satisfacer las expectativas del cliente.

custom manufacturing *fabricación personalizada* El proceso que se usa para diseñar y fabricar un producto único para satisfacer las necesidades específicas del comprador.

D

data *datos* Cifras y hechos originales que generan los negocios.

database *base de datos* Una colección de datos organizados de manera que facilita encontrar, actualizar y administrar los datos.

data-based decision *decisión basada en datos* El resultado de utilizar hechos y medidas como la base principal para elegir entre alternativas.

data mining *minería de datos* El proceso de utilizar datos en bases de datos para encontrar las relaciones entre los individuos y sus comportamientos o preferencias.

data set *conjunto de datos* Todas las cifras y hechos que se han acumulado para un estudio.

data processing *procesamiento de datos* El conjunto de actividades que consiste en obtener, registrar, organizar y mantener la información financiera de una organización.

debentures *bono de deuda* Bonos que no están asegurados por activos, pero que se basan en la fe y crédito de la corporación que los emite.

debit card *tarjeta de débito* Una tarjeta que se utiliza para transferir fondos electrónicamente de la cuenta chequera del titular a la cuenta del negocio en donde se hizo la compra.

debt capital (creditor capital) *capital adeudado (capital del acreedor)* Dinero que otros prestan a un negocio.

decentralized organization *organización descentralizada* Un negocio dividido en unidades operativas más pequeñas, y los gerentes que encabezan las unidades tienen casi toda la responsabilidad y la autoridad de las operaciones.

decision support system (DSS) *sistema de apoyo a la decisión (DSS)* Un sistema que ayuda a los gerentes a considerar alternativas al tomar decisiones específicas.

decline stage *etapa de caída* La etapa del ciclo de vida del producto cuando un producto nuevo sale al mercado que es mejor y más fácil de usar y los clientes comienzan a cambiar del producto antiguo al nuevo.

deductible *deducible* La cantidad que el asegurado asume por la pérdida antes de que la compañía de seguros pague algo.

deductive reasoning *razonamiento deductivo* El uso de principios generales para hacer predicciones acerca de situaciones o circunstancias específicas.

defined benefit plan *plan de beneficios definidos* Un plan de retiro que provee un beneficio mensual específico a los empleados jubilados, y que es determinado por sus años de servicio y la cantidad de ingresos durante su empleo.

defined contribution plan *plan de contribuciones definidos* Un plan de retiro que requiere pagos fijos a una cuenta de retiro para el empleado pero que no garantiza un beneficio mensual específico que se pagaría al jubilarse.

demand *demanda* El número de productos que serán comprados en un tiempo determinado a un precio determinado.

demand deposit *depósito a la vista* Dinero que se guarda en una institución financiera y el que se puede retirar en cualquier momento sin penalización.

democratic leader *líder democrático* Alguien que promueve a los trabajadores a compartir en la toma de decisiones sobre su trabajo y problemas relacionados con el trabajo.

depreciation *depreciación* La pérdida gradual en el valor de un activo debido a su antigüedad y uso.

depression *depresión* Una larga y severa caída en el producto doméstico bruto (GDP).

descriptive statistics *estadísticas descriptivas* Resumen significante de datos para asistir en la explicación de una situación actual.

digital dashboard *tablero digital* Un sistema de mantenimiento de información que permite que varias fuentes de información sean presentadas gráficamente por medio de una computadora.

direct deposit *depósito directo* La transferencia electrónica de un pago directamente a la cuenta bancaria del beneficiario.

direct distribution *distribución directa* Cuando los fabricantes venden directamente al consumidor.

direct marketing *mercadeo directo* El ofrecimiento de productos al consumidor por medios tales como catálogos, correo, telemercadeo, mercadeo por medio de correo electrónico, y páginas web.

disability insurance *seguro por discapacidad* Seguro que ofrece pagos a empleados que ya no están aptos para trabajar debido a accidentes o enfermedades.

discharge *despido* El despedir a un empleado de una compañía debido a conducta inapropiada en el trabajo.

discounts *descuentos* Reducciones del precio de mercado del producto para promover a los clientes a comprarlo.

distortion *distorsión* La manera consciente o inconsciente de cómo las personas cambian mensajes.

distraction *distracción* Cualquier cosa que interfiere con el mensaje creado y enviado por el emisor y el mensaje que recibe e interpreta el receptor.

distribution (place) *distribución (lugar)* El conjunto de actividades requeridas para transportar y almacenar productos y hacerlos disponibles para los clientes.

distribution center *centro de distribución* Un edificio grande diseñado para acumular y redistribuir productos eficazmente.

diversify *diversificar* La distribución de riesgo de inversión al colocar dinero en diferentes categorías de inversión.

domain name *nombre de dominio* Nombre exclusivo del titular el cual identifica su sitio web.

domestic goods *bienes domésticos* Productos hechos por empresas en Estados Unidos.

downsize *reducción* Reducir la cantidad y variedad de productos y servicios producidos y el número de empleados necesarios para producirlos.

dumping *dumping (inundar el mercado)* La práctica de vender mercancías en un mercado extranjero a un precio por debajo del costo o por debajo de lo que el negocio cobra en su propio país.

E

e-business *comercio electrónico* El uso de la comunicación electrónica para apoyar las operaciones de un negocio.

economic discrepancies *discrepancias económicas* Las diferencias entre los ofrecimientos de un negocio y los requisitos de un consumidor.

economic growth *crecimiento económico* Situación en la cual la producción de un país excede su crecimiento en población.

economics *economía* Base de conocimiento que se relaciona con la producción y el uso de bienes y servicios que satisfacen los deseos humanos.

economic system *sistema económico* Una forma organizada para que un país decida cómo usar sus recursos de producción; es decir, de decidir qué, cómo y para quién se producirán los bienes y los servicios.

economic utility *utilidad económica* La cantidad de satisfacción recibida del uso de un producto o servicio.

economic wants *deseos económicos* El deseo de escasos bienes materiales y servicios.

effectiveness *efectividad* El tomar las decisiones correctas sobre qué productos o servicios ofrecer a clientes y las mejores maneras de producir y entregarlos.

efficiency *eficiencia* El producir productos y servicios rápidamente, a precio económico sin desaprovechar el tiempo y los materiales.

electronic funds transfer (EFT) *transferencia electrónica de fondos (EFT)* Transferir dinero mediante una computadora.

electronic shopping carts *carritos para la compra electrónicos* Programas que llevan el registro de las selecciones de los consumidores mientras hacen compras, les proveen formularios de pedido para completar y enviar a la compañía a través de la Internet.

embargo *embargo* El proceso en el cual el gobierno les prohíbe a compañías de hacer negocios con ciertos países.

empathy *empatía* Dimensión de *SERVQUAL* (también RATER o evaluador de servicio y calidad); el afecto y la atención individual que el negocio le provee al cliente.

employee assistance program *programa de asistencia a empleados* Programa para el empleado que provee asistencia confidencial e individual, incluyendo asesoría y servicios de apoyo a empleados que están pasando por asuntos serios ya sean personales o familiares.

employee benefits *prestaciones a empleados* Todo tipo de compensación y servicios que provee la compañía a los empleados además de salarios y sueldos.

employee stock ownership program (ESOP) *plan de compra de acciones para empleados* Un plan de beneficio que permite a los empleados hacerse dueños de la compañía para la que trabajan por medio de la compra de acciones.

employee turnover *rotación de empleados* El índice en que las personas entran y dejan un empleo en un negocio durante un año.

empowerment *empoderamiento (otorgamiento de poderes)* (1) Autoridad que se le otorga a empleados individualmente para tomar decisiones y resolver problemas que se dan en su trabajo con los recursos disponibles; (2) el dejar que los trabajadores decidan cómo desempeñar sus tareas y aportar ideas de cómo mejorar el proceso del trabajo.

endorsement *endoso* La firma del beneficiario al dorso del cheque transfiriendo legalmente la titularidad.

enhanced product *producto mejorado* Un producto que ofrece diferentes características y opciones para el consumidor.

entrepreneur *empresario* Una persona que empieza, administra y es dueño de un negocio.

entry-level occupations *oficios a nivel de principiante* Oficios que normalmente consisten de rutinas comunes y requieren poco entrenamiento.

equity capital (owner capital) *capital social (capital del dueño)* Contribuciones personales financieras al negocio por parte del dueño.

ergonomics *ergonomía* La ciencia de adaptar equipos de trabajo a las necesidades del trabajo y la salud de las personas.

ethics *ética* Estándares de conducta moral que se establecen a si mismo los individuos y grupos, definiendo lo que valoran como bien o mal en el comportamiento.

Euro *Euro* La moneda de la Unión europea.

European Union (EU) *Unión europea (UE)* Un bloque de intercambio de países europeos.

exchange rate *tasa de intercambio* El valor de la moneda de un país expresado en la moneda de otro.

excise tax *impuesto de consumo* Impuesto sobre la venta que se aplica solamente a bienes y servicios selectos como la gasolina.

executive information system (EIS) *sistema de información para ejecutivos* Sistema de información que combina y resume las transacciones en proceso dentro de la compañía para proveer a los altos ejecutivos la información necesaria para tomar decisiones que afectan las metas y dirección de una organización.

executive summary *resumen ejecutivo* Un resumen escrito de un reporte más largo que incluye análisis conciso, recomendaciones y conclusiones.

executive *ejecutivo* Un gerente de alto nivel que pasa casi todo su tiempo en funciones administrativas y decisiones que afectan a la compañía entera.

executive/entrepreneur occupations *ocupaciones del ejecutivo/empresario* Ocupaciones en las cuales las personas son totalmente responsables por el éxito o fracaso de la compañía.

exit interview *entrevista de salida* Una entrevista formal con un empleado que deja la compañía para determinar las actitudes y opiniones de esa persona sobre la compañía, y sus sugerencias para la mejora de la compañía.

expert power *poder externo* Poder otorgado a personas por su conocimiento superior sobre el trabajo.

exporting *exportación* Cuando una compañía vende sus bienes y servicios a compradores en un país extranjero.

extended product *producto más extenso* Un producto que incluye características adicionales que no son parte del producto físico pero que aumentan su utilidad.

extranet *extranet* Una red privada que usan las compañías para compartir cierta información con personas selectas fuera de la organización, tal como proveedores y clientes mayores.

F

factor *factor* Una empresa que se especializa en prestar dinero a negocios en base a las cuentas por cobrar del negocio.

factors of production *factores de producción* Terreno, trabajo, bienes del capital y la administración – los cuatro recursos básicos que se combinan para crear bienes y servicios útiles.

Fair Labor Standards Act (FLSA) *La Ley de Normas Razonables de Trabajo* Ley federal que establece estándares para sueldos y pago de tiempo extra.

false advertising *publicidad engañosa* Publicidad que es engañosa en algún sentido importante, incluyendo la falta de revelar detalles sobre los posibles resultados que se dan por el uso de los productos publicados.

Family Medical Leave Act (FMLA) *La Ley de Ausencia Familiar y Médica* Ley federal que les da derechos a los empleados que califiquen de tomar una ausencia sin paga del trabajo por razones familiares y médicas específicas.

Federal Deposit Insurance Corporation (FDIC) *Corporación Federal de Seguro de Depósitos* Una agencia federal que asegura los depósitos en bancos e instituciones de ahorro.

Federal Reserve System (FED) *Sistema de la Reserva Federal* El banco central de los Estados Unidos.

feedback *reacción o retroalimentación* La respuesta de quien recibe el mensaje para la persona que lo manda.

finance *finanzas* Actividad de negocios que trata con todos los asuntos monetarios relacionados con operar un negocio.

financial institution *institución financiera* Una organización que cobra dinero de los clientes y lo utiliza para inversiones que benefician tanto a la organización como al cliente.

financial records *registros financieros* Resúmenes organizados de la información financiera y actividades de un negocio.

financial statements *estados financieros* Informes que resumen los datos financieros por un plazo de tiempo.

financing *financiar* El proveer dinero necesario para desempeñar varias actividades de mercadeo.

firewall *firewall (cortafuegos)* Software especial que revisa a las personas que entran a una red solicitando información especial como claves de acceso.

fixed assets *activos fijos* Activos caros de un negocio los cuales se espera que duren y se utilicen por largo tiempo.

fixed interest rate *tasa de interés fijo* Una tasa de interés que no cambia durante el plazo del préstamo.

flame *flamear* Un mensaje electrónico cuyo contenido es abusivo, amenazador u ofensivo el cual puede violar la política de una compañía o las leyes públicas.

flattened organization *organización nivelada* Una organización que tiene menos niveles administrativos que las estructuras tradicionales.

flex-time *horario flexible* Un plan que permite a los empleados escoger sus propias horas de trabajo, dentro de límites específicos.

foreign goods *bienes extranjeros* Productos hechos por empresas en otros países.

formal communication network *red de comunicación formal* Sistema de medios oficiales que llevan mensajes aprobadas por la organización; fluye hacia arriba, hacia abajo, y a través de toda la compañía de manera establecida.

formal training *capacitación formal* Instrucción cuidadosamente planeada con un currículum e instructor específico.

fraction *fracción* La parte de un número entero expresado como una porción.

franchise *franquicia* Un acuerdo legal en el cual un individuo o un grupo pequeño de inversionistas compra los derechos para vender el producto o servicio de una compañía bajo el nombre y la marca registrada de la compañía.

franchisee *franquiciado o concesionario* El distribuidor de un producto o servicio bajo franquicia.

franchisor *franquiciador* La compañía matriz de un acuerdo de franquicia que provee el producto o el servicio.

free trade agreements *acuerdos de libre comercio* Tratados entre dos o más países que eliminan casi todas las restricciones de comercio y subsidios entre los países.

frequency distribution *distribución de frecuencia* La lista de los valores dentro del rango de una característica y el número de veces que el valor aparece en el conjunto de datos.

Frost Belt *Cinturón de hielo* Los estados más fríos en el norte y noreste de los Estados Unidos.

full disclosure *declaración completa* El proveer toda la información necesaria a los consumidores para que tomen una decisión informada.

G

Generation X *Generación X* La gente nacida durante el período de baja natalidad entre 1960 y 1980.

Generation Z *Generación Z* La gente nacida entre 1991 y el fin del milenio; también se les llama generación del milenio.

glass ceiling *barrera invisible* Una barrera invisible para el avance en el trabajo.

global competition *competición global* La habilidad de negocios de un país de competir con otros negocios similares en otros países.

goal *meta* Declaración específica de un resultado que el negocio espera lograr.

goods-producing business *negocios de producción de bienes* Empresas que producen bienes que usan otros negocios, organizaciones, o consumidores.

grading and valuing *clasificar y evaluar* El agrupar los bienes de acuerdo al tamaño, la calidad y otras características y determinar un precio apropiado por los productos y servicios.

grapevine *información informal o chismorreo* La transmisión informal de información entre los trabajadores.

graph *gráfica* Una representación visual de datos que muestra sus cambios a lo largo del tiempo.

gross domestic product (GDP) *producto doméstico bruto* El valor total de mercado de todos los bienes producidos y servicios provistos en un país en un año.

gross profit *ganancia bruta* La cantidad sobrante después de restar de los ingresos el costo de los bienes vendidos.

growth stage *etapa de crecimiento* La etapa del ciclo de vida del producto cuando varias marcas del nuevo producto están disponibles.

H

health insurance *seguro médico* Seguro que provee protección contra los gastos del cuidado de la salud.

high-context culture *cultura de alto contexto* Una cultura en la cual la comunicación ocurre a través de signos no verbales y sugerencias indirectas.

home country *país de origen* El país en el que una corporación multinacional tiene sus oficinas centrales.

host country *país anfitrión* País extranjero donde una empresa multinacional tiene plantas de producción y servicio.

human capital *capital humano* El conocimiento acumulado de los seres humanos; el valor total de la educación y habilidades adquiridas por cada persona.

human relations *relaciones humanas* Lo bien que se llevan las personas cuando trabajan juntas.

human resources management (HRM) *administración de recursos humanos* Todas las actividades involucradas con la adquisición, desarrollo y compensación de las personas que desempeñan el trabajo de la compañía.

human resources planning *planeamiento de recursos humanos* El determinar los tipos de trabajos que se requieren para cada fase del procedimiento de producción, el número de personas que se necesitan para cada trabajo, y las habilidades que cada persona necesitara para desempeñar el trabajo.

hygiene factors *factores de higiene* Los factores del trabajo que contribuyen a la insatisfacción cuando no están presentes pero que no contribuyen a la satisfacción cuando están presentes.

I

identity power *poder de identidad* El poder otorgado a las personas porque otros se identifican y quieren ser aceptados por ellos.

identity theft *robo de identidad* El uso de información de identificación personal no autorizada, tal como nombre, número de seguro social, o número de tarjeta de crédito para cometer fraude y otros crímenes. Además del impacto en las víctimas, el robo de identidad crea problemas para negocios.

implementing *implementación* El llevar a cabo los planes y ayudar a los empleados a trabajar eficientemente.

importing *importar* Comprar bienes o servicios hechos en un país extranjero.

income statement (profit and loss statement) *declaración de ingresos (declaración de ganancias y pérdidas)* Un estado financiero que reporta información de los ingresos y gastos de una compañía dentro de un plazo específico.

income tax *impuesto sobre los ingresos* Un impuesto sobre las ganancias de negocios y los ingresos de individuos.

indirect distribution *distribución indirecta* La distribución que se hace a través de los miembros del canal (de distribución).

individual career plan *plan individual de la carrera* Una estrategia que identifica a los empleos que son parte de la trayectoria profesional, la capacitación necesaria para avanzar durante la trayectoria, y el horario provisional de las actividades del plan.

inductive reasoning *razonamiento inductivo* El análisis de datos específicos para sacar conclusiones más extensas.

industrial goods *bienes industriales* Productos diseñados para que otros negocios los usen.

industrial revolution *revolución industrial* La época de los siglos dieciocho y diecinueve en que el poder de la maquinaria reemplazó al poder humano y animal en el proceso de producción que llevó a grandes cambios tanto sociales como en negocios.

industry *industria* Palabra que se usa con frecuencia para referirse a todos los negocios dentro de una categoría desempeñando trabajos similares.

inferential statistics *estadística deductiva* El análisis de información utilizada para hacer predicciones sobre circunstancias similares futuras.

inflation *inflación* Un incremento rápido en los precios causado por un suministro inadecuado de bienes y servicios.

informal communication network *red de comunicación informal* Maneras no oficiales de compartir información en una organización.

informal training *capacitación informal* Capacitación y educación sin estructura, desarrollada para situaciones e individuos específicos.

information *información* Datos que son procesados de manera significativa.

information liability *responsabilidad de información* Responsabilidad por daño físico o económico como resultado de datos incorrectos o uso erróneo de datos.

information system *sistema de información* Un sistema de computadora que procesa datos generando información con sentido.

initial public offering (IPO) *oferta pública inicial* La primera vez que una compañía vende acciones al público.

innovation *innovación* Algo completamente nuevo.

installment credit *crédito a plazo* Crédito que se usa cuando un cliente hace una compra costosa y está de acuerdo a hacer pagos sobre un plazo de tiempo largo, pero fijo.

insurable interest *interés asegurable* La posible pérdida financiera que pudiera sufrir el asegurado si la propiedad llega a ser dañada o destruida.

insurance *seguro* Una herramienta de administración de riesgo que intercambia la inseguridad de una posible pérdida financiera a cambio de pagos menores.

insurance agents *agentes de seguro* Personas que representan la compañía de seguro y venden pólizas a individuos y negocios.

insurance rate *cuota de seguros* La cantidad que una compañía de seguros le cobra al asegurado por un cierto valor de seguro.

insured *asegurado* Personas o una organización bajo la protección de una póliza de seguro.

insurer *asegurador* Compañía que vende seguros.

intangible *intangible* Cuando se refiere a servicios, no tiene forma física, visible o de existencia después de que el consumidor ha utilizado el servicio.

intermittent processing *proceso intermitente* Proceso de fabricación que utiliza períodos cortos de producción para fabricar cantidades predeterminadas de diferentes productos.

international business *negocio internacional* Actividades de negocio que ocurren entre dos o más países.

international licensing *adquisición de licencia internacional* Acuerdo en el cual una compañía permite a una compañía diferente en otro país de fabricar y vender sus productos de acuerdo a ciertas especificaciones.

International Monetary Fund (IMF) *Fondo monetario internacional* Instituto internacional que ayuda a países que enfrentan graves dificultades financieras de pagar por sus importaciones o a pagar los préstamos.

Internet (Net) *Internet (Red)* Red mundial de computadoras conectadas que permite a los usuarios transferir datos e información de una computadora a otra en cualquier lugar del mundo.

interstate commerce *comercio interestatal* Operaciones de negocios y transacciones que cruzan las fronteras estatales.

intranet *intranet* Una red de comunicación privada dentro de una compañía que permite a los empleados compartir recursos sin importar en donde se encuentren.

intrapreneur *intrapreneur (empresario interno)* Un empleado a quien se le otorga fondos y la libertad para crear una unidad especial o departamento dentro de una compañía para que desarrolle un producto, proceso o servicio nuevo.

intrastate commerce *comercio dentro de un estado* Negocio que se hace dentro de un estado.

introduction stage *etapa de introducción* Etapa del ciclo de vida de un producto cuando un producto nuevo entra al mercado.

inventory *inventario* Todo el producto y material un negocio tiene a la mano para uso en la fabricación y disponible para la venta.

inventory management *administración de inventario* Planificación de las cantidades de materiales y abastecimientos necesarios para la producción y la cantidad de productos terminados requeridos para llenar pedidos del consumidor.

investment *inversión* El uso de dinero para generar más dinero.

investment bank *banco inversionista* Una organización que ayuda a negocios a recaudar capital mediante la venta de acciones y bonos.

J

job description *descripción de trabajo* Una lista de deberes y responsabilidades que constituyen un empleo.

job design *diseño de trabajo* Los tipos de tareas que constituyen un trabajo y la manera en que los empleados desempeñan estas tareas al hacer su trabajo.

job enlargement *ampliación de trabajo* El hacer un trabajo más interesante al añadir una variedad a las tareas.

job enrichment *enriquecimiento laboral* El estimular la participación de los empleados en la toma de decisiones.

job security *seguridad laboral* La probabilidad de tener un empleo futuro con la misma compañía.

job sharing *empleo compartido* Un plan de empleo que permite que dos personas compartan un trabajo de tiempo completo.

job specification *especificaciones de trabajo* Una lista de los requisitos y habilidades que necesita un obrero para realizar un trabajo.

joint venture *empresa conjunta* Dos o más negocios que están de acuerdo en proveer un bien o servicio compartiendo los gastos y ganancias del negocio.

just-in-time (JIT) inventory controls *control de inventario a tiempo* Un método por el cual la compañía mantiene inventarios pequeños y obtiene materiales a tiempo para su uso.

K

knowledge workers *trabajadores con conocimiento* Las personas que trabajan con información.

L

labor *labor* El esfuerzo humano, ya sea físico o mental, necesaria para la producción de bienes y servicios.

labor agreement *acuerdo laboral* El contrato entre la gerencia y el sindicato que identifica los derechos y responsabilidades del negocio y sus empleados.

labor force *fuerza laboral* La mayoría de las personas mayores de 16 años que están disponibles para trabajar estén o no empleadas.

labor participation rate *índice de participación laboral* El porcentaje de la población adulta que está en la fuerza laboral.

labor union *sindicato laboral* Una organización de trabajadores que se forma para representar sus intereses en común de mejorar sueldos, prestaciones y las condiciones de trabajo.

layoff *despido* Una reducción temporal o permanente en el número de empleados a causa de un cambio en las situaciones del negocio.

leader *líder* Un gerente que se gana el respeto y cooperación de los empleados para que realicen satisfactoriamente el trabajo de la organización.

leadership *liderazgo* La habilidad de influir en los individuos y grupos para que cooperativamente logren las metas comunes.

leadership style *estilo de liderazgo* La manera general en que un gerente trata y supervisa a los empleados.

lease *contrato de arrendamiento* Un contrato que permite el uso de un activo a cambio de una cuota que se paga según un horario.

liabilities *responsabilidades* Los reclamos en contra de activos o cosas que se deben – las deudas de un negocio.

liability insurance *seguro de responsabilidad civil* Seguro que provee protección en contra de riesgos de pérdida debido a lesión a la gente o su propiedad que resulta de los productos, servicios u operaciones de un negocio.

licensing *adquisición de licencia* Una manera de limitar y controlar a quienes planean entrar a ciertos tipos de negocio.

life insurance *seguro de vida* Seguro que paga dinero a la muerte de un asegurado a una persona o personas identificadas en la póliza de seguro.

limited liability company (LLC) *compañía con responsabilidad legal limitada* Un tipo especial de corporación con permiso del estado a la que se le cobra impuesto como si fuera de un solo dueño o sociedad.

limited liability partnership *sociedad con responsabilidad limitada* Una sociedad en la que la responsabilidad de cada socio está limitada a su inversión individual en la sociedad.

limited partnership *sociedad limitada* Sociedad con al menos un socio general que tiene responsabilidad ilimitada y al menos un socio limitado cuya responsabilidad está limitada a su inversión propia.

line-and-staff organization *organización de línea y personal* El añadir personal especializado a la organización lineal.

line of credit *cuenta de crédito* La autorización de tomar prestado hasta una cantidad máxima por un plazo específico.

line organization *organización lineal* Estructura de negocio en la cual toda autoridad y responsabilidad debe seguirse en línea directa desde el ejecutivo más alto hasta el empleado en el nivel más bajo.

liquidity *liquidez* La facilidad de cambiar una inversión en efectivo sin pérdidas significativas.

list price *precio de lista* El precio inicial que un vendedor le pone al producto.

local area network (LAN) *red de comunicación del área local* Red de computadoras interconectadas que utilizan los usuarios de *servers* (servidores de computación) en un solo edificio o complejo de edificios.

long term debt *deuda a largo plazo* Capital que es prestado por más de un año.

low-context culture *cultura de bajo contexto* Una cultura en la cual las personas se comunican directa y explícitamente.

M

malpractice insurance *seguro por negligencia profesional* Un tipo de seguro de responsabilidad que protege contra pérdida financiera como resultado de demandas por negligencia al ofrecer servicios profesionales.

management *administración* El proceso de lograr las metas de una organización mediante el uso efectivo del personal y otros recursos.

management information system (MIS) *sistema de administración de información* (1) Un sistema de computación que archiva, organiza, y provee información sobre un negocio. (2) Un sistema que integra los datos de varios departamentos para que estén disponibles para ayudar a los gerentes con las operaciones diarias del negocio.

management principles *normas administrativas* Los principios fundamentales para las decisiones y acciones de los gerentes.

management role *papel administrativo* Un conjunto de actividades comunes que forman parte importante en el trabajo de un gerente.

management science *ciencia administrativa* El estudio objetivo y cuidadoso de las decisiones y procedimientos administrativos para poder mejorar las operaciones de negocios y empresas.

management strategy *estrategia administrativa* Un método completo cuidadosamente desarrollado para dirigir una empresa.

manager *gerente* Persona que cumple regularmente las cuatro funciones administrativas y que tiene autoridad sobre otros trabajos y personas.

manufacturing *fabricación* Manera de producción mediante la cual el material bruto y el semifinalizado se procesan, ensamblan y se convierten en productos terminados.

margin (gross profit) *margen (ganancia bruta)* La diferencia entre el precio de venta y el costo de mercancías vendidas.

markdown *rebaja* Cualquier cantidad por la que se reduce el precio original de venta antes de que el artículo se venda.

market *mercado* Los tipos de compradores que un negocio desea atraer y dónde están localizados estos compradores.

market economy *economía de mercado* Un sistema económico en el cual las decisiones de compra individuales en el mercado conjuntas determinan qué, cómo y para quién serán producidos los bienes y los servicios.

marketing *mercadeo* (1) Las actividades entre negocios y clientes que involucran comprar y vender bienes y servicios. (2) Un conjunto de actividades que mueve productos del fabricante a los consumidores.

marketing concept *concepto de mercadeo* El mantener las necesidades del consumidor primordialmente en mente durante el diseño, producción y distribución de un producto.

marketing managers *gerentes de mercadeos* Gerentes responsables de coordinar las funciones de mercadeo de todos los departamentos en general para satisfacer las necesidades de los clientes.

marketing mix *combinación de mercadeo* La mezcla de todas las decisiones relacionadas con los cuatro elementos de mercadeo.

marketing plan *plan de mercadeo* Una descripción por escrito y detallada de todas las actividades de mercadeo que un negocio debe lograr para poder vender un producto.

market research *estudio de mercado* El estudio de los actuales y posibles clientes de una compañía.

market value *valor de mercado* El valor al que se compra y vende un acción en cualquier día determinado.

markup *margen de ganancia* La cantidad añadida al costo de mercancías vendidas para determinar el precio de venta.

mass production *producción masiva* Proceso de ensamblaje por medio del cual se producen gran cantidad de productos idénticos; casi siempre consiste en una línea de ensamble.

matrix organization *organización matriz* Una organización que combina a los empleados en equipos de trabajo temporales para completar proyectos específicos.

maturity stage *etapa de madurez* La etapa del ciclo de vida del producto cuando hay muchas marcas competitivas con muchas características similares.

mean *promedio* La suma de todos los valores dividido por el número de valores.

median *término medio* El número del centro en un rango de valores.

Medicare *Medicare* Seguro médico para la gente mayores de 65 años y para la gente menor de 65 años con discapacidades.

merchandise inventory *inventario de mercancía* El valor de las mercancías que se compran para vender a clientes sacando ganancia.

merchant account *cuenta comercial* Una cuenta bancaria especializada establecida por un negocio para poder procesar créditos y pagos de sus clientes.

merchant account provider *proveedor de la cuenta comercial* Una compañía privada que participa como intermediario entre los negocios y uno o más compañías de tarjetas de crédito para establecer y administrar servicios de crédito.

metric system *sistema métrico* Método para medir basado en el sistema decimal en el cual todas las medidas están comúnmente en unidades de diez.

middle manager *gerente de nivel medio* Un gerente quien ejecuta todas las funciones administrativas pero pasa la mayoría del tiempo desempeñando trabajo especializado en una de las funciones administrativas o uno que es responsable de una parte específica de las operaciones de la compañía.

minimum wage law *la ley del salario mínimo* Una ley que especifica que es ilegal que los empleadores paguen menos de un índice de salario establecido a sus empleados.

mission *misión* Una declaración corta y específica del propósito y dirección del negocio.

mixed economy *economía mixta* Un sistema económico que utiliza aspectos de un mercado y una económica planificada para tomar decisiones sobre qué, cómo y para quién se producen bienes y servicios.

mode *medio* El valor que aparece con más frecuencia dentro de un rango de valores.

modified rebuy *hábitos de compra modificados* La compra de un producto nuevo o modificado de proveedores establecidos.

money market account *cuenta de mercado de valores* Un tipo de cuenta de ahorros en la cual los depósitos son invertidos por la institución financiera en valores bursátiles a corto plazo, respaldados por el gobierno.

monopoly *monopolio* Situación que ocurre cuando solamente una compañía provee un producto o servicio sin la competencia de otras compañías.

Moore's Law *Ley de Moore* La predicción de que la cantidad de datos que un chip de una computadora se duplicara aproximadamente cada 18 meses.

mortgage bond *bono de hipoteca* Un bono de plazo largo asegurado por activos especificados del emisor.

motivation *motivación* El conjunto de factores que causan que una persona actúe de cierta manera.

motivators *motivadores* Factores de trabajo que aumentan la satisfacción del trabajo.

multinational firm *empresa multinacional* Un negocio que es dueño o controla las instalaciones de producción o servicio fuera del país en donde está basada.

mutual fund *fondo mutuo* Una compañía que acumula el dinero de muchos inversionistas pequeños para la compra de acciones y bonos.

N

natural monopoly *monopolio natural* El tipo de monopolio que comúnmente consiste en proveer servicios públicos, tales como utilidades públicas, las cuales tienen una demanda estable y son costosos de producir.

natural resources *recursos naturales* Cualquier cosa que provee la naturaleza y que afecta la habilidad de producción de un país.

need for esteem *necesidad de aprecio* En la jerarquía *Maslow* de las necesidades, la necesidad del reconocimiento y respeto de los demás.

net profit *ganancia neta* (1) La cantidad restante después de restar todos los gastos de los ingresos, con la excepción de los impuestos. (2) La diferencia entre el precio de venta y todos los costos y gastos del negocio.

new task purchase *compra de nueva asignación* Proceso que ocurre cuando un negocio está comprando un nuevo producto, artículo para el inventario, o provisión por primera vez.

no-fault insurance *seguro de protección de no culpabilidad* Seguro que requiere que cada compañía de seguros pague por las pérdidas de sus asegurados cuando ocurre un accidente, independiente de quien pueda haber sido responsable por las pérdidas.

nominal group technique (NGT) *técnica nominal en grupo* Método de resolución de problemas en grupo, en la cual miembros del equipo escriben y evalúan ideas para compartirse con el equipo.

nonbank *banco de función única* Institución financiera cuya función principal es de ofrecer productos y servicios financieros no incluyendo los depósitos y préstamos.

noneconomic wants *necesidades no económicas* Deseo por cosas inmateriales que no escasean.

nongovernmental organizations (NGOs) *organizaciones no gubernamentales* Grupos independientes que influyen en los negocios a través de cabildeo, publicidad y tácticas de presión para alterar sus actividades.

nonprofit corporation *corporación sin fines de lucro* Una organización que no paga impuestos y no existe para generar una ganancia.

nontariff barriers *restricciones sin impuesto* Restricciones además de impuestos que limitan las importaciones.

nonverbal communications *comunicación no verbal* Entrega de mensajes por medios aparte de los hablados o escritos.

North American Free Trade Agreement (NAFTA) *Tratado de libre comercio de Norte América* Una unión de intercambio entre Estados Unidos, Canadá y México.

O

objections *objeciones* Preocupaciones o quejas que expresa el cliente.

obsolescence *obsolescencia* La situación de estar antiguo o inadecuado para un propósito en particular.

Occupational Safety and Health Act *Ley de Seguridad y Salud Ocupacional* Ley federal que regula las condiciones de seguridad y salud en la mayoría de los negocios.

officer *director* Ejecutivo más alto que se emplea para administrar el negocio.

open corporation *corporación abierta* Una corporación que ofrece sus acciones para la venta pública.

open leader *líder de autoridad abierta* Gerente que da poca o ninguna dirección a los empleados.

operating budget *presupuesto de operaciones* Un presupuesto mostrando las ventas planeadas, costos, gastos, y ganancias para la continua operación del negocio.

operating expenses *gastos operativos* (1) Todos los gastos no directamente asociados con la producción o compra de mercancía que el negocio vende. (2) Los costos de operar un negocio.

operational planning *planificación operacional* Planificación a corto plazo que identifica las actividades específicas de cada área del negocio.

operations *operaciones* Las actividades mayores continuas del negocio.

operations management *administración de las operaciones* Dirigir efectivamente las actividades mayores del negocio para lograr sus metas.

organizacional culture *cultura organizativa* El conjunto de creencias y patrones de comportamiento que son compartidas por la gente dentro de la organización.

organizational development *desarrollo organizativo* Los cambios cuidadosamente planificados en la estructura y operación de un negocio para adaptarse al ambiente competitivo.

organization chart *organigrama* Una ilustración de la estructura de una organización, la clasificación mayor de los trabajos, y las relaciones de mando entre el personal de la organización.

organizing *organizar* El determinar cómo se pueden lograr los planes más eficientemente y organizar los recursos para completar el trabajo.

output *rendimiento* La cantidad que se produce dentro de un plazo determinado.

outsourcing *externalización* Contratar a una empresa externa para que realice tareas especializadas.

P

par value (stated value) *valor nominal (valor establecido)* Valor en dólares mostrado en una acción, la cual es una cantidad asignada arbitrariamente que se usa para propósitos de contabilidad.

parent firm *empresa matriz* Una compañía que controla otra compañía.

partnership *sociedad* Un negocio del cual son dueños dos o más personas.

partnership agreement *contrato de sociedad* Un acuerdo por escrito entre dos o más personas que identifica cómo los socios aportaran capital, trabajo, y otros activos y cómo dividir las ganancias.

patent *patente* Un acuerdo por el cual el gobierno federal otorga el derecho único por 20 años a un inventor de hacer, usar y vender un invento.

pension plan *plan de pensión* Un plan de retiro que patrocina la compañía que hace pagos regulares a los empleados después de jubilarse.

percentage *porcentaje* Una parte de un entero expresado en décimos.

performance review *evaluación de desempeño* (1) Un proceso que evalúa el trabajo y el cumplimiento de un empleado y provee retroalimentación sobre el desempeño. (2) El proceso de evaluar qué tan bien están desempeñando su trabajo los empleados.

performance standards *estándares de desempeño* Declaraciones específicas de los resultados que se esperan de las actividades críticas de un negocio.

peril *peligro* Causa de la pérdida de una persona u organización. Peligros comunes son el fuego, los accidentes, la enfermedad, el fallecimiento, y el robo.

personal property tax *impuesto sobre los bienes personales* Impuestos en artículos movibles tal como muebles, maquinaria y equipo.

personal selling *venta personal* Promoción a través de contacto directo y personal con un cliente.

physiological needs *necesidades fisiológicas* En la jerarquía *Maslow* de las necesidades, las cosas necesarias para sustentar la vida, tal como comida y albergue.

piece-rate plan *plan de pago por pieza* Un plan de compensación que paga al empleado una cuota fija por cada unidad producida.

piggyback service *servicio piggyback (sobre de)* Método de distribución donde los camiones remolques se cargan y se colocan en los vagones del ferrocarril para enviarse cerca de su destino final.

place utility *utilidad locacional* Significa la utilidad de un producto estando en un lugar en donde los clientes lo necesitan o desean.

planning *planificar* Analizar información y tomar decisiones sobre lo que es necesario hacer.

policies *política* Normas en general que se usan para tomar decisiones en cuanto a situaciones específicas repetitivas.

policy *póliza* Un acuerdo por escrito o contrato entre la compañía de seguros y el asegurado.

policyholder *asegurado* Persona o negocio que compra un seguro.

population *población* Todas las personas y objetos dentro de una característica similar o características siendo analizadas.

positioning chart *gráfica de posicionamiento* Gráfica utilizada para identificar segmentos de mercado alternativos con necesidades únicas en base a un mayor criterio de opciones.

position power *posición de autoridad* La autoridad que viene de la posición que tiene el gerente en la organización.

power *autoridad* La habilidad de controlar el comportamiento.

power need *necesidad de autoridad* En la teoría de McClelland, el deseo de influir y tener control sobre otros y ser responsable de las actividades de un grupo.

preferred stock *acciones preferidas* Titularidad que le da preferencia a los accionistas comunes al distribuir dividendos y activos.

premium *prima* Pago del asegurado al asegurador para la protección contra el riesgo.

price *precio* La cantidad de dinero que se da por adquirir un producto.

price discrimination *discriminación en precio* El imponer diferentes precios para diferentes clientes.

prime rate *tasa de interés preferencial* La tasa de interés a la que bancos grandes prestan grandes sumas a los mejores y más calificados prestatarios.

principal (par value) *capital (valor nominal)* La cantidad que la compañía pide prestado cuando usa un bono.

private property *propiedad privada* Artículos de valor que los individuos pueden poseer, usar y vender.

privatization *privatización* La transferencia de autoridad para proveer un bien o servicio a individuos o negocios privados.

probability *probabilidad* La probabilidad de que cierto resultado ocurra.

problem *problema* Una situación difícil que requiere una solución.

procedure *procedimiento* Secuencia de pasos a seguir para realizar trabajos específicos.

processed data *datos procesados* Datos que han sido checados para su precisión y organizados de manera de que se entienda y se pueda utilizar.

process improvement *mejoras del procedimiento* Esfuerzos para aumentar la efectividad y eficiencia de operaciones específicas de negocio.

producer *productor* Cualquiera que crea un producto.

product *producto* Todos los atributos, tanto tangibles como intangibles, que reciben los clientes a cambio de precio de compra.

product assortment *variedad de producto* El conjunto total de todos los productos que ofrece un negocio al mercado.

product development *desarrollo de producto* Proceso de desarrollar o mejorar un producto o servicio.

production *producción* Elaborar un producto o proveer un servicio.

production-oriented firm *empresa enfocada en la producción* Empresa que está enfocada en qué y cómo producir.

production scheduling *planificación de producción* El identificar los pasos requeridos en el proceso de fabricación, el tiempo necesario para completar cada paso, y la secuencia de los pasos.

productivity *productividad* Producir la mayor cantidad en el mínimo tiempo posible utilizando métodos eficientes y equipo moderno.

product life cycle *ciclo de vida del producto* Las cuatro etapas de venta y rendimiento de ganancias a través de las cuales todas las marcas de un producto progresan.

product life cycle theory *teoría del ciclo de vida del producto* Teoría declarando que las compañías busquen nuevos mercados cuando los productos están en sus etapas de madurez y caída del ciclo de vida del producto.

product line *línea de un producto* Un grupo de productos similares con variaciones obvias en el diseño y calidad para satisfacer las necesidades de grupos de clientes distinguidos.

profit *ganancia* (1) Los ingresos menos los costos. (2) El incentivo así como la recompensa para producir bienes y servicios.

profit-sharing plan *plan de participación en los beneficios* Un plan de beneficio que le paga a los empleados un porcentaje pequeño de las ganancias de la compañía al final del año.

progressive tax *impuesto progresivo* El impuesto basado en la habilidad de pagar.

promissory note *pagaré* Una promesa incondicional por escrito de pagar al prestamista una cierta suma de dinero a un tiempo determinado o a su petición.

promotion *promoción* (1) Proveer información a los clientes que les ayudará a tomar una decisión para comprar un producto o servicio, (2) La progresión de un empleado dentro de una compañía a una posición con más autoridad y responsabilidad.

property tax *impuesto sobre los bienes* Impuestos sobre bienes materiales que se poseen.

proportional tax (flat tax) *impuesto proporcional (impuesto fijo)* Tarifa de impuesto que permanece igual sin importar la cantidad en la cual se basa el impuesto.

proprietor *propietario* Persona que es dueña de y administra un negocio de y a menudo desempeña las actividades diarias con la ayuda de empleados contratados.

proprietorship *propiedad exclusiva* Negocio que es adueñada y administrada por una persona.

public franchise *franquicia pública* Un contrato que permite a una persona u organización usar la propiedad pública para ganancia privada.

pure research *investigación en general* Investigación que se hace sin un producto específico en mente.

Q

quality control *control de calidad* El proceso de asegurar que el trabajo cumple con estándares aceptables.

quality management *administración de calidad* (1) El proceso de asegurar la calidad del producto al desarrollar estándares para toda operación y producto y comparar esos resultados con esos estándares. (2) Un compromiso total de todos en la organización para mejorar la calidad de procedimientos y productos al reducir desperdicios, errores, y defectos.

quality standard *estándar de calidad* Una medida específica que describe la expectativa de la consistencia en producción o desempeño.

quantity discount *descuento por cantidad* Una reducción en el precio ofrecido a los clientes que compran en cantidades más de un mínimo especificado.

quantity standard *estándar de cantidad* Una medida específica que establece la cantidad de trabajo completado que se espera.

quasi-public corporation *corporaciones casi públicas* Un negocio que es importante para la sociedad, pero que carece el potencial de ganancias para atraer a inversionistas privados y que frecuentemente es operado por el gobierno local, estatal o federal.

quotas *cuotas* Límites impuestos en la cantidad o el valor de las unidades que se permiten entrar a un país.

R

range *alcance* Todos los valores posibles de una característica desde el menor al mayor.

ratio *proporción* La relación entre dos cantidades.

raw data *datos en bruto* Cifras o hechos originales que no han sido procesados par uso significativo.

real property tax *impuesto a bienes raíces* Impuesto de inmuebles, tal como la tierra y edificios.

recession *recesión* Un descenso del GDP (producto doméstico bruto) que continúa por seis meses o más.

record-keeping system *sistema de llevar registros* Un proceso manual o automático de colectar, organizar, y administrar la información financiera de un negocio.

recycling *reciclar* El volver a usar productos o empaque de productos.

regressive tax *impuesto regresivo* Imposición de impuestos cuando disminuye la tarifa del impuesto actual cuando aumenta la cantidad a la que se le cobra el impuesto.

reinsurance *reaseguro* Otra compañía de seguros cobra una prima para cubrir parte del riesgo que enfrenta la aseguradora original.

reliability *confiabilidad* Dimensión de *SERVQUAL* (también RATER o evaluador de servicio y calidad); la habilidad de desempeñar confiable y exactamente el servicio prometido.

repetitive production *producción repetitiva* El tipo de producción masiva en la cual se hace la misma cosa una y otra vez para producir un producto.

representative *representante* Consistente con otros datos similares que pueden recolectarse.

researching *investigación* El estudiar los intereses y las necesidades de los clientes, poner a prueba los productos y reunir los datos necesarios para tomar buenas decisiones de mercadeo.

responsibility *responsabilidad* La obligación de hacer un trabajo asignado.

responsiveness *grado de reacción* Dimensión de *SERVQUAL* (también RATER o evaluador de servicio y calidad); la voluntad propia de ayudar a los clientes y proveer servicio rápido.

retailers *minoristas* Los negocios que venden directamente al público.

retained earnings *ingresos retenidos* Las ganancias que no son retiradas del negocio, más bien son guardadas para uso del negocio.

revolving credit *crédito rotativo* Un plan de crédito que permite a los clientes hacer compras a crédito en cualquier momento mientras que el saldo no exceda el límite en dólares especificado.

reward power *autoridad de recompensa* Autoridad que se basa en la habilidad de controlar recompensas y castigos.

risk *riesgo* La incertidumbre de que una pérdida pueda ocurrir.

risk taking *arriesgarse* Asumir el riesgo de pérdidas que puedan ocurrir por incendios, robo, daño u otras circunstancias.

rules *normas o reglas* Guías prescritas para las acciones y la conducta.

Rust Belt *Cinturón Industrial* Los estados del noreste y norte central donde una vez dominaban los centros mayores de fabricación.

S

salary *sueldo* Una cantidad fija de pago en horario habitual, tal como semanal y mensual.

sales budget *presupuesto de ventas* Un pronóstico de los ingresos por ventas que anticipa recibir una compañía en un mes, un trimestre, o un año.

sales finance company *compañía financiamiento de ventas* Empresa que provee capital a un negocio basado en contratos de ventas a plazos.

sales-oriented firm *empresa en base de ventas* Empresa enfocada ampliamente en la distribución y promoción.

sales promotions *promociones de venta* Cualquier actividad promocional además de la publicidad y las ventas personales con la intención de motivar al cliente para que compre.

sales tax *impuesto sobre las ventas* Impuesto sobre el precio de venta de bienes y servicios en el momento en que se venden.

sample *muestra* Una pequeña parte que representa la población seleccionada para ser estudiado.

sanctions *sanciones* Forma de embargo un poco más leve que prohíbe vínculos de negocio específicos con un país extranjero.

savings account *cuenta de ahorros* Una cuenta de depósitos a la vista que permite a los clientes hacer depósitos, ganar intereses y hacer retiros en cualquier momento sin penalizaciones financieras.

savings bond *bono de ahorro* Valores no negociables vendidos por la tesorería de los Estados Unidos.

schedule *horario* Un plan del uso de tiempo en que deben lograrse objetivos.

search engine *buscador* Un programa que asiste en localizar información en las redes.

seasonal discount *descuento de temporada* Una reducción del precio que se ofrece por ordenar o aceptar la entrega de bienes antes del período normal de compra.

secured loan (collateral loan) *préstamo asegurado (préstamo con garantía)* Un préstamo respaldado con algo de valor que le pertenece al prestatario.

security (security collateral) *garantía (colateral garantizado)* Algo de valor prometido para asegurar el cumplimiento de una obligación.

security needs *necesidades de seguridad* En la jerarquía *Maslow* de las necesidades, las cosas requeridas para asegurar que tú y tus queridos estén a salvo y libres de peligro.

self-actualization *auto-actualización* En la jerarquía *Maslow* de las necesidades, la necesidad de crecer emocional e intelectualmente, de ser creativo, y de realizar tu potencial total.

self-directed work team *equipo de trabajo auto-dirigido* Un equipo en el cual los miembros conjuntamente son responsables por el trabajo asignado al equipo.

self-service merchandising *mercancía de auto-servicio* Los clientes seleccionan los productos que desean, los llevan a la registradora o cajeros y pagan por ellos, sin mucha ayuda de la persona de ventas.

self-understanding *auto-entendimiento* Estar consciente de tus actitudes y opiniones, tu estilo de liderazgo, tu estilo de toma de decisiones, y tu relación con otras personas.

selling *vender* El proveer información personalizada y persuasiva a los clientes para ayudarlos a que compren los productos y servicios que necesiten.

selling price *precio de venta* El precio actual que el cliente paga por los productos.

server *servidor* Una computadora en una red de computadoras que archiva datos y programas de software para todas las terminales de trabajo.

service businesses *negocios de servicios* Negocios que utilizan en su mayor parte mano de obra para ofrecer principalmente productos intangibles para satisfacer las necesidades de los clientes.

shopping goods *mercancías para compra* Mercancías que se compran con menos frecuencia que las mercancías de conveniencia, generalmente tienen un precio más alto y requieren que se piense antes de comprarse.

short-term debt *deuda a corto plazo* Un préstamo que debe pagarse en menos de un año.

significant *significante* Con sentido y que no ocurre al azar.

situational leader *líder situacional* Uno que entiende a los empleados y los requisitos de empleo y corresponde las acciones y decisiones con las circunstancias.

small business *negocio pequeño* Compañía que la opera uno o pocos individuos.

Small Business Administration (SBA) *Agencia Federal para el Desarrollo de la Pequeña Empresa* Una agencia del gobierno federal que provee información, consejo, y asistencia en obtener crédito y otros apoyos financieros para los negocios pequeños.

smart card *tarjeta inteligente* Una tarjeta de plástico con un microprocesador incorporado que puede almacenar y procesar una gran cantidad de información que puede ser leída por las computadoras.

socialism *socialismo* Un sistema político-económico en el cual el gobierno controla el uso de los factores de producción del país.

social needs *necesidades sociales* En la jerarquía *Maslow* de las necesidades, la necesidad de pertenecer, de interactuar con otros, de tener amistades, y de amar y ser amado.

social networking *interconexión social* Comunidades virtuales que permiten a los usuarios publicar información de sí mismos y compartir esa información con otros.

social responsibility *responsabilidad social* El deber de un negocio de contribuir al bienestar de la sociedad.

Social Security *Seguro Social* Un programa de seguro tipo social financiado por contribuciones de nómina.

sole proprietorship *empresa de propietario único* Negocio de propiedad y administrado por una persona.

spam *spam (correo basura)* La publicidad no solicitada por el e-mail.

span of control *límite de control* El número de empleados que un gerente supervisa directamente.

specialist occupations *ocupaciones de especialista* Ocupaciones que requieren una variedad de habilidades en una o más funciones de negocio y un extenso conocimiento de las operaciones de una compañía o industria específica.

specialty goods *mercancías especializadas* Los productos que los clientes insisten en tener y están dispuestos a buscar hasta que los encuentren.

stakeholders *interesados* Los dueños, clientes, proveedores, empleados, acreedores, gobierno, público en general y otros grupos que se afectan por la acción de una empresa.

standard *estándar* Una medida específica por la cual algo es juzgado.

start-up budget *presupuesto inicial* Un presupuesto que pronostica los ingresos y gastos desde el comienzo de un negocio nuevo hasta que se anticipe que sea productivo.

statistics *estadísticas* Herramientas en matemáticas que utilizan información numérica cuidadosamente seleccionada para describir una situación siendo analizada o para pronosticar circunstancias futuras similares.

sticky-floor syndrome *síndrome de inamovilidad* La inhabilidad de que trabajadores avancen de puestos de bajo salario que requieren poca habilidad y capacitación.

stockholders *accionistas* Los propietarios de una corporación.

stock index *índice de la bolsa* Un promedio de los precios de acciones elegidas que se consideran representativas de una cierta clase de acciones de la economía en general.

stock option *opción a derechos de acciones* Un derecho otorgado por una corporación que permite a los accionistas comprar acciones adicionales cuando sean emitidas a un precio fijo por un plazo especificado.

storing *almacenar* Guardar los productos hasta que los necesiten los consumidores.

straight rebuy *recompra directa* Una compra de los proveedores anteriormente utilizados.

strategic alliances *alianzas estratégicas* Acuerdos en los que las empresas acuerdan en cooperar en ciertos aspectos del negocio mientras que permanecen competidores en otros aspectos.

strategic planning *planificación estratégica* Planificación a largo plazo que provee metas amplias y direcciones para todo el negocio.

subordinate *subordinado* Alguien que está sujeto a la autoridad y control de otra persona.

subsidiaries *filiales* Sucursales extranjeras de un negocio, que están registradas como entidades legales e independientes.

substantiation *justificación* Evidencia de todas las reclamaciones hechas sobre productos y servicios en promociones.

Sun Belt *Zona soleada* Los estados más cálidos en el sur y suroeste de los Estados Unidos.

supervisor *supervisor* Un gerente cuyo trabajo principal es dirigir el trabajo de los empleados.

supervisor/management occupations *Deberes del supervisor/gerente* Ocupaciones que consisten en la responsabilidad por unidades específicas en un negocio y por las decisiones sobre las operaciones y el personal.

supply *oferta* El número de productos similares que se ofrecerán a la venta en un tiempo determinado y a un precio en particular.

sustainability *sostenibilidad* La consideración de las necesidades ambientales, de la sociedad, y de la economía, para cumplir con las necesidades del presente sin comprometer la habilidad de que las generaciones futuras logren sus necesidades.

SWOT analysis *análisis DAFO (Debilidades, Amenazas, Fortalezas y Oportunidades)* Un análisis de los puntos fuertes y débiles internos de una organización así como las oportunidades y amenazas externas.

symptom *síntoma* Una señal o indicación de algo que parece ser el problema.

T

360-degree feedback *proceso circular de retroalimentación* Un método para evaluar el rendimiento que usa la retroalimentación del desempeño adquirido de una amplia variedad de personas con quienes el empleado trabaja, tanto fuera como dentro de la organización.

table *tabla* Una presentación de información organizada en columnas y renglones.

tally *cuenta (de contar)* Cualquier forma de marcar o señalar que se utiliza para recordar.

tangibles *tangibles* Dimensión de *SERVQUAL* (también RATER o evaluador de servicio y calidad); la presencia física de las instalaciones, equipo, personal, y material promocional.

target markets *mercados determinados* Grupos de clientes con necesidades muy similares a quienes la compañía piensa vender sus productos.

tariff *tarifa* Un impuesto sobre bienes extranjeros para proteger a las industrias domésticas y generar ingresos.

tax-deferred *impuesto diferido* Término que se refiere a las contribuciones de un plan de retiro hechas antes de que sean calculados los impuestos sobre los ingresos del empleado.

team building *fomentación en equipo* Conseguir que la gente apoye las mismas metas y que trabajen bien juntos para lograrlas.

team organization *organización en equipo* Estructura de negocio que divide a los empleados en equipos permanentes de trabajo.

telecommunications *telecomunicaciones* El movimiento vía electrónica de información de un lugar a otro.

telecommute *trabajar a distancia* El mantenerse en contacto con el empleador vía electrónica mientras se trabaja de casa o de viaje.

teleconferencing *teleconferencia* Una junta mediante audio o video con los participantes en dos o más localidades.

telemarketing *telemercadeo* El mercadear bienes y servicios por teléfono.

term loan *préstamo a plazo* Financiamiento a plazo mediano o largo utilizado para los fondos operativos o la compra o mejora de activos fijos.

time deposits (certificates of deposit or CD's) *depósitos de plazo (certificados de depósito o CDes)* Depósitos que se hacen por un plazo específico los cuales no se pueden retirar antes de tiempo sin una penalidad financiera.

time management *administración del tiempo* El administrar los horarios de trabajo para lograr la productividad máxima.

time plan *plan de tiempo* Un plan de compensación que paga una cierta cantidad por un período de tiempo especificado de trabajo.

time standard *estándar de tiempo* Una medida específica que establece la cantidad del tiempo necesario para completar una actividad.

total quality management *administración de calidad total* Un compromiso a la excelencia que se logra trabajando en equipo y con el mejoramiento continuo de los procedimientos de trabajo y productos.

trade credit *crédito comercial* Financiamiento a corto plazo que se obtiene mediante la compra de bienes y servicios que no requieren de pago inmediato.

trade discount *descuento comercial* Una reducción de precio que los fabricantes otorgan a sus socios distribuidores, tales como mayoristas o minoristas, a cambio de servicios adicionales.

trademark *marca registrada* Un nombre distintivo, un símbolo o una marca especial que se coloca en la mercancía o servicio y que está legalmente reservada para el uso exclusivo del dueño.

trading bloc *bloque comercial* Grupo de dos o más países que acuerdan en eliminar todas las restricciones en las ventas de bienes y servicios entre ellos, mientras que imponen restricciones para comerciar e invertir con países que no forman parte del bloque.

transfer *transferencia* La asignación de un empleado a otro trabajo en la compañía con el mismo nivel de responsabilidad y autoridad como su empleo actual.

transporting *transportar* Mover mercancías de donde fueron hechas a donde el cliente las puede comprar.

Treasury instruments *instrumentos de la tesorería* Valores bursátiles emitidos por el gobierno de los Estados Unidos.

trend *tendencia* Una dirección en general en la cual algo se está desarrollando o cambiando.

U

underground economy *economía clandestina* Ingresos que no están registrados en el GDP (producto doméstico bruto).

unemployment insurance *seguro de desempleo* Un programa administrado por el estado que provee ingresos temporales a individuos que han sido recortados en su empleo.

unity of command *unidad de mando* Una ley o norma en general que declara que ningún empleado tiene más de un supervisor a la vez.

unlimited financial liability *obligación financiera ilimitada* Cuando cada socio es personalmente responsable de todas las deudas incurridas por la sociedad.

unsecured loan *préstamo no asegurado* Un préstamo que no está respaldado por un colateral.

unsought goods *mercancías sin demanda* Productos que muchos clientes no buscan porque no tienen una verdadera necesidad del producto.

utility *utilidad* La habilidad de un bien o servicio para satisfacer un deseo.

V

values *valores* Creencias y actitudes fundamentales.

variable interest rate *tasa de interés variable* Una tasa de interés que puede incrementar o disminuir basado en los factores utilizados para ajustar la tasa.

variance *variación* La diferencia entre el rendimiento actual y el estándar.

venture capital *capital de riesgo* Financiamiento que se adquiere de un inversionista o grupo inversionista que presta grandes sumas de dinero a pequeñas compañías nuevas con potencial de expansión.

vision *visión* Una perspectiva amplia, duradera, y a veces inspiradora de la razón de existencia de una compañía.

Voice over Internet Protocol (VoIP) *voz a través del Internet* Utilizar el Internet para servicios telefónicos.

W

wage *sueldo* Pago basado en una tarifa por hora o por la finalización de una cantidad de trabajo especificada.

warehouses *almacenes* Edificios que se usan para almacenar grandes cantidades de productos hasta que se vendan.

web server *servidor de Internet* Una computadora que contiene el software y almacena datos para las redes.

web-hosting service *servicio de alojamiento de sitios/páginas web* Un negocio privado que mantiene los sitios Web de individuos y organizaciones en sus computadoras por una cuota.

what-if analysis *análisis del ¿qué pasaría si?* Una manera sistemática de explorar las consecuencias de decisiones específicas utilizando software de computadora.

wholesalers *mayoristas* Negocios que compran productos de los negocios y los venden a los minoristas o a otros negocios.

wholly-owned subsidiary *subsidiaria de propiedad absoluta* Cuando una empresa establece un negocio en el extranjero por sí misma sin socios.

wide area network (WAN) *red de área extensa* Una red de computadoras que cubre una área geográfica extensa.

win/lose strategy *estrategia de ganar/perder* Una estrategia en que la cual nadie llega a un acuerdo, así resultando en que una persona gana y otra pierde.

work coach *aconsejador de trabajo* Un gerente con experiencia que se reúne regularmente con un gerente nuevo para proveer retroalimentación y consejo.

work rules *reglas del trabajo* Regulaciones que se crean para mantener un ambiente efectivo de trabajo en un negocio.

work schedules *horarios de trabajo* Horarios que indican las labores que se deben hacer, los empleados asignados al trabajo, y el plazo para completar cada trabajo.

work team *equipo de trabajo* Un grupo de individuos que cooperan para lograr una meta común.

workers' compensation *indemnización laboral* Seguro proveído por los empleadores por el fallecimiento, lesión, o enfermedad de los empleados que resulta de su trabajo.

working capital *capital activo neto* La diferencia entre activos actuales y obligaciones actuales.

World Bank *Banco mundial* Instituto internacional que provee préstamos a largo plazo a bajo costo, a países menos desarrollados para el desarrollo de sus industrias e instalaciones básicas.

World Trade Organization (WTO) *Organización mundial de comercio* Organización internacional que crea y hace cumplir las reglas que gobiernan el comercio entre países.

World Wide Web (WWW, Web) *Red mundial (WWW, web)* Un conjunto de estándares que permite que la Internet sea accesible a la persona común.

Z

zoning *zonificación* Regulaciones que especifican cuáles áreas de terrenos se pueden usar para casas y cuáles se podrían usar para diferentes tipos de negocios.

Index

Health insurance, 503–504
Health maintenance organizations (HMOs), 504
Herzberg, Frederick, 119
Herzberg's two-factor theory, 119–120
Hidalgo Tortilla Company, 245
High-context cultures, 232
Hispanic population, growth of, 16, 170
History Academic Connections, 24
Home countries, of multinational firms, 229
Honesty, in leadership, 56
Hoovers, 316
Host countries, of multinational firms, 229
"Hot stove principle," 72
Human capital, 194
Human Development Index (HDI), 157
Human relations management, 12–13, 54, 60–62
Human resources
  careers in, 699
  in effective organizations, 673–675
  employee assistance activities in, 627
  employee relations activities in, 625
  employment activities in, 623, 627
  health and safety activities in, 625–626
  mathematics for, 362
  need for, 622–623
  overview, 62
  performance activities in, 624–627
  planning for, 528
  research in, 42
  service improvement in, 656–657
  social and ethical issues in, 169–175
  wages and benefits activities in, 624
  See also Employees; Employment
Human Resources Management Event, 701
Hurricane Andrew, 502
Hurricane Katrina, 248, 502
Hygiene factors (Herzberg), 119

I

IBM, Inc., 253
"Idea factory," 686
Identity power, 57–58
Identity theft, 133, 290
Illegal aliens, 248
Illegal pricing strategies, 197
Image, business, 668
Immigration, 170
Implementing, in management, 113–123
  activities, 114–117
  challenge of, 113–114
  change management in, 120–123
  definition of, 6
  motivation theories in, 118–120

resources for, 30–31
  time allocated for, 8
Imports and exports, 224, 228
Incas (South American), 9
Income
  balancing expenses with, 145
  distribution of, 206–207
  fixed, 211
  taxes on, 297
Income statement, 408–410
"Incubation" period, 45
Index of Leading Economic Indicators, 211
India, economy of, 208
Indirect distribution, 573–574
Indirect suggestions, 232
Individual well-being, 157
Inductive reasoning, 359
Industrial goods, 555
Industrial Revolution, 10
Industry, definition of, 147–148
Inferential statistics, 369, 371–372
Inflation, 211, 467, 469
Influencing people, 57–59
Informal communication networks, 339–340
Informal training, 661
Information
  from data, 306
  for decision making, 218
  distribution of, 308–309
  financial, 416–417
  for management, 41–46
  security of, 499
Information liability, 290
Information literacy, 453
Information management systems, 329
Information systems, 310–311
ING, Inc., 457
Initiative, 56, 488, 683
Innovation
  business affected by, 149
  efficiency improved by, 152–153
  integrating, 632
  international business on Internet, 233
  overview, 15
  See also Focus On...Innovation feature
Installment credit, 483
Insurable interest in property, 498
Insurance
  business operations, 505
  concepts of, 496–499
  disability, 503–504
  as employee benefit, 653
  health, 133–134, 503–504
  international operations, 506
  life, 504–505
  need for, 512

noninsurable risks, 499–500
  property, 501–502
  risk reduction and, 495–496
  theft, 133
  unemployment, 637–638
  vehicle, 503
Insurance companies, 271, 456
Intangible, services as, 533
Integrated marketing channels, 574–575
Intellectual property protection, 287–289
Intelligence, in leadership, 56
Interest
  business financing and, 440
  on checking accounts, 466
  as income, 206
  on loans, 462
Intermittent processing, 524
Internal factors, in SWOT analysis, 83
Internal motivation, 115
Internal Revenue Service (IRS), 272, 298, 396
International Bureau of Weights and Measures, 366
International environment of business. See Business, international environment of
International Exhibition (London, 1862), 10
International Monetary Fund (IMF), 226, 238
International stock indexes, 470
International System of Units (SI), 366
Internet
  business affected by, 149
  cookies from, 290, 293, 313
  e-commerce on, 18, 80
  financial programs on, 401
  fraud on, 133
  high-speed, wireless access to, 306
  India affected by, 208
  international business on, 233
  manufacturing and, 530
  overview of, 307–308
  privacy on, 293
  to recruit employees, 630
  shopping on, 556
  small business and, 158
  telecommuting and, 178
  virtual employees and, 18
  See also Technology
Internet Advertising Bureau, 600
Internet Protocol (IP) platform, 307
Interpersonal skills, 17, 195
Interstate commerce, 290–291
Interviewing, 632, 634
Intranets, 308–309
Intrapreneurs, 252–253
Intrastate commerce, 291